How Parliament Works

Parliament is constantly in the news and televised daily, but much of its work remains a mystery to outsiders and is sometimes perplexing even to its own members. Written by expert insiders, *How Parliament Works* is a straightforward and readable analysis of one of the country's most complex – and often misunderstood – institutions. Covering every aspect of the work, membership and structures of both Houses, this key text provides a unique insight into the work and daily life of Parliament. It explains not only what happens but why and analyses the institution's strengths and weaknesses, as well as opportunities for Parliament to be more effective.

The eighth edition has been substantially revised to take account of recent changes in both Houses, and to cover all the key issues affecting Parliament and politics, such as:

- Parliament, Brexit and Europe – the impact of the referendum vote on Parliament to date, Parliament's role in implementing Brexit and its role thereafter;
- Questions about how much Parliament is a genuinely representative body of the population at large in its diversity;
- The latest developments in the legislative process, party discipline and rebellion;
- The 'English votes for English laws' procedures;
- The effects of a minority government;
- Changes to the Budget cycle;
- Updates on the arrangements for the internal management of both Houses, reflecting governance reviews, with all statistics and examples fully updated throughout.

How Parliament Works is essential reading for anyone who has anything to do with the Westminster Parliament: journalists, civil servants, lawyers, lobbyists, business and trade associations, diplomats, overseas parliaments and international bodies – and indeed members of both Houses. *How Parliament Works* is also an invaluable companion to the study of politics at AS, A2 and university level, and provides a wealth of source material for teachers.

Nicolas Besly became a clerk in the House of Lords in 2002. He has worked in the Committee Office, Public Bill Office, Table Office and Journal Office. He became the first private secretary to a Lord Speaker and edited *The Table*, a journal on Commonwealth parliaments. He is currently a Clerk of Select Committees, overseeing five permanent Lords committees.

Tom Goldsmith became a clerk in the House of Commons in 1996. He has worked in the Public Bill Office, the Table Office and the Overseas Office. He headed the Governance Office and has served as Secretary to the House of Commons Commission. He has worked for a number of select committees and is currently the Clerk of the Foreign Affairs Committee.

Robert Rogers (now Lord Lisvane) and **Rhodri Walters** retired from the service of the House of Commons and the House of Lords respectively, in 2014. Their careers covered every aspect of the work of both Houses and between them they ama

Parliament.

How Parliament Works

Eighth edition

Robert Rogers and Rhodri Walters
New edition by Nicolas Besly and
Tom Goldsmith

LONDON AND NEW YORK

Eighth edition published 2019
by Routledge
2 Park Square, Milton Park, Abingdon, Oxon OX14 4RN

and by Routledge
711 Third Avenue, New York, NY 10017

Routledge is an imprint of the Taylor & Francis Group, an informa business

First edition published by Pearson Education Limited 1987
Seventh edition published by Routledge 2015

British Library Cataloguing-in-Publication Data
A catalogue record for this book is available from the British Library

Library of Congress Cataloging-in-Publication Data
Names: Rogers, Robert, 1950– author. | Walters, R. H. (Rhodri Havard), author. | Besly, Nicolas, author. | Goldsmith, Tom, author. | Walters, R. H. (Rhodri Havard). How Parliament works.
Title: How parliament works / Robert Rogers and Rhodri Walters ; new edition updated and revised by Nicolas Besly and Tom Goldsmith.
Description: Eighth edition, New updated and revised edition. | New York : Routledge, [2018] | "Seventh edition published by Routledge 2015"—T.p. verso. | Includes bibliographical references and index.
Identifiers: LCCN 2018025949 | ISBN 9780815369639 hardback | ISBN 9780815369646 paperback | ISBN 9781351251822 ebook
Subjects: LCSH: Great Britain. Parliament.
Classification: LCC JN550 .W35 2018 | DDC 328.41—dc23
LC record available at https://lccn.loc.gov/2018025949

ISBN: 978-0-8153-6963-9 (hbk)
ISBN: 978-0-8153-6964-6 (pbk)
ISBN: 978-1-351-25182-2 (ebk)

Typeset in Galliard and Frutiger
by Apex CoVantage, LLC

Printed and bound in Great Britain by
TJ International Ltd, Padstow, Cornwall

To those who believe that
Parliament matters

Contents

Foreword

THIS EIGHTH EDITION OF *How Parliament Works* is under new management. We are delighted to have taken on its authorship from our illustrious predecessors, Robert Rogers (now Lord Lisvane) and Rhodri Walters. While this edition has been comprehensively revised and updated our aims remain the same: to explain a complex and constantly evolving national institution in straightforward language; to give an insider's feel for how and why things happen; to analyse strengths and weaknesses; and to examine ways in which Parliament might develop. Parliament's ancient functions of legislating, controlling expenditure, representing the citizen and calling government to account have never been more important; and the more effective Parliament is, the better it will serve its real owners – the people of the United Kingdom.

We hope that our readers will include those who have anything to do with Parliament in their daily lives: journalists, lawyers, civil servants, lobbyists, academics, researchers, students and teachers, and, indeed, parliamentary candidates and members of both Houses; and those who simply want to find out how their Parliament works, and what it can do for them.

The previous edition was published only four years ago, but a lot has changed since then. Two general elections have been held, the first bringing to an end a period of coalition government and the second introducing one of minority government; the House of Commons now has procedures to give English MPs a veto over legislation that affects England only (or England and Wales and Northern Ireland, as appropriate); and, most dramatic of all, the referendum result determining that the UK would leave the EU has meant that legislating for departure, planning for its aftermath and scrutinising the government's implementation of Brexit has dominated the work of both Houses. If all those developments were not enough for parliamentary adrenalin-junkies, both Houses have also given their agreement to a programme of restoration and renewal of the Palace of Westminster which will see Parliament decanted to alternative homes for something like six years.

We are very grateful for the help of friends and colleagues in preparing this edition. Our thanks go to Amanda Colledge, Nigel Evans MP, Catherine Fogarty, Anne-Marie

Griffiths, Mike Hennessy, Larry Honeysett, Tahiyya Jurdine, David Lloyd and Tony Lloyd MP. We are especially grateful to Sean Kinsey for the time-consuming task of sourcing all the images in the book. Any mistakes or omissions are our responsibility and any views expressed are those of the authors alone.

We are also grateful for the help and support of our agent, Charlotte Howard; and the assistance (and patience!) of Andrew Taylor and Sophie Iddamalgoda at Taylor & Francis.

Finally, our deepest thanks go to our predecessors. While we have updated the book comprehensively, this edition draws heavily on their work on earlier iterations, both in structure and content. Our gratitude to Robert and Rhodri goes beyond their work on this book: we thank them for their long and distinguished service to Parliament, and more personally for being delightful and inspiring colleagues and friends. We are honoured that they asked us to continue *How Parliament Works* and hope you enjoy reading it.

Nicolas Besly
Tom Goldsmith

1

Parliament: its home and origins

Mid-Victorian masterpiece: Parliament in its setting

The Palace of Westminster is probably the United Kingdom's most famous landmark. Like the Parliament it houses, the palace comprises mediaeval origins, Victorian reinventions and modern flourishes. Just as Parliament itself has developed, the palace has grown and changed over nearly a thousand years. Much of the change has been evolutionary and incremental, sometimes even make-do-and-mend. At other times the change has been drastic.

Almost two centuries after the fire of 1834 which ravaged most of the palace, the Victorian Gothic masterpiece which was built in its aftermath is in pressing need of restoration. The precise scope and nature of that renewal is yet to be determined, but some urgent work has already started. Hence, in early 2017 a four-year renovation started of the Elizabeth Tower at the north end of the palace. The Tower, which houses the iconic Great Clock, will remain covered in scaffolding throughout the works; and the most famous bell in the world, Big Ben, fell silent. Cynics seeking a metaphor for the political tumult of Brexit and minority government did not have to look far. Yet, for all that it needs renewal, the palace is one of the greatest achievements of nineteenth-century architecture and art, and even those who work there every day remain awed by its power and confidence. It is at least arguable that that confidence has been reflected in recent years in the work of Parliament itself, for example in the renewed willingness of committees and independent-minded backbenchers to hold the government to account.

If the Palace of Westminster were empty, it would still be one of the great tourist attractions of Europe. But this Grade I listed building, part of the World Heritage site that includes Westminster Abbey, contains a Parliament that is one of the biggest and busiest in the world. This is a source of many tensions. Whatever its working methods, and however effective it may be, it is very difficult for a Parliament housed in a heritage icon to *look* modern and efficient. And the constraints of conserving and caring for such a building mean that any structural change for parliamentary purposes – from new door locks to constructing an education centre – must run the gauntlet of English Heritage, the planners of Westminster City Council, and countless others who love the building for its art and history. The building is expensive to maintain precisely because everything must be done to the highest standards for the benefit of future generations. Finally, the palace is a perfect example of how buildings shape the activity within them. As we shall see, the nature of the buildings of Parliament has a powerful influence on how business is conducted and the way that members of both Houses work.

The King's palace

It may seem odd that a Parliament should meet in a palace; but the Palace of Westminster has been a royal palace for well over 1,000 years. Before the Norman Conquest it was the residence of Edward the Confessor, and it continued to be used by the monarch until the reign of Henry VIII, who bought Whitehall from Cardinal Wolsey in 1529 and then built St James's Palace in 1532. Although Westminster was thereafter no longer a royal residence, it continued to be a royal palace. Property in what is now London SW1 was clearly as much in demand in the sixteenth century as it is now, and the buildings huddled around the great bulk of Westminster Hall were rapidly taken up for use by the two Houses, the law courts (which remained at Westminster until they moved to the Strand in 1882), courtiers, placemen and shopkeepers – and others plying less reputable trades.

The King's summons

Although Parliaments have met at Westminster for some 750 years, there is no requirement to do so. Parliament has met, and could meet, elsewhere and still conduct its business with constitutional and legal propriety. Second World War bomb damage forced the two Houses from their own chambers; and today Parliament could meet elsewhere with the minimum of infrastructure – indeed, there are plans to do so.

The word 'parliament', from the French *parler*, to speak or talk, was first used in England in the thirteenth century, when it meant an enlarged meeting of the King's council, attended by barons, bishops and courtiers, to advise the King on law-making, administration and judicial decisions. The origin of the modern institution can be traced back to the parliament summoned on Henry III's behalf by Simon de Montfort in 1265, when representatives from the towns were present for the first time. Parliaments still meet in response to a royal summons; the parliament that met after the 2017 general election was summoned by a proclamation from the Queen, which in part said:

> *And We . . . being desirous and resolved, as soon as may be, to meet Our people and to have their Advice in Parliament . . . do hereby make known unto all Our loving Subjects Our Royal Will and Pleasure to call a new Parliament.*

Those words may fall strangely on a modern ear, but the purport of Elizabeth II's proclamation was the same as those issued in the reigns of 34 of her predecessors.

The development of the two Houses

By the middle of the fourteenth century the King's parliaments were attended by knights of the shire and burgesses from the cities and boroughs (the Commons), the magnates (the Lords Temporal) and the bishops and abbots (the Lords Spiritual). At this time, the reign of Edward III, the Commons began to claim that their agreement was required for any taxation by the monarch, in particular the tax on wool. By now the Commons and Lords had emerged as two distinct houses. Once settled at Westminster, the Commons met in the Painted Chamber or in the refectory or the chapter house of Westminster Abbey, and they moved to St Stephen's Chapel in 1547. The Lords settled in the White Chamber of the old palace, moving to the larger White or Lesser Hall in 1801 when the Union with Ireland introduced extra members into the House. After the fire of 1834 they moved to the re-roofed Painted Chamber until they were able to move into their present accommodation in 1847.

The fire

The night of 16 October 1834 was fine, with some high cloud. By seven o'clock that evening the London sky was lit by flames. Two workmen had been told to dispose of large quantities of Exchequer tallies – notched hazel sticks used from early mediaeval times to show what each taxpayer owed; the stick could be split to provide both a record and a receipt. The workmen burned the tallies in the furnaces that heated the flues under the floor of the House of Lords. Their enthusiasm, or possibly their impatience, led to the destruction of the mediaeval palace and the meeting places of both Houses. Thousands watched. One contemporary observer wrote:

> *An immense multitude of spectators assembled at Westminster to witness the ravages of the fire, the lurid glare of which was visible for many miles around the metropolis. Even the river Thames . . . was covered with boats and barges . . . and the reflections of the wavering flames upon the water, on the neighbouring shores and on the many thousands thus congregated, composed a spectacle most strikingly picturesque and impressive.*

The winning design

The destruction of a large part of the old palace and of much of its contents, including irreplaceable manuscripts, paintings and tapestries, was a great loss. Westminster Hall survived, as did other parts of the building that today would undoubtedly have been preserved or restored. But the authorities of the day saw the fire as an opportunity to start afresh. A competition was held for the design of a completely new parliamentary building, which resulted in an extraordinary architectural and artistic partnership. The scheme produced by the architect Sir Charles Barry and the interior designer Augustus Welby Pugin was chosen from among 97 designs submitted, and the foundation stone was laid on 27 April 1840. The palace that was built over the next 20 years is huge. It covers eight acres (3.24 hectares), and has 1,100 rooms, 100 staircases and three miles (4.8 km) of passages.

A Victorian Parliament

The Barry and Pugin palace had, apart from its visual merits, one great advantage: it was a purpose-built parliamentary building. As well as the two chambers, it provided residences for the principal officers and officials, dining rooms, smoking rooms, writing rooms, committee rooms, libraries and all the paraphernalia of a grand country house and London club combined.

This was all a mid-Victorian Parliament needed. There were 658 members of the Commons and some 500 members of the Lords, no more than 350 of whom turned up to speak in any session; but an MP or peer wrote his correspondence in longhand, and if he wanted to find something out, he went and looked it up, just as he would have done in his library or study at home. Members of the Commons were careful to keep on the right side of local political magnates, but modern constituency pressures were unknown. Indeed, illuminated addresses survive that were presented to the local MP 'on his visit [sometimes *annual* visit!] to the Constituency'.

The new palace today

Sadly, the ever-present threat of terrorism has meant that public access to the Palace of Westminster has to be closely controlled. During term time, the parties of constituents and other visitors who tour the principal parts of the palace must be sponsored by an MP or peer, although visitors may pay to take a guided tour of the palace (in nine different languages, or a tactile tour for blind and partially sighted visitors) during the commercial opening on Saturdays, during most summer recesses and on non-sitting days at other times of the year (see page 430).

Those who visit the Palace of Westminster follow the Queen's route at the State Opening of Parliament, in the part of the palace still devoted to the monarch. With the exception of the Commons chamber, much of what they see has changed little and would have been familiar to Gladstone or Disraeli. A plan of the palace is on page 5.

The Robing Room and Royal Gallery

When the Queen opens Parliament in state, her state coach drives under the great archway of the Victoria Tower, the 323-foot (98.5-m) tower at the south end of the palace that houses the parliamentary archives. She then ascends the Royal Staircase and passes through the Norman Porch (so called because it was intended to place statues of the Norman kings there, but somehow Victorian prime ministers supplanted them) to the Robing Room, where she puts on the state robes and Imperial State Crown before walking in procession through the 110-foot (33.5-m) long Royal Gallery, into the Prince's Chamber and then into the chamber of the House of Lords. This ceremony

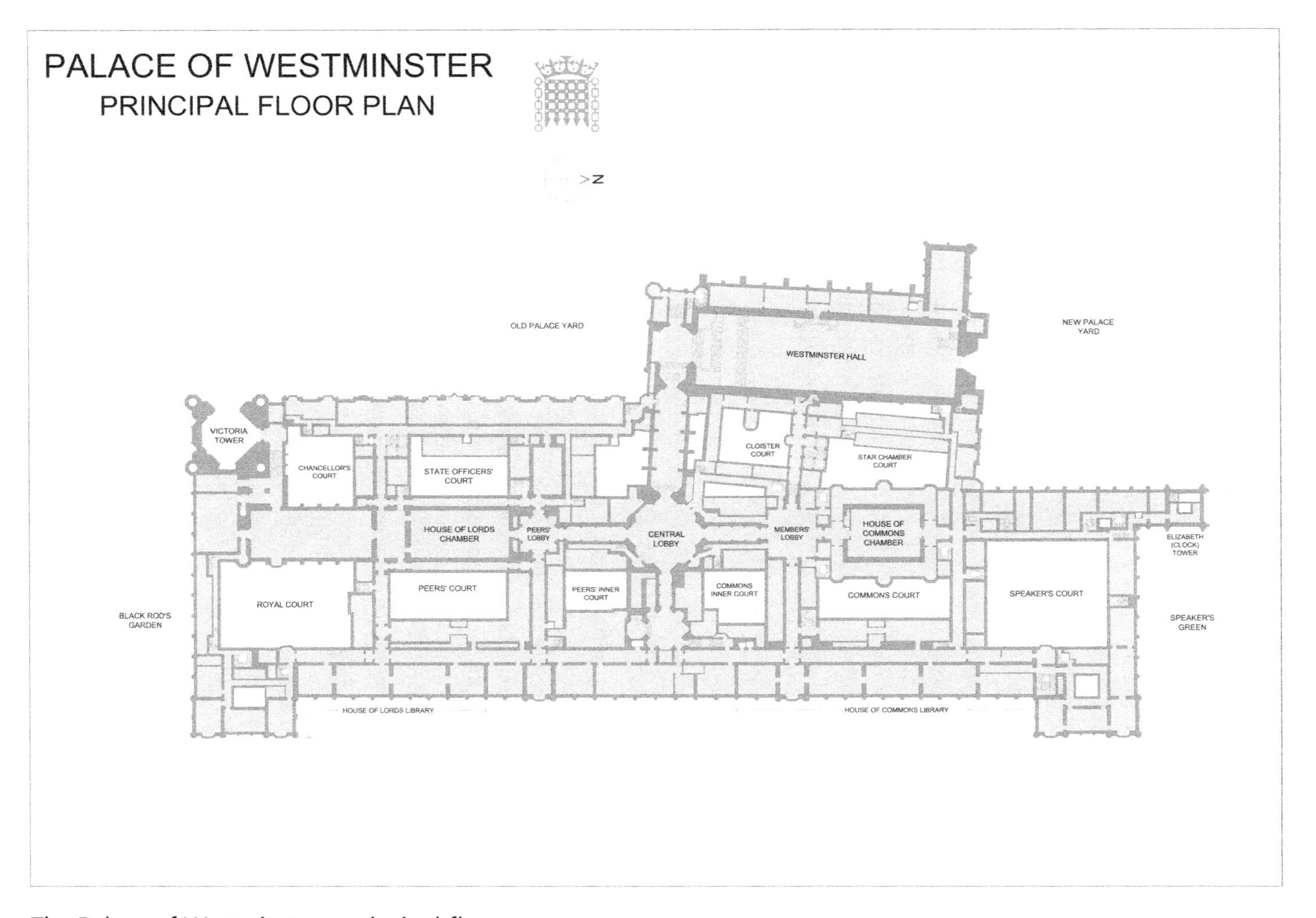

The Palace of Westminster – principal floor

Source: Copyright House of Commons, 2014. Artwork by Jonathan Rix

was modified when the Queen opened Parliament after the unexpected general election in 2017. On that occasion she arrived by car and not a state coach; she did not wear the state robes and crown, though the procession still took place.

This southern end of the palace is magnificent and ornate – deliberately conceived as a backdrop to state ceremonial. The perfect proportions of Barry's rooms are complemented by the sumptuousness of Pugin's decoration. His themes of portcullis, rose, lily and lion, together with Queen Victoria's VR cipher, run throughout the palace's decoration, with its Gothic features and linenfold panelling, but his 'graceful fancy' is nowhere more evident than at the south end of the building – the Robing Room and the Royal Gallery.

Although the chief purpose of these two great rooms was to impress, they can be used for other purposes. Following the destruction of the Commons chamber by enemy bombing the House of Lords sat in the Robing Room between 1941 and 1949 to enable the Commons to use the Lords chamber. Both rooms are used when a visiting head of state – or occasionally head of government – addresses members of both Houses of Parliament. As there is no concept of joint sittings of the two Houses, the Royal Gallery and Robing Room provide a convenient place for such events – such as in 2017 when King Felipe VI of Spain gave an address in the Royal Gallery and in 2016 when Colombia's President Juan Manuel Santos addressed both Houses in the Robing Room.

The chamber of the House of Lords

The visitor then moves to the chamber of the House of Lords, which is fitted out in the same rich style. At one end, the throne faces north under a gilded canopy and Cloth of Estate. In front of it is the Woolsack, on which sits the Lord Speaker as presiding officer of the House of Lords. The Woolsack is a seat stuffed with wool from the different countries of the Commonwealth. Stuffed sacks or cushions were a standard form of mediaeval furniture but tradition has it that Edward III decided that a sack of wool would be a useful reminder to their lordships of the pastoral basis of the country's economy – and the chief source of his revenue – and the practice has persisted. In front of the Woolsack are the two judges' woolsacks. These remind us that Court of Appeal and High Court judges still receive Writs of Assistance to attend the House. Nowadays they attend only in a representative capacity on the day of the State Opening. To the left and right of the Woolsack are four rows of red benches for peers, divided into three sections. In the centre of the floor is the Table of the House, and on the far side of the Table from the Woolsack there are three further benches.

Looking from the throne, the right of the House is known as the *spiritual side*, because the bishops sit there, in the front two rows of the section nearest the throne. The left is called the *temporal side*, while beyond the Table are the crossbenches. As well as the bishops, government peers sit on the spiritual side, with ministers in the front row of the central section. Opposition parties sit on the temporal side. Peers who do not belong to a party sit on the crossbenches. A labelled view of the chamber and a photograph of the House in session are shown opposite.

The chamber of the House of Lords

Source: Copyright House of Lords, 2018.

The House of Lords in session

Source: Copyright House of Lords, 2018. Photography by Roger Harris

Beyond the Lords chamber, the visitor passes through Peers' Lobby to the Central Lobby, a large octagonal room at the very centre of the palace, beneath the third-largest of the palace's towers. Almost all visitors on business come to the Central Lobby; it is the place where constituents who wish to lobby an MP come to fill in a green card requesting an interview. It lies directly between the two chambers; and when on State Opening day all the doors are thrown open, the Queen sitting on the throne in the Lords can see the Speaker presiding over the House of Commons more than a hundred yards (91m) away.

Members' Lobby and the chamber of the House of Commons

Moving towards the Commons chamber, the visitor passes into Members' Lobby. This is a much larger space than Peers' Lobby. When the House is busy, especially before and after votes, it is thronged with MPs and is the haunt of 'lobby' journalists; it is then a clearing-house of opinion, news and rumour. It contains a message board with a slot for each member's messages (less used in these days of mobiles), pigeonholes for members' select committee papers (also less used now that committees are predominantly paperless), a counter where members can get a wide range of parliamentary and government papers, and a post office that deals with some 50,000 items every sitting day. The whips' offices of the major parties (see page 88) adjoin the Members' Lobby.

The Commons chamber was destroyed in an air raid on the night of 10 May 1941. Barry's original chamber was less ornate than that of the Lords; and the rebuilt Commons chamber, designed by Sir Giles Gilbert Scott, is austere by comparison with that of the Lords. A labelled view of the chamber and one of the House in session are shown on pages 9 and 10. From the public gallery one now looks down through a massive seven-tonne glass screen, installed in September 2005 on security advice. Below, the Speaker's canopied Chair is the focal point. During Question Time and ministerial statements, the Speaker's Secretary stands to the right of the Chair (as seen from the gallery) helping the Speaker to identify members and keeping a record of those he has called. To the left of the Chair, against the far wall, is the officials' box for civil servants advising ministers. In front of the Chair is the Table of the House, at which sit the clerks at the Table, who advise the Speaker and his deputies, whips and any other member, on the conduct of proceedings, and who also compile the legal record of the House's decisions.

On each side of the chamber are five rows of green benches, divided by a gangway into two sections. On the left, as seen from the gallery, are the benches occupied by the government party. On the right, as seen from the gallery, are the opposition parties, with the smaller parties sitting nearest to the gallery. Ministers sit on the front bench by the Table, and the main opposition party's spokesmen and women (or shadow ministers) sit opposite them. Ministers and their shadows are thus known as frontbenchers; all other MPs are backbenchers.

The Chamber of the House of Commons, looking down from the public gallery

Source: Copyright House of Commons, 2014. Photography by Deryc R. Sands

The House of Commons in session, 2017
Source: Copyright House of Commons, 2017. Photography by Jessica Taylor

On each side of the Table are the despatch boxes at which ministers and their counterparts from the main opposition party speak; and at the near end of the Table is the Mace, which symbolises the authority of the House.

At our observer's eye level, above the Speaker's Chair, is the Press Gallery, with seats in the centre for the *Hansard* reporters who compile the record of what is said. Other galleries are for members of the House of Lords and distinguished visitors, as well as for the general public. Two galleries are reserved for MPs and are technically part of the floor of the House, although Speakers have indicated that they will not call members to speak from there (and there are no microphones). Down below, but not visible except from the front of the gallery, sits the Serjeant at Arms, responsible for order around the House and in the galleries. There, too, are the crossbenches; but as there are, apart from the occupants of the Chair, few members with no party allegiance (since 1997 no more than three in any parliament, and at present two), these are in practice extensions of the seating for government and opposition members (although MPs may not speak from them).

Westminster Hall

This brief description of the Palace of Westminster would be incomplete without reference to what is one of the finest rooms in Europe – Westminster Hall, the great hall of the mediaeval palace and, along with the crypt Chapel of St Mary Undercroft, the only part of the original building to remain. The hall has been much restored over the years including, in 2017–18, work to clean and conserve the internal roof, install a fire detection system and improved lighting, and to repair the lead lantern. At its core, however, it remains an eleventh-century building with a late fourteenth-century hammerbeam roof. It is used today for ceremonial occasions. The Lying in State of the Queen Mother took place in Westminster Hall in April 2002; and the Queen received the Humble Addresses of the two Houses of Parliament there on the occasion of her Diamond Jubilee in 2012. The Hall is sometimes also used instead of the Royal Gallery to hear addresses from visiting Heads of State – Pope Benedict in 2010 and President Obama in 2011 – or other figures, such as Aung San Suu Kyi in 2012. The regular sittings of the House of Commons 'in Westminster Hall' (see page 278) take place not in the Hall itself, but in the Grand Committee Room at the north end.

The palace and parliamentary vocabulary

The layout of the chambers, derived from earlier meeting rooms of the two Houses, is reflected in the vocabulary of Parliament, which in many cases has passed into general everyday use and has been adopted around the world with the spread of the Westminster model of parliamentary government.

The *opposition* parties sit physically opposite the government party (as well as opposing it). A meeting of the House is a *sitting*, at the end of which the House *rises*. Matters considered by either House are debated *on the floor*. If a member changes parties, he or she is said to have *crossed the floor*. When MPs and peers hand in questions, amendments to bills or notices of motions, or when ministers place documents formally before either House, they are said to have *tabled* them, even if they do not place them on the massive Table in either House. If a bill has its committee stage in a Commons public bill committee, it is said to be taken *upstairs* because most of the palace's committee rooms are on the first floor. When either House votes, it is said to *divide*, because those voting divide physically into two groups ('ayes' and 'noes' in the Commons, 'contents' and 'not contents' in the Lords) and walk through separate lobbies on either side of both chambers to be counted. Securing something *on the nod* – that is, without debate or division – may derive from a member's brief bow to the Chair when moving a motion formally.

Some supposed parliamentary derivations are bogus. *In the bag* stems not from the petition bag on the back of the Speaker's Chair but from the much older idea of a game bag. It is just as fanciful as the myth that the red lines on the floor of the Commons chamber are two sword lengths apart, although there is a rule that a member speaking from the front row of benches (above or below the gangway) should not step over the lines. And *toe the line* has nothing to do with these lines; it comes from the Royal Navy of Nelson's time, when barefooted seamen lined up for inspection on the seams, or lines, in the deck planking. A more frequent error is the description of Westminster as 'the mother of parliaments'. When John Bright coined the phrase in 1865 he was referring to *England* as the mother of parliaments; but, given the immense influence

Westminster has had on the development of parliaments around the world, perhaps the mistake is understandable.

'We shape our buildings, and afterwards our buildings shape us'

From the start, the club-like rooms and communal spaces of Barry's palace have encouraged members of both Houses to congregate and meet informally. In the Commons, the Smoking Room (like the rest of the palace, now a no-smoking area), the Tea Room and Members' Lobby after a big vote (as well as the division lobbies themselves during it) are places where opinions are formed and exchanged, support is canvassed and tactics planned. This informality and personal contact also produces volatility: rumours travel quickly, even through so large a membership; views – and perhaps backbench rebellions – can gather momentum with surprising speed. The use of social media has only increased the speed with which such views are disseminated.

A first-time visitor almost always finds the Commons chamber smaller than expected; for an assembly of 650 members, it is surprisingly intimate – its floor area is not much more than that of a tennis court. Its seating capacity (together with the galleries reserved for members) is usually said to be 427; but as there are no individual seats and members inevitably take up varying amounts of the green leather, this is an approximation.

There are no individual places, so also no desks, telephones or computer terminals; and members speak from their places, not from a podium. When the House is full, perhaps towards the end of a major debate or during Prime Minister's Questions, the atmosphere is made tense by the crush of MPs, and one can appreciate the way in which the House can become great political theatre. On such occasions the noise can be overwhelming, with members straining to hear what is being said, often leaning close to the small speakers in the benches behind them. The small size of the chamber also means that, even when only a few MPs are present for some abstruse debate, the feeling of speaking to empty space, which is a problem in many foreign parliaments, is minimised.

It is likely that the rows of benches facing each other derive from the use by the Commons of St Stephen's Chapel in the old palace. The clergy faced each other in choir stalls on each side of the altar, and the arrangement was unchanged when the Tudor House of Commons took over the chapel. Some feel that this encourages adversarial politics (and even, perhaps fancifully, a two-party system). The Commons, unlike the Lords, has no crossbenches spanning the width of the chamber. It may be significant that public bill committee rooms, where legislation is debated in the same way as in the House, are laid out as in the chamber; but for select committees, where there is a more consensual approach, members sit around horseshoe tables, and MPs and peers do not necessarily sit on party lines.

Certainly, the idea of replacing the chamber with a hemicycle, of the sort found in many continental parliaments and in the European Parliament, has its supporters, especially among those who shun confrontational politics. A hemicycle would almost certainly bring with it individual desks and seats, but accommodating a chamber of that size in Barry's palace would be next to impossible. The House of Commons had a chance to make the change after the old chamber was destroyed in 1941. However, neither a hemicycle nor a larger traditional chamber found favour. Churchill represented the majority view in the House when he said in the debate on the rebuilding:

> *if the House is big enough to contain all its members, nine-tenths of the debates will be conducted in the depressing atmosphere of an almost empty or half-empty chamber . . . We wish to see our Parliament as a strong, easy, flexible instrument of free debate. For this purpose a small chamber and a sense of intimacy are indispensable . . . The conversational style requires a fairly small space, and there should be on great occasions a sense of crowd and urgency . . . We shape our buildings, and afterwards our buildings shape us.*

Time and space

In an echo of metaphysics, the way any parliament operates is dictated by time and space. *Time*: to allow full scrutiny of government, examination of draft legislation, airing of concerns affecting constituencies and constituents, and the political causes pursued by political parties and individual members. *Space* is almost as important: space to provide meeting rooms for committees, political parties and lobby groups; space for library and research facilities; adequate office accommodation for MPs and their staff to provide the service that their constituents expect, and for members of both Houses to support their parliamentary duties.

Add to that the space that is needed for the infrastructure of Parliament: support for the work of the two chambers and of legislative and investigative committees; provision of IT, security, catering, housekeeping, maintenance, and administration of pay and personnel. Then there are those who are in Parliament but not of it: TV, radio and print journalists, and civil servants supporting ministers. Last, but emphatically not least, are the owners of Parliament: constituents and taxpayers and their families, who may want to bring problems to their local MP, or have a cause taken up by a member of either House, or who may simply want to see Parliament at work.

These demands fluctuate. Parliament must react to expectations of it, as well as to events. The creation of a new government department will need a new select committee to scrutinise it in the Commons; some major issue of the day may lead to the establishment of a new select committee in the Lords. More draft bills will need more select committee consideration, and in turn space for the staff to support the process; and proposals to change the number of members in each House may have a significant effect. We consider below how the two modern Houses have tried to cope with the constant pressure on their accommodation.

The shoe pinches

The new Palace of Westminster was largely completed by 1852, although it was not finally finished until 1860. The Lords occupied their chamber on 15 April 1847; the Commons first sat in theirs on 30 May 1850 but did not move in permanently until 3 February 1852. In 1854 Sir Charles Barry produced plans to build additional offices surrounding New Palace Yard, but these were never pursued. By 1867 a select committee was examining how the size of the Commons chamber could be increased and, in 1894, another Commons select committee was looking at the adequacy of accommodation more generally.

The pressures

The shortage of accommodation was a recurring theme over the next 100 years. In the Commons it became particularly acute during the last 20 or 30 years of the last century with the increasing burdens of constituency work, the need to house larger numbers of MPs' own staff, and the growth in select committee work and in research facilities. The administration and support of the House became more professional and better resourced, needing more staff and office accommodation. Every new facility, however desirable in itself, has imposed new strains, from the introduction of broadcasting (with its need for control rooms and archive space) to the establishment of information offices for the public, and educational facilities. The apparently relentless growth in the use of IT has resulted in a dramatic increase in the numbers of officials working in that area.

A visitor following the route from the Victoria Tower to the Commons chamber has an impression of lofty ceilings and spacious rooms, but on the floors above and below (except along the Committee Corridor on the river front) the story is rather different and includes subdivided rooms, mezzanine floors and even temporary huts on flat roofs.

For many years in the Commons, members were prepared, however reluctantly, to share offices – even with nine or ten of their colleagues – or to do much of their constituency work around the House, writing letters in the library or dictating to their secretaries in the Committee Corridor while waiting to vote. That this did not lead to changes may have been partly because of the 'never did me any harm' principle, but also because the scope for change was limited.

New buildings

The only realistic possibilities lay to the north of the palace, across Bridge Street towards Whitehall. Various schemes blossomed, were rejected and withered. Between 1984 and 1991, however, the buildings in 1 Parliament Street, at the end of Whitehall, were converted to provide some 90 offices for MPs, together with library, catering and meeting facilities. Nearby, the old Scotland Yard police headquarters (the Norman Shaw buildings) were taken over and the next-door Canon Row buildings adapted for office accommodation. In 2018 Richmond House, opposite the Cenotaph on Whitehall and until recently home to the Department of Health, began to be used by Commons staff. At the other end of the palace, Westminster House at 7 Millbank contains officials; and to the west 14 Tothill Street contains most of the staff of Commons select committees and most of the library's researchers.

Portcullis House

However, if MPs and their staff were to have proper modern office accommodation that would allow them to give a proper service to their constituents, the key site was that overlooking the river. Here, between 1998 and 2000, Portcullis House was constructed to provide offices for 210 MPs and 400 of their staff, together with a variety of meeting rooms. Designed by Michael Hopkins and Partners (now Hopkins Architects), from the outside the building appears austere, even forbidding, but inside it shows a confident and innovative style that has won a string of awards.

Although at the time it was built the cost was controversial, the building has now become a thriving part of the House of Commons. It contains modern, relatively spacious, offices for MPs and their staff, committee rooms and smaller meeting rooms, and support services such as an IT centre and a 'one-stop shop' for MPs. Perhaps just as significantly, the open-plan, airy atrium containing contemporary eateries and

Portcullis House

Source: Copyright UK Parliament

a coffee shop is home to a café-style culture quite different from the narrow corridors and grand restaurants in the palace.

It is safe to say that those who commissioned the new palace after the fire of 1834 would not have recognised any part of this description of the uses of a parliamentary building.

Lords accommodation

As with the Commons, the House of Lords has outgrown the 40 per cent of the original palace that it occupies and, rather late in the day compared with the House of Commons, has started to acquire office space for staff and members in nearby streets. In 1994, 7 Old Palace Yard – an elegant Georgian house opposite the west front of the palace – was returned by the Commons to Lords use; and, in 2005, Fielden House, an office building in Little College Street, was occupied. From 2001 Millbank House was gradually occupied for mixed member and staff use – starting with 2 Millbank then, from 2011, 1 Millbank and, from 2018, the remaining portion of 5 Great College Street. This requirement for space reflects the increased level of activity of the Lords. As we shall see in Chapter 2, average daily attendance is now higher than ever. In addition, members' expectations of desk space, IT facilities, research and information, and procedural support are always rising. Unsurprisingly, as in the Commons, this scattering of staff and members' offices has made the Lords seem less of a homogeneous organisation.

Restoration and renewal

There has been little modernisation of the Palace of Westminster over the 160 years of its existence. As, over a century and a half, new requirements and new technologies have emerged, they have been accommodated somehow, but with no strategic plan; and the fabric of the palace is showing its age. Although the visitor to the main or Principal Floor of the palace would not guess it, the services in the basement and in the 98 'risers' between floors (water, air-conditioning, steam, sewage, electricity, communications, IT), carried by many miles of pipes and wires, are in poor condition, and the possibility of a catastrophic failure, which could make it impossible for either House to sit, is increasing. Over the years, the fabric has deteriorated, and roofs and stonework need attention.

In 2013, following a preliminary study by officials, an independent options appraisal was commissioned from a team of consultants led by Deloitte Real Estate to assess the state of the building and its services, and to consider how to set about a programme of restoration and renewal. Two options were ruled out from the beginning: doing nothing; and constructing a new parliamentary building. Three options remained: first, tackling the problems while the business of both Houses continues, which might mean decades of work; second, 'decanting' first one House, its members and staff to another building acquired for the purpose; and third, decanting both Houses and all the occupants of the palace for five or six years.

In 2015 the consultants' Independent Options Appraisal was published. It found that option 1 – continuous occupation but with 12 areas of the palace fully decanted one by one – would cost the most (estimated at £5.67 billion) and take the longest (estimated at 32 years). Option 2 – one chamber decanted at a time – was estimated to cost around £4 billion and take 11 years. Option 3 – full decant – came in at an estimated £3.5 billion and six years. In each case the cost and time involved would vary according to the level of improvements made.

Following the 2015 general election the Joint Committee on the Palace of Westminster was established to consider these three options. It was co-chaired by the then Leaders of both Houses (incidentally the concept of co-chairs of a committee was an innovation in Westminster) and comprised their opposition 'shadows' in each House and senior backbenchers. After hearing evidence and deliberating for a year, in September 2016 the joint committee reported. It found that there was a 'clear and pressing need to tackle the work required to the Palace of Westminster . . . to prevent catastrophic failure in the next decade'. It concluded that in principle full decant of the palace was the best option, but that an arm's-length delivery authority should be established to validate the preferred option and then to oversee the work.

If both Houses are to move out from the Palace of Westminster they need somewhere to go. The joint committee recommended that, subject to further feasibility work, the House of Commons should occupy Richmond House. The House of Lords could meet in the Queen Elizabeth II Conference Centre, opposite Westminster Abbey.

The joint committee recommended that the next step should be for each House to pass a motion endorsing, among other things, the recommendation for a full decant.

After that progress slowed, with a date for debating the report being promised but not delivered. But in early 2018 it was finally debated, and both Houses agreed that the 'best and most cost-effective way' to carry out the restoration and renewal of the building was to move out temporarily and allow the works to be carried out in one single phase. The Houses also gave their approval for the establishment of a shadow Olympic-style Delivery Authority and Sponsor Board. They are shadow because legislation is needed to establish them as statutory bodies with full powers. In July 2018 the Prime Minister announced that a draft bill would be introduced later in 2018 for pre-legislative scrutiny. The thinking is that a decant will not happen until 2025 but in the meantime extensive preparations will be needed.

Few dispute the necessity and urgency of making substantial repairs to the palace. But the politics of it are fraught. Even with both Houses having set out their preference for the cheapest option, the cost will be in the billions, at a time of continuing pressure on the public finances. Given the history of large public-sector infrastructure projects, it is feared that the forecast cost and time will end up being significant underestimates. Some point – with varying degrees of accuracy or relevance – to other old buildings which have been comprehensively renovated while maintaining continuous occupation.

Meanwhile, major programmes to re-roof the palace, to clean stonework, to support the mechanical and electrical services, and to replace the thousands of worn and damaged encaustic floor tiles continue. In August 2017 the Elizabeth Tower's major refurbishment began, which involves pausing the ringing of Big Ben for four years

Elizabeth Tower under scaffold, 2017

Source: Copyright House of Commons, 2017. Photography by Mark Duffy

(with exceptions made for Remembrance Sunday and New Year's Eve). This attracted considerable attention, with some politicians regretting the lack of forewarning or approval for the extent of the works.

The parliamentary estate

Today's parliamentary estate is akin to a small town. It covers 209,023 square metres in 14 buildings, excluding residences, retail and storage facilities, housing well over 6,000 people – and this population is more than doubled by those from outside Westminster who have business in Parliament each day. A plan of the parliamentary estate appears overleaf.

We now move on to consider the institution housed in those buildings.

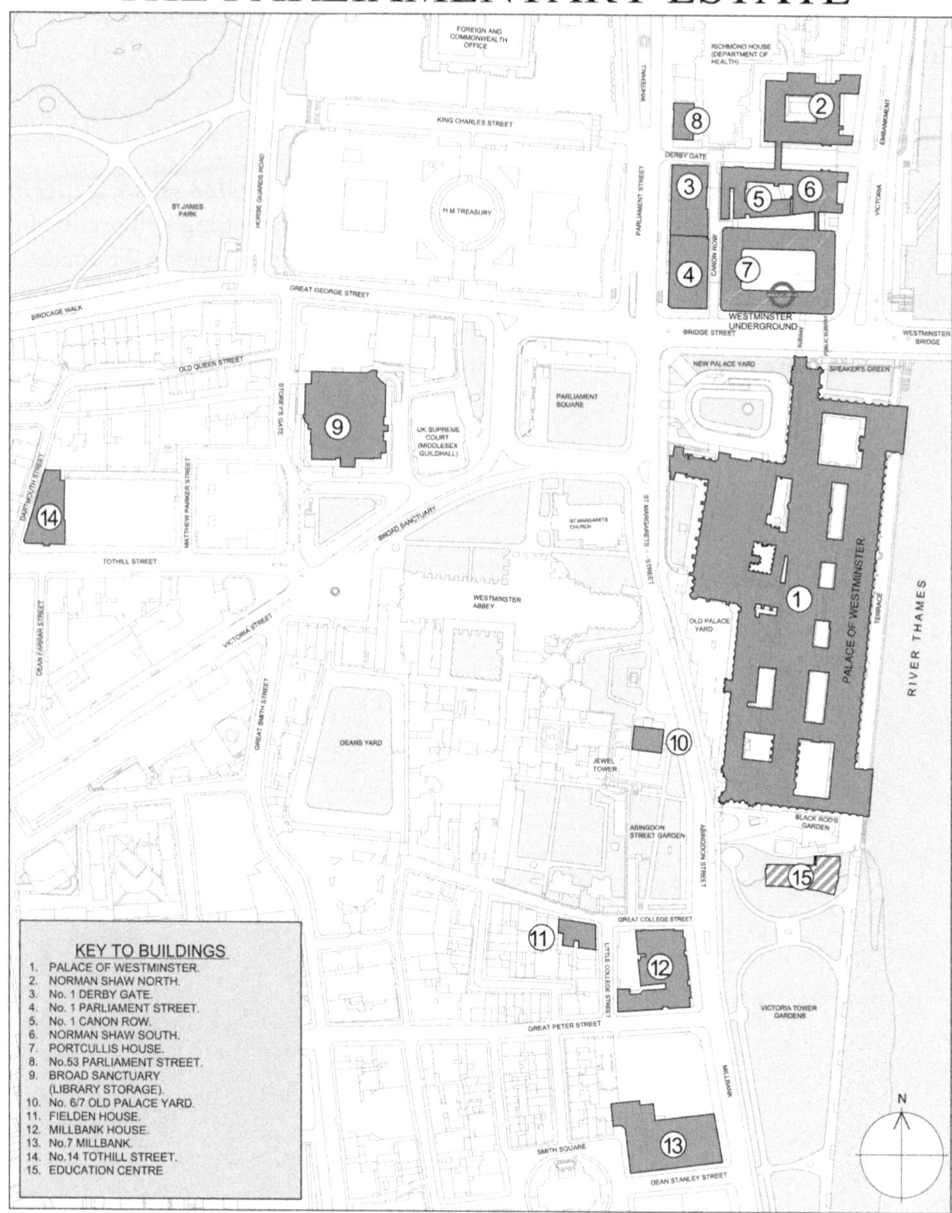

The Parliamentary Estate and its surroundings

Source: Copyright House of Commons, 2014. Artwork by Jonathan Rix

2

Who is in Parliament?

The Commons

The size of the Commons

Even in the early fifteenth century, there were more than 250 members of the Commons – two knights from each of 37 counties, two citizens or burgesses from each of the 80 or so cities and boroughs, and 14 members from the Cinque Ports. More were steadily added by statute and royal charter, and by 1673 the membership of the House – at that time only from England and Wales – stood at 513. Union with Scotland in 1707 added 45 members, and a further 100 came from Ireland with the Union of 1801, making 658.

The House grew to 670 members in 1885, and to 707 – the most at any stage – in 1918. Irish independence reduced the numbers to 615 by 1922. The upward trend during the rest of the twentieth century produced a House of 659 members by 1997; but the post-devolution reduction in Scottish seats at Westminster from 72 to 59 meant that there were 646 members of the Commons in 2005. This was increased to 650 by the boundary review that took effect at the 2010 general election. The number sitting for constituencies in England is now 533: 59 in Scotland, 40 in Wales and 18 in Northern Ireland. There is thus one MP for every 100,415 people (or for every 72,067 people entitled to vote).

Too big?

Even for a population of some 65.6 million, this is a large House. By comparison, the Italian Camera dei Deputati has 630 members, or one for every 94,197 people, the French Assemblée nationale has 577 members (one for every 112,715 people) and the Spanish Congreso de los Diputados has 350 members (one for every 132,468 people). A comparison with the US House of Representatives is even more striking

(435 members, one for every 749,256 people) but of course in the USA representation at state level also has to be taken into account.

A big House of Commons has some disadvantages – at least from the point of view of the individual member. Parliamentary time is at a premium. The backbencher must compete with colleagues to ask questions or to be called in debate, and the individual's share of both influence and parliamentary resources is less than in a smaller House.

However, from the point of view of the electorate, a large House means that an individual MP represents a relatively small number of people. An MP's focus on the constituency is very sharp, not only because it is a power base, and he or she must woo the electors to be re-elected, but also because, especially in the social media age, the expectations of members to respond quickly and constructively to their constituents' problems are greater than ever. Your chances of engaging an MP's attention on an issue are much greater if it is something that directly affects his or her constituency. The close and valued relationship between a single MP and a single constituency has undoubtedly been a factor in opposition to some forms of proportional representation.

In addition, the historically large numbers of MPs have led to a large number of ministers. Following the June 2017 general election, 93 ministers sat in the Commons out of a total of 118 in both Houses. (The maximum number of MPs who may be ministers is set by law at 95; the total number of ministerial salaries that may be paid is 109, so there were nine unpaid ministers.) This means that many individual members get ministerial experience (although the proportion – 14 per cent – might well be the same in a smaller House). A large House provides more backbenchers to undertake the scrutiny of government through select committee work; in the 2016–17 session, 382 MPs were members of select committees.

The constituencies

Legislation passed under the coalition government in 2011 sought to reduce the size of the House of Commons to 600 members. Four Boundary Commissions, one for each part of the UK, keep under review the size, boundaries and numbers of parliamentary constituencies, making recommendations for changes which then require parliamentary approval before implementation. The Parliamentary Voting System and Constituencies Act 2011 required the Commissions to ensure in their recommendations that the House of Commons has 600 members and that the electorate of each constituency is within 5 per cent of the electoral quota for the UK (currently 74,769). Four island constituencies (Orkney and Shetland, Western Isles and two seats on the Isle of Wight) are exempt from this parity rule.

However, the changes have not been implemented and it is not clear that they will be. The anticipated reduction in the number of constituencies, along with significant changes to constituency boundaries, was postponed in 2013 after a disagreement between the two parties in the then coalition government. Following the publication of revised proposed boundary changes in October 2017, the issue remains disputed. The Labour and Liberal Democrat parties are opposed to the proposed changes, citing amongst other reasons the fact that significant powers would be 'repatriated' to

Westminster following Brexit. The increasing size of the House of Lords (see page 399 below) is another argument put forward against reducing the number of MPs. Following the consultation final recommendations, on the basis of 600 seats, will be put forward. However, given the reaction of the opposition parties to the proposals being consulted on, it is far from certain that Parliament will approve those final recommendations. Despite an unambiguous legislative intent to reduce the number of MPs to 600 in the 2011 Act, the House could therefore still end up with 650 MPs after the next election.

One of the objectives of the Parliamentary Voting System and Constituencies Act 2011 was to create greater uniformity in the number of people represented in each constituency. In 2017 the largest constituency was the Isle of Wight at 107,572. The smallest was Na h-Eileanan an Iar (the Western Isles of Scotland) at 20,887, where the identity of the islands is so distinct that combining them with a mainland constituency is not an option. Those constituencies are statistical outliers; their unusual circumstances are acknowledged by the exemptions in the 2011 legislation for them, and Orkney and Shetland, to be within 5 per cent of the electoral quota. However, there are still significant discrepancies within the 646 'non-exempt' constituencies, with Wirral West, for example having 53,877 electors and North West Cambridgeshire 90,993. It was disparities in the size of constituencies such as these that encouraged changes to the electoral quota per constituency.

The boundary review that was not implemented would have changed the constituency boundaries much more than previous reviews; in the fifth review, implemented at the 2010 general election, only 77 of the 533 constituencies in England were changed by 50 per cent or more; in the sixth review, 203 constituencies would have changed to this extent. The 2017 proposed changes would also have a significant effect, with nine seats being created, 50 current seats disappearing and many more being redrawn.

The time-lag between population change and constituency change has in the past benefited the Labour Party. In 2010 the average size of the electorate in Labour seats was 68,487, compared with 72,418 in Conservative seats. The changes to the rules were seen as a means of addressing this difference. (It was estimated that if the 2017 proposed changes had been in place at the time of the 2017 general election, the Conservative Party would have achieved an overall majority of four seats.)

The candidates

Anyone may stand for election to the Commons if he or she is a British subject or citizen of the Republic of Ireland, is aged 18 or over, and is not disqualified. Those disqualified include those subject to bankruptcy restrictions orders (or, in Scotland, those against whom sequestration of estates is awarded), people sentenced to more than one year's imprisonment, members of the House of Lords (but hereditary peers not sitting in the Lords are eligible; one, Viscount Thurso, was an MP from 2001 to 2015, and two who left the Commons in 2010, Douglas Hogg and Michael Ancram, succeeded to peerages while MPs but did not lose their seats) and holders of offices listed in the House of Commons Disqualification Act 1975. These last, often described as those 'holding an office of profit under the Crown', include civil servants, judges, members of the regular armed forces and police, some local government officers and members of some public bodies.

Independent candidates are occasionally elected. The first for many years was Martin Bell as the 'anti-sleaze' candidate in Tatton in 1997, followed by Richard Taylor in Wyre Forest in 2001 on a platform of saving Kidderminster Hospital (beating a sitting member, who was also a minister, by the large majority of 17,630). Remarkably, Taylor held the seat in 2005, although with a reduced majority of 5,250, but lost in 2010 to the Conservatives. But these results are very much the exception. Bell was a respected former TV journalist, Taylor a local doctor, and each had a clear-cut campaign issue with striking local relevance.

Two other candidates caused upsets in the 2005 general election. Peter Law stood as an independent in Blaenau Gwent after the imposition of an all-women shortlist prevented him standing as a Labour candidate, and won with a majority of 9,121; and in Bethnal Green and Bow, the maverick former Labour MP George Galloway, who had founded his own 'Respect' party but was in effect an independent, beat the sitting Labour MP Oona King by 823 votes. Galloway lost his seat at the 2010 general election but returned to the Commons at a by-election in Bradford West in 2012, standing as a Respect candidate; he lost the seat in 2015. In 2010, shortly before the general election, Sylvia Hermon (Lady Hermon) left the Ulster Unionist Party but retained her North Down seat in the election as an Independent (and has continued to do so since).

Normally, you need to be the adopted candidate of a major political party to have a realistic chance of election to the House of Commons. In the 2017 general election there were 3,304 candidates altogether; 1,898 of these were from the three major UK-wide parties. UKIP and the Green Party fielded hundreds of candidates each and the SNP, Plaid Cymru and the various Northern Ireland-based parties contested all (or almost all) of the seats in their respective nations. A few dozen parties were represented by a smattering of candidates – for example, the Monster Raving Loony Party (12 candidates), the Pirate Party (10) and the BNP (10). There were 187 independent candidates, as well as 34 'parties' represented by just one candidate (including the Church of the Militant Elvis Party (195 votes), the Space Navies Party (81) and the Realists' Party (61)).

In 2017 Caroline Lucas held the Brighton Pavilion seat, which she originally won in 2010, when she became the first Green Party candidate elected to the House. Douglas Carswell stood down in Clacton: having originally been elected as a Conservative in Harwich (2005), then Clacton (2010), Carswell 'crossed the floor' to become a UKIP MP in 2014, triggering a by-election, which he won as a UKIP candidate. Re-elected as a UKIP candidate in the 2015 election, Carswell then quit the party in March 2017, serving briefly as an independent MP before deciding not to contest the general election.

Candidates are chosen by the party organisations in the constituency concerned. Commonly both the Labour and Conservative parties give a committee of the local party the power to draw up a shortlist of five or six candidates from as many as 100 names, who will usually also be on the party's 'approved' list. Candidates are interviewed at a meeting of local party members and then selected by eliminating ballots.

However, the central party organisations have considerable power, and it is possible for them to impose their own shortlists. The Conservative Party did this in 2017, when the unexpected election gave little time to select candidates where there were vacancies; in the Labour Party, the central National Executive Committee selected candidates, with local branches losing their usual powers due to the 'exceptional general election circumstances'. The Labour Party uses all-women shortlists for some seats. Following the election of Jeremy Corbyn as Leader of the Labour Party there have been various proposals for strengthening the influence of 'rank and file' members. There has been speculation that a review of the party's internal democracy will propose changes to the process of candidate selection to give individual members more of a say. All parties have tended to exercise greater control over by-election selections, where candidates usually have to be able to withstand extensive media coverage.

The selection of candidates is thus normally subject to local control. Although no procedure as elaborate as the primary system in the United States of America has evolved, the Conservative Party experimented with holding primaries for some candidate selections during the run-up to the 2010 general election – a process that was not widely repeated for subsequent elections. However, unlike in the USA, it is not necessary for a would-be MP to have considerable personal means. The election deposit is £500 and is forfeited only if the candidate receives less than 5 per cent of the votes cast. In any case, it is funded by the party, as are most of the candidate's expenses (see page 28). Once elected to the Commons, an MP can usually expect to remain the party's candidate at the next election. However, sometimes sitting MPs are deselected: Robert Wareing (Labour) in Liverpool, West Derby, was deselected before the 2010 general election. Anne McIntosh (Conservative, Thirsk and Malton) and Tim Yeo (Conservative, South Suffolk) were deselected before the 2015 election; after their local associations' executives refused to endorse them, all association members voted on whether they should be re-selected. The Labour Party requires sitting MPs to be re-selected by a 'trigger ballot' of their local party, although that process has resulted in the overwhelming majority of sitting MPs being re-selected, leading to pressure for a more testing mandatory reselection process.

Elections: when?

General elections used to be held after Parliament had been dissolved, either by royal proclamation on the advice of the Prime Minister or because the maximum life of a parliament – five years – had expired. Between 1945 and 2010 no parliament ran its full term, although the 1992–97 parliament came within a fortnight of doing so. The average length of parliaments between 1945 and 2010 was a little over three years and seven months. This contrasted with the fixed terms of the US Congress or the practice in countries such as Belgium or Germany, where parliaments are dissolved early only in exceptional circumstances. The ending of a parliament by royal proclamation, in effect, by decision of the Prime Minister, gave him or her a tactical advantage in the timing of the election, although this did not profit the party in government in June 1970 or February 1974. The coalition government in 2011 introduced the Fixed-term Parliaments Act, which ended the prerogative power of dissolution and instead stipulated that a parliament runs for a five-year fixed term, unless a parliamentary procedure for an early election was used. A general election duly took place on 7 May 2015, as stated by the Act. It was expected that the next election would take place five years later, but on 19 April 2017 Parliament voted by the necessary two-thirds majority for an early election, which took place on 8 June 2017. Unless there is another early election, the next one will be on 5 May 2022. We examine the Fixed-term Parliaments Act 2011 in more detail in Chapter 5 (page 125).

A by-election takes place when a seat becomes vacant because the MP dies or is otherwise no longer eligible to sit (see 'The candidates', page 23). A by-election is not required if an MP changes party, although there have been recent instances where MPs changing parties have voluntarily triggered by-elections. An MP cannot, in terms, resign from the House but, in effect, does so by accepting one of the 'offices of profit' of steward or bailiff of Her Majesty's three Chiltern Hundreds of Stoke, Desborough and Burnham, or of the manor of Northstead, which are in the gift of the Chancellor of the Exchequer. These are not real jobs but purely symbolic offices used to allow an MP to stand down. Unusually, in 2011 Sinn Fein's Gerry Adams sought to resign by writing to the Speaker. Adams was made steward and bailiff of the Manor of Northstead without his having requested the post or, indeed, having accepted it. He wished to leave the Commons and so was content with the disqualification that flowed from his 'appointment', but denied that he had, in fact, accepted an office of profit under the Crown.

By convention, a by-election normally takes place within three months of the vacancy occurring and the process ('moving the writ') is initiated by the Chief Whip of the party which had the seat (although any MP may move a writ). Until a new MP is elected, constituency matters are normally handled by a neighbouring MP of the same party.

Elections: who can vote?

The United Kingdom has a wider franchise than many for its parliamentary elections. There is no property qualification, since 1928 no sex discrimination, and there are voting rights for Britons who live abroad and choose to register. Commonwealth and Irish citizens resident in Britain are entitled to vote, and the only main categories excluded are those under 18, convicted offenders still in prison, people detained under mental health legislation for criminal activity, and members of the House of Lords. European Union citizens living in the UK who are not Irish or Commonwealth nationals may not vote in parliamentary elections. You do not have to have an address in order to vote; homeless people may make a 'declaration of local connection'. However, you must be on the register of parliamentary electors in a constituency. A new system of individual electoral registration was introduced in 2014; instead of being registered as part of a household, voters are now registered individually. The new system was introduced to ensure greater integrity of the register after some high-profile electoral fraud cases that involved false registration. Voters' personal details are verified by cross-checking against the Department for Work and Pensions' database. Critics of the new system have argued that more effort should be made to try to increase registration rates among the groups least likely to register; these include the young and those in privately rented accommodation who move frequently. The Electoral Commission estimated that around 1.1 million new voters registered in 2016, following a surge of registrations in the run-up to the referendum on EU membership. Nonetheless it is estimated that there are still several million people who should be on the electoral register but are not.

Elections: the timetable

The timetable between parliament being dissolved and a general election taking place was lengthened in 2013 from 17 to 25 working days. The timetable is set out in the Representation of the People Act 1983, as amended by the Electoral Registration and Administration Act 2013. In part, this was in response to the increasing practice of combining parliamentary with local elections, which already had a timetable of 25 days, but a longer timetable allows more time for late registration of voters and to apply for and receive and return postal votes.

In 2022, dissolution will need to take place on Monday 28 March to allow polling day to be on Thursday 5 May 2022, the date fixed for the next general election by the Fixed-term Parliaments Act 2011. In the past, the date of the general election was decided by the Prime Minister and, although the timetable for the election was much shorter, at 17 days, Parliament was frequently prorogued before dissolution.

In 2017, the Prime Minister announced her intention to call the general election on 18 April 2017, and thereafter the timetable ran as follows:

Wednesday 19 April 2017	House of Commons voted by necessary two-thirds majority that there should be an early election
Tuesday 25 April 2017	Royal Proclamation set polling day as 8 June 2017
Thursday 27 April 2017	Parliament prorogued
Wednesday 3 May 2017	Parliament dissolved
Friday 5 May 2017	Royal Proclamation summoned meeting of new parliament on 13 June 2017
Thursday 8 June 2017	Polling day
Tuesday 13 June 2017	Parliament met to swear in members and, in the Commons, to elect a Speaker
Wednesday 21 June 2017	Opening of Parliament and Queen's Speech

Election expenses

We have seen that personal wealth is not a prerequisite for standing for Parliament. Indeed, however well-off a candidate or party may be, the law limits what may be spent in each constituency during an election. The general election limits in 2017 were £8,700 plus 9p per elector in a county constituency (that is, one which is partly rural) and £8,700 plus 6p per elector in a borough constituency. For a by-election, the overall limit is £100,000.

The total of a party's campaign expenditure over the 365 days before a general election is £30,000 times the number of constituencies that party is contesting: a maximum of £19.5 million, if all 650 constituencies are contested. A general election also involves public expenditure; the government has stated that the cost to the public purse of the 2017 election was £140 million.

In 2014 new limits were introduced on third-party campaigning at general elections, and a wider range of activities was counted under the limits. The level at which third parties must register with the Electoral Commission, providing accounts and so on, is £20,000 in England, or £10,000 in Scotland, Wales and Northern Ireland. The maximum expenditure by non-party campaigners at UK general elections is £319,800 in England, £55,400 in Scotland, £44,000 in Wales, and £46,100 in Northern Ireland.

Voting patterns in the 2017 general election

In the 2017 general election, 32,204,124 votes were cast. Of those 28,886,403 (89.7 per cent) were for one of the three main UK-wide parties.

These parties share the vote with nationalist parties in Scotland and Wales, and with a variety of smaller parties across the UK. The Labour and Liberal Democrat parties do

Table 2.1 Voting patterns in the 2017 general election

Party	Votes received	Vote share (%)	Seats won	Seats in proportion to votes received
Conservative	13,636,684	42.3	317	275
Labour	12,877,858	40.0	262	260
Liberal Democrat	2,371,861	7.4	12	48
Scottish National Party	977,568	3.0	35	20
UK Independence Party	594,068	1.8	0	12
Green	525,665	1.6	1	11
Democratic Unionist Party	292,316	0.9	10	6
Sinn Féin	238,915	0.7	7	5
Plaid Cymru	164,466	0.5	4	3
Social Democratic and Labour Party	95,419	0.3	0	2

Note: Seats do not sum to 650 because two seats are not reflected in the table: Buckingham (held by the Speaker, John Bercow) and North Down (held by the Independent MP, Lady Sylvia Hermon)

not stand in Northern Ireland, although the Labour Party enjoys a close relationship with the Social Democratic and Labour Party, whose MPs informally accept the Labour whip. The Conservative Party historically had close ties to the Ulster Unionist Party (which failed to win any Westminster seats in 2017), including fielding joint candidates in 2010. Since then, the party has fielded its own candidates (as NI Conservatives) in 16 of the 18 constituencies in Northern Ireland in 2015 and in seven constituencies in 2017 (winning 3,895 votes and no seats).

The number of votes received, share of vote and number of seats won for the 10 most successful parties (in terms of numbers of votes) in the 2017 election are in Table 2.1. The table also shows the number of seats that each party would have won had the numbers of MPs corresponded exactly to the votes cast.

For the second time in three general elections, no party gained enough seats for a working majority. Following negotiations, the Conservatives, the largest party with 317 seats, entered into a 'supply and confidence' agreement with the Democratic Unionist Party (DUP), with 10 seats, in order to secure a majority in the Commons.

First past the post and calls for reform

Electoral law on the timing of campaigns is clear, the franchise is wide and elections are frequent. But whether an election result is representative and properly reflects the views of the voters depends on the voting system. The British system is based on the relative majority method, usually called first past the post (FPTP). The voter marks a ballot paper with one X against the name of his or her favoured candidate – hedging bets with two Xs will mean that the ballot paper is spoiled and will not be counted – and the candidate with the most votes wins. In this system there are no prizes for coming second; it also means that the proportions of MPs of each party are not the same as the parties' shares of the votes cast across the nation as a whole. It has the merit of creating clear winners and losers, and giving the elected MP a decisive link with the local electorate. The system is, in essence, descended from the historical composition of the Commons as a set of local representatives.

Calls for reform of the voting system and for its replacement with a system of proportional representation – where the number of seats awarded to a party more closely reflects the total number of votes received by that party – have been made for many decades. Those arguing for change say that FPTP unfairly rewards some parties with more seats than their share of the vote alone would merit, while other parties have fewer seats than they would be entitled to if seats reflected votes cast proportionately. So, as Table 2.1 above shows, in 2017 the Conservatives won 317 seats while their share of the vote would have translated to only 275 seats under an entirely proportionate system. The Liberal Democrats, on the other hand, won 12 seats, but would have been entitled to 48 under a proportionate system. UKIP, which won no seats, would have merited 12. So while the headline result of the election would have been similar under a fully proportionate system – no party would have had an overall majority – the composition of any deal or coalition formed to establish a working majority might have looked very different to that which actually came about in June 2017.

The other side of the story is what is sometimes known as the 'wasted vote'. For example, in 2017 the constituency of Lanark and Hamilton East was within the grasp of three parties. The result was:

SNP	16,444 (32.6%)
Conservative	16,178 (32.1%)
Labour	16,084 (31.9%)
Liberal Democrat	1,214 (2.4%)
UK Independence Party	550 (1.1%)

Angela Crawley won the seat for the SNP with only 32.6 per cent of the votes cast; 34,026 people voted for other parties, but their votes were not reflected in the result. However, the *potential* power of each voter in Lanark and Hamilton East (by switching parties as a 'floating voter') was much greater than that of a voter in Liverpool Walton who did not wish to vote for the Labour candidate. There Dan Carden (Labour) won the safest seat in the country with 85.7 per cent of the vote – 36,175 votes compared with his closest rival, the Conservative, with 3,624 votes. In the country as a whole, the different effect of votes cast for the three main parties was striking. It took 197,000 votes to elect a Liberal Democrat MP, but only 43,000 to elect a Conservative MP and 49,000 to elect a Labour MP. Despite receiving almost 600,000 votes nationally, UKIP did not gain a single MP.

One of the strongest arguments advanced in favour of first past the post is that it is a simple system – no preferences, or second and third choices – which is easily understood by voters. The other main arguments traditionally put forward– it usually produces clear results, with one party having a strong mandate to govern; it avoids 'smoke-filled rooms', where political choices are made by negotiation between parties after an election, where deals are made and policies agreed that have not been put before the electorate – are less convincing given that the 2010 and 2017 elections resulted in just that kind of deal-making. Proponents of FPTP might counter that adopting a system of proportional representation would almost inevitably lead to such back-room deal-making after every election.

In 2010, when no party had enough seats to govern on its own, a series of negotiations between the parties resulted in the Conservatives (as the party with the most seats) forming a coalition with the Liberal Democrats, with a formal coalition agreement and 'Programme for Government', and ministers from both parties serving alongside each other. The Liberal Democrats made it a condition of entering into the coalition government that there should be a referendum on a proportional electoral system: the alternative vote (AV) method, also known as ranked choice voting. Under it, the voter ranks candidates in order of preference; a candidate with more than half the first preferences is elected outright, but otherwise in successive rounds of counting the lowest-scoring candidates are eliminated and their preferences redistributed among the surviving candidates. The referendum was held on 5 May 2011 when voters rejected a move to AV by a decisive 67.9 per cent to 32.1 per cent. The No vote was in the majority in every UK region and was above 70 per cent in five of the nine English regions. Out of 440 vote counting areas, the No vote was in the majority in 430. Of the ten areas that had a majority of Yes votes, six were in London.

Are the members of the Commons representative?

Despite a local democratic element in the choice of candidates, the MPs who sit in the Commons are not a microcosm of the electorate as a whole.

Age

The House of Commons is overwhelmingly middle-aged. The average age of MPs elected to the House in 2017 was 50.5; in fact the average age of MPs has remained remarkably constant since 1979 (when it was 49.6). In the House elected in 2017, 387 MPs were aged between 40 and 59 (59 per cent of the total compared with approximately 30 per cent of the population of the UK as a whole). Fourteen MPs were younger than 30 when elected in 2017, and 28 aged 70 or over. The youngest MP elected in 2017 was Mhairi Black, aged 22, and the oldest was Dennis Skinner, aged 85. The average age of the House is perhaps not surprising. Few young aspiring politicians are lucky enough to be selected for a winnable seat; constituency parties often prefer candidates with some experience outside politics. Nevertheless, although the average age of the population as a whole is rising, the age profile of the Commons may be a factor in distancing younger voters from the political process.

Occupation and education

Of those elected in 2017, 29 per cent of MPs had been privately educated, compared to seven per cent of the UK population. Fifty-one per cent went to comprehensive schools and 18 per cent to state grammar schools. Eighty-eight per cent of SNP MPs attended a comprehensive school, compared to 67 per cent of Labour MPs and 38 per cent of Conservative MPs. Eighty-nine per cent of MPs are graduates and 23 per cent studied at Oxbridge (compared to an estimated 1 per cent of the UK population).

The vast majority of MPs worked in white collar jobs before being elected. In 2015, 31 per cent of MPs had previously been in one of the professions, with 14.2 per cent having been lawyers. Just over 30 per cent of MPs had previously been business people, an increase from 22 per cent in 1979. However, perhaps the most striking rise is that of the 'professional politician': in 1979, just 3 per cent of MPs defined their previous job as 'politician/political organiser'; in 2015, that figure was 17 per cent. Conversely, in 1979, 16 per cent of MPs had previously been employed in manual jobs; by 2015, only 3 per cent of MPs had such jobs before being elected.

There are many reasons why certain occupations produce a disproportionate number of MPs while others are less well represented. Other than those in very safe seats, MPs do not have secure jobs in Parliament and may want to retain part-time work in their old professions – something criticised by those who believe that election as an MP with a salary of more than £77,000 demands full-time attention. Some jobs are communicative and more likely to appeal to those who want to enter politics. In some jobs it is impossible to devote large amounts of time to politics – normally essential if one intends to stand for Parliament. And despite the fact that an MP's pay is more than two-and-a-half times the national average wage of £27,271, some who might consider standing would have to take a substantial pay cut.

Women in Parliament

After decades of campaigning, culminating in the suffragette movement, the bill to allow women to stand for Parliament was passed on the day that Parliament was dissolved for the 1918 general election. Paradoxically, it allowed women to be candidates at the age of 21, although women did not then have the right to vote until the age of 30 (reduced to the same age as men, then 21, in 1928).

The first woman elected to the Commons, Countess Markievicz, was elected in 1918 for the St Patrick's division of Dublin as a Sinn Féin member but, in protest against British policy on Ireland, never took her seat. It was ironic that the first woman to do so, Viscountess Astor, who was elected at a by-election on 15 November 1919, had never campaigned for women's rights. Since 1918, 489 women have been elected as members of the House of Commons. The numbers of women MPs remained very low for 70 years, passing 5 per cent only at the 1987 general election, rising to

The Labour Party benches, 2017

Source: Copyright House of Commons, 2017. Photography by Jessica Taylor

9.2 per cent in 1992 and sharply to 18.2 per cent in 1997, the steep increase resulting primarily from the use of all-women shortlists by the Labour Party. The 208 women elected in the 2017 general election was the most ever – 32 per cent of all MPs – but still a low proportion compared to women making up 51 per cent of the population. The devolved parliaments do better: just over one-third (35 per cent) of members in the Scottish Parliament are women, and 42 per cent of members of the National Assembly for Wales are female.

Data from the Inter-Parliamentary Union show the proportion of women in the lower (or single) House of different countries' legislatures following the most recent elections. The UK is ranked 39th. Rwanda is first, followed by Bolivia, Cuba and Iceland. Five countries in the ranking have no women in their lower or single House, while 31 have fewer than 10 per cent women.

Ethnic minorities

There were non-white members of the House of Commons a century or more ago (a Liberal, a Conservative and a Communist, who each sat for brief periods between 1892 and 1929) but, despite the substantial immigration into the United Kingdom from its former colonies in the West Indies and from the former Indian Empire in the 1950s and later, no representative of these communities was elected to Parliament until 1987 (although several had been created life peers). Efforts have been made in all parties to nominate ethnic minority candidates, but not with great success. In the 1992 parliament there were six MPs who described themselves as being from an ethnic minority. This increased to nine in the 1997 parliament; 12 (1.8 per cent) in the 2001 parliament; 15 (2.3 per cent) in 2005; 27 (4.2 per cent) in 2010; and 41 (6.3 per cent) in 2015. After the 2017 general election there were 52 minority ethnic MPs in the House of Commons: 8 per cent of the total. The UK population is becoming increasingly diverse in terms of ethnicity and the 2011 census showed 18 per cent of the UK population reporting a non-white background, compared with 8 per cent 10 years earlier. However, despite increases in the number of minority ethnic MPs over the last two decades, the diversity of MPs remains disproportionate to the population as a whole. If the non-white population were represented proportionally in the House of Commons, there would be around 117 minority ethnic MPs.

LGBT MPs

In 2017, 45 openly LGBT people were elected to the House of Commons, equating to 6.9 per cent of all MPs. (Figures for the general population are disputed: according to the Office for National Statistics, 2 per cent of people identified as LGB in 2016; the campaigning group Stonewall says that the figure is likely to be between 5 and 7 per cent, as many people do not come out.) When 32 LGBT MPs were elected in 2015 the House of Commons was reported to have the highest number of openly LGBT MPs of any legislature in the world.

Does it matter?

In one sense, it can be argued that it matters little that the make-up of the membership of the House of Commons does not reflect the population as a whole. Every MP is there to represent all the people in a constituency, whether they voted for the MP, or one of the other candidates, or did not vote at all. A man, or a woman, or someone from an ethnic minority, or a single parent, may perhaps be thought to have a better understanding of the outlook of men, of women, of ethnic minorities, or of single parents. Nevertheless, the MP's job is to represent the diversity of the people in the constituency in a conscientious and professional way. Understanding your constituents is part of doing the job well, whether or not you have a particular affinity with one group or another. However, recognising that the House of Commons failed to reflect the population it served in some respects, steps have been taken in recent years to help broaden the membership of the House. For example, a Speaker's Conference on parliamentary representation was established in 2008 following a proposal by Gordon Brown as Prime Minister which made a range of recommendations about steps which could be taken by the parties, the House administration and others to increase diversity. The most important recommendation to be acted on was probably the extension of the ability to use all-women shortlists until 2030, legislated for in the Equality Act 2010. In 2016 Speaker Bercow convened the Commons Reference Group on Representation and Inclusion, which is overseeing the implementation of many recommendations made by Professor Sarah Childs in her *Good Parliament* report, with the aim of making the House more representative and effective.

The reputation of Parliament

Another factor is how the House of Commons is seen by the people it represents. For most of the three decades before the 2010 election, from the victory of Margaret Thatcher's Conservatives in 1979, and then from 1997 when the Labour Party won the first of three consecutive large majorities, a powerful executive and a large parliamentary majority for one party conditioned the perception of Parliament's powers and what it can do for the citizen. (The exception was the 1992–97 parliament, when an overall majority of 21 for the Conservatives was gradually whittled down through defections and by-election defeats until the government lost its overall majority.) Since 2010 three general elections have resulted in, first, a coalition, followed by a government in 2015 with a small overall majority of 12, and in 2017 a Conservative government with no overall majority which requires the support of the DUP. The absence of a large majority, combined with greater independence of mind among MPs, means that recent governments have not been able to assume that the House will back their proposals: however, it is not clear how that refined relationship, and the relative strengthening of the House's hand against the government's, has affected public perceptions.

The expenses scandal of 2009 dealt a savage blow to the reputation of Parliament, but most insiders saw the 2010 election as a turning point. There were 227 new MPs elected – some 35 per cent of the House. They knew what they were getting into, and came to Westminster with an evident determination to do things differently. Unfortunately it is much quicker and easier to damage a reputation than to restore it. The behaviour, and thus the standing, of individual MPs is another factor. Financial, sexual and other allegations against individual MPs have been a sporadic feature of the political scene since at least the 1960s. Towards the end of the 1992–97 parliament John Major's 'back to basics' campaign was followed by a slew of sexual allegations against Conservative MPs in particular. More recently, in 2017, a range of claims of sexual and other harassment were made against MPs. The allegations resulted in ministerial resignations (including that of the Secretary of State for Defence) and calls for new structures to be put in place to protect staff working on the parliamentary estate. It is not yet clear whether the reputational damage of those claims will be confined to those against whom the allegations were made or whether there will be long-term damage to Parliament as an institution.

Despite increasing direct access to Parliament and its work, through Parliament's own outreach programme and through the BBC Parliament channel, webcasting on www.parliamentlive.tv and the parliamentary website www.parliament.uk, most people hear about Parliament through the media. *Political* reporting in the UK is of a generally high standard, but *parliamentary* reporting, requiring a knowledge of the institution and the way it works, is less so.

A useful barometer of public perceptions of Parliament is the Hansard Society's *Audit of Political Engagement*, which has tracked opinion over the last 14 years. The 2017 *Audit* showed high scores for Parliament being 'essential to democracy' (73 per cent of those polled) and that it 'debates and makes decision that matter to me' (56 per cent). However, only 28 per cent agreed that Parliament 'encourages public involvement in politics' and only 46 per cent saw Parliament as holding government to account – though this is a higher proportion than for the media (34 per cent), the judiciary (30 per cent) or the House of Lords (23 per cent). Fifty-three per cent said they were 'very' or 'fairly' interested in politics and 45 per cent thought they had at least 'a fair amount' of knowledge of Parliament. Fifty-nine per cent said that they were certain to vote in a general election. Turnout is not the only measure of public engagement with parliamentary politics, but it is probably the single most significant one.

Turnout: reconnecting Parliament with the people

In the general election of 1992, nearly 78 per cent of those registered to vote did so. The turnout fell to 71.5 per cent in 1997, perhaps because so many people assumed that Labour would win. Even though the result of the 2001 election was also widely predicted, the fall in the turnout – to just over 59 per cent – was dramatic. It was lower than at any election since the introduction of the universal franchise, and it seemed to signal a loss of interest in the country's central democratic institution. In the 2005 general election turnout went up slightly to 61.5 per cent. It rose again in the 2010 general election, to 65.1 per cent. The trend continued in 2015 and 2017 with turnouts of 66.2 per cent and 68.8 per cent respectively.

Despite turnout increasing in each of the last four elections, it remains lower than at any general election between 1922 and 1997. Does an adversarial style of politics put voters off? Did the generally large majorities of the three decades from 1979 make some people think their vote would make no difference? Will the 'shocks' to the political system of the Brexit vote and the election of Jeremy Corbyn as Leader of the Labour Party galvanise people to vote? If there has been no agreement on the reasons for fluctuations in turnout, there is no agreement on how the recent upward trend can be sustained. A change in the electoral system? No, because the 2011 referendum on the introduction of AV for parliamentary elections showed that the public had little enthusiasm for ditching the first-past-the-post system. More access to the political process, through online consultations, draft bills and the work of select committees? Fostering a wider understanding of what Parliament does and how it works? We will have a closer look at the possibilities in Chapter 12.

The Lords

Unlike the House of Commons, the House of Lords has never been representative. From its earliest times it was a chamber of individuals. Originally, members of the House were mainly the rich and powerful landed magnates on whom the king relied for his support and whose retainers would turn out to assist him (or when things went wrong, oppose him!) on the battlefield. From the late seventeenth century the House came to include members whose influence lay elsewhere – in money, commerce and political patronage. During the twentieth century this changed as new members were increasingly drawn from the ranks of former MPs and others without landed or moneyed connection – such as trade unionists, academics, former public servants, local councillors and so forth. But members continued to have one thing in common throughout the ages: they represented no one but themselves.

Current membership

Membership of the House in February 2018 was 793, exclusive of those members who were on leave of absence – that is to say, they had been granted leave of the House not to attend in response to their writs of summons to Parliament – and those who were disqualified. The categories of membership were as follows:

Archbishops and bishops	25
Life peers	677
Hereditary peers under the House of Lords Act 1999	91
Total	793

Let us take a closer look at these different categories. Who are they and how are they selected?

Archbishops and bishops

The Anglican Archbishops of Canterbury and York, the Bishops of Durham, London and Winchester and the 21 senior diocesan bishops from other dioceses of the Church of England sit in the House as 'Lords Spiritual'. All the other Lords are known as 'Lords Temporal'. In the mediaeval Parliament the Lords Spiritual (bishops and mitred abbots) made up about half the membership. Currently they represent about one in 30. Following the Church of England beginning to allow women bishops, until 2025 a vacancy among the 21 Lords Spiritual is filled by a woman bishop in preference to a more senior male bishop.

Only the Church of England is represented. The other established church, the Church of Scotland, has no nominees; nor do other religious denominations, non-Christian religions or the Anglican churches outside England. When the then Chief Rabbi, Lord Sacks, was made a peer in 2009, it was personal to him. When bishops retire, they lose their seat in the Lords, though it has been the practice to give life peerages to retiring Archbishops.

Life peers under the Life Peerages Act 1958

Most members of the House of Lords are life peers, appointed to the House under the Life Peerages Act 1958. Under this legislation men and women are created peers for life and the titles they hold cease on their death. Until the passing of the Act, the House was a largely hereditary institution but the arrival of life peers changed that: within a short time new hereditary peerages had virtually ceased, and the activities of the House were much invigorated. Following the exclusion of all but 92 of the hereditary members in 1999, the House has in effect become a predominantly appointed senate-like body, unlimited in number. In general, temporal peers remain members until they die, thus the average age of the House is 69 years.

The granting of life peerages allowed members to be appointed from a wide range of backgrounds and facilitated greater diversity by gender and ethnic background. The professional background of new appointments to the House since 1958, based on the 10 years preceding their appointment, is as follows:

Table 2.2 Professional background of new appointments to the House of Lords since 1958

	1958–97	1997–2010	2010–14
MPs	38.3	28.0	24.7
Other politics/unions	4.5	9.4	16.7
Industry/trade	14.1	14.7	14.2
Military	1.4	1.4	1.9
Public service	6.1	12.4	8.6
Law	9.6	7.3	4.3
Academic/medical	10.4	7.8	4.9
Voluntary	2.3	5.0	5.6
Local government	4.2	3.6	6.8
Other	9.1	10.4	12.4

Closer scrutiny shows a continuing predominance of national and local politicians and their advisers among new members: in the period to 1997 they numbered 47 per cent and in the period from the 2010 general election to June 2014, 48.2 per cent. Recently there have been proportionately fewer former MPs, which goes against conventional perceptions. And there has been a falling off in appointments from the professions, which represented 20 per cent of new appointments in the period to 1997, and only 9.2 per cent between 2010 and 2014. Professional diversity in the House clearly has its boundaries. Gender diversity has certainly improved in recent years. In 2005, 18 per cent of members were women; by 2017 this had risen to 26 per cent. Figures are not maintained on ethnic diversity but a much more ethnically diverse chamber than ever before is visible on all benches.

How are members of the House of Lords appointed? The power to create new peerages belongs to the Crown, but in effect is exercised by the Prime Minister. She is the gatekeeper who decides when a list of new members is announced and the number of names it contains. By convention other party leaders are asked to make nominations from among their own party faithful – a reality recognised formally by the Prime Minister in February 2018. This gives party leaders considerable patronage. Until relatively recently it was possible to separate these lists into different categories – dissolution and resignation lists, honours lists and 'working peers' lists. But the award of a peerage through the honours system is now rare: neither Tony Blair nor Gordon Brown had resignation lists. There was a dissolution list of former MPs of all parties following the 2015 election but not after the 2017 election. It is fair to say that at present all lists of new members are for 'working peers', given the parties' presumption that members will attend regularly. Occasionally a single person may be nominated – for example, if he or she is required to serve as a minister in the Lords.

In addition to these party-political nominations, a non-statutory House of Lords Appointments Commission makes recommendations for non-political (i.e. crossbench) members and vets for propriety all other nominations. Following the establishment of the commission in May 2000, a public nomination system was launched. In 2001, 15 'people's peers' were announced, with a further seven in 2004. The rate of nomination has now settled at two new crossbenchers a year. In addition, the Prime Minister can award a non-political peerage in recognition of public service – for example, when a Chief of the Defence Staff or Cabinet Secretary retires. Prime Ministers have limited themselves to 10 of these appointments in a Parliament. In 2014 the then Prime Minister widened the eligibility criteria for such public service peerages, resulting in (among others) the appointment of a distinguished former Clerk of the House of Commons. However, in February 2018 the Prime Minister stated that there would be no automatic entitlement to a peerage for any holder of high office in public life – a strong hint that those office holders who previously could expect a peerage on retirement could no longer do so.

There is in this process no attempt to pace the introduction of new members over time and, among those who make the nominations, no concept of what constitutes an ideal size for the House. As a result there are times, particularly following a change of administration, when the Lords must absorb large numbers of new members as supporters of the outgoing regime are rewarded and supporters of the incoming regime are found places. Thus, in the months following the 2010 election, 111 party nominees became members.

Life peers under the Appellate Jurisdiction Act 1876

Before the establishment of the Supreme Court as a separate institution in 2009, the House of Lords acted as the final court of appeal for the whole of the United Kingdom in civil cases and for England, Wales and Northern Ireland in criminal cases. The judges who heard these appeals, mostly sitting as a committee called the Appellate Committee, were specially appointed to the House as Lords of Appeal in Ordinary, or Law Lords, under the 1876 Act. These were the first life peers and they were able to engage in the wider parliamentary functions of the House too, though latterly many of them did not. In 2009 the serving Law Lords who became Justices of the Supreme Court were disqualified from sitting under the Constitutional Reform Act 2005. But, on retirement, that disqualification ceases and they can resume their seats. And of course the retired Law Lords never left. They are a dying breed as the 1876 Act has now been repealed, but there are currently 13 members in this category. It has yet to be decided whether Justices of the Supreme Court who were not already peers will become so on their retirement. Some are pressing for that in order to maintain the level of legal expertise in the House, but the attendance record of retired judges is variable.

Hereditary peers

Until the passing of the Life Peerages Act 1958 all members of the House of Lords, except for the bishops and Lords of Appeal in Ordinary, were hereditary. The principle of a hereditary peerage is that, at some historical point, an individual is created a peer or lord (in one of the different ranks of dukes, marquesses, earls, viscounts or barons), and the legal document conferring that peerage (the 'letters patent') stipulates that his heirs (normally only the males) may inherit his title and with it the right to sit in the House of Lords. Some peerages descend through the female line, as well as the male, and after 1963 women holders of hereditary peerages were also able to take their seats in the Lords.

Current membership of the House of Lords includes up to 92 hereditary peers who have seats as a result of the House of Lords Act 1999. This Act reformed the House's membership by excluding hereditary peers from sitting, but following an agreement between the government and the then Leader of the Opposition in the Lords, Viscount Cranborne, the bill was amended so that 75 hereditary members were excepted from the general provisions of the Act by election from among their own party or group, a further 15 by election by the whole House to serve as Deputy Speakers and committee chairmen, and two (the Earl Marshal and the Lord Great Chamberlain) *ex officio*.

These arrangements were expected to be transitional pending further reform of membership (see Chapter 12), but 19 years later they continue, sustained by a system for replacing deceased or retired hereditary members. From the passing of the House of Lords Act until the end of the 2001–02 session, vacancies among one of the 90 elected members were filled by the runners-up in the relevant category with the most votes. Two crossbench vacancies were filled in this way. Thereafter a system of by-elections came into force. Anyone in receipt of a writ before the passage of the Act, or anyone who has subsequently established a right to be included, may ask to be on the register of eligible candidates maintained by the Clerk of the Parliaments. The electors are the whole House in the case of the 15 Deputy Speakers or chairmen but only the hereditary peers in a party or group in respect of the 75 elected by party or group. The Labour Party currently has four excepted hereditary members, and thus three electors! The first such election was held in March 2003, using a preferential voting system, and elections have since become commonplace.

Before the 1999 Act the House of Lords was on paper at least a predominantly hereditary body, although in terms of regular attendance the hereditary element was just under 50 per cent. Now, the 92 hereditary members represent just 11 per cent of membership.

Attendance

We have already noted that members of the House are not representative. They are also part-time and do not always attend. Thus, in the 2016–17 session, of those eligible to attend, just over 40 per cent of members attended 75 per cent or more of the sittings; and 65 per cent attended 50 per cent or more of the sittings. Average daily attendance is as high as it has ever been, having risen steadily since 1999. The numbers for selected sessions between 1999 and 2017 are shown below:

Session	*Attendance*	*Rate of attendance*
1999–2000	352	51%
2004–05	388	56%
2010–12	475	59%
2015–16	497	62%
2016–17	484	60%

Rates of attendance vary widely by political group. In the 2016–17 session, the mean daily attendance per member was 67 per cent for Labour, 61 per cent for Conservatives, 75 per cent for Liberal Democrats and 50 per cent for crossbenchers. Thus two key facts emerge: first, attendance has generally increased; and second, there are still wide differences in individual behaviour, indicating that members interpret their obligations to attend Parliament in response to the Queen's writ of summons – and, indeed, the promises they may have made to their political sponsors or the Appointments Commission before their appointment – in a variety of ways. In many respects the rate of attendance matters more than the overall size of the House; it is only those who turn up who compete for limited speaking time in the House, use the facilities of the House and claim the daily allowance.

Politics

Although members of the House are not representative and are unelected, they are nearly all political animals. Most members of the House take a party whip, and of course most of the life peers owe their membership of the House to political patronage. The non-aligned crossbench members have political opinions on issues, and although none of them takes a party whip a small number have a remarkably consistent record of voting against (or sometimes for) the government. Party political allegiance in February 2018 is set out in Table 2.3.

It is apparent from Table 2.3 that the Conservatives have a plurality of members but nowhere near a majority. The Conservatives are far more dependent on excepted hereditary members than are Labour; if they were removed the numbers would be almost equal. The number of crossbenchers is significant – far higher than the number of independent members in most comparable legislatures. Perhaps most striking, though, is the number of Liberal Democrat members – 100, compared to its 12 MPs. This is a stark example of the effect of membership of the Lords generally being for life. The Liberal Democrats received 51 peerages when they were in government in the 2010–15 parliament (including the 2015 dissolution list), and those members remain in the House after their party's electoral fortunes have declined.

Party loyalty is much stronger in the House of Lords than is often imagined. Party cohesiveness, as measured in voting habits, is very high – about the same as in the Commons. Few rebel against the party whip. Thus, in whipped votes in the 2015–16 session the Labour Party achieved 96 per cent cohesion, the Conservatives 99 per cent and the Liberal Democrats 99.6 per cent. But what the whips cannot always enforce is attendance, and it is likely that peers who are unhappy with their party's policy on an issue simply do not turn up to vote for it, rather than rebel.

There is evidence that members' readiness to turn out to vote has increased greatly in the last few years. Between the 2008–09 and 2016–17 sessions, average daily attendance rose by just over 24 per cent from 400 to 484 but the average number of members voting in divisions rose by 104 per cent, from 194 to 396.

It has been maintained that the relative size of the political parties in the Lords broadly reflects their relative share of votes cast at the last general election and that this accords the House as it is presently composed a form of legitimacy. To the extent that

Table 2.3 Composition of the House of Lords, February 2018*

	Life	Hereditary	Bishops	Total
Conservative	199	49	–	248
Labour	193	4	–	197
Liberal Democrat	96	4	–	100
Crossbench	151	32	–	183
Bishops	–	–	25	25
Other	38	2	–	40
Total	677	91	25	793

*Excludes members on leave of absence, disqualified or suspended

this may be true it is largely coincidental and as a proposition might well not survive a substantial swing from one party to another or a voting collapse. Although the coalition agreement of 2010 proposed that Lords appointments would be made so that the House is 'reflective of the share of the vote secured by the parties at the last general election', since the 2015 election there has been no guidance on what should be the party balance in the House. Options for changing the membership of the House are explored further in Chapter 12.

Leaving the Lords

Until 2014 it was not possible for a member of the House of Lords – other than a bishop – ever, formally, to leave it. Life meant life. In 1957, in the days of the hereditary House, a scheme was instituted whereby a member who could not attend may apply for leave of absence for the remainder of a parliament. At the end of the 2015–17 parliament, 25 members had taken leave. Such leave may be rescinded on three months' notice. Since 2016 members applying for leave of absence must state that they have a reasonable expectation of returning as an active member in future. Thus leave of absence is now intended to cater for temporary circumstances, such as a member working abroad or being temporarily ill. However, there is currently no means of ensuring that it is used only in those cases.

A small but significant change to membership was effected when the House of Lords Reform Act 2014 was passed. The Act allowed members to retire permanently and cease to receive a writ of summons. It is irreversible; a retired member may not subsequently re-enter the House. Retirement is voluntary, and at first few members opted for it. However, the dissolution for the 2015 general election saw a flurry of retirements, which has been followed by a steady flow. By October 2017, 68 members had retired – an average of just over 20 per year. However, nearly a quarter of those who have retired have since died, many were inactive in the House and the five hereditary peers who retired were replaced in by-elections – so the net effect on active membership is limited. There are incentives to encourage retirement: retirees are thanked in the chamber, may have a reception hosted in their honour (not paid for by the taxpayer!) and may make limited use of the House's facilities after retiring. Many members talk about retiring in the future, and some senior figures in the House have been vocal in encouraging it. But the fact remains that, in the absence of any agreement between the parties, the retirement of a member means one less vote for their party.

The House of Lords Reform Act 2014 also removed members who do not attend the House at any time in a session lasting six months or more. Four members duly left the House at the end of the 2015–16 session, and two after the 2016–17 session.

The final incremental reform in the 2014 Act was to remove permanently members convicted of a serious offence carrying a term of imprisonment of over one year, thus bringing the Lords into line with the Commons. This was not retrospective and so has yet to be deployed. The change was supplemented by the House of Lords (Expulsion and Suspension) Act 2015, which granted the House power to expel members for misconduct – a power also hitherto unused.

The Queen

It is easy to think of Parliament as consisting simply of the two Houses; but the sovereign is also part of the institution. Indeed, the words that precede every Act of Parliament remind us that, to become law, a bill must be approved by the Queen, as well as by both Houses:

> *Be it enacted by the Queen's most Excellent Majesty, by and with the advice and consent of the Lords Spiritual and Temporal, and Commons, in this present Parliament assembled, and by the authority of the same, as follows:*

The Queen's name appears again and again in the proceedings of Parliament. Bills go for royal assent; if a bill affects the royal prerogative or the Queen's personal interests, then the Queen's consent must be signified before it is passed; the spending of taxpayers' money in connection with a bill must have the Queen's recommendation; the government's legislative programme is set out at the beginning of a session in the Queen's Speech; many papers presented formally to the two Houses are presented 'by

The Queen Walks with the Speaker, John Bercow, in 2012

Source: Copyright UK Parliament, 2012. Photography by Catherine Bebbington

command of Her Majesty'; Orders in Council – a category of delegated legislation – are made in her name; the government is 'Her Majesty's Government'; and ministers are 'Ministers of the Crown'.

This terminology may seem more appropriate to the mediaeval relationship between the monarch and his fledgling parliament, and in the early twenty-first century the language is entirely symbolic. The Queen does, indeed, give her assent to bills – by signing a list of bills passed rather than each one – but she has no practical power of refusal. The last sovereign to refuse royal assent (to a bill for settling the militia in Scotland) was Queen Anne in 1707–08, and in subsequent centuries sovereigns have progressively distanced themselves from the business of politics.

Above politics: political neutrality

The conventional phrase is that the Queen is 'above politics' or, as Walter Bagehot said of royalty and Queen Victoria, 'Its mystery is its life. We must not let in daylight upon magic. We must not bring the Queen into the combat of politics, or she will cease to be reverenced by all combatants; she will become one combatant among many'. Some 150 years after Bagehot's *The English Constitution*, the Queen's political neutrality is still of constitutional importance. On the one hand, most people would regard it as unacceptable for the monarch to be identified with a particular political party (even a political party that they themselves supported); on the other hand, the Queen may have to perform a crucial constitutional task: deciding who should form a government after a general election.

Choosing a Prime Minister

Normally this is straightforward. The day after polling day the leader of the party with the most seats in the House of Commons – and so able to command the House and get the business of government through – is summoned to Buckingham Palace and asked as Prime Minister to form a government, which in practice means appointing the members of the cabinet and other ministers and taking responsibility for the administration of the country.

Similarly, when a sitting Prime Minister resigns – as Tony Blair did in 2007 and David Cameron in 2016, having lost the EU referendum – the sovereign's task is easy. The government party will choose a new leader under the procedure required by its party rules, and – assuming that that party still has a majority in the House – the Queen will invite the winner to form a government.

A hung parliament

However, in a hung parliament after a general election, where no one party has a majority, the Queen's task may be more difficult. When the final tally of seats is clear, there will probably be intense negotiation between the parties to see how much common ground there might be for the formation of a coalition (where ministers would be drawn from two or more parties) or for one party to govern with the formal support of another. When the Conservative Party lost its majority in the general election of February 1974, Edward Heath negotiated with the Liberal Party in an attempt to continue in government with Liberal support. When it was clear that he would be unsuccessful, the Queen asked Harold Wilson to form a minority government, which struggled on until a general election in October that year, at which Wilson won a narrow overall majority of three seats. In May 2010 the Conservative Party under David Cameron was the largest party but 20 seats short of an overall majority (306 seats to Labour's 258). However, the coalition agreement between the Conservatives and the Liberal Democrats (with 57 seats), negotiated between 7 and 12 May 2010, meant that the coalition had an overall majority and the Queen's task was straightforward. The 2017 general election left the Conservatives eight seats short of an overall majority. The morning after the election Theresa May announced that she would seek an arrangement with the Democratic Unionist Party, which had 10 seats. With those MPs' support added to the Conservatives' tally, Theresa May advised the Queen she could command a majority in the House of Commons. The deal between the two parties is an example of a confidence and supply arrangement. It falls short of a full coalition (so there are no DUP ministers, for example) but the smaller party commits to supporting the government in any votes on confidence motions; on the Queen's Speech; and on the parliamentary means by which the government can tax and spend (the budget, finance bills, money bills, supply and appropriation legislation and estimates – see Chapter 7).

More difficult for the sovereign would be a situation where a general election produced a three-way split in seats in the Commons but very little common ground between any of the three parties. If it was quickly clear that the party leader first asked to form a government could not sustain it – for example, by losing the vote on the proposed legislative programme in the Queen's Speech – she would probably invite another party leader to attempt to form a government.

It would be a matter of judgement as to how long this process could be allowed to go on. On the one hand, the argument goes, the people have spoken (as former President Clinton famously said of the 2000 US presidential election, 'but we're not sure yet what they've said') and it is for politicians to agree a constructive way forward. To force another poll so soon after the first would inflict another general election on a weary electorate, with no guarantee that it would produce any different result (and anyway holding it may be complicated by the Fixed-term Parliaments Act 2011). On the other hand, the business of government needs to be carried on and a second general election might be preferable to months of inter-party squabbling and horse trading.

In these circumstances, the sovereign's political neutrality is crucial. While others may be concerned about party advantage, she must consider only the national interest. The process is not risk-free: when in Australia in 1975 the Governor-General dismissed the Prime Minister on the grounds that the two Houses of Parliament could not reach agreement on the budget and the business of government could not be carried on, that undoubtedly fuelled the flames of republicanism. By contrast, in Belgium, where coalition governments are the norm, there was little criticism of the King in 1985 when he refused the Prime Minister a dissolution because the coalition government had broken down.

The sovereign as statesman

To quote Bagehot again: 'the sovereign has, under a constitutional monarchy such as ours, three rights – the right to be consulted, the right to encourage, the right to warn'. He was speaking of Queen Victoria, who perhaps exercised more influence than does her great-great-grand-daughter, but those principles hold good today. It is worth remembering that the present Queen has more experience of the nation's affairs than anyone in politics. She sees a wide range of state papers and is briefed frankly by the government on the issues of the day. British ambassadors ('Her Majesty's Ambassadors') and high commissioners call on her when they leave to take up their posts and when they return, and she sees their most important despatches.

She has known thirteen Prime Ministers, from Churchill to May, and at weekly audiences has discussed with them the crises and dilemmas that they have faced. Almost all have had an excellent relationship with her, and some have described the weekly audiences in terms almost of therapy: being able to talk about major problems in total confidence with someone of immense political experience who is neither a political opponent nor a rival. The role of the present Queen demonstrates that Bagehot's rights of the sovereign are still invaluable.

3

Running Parliament

The House of Commons

The Speaker

The Speaker of the House of Commons is the most visible player on the parliamentary stage. His 'Order, order' opens every parliamentary day in the chamber; he is usually in the Chair for the stormiest parliamentary events, and he is the representative of the House on occasions of state ceremony, sorrow and rejoicing.

Not only does the Speaker have the task of chairing the House; he is also an influential figure in most aspects of the way that the House and its administration are run. As the presiding officer of the Commons he may seem the exact counterpart of the Lord Speaker as the presiding officer of the Lords; but, as we shall see, their functions are very different.

The office of Speaker

The first member known as Speaker was Sir Thomas Hungerford in 1376, although it seems clear that individual members presided over the early mediaeval House before then, perhaps as early as Peter de Montfort in Henry III's 'Mad Parliament' at Oxford in 1258. The title of Speaker (Mr Speaker or Madam Speaker, as he or she is always referred to in the House) comes from the ancient position of official spokesman of the Commons to the monarch. In the days when sovereign and Commons were frequently at odds, this aspect of the job was rather more arduous than today, and more hazardous: between 1471 and 1535, six Speakers were executed.

Some of the ancient functions of the Speaker survive in more symbolic form. Once elected by the Commons, he makes claim to the Crown of the House's:

> *ancient and undoubted Rights and Privileges, particularly to freedom of speech in debate, freedom from arrest, freedom of access to Her Majesty whenever occasion may require, and that the most favourable construction should be placed on all its proceedings.*

Commons Speaker, John Bercow, 2014

Source: Copyright House of Commons, 2014. Photography by Jessica Taylor

Although this may perhaps appear a little at odds with the modern relationship between the monarch and a House elected by universal suffrage.

The Speaker still occasionally acts as the House's spokesman and representative. After the terrorist atrocities on 11 September 2001 he expressed the House's condolences to the US Congress; and on the occasion of the Diamond Jubilee in 2012 he presented an Address of the House to the Queen in Westminster Hall. When parliaments around the world responded to the terrorist attack in London of 22 March 2017 it was to the Speaker that they sent their messages of sympathy.

The independence of the Speaker

In many foreign parliaments the presiding officer is a party politician. In the US House of Representatives, for example, the Speaker is a leading party politician and frequently takes part in controversial debate. In Germany, the president of the Bundestag is normally a senior member of the government party who continues to play an active part in his party's affairs, and the same is true of the president of the French Assemblée nationale.

However, in the House of Commons there is a long tradition of impartiality, which began with Arthur Onslow (Speaker for 33 years from 1728) and which is so strong that there is a powerful expectation that all Speakers should be seen as genuinely independent of party. In practice, this means that the Speaker resigns from his party – perhaps after having been a party member for many years – and has nothing more to do with its internal affairs. When he stands at a general election, it is not under a party banner but as 'the Speaker seeking re-election'; and he is usually unopposed by the major parties. Some controversial matters do not necessarily divide neatly on party lines however, and in early 2017 Speaker Bercow attracted criticism from some for telling a group of students how he had voted in the Brexit referendum. A week earlier he had voiced his strong opposition to any proposal for President Trump to address both Houses in Westminster Hall. That stance was supported by many MPs (attracting a less than orderly round of applause in the chamber) but others felt it strained the bounds of the Speaker's impartiality. However, a motion of no confidence in the Speaker, tabled following his comments on President Trump, was supported by only five MPs.

The Speaker draws the salary of a cabinet minister and can look forward on retirement to a generous pension and a peerage. The dress worn by the Speaker in the chamber has grown somewhat less formal according to the preference of recent incumbents. Speaker Boothroyd abandoned the full-bottomed wig and, since Speakers Martin and Bercow followed suit, that particular tradition has probably ended for good. Speaker Bercow has gone further and now simply wears a gown over a lounge suit when in the Chamber. When the Speaker goes to and from the chamber he is preceded by a train-bearer. Warned by cries of 'Speaker!' from the doorkeepers, even the most senior MPs are expected to stop what they are doing and bow as he goes by.

In the Palace of Westminster the Speaker has a personal staff to support him and splendid state apartments, which are his official residence, with a comfortable and less formal flat above. He no longer eats with other MPs in the dining rooms or takes part in the political gossip of the Tea Room. Members now come to him. Every Speaker must keep a finger on the pulse of the House and the concerns of its members, and much of his time is taken up with meetings not only with, for example, the Leader of the House or the Chief Whips, but also with a wide variety of MPs with concerns, problems – or bright ideas.

The Speaker is also the embodiment of the House as far as the outside world is concerned. He receives ambassadors, Speakers and ministers from other parliaments, delegations of all sorts, and he presides over a number of parliamentary associations and other bodies.

The Speaker still carries out constituency work and duties in the same way as any other MP. It is sometimes suggested that the Speaker should sit for a notional constituency, perhaps called St Stephen's – but this idea has never found much favour and has been rejected by the House's Procedure Committee. Speakers rightly want to understand and share at first hand the constituency pressures and problems faced by other MPs; and their own constituents are fortunate in having the Speaker for their Member of Parliament as ministers understandably give special attention to constituency cases raised by the Speaker.

The election of the Speaker

Since 1945, some Speakers have been former ministers (Morrison, Lloyd and Thomas had all been cabinet ministers, while Hylton-Foster had been Solicitor-General and

Weatherill had been government Deputy Chief Whip); the careers of others had been mainly on the backbenches (King and Martin; Boothroyd had been a government assistant whip for two years; Speaker Bercow had briefly been an opposition frontbencher). However, since 1965 five out of the seven Speakers have been former Deputy Speakers (King, Thomas, Weatherill, Boothroyd and Martin); not only did they come to the Speakership with experience in the Chair, but also the House had been able to make some assessment of them in that role.

Perhaps surprisingly in view of the rigid political independence of the office, all post-war Speakers except Betty Boothroyd and John Bercow have come from the government side of the House, whichever party has been in power. Given that one of the roles of the Speaker is to protect the House's interests when they conflict with those of the executive, this may have required a rapid reorientation; but it is often said that, particularly at the outset, Speakers tend to be harder on their former party than on the other side of the House.

Since 1992 there have been elections for the Speakership each time it has come vacant. In 1992 the former cabinet minister, Peter Brooke, was defeated by 372 votes to 238, and Betty Boothroyd was elected. She was re-elected unopposed at the start of the 1997 parliament.

On her retirement in 2000 there was an unprecedented election for the Speakership, with no fewer than twelve candidates standing. Propositions are normally put to the House in the form of a motion to which amendments may be moved, and this had always been the procedure for the election of the Speaker, where the motion 'That X do take the Chair of this House as Speaker' could be amended by leaving out 'X' and inserting 'Y'. Thus in 2000 the motion named Michael Martin, and the other candidates were put to the House one by one in a series of amendments. Speeches proposing and seconding the candidates, and by the candidates themselves, together with the votes on each amendment and the final decision, took nine hours. As of course there was no Speaker, the member with the longest continuous service (the then Father of the House), Sir Edward Heath, presided.

In one sense, a day's sitting to fill a post of such importance to every single MP and to the House as a whole was not excessive; but there was understandable pressure to see whether matters could be handled differently. Following a report from the Procedure Committee, in 2001 the House agreed new arrangements. These favoured a Speaker who returns to the House after a general election; only if a motion that he or she should take the Chair is defeated does the new procedure for a contested election come into play.

In a contested election, nominations (supported by 12 to 15 MPs, at least three of whom cannot be from the candidate's own party) are submitted to the Clerk of the House on the morning of the election. When the House meets later that day, the candidates address the House in turn, in an order chosen by lot, and MPs then vote by secret ballot. If one candidate gets more than half the votes, his or her name is put to the House straight away; but if not, the lowest-scoring candidate and any candidate with less than five per cent of the votes are eliminated, a second ballot is held, and so on until one candidate gets more than half the votes. The system is designed to be as fair as possible and not to give an advantage to the candidate who is proposed first (as did the previous system). It is unlike any voting system used in any of the House's other decisions and was first used in June 2009, following the resignation of Speaker Martin in the wake of the expenses scandal.

The 2009 election for Speaker was unprecedented for a number of reasons. It not only followed the new process outlined above, but the *behaviour* of the candidates was novel: the traditional air of reluctance adopted by putative Speakers was cast aside as the contenders set out their stalls in a series of hustings, including one that was televised. Debate about the role focused not just on the candidates' distinctive approaches, but in some cases on their proposals for innovation or reform of the House's practices.

On the day of the election, after the 10 candidates had each addressed the House, the first round of voting failed to achieve an outright winner; the candidate with the fewest votes and three other candidates with fewer than five per cent of the votes were eliminated. The second round also failed to produce a winning candidate with more than half the votes; again, the candidate with the least support was eliminated and the three other lowest polling candidates each withdrew from the contest. Therefore, only two candidates went into the final round; John Bercow gained 322 votes compared with 271 for Sir George Young, the 50 per cent threshold was crossed and the House had a new Speaker. A subsequent review of the arrangements by the Procedure Committee concluded that they had generally worked well, although some minor changes were made.

The procedures have been questioned, however, as they relate to the case of an incumbent Speaker seeking re-election at the start of a parliament. In those circumstances, once the incumbent has indicated that he is willing to continue to serve, MPs decide whether he should be allowed to do so. There was speculation in 2010, 2015 and 2017 that some MPs would oppose Speaker Bercow being able to continue in the role after the elections in those years, although in the event the House agreed that he should continue in each case without a vote. However, any vote held on that question would be conducted not by secret ballot, but in the House's usual way, with MPs' votes recorded by name in *Hansard*. On the final day of the 2010–15 parliament, the government unexpectedly brought forward proposals to change this procedure, so that any vote on whether an incumbent Speaker should be able to continue in post would be determined by a secret ballot. Explaining the proposal, the then Leader of the House said that the case for the existing arrangements was that they were familiar and quick, and that the incumbent Speaker is re-elected by his constituents on the assumption that he will continue in the role. The arguments for moving to a secret ballot were that this was how the House now elected a new Speaker as well as select committee chairs, and that secret ballots reflected the principle that 'whenever voters elect someone to a position of power and authority over them . . . they should be able to do so without fear or favour'.

Regardless of the strength of the arguments, the government's move was interpreted by many as having been motivated by an ad hominem desire to make it easier to remove Speaker Bercow. The manner in which the debate was proposed, with very little notice at the last possible opportunity in the parliament on a day when many MPs would have planned to be back in their constituencies, was widely criticised, with the

Shadow Leader of the House describing it as an 'appalling and shabby way to treat the House'. The government's proposal was defeated and the status quo maintained.

The roles of the Speaker

Maintaining order

Perhaps the most obvious function of the Speaker and his deputies is to maintain order when the House is sitting. All speeches made in the chamber are addressed to the Chair, and the Speaker 'calls to order' any MP who offends against the rules of the House. Some of these are conventions, and others are laid down in standing orders or in past resolutions of the House. The definitive guide to them is *Erskine May's Treatise on the Law, Privileges, Proceedings and Usage of Parliament*, usually known as *Erskine May*. Sir Thomas Erskine May, Clerk of the House from 1871 to 1886, edited the first nine editions, and 15 more have been edited by his successors.

The House's rules range from the relatively trivial, such as requiring members to refer to each other by constituency rather than name, to the more serious, such as the *sub judice* rule (see page 283), which is designed to prevent criminal trials or civil actions in the courts being prejudiced by comment in the House. Other rules require speeches to be relevant to the matter before the House (and supplementary questions to be relevant to the subject of the question on the Order Paper), forbid the use of insulting words or 'unparliamentary expressions' (see page 283), specify when an MP may speak a second time in a debate, regulate the proper conduct of votes, and so on. The Speaker has both to make sure that these rules are observed and to give his rulings when MPs raise points of order about the application or interpretation of these rules.

In a democratic assembly passions can run high and tempers flare. It is then that the Speaker and his deputies need to be most sensitive in gauging the mood of the House. Will a humorous intervention from the Chair defuse the situation, or is there serious trouble that must be dealt with firmly from the outset? At need, they have powers to discipline individual MPs, either by ordering them to resume their seats, to leave the chamber for the day or, for more serious offences (usually involving a disregard for the authority of the Chair), naming them. After a member has been named, a motion is moved by the senior minister present, to which the House invariably agrees, and which has the effect of suspending the MP, so barring him or her from the building for five sitting days on the first occasion, 20 sitting days on the second and indefinitely on the third (and stopping payment of the member's salary for those periods). If there is general disorder in the chamber, the Speaker can suspend the sitting.

These are powers used with great reluctance by the Speaker. He does not want to create martyrs or give an individual MP's political protest added force by expulsion from the chamber; but he has also to protect the reputation of the House and the business before it. Precipitate disciplinary action can rebound upon the Chair, as with the Victorian Speaker who was foolish enough to have the police called to deal with disorder in the chamber. Thereafter, whenever the House was rowdy, his authority was routinely undermined by shouts of 'send for the police'.

Holding the ring

The Speaker and his deputies have absolute discretion over which members they call to speak. There may be some fixed points in a major debate: perhaps a cabinet minister will open the debate, responded to by his or her opposition shadow and the winding-up speeches at the end might be made by another member of the shadow cabinet and by another cabinet minister.

In between, the character of the debate is shaped by which MPs the Chair calls to speak. Balancing their claims is no easy task. Let us suppose that there is a full day's debate on policy towards asylum seekers: in practice, five or six hours' debating time. The opening and closing frontbench speeches might leave no more than three or four hours for everyone else who wishes to take part. Let us also suppose that pressure on existing reception centres for asylum seekers has led the government to propose a number of additional sites. Unrest in two or three centres has been followed by violence and extensive damage. There will be MPs with asylum centres in their constituencies; those who represent people who are up in arms that a new centre might be located near them; those who represent Channel ports; those who are close to the unions representing asylum centre staff; perhaps the chair and members of the Home Affairs Select Committee, who have just produced a critical report on asylum policy. And, as well as juggling these urgent claims to speak, the Speaker and his deputies have to ensure that the party balance is maintained. Even with the imposition of time limits on backbench speeches (see page 281) it can sometimes be impossible to call all those who wish to speak in a debate, although the Speaker and his deputies try to do so.

During Question Time (see Chapter 9), the Speaker's ability to shape events is even more marked. He can cut short over-long supplementary questions (and ministerial answers), but he can also decide how long to go on calling MPs to ask supplementaries on a particular question. If the subject is one on which the government is vulnerable, eight supplementary questions – perhaps including some hostile ones from the minister's own side – instead of two or three may give a minister a torrid time at the despatch box. Similarly, if political and media pressure has forced a ministerial statement or urgent question (see pages 144 and 307) on some high-profile problem, the government's exposure will be much greater if questions run for one hour instead of half an hour, and the present practice is to allow every MP who wants to ask a question to do so, even though the later questioning may add little to what has already been elicited. When David Cameron made a statement in the run-up to the 2016 referendum on EU membership the Speaker allowed 103 MPs to ask supplementary questions, keeping the Prime Minister at the despatch box for 2 hours 40 minutes.

The Speaker's powers in the chamber

In sharp contrast to the House of Lords, the Commons has given its presiding officer extensive powers. The House of Lords may largely regulate itself, but in the much more contentious and politically polarised Commons the Chair has a considerable armoury.

First, as we have seen, there is the power to *call MPs to speak in a debate or to ask a question*, described by Speaker Thomas as his most potent weapon. Although Speakers strive to be fair to every MP, the member who is disruptive or abusive, or disregards the authority of the Chair, may find it difficult to catch the Speaker's eye at Prime Minister's Questions for some little while thereafter. Allied with this is the power to *decide how long questioning on a particular topic may continue.*

In most debates, the Speaker also has the power to *limit the length of backbench speeches.* He can also intervene to *prevent deliberate time-wasting* by MPs either speaking repetitiously or calling for unnecessary votes. The decision on whether to accept the closure – in other words, to *allow the House to decide whether a debate should end and a vote be taken on the subject under discussion* – is entirely in the hands of the Chair.

The Speaker also has discretion on *whether amendments to bills or to motions before the House should be debated and voted upon.* This can be of great significance. For example, on 26 February 2003 the Commons debated a government motion calling upon Iraq to recognise this as its final opportunity to comply with its 'disarmament obligations'; the Speaker selected a Labour backbench amendment to the effect that the case for military action against Iraq was 'as yet unproven'. The amendment was defeated by 393 votes to 199, but the 199 included 122 Labour MPs voting against the government's policy – a rebellion of huge political significance.

Less than a month later, the government put before the House of Commons a motion authorising the use of all means necessary to ensure the disarmament of Iraq's weapons of mass destruction – in effect authorising war. Again, the Speaker selected a Labour backbench amendment asserting that 'the case for war against Iraq has not yet been established, especially given the absence of specific United Nations authorisation'. This time the amendment was defeated by 396 votes to 217; the 217 included 139 Labour MPs (29 of whom had not rebelled on the previous occasion), again a seismic political event.

The number of amendments selected for voting upon by the Speaker can be a matter of controversy. In May 2013, at the end of the debate on the Queen's Speech, the Speaker allowed separate divisions to be held on three amendments (in addition to one held on the penultimate day). The government viewed this as a break with precedent, as previously only two amendments had been called on the final day and they argued that the House would be in a confused position if the Speaker felt able to select an unlimited number of amendments to put to the vote. They also argued that the phrasing of the relevant standing order ('*a* further amendment') could be interpreted only as singular. Eventually, the situation was clarified by a change in the standing orders of the House which set out that up to four amendments in total could be selected (with an assumption that one of these would be voted on during the penultimate day of the debate).

The Speaker can set part of the political agenda, and allow the House to call the government to account, through urgent questions (or UQs), formerly called private notice questions because they are applied for to the Speaker privately rather than being printed on the Order Paper. If the Speaker thinks a matter is sufficiently urgent or important, and there is unlikely to be another way of raising it in the House in the next day or so, he allows a question to be put to a minister (often by the opposition spokesman on the subject) at the end of Question Time. Although ministerial statements are made voluntarily by the government, urgent questions are granted when, in the Speaker's view, the House needs to be informed but no ministerial statement is forthcoming. Speaker Bercow has allowed many more UQs than did his predecessors, as shown below:

Table 3.1 Number of urgent questions allowed since 2006

Session	Number of urgent questions
2016–17	74
2015–16	77
2014–15	45
2013–14	35
2012–13	38
2010–12 (a notably long session)	73
2009–10	26
2008–09	11
2007–08	4
2006–07	9

Urgent questions are described in more detail in Chapter 9 (page 307).

The Speaker also has the power to decide whether *a complaint of privilege* – in other words, an allegation that an MP, or a servant of the House, or perhaps a select committee, has been obstructed or threatened – should be put to the House. If the Speaker believes that there may be grounds for action, he allows the matter to take precedence over other business and a motion to be moved either referring the complaint to the Committee on Privileges for investigation or proposing some other means of dealing with the complaint without recourse to the committee. Such complaints are rare, although in November 2017 the SNP MP Pete Wishart told the House that he had written to the Speaker to complain that the government was in contempt of the House by not producing in a timely way documents analysing the effect of Brexit on different sectors which had been demanded by the House. Privilege is described in more detail in Chapter 5 (page 168).

The casting vote

Once put to the vote in the House, a matter must be decided; it cannot be left as a draw. If the numbers of 'ayes' and 'noes' are equal, then the occupant of the Chair must decide the question by casting a vote; and it is only on these occasions that the Speaker or his deputies vote. However, the Chair is protected from controversy by clearly established historical principles. These are, broadly, that a decision should be taken by a majority of the House, not just on the basis of a casting vote; and that there should be opportunity for further discussion. Thus the Chair will vote 'aye' on a casting vote on the second reading of a bill, because the bill can continue its progress and be amended if the House wishes. But the Chair will vote 'no' if the vote on the third reading is tied, because that is the moment at which the Commons approves the bill, and the law should not be changed except by a majority of the House. If the vote is on a motion for the adjournment, the Chair votes 'no' in order to allow the House to proceed with other business.

In the Thatcher and the Blair years, big government majorities made the need for casting votes much less (although on issues of conscience, or unwhipped votes on private members' bills the possibility was always there). However, when the government has a small majority the more likely is the need for a casting vote; it was used seven times between 1974 and 1979. It was almost needed when the Callaghan government fell as a result of losing a vote of confidence on the night of 28 March 1979; 311 MPs voted against the government, and 310 for.

Had the casting vote been needed then, it would have been 'no' on the principle that the decision had to be taken by a majority and not on a casting vote. So clear is the principle that, even in the greatest political controversy, there is no question of political bias. The most recent casting vote is a good example. On 22 July 1993, the House was voting on the Leader of the Opposition's amendment to a motion on the Social Protocol of the Maastricht Treaty. The votes were 317 ayes and 317 noes. Speaker Boothroyd voted 'no' on the basis that the decision should be taken only by a majority. The government lost the vote on the motion itself and put a motion of confidence before the House the next day, which it won comfortably, without the need for a casting vote.

Recalling the House

There have been 27 occasions since the Second World War when, because of some grave event, the House was recalled during a recess. There have been 11 such instances in the last two decades, as shown below:

Table 3.2 Occasions when the House has been recalled during a recess

Date of recall	Subject matter
31 May 1995	Bosnia
2–3 September 1998	Omagh bombing: Criminal Justice (Terrorism and Conspiracy Bill)
14 September, 4 and 8 October 2001	International terrorism and attacks in the USA
3 April 2002	Death of Her Majesty Queen Elizabeth the Queen Mother
24 September 2002	Iraq and Weapons of Mass Destruction
20 July 2011	Public confidence in the media and police
11 August 2011	Public disorder (additional statement on global economy)
10 April 2013	Death of Baroness Thatcher
29 August 2013	Syria
26 September 2014	ISIL and Iraq
20 June 2016	Death of Jo Cox MP

At such times the media normally report that the Prime Minister has recalled Parliament. In fact, the standing orders provide that ministers may represent to the Speaker that the public interest requires an earlier meeting of the House; and, if the Speaker agrees, he appoints a time for the House to sit. This may be a distinction that is not much of a difference because, following precedent, the Speaker always agrees to the government's request. However, revisiting an idea previously mooted in Gordon Brown's Green Paper *The Governance of Britain*, in October 2017 Speaker Bercow made the case for introducing a procedure by which MPs could call for a recall. He noted that in order to avoid any such procedure being exploited simply for partisan ends, rather than genuinely urgent need, a mechanism would be needed to ensure that any proposed recall had widespread support from both government and opposition MPs.

Statutory and other functions

The Speaker is *ex officio* chairman of each of the Boundary Commissions mentioned in Chapter 2, although the work falls to the other members, led by a High Court judge (or Scottish equivalent). He also chairs the Speaker's Committee on the Electoral Commission and the Speaker's Committee for the Independent Parliamentary Standards Authority.

The most important and time-consuming of the Speaker's statutory responsibilities is as chair of the House of Commons Commission, which is the financial and employing authority for the House administration, and whose work we describe on page 64.

The voice of the House

The Speaker's role as official spokesman of the Commons to the monarch may survive only in ceremonial form, but the core of his job is still protecting and expressing the interests of the House. He must protect the interests of the House through securing orderly proceedings, the courtesies of debate, and consistent and fair rulings on points of order and matters of contention. Expressing the interests of the House is more complex and potentially more politically exposed, as it centres upon the House's relationship with the government of the day. The Speaker can grant urgent questions, select unwelcome amendments, allow questions to run on, and ensure that a wide spectrum of opinion is called in debate if this helps Parliament better to air issues and hold the government to account.

One key area on which successive Speakers have expressed strong views is that the House is the first to hear of important developments in government policy. This is a sensitive area; governments of both political parties have wanted to set the media agenda outside the House, to brief selected journalists, perhaps to prepare public opinion for unwelcome news. But if Parliament is to be the focus of national attention then, whether the news is momentous or not, the principle that the nation's representatives in Parliament are told first is an important one; and the

Speaker must be its main advocate. The increased use of urgent questions, noted on page 55 – where ministers can be compelled to come to the House – has meant that the government must now routinely expect that the Commons will require an explanation about urgent and important matters, even when they had not planned to make a statement.

Conferences and commissions

Between 1916 and 1978 there were five Conferences on Electoral Law, held at the request of the Prime Minister and chaired by the Speaker. The first of these, in 1916–17, chaired by Speaker Lowther, paved the way for the franchise to be extended to women. In September 2007 Gordon Brown revived the practice, and called on the Speaker to chair a conference looking at voter registration and turnout, weekend voting, the representation of women and ethnic minorities in the House of Commons, and the possibility of extending the franchise to 16-year-olds. The Conference was established as a committee of the House and reported in January 2010.

In November 2013 the Speaker announced he was setting up a Commission on Digital Democracy, the aim of which was to 'consider the effect of the digital revolution' on representative democracy. The Commission reported in February 2015 and examined the opportunities presented by digital developments to enhance scrutiny of government, pass legislation, represent citizens and promote dialogue among them, and encourage engagement with the political process.

Precedent and change

Precedent provides the framework within which any Speaker operates. It is a powerful ally in making rulings robust against challenge and – as with casting votes – emphasising the impartiality of the Chair. But no Speaker can simply rest on precedent. Parliament is constantly changing – not only internally in terms of its membership and political complexion, but also in terms of the influences and pressures on it. There are always new problems and situations with which a Speaker must grapple, and set new precedents in the process. These may be as far-reaching as the procedures adopted by Speaker Brand in the 1870s and 1880s to deal with the Irish Home Rule MPs who were obstructing the House's business; before his unilateral action to limit MPs' rights to speak by the introduction of the closure, members could speak for as long as they liked on any question before the House. More often, changes come about almost imperceptibly as a result of a series of Speaker's rulings.

The Speaker can draw on the professional knowledge and long experience of the Clerk of the House and the Clerk's senior colleagues, and has the political and professional advice of often highly experienced deputies. But the decisions are for him alone. Members may criticise the Speaker only by putting down a substantive motion for debate; if necessary, the government quickly finds time for a debate in order to resolve the matter. It was the tabling of such a motion in 2009 that triggered the resignation of Speaker Martin (before the motion was debated). Only three such motions have actually been debated since the Second World War. The most recent motion, tabled as an Early Day Motion in February 2017, attracted only five signatures and was not debated.

The Deputy Speakers

The Speaker is assisted by three deputies – the Chairman of Ways and Means and two Deputy Chairmen. Before 2010 they were appointed by the House for the duration of the parliament, normally all at the same time on the first business day of a new parliament, and in a far less elaborate way than the Speaker; after informal soundings were taken, a motion to appoint them appeared in the name of the Prime Minister or the Leader of the House. This rather informal procedure was replaced in 2010 by elections of the Deputy Speakers. After consideration by the Procedure Committee, and agreement by the House, the first elections for the jobs were held in June 2010. The elections are held under the Single Transferable Vote (STV) system, with provisos that the Chairman of Ways and Means (the senior Deputy) and the Second Deputy Chairman must be a candidate from the opposite side of the House from which the Speaker was drawn; the First Deputy Chairman of Ways and Means must be drawn from the same side of the House from which the Speaker came; and that, across the four posts of Speaker and three Deputies, at least one woman and one man shall be elected. Under the STV system, candidates do not need a majority to be elected, only a known 'quota' or share of the votes, determined by the size of the electorate and the number of positions to be filled. Nine candidates stood in the 2010 election, and Sir Lindsay Hoyle was elected as Chairman of Ways and Means, a post he still holds. The other two Deputies are Dame Eleanor Laing (First Deputy Chairman) and Dame Rosie Winterton (Second Deputy Chairman).

The Chairman of Ways and Means is so called because, since the late seventeenth century, he presided over the Committee of Ways and Means (dealing with taxation), as well as the Committee of Supply (dealing with government expenditure), at that time the only two permanent committees of the House. It was not until 1853 that the Chairman began formally to deputise for the Speaker.

Today, the Chairman of Ways and Means exercises most of the powers of the Speaker in the chamber (and has the power to select amendments in the Committee of the whole House, when the Speaker never presides). The Chairman also has three other distinct roles. He oversees the consideration of private bills (as distinct from private members' bills) (see page 235); he supervises arrangements for sittings in Westminster Hall (see page 278); and through his chairmanship of the Panel of Chairs (see page 197), he has general responsibility for the work of legislative committees. From 1902, a Deputy Chairman of Ways and Means was appointed, and a Second Deputy Chairman from 1971. They exercise the same powers in the chamber as the Chairman of Ways and Means. No decision of any of the three may be appealed to the Speaker.

The three Deputy Speakers come from both sides of the House and, together with the Speaker, cancel out the loss of numbers from government and opposition sides of the House. Thus, Speaker Bercow came from the government (Conservative) side; Sir Lindsay Hoyle, the Chairman of Ways and Means, from the opposition (Labour) side; Dame Eleanor Laing, the First Deputy Chairman, from the government (Conservative) side; and Dame Rosie Winterton, the Second Deputy Chairman, from the opposition (Labour) side. The deputies are rigidly impartial in the Chair and other House duties, and they do not vote (except to resolve a tied vote). However, unlike the Speaker they remain members of their parties, they fight general elections on a party basis, and after serving as a deputy they may return to the backbenches taking the party whip.

The Speaker and the deputies have a rota of duty in the Chair; normally, the Speaker takes the first two hours, disposing of Question Time, one or more ministerial statements thereafter, and any points of order before the main business of the day begins. The deputies do stints of two hours or so, although the Speaker may return to preside over the end of the main business and any votes that take place.

In 2002 the Procedure Committee attempted a job description for the deputies:

> *an ability swiftly to command the respect of the whole House . . . a demonstrable knowledge of procedure and its application, as well as wider experience of the House and the way it works, together with an ability to chair the most challenging debates with demonstrable fairness and authority . . . a good team player. An appetite for hard work, unremitting punctuality and a sense of humour and proportion are also highly desirable.*

The Leader of the House

The Leader of the House of Commons – from June 2017, Andrea Leadsom – is a key figure in both government and Parliament. She is a cabinet minister, as well as an MP; but although the Leader has collective Cabinet responsibility for defending the government's policies in the House, she also has the wider task of upholding the rights and interests of the House. With the Chief Whip, the Leader is responsible for the arrangement of government business in the Commons, and for planning and supervising the government's legislative programme as a whole by chairing the Parliamentary Business and Legislation Committee of the Cabinet (known as PBL). She is also a member of several Cabinet sub-committees.

The Leader reports weekly to Cabinet on forthcoming parliamentary business. She announces that business – firm for the following week, provisional for the week after – to the House every Thursday, an event that emphasises the control that the government of the day has over the time of the House of Commons. She also answers oral questions once a month on her wider responsibilities as Leader.

The Leader usually moves (and defends) motions to determine how Commons business is to be dealt with, or to introduce procedural change, and often winds up at the end of major debates on behalf of the government. She also plays a role in House administration as an ex officio member of the House of Commons Commission and as the minister responsible for the Members Estimate (see page 65).

Leaders of the House also have a role in helping to resolve issues affecting the House as a whole, especially those which might threaten its reputation. Thus, the current Leader chaired a cross-party working group, convened by the Prime Minister, set up in response to allegations of sexual harassment and bullying in Parliament. The group made a range of recommendations in February 2018, including that everyone working in Westminster should abide by a 'behaviour code' for Parliament; that a new complaints and grievance procedure independent of political parties should be established; and that MPs' staff should have access to human resources advice.

The Clerk of the House

The Clerk of the House of Commons is the House's senior official and combines a variety of roles. He is the House's principal constitutional adviser, and adviser on all aspects of its business, procedure, practice and privilege; the editor of *Erskine May*; and a frequent witness before select committees and joint committees. He is the Speaker's and Deputy Speakers' principal adviser on a wide range of issues, but he answers not to the Speaker but to the House as a whole, and advises government and opposition, as well as any individual member of the House. He is Head of the House of Commons Service and a member of the House of Commons Commission (see page 64). He is Accounting Officer for the House of Commons Administration Estimate and the Members Estimate and so is personally responsible for the propriety and economy of expenditure. He is the House's Corporate Officer and so formally holds property (including the Commons part of the Parliamentary Estate) and enters into contracts on the House's behalf, and is legally responsible for the actions of the House Administration. He is the Data Controller and so legally liable for the proper handling of information under the Data Protection Act 1998. In addition, he is the professional head of the cadre of Clerks in the House, most closely concerned with the work of the House and its committees.

It may seem strange that the Clerk combines the somewhat academic precision of procedural matters with overall responsibility for the management of the House's services. A Select Committee on House of Commons Governance which reported in December 2014 considered this question and concluded that, while the Clerk should remain head of the House Service (as well as Accounting Officer and Corporate Officer), he should no longer be the chief executive, and that a new post of Director General should be established, reporting to the Clerk, but with significant responsibilities for the delivery of services. It also recommended that the Clerk and Director General should serve as official members of the House of Commons Commission (see page 64).

Commons clerks in the chamber, 2017

Source: Copyright House of Commons, 2017. Photography by Jessica Taylor

The first known Clerk of the House – formally styled 'Under-Clerk of the Parliaments, to wait upon the Commons' – was appointed in 1363; there has been an unbroken line since. The title 'Clerk' probably derives from the fact that in early mediaeval times literacy was by no means universal and was most widely found among priests, or clerks in holy orders. The Clerk of the House is appointed by the Queen by Letters Patent, which underpins his independence and ability to give advice no matter how unpopular that advice might be. For the first time, a competition open to staff from the UK's parliaments and assemblies was run for the role of Clerk and Chief Executive in 2011; and an open competition was run in 2014, but abandoned amid some controversy. That controversy prompted the establishment of the Governance Committee referred to above, which led to a number of reforms.

The House of Commons Service

The permanent staff of the House (some 2,500 people) are not civil servants but employees of the House of Commons Commission. This distinction may not be of great importance for those staff who are responsible for the upkeep of the buildings or for catering services, but for many it is of constitutional importance. The clerk of a departmental select committee who manages a committee's inquiry into something that has gone wrong within government and then has to draft a report strongly critical of ministers and civil servants would face an intolerable conflict of loyalties if he or she owed allegiance to the Civil Service. To take another example, analysis prepared by the subject experts in the Library's research services is expected to be rigorous regardless of the possibility that their findings may not be palatable to the government of the day.

The House of Commons Service must also be politically impartial. Again, this is more important in some areas of work than in others. Staff in the Chamber and Committees Team may find themselves in quick succession advising both government and opposition on procedural tactics for highly contentious business in the House, or within the space of a few minutes advising both the member in charge of a private member's bill and those MPs who want to scupper its chances of proceeding any further. If they are to retain the confidence of MPs, it is essential for their credibility that clerks giving that advice are seen to be absolutely impartial as to both parties and issues.

The House administration

The administration of the House of Commons is fairly complex. This is not surprising; on the one hand, it has to deliver a wide range of disparate services, from regilding Pugin decoration in a Grade I listed building to supporting select committee work that covers every aspect of public life, to producing overnight a record of all the proceedings in the House and in Westminster Hall. On the other hand, professional management and planning must take into account the changing, and not always consistent, wishes of MPs, as well as the unpredictable pressures on Parliament itself.

A 1999 review of the way the House services were run summed up the problem.

> *The effective operation of the House is of enormous constitutional and public importance. The elector (and taxpayer) expects Governments to be held to account; constituents to be represented and their grievances pursued; and historic Parliamentary functions to be extended and adapted to changes in the wider world.*
>
> *These things do not come cheap, and no-one should expect them to. Seeking to hold to account a complex, sophisticated and powerful Executive; dealing with an unremitting burden of legislation; and meeting ever-increasing expectations on the part of constituents; all this requires substantial, high-quality support. . . .*
>
> *There is no shortage of complicating factors. Each Member of Parliament is an expert on what he or she wants from the system, and what the system should provide. With their staffs, Members are in effect 659* [now 650] *small businesses operating independently within one institutional framework. Managers in both the public and private sectors have to meet the needs of demanding customers; but they do not*

> *have customers every one of whom can take a complaint to the Floor of the House of Commons – perhaps televised nation-wide.*
>
> *At the same time the House and its Members are funded by the taxpayer. This spending is inevitably high-profile, exposed to media interest which is not always friendly and which may not pause to assess the wider value of Parliamentary expenditure. The House must be able to demonstrate proper stewardship of public money, and to show that expenditure is efficient, effective and economical.*

Although that report is now almost 20 years old, it remains a valid description of the task facing the House administration. If anything, the pressure on the House service is greater now – with the need to restore the palace's buildings more urgent, enhanced security demands, a more complex IT infrastructure and greater levels of transparency since the implementation of the Freedom of Information Act.

The House of Commons Commission and the Members Estimate Committee

The Commission is the supervisory body of the administration, responsible for the House's finances and the employer of almost all its staff. Set up under the House of Commons (Administration) Act 1978, it is chaired by the Speaker; its other members are the Leader of the House, a member nominated by the Leader of the Opposition (in practice, always the Shadow Leader of the House), four senior backbenchers, two official members (the Clerk and Director General), and two external members. The Commission operates in a wholly non-party way; in any event, it has never had a majority of government members. Established in 1978, the House of Commons Commission Act 2015 updated its composition following the review of governance in the House of Commons. It also provided for an additional statutory function of setting the strategic priorities and objectives of the House administration.

The Commission meets monthly or more frequently when the House is sitting. Its meetings are private, usually with senior staff who are responsible for the subject under discussion; but it posts its agendas and decisions on the internet, and also publishes an annual report that is a mine of information about the activities of the House administration, its plans and performance. One member of the Commission acts as its spokesman and answers written parliamentary questions on its behalf, as well as oral questions in the chamber once a month. The MPs who sit on the Commission comprise the Members Estimate Committee (the Commission's official and external members are not members of the MEC), and its role is to oversee the Members Estimate (see below).

The Commission is advised by two select committees of MPs: the Finance Committee considers major items of expenditure, and financial and business plans; the Administration Committee advises on services more generally. In addition, the Speaker's Advisory Committee on Works of Art, although not a select committee, advises Mr Speaker and officials on the Parliamentary Art Collection and takes decisions about acquisitions.

Strategic planning

The House of Commons itself may not have a mission statement, but the House administration is subject to normal public sector disciplines. In 2016 the Commission endorsed a five-year strategy for the House Service which included the following objectives:

- Facilitating effective scrutiny and debate
- Involving and inspiring the public
- Securing Parliament's future.

The Executive Board

Responsibility for running the House services, and for employing staff, is delegated by the Commission to the Executive Board, which comprises the Clerk of the House, the Director General and the heads of the main teams within the House Service. It is chaired by the Director General.

Estimates and the Audit Committees

The activities of the House of Commons are funded under two budgets or Estimates, which provide the legal authority for the House to finance its activities. The House of Commons Administration Estimate covers the staff of the House and its running costs, and the Members Estimate covers certain expenditure relating to MPs. Much of the expenditure previously authorised under the Members Estimate, including members' pay and allowances, was transferred to the Independent Parliamentary Standards Authority in 2010.

The Administration Estimate Audit and Risk Assurance Committee and the Members Estimate Audit Committee (MEAC) support the Clerk as Accounting Officer in discharging his responsibilities under the relevant estimate. In particular, the committees advise on: the effectiveness of the system of governance, risk management and internal control; the integrity of the accounts; the work of the internal audit service and the external auditor, the National Audit Office (NAO); and other matters referred to them by the Accounting Officer or the Commission/MEC. The committees have identical membership, comprising three MPs and three external members, one of whom chairs the committees.

House teams

For reasons of good governance and economy, the House administration must operate as a corporate whole. There are also issues such as financial planning, the use of accommodation, information and communications technology (ICT), health and safety, data protection, human resources and so on that can be dealt with effectively only across the board. Some of the functions provided have been required by the House for centuries, such as procedural advice; others are more recent additions. The organisational structure through which those services are provided has been subject to several reviews over the last 20 years. Following the most recent review, by the Director General in 2016, staff of the House have been brigaded into seven functional teams, as described below.

Chamber and Committees Team

The Chamber and Committees Team (CCT) comprises the staff who give procedural advice to the Speaker and other members; the secretariats of the House's select committees; and staff of the *Official Report*, better known as *Hansard*, who record what is said in the House of Commons chamber, Westminster Hall and various committees. Senior members of the CCT, along with the Clerk of the House, are perhaps the most visible of all the House staff; in television coverage of the chamber, they are seen sitting at the Table of the House in front of the Speaker, wearing gowns and bowties. (Until 2016 they dressed as a QC would be in court: court coat, wing collar, but with a white tie rather than barrister's bands, wig and gown.) Their task there is to advise the Chair, ministers, whips and any other MP on the business the House is transacting; to record the decisions the House has taken (but not what has been said, which is taken down by the *Hansard* reporters in the gallery above them) and to help to conduct votes. The Clerks at the Table have other roles as well, usually as head of one of the offices of the CCT, including: the Public and Private Bill Offices, which administer all business relating to legislation before the House, provide the staff for public bill committees and other legislative committees, and advise members and others on legislation; the Journal Office, which advises on parliamentary privilege and procedure generally and compiles the daily permanent legal record of proceedings; and the Table Office, which prepares the Order Paper and processes parliamentary questions.

The CCT also includes: the Overseas Office, which is responsible for the House's relations with other parliaments and international assemblies; the Vote Office, which provides official papers to MPs; and the Ways and Means Office which supports the Chairman of Ways and Means and his deputies. The Office of Speaker's Counsel and the Office of the Parliamentary Commissioner for Standards are within the CCT for budgetary purposes, though they are operationally independent.

Participation Team

The Participation Team's functions relate to those who visit Parliament or who otherwise engage with it. The Outreach and Engagement Service works to increase public understanding of, and engagement with, Parliament. It is a bicameral team which provides services for the House of Lords as well as the House of Commons. The Education Service runs educational programmes and activities and helps members of both Houses in their work with young people. Around 100,000 school pupils visit

Parliament annually via the service's programmes and in 2015 a dedicated Education Centre was opened at the north end of Victoria Tower Gardens. The centre features an immersive experience using state-of-the-art augmented reality technology. As well as visits to Parliament, the service runs an outreach programme in schools which provides a range of resources to support teaching about Parliament. The Participation Team's visitor assistants welcome visitors to Parliament and provide tours. The team also runs a number of retail outlets selling gifts to those who work in and visit Parliament. The Participation Team also answers queries from members of the public as well as making sure that relevant information is available on Parliament's website.

Research and Information Team

The largest part of the Research and Information Team is the House of Commons Library. Although the grand rooms running along the river front of the palace may seem reminiscent of the sort of Victorian library mentioned in Chapter 1, the daily work of the Library is modern and varied. As well as offering the library and reference facilities one might expect, it provides MPs with high-quality, impartial research and information services.

The researchers are highly qualified, and their work is respected inside and outside the House. When a member says in the chamber 'the Library have told me', what they have said is unlikely to be challenged. Library staff undertake research in response to specific requests from MPs, as well as producing research papers on bills and other current issues. This research back-up is highly valued by MPs, and especially by opposition spokespeople in shadowing ministers, when the latter can call upon the extensive resources of government departments. Much of the briefing work produced by the Library is available on parliament's website, and is therefore a valuable resource for those outside parliament as well as the members in it.

In House Services Team

IHS manages the day-to-day care of the parliamentary estate, and hosts its maintenance team and the Accommodation and Logistics Service which, amongst other things, works with the party whips to ensure that MPs are provided with functioning offices and that moves go smoothly. The team runs the House's food and drink outlets, serving an estimated 1.5 million meals each year. IHS also includes the Curator's Office, which manages the impressive Parliamentary Art Collection on behalf of both Houses. The collection comprises 7,100 paintings, drawings, prints and photographs, 700 sculptures, 600 coins and medals, 50 textiles, and 20 original wallpaper fragments, with an historical range running from the fourteenth-century statues of monarchs which stand in Westminster Hall to specially commissioned portraits of contemporary parliamentarians.

The Serjeant at Arms is based within IHS and is responsible for maintaining order within the Commons part of the estate (although responsibility for security has moved to the Parliamentary Security Department). The first recorded Serjeant at Arms was given office by King Henry V in 1415, the year of the Battle of Agincourt. In previous centuries, he was responsible for carrying out orders of the House, including making arrests; the splendid silver gilt Mace that the present Serjeant carries in the Speaker's procession every day, and which then lies on the Table while the House is sitting, was in times past a necessary symbol of the House's authority outside the precincts.

Strategic Estates Team

The Strategic Estates Team is responsible for the extensive capital investment required to keep Parliament's estates working. At any time, it is undertaking around 140 'business as usual' projects as well as tackling extensive renewal work required across almost the entire estate, including preparatory work for the hugely expensive and challenging task required for restoration and renewal of the palace itself (see page 16).

Corporate Services Team

The Corporate Services Team manages the House's finances and provides its HR functions. It coordinates the House Service's strategic planning and the House's Diversity and Inclusion Team is based in it.

Parliamentary Security Department

The Parliamentary Security Department (PSD) is responsible for the physical, personnel and cyber security of both Houses of Parliament. It sets security strategy, provides expert advice and delivers an operational service. PSD's staff (including a large number of uniformed civilian security officers who formerly worked for the Metropolitan Police Service) are employed by the House of Commons but serve both Houses.

Services shared between the Lords and the Commons

Many of the functions described above are managed by the House of Commons but serve both Houses; similarly, some functions are hosted by the House of Lords but provide a bicameral service. However, in 2005, the first – and, to date, only – joint department of the two Houses, the *Parliamentary Information and Communications Technology Service* (PICT) was established, charged with providing ICT support to peers, MPs, their staff and staff of both Houses. Following an externally commissioned independent review, in 2014 a new Parliamentary Digital Service (PDS) was established, which brought together the management of all online and ICT services into a single organisation, with an aim of putting digital delivery at the forefront of the work done to support both Houses, prioritising the needs of users.

MPs' pay, allowances and IPSA

MPs' pay and allowances

As we saw in Chapter 2, the expenses scandal of 2009 was a hammer blow to the public reputation and self-confidence of MPs and the House. Members of Parliament were first paid in 1911, when the rate was £400 a year. Ever since, their pay levels have been controversial, not least because, until the recent reforms, MPs were one of the few groups of people who could in effect set their own salaries. In order to provide an objective assessment, pay and allowances had, since 1970, been referred to an outside organisation, latterly the Senior Salaries Review Body (SSRB). The SSRB based its recommendations on general principles: that pay should not be so low as to deter or so high as to make it the main attraction; that, although some MPs take on work outside Parliament, pay should be at a level reflecting the full-time job that it is for most MPs; that there should be no compensation for job insecurity or reflection of length of service; and that there should be a clear distinction between pay and expenses.

However, the political fall-out of the expenses scandal meant that earlier attempts at objectivity were perceived as insufficient and the system in place for determining MPs' pay and allowances politically unsustainable. The Independent Parliamentary Standards Authority (IPSA) was established by the Parliamentary Standards Act 2009 with the intention of shifting the parliamentary allowances system in the House of Commons from a system of self-regulation to one of regulation by an independent body. While IPSA was originally given responsibility to pay members' salaries, and to determine the level of and to pay members' allowances, it was in 2011 given the additional responsibility of determining pay, as well as allowances. In 2013, it conducted a review of MPs' remuneration and found that 'past increases in MPs' pay, judged to be justified and appropriate by review bodies, have been set aside or diluted because of concerns about the political consequences of their implementation. Quite simply, there is never a good time to determine MPs' pay'. It recommended a package that, without increasing the cost to the taxpayer, it said would involve five elements: 'a one-off pay rise, thereafter linking MPs' pay to what everyone else is paid; overhauling MPs' generous pensions; scrapping resettlement payments worth tens of thousands of pounds; further tightening expenses; and calling on MPs to produce an annual report to help constituents understand their work'. Following the statutory review it is required to do at the start of each Parliament, IPSA announced that MPs' salaries would be increased to £74,000 with effect from 8 May 2015. It determined that subsequent annual increases should be in line with changes in public sector average earnings (not whole economy average earnings). The most recent annual adjustment to MPs' basic pay was an increase of 1.8 per cent, bringing the overall salary to £77,379 from April 2018.

Even after the anger aroused by the expenses scandal, it is generally accepted that MPs need to be able to claim certain expenses – in order to be able to hire staff, to travel between Westminster and their constituencies and, where necessary, to rent accommodation to allow them to be able to live and work both in Westminster and their constituencies, for example. The amounts available are as follows:

Table 3.3 IPSA summary of MPs' available allowances in 2017–18

Budget heading	Area/eligibility	Returning MPs (*full 2017–18 budget*)	Departing MPs (*3 months pro-rated*)	New MPs (*10 months pro-rated*)
Accommodation expenditure – rental costs	London area	**£22,760**	**£5,690**	**£18,967**
	Outside London area	**£15,850**	**£3,963**	**£13,209**
Accommodation – associated expenditure only	(Non-London area MPs only)	**£5,963** 3 months @ £8,850 per year pre-election; 9 months @ £5,000 per year post-election	**£2,213**	**£4,167**
Office costs	London area MPs	**£26,850**	**£6,713**	**£28,375** incl. £6,000 start-up supplement
	Non-London area MPs	**£24,150**	**£6,038**	**£26,125** incl. £6,000 start-up supplement
Staffing	London area MPs	**£161,550**	**£40,388**	**£134,625**
	Non-London area MPs	**£150,900**	**£37,725**	**£125,750**
Winding-up	London area MPs	N/A	**£57,150**	N/A
	Non-London area MPs	N/A	**£53,950**	N/A
London Area Living Payment (LALP)	London area MPs	**£3,820**	**£955**	**£3,184**

Regardless of the amounts available to help MPs function, there is now greater transparency about what claims are made by them. Before responsibility moved to IPSA, the House had, for many years, published the total amounts claimed by each MP against the main allowances. IPSA continues to publish such information, but it also publishes individual claims submitted by each MP (other than those relating to security and disability assistance). Constituents are thus able to see exactly what their MP has claimed (and compare those claims with those of other MPs).

The reputational hangover of the expenses scandal persists, and evidence suggests that many people still do not trust their MPs. However, whether MPs are paid too much or too little, and whether their allowances regime is overly generous or penny-pinching, it has never been easier to see exactly what payments have been made to them; and they no longer take decisions about the levels of those payments.

MPs' staff

MPs are the employers of their staff, although staff are paid centrally by IPSA and are hired on standard contracts. In recent years, there has been a substantial increase in MPs' paid staff, from 1,850 in 2001 to 2,580 in 2005, to around 3,150 in 2016 (in addition to unpaid staff).

There is no one pattern of the way an MP uses staff, and there are many permutations. Some MPs, particularly those with a heavy constituency caseload, base all their staff in the constituency. This makes practical sense: staff in constituency offices can network more easily with local agencies and more conveniently make arrangements for surgeries, visits and so on, and staff costs are lower outside London. Others, especially London members, whose constituencies are not far away, have all their staff at Westminster (where they also have the advantage of free office accommodation and other services). In the country as a whole, staff are split about one-third at Westminster and two-thirds in constituencies. There is concern that the structure of IPSA's staffing allowances provides a perverse incentive for MPs to base staff at Westminster rather than in their constituencies. Not only does this put additional pressure on the House administration and the Parliamentary Estate, it would be perverse if MPs' staff unnecessarily based at Westminster cost the taxpayer more per head than those in constituencies.

The types of people that MPs employ, and what they expect from them, vary from member to member, reflecting the fact that there is no standard way of doing the job of an MP. Some need caseworkers; some need a PA to organise a diary and act as their right hand; others need researchers to support work on their specialist subjects; yet others need a 'deputy MP' in the constituency, someone they can trust to handle their local profile and press relations, combined with a sure touch on constituency cases.

Opposition frontbenchers have a particular need for specialist support because they are taking on ministers who can draw on the non-party-political, but nevertheless substantial, resources of government departments. Sometimes, MPs pool their staff; for example, in opposition the Conservative Party established its own parliamentary research unit of a dozen or so graduates who researched topics in depth on request from subscribing MPs. Opposition frontbenchers are also heavy users of the independent researchers in the House of Commons Library.

Some MPs have worked at Westminster before winning a seat of their own, and a post as a researcher is a recognised apprenticeship in a political career. But it is also not unusual to find staff who do not identify fully with their MP's political views and see themselves as servants of the constituency as much as of a party politician.

Some, especially the traditional secretary or PA, spend much of their working lives in the job. For others, such as the 'interns' in the US model, working for an MP may be more for the experience than the pay, as a prelude to a career in a different field. A few universities now have a sandwich year as a formal part of a politics degree.

Just as the use made of staff varies, so too does its effectiveness. Having personal staff is a new experience for many newly elected MPs. Some take to it readily and use staff to add real value to their work. However, there are also MPs who allow researchers to operate with a good deal of independence, which leads to criticisms that these are surrogate members pursuing their own agendas and encouraging MPs to commission Library research or table parliamentary questions that are more for the benefit of researcher than member.

The recent harassment scandal, where allegations were made about the treatment of staff by some MPs, highlighted an apparent lack of support for those staff. Concerns that some staff – particularly younger people, and those keen to pursue a political career and so wanting to avoid being seen as 'trouble makers' – were vulnerable to abuse or harassment resulted in the setting up of the working group mentioned earlier (page 61). While the party leaders have signed up to the recommendations of that group, much of the detail of their implementation remains to be fleshed out. The report certainly signals the intent of the party leaderships to tackle the problem.

Finance for opposition parties

'Short money': parties in the House of Commons

Since 1975 there has been financial support for opposition parties in the Commons (often called Short money, after Edward Short, Leader of the House at the time) to go some way towards redressing the imbalance between the support available to opposition parties and that available to the government through the Civil Service. In order to qualify, a party must have at least two MPs – or one MP, provided that the party also polled 150,000 votes nationwide. In either case, the MPs must have been elected for their party at the previous general election, which disqualifies new party groupings formed in the current parliament from claiming financial support.

There are three categories of support: the basic funding established in 1975; travel and associated expenses, introduced in 1993; and support for the Leader of the Opposition's Office, which began in 1999. All are up-rated annually. In 2016 new reporting requirements were imposed on parties to publish audited accounts showing how the funding was used. Changes designed to reduce the cost of Short money (by updating it line with CPI rather than RPI) and new floors and ceilings in the amounts payable to the smallest parties (those with five or fewer MPs) were also introduced.

The current amounts for basic funding are £16,938 per MP and £33.83 for every 200 votes cast for the party in the last general election. The 2016/17 allocations were:

Labour	£5,510,661
SNP	£1,194,540
Liberal Democrats	£544,170
Green	£212,100
UKIP	£212,100
DUP	£166,661
Plaid Cymru	£81,532
SDLP	£70,700
UUP	£70,700

For travel expenses, the opposition parties shared a total of £186,073 in the same proportions as their basic funding. Support for the Leader of the Opposition's Office was £789,146.

The basic funding may be used only for parliamentary business, which includes research to support shadow ministers and their work, and developing and communicating alternative policies. The money may not be used for political campaigning, fund raising or membership drives. In February 2006, the government's proposal to give the Sinn Féin MPs financial support along the same lines as Short money, although they had not taken their seats, was approved despite fierce opposition in some quarters.

Opposition salaries

Six opposition members in the two Houses receive a salary by virtue of the posts they hold. In the Commons, the Leader of the Opposition gets £63,762 a year, the Opposition Chief Whip gets £33,350 and his deputy and one other whip get £19,441 – in each case, in addition to their salaries as MPs. In the Lords, the Leader of the Opposition receives £68,710 and the Opposition Chief Whip £63,537 a year.

Why subsidise the opposition?

It may seem reasonable for a taxpayer to say: 'I'm prepared to fund hospitals, or the education system; but why should I pay for party politicians?' Fair enough; but there is a powerful counter-argument. Ministers are not allowed to use their civil servants for overtly party political purposes, although they can still use the huge resources of their departments to research, develop and present new policies. But no government has a monopoly of truth and right. It must surely be to the advantage of the country as a whole when opposition parties have the resources to test and challenge those policies in a reasoned, well-researched way, and to put forward credible alternative proposals.

This was recognised in the Political Parties, Elections and Referendums Act 2000, which made provision for 'policy development grants'. The sum of £2 million a year is available for work on policies for inclusion in a party's manifesto. Under the supervision of the Electoral Commission, the money is divided between parties with at least two MPs at Westminster (who have taken their seats, so Sinn Féin are not eligible). The money is allocated in a similar way to Short money: £1 million is split in proportion to numbers of MPs; and £1 million in proportion to votes cast at the last election.

State funding for political parties?

More generally, the extent to which the non-parliamentary activities of political parties should be publicly funded remains contentious. Membership of the Labour party has increased greatly since 2015 (to about 550,000); the Conservatives have around 125,000 members. The increasing costs of election campaigns and day-to-day running of parties cannot be met by membership subscriptions alone. This inevitably means parties look to major donations by trade unions or wealthy individuals; but these, in turn, give rise to suspicions of peddling influence and politicians in hock to vested interests.

Although there are no caps on the amounts that may be donated to parties, they are required to report to the Electoral Commission all donations and/or loans from any single source which total £7,500 or more in any one year, and their accounts must be lodged with the Electoral Commission. In 2016, Labour was the best-funded party with an income of £49.8 million (including 'Short money'), the Conservatives were in second place with £28.3 million and the Liberal Democrats third with £8.5 million. The other parties received: SNP, £4.9 million, UKIP, £3.4 million, the Green Party £2.1 million and Sinn Féin, £1.2 million.

A review of party funding, chaired by Sir Hayden Phillips, was launched in 2006 and reported the following year. However, the parties were unable to agree on reforms, and so talks were suspended. Following the 2010 election, the coalition government said that it wanted to return to the issue and the Deputy Prime Minister was given responsibility for this. The Committee on Standards in Public Life reported on the financing of parties and the government accepted, in principle, the case for caps on donations and for funding of parties by trades unions to be reviewed. However, the cross-party talks that followed were not successful and the government said that the full package of reforms would not proceed. However, the Transparency of Lobbying, Non-Party Campaigning and Trade Union Administration Act 2014 tightened the controls in place for non-party campaigning (for example, charities and unions) in the run-up to elections, and placed certain caps on what could be spent. And the Trade Union Act 2016 requires new trade union members to opt-in to making donations to a union's political fund (used to donate to a political party, usually the Labour Party), a change from an opt-out system. The Act was watered down from the government's original proposals, and was criticised for addressing only one aspect of party funding.

There is considerable opposition in some quarters to the state funding of *all* the activities of political parties (in contrast to the parliamentary functions of challenge referred to on page 72). There are also the arguments that state funding tends to make recipient parties complacent and – because the obvious way of setting levels is to base them on the previous election results – that it over-rewards those who do well. Meanwhile neither the Conservative nor the Labour manifestos for the 2017 general election made any mention of reforming party funding (beyond Labour's commitment to repeal the Trade Union Act 2016).

The House of Lords

The Lord Speaker

Since July 2006 the House of Lords has elected its own presiding officer in the form of the Lord Speaker. The speakership had, until then, been held *ex officio* by the Lord Chancellor but the role ended with the passage of the Constitutional Reform Act 2005 and the effective dismemberment of that ancient office. The Lord Speaker is elected by the whole House using the alternative vote system and has assumed the parliamentary duties formerly performed by the Lord Chancellor, along with other functions befitting a full-time, salaried office. The current Lord Speaker, Lord Fowler, was a Conservative peer (having been an MP and a cabinet minister) and was elected in 2016. He is the third holder of the office.

First and foremost, the Lord Speaker presides in the chamber of the House, seated upon the Woolsack or at the Table of the House when the House is in Committee. But the powers of the Lord Speaker in the chamber are relatively limited. The Lord Speaker does not arbitrate on rules of order. The preservation of order in the House is the responsibility of all the Lords who are present, and any Lord may call the attention of the House to any breaches of order or laxity in observing its customs. If the House is in need of advice on matters of procedure and order, it is to the Leader of the House (also a government minister) that they look. And the Leader – or, in her absence, the Government Chief Whip – will often intervene to interpret and give voice to what he or she considers to be the wish of the House when procedural difficulties occur.

The Lord Speaker and Deputy Speakers do not call lords to speak. As we will see on page 288, the order of speaking in debates is prearranged and set out in lists prepared by the Government Whips' Office. Each item of the day's business set out on the Order Paper is called on by the Clerk at the Table. The Lord Speaker or his deputies will call members to speak to their amendments when the House is considering legislation, but no one calls the subsequent speakers in a debate on an amendment. The Lord Speaker cannot curtail debate, and when debate is concluded, the function of this role is limited to putting the question – announcing what it is on which the Lords are about to vote – and then declaring the result of the vote. The Lord Speaker is expected not to vote in the House, even if a vote is tied. In such cases, the standing orders of the House decide the result and the amendment falls. The Lord Speaker decides whether to grant leave for an urgent (private notice) question to be asked at Question Time, and also in exercising discretion in the application of the *sub judice* rule.

A significant function is to chair the House of Lords Commission, which is the House's chief administrative body (see page 79). This gives the Lord Speaker a major role in most aspects of the internal administration of the House. Together with the Speaker of the Commons (and the Clerks of the two Houses as Corporate Officers), the Lord Speaker has responsibilities for the security of the precincts and meets regularly with the Speaker to discuss matters of joint concern. The Lord Speaker is empowered to recall the House of Lords whenever it stands adjourned if public interest requires it; as in the House of Commons, in practice this happens only when requested by the government.

The representative role of the Lord Speaker has blossomed since the post became elected, both in promoting the work of the House to audiences at home, representing the House at meetings of conferences of Speakers overseas, and fulfilling bilateral visits to overseas parliaments. The Lord Speaker also represents the House on ceremonial occasions – hosting and, together with the Commons Speaker, making a speech of welcome to visiting heads of state and others; presenting Humble Addresses to The Queen, as on the occasion of her Diamond Jubilee in 2012; as a member of Royal Commissions for Prorogation; and at the State Opening of Parliament.

The Lord Speaker, Lord Fowler, 2017

Source: Copyright House of Lords

The Senior Deputy Speaker, Deputy Speakers and Deputy Chairmen

The Lord Speaker is assisted in his duties presiding over the House by a panel of 20 deputy speakers. Unlike in the Commons, these deputies carry on as normal party (or cross-bench) members when not on the Woolsack – speaking in debates and voting in divisions.

The team of deputies is led by the Senior Deputy Speaker, currently Lord McFall of Alcluith. He is appointed by the House at the beginning of every session to take the chair in all Committees of the whole House. The Senior Deputy Speaker is an influential figure in the Lords and is paid the salary of a minister of state in consequence. He organises the panel of Deputy Speakers and Deputy Chairmen and assigns them their duties week by week. He has considerable powers in the field of private legislation (see page 236) by selecting opposed private bill committees and presiding over unopposed bill committees. During the nineteenth century – the heyday of private legislation – this gave the holder of the post immense power and influence over many of the greatest public works projects of the day. This aspect of his work takes up far less of the Senior Deputy Speaker's time today.

The post of Senior Deputy Speaker was created in 2016 following a review of domestic (i.e. inward-facing) committees in the House of Lords. It replaced the role of Chairman of Committees, though that title remains in legislation. The Senior Deputy Speaker acts as the House of Lords Commission's spokesman in the House. He chairs the Liaison Committee, which meets from time to time to review and allocate resources to the policy select committees of the House; the Privileges and Conduct Committee; and the Procedure Committee. He also chairs an informal group of select committee chairmen who meet to co-ordinate committee activity on Brexit. Before the 2016 reforms to the office the Chairman of Committees chaired the domestic committees concerned with the administration of the House of Lords – covering works, catering, etc. Now those matters are overseen by the Finance Committee and the Services Committee, which have their own chairmen and which report to the House of Lords Commission.

The Leader of the House of Lords

The Leader of the House of Lords, currently Baroness Evans of Bowes Park, is a government minister and a member of the Cabinet. The allegiance of this role is to the government and its policies, but the Leader of the House of Lords also has a wider task of upholding the rights and interests of the House as a whole. It is the Leader of the House, for example, who assists the House in keeping its own order during proceedings – particularly during Question Time – and who makes representations on behalf of the House to fellow ministers.

The Leader of the House of Lords works closely with the Leader of the House of Commons in planning and supervising the government's legislative programme; she is a member of the Parliamentary Business and Legislation Committee of the Cabinet, together with the Government Chief Whip; and reports to the Cabinet itself on business in the Lords. The role is responsible for delivering the government's business in the House, although most of the planning of this is undertaken by the Government

Chief Whip and, in particular, by the Chief Whip's principal private secretary, a clerk on secondment to the Cabinet Office, who also assists the Leader of the House in her parliamentary work.

Much of the Leader's influence is exerted behind the scenes – for example through meetings of the business managers (as the Leaders and Government Chief Whips of the two Houses are known). Within the Lords, the Leader of the House of Lords secures agreement on matters relating to the business of the House and other matters by discussions with other party leaders. Similar negotiations are held by the Chief Whip with other party whips. As in the Commons, these contacts are known as 'the usual channels'. They are entirely informal and by their very nature devoid of any ground rules, save perhaps one – that a deal struck through the usual channels will normally stick. The Leader of the House, together with other party leaders, sits on all key decision-making bodies within the House – such as the House of Lords Commission, the Liaison Committee and the Procedure Committee.

The Clerk of the Parliaments and the staff of the House

The most senior official of the House of Lords is the Clerk of the Parliaments. In the same way as the Clerk of the House of Commons, he combines a variety of roles. He is the principal adviser to the House on all aspects of parliamentary practice and procedure, and the daily business of the House proceeds on the basis of briefs prepared by the clerks in the procedural offices. But he also has wide administrative responsibilities as chief executive of the House administration and chair of the Management Board (see page 79) – a pre-eminence derived from his position as Accounting Officer for money spent under the two Lords Requests for Resources (formerly Votes), and as the employer of all House of Lords staff under the Clerk of the Parliaments Act 1824 and the Parliamentary Corporate Bodies Act 1992. The 1992 Act makes the Clerk of the Parliaments Corporate Officer of the House of Lords, and in this capacity he gives the House legal personality and enters into contracts on its behalf. The Clerk of the Parliaments is appointed by the Crown under Letters Patent, usually from among the longer-serving clerks of the House, following advertisement and interview by the party leaders and Convenor. His immediate deputies, the Clerk Assistant and the Reading Clerk, are appointed by the Lord Speaker following a similar process.

Different offices of the House's administration deal with finance, committees, legislation, human resources, facilities (including works and accommodation), the Journal of the House, overseas business, the official report or *Hansard*, catering services, the Library and Parliamentary Archives. Black Rod's Department deals with ceremonial events and access to the House. The total number of staff employed in these offices is about 480. This figure excludes staff in services shared with the Commons – for example, in the Parliamentary Estates Directorate; the Parliamentary Digital Service; the Visitor, Education and Outreach Services; and the Parliamentary Security Department.

House of Lords administration

The chief decision-making body in the administration of the Lords is the House of Lords Commission, a select committee of 10 members, including the Leader of the House and other party leaders and the Convenor of the Crossbench Peers, and two external members. The Clerk of the Parliaments attends and other senior officers attend as required. The Commission was created in 2016, replacing the House Committee. Its role is to provide high-level strategic and political direction to the House of Lords administration on behalf of the House. In addition it develops and approves the House's strategic, business and financial plans; agrees the annual estimates and supplementary estimates; and supervises the arrangements relating to members' expenses. Its work is assisted by a management board of senior officers of the House and external members, chaired by the Clerk of the Parliaments. The House of Lords Commission meets monthly when the House is sitting; the Management Board meets fortnightly. Both of their agendas and minutes are published on the internet.

The House of Lords Commission is advised by the Finance Committee and the Services Committee. It delegates certain functions to them, and their chairmen sit on the Commission. Any decision requiring major unauthorised expenditure requires the agreement of the House of Lords Commission.

The administration is also assisted by an Audit Committee, whose membership – unusually – is determined by the House of Lords Commission. It consists of five members of the House, none of whom holds any other office in the House, and two external members, one of whom also currently attends meetings of the management board. The Audit Committee oversees the House's internal financial controls, management responses to internal audit reports and risk management.

Completing the picture is the Lord Speaker's Advisory Panel on Works of Art, which advises the Lord Speaker on matters relating to works of art in the House of Lords. It comprises 12 members and, although not formally a select committee, it acts much like one.

Expenses

Members of the House of Lords are unpaid, in the sense that, with the exception of certain office holders, they do not receive a salary. But they do have their travel to and from Westminster paid for, and they may receive financial support in respect of each day of attendance at the House or on other prescribed business. This may be claimed at one of two rates – £153 or £305, though a few members make no claims at all. This payment is tax free because members of the House of Lords, unlike MPs, are deemed to hold a 'dignity' rather than a paid 'office'. The current scheme was adopted in May 2010 and replaced a more elaborate scheme of day and overnight subsistence, and other allowances. The flat rate was introduced after it had emerged in 2009 that the allowances – the overnight allowance, in particular – were in some cases being improperly claimed. The rate of financial support is increased each year in line with the percentage increase in MPs' pay.

Finance for political parties in the Lords: 'Cranborne money'

For many years, the chief opposition parties in the Lords received funding from money made available from public funds to opposition parties in the Commons (see page 72). Since 1996, the Official Opposition and the second-largest party have been provided with a separate allocation, funded by the House. Since 1999, the Convenor of the Crossbench Peers has received similar funding to provide secretarial support. These sums are determined by resolution of the House and are up-rated annually in line with inflation. For 2016–17, the amounts available were £587,117 to the Labour Party as Official Opposition, £293,142 for the Liberal Democrats and £89,165 to the Convenor.

House of Lords funding

The House of Lords is funded directly from the Treasury on the same lines as a government department, but for constitutional reasons – and unlike a department – the House is not cash-limited. That does not mean that it can spend what it wants. Great self-restraint is, in fact, exercised on the demands made upon the public purse, and a savings programme that was put in place in 2010 has had a considerable downward effect on spending. The House has two Estimates, one for resource costs of the administration (including members' financial support) and one for capital spending, chiefly works, which is more liable to fluctuation according to the projects in hand. Overall financial control rests with the House of Lords Commission; the Clerk of the Parliaments, who is head of the Lords administration, is the Accounting Officer and is responsible for all its expenditure, including its propriety and effectiveness. The House of Lords accounts are examined and certified each year by the NAO.

How much does Parliament cost?

Parliament operates on the same resource accounting basis as central government, so the costs of Parliament include not only what is paid in cash – such as salaries, rates and electricity – but also notional costs for the use of buildings and other assets.

On this basis, in 2016/17 the House of Commons administration cost some £227 million, including capital expenditure. In the same year, IPSA was forecast to cost approximately £188 million, including the salaries of all MPs and their staff. In 2016/17, the House of Lords cost £98 million, including expenditure on works. The total cost of Parliament was considerably less than one-tenth of 1 per cent of total government spending.

4

Influences on Parliament

The House of Commons

The job is what you make it

Almost everyone in employment in the United Kingdom has a job description. And those who are self-employed – perhaps running a shop or other small business – have pretty clear indications of what constitutes success or failure. Members of Parliament have neither, unless it is to be re-elected at the next election. As we shall see, there is no shortage of people who will tell the newly elected MP what he or she should be doing; but there is no formal statement of what the job involves.

There are many good descriptions of 'what MPs do', but they are strictly *descriptions*, drawn from observing the many, and not *definitions*. The truth is that no definition exists. As a new MP, it is entirely up to you to decide how you do the job. In 2001 the Senior Salaries Review Body attempted to draft a generic MP's job description, and listed the following 'principal accountabilities':

1. *Help furnish and maintain government and opposition so that the business of parliamentary democracy may proceed.*
2. *Monitor, stimulate and challenge the executive in order to influence and where possible change government action in ways which are considered desirable.*
3. *Initiate, seek to amend and review legislation so as to help maintain a continually relevant and appropriate body of law.*
4. *Establish and maintain a range of contacts throughout the constituency, and proper knowledge of its characteristics, so as to identify and understand issues affecting it and, wherever possible, further the interests of the constituency generally.*
5. *Provide appropriate assistance to individual constituents, through using knowledge of local and national government agencies and institutions, to progress and where possible help resolve their problems.*

6. *Contribute to the formulation of party policy to ensure that it reflects views and national needs which are seen to be relevant and important.*
7. *Promote public understanding of party policies in the constituency, media and elsewhere to facilitate the achievement of party objectives.*

It is a daunting list, and each MP must decide the balance of time and energy they will expend on each area. Will you devote yourself entirely to your constituents and their problems? (Unless you are both selective and realistic, you will rapidly discover that you could easily spend 24 hours in every day on this.) Will you become a standard bearer for some product of your constituency – apples, computer software, shellfish, sports cars? Will you pursue an abiding political interest that you had before you came into the House: perhaps debt in the developing world or renewable energy? Possibly you are attracted by select committee work, the business of calling the government to account, and making yourself an expert on a particular area of policy. Perhaps you might set yourself to contribute to better understanding between the United Kingdom and the Arab world, or to ensuring that the UK makes the most of commercial opportunities on the Pacific Rim. If you are in the party of government, might your ambitions be focused on ministerial office and getting a foot on the first rung of the ladder as a parliamentary private secretary (PPS; see page 84)?

In practice, most MPs will do some or all of these various aspects of the job. But few will do exactly what they expected when first they came into the House. The main reason for that is the complex web of influences on the House and its members.

The government's control of the House of Commons

We saw in Chapter 2 how, in order to be invited to form a government, a prospective Prime Minister must have control of the House of Commons – that is, for his or her party (together, if necessary, with other parties) to have a sufficient parliamentary majority to be certain of getting approval for the legislative programme (announced in the Queen's Speech) and for government taxation and spending (through the Finance Bill and the Estimates). But having a numerical majority in order to be able to win votes and secure government business is only one kind of control; control of the House's time and agenda – what is debated, for how long, and on what terms – also matters. And while the government retains very significant control of what the House debates and when, this control was weakened in the 2010–15 Parliament by backbenchers being given greater influence over the House's time and agenda.

Control of time

Every Thursday, the Leader of the House announces what the business will be – that is, what items will be taken on each day – for the next fortnight. In many parliaments, particularly those on the continental model, there is a business committee or *bureau*, involving not only the business managers and other party representatives, but also the president of the assembly and his deputies, who decide what business to propose. And even then, that draft agenda is subject to approval by the assembly as a whole. At the start of the 2010 Parliament, it seemed that the House might soon adopt a similar approach: the Coalition Agreement included a commitment to implement in full the proposals of the Reform of the House of Commons Committee – or 'the Wright Committee' as it was better known, after its chair, Dr Tony Wright, the former MP for Cannock Chase – including plans for a House Business Committee, which would have carried out *bureau*-style functions. In 2014, however, the Leader of the House said that there was as yet no basis of agreement on the proposal, and it has not been pursued since.

The absence of a House Business Committee in the Commons means that it remains primarily for the government of the day to propose and to dispose. Ever since the Balfour reforms at the turn of the nineteenth/twentieth centuries, all House of Commons time that is not ring-fenced is at the disposal of the government of the day. This meant, before the 2010–15 parliament, that in 150 or 160 sitting days in a parliamentary session, only 20 'opposition days', 13 days for private members' bills, some time for private bills, three 'estimates days' for debates on select committee reports, the daily half-hour adjournment debate, urgent questions and the daily Question Time were not in the gift of the government. Even then, it was for the government to decide *when* the opposition days, private members' bill days and estimates days were to be taken.

It is still the case that non-ring-fenced time is at the government's disposal, but the big change introduced in the 2010–15 parliament was the appointment of the Backbench Business Committee (BBCom) (see also page 276) and its allocation of 35 days (27 in the chamber, and the remainder in Westminster Hall) of backbench business. This has loosened the (still formidable) grip of the government on the timetable and agenda of the Commons. The statistics bear this out: the amount of time spent on business initiated by the government has fallen from nearly three-fifths in the 2003–04 and 2004–05 sessions to around one-third in 2016–17, while time on business initiated by backbenchers has risen in the same period from around one-tenth to nearly one-quarter.

The 35 days available for backbench business, 20 for opposition days and 13 for private members' bills are set out in the House's standing orders as a per-session quota. However, while most parliamentary sessions run for approximately a year, they can run for longer or shorter periods, at the government's instigation; in those circumstances there is no automatic re-allocation of days for non-government business on a pro rata basis. Following the 2017 election, the government announced that there would a long, two-year session. Opposition parties protested that there was no proportionate increase in the number of days available for non-government business and pointed to the example of the long 2010–12 session when additional days were allocated for opposition debates and private members' bills.

The 'elective dictatorship'?

A former Conservative Lord Chancellor, Lord Hailsham of St Marylebone, described the Westminster system of parliamentary government as an 'elective dictatorship': that is, one in which a government, once elected, is free to do very much what it wants. To an extent, Lord Hailsham was and is right. The Westminster system is not government by Parliament but government through Parliament and (perhaps especially obvious when the government has a large parliamentary majority) one of the roles of Parliament is to legitimise what the government does. The difference between debating policies and enshrining them in legislation is important: while the recent changes to backbench business have increased the ability of backbenchers to initiate debates in the House, it remains the case that the vast majority of legislation passed by Parliament is government legislation, and even private members' bills stand little chance of enactment unless they have government support.

Government patronage and collective responsibility

The government's position is further entrenched by the Prime Minister's ability to choose ministers and for ministers to choose parliamentary private secretaries (PPSs), who are not ministers but who act as unpaid aides to secretaries of state or ministers of state. Collectively, these people make up the payroll vote: those individuals expected to vote with the government – a total of some 140 MPs in the Commons.

Not only is the power of ministerial appointment a key prime ministerial weapon, but it is also allied to the constitutional doctrine of collective responsibility, under which all the members of a government publicly support all the government's policies. Ministers may (and often do) disagree privately and seek to change or modify their colleagues' minds and policies, but if they disagree publicly they are expected to resign (as did the Leader of the House, Robin Cook, in 2003 over the government's proposed military action against Iraq; the Work and Pensions Secretary, Iain Duncan Smith, in 2016 over the government's approach to welfare cuts; and the Foreign Secretary and DEXEU Secretary in 2018 over the handling of Brexit) or face the sack from the PM of the day. The essence of collective responsibility is accountability to Parliament: each House is entitled to an explanation of the government's position on an issue, such that it may hold the government as a whole to account. It also has political benefits for the government of the day: the media rarely respect a government which bickers in public.

This concept came under strain under the coalition government of 2010–15. From the outset exceptions to the convention were agreed in the coalition's *Programme for Government*. This stated that the governing parties might adopt opposing positions on: the referendum to be held on the alternative vote system (but not the bill setting up the referendum); university funding; the renewal of Trident; and tax allowances for married couples. Such explicit 'agreements to differ' were not a constitutional novelty. In 1975, the Labour government agreed that its ministers could (outside Parliament) campaign against the collective line in the referendum on membership of the (then) European Economic Community; two years later, the government decided that ministers could vote against laws establishing direct elections to the European Parliament. There is a coalition precedent, too: on 23 January 1932, *The Times* published the then coalition government's agreement to differ on the issue of tariff reform. Ten days later, in the House, the Conservative Chancellor, Neville Chamberlain, introduced the government's policy, subsequently to be opposed by the Liberal Home Secretary, Sir Herbert Samuel.

In addition, over the course of the parliament further disagreements other than those anticipated during the drafting of the *Programme for Government* emerged. In 2012, collective responsibility was suspended on an amendment to the Electoral Registration and Amendment Bill which delayed a review of parliamentary constituency boundaries. This was after the Deputy Prime Minister instructed Liberal Democrats to vote against it in response to the failure of House of Lords reform – a favourite policy of the Liberal Democrats, included in the Coalition Agreement – because sufficient numbers of Conservatives did not support such reform.

Another high-profile disagreement between the two parties took place over the report by Lord Justice Leveson on *The Culture, Practices and Ethics of the Press*. Following publication of the report in 2012, the Prime Minister and the Deputy Prime Minister made separate, successive statements in the House of Commons in response to it, each answering questions from backbenchers. In that case, however, there was no collective government position on how to respond to the report and so, formally at least, the concept of collective responsibility was preserved. In the event the two sides of the coalition reached a collective position on how to implement (or not) the report's recommendations.

A more egregious departure from the convention concerned the 2013 Queen's Speech. Conservative MPs tabled an amendment regretting that an EU referendum bill was not included in the Speech. The Queen's Speech, in setting out the government's legislative intentions for the forthcoming session (see page 131), may be seen as the epitome of collective responsibility. Therefore, when the Prime Minister indicated that ministers would be able to abstain on the vote and PPSs allowed to vote for the rebel amendment, this appeared to represent a flouting of the convention of collective responsibility as generally understood.

However high-profile these disagreements, they represented a tiny fraction of the government business conducted under the coalition. In that sense, perhaps it is more remarkable that the concept of collective responsibility survived coalition government as well as it did, rather than that it occasionally broke down.

Another notable departure from collective responsibility happened in 2016 over the EU referendum. Individual ministers were permitted during the referendum campaign to express a different view from the government's collective stance of recommending a 'remain' vote. Thus five cabinet ministers (Michael Gove, Chris Grayling, Priti Patel, Theresa Villiers and John Whittingdale) and several junior ministers supported 'leave' while keeping their ministerial posts – though in some cases not for long after the referendum result and change of Prime Minister.

Theory and practice

It might appear that little stands in the way of the government doing what it wants (or, perhaps more precisely, what the Prime Minister with the backing of the Cabinet wants). But the picture is more subtle than that. There is, indeed, an expectation that a government having won a mandate at a general election, with a majority in the House of Commons, will be able to get its business through. However, in practice this depends on a number of factors. A government must retain the support of its backbenchers; and, as we shall see, it is not enough to issue orders; persuasion is often needed. Public and media opinion needs to be benign – or, at least, not so critical as to give government backbenchers cold feet.

In addition, all governments are aware of the fact that, perhaps not too long distant, they may be on the opposition benches. In the heady days after a big election victory, or with the insulation of a large parliamentary majority, this recollection may be sometimes less vivid, but it underpins any government's need to maintain a working relationship with the opposition, and especially with the largest opposition party ('the Official Opposition'). New MPs who have known only the government benches may want to press on regardless, but their enthusiasm tends to be tempered by longer-serving MPs who remember all too many occasions when in opposition they won the arguments but lost the votes.

This working relationship with the opposition means, in House terms, general agreement on the arrangement and timing of business, and accord on less contentious matters such as the dates of parliamentary recesses, normally through 'the usual channels' (see page 90). The opposition, too, has a considerable interest in maintaining this working relationship. The traditional statement that the opposition's power is one of delay is now out of date, given the routine programming of government bills (see page 185). However, cooperation with the government in the arrangement of business will give the opposition the chance to express (and sometimes secure) priorities for debate, and to trade time and tactics, perhaps along the lines of 'no division on second reading of bill X and only half a day on its report stage', but in return 'an extra day on the report stage of bill Y'. The opposition gets the extra day on bill Y, which it sees as more important; the government saves some time on bill X and also knows that it can slacken the voting requirements for its MPs on the second reading of that bill.

Accountability and responsibility

A distinction is sometimes made between ministerial accountability (being answerable to Parliament for the government's actions) and ministerial responsibility ('taking personal responsibility for what has been done in the minister's name – even without the minister's knowledge – and, if necessary resigning') but, in practice, the second is really an extension of the first.

Arthur Balfour (Prime Minister 1902–05) described democracy as 'government by explanation'. Even if it is likely that the government will eventually get its way, Parliament is the forum in which it must explain itself and be held to account. Explanation may take various forms: responding to criticisms of proposed legislation at the second reading of a bill, or on detailed amendments put forward at report stage; explaining and defending a broader policy, perhaps on education reform or NHS funding, as part of a full day's debate initiated by the opposition or backbenchers; or giving a detailed account of its actions to a select committee. A minister may decide to come to the House of Commons to make a statement on a topical matter; if not, they might find themselves having to attend to answer an urgent question on the same matter (see page 307). The requirement on governments to explain and justify can, in itself, be a brake on executive power; but it is up to members in both Houses to make this process effective.

Ministerial accountability is a concept that it is easier to recognise than to define. There is extensive case law covering a number of years, beginning with the Crichel Down affair in 1954, when the Minister of Agriculture, Sir Thomas Dugdale, resigned apparently because he was taking responsibility for errors made by his civil servants (but more likely because he was left high and dry by a change in government policy); the Westland affair in 1986; and the special adviser Jo Moore 'burying bad news' in 2001, which led eventually to the resignation of Stephen Byers as Secretary of State for Transport, Local Government and the Regions. On Westland, Leon Brittan resigned as Secretary of State for Trade and Industry, taking responsibility for errors by officials but refusing to explain exactly what had happened. The Defence Select Committee, which investigated the saga, remarked drily: 'A Minister does not discharge his accountability to Parliament merely by acknowledging a general responsibility and, if the circumstances warrant it, by resigning. Accountability involves accounting *in detail* for actions as a Minister'.

The principle of accountability to Parliament is now underpinned by resolutions of both Houses in March 1997 (following the Scott inquiry into the supply of arms to Iraq) on how ministers should behave towards Parliament:

> *Ministers of the Crown are expected to behave according to the highest standards of constitutional and personal conduct in the performance of their duties. In particular, they must observe the following principles of Ministerial conduct:*
>
> *i* *Ministers must uphold the principles of collective responsibility;*
> *ii* *Ministers have a duty to Parliament to account, and be held to account, for the policies, decisions and actions of their Departments and Next Steps Agencies;*
> *iii* *It is of paramount importance that Ministers give accurate and truthful information to Parliament, correcting any inadvertent error at the earliest opportunity. Ministers who knowingly mislead Parliament will be expected to offer their resignation to the Prime Minister;*
> *iv* *Ministers should be as open as possible with Parliament and the public, refusing to provide information only when disclosure would not be in the public interest, which should be decided in accordance with relevant statute and the Government's Code of Practice on Access to Government Information;*
> *v* *Similarly, Ministers should require civil servants who give evidence before Parliamentary Committees on their behalf and under their directions to be as helpful as possible in providing accurate, truthful and full information in accordance with the duties and responsibilities of civil servants as set out in the Civil Service Code.*

In Chapters 9 and 10, we will look more closely at the ways in which the government is called to account.

The party

However close an MP's relationship with the constituency, for most MPs the party to which he or she belongs is the key element in an MP's parliamentary life. This is not surprising; as we saw in Chapter 2, in general the only realistic prospect an aspiring politician has of being elected to the House of Commons is to join a political party and then have the backing of that party to fight an election. But for most MPs their relationship with their party has an element of compromise about it. No party is ever in the happy position that every one of its MPs would sign up to every detail of all of its policies. Some would prefer to see greater emphasis in this or that direction; others are uneasy about the party committing itself on something else. However, just as the collective responsibility of ministers has its strength in public unity, so MPs are content to exchange occasional disagreements or private doubts for the shelter and support of the party that best represents their political outlook.

Given the enormous importance of political parties in Westminster politics, it is perhaps surprising that they are not more explicitly recognised in the rules of the two Houses. In the Commons, the standing orders notice parties only so far as 'committee memberships reflect the composition of the House', that smaller opposition parties have a share of opposition day debates, that a small number of posts are reserved for (or have to be divided between) parties, and that one MP speaking for the second largest opposition party is exempted from any limit that may be imposed on speaking time for backbenchers in a particular debate. In a formal sense, party structures and disciplines exist in parallel with the regulation of the House and its proceedings although, in practice, they interlock at every level.

By contrast, in some parliaments – for example, the Canadian House of Commons – the role of parties is explicitly recognised in the allocation of oral questions and speaking time, which means that the Speaker plays a smaller role in allocation than at Westminster.

The whips

The whips are key players in party organisation and discipline, and in the arrangement and timing of business, on both sides of the House. The title derives from 'whippers-in' or 'whips' in the hunting field. Whips act as a two-way channel of communication between the party leadership and the backbenches; on the one hand feeding back MPs' views and warning of areas of possible difficulty or dissent and, on the other, making clear to backbenchers what the leadership wants from them.

An effective whip needs to be a strong character and a shrewd operator, but also has to balance personal authority with an understanding of the pressures on the MPs for whom she or he is responsible. Much is written, and more speculated, about the black arts of the whips – their techniques for bringing recalcitrant MPs into line – and of their intelligence gathering. There is no doubt that whips can, on occasion, be fearsomely effective, whether by use of stick or carrot, in persuading potential rebels to live with their doubts rather than express them; and there is no doubt, either, that a good whips office knows more about the views and foibles of its backbenchers than it would ever wish to see made public.

Someone who should know – the former Liberal Democrat Chief Whip, Don Foster – claimed that these days the job of the whips involves more carrots than sticks. He said:

> *In the past, the so-called black arts, the revealing of personal secrets, denying office space, denying membership of the committee, denying chairmanship of the committee, all these levers that were part of the [whips'] bag of black arts: they don't exist any more. Parliament has got sufficient office space for MPs, Parliament itself decides its membership of committees . . . so the power of the whips has been stripped away by quite rightly handing those powers back to Parliament itself . . . So what you've got to do is to persuade people of the importance of collegiality.*
>
> *But you've also got to make sure that you bring legislation before Parliament that's not going to cause great friction. The job of the whip, the whole whips' operation, has changed dramatically in recent years.*

Whips also need to be good personnel managers. New (and some more experienced) MPs may find life at Westminster difficult and frustrating; and spending much of the working week perhaps hundreds of miles from home and family, possibly combined with constituency casework that is especially tragic or emotionally draining, can impose real strains. In such circumstances a good whip is a source of advice and support.

Whips are ever-present in proceedings in the House and general committees (see Chapter 5, page 195). In the House, there is always a government and an official opposition whip sitting on the frontbenches keeping an eye on proceedings, jotting down notes on speeches (and speakers) in the debate and alert for any procedural or political difficulty that may arise. Whips have a talent-spotting role, and their good opinion (and especially that of the Chief Whip) may lead to ministerial office or a shadow post.

The Government Chief Whip is known formally as the Parliamentary Secretary to the Treasury (and sometimes as the Patronage Secretary – a reminder of the carrot rather than the stick of parliamentary discipline). It is his responsibility to get the government's business through the Commons with the greatest efficiency and the least dissent from government backbenchers. He normally attends Cabinet meetings and advises the Prime Minister and his senior colleagues on opinion within the parliamentary party, and how proposed policies are likely to play with backbenchers. On the government side, the next three senior whips carry formal titles of posts in the Royal Household: the Treasurer of HM Household, followed by the Comptroller and the Vice-Chamberlain. Traditionally, the Treasurer has also been the Deputy

Chief Whip. There are six other whips (known as Lords Commissioners of the Treasury) and usually seven assistant whips.

The Labour Official Opposition has a Chief Whip and a deputy (who receive additional salaries even though they are in opposition) and 12 or 13 other whips (one of whom receives an additional salary). The smaller parties each have someone who acts as a Chief Whip, although with relatively few MPs their role is more as their parties' voice in the arrangement of business than as organisers and disciplinarians. In the major parties, the whips have regional and subject responsibilities; for example, one may be responsible for both MPs representing constituencies in the North-East and defence.

The usual channels

This is deliberately vague shorthand for the informal discussions that take place between the business managers on both sides of the House. It embraces the Leader of the House and shadow Leader, and the government and opposition Chief Whips (and of other parties as circumstances require), but it also includes day-to-day and minute-to-minute conversations and arrangements between whips on both sides. A key player is the private secretary to the Government Chief Whip who, although a civil servant, plays a highly political role as a go-between.

The usual channels deal with a wide range of business, from issues such as the amount of time to be spent on a government bill in committee and which party should get which select committee chair, to extempore arrangements in which a whip will go round the chamber asking his side's last two or three speakers to limit their speeches so that the 'winding-up' speeches from the frontbenches can start at the time agreed. Off-the-cuff arrangements are sometimes referred to as being done 'behind the chair' – which is, indeed, where they happen when whips from both sides have whispered conversations behind the Speaker's chair.

Discussions through the usual channels are private – were they to be made public, it is unlikely that they would take the same form or be so effective (this is the tension at the heart of proposals for a House Business Committee). But this secrecy, and the feeling on the part of some that deals cooked up behind the scenes may be more for the convenience of the participants than that of backbenchers on one side or another, has led to criticism: Tony Benn, for example, described the usual channels as 'the most polluted waterway in Europe'; and the current Speaker, John Bercow, has frequently criticised the whips.

The Whip

A vital document for every MP is *The Whip*. This is circulated weekly by the whips of each party to their own members and lists the business for the following two weeks, together with the party's expectations as to when its MPs will vote. The importance of the business was formerly reflected by the number of times it was underlined – hence the phrase 'a three-line whip' for something seen as an unbreakable commitment. An example is overleaf.

By arrangement with the whips, an MP may miss even an important vote if he or she is paired – that is, if an MP from the other side makes a formal arrangement not to vote, so that the effect is neutral. For example, it allows the Foreign Secretary to be at the UN, or other ministers to take part in crucial negotiations in Brussels, rather than being called back to vote. This is of less importance when the government of the day has a very large majority; then the government party will normally excuse some of its MPs from voting, on a rota basis, so that they can spend time in their constituencies.

Occasionally the usual channels break down and the opposition withdraws pairing arrangements. This can be a great inconvenience to the government, which must keep many more of its MPs in the precincts or nearby in case of a snap vote.

Party discipline

The whips are responsible for delivering the votes to give effect to their parties' policies and intentions. On matters that are likely to be contentious within the party, the leadership normally takes care to trail proposals in advance to assess whether there is likely to be dissent. It follows that, for the whips, a backbencher's cardinal sin is to abstain, or worse, vote against his or her party without giving any warning. An MP who expresses doubts about being able to support the party will normally be asked to discuss those doubts with his or her own whip, and probably also with the Chief Whip. For crucial votes, the Prime Minister (or other party leader) may want to try to change minds by meeting waverers, as in the vote on military intervention in Syria in August 2013.

A former Cabinet minister once advised his new MP colleagues 'to tread that narrow path between rebellion and sycophancy'. Although, as we shall see below, MPs have become more rebellious in recent Parliaments, party discipline is normally not a problem for most MPs. They accept that membership of a party, with all the advantages that its structures and organisation bring, involves compromise; and they are usually content to vote as the party wishes, especially in subject areas of which they have no close knowledge. They are also well aware that a divided party is a parliamentary, and certainly an electoral, liability. It is ironic that, on the one hand, there is public pressure for MPs to be more independent but, at the same time, a feeling that a party that cannot keep its own members on side has somehow failed.

Dissent and rebellion

An MP will think very carefully before voting against the party, or even abstaining, in an important vote. Unless it is unassailably on a matter of personal conscience, the

THE BUSINESS FOR THE WEEK COMMENCING 23RD JUNE WILL INCLUDE:

MONDAY 23RD JUNE
Last day for tabling: Business, Innovation and Skills
The House meets at **2:30pm** for **Work and Pensions Questions**
Conclusion of the Remaining Stages of the Deregulation Bill (Whip in Charge: Gavin Barwell)
THERE WILL BE A RUNNING 3-LINE WHIP FROM 3.30PM

TUESDAY 24TH JUNE
Last day for tabling: Communities & Local Government and Scotland
The House meets at **11:30am** for **Treasury Questions**
Remaining Stages of the Wales Bill (Whip in Charge: Stephen Crabb)
THERE WILL BE A RUNNING 3-LINE WHIP FROM 12:30PM

WEDNESDAY 25TH JUNE
Last day for tabling: Justice
The House meets at **11:30am** for **Cabinet Office Questions**
At 12 noon: Prime Minister's Questions
Opposition Day (2nd Allotted Day). There will be Debates on Opposition Motions, including on the Subject of the Private Rented Sector (Whip in Charge: Claire Perry)
THERE WILL BE A 3-LINE WHIP AT 3PM FOR 4PM AND 6PM FOR 7PM

THURSDAY 26TH JUNE
Last day for tabling: Prime Minister
The House meets at **9:30am** for **Business, Innovation and Skills Questions**
At 10:30: Business Questions
General Debate on the Programme of Commemoration for the First World War (Whip in Charge: Harriett Baldwin)
THERE WILL BE A 1-LINE WHIP

FRIDAY 27TH JUNE
The House will not be sitting.

A political party's 'Whip', which tells its MPs when they should be present for votes in the Commons

Source: Government Chief Whip's Office, 2014

action will be seen as disloyal and will often have an effect on the prospects for preferment; whips have long memories.

The reasons for rebellion are varied: the issue may be one of general principle, such as limiting the right to jury trial, or the prospect of military action. It may be on an issue that is seen by some of its members as contrary to a party's traditions and best interests; for example, for the Conservatives on the Maastricht treaty in the 1992 parliament and on continued membership of the EU in the 2010–15 parliament, and for the Labour Party on university tuition fees in the 2001 parliament.

The size of a government's majority is obviously an important factor. In 1992 the Conservatives under John Major were returned with an overall majority of 21. By the end of the parliament, by-election defeats and defections to other parties had reduced this to a minority of three. Rebellions among Conservative MPs resulted in nine defeats for the government during that parliament. By contrast, in 1997 Tony Blair had an extraordinarily high majority of 179 over all other parties. The government suffered no defeats in the 1997–2001 and the 2001–05 parliaments, but rebellions were still concerning to the leadership. In the 2010–15 parliament coalition government made dissent an issue for party leaders and whips. Each side wanted to be able to 'deliver' its MPs in support of coalition policy, such that policies more favoured by one side of the coalition would be supported by MPs of the other side. In the current parliament, with a minority government, government whips will have to work hard to win every vote, and will not be able to afford dissent.

Dissent in recent parliaments

1997–2010

In the 1997–2001 parliament, the level of dissent on the government backbenches was less than in previous parliaments. Nevertheless, there were 104 occasions on which Labour members voted against the government on the floor of the House. The biggest rebellions during the Labour administrations between 1997 and 2010 – and, in fact, the biggest for more than a quarter of a century – took place over the government's policy on military action against Iraq. On 26 February 2003, 122 Labour MPs voted against the government on an amendment asserting that the case for military action was 'as yet unproven'; and on 18 March 2003, 139 Labour MPs voted for an amendment to the effect that the case for war had not been established.

In general, levels of dissent amongst government backbenchers increased following the 1997 parliament. In the 2001–05 parliament, Labour MPs voted against their government in 21 per cent of divisions; the figure increased to 28 per cent (365 divisions) in the 2005–10 parliament – a post-war high. (The most rebellious Labour MP during those years, voting against his party's whip 364 times across the two parliaments was Jeremy Corbyn.) The upward trend of backbench rebellion continued under the coalition government in the 2010–15 parliament.

2010–15

The scale of rebellions increased yet further in the 2010–15 parliament. Conservative and Liberal Democrat backbenchers voted against the government in more than one in three divisions (35 per cent). The 2010–15 parliament was therefore the most rebellious since the Second World War. Given the scale of dissent, it is perhaps surprising that this did not translate into more government defeats. In fact, the government could really only be said to have lost a vote as a result of backbench dissent on two occasions. The first, in October 2012, saw 53 Conservative rebels vote for an amendment tabled by a Conservative MP, Mark Reckless, calling for a reduction in the EU budget. The amendment was supported by the Labour opposition and the government lost by 307 to 294 votes. The second defeat sustained as a result of backbench dissent was of greater consequence, causing the government to shelve plans for likely military intervention.

The government recalled parliament on 29 August 2013 to debate the situation in Syria. Responding to the evident disquiet among their own backbenchers, the government committed not to engage in military action without a further vote. Despite that stance, 30 Conservative and nine Liberal Democrat MPs voted against the government motion, which was defeated by 285 to 272.

The government lost a further vote on 18 November 2014 about the control big breweries have over pub landlords. What was noteworthy about that vote however, was that it was on an amendment brought forward by a coalition backbench MP (the Liberal Democrat Greg Mulholland) to a government bill (the Small Business, Enterprise and Employment Bill) which attracted support from both Conservative and Liberal Democrat rebels, and was passed by 284 votes to 259.

What the small number of defeats did not expose was the sometimes quite dramatic steps taken by the coalition government in order to avoid such defeats. We noted (page 84) that the coalition's *Programme for Government* indicated that there would be an agreement to differ between the two governing parties on matters such as university funding, the renewal of Trident and tax allowances for married couples: all issues on which, in previous post-1945 non-Coalition governments, it would be very difficult to imagine circumstances in which government MPs would not be expected to vote as directed by their whips. We also saw how (page 85), on a rebel amendment to the Queen's Speech, in the knowledge that the alternative was a humiliatingly large rebellion, the Prime Minister sanctioned abstentions by ministers and votes for the amendment by PPSs.

But the most dramatic volte-face by the government as a result of near-inevitable rebellion was the abandonment of the House of Lords Reform Bill in 2012. Although the government achieved a large majority at second reading, it did so because of Labour support, and despite the 91 Conservative MPs who voted against the bill. Knowing that a similar number of rebels would also vote against a programme motion for the bill – crucial, if the Commons was not going to get bogged down in the minutiae of the bill, to the near exclusion of all other legislation – and that Labour would not support such a motion, the government abandoned the motion and the bill. So, while the government was not defeated in a vote, its policy was jettisoned because of the likelihood of such a defeat. The prospect of rebellion can be just as disruptive for government as the reality.

Dissent since 2015

The small working majority achieved by the Conservatives at the 2015 election changed the context of dissent, but it did not alter the willingness of rebellious MPs to vote against the government on certain issues. The first major test came on 16 June 2015, just over a month after the election, when 27 Conservative MPs voted against the government's proposals to change the 'purdah' rules regarding the prospective EU referendum. The government sought to remove the usual purdah arrangements – the restrictions which apply to initiating and publicising longer-term policies during an election campaign – in the European Union Referendum Bill. The government won the vote on that occasion, in Committee of the Whole House, as the official opposition voted with them, but when the House returned to the issue at report stage, on 7 September 2015, 37 Conservatives rebelled, and the Labour Party opposed the government, which meant they lost the vote by 312 to 285.

The government suffered an unrelated defeat on 9 March 2016 when it attempted to give powers to English and Welsh councils to extend Sunday trading opening hours as part of the Enterprise Bill. The government was defeated by 317 votes to 286, with 26 Conservative rebels.

Following the loss of the Conservative's majority in the 2017 election, the party has had to rely on DUP votes to sustain a majority in the House of Commons. Even so, the tightly balanced composition of the House means that a small number of Conservative rebels has potentially had the ability to derail the government's plans. This has been particularly evident during the passage of the European Union (Withdrawal) Bill, when last-minute concessions were made by ministers to head off defeat on amendments. This did not, however, prevent the government losing a vote at committee stage to allow ministers to use delegated powers to implement any withdrawal agreement with the EU only if Parliament had passed an Act approving the final terms of withdrawal. The amendment was moved by the Conservative former Attorney General Dominic Grieve; the support of 11 Conservative MPs meant the government suffered its first defeat of the parliament.

The dynamics of dissent

The reasons why MPs vote against their parties vary. Quite apart from their views on matters of principle or what is in the interests of their constituency, MPs may want to make a point about being consulted by the party leadership. They may want to establish their credentials, both within the party as a whole and with their constituents, on a major issue.

Especially if the government's majority is small, a threatened revolt may secure substantial changes in policy. But small majorities work both ways; when the boat is low in the water, people are less inclined to rock it, and, however strongly they feel, government MPs will be reluctant to risk the 'nuclear option' of defeating their party on a major issue and perhaps triggering a vote of confidence (as happened when, in July 1992, the Conservative government was defeated by 324 votes to 316 over the Social Protocol to the Maastricht Treaty – even though it won the confidence motion the next day by the luxurious margin of 110 votes).

Dissent and rebellion can become a habit for some MPs. In the 2010–15 parliament the five most rebellious Conservative MPs (Philip Hollobone, Philip Davies,

Christopher Chope, David Nuttall and Peter Bone) all voted against the majority of their party colleagues in 15 per cent to 20 per cent of votes. (Although not all of those votes would have been rebellions against the party whips, as the figures include instances where those members voted in a different lobby to the majority of their colleagues on free votes.) Repeated rebellion sometimes indicates a growing disenchantment with the mainstream views of the party – for a few, this may be the first step towards defection to another party (see 'Crossing the floor' on page 97). It is also the case that rebellion becomes easier; an MP may think that, having damaged his prospects by voting against the government several times, full membership of the 'awkward squad' will not make things much worse. The presence of a major figure, perhaps a former Cabinet minister who is on the backbenches because he or she resigned over a major policy difference, may also be a potential focus of dissent. The number of sacked ministers and MPs who are unpromoted and resentful (the 'ex-would-be-ministers') is also contributory.

Because of their wish to present a united front to the electorate and the media, political parties tend to undervalue dissent – or, at least, dissent in public. In most organisations and businesses, challenge is seen as a healthy process, leading to better decision-making.

Punishment

Voting against the party is not normally a good career move – at least in the short term – as most parties are unwilling to reward rebels with promotion. There are more formal sanctions. The Parliamentary Labour Party (PLP) has a code of conduct that requires its MPs to behave in a way that is consistent with the policies of the party, to have a good voting record and not to bring the party into disrepute. However, it does contain a 'conscience clause', which recognises a right of dissent on 'matters of deeply held personal conviction'. The Chief Whip may reprimand an MP in writing (which may also be reported to the member's constituency party). The PLP as a whole may 'withdraw the whip' from one of its MPs – in effect expelling them from the party.

The Conservative Party has similar rules, also with 'conscience' provisions. But, in the 1992–97 parliament, eight eurosceptic Conservative MPs had the whip withdrawn from them for six months because of their repeated voting against the party on European issues, and crucially on the Maastricht Social Protocol, which became an issue of confidence for the government.

Whether to make an example of rebels is a matter of judgement. There is a balance between doing so *pour encourager les autres* and the risk of creating martyrs. And, if dissent is on a large enough scale, the whips may have little practical power; the solution then is for the party to re-examine its policy. The election of Jeremy Corbyn as Labour leader – previously his party's most rebellious backbencher (see page 93) – has arguably made party discipline a harder sell to his own backbenchers. For the Conservatives, the absence of a working majority means it can ill afford to remove the whip from those who vote against the party line. This explains why in recent parliaments, the whip has tended to be removed as a result of personal behaviour rather than because of rebellions arising from policy differences. For example, in 2017, in the wake of a spate of allegations about harassment and other misbehaviour at Westminster, three Labour MPs had the whip suspended, as did one Conservative MP (who claimed that he had not been told the nature of the allegations against him). Financial misconduct has also been a reason for withdrawing the whip: in 2009 three Labour MPs had the whip removed as a result of allegations about expenses, and in the following year three former Cabinet ministers lost the whip because of claims about lobbying.

Crossing the floor

In an extreme case, an MP who falls out with his or her party may leave altogether and join another party. This is relatively rare; there were eight in the period 1992–2005. Since then, one Conservative MP became an Independent UKIP MP briefly, and in August 2014 Douglas Carswell, and in September 2014 Mark Reckless, defected from the Conservatives to UKIP, but no MP has crossed the floor between any of the major parties. An MP changing parties does not normally trigger a by-election, as he continues to represent constituents whether or not they voted for him; but there is usually some local pressure for the defector to resign so that a new candidate can be chosen. Douglas Carswell and Mark Reckless resigned their seats in order to fight by-elections in Clacton and in Rochester and Strood, both of which they won decisively. But Mark Reckless lost his seat at the 2015 general election and Douglas Carswell stood down at the 2017 general election, having left UKIP earlier that year.

Large-scale defections may rewrite part of the political map, as in 1981 when 27 Labour MPs and one Conservative joined the newly formed Social Democratic Party founded by the 'Gang of Four' – former Labour ministers Roy Jenkins, David Owen, Shirley Williams and William Rodgers. The importance of established party backing was demonstrated by the fact that only four of the 28 survived the 1983 election (and one of those lost in 1987).

Party organisation in Parliament

The whips do not spring political surprises on MPs, for MPs are themselves part of the decision-making processes in their party, and their influence is felt in the committees and groups in each party. The smaller parties' MPs meet regularly to discuss tactics and, for example, decide which of their number will speak in specific debates. Such organisation is obviously more complex in larger parties, and the arrangements for the two largest parties are described below.

The Parliamentary Labour Party (PLP)

All Labour MPs, backbench and frontbench, and Labour peers, are members of the Parliamentary Labour Party. The PLP meets at 6.00 pm every Monday for between 45 and 90 minutes. A standard agenda item is next week's business in the House, and the Chief Whip tells MPs what the whipping will be. The meeting also receives reports from the Cabinet or Shadow Cabinet or the PLP's departmental or regional groups and a (shadow) Cabinet minister will normally be a guest speaker, reporting on plans and current issues (with a chance to shine in front of the party's rank and file). An important agenda item may be a topical subject raised under 'any other business'. Individual MPs may move motions to make a point or to test opinion; notice of these must be given at least a week before the meeting unless deemed to be an emergency by the Chair. Attendance at the weekly PLP meetings is usually between 100 and 150. The chair of the PLP (since 2015, John Cryer) is elected by a ballot of all Labour MPs (not just backbenchers) and is a key party figure.

The Parliamentary Committee

The Parliamentary Committee is the executive of the Parliamentary Labour Party. It consists of the four officers of the PLP (Leader and Deputy Leader of the Labour Party, Chair of the PLP and Chief Whip), six backbench Commons members, one backbench Lords member and four other members of the Shadow Cabinet, one being from the Lords.

Departmental groups

Departmental groups monitor the work of government departments from a party point of view; there is also a Women's Group, which consists of women members only. The Chair of each departmental group is a backbencher elected by Commons members and one vice-chair of each group is a Labour peer. Attendance at departmental groups is open to all Labour MPs and peers.

Attendance in meetings varies greatly according to the interest of the agenda, down to half a dozen or so. When the party is in government, the chairman and officers of a subject group keep in close touch with the ministers of the relevant department, they are consulted about forthcoming policy initiatives and legislation, and ministers report to the relevant groups on the work and plans of their departments.

Regional groups

Every Labour MP belongs to the appropriate regional group corresponding to the Labour Party's regional structure: for example, Greater London, the North or Wales. These usually meet fortnightly and focus on issues of particular local concern or interest. They can play an important part in setting the broader agenda within the party, and they are also a target for local government, agencies and institutions that want to shape opinion among the MPs for their area.

The 1922 Committee

The Conservatives' equivalent of the PLP is the 1922 Committee, which was founded in 1923 by MPs who came into the House for the first time at the 1922 general election. Despite its former formal title of 'the Conservative Private Members' Committee', it has always been known as 'the 1922 Committee' or 'the '22'. Every Conservative MP may attend meetings of the '22', although only backbenchers may vote. Conservative members of the European Parliament (MEPs) and peers may attend but do not vote. The 1922 Committee meets on Wednesdays at 5.00 pm; the business taken is similar to that in the PLP. The Chairman of the 1922 Committee (since 2010, Sir Graham Brady) plays an important role in the party as the representative of the interests of backbenchers, with direct access to the leader of the party; he also sits on the Conservative Party Board, the governing body of the party.

The Executive Committee of the 1922 Committee

This consists of the Chairman of the 1922 Committee, two vice-chairmen, a treasurer, two secretaries and 12 other backbenchers, elected each year. The Executive Committee has always had a significant influence on party policy and direction.

Policy committees

The 1922 has five elected backbench policy committees, with each committee covering the work of a number of government departments.

Political groups

We said earlier that membership of a party involved a degree of compromise, that some MPs would prefer to see greater stress placed on some areas of policy or might be uneasy about other areas. For many years, in all political parties, these differences of emphasis have led to the formation of political groups within parties that more closely represent particular currents of opinion. The Conservative Party's dining clubs come and go, but the more enduring include the No Turning Back group, which is to the right of the party and the Cornerstone Group, which is sometimes described as 'the religious right' and whose MPs have been vocal on Brexit issues. In Labour the Momentum group was founded outside Parliament to support Jeremy Corbyn's 2015 leadership campaign but has attracted support from MPs.

Party leadership

No assessment of influences on MPs within their own parties (and the influence that they, in turn, can exercise) would be complete without a mention of the way in which party leaders are elected. Dissatisfaction with a party leader, or the perception that there is a leader-in-waiting, can produce blocs of opinion within a party – as witness the press's enthusiastic labelling of Labour ministers between 1997 and 2010 as 'Blairite' or 'Brownite'.

It can also give rise to an extreme form of dissent, as when in 1990 Margaret Thatcher was deposed as party leader (and so as Prime Minister) following a leadership challenge by Michael Heseltine, who had resigned from the Cabinet over the Westland affair almost five years before. Thatcher won the ballot by 204 votes to 152, but the scale of support for Heseltine led her to withdraw from the contest. In the early part of the 2005 parliament, the dissent of some Labour MPs seemed to be aimed at Tony Blair's premiership almost more than the issues on which they voted against him.

In the Conservative Party, a challenge to the leadership may be triggered only if 15 per cent or more of Conservative MPs (in the present parliament, at least 48) ask the Chairman of the 1922 Committee for a vote of confidence in the leader. If the leader then receives a majority of the votes cast, there can be no further challenge for a year. If the leader loses, votes of all Conservative MPs then reduce the number of candidates for the leadership to two, and the contest is decided by a ballot of all party members in the country at large (despite an unsuccessful attempt by Michael Howard in 2005 to make the views of party members advisory, and that of Conservative MPs decisive). In 2003, Iain Duncan Smith lost the party leadership following a vote of no confidence among Conservative MPs (90 votes to 75); Michael Howard was the only candidate to succeed him, and became leader with neither a further vote by MPs, nor a ballot of party members. In 2005, after ballots of Conservative MPs had eliminated Kenneth Clarke and Liam Fox, it was on a vote of party members, by 134,446 to 64,398, that David Cameron beat David Davis for the leadership. In 2016, after David Cameron resigned, ballots of Conservative MPs eliminated Stephen Crabb, Liam Fox and Michael Gove. Theresa May and Andrea Leadsom were due to be put to a vote of all party members but four days into the race Andrea Leadsom withdrew, citing the need for stability.

In the Labour Party, in March 2014 rule changes were agreed so that in leadership contests candidates would need to be nominated by 15 per cent of Labour MPs and all members (including affiliated and registered supporters) would then vote on a one-member-one-vote basis. This replaced the previous system, under which the leader and deputy leader were elected by three elements of the party: Labour MPs and MEPs, party members, and affiliated organisations (mainly trade unions), each element disposing of one-third of the vote. Thus in 2015, after Ed Miliband stood down as leader following the general election, despite having achieved the necessary nominations from his fellow MPs by the narrowest of margins, Jeremy Corbyn won 59.5 per cent of the votes of members, giving him a comfortable victory in the first round. His closest challenger was Andy Burnham (19 per cent), then Yvette Cooper (17 per cent) then Liz Kendall (4.5 per cent). In 2016 Jeremy Corbyn was challenged for the leadership after the EU referendum and a large vote of no confidence in him by the parliamentary party. The no-confidence vote itself had no formal status, but as a challenge had been launched the National Executive Committee decided that a leadership election would be held. It further decided that as the incumbent Mr Corbyn would automatically be on the ballot paper (i.e. he would not require the support of 15 per cent of the parliamentary party). The challenger was Owen Smith, who won 38 per cent of the membership votes to Mr Corbyn's 62 per cent. In 2017 the Labour conference lowered the threshold for an MP to run for the leadership. Now each candidate requires the support of 10 per cent of the parliamentary party, not 15 per cent.

The Liberal Democrat leader is elected by a ballot of the party in the country as a whole under the alternative vote system. An election can be triggered by a vote of no confidence in the incumbent leader by MPs or by 75 local parties writing to the President of the party to request a contest. Candidates must be Liberal Democrat MPs, and they must have the support of 10 per cent of MPs in the parliamentary party, and of 200 party members in at least 20 local parties. In 2015 Tim Farron won 56.5 per cent of the vote to Norman Lamb's 43.5 per cent. When Mr Farron stood down after the 2017 general election the only candidate to replace him was Sir Vince Cable, who was duly declared leader.

The party: conclusion

Political parties consist of much more than members of Parliament, but MPs are at the forefront of political activity, and they have an important role in determining and presenting their parties' policies. The multifaceted organisation of parties in Parliament is a constant influence on the individual MP, in terms of voting expectations, exposure to the views of other MPs and changing currents of opinion, and, in the major parties, interaction with ministers when the party is in government and with shadow ministers when it is not.

In turn, MPs have the opportunity to take part in the development of party policies through formal committee and group structures, and through informal personal contacts and relationships – the newest MP may spark off an important new idea with the leadership in a three-minute conversation in the Tea Room or the division lobby.

Personal influences

People are shaped by their experiences, and MPs are no exception. They bring with them into the House what they have acquired in previous careers, whether as teachers, lawyers, social workers, as craftspeople or in other fields, such as the Labour MP who was deployed with the Parachute Regiment in Kosovo, Iraq and Afghanistan, the SNP MP who was a breast cancer surgeon or the Conservative who was a firefighter. MPs are also influenced by more personal experiences. In recent years, members' contributions have reflected, for example, the death of a child, and personal experiences of mental health issues. Many of these experiences will condition how an MP reacts to some of the myriad issues of parliamentary life.

The constituency: the MP's relationship

The constituency is a vital part of the life of every MP. As we noted in Chapter 2, it is a power base, and its voters must be wooed to maximise the chances of being elected. An MP's identification with the interests and concerns of a constituency is also sharpened by the fact that UK constituencies are small enough often to be fairly homogeneous in terms of character, population and economic activity.

An MP represents all the people in a constituency, whether or not they voted for him or her – or, indeed, whether they were old enough to vote; an average constituency in England may have 76,000 electors but a total population of 90,000 if you count those under 18. This non-party representation of a constituency is emphasised by the fact that in most cases the majority of people entitled to vote will not have voted for the person elected as an MP. This is especially true in safe seats (where turnout tends to be lower). In 2017 the lowest turnout was 52 per cent in Wolverhampton South East, a safe Labour seat in all 12 elections since its creation.

The closeness of an MP's relationship with the constituency, and the extent of its influence on the MP's actions in Parliament, has steadily increased. The classic statement of the relationship of member and constituency is in Edmund Burke's speech to the electors of Bristol in 1774:

> *It ought to be the happiness and glory of a representative to live in the strictest union, the closest correspondence, and the most unreserved communication with his constituents. Their wishes ought to have great weight with him; their opinion, high respect; their business, unremitted attention. It is his duty to sacrifice his repose, his pleasures, his satisfactions to theirs – and above all, ever, and in all cases to prefer their interest to his own. But his unbiased opinion, his mature judgement, his enlightened conscience, he ought not to sacrifice to you, to any man, or to any set of men living. . . . Your representative owes you, not his industry only, but his judgement; and he betrays, instead of serving you, if he sacrifices it to your opinion.*

The first part of this antithesis – the close relationship with and unremitting attention to the constituency – may be seen as years before its time, even though Burke was speaking to electors a century and a half before universal suffrage. For the whole of the nineteenth century, and in many cases into the twentieth, constituencies were simply platforms on which MPs stood to take part in public life and that they visited rarely. Such absenteeism would not wash today, and we will shortly describe some of the constituency pressures on the modern MP.

The second part – the assertion that an MP is the representative of a constituency who votes according to his judgement and conscience, and not a delegate who votes according to constituents' instructions – has undergone a transformation. An MP may still exercise judgement and conscience, and in doing so may represent a minority of opinion in the constituency – for example, many Labour MPs opposed Brexit even though it was supported by a majority in their constituency – but, as we saw earlier in this chapter, the main constraint on the way an MP *votes* is now the party to which he or she belongs.

Listening to constituents

Almost every MP has a constituency office to deal with matters raised by constituents and to have a presence close to local issues; and many MPs base some or all their support staff in constituencies rather than at Westminster.

In recent years, the core of an MP's work on behalf of constituents has been the 'surgery', when the MP's availability to discuss problems is advertised on their websites, in the local press and elsewhere. In a small constituency, this may be at a central constituency office; in a larger one, it may be in a succession of town and village halls during the day, or even in a caravan that the MP tows around. Surgery work is on the increase; many MPs have moved to twice-weekly surgeries, and the changed sitting patterns of the Commons since 2002 have included many more non-sitting 'constituency Fridays'.

Constituents also raise issues and problems with their MP by letter. While MPs still receive many letters each day, evidence suggests the numbers are declining: in 2006, almost 4.8 million items of correspondence were delivered to the Palace of Westminster; by 2016, that number had dropped to 1.6 million. However, that falling off in the number of letters sent appears to have been more than counterbalanced by the huge numbers of emails received by MPs. This brings its own challenges: the speed of communication leads many constituents to expect an equal speed of reply on what may be a hideously complicated problem. One inner London MP estimated that she received between 300 and 400 emails each day.

MPs are also increasingly communicating via social media. By December 2017 it was estimated that MPs collectively were tweeting more than 1,000 times each day and 86 per cent of MPs (559) had Twitter accounts, including all SNP, Liberal Democrat, and Plaid Cymru MPs. The Conservatives, with 79 per cent of MPs with accounts, lagged a little behind the Labour Party with 92 per cent. Of course, MPs do not use Twitter to communicate exclusively about constituency matters – on one day in December 2017, one Conservative backbencher's tweets encompassed tax policy, President Trump's foreign policy and the winner of a constituency primary school Christmas card competition, for example – but it provides another means by which MPs can communicate with constituents about local, national and international issues. The social media reach of the most-high profile MPs goes well beyond their constituents alone. The MPs with the three most followed Twitter accounts in December 2017 were Jeremy Corbyn (1.6 million followers), Ed Miliband (730k) and Theresa May (440k). While those at the top (or formerly at the top) of their parties tended to have the most followers, backbenchers who use the medium effectively also had many followers, for example David Lammy (260k followers) and Jacob Rees-Mogg (80k). While Twitter gives MPs an easy means of communicating with constituents and others, it also provides an easy opportunity for offensive (and worse) users to attack MPs. Abuse and attempted intimidation of female MPs in particular is a problem, with some female MPs subjected to hundreds of abusive tweets in the run-up to the 2017 election and beyond. This led to a report by the Committee on Standards in Public Life on *Intimidation in Public Life*, which among other things recommended a new electoral offence of intimidating parliamentary candidates and party campaigners.

Constituents' problems

People will raise literally any subject with their MP. They do so for a variety of reasons: they think the MP will be able to get action; they have exhausted all other possibilities;

they do not know who to approach and so start with the MP; or they go to the MP as a personification of an establishment that they see as being the problem itself. This last category inevitably includes the desperate and the disturbed, and at surgeries security is often an issue. Jo Cox MP was murdered outside a constituency surgery in 2016, in an event which shocked the country and led to soul-searching about the treatment of MPs – such reflections alas proving too brief. In 2000, an MP's researcher was killed and the MP himself badly injured. Other MPs have been attacked and occasionally seriously injured.

When a constituent seeks help, the MP must first establish exactly what is the problem. This is often much more difficult than it might seem. The constituent may be coming to the MP only after months or years of struggle with some organisation or agency, and his or her opening gambit may be to present a box file overflowing with documents of all sorts, some more legible than others. Unravelling the tangled skein to find out exactly what has happened, whose fault it was and what can be done about it can be enormously time-consuming. On the other hand, the problem – perhaps 'neighbours from hell' – may be very straightforward, but what can be done without legal action, which the constituent cannot afford, may be much more difficult.

People often assume that an MP can do something about anything but, strictly speaking, an MP's role is limited to matters for which ministers are answerable to Parliament – in general, the responsibilities of government departments or executive agencies. This nevertheless covers a huge range of things that give rise to constituents' problems: immigration and asylum, pensions and social security, income tax, child maintenance, the National Health Service, and animal health and farming subsidies being just a few.

The MP does not have a direct role in matters that are the responsibility of a local authority – the running of local schools, rubbish collection and recycling, council housing, council tax, and so on, as 'constituency cases' here are the responsibility of local councillors. But although an MP will usually be careful not to step on the toes of councillors (whether of the same party or not), he or she may on the basis of local difficulties pursue a broader issue of principle for which central government *is* responsible: for example, in the extent of central government funding for local authorities and what is taken into account in setting the level of that funding. In addition to respecting the remit of local councillors, one impact of devolution is that a wide range of issues are now the responsibility of members of the relevant devolved body, rather than Westminster MPs. A constituent may bring to the MP a 'private sector' problem: perhaps the mis-selling of pensions, rogue builders, or rocketing insurance premiums in an area prone to flooding. A letter from an MP may or may not have any influence directly with the company concerned, but in such cases the MP's best bet is to engage the responsibilities of ministers for regulating these sectors of industry in the public interest, or perhaps to seek the assistance of an industry's own watchdog body, which has an interest in the reputation of the industry as a whole. If the problem is a failing company and job losses, the MP may be looking for money for retraining redundant workers.

Even if the MP really has no direct role, and the possibility of doing something constructive is very limited, there is always the risk that an honest answer to this effect may be misrepresented by the constituent, the press or a political opponent as 'Ms X doesn't care' or 'Mr Z isn't prepared to put himself out'. There is thus a good deal of pressure on the MP to make some sort of positive or helpful response, even if it is only to suggest some other person or agency to approach.

MPs are extremely careful to check that the person raising a problem is, indeed, their constituent and not that of a neighbouring member (you can find out who your MP is on the parliamentary website: www.parliament.uk/mps-lords-and-offices/mps/). Occasionally, an MP faced with a case in which he or she might be thought to have a personal interest may ask another MP to take it on. This also happens from time to time when an MP has taken a strong public stand on an issue, in order to avoid a constituent with a contrary view feeling that there might be a conflict of interest. If an MP dies or resigns, it is usual for constituents' problems to be dealt with by one or more neighbouring MPs until the election of a successor.

A new MP is always warned by colleagues not to take up planning cases; planning has its own quasi-judicial machinery at both local and national levels, and the applicants and the objectors are usually all constituents; to favour one is to disadvantage another. Similarly, although the 'neighbours from hell' may be a public nuisance for a whole local area, MPs are generally reluctant to take up neighbour or family disputes; all concerned are likely to be constituents.

What can the MP do?

An MP does not have executive power but is an analyst and advocate. In taking up a constituent's case, the MP must identify what the problem is and who is responsible (or direct the constituent elsewhere if someone else is more likely to be able to take effective action). Then, it is a matter of exposure and persuasion. A letter on House of Commons writing paper or an email from a parliamentary address may be enough to break a bureaucratic log jam or to persuade a company that it has treated someone unfairly.

On most things for which central government is responsible, the most usual first step is a letter to the minister. This may ask for a case to be reviewed, for the minister's observations on the problem or simply for a clear statement of the department's policy on the point at issue. We return to MPs' letters to ministers in Chapter 9.

If the minister's response does not solve the matter, and the constituent has a good case that the MP is determined to take forward, the possibilities are limited only by energy and ingenuity. The MP may seek a meeting with the minister. If the problem is a wider one within the constituency – perhaps involving mass redundancies, or a manufacturing or farming sector in crisis, this may take the form of leading a deputation to a formal meeting in the department, with the minister and civil servants present. The MP may make an informal approach – the classic way is to corner a minister in the division lobby during a vote in the House. Perhaps there are other members who have had similar problems in their constituencies, who can make common cause. Maybe the issue can be given a higher profile through parliamentary questions or an early day motion (EDM) (see page 280); or the MP may apply for a debate in the House or

Westminster Hall via the Backbench Business Committee (see page 276) or for one of the daily half-hour adjournment debates in the House, when there will be an opportunity to set out the case in detail and the responsible minister will have to reply. Sometimes an MP might raise an issue with the relevant select committee, although that is more likely to lead to an investigation of the generic issue, rather than the individual case. A case of maladministration may be referred to the Ombudsman (see page 325). At any of these stages, the support of the local – or, possibly, the national – media may be enlisted.

However good the constituent's case, success is not guaranteed. But, as with so many issues in parliamentary and political life, a good argument, persuasively and energetically deployed, the support of sympathisers and, above all, persistence and determination offer the best chance of success.

Constituents' views

The issues raised with MPs at surgeries and in correspondence vary with the political agenda but a survey conducted of 40 surgeries in 2017 found that housing was the subject most frequently raised (37 per cent), followed by immigration (23 per cent) and welfare benefits (13 per cent). In most cases an MP's response will reflect party policy or personal views. However, the strength of popular opinion shown by the size of the postbag – provided that it consists of individually written letters and not duplicated campaign mailings – may influence both individual MPs and their parties.

Constituency profile

A new Labour MP for a Welsh valley constituency had previously been an energetic local councillor. Within weeks of being elected to Westminster, he was stopped in the street by a constituent he had known for a long time. 'We don't see much of you now', she said. He replied that he had been elected as an MP. 'Yes', she said. 'I voted for you. But we still don't see much of you'. He explained that he was very busy in the House for most of the week. 'So you're not going to be here as much as you were?' 'No', he said. 'I'm sorry, but I'm not'. 'Oh', she said. 'If I'd known that, I'd never have voted for you'.

This anecdote (not apocryphal) illustrates a tension in the life of the constituency MP. The centre of parliamentary life is Westminster, and to satisfy the requirements of the parliamentary party and the whips, to promote constituency interests and to take part in select committee work, as well as to pursue personal political priorities, that is where the MP needs to spend a good deal of time. But there is a strong gravitational pull from the constituency as well. The local MP is expected to be on the spot: to open bazaars and fairs; to speak to working men's clubs and the WI; to put in an appearance at school prize-givings or road safety days; to comment knowledgeably on livestock at an agricultural show or present quality awards at the diesel engine works; to read the lesson at the civic service; to attend the Remembrance Day parade; or to draw the fund-raising raffle.

Those activities are public duty rather than party duty; but an MP must also spend time cultivating local party links and support. This may involve party social events, from wine and cheese to beer and crisps, and a round of dinners and lunches (the so-called 'rubber chicken circuit'), as well as reporting back on the MP's work at Westminster.

For many MPs, constituency activity fills up the rest of the week not occupied by work at Westminster. Some constituencies are within easy reach of Westminster and the distinction is less sharp, but, for most members, the Westminster week finishes on Thursdays; they travel to their constituencies that afternoon, and Friday, the weekend and Monday mornings are given over largely, or even entirely, to activity in the constituency; they then travel back to Westminster on Monday in time for votes in the evening.

Fighting the corner

Dealing effectively with constituents' problems is only half of being a 'good constituency MP'. The local member is also expected to be an advocate and ambassador for the constituency as a whole. This may involve ensuring that ministers do not forget how a crisis in farming is hitting the constituency or perhaps (for some Scottish MPs with distilleries) making the case against a Budget tax rise on spirits. As well as direct approaches to ministers and the media, subject debates and, particularly, Question Time are good opportunities for this; but there is a convention (not always observed) that members should not use select committee work to make the constituency case.

In the last analysis, constituents expect important constituency matters to be paramount for the MP, even if that means rebellion against the party line. For example, more than 30 Conservative MPs voted against the HS2 High Speed Rail Bill, in large part because of its impact on their constituencies.

The constituency comes to Westminster

The closer a constituency is to London, the more likely an MP is to see his or her electors at Westminster. This may be an individual visit to put a problem to the MP; it may be an organised party to see around the Palace of Westminster and perhaps listen to a debate; it may be a school visit; or it may be tea on the Terrace for senior members of the party in the constituency and their spouses. MPs value these connections; they give constituents a chance to see the other side of an MP's life and understand more about Parliament – and it may be a special day out that demonstrates the MP's regard for his or her constituents.

All-party parliamentary groups

'All-party parliamentary groups' (APPGs) bring together MPs and peers to discuss issues of common interest. They must contain at least four members from different parties, and, as the rules are administered by the Commons, the Chair must be an MP.

Many such groups also involve outsiders, though they cannot vote. Most notably, the Parliamentary and Scientific Committee brings together MPs, peers, scientific organisations, science-based companies and universities.

APPGs can be divided into subject groups, and country groups. The subject groups are numerous – in September 2017, there were over 400 such groups, covering subjects from adult education to Zoroastrianism.

States such as Kyrgyzstan and Belize, as well as many more familiar countries, have their own country group; there are also groups covering regions or sub-state entities. Most groups receive briefings from the embassies of the countries in which they are interested, and their members are sometimes invited to visit or to receive overseas delegations to the UK. Country group members do not normally see themselves as defenders of the governments of the countries concerned but as people who know something of the politics, culture, economics and history, and so are able to make some contribution to the UK's relationship with that country. Most country groups cooperate with the Inter-Parliamentary Union or the Commonwealth Parliamentary Association.

APPGs meet as often as enthusiasm sustains them; they elect their own officers and (because they are often seen as potential lobbying targets and, in some cases, receive outside funding) they are officially – and publicly – registered. The principal groups are Westminster fixtures; others are established or disappear as the mood takes. Some have formal secretariats and planned programmes; others may simply have a social event from time to time, perhaps with a guest speaker.

The extent and variety of activity is exemplified by the meetings advertised in the *All-Party Group Notices* for the last full week in October 2017. On Tuesday 24 October, there were meetings of country or region groups for Africa (holding a panel discussion on Cameroon), Georgia (with the Georgian minister of foreign affairs), 'Friends of Syria' (to discuss the fight against ISIS) and North Korea. The APPG on Charities and Volunteer Fundraising heard from fundraising regulators; the APPG for South West Rail heard from Network Rail executives; the (separate) APPG for Rail Group also heard from Network Rail; the APPG for Women and Work discussed 'gig' work and disruptive industries; the APPG for the Packaging Manufacturing Industry heard from the Paper Cup Alliance; and the APPG on American Football had a guest speaker from the British American Football Association. There were also meetings of the APPGs on Prostitution and the Global Sex Trade, Taxation, School Food, Women in the Penal System, Parliamentary Internet, Communications and Technology, Integrated Healthcare and Road Passenger Transport. Finally, there were AGMs (APPGs are required to hold one) of the APPGs on Climate Change and Arrhythmia Alliance.

All-party parliamentary groups give MPs and peers the opportunity to discuss a wide range of issues, often with major players. They give members the chance to develop policy, to focus opinion and, in turn, to influence ministers. APPGs driven by committed and knowledgeable members can help bring about change: the APPG for Smoking and Health, for example, has been very influential.

Lobby groups and lobbyists use such groups to assess and influence parliamentary and political opinion. While some APPGs are shoestring operations, run from a member's office, others have secretariats supported by external organisations, such as charities, industry associations or learned societies. Opinion is divided over the relationship between APPGs and lobbying; lobbying is seen as part of the parliamentary process, but external funding imports a degree of risk. Even so, it should be noted that the rules prohibiting paid lobbying by members extend to APPG activity, and the fact that in 2014 an MP was forced to resign for attempting to set up an APPG in return for payment demonstrated that this rule could and would be enforced.

In response to such concerns the rules on APPGs were reformed in 2015. There are now enhanced requirements for transparency, including on income and expenditure, and parliamentarians are clearly responsible for the activities and governance of APPGs.

Lobby groups and lobbyists

The word 'lobby' used in the sense of a House of Commons ante-room first appears in 1640. It later crossed the Atlantic to be applied to the geography of the US Congress. But 'to lobby' (meaning to seek to exert influence on parliamentarians) and 'lobbyist' (one who does so) are American coinages first appearing in 1850 and 1863, respectively. By the end of the nineteenth century, both had crossed the Atlantic the other way and became commonly used in the Westminster Parliament.

The term 'lobby group' is usually used of political pressure groups that might, for example, be campaigning for more resources to provide clean water in the developing world, or for healthier children's diets, or homeopathy – or for the ordering of new fighter aircraft, or lower taxes on electric cars. 'Lobbyist' is usually used of the professional advocate whose skills in presentation, making contacts and persuasion are for hire.

Modern lobbying is mainly directed at governments, whose executive power and power of initiative make them obvious targets, and covers the whole field of government activity. Political pressure groups, charities or commercial interests may try to have particular provisions included in (or, just as often, excluded from) forthcoming legislation, or seek favourable tax treatment in a forthcoming budget. The government is a huge contractor and purchaser (for example, of defence equipment), and selling to government is a major area of lobby activity.

Single-issue politics – embracing campaigns such as those on, for example, animal rights and anti-globalisation, often with an international dimension – have become more prominent in recent years. They tend not to use traditional lobbying methods but use the internet, especially social media, both to bring their supporters together and to target politicians who are seen as opponents, often running campaigns against those with slim majorities. Some organisations that have used more traditional techniques in the past are either switching to this approach or are running both methods in tandem. Lobby groups and lobbyists are interested in MPs for two main reasons. First, if they espouse a cause they can give it a high profile through writing to ministers, parliamentary questions, early day motions or tabling of helpful amendments to legislation. Second, they can influence opinion, both outside the House through the media and, more important, with their colleagues, both backbench and frontbench. This influence will usually be greater if their party is in government.

Effective lobbying means effective targeting, either through knowledge of an MP's interests and experience, or by exploiting the vital constituency link. Too many would-be lobbyists have an entirely unrealistic idea of how interested most MPs will be in what they have to say. In the view of the Conservative MP for North Wiltshire, who had been a director of one of the larger lobbying consultants:

> *Bombarding decision-makers with excess and useless information will often be counter-productive. Those people who believe that they are achieving something useful by sending their annual accounts out to MPs with a stereotyped covering letter with 'Dear James Gray' at the top (only worse is 'Dear James Gray, Esq., MP', which happens all too often) are mistaken . . . waste paper baskets round Westminster will be the only beneficiaries.*
>
> *By contrast, a simple letter along the following lines will hit the mark every time: Dear Mr Gray* [preferably handwritten], *the widget-makers of North Wiltshire are very concerned about the effects of a forthcoming government Statutory Instrument about widget specifications, which may put 25 jobs in your constituency at risk. I know that Mr Blodgett, the managing director of Widgets to the Gentry, Bumpers Farm, Chippenham, would very much welcome the opportunity of meeting you to explain the matter and to introduce you to his workforce if you could spare an hour or so, perhaps one Friday, in the near future.* [Handwritten:] *Yours sincerely, Fred Plunket, National Association of Widget-Makers.*

This description of an MP's reactions is reinforced by Lord Tyler, the former Liberal Democrat MP, who had run a public affairs consultancy:

> *Anything that looked like a real message from a real constituent – preferably a local postmark – got priority attention . . . Targeting from a constituency viewpoint, and timing to coincide with the parliamentary agenda, has always seemed to me to be much more likely to achieve impact than the most elaborate hospitality or printed material.*

Although lobby groups and lobbyists influence MPs, they are also extremely useful to MPs – and to others – as well. James Gray again:

> *Those of us in Parliament, and no doubt in government, find truly professional lobbying very useful indeed. A shadow minister handling an obscure statutory instrument debate; a back-bencher searching for an original line in a select committee or during oral questions; a journalist looking for a new perspective on legislation; a civil servant seeking to summarise an industry or public response to a ministerial initiative – all of these and others will value a truly professional, concise and targeted exposition of a particular argument.*

Good lobbying (objective, factual, well-argued) provides some of the research resource that many MPs feel they lack, despite the support of their own staff and the work of the researchers in the House of Commons Library. If it obeys the golden rule of being on an MP's particular political interest, or relating to the constituency, it is likely to be used.

Lobbyists, or parliamentary or public affairs consultancies, are used by many organisations and interest groups. Some simply want to have parliamentary and government activity monitored in order to have early warning of what is coming forward. Others feel they need help in making their case. A typical assignment might be to attempt to head off a policy proposal that the client believes might damage his business. The lobbyist will need to understand the proposal and its context and master the arguments against it.

Contacts between ministers, MPs, civil servants, journalists and others must then be used, or new ones developed, to get the message over. The earlier a problem is tackled, before political capital is invested and it quickly becomes much harder to get a proposal modified or dropped, the better.

One fundamental difference between lobbying in the USA and in the UK is that lobbyists in Washington are advocates for their clients; US politicians seem to prefer dealing with a 'hired gun' than directly with the client. In the UK, however, parliamentarians prefer to hear the message direct, and lobbyists prepare their clients for meetings rather than being the principal actors.

In the late 1980s and 1990s, some types of lobbying acquired a doubtful reputation, becoming associated with parliamentary sleaze and appearing to be based more on lavish entertainment than strength of argument. In the 1990s, there were attempts to brighten the industry's rather tarnished image by promoting high ethical standards through voluntary codes of conduct and registers. In 2014, registration of lobbyists was put on a statutory footing by the Transparency of Lobbying, Non-Party Campaigning and Trade Union Administration Act 2014 which prohibits lobbying by unregistered consultant lobbyists (those who are paid to lobby for third parties). Registration is required only for lobbying ministers and permanent secretaries, not parliamentarians or more junior civil servants.

There are also organisations that make it easier for members of the public to email MPs on a variety of topics, such as 38 degrees and Change.org. This can give MPs an indication of the strength of opinion on a particular topic, but is rarely as effective as a more personal approach, except where a member is already concerned about a particular subject. Members are well aware of the amount of effort and engagement needed to click a mouse rather than write a letter. As a result, they may respond to mass campaign tools in kind through standardised responses, often on websites, sometimes prepared centrally by party organisations or groups of MPs.

Parliamentary standards

Self-regulation and privilege

The House of Commons has long regarded its independence as paramount. Over the centuries, the House has evolved into a body that can, if it wishes, control the executive rather than one that was summoned by the Crown only when necessary, and was largely controlled by the Crown. The right of members to speak freely, and of the House to control its own precincts, was a key part of this evolution, and was fiercely fought for. It is enshrined in 'parliamentary privilege', which we examine in greater detail on pages 168 to 173.

Parliamentary privilege is not immunity. MPs are subject to the law of the land in the same way as anyone else. If they engage in criminal conduct, they can be (and have been) prosecuted. Civil suits can be brought against MPs. This is in itself a mark of British confidence in its judicial system. In many other countries, members of Parliament have complete immunity from criminal proceedings while they are MPs, unless the Parliament concerned chooses to waive it. In such countries, parliamentary immunity is often defended on the ground that politically motivated prosecutions could be used to remove an awkward MP.

The principle of 'exclusive cognisance' means that only the House can regulate what is said or done in proceedings in the House. That does not mean there are no external sanctions: a political party may decline to select a sitting MP as its candidate in the next election or the electorate may choose to reject him or her. But the disciplinary powers for what is said and done in the House rest with the House itself, and it is for the House to decide the rules that should govern MPs' behaviour.

Although there is a constitutional principle behind it, the lack of parliamentary immunity means that the House's self-regulation is broadly similar to the self-regulation exercised by many professions. Nonetheless, parliamentary self-regulation has become a matter of some controversy.

The Committee on Standards in Public Life

The evolution of the disciplinary system in each House of Parliament – and, indeed, in many walks of public life – has been greatly influenced by the Committee on Standards in Public Life (CSPL). This was established in October 1994 by the then Prime Minister, John Major, in response to scandals about 'sleaze' – in particular, cash for questions.

The committee has eight members; it has no parliamentary character (although two MPs and two peers, including its chair, are members); it is appointed by the Prime Minister and reports to her. It covers the whole of the public sector, but has produced several reports on parliamentary standards, prompted first by the difficulties of the 1990s, and subsequently by the expenses scandal.

Following the first report of the CSPL in 1995, the House of Commons set up a Select Committee on Standards in Public Life to consider the Committee's findings and to recommend how they should be reflected in the rules of the House. The main changes made in 1995 were:

- the appointment of a Parliamentary Commissioner for Standards (PCS);
- the setting up of a new Committee on Standards and Privileges to replace the separate Committees on Privileges and on Members' Interests; and
- the drawing up of a Code of Conduct for MPs.

Subsequent changes have included:

- making provision for an investigatory panel to assist the Parliamentary Commissioner for Standards in making findings of fact in serious cases (this has not been used);
- introducing a non-renewable fixed term for the PCS as a guarantee of independence; and, most recently
- the involvement of lay members in House of Commons disciplinary processes.

Regulating influence: a history

It is clearly of the greatest importance for public confidence in Parliament that MPs act in the national and constituency interest rather than with the expectation of private gain. In 1695, the House of Commons passed a resolution 'Against offering bribes to Members', stating that the offer of money or 'other Advantage' in respect of a matter that was to be transacted in Parliament was 'a high Crime and Misdemeanour and tends to the Subversion of the Constitution'. Although the seventeenth- and eighteenth-century approach seems to have been rather more relaxed about the acceptance of favours, when Sir John Trevor as Speaker received the then colossal bribe of £1,050 from the Common Council of London for helping to get a bill passed, the House expelled him in short order.

The Victorian House of Commons recognised the importance of MPs' advocacy in the House being divorced from private gain and, in 1858, resolved that:

> *It is contrary to the usage and derogatory to the dignity of this House that any of its Members should bring forward, promote or advocate in this House any proceeding or measure in which he may have acted or been concerned for or in consideration of any pecuniary fee or reward.*

This was aimed especially at MPs who were practising barristers, but it was reinforced in 1947 by a further resolution forbidding contractual arrangements under which, for any benefit, a member promoted any point of view on behalf of an outside interest. In 1974, the House agreed that MPs should be required to declare any financial interest that they might have in matters being debated or otherwise before the House or its committees, and that they should register their financial interests. A Select Committee on Members' Interests was established to supervise this process.

In the late 1980s and early 1990s there was a steady growth in professional lobbying firms on the US model, many with multi-million or multi-billion pound businesses as clients. They saw parliamentary influence as a valuable commodity and, by 1995, more than one-quarter of MPs had paid consultancies with lobbyists (26) or with other bodies outside the House (142).

Whether or not this was against the public interest, public unease was greatly increased by some high-profile incidents: the 1994 'cash for questions' affair, in which *Sunday Times* journalists approached 20 MPs offering £1,000 for simply tabling parliamentary questions (which was accepted by two of them); and the allegations by the businessman and then owner of Harrods, Mohamed al-Fayed, that he had rewarded MPs for lobbying on his behalf.

At the same time, there was a growing public suspicion – both reflected in and, to an extent, fuelled by a high media profile – of the uses that certain individuals made of their position or wealth. Donations to political parties to buy influence, newly retired or resigned ministers and senior civil servants obtaining lucrative directorships, important public appointments being made on the basis of personal connections rather than merit – however widespread (or not) this might have been, the important thing was that it was widely believed.

It was this unease that led to the establishment of the CSPL, and a great part of the Code of Conduct for MPs is aimed at preventing improper use of influence.

The expenses scandal

The Code of Conduct had prohibited misuse of resources from its inception, and the Committee on Standards and Privileges had dealt with a number of cases related to misuse of public money that caused public concern, including the case of a member who was found to have employed his son and paid bonuses when that son had, in fact, done no work. But the issue really ignited as a result of the publication of unredacted expenses claims by *The Daily Telegraph* starting in May 2009. There were three aspects to this. First, some MPs and peers had been acting in ways that were subsequently judged to be criminal; second, many MPs had claimed for money to which they were not entitled, either inadvertently or to obtain maximum benefit from the system; and third, the expenses system itself was seen as much too generous. The seeds of disaster had probably been sown in the early 1980s, when Margaret Thatcher's government backed down on a justified pay rise for MPs but contrived to imply that the difference could be made up on expenses.

As a result of the expenses scandal, a new statutory body, the Independent Parliamentary Standards Authority (IPSA) was established to set and administer MPs' pay and expenses. It is theoretically possible that if an MP claimed expenses in a way that was not criminal, but was felt to be improper, the IPSA Compliance Officer could refer the matter to the Parliamentary Commissioner to consider whether there had been a breach of the Code of Conduct. In fact, this has never arisen so the House has not yet had to consider complaints of misuse of expenses under the new system.

A further result of the expenses scandal was that the Committee on Standards and Privileges put it on record that criminal proceedings against members should take precedence over the House's own disciplinary proceedings. This principle has been reiterated by the successor Committee on Standards.

The rules

The House has agreed two distinct but overlapping and interdependent mechanisms for the disclosure of personal financial interests; these aim to 'provide information about any financial interest that might reasonably be thought by others to influence their parliamentary conduct or actions'. The first is registration of interests: information about certain financial interests has to be registered within four weeks of acquiring the interest. The Register of MPs' Financial Interests is updated online once a fortnight when the House is sitting. There are 10 categories of interest. Members are required to register information about remunerated employment, including details of any client for whom they work directly; donations they may have solicited to their constituency party or association; gifts, benefits and hospitality above a certain threshold; land and property other than that used as a residence; significant shareholdings; and details of family members whom they employ or who are engaged in lobbying. Journalists and members' staff also have to register financial interests that might be advantaged by their position.

The Register is intended as a register of interests, not a declaration of wealth. The thresholds for registration and the registration categories are changed from time to time by the House. Indeed, during the expenses scandal, there were frequent changes to rules and thresholds – first, in an attempt first to tighten up rules that were deemed inadequate and, subsequently, to correct overreactions.

An MP must disclose a financial interest when speaking in a debate, in a way sufficiently informative to allow a listener to understand the nature of the interest. Interests must also be declared when tabling parliamentary questions, when tabling early day motions or amendments to bills (or adding names to them), and when introducing private members' bills. When an interest is declared, the symbol [R] appears on the Order Paper beside the name of the member concerned.

An MP must also declare if he or she has a reasonable expectation of future financial advantage – for example, an MP whose family business made industrial cleaning equipment would be expected to declare an interest when speaking on a bill that would set up an inspectorate to monitor standards of cleanliness in schools and hospitals.

In select committees, all members declare their registrable interests before standing for election as chair, on the ground that this aspect of an MP's independence is a factor in his or her suitability for the chair. Thereafter, members of a select committee must declare any relevant interest, or even withdraw from an inquiry completely if there is a conflict of interest.

Lobbying for reward and paid advocacy

This rule, based on the 1858 and 1947 resolutions (see page 113) and borrowing some of their language, takes the declaration of interests several steps further. It outlaws paid advocacy – that is, doing anything in the House (speaking, voting, tabling amendments or urging other MPs to do so, or approaching ministers or civil servants) directly for payment. In practice, this means that an MP who is a director of a company, or a paid adviser for an organisation, may not try to get any preferential treatment for that company or organisation (for example, in tax relief, subsidies or some special treatment or opportunity) in any use of his or her functions as an MP.

Voting and interests

The classic rule was stated from the Chair almost two centuries ago, when Speaker Abbott ruled that 'no Member who has a pecuniary interest in a question shall be allowed to vote upon it'. In modern times, this is interpreted as a direct financial interest, and in the context that an MP's interests have been declared. To take two examples: in 1983, the Speaker ruled that MPs who were solicitors might vote on a bill that removed their exclusive rights on conveyancing, as the bill was a matter of public policy; however, in 1981 MPs who were also members of Lloyd's were advised not to vote on a bill to regulate the Lloyd's insurance market.

The Ministerial Code

MPs (and peers) who are ministers are subject to the Code of Conduct of the relevant House. They are also covered by the Ministerial Code laid down by successive prime ministers with the aim of ensuring that there is no actual or apparent conflict between their private interests and their public duties as ministers. The Prime Minister appoints an independent adviser on the Code, currently Sir Alex Allan, to provide advice on it and to investigate allegations of breach at the request of the Prime Minister. Between 2011 and 2016 there was only one such investigation. In December 2017 Theresa May asked Sir Alex Allan to review the finding of an internal Cabinet Office inquiry which found Damian Green in breach of the Ministerial Code by being untruthful about a police investigation. After Sir Alex upheld the finding the Prime Minister insisted on the resignation of Mr Green as First Secretary of State, thus proving that ultimately the Prime Minister decides whether an investigation is warranted and judges whether a minister has breached the Code.

The Committee on Standards and the Parliamentary Commissioner for Standards

Two institutions are key to setting and enforcing standards: the Parliamentary Commissioner for Standards and the Committee on Standards (formerly Standards and Privileges), which oversees the work of the Parliamentary Commissioner. The current Commissioner is Kathryn Stone, who had been Chief Legal Ombudsman of England and Wales. She is supported by a small secretariat, which includes the Registrar of Members' Financial Interests.

The role of Parliamentary Commissioner for Standards was intended to introduce an element of independence to the system. She is appointed for a fixed term, non-renewable contract to ensure she cannot be threatened with loss of office, or influenced by the prospect of a further term. Although the Parliamentary Commissioner is overseen by the Committee on Standards, the committee neither manages her work, nor what she chooses to say in her memoranda or annual reports. The Commissioner's power to propose changes in the rules is not limited in any way; Commissioners have, for example, consulted publicly on potential revisions to the Code and Guide.

Much of the work of the Parliamentary Commissioner, and of her office, is in maintaining the register, offering advice to members individually and collectively, and keeping the system under review. The Commissioner is required to monitor the operation of the Code and registers, and to make recommendations to the committee. The committee's role is to approve or modify the arrangements proposed by the Commissioner or the Registrar, and to support the Commissioner and her office in their work. So, for example, the chair of the committee has written to members advising them about how particular rules should be interpreted, or reminding them to check their register entries.

The Commissioner's independence provides a check on the self-regulatory system, while the committee's oversight of her work means that the Commissioner cannot make unilateral recommendations or findings that could be unreasonable.

The Committee on Standards contains seven MPs and seven lay members. The lay members are people who have never been MPs and were selected on the basis of fair and open competition. Their tenure is limited to the Parliament in which they were first appointed plus a possible further term of up to two years. This regular turnover should have the effect of avoiding 'organisational capture'. As for the MPs, although the party balance on the committee reflects the party balance in the House, no one party has a majority, and committee members are expected to set aside their party loyalties. The committee is usually chaired by a member of an opposition party.

The lay members do not have a vote because if they were full members – not being MPs but, in effect, co-opted – the committee would not be a proper select committee and its proceedings (and its members) would not be protected by parliamentary privilege. Nonetheless, they play a full part in the discussions of the committee and, as the committee normally proceeds by consensus, they have at least as much influence over proceedings as any MP. Arguably, they have more influence, in that they have the formal power to add an opinion to a report, setting out their views. If they wish to do this, the committee report cannot be published until the opinion is ready, and there are no restrictions on what the opinion may cover. The power to append an opinion gives lay members the opportunity to set out their views in a freestanding and public way. In contrast, an MP who disagrees with some or all of a draft report will simply have his or her dissent recorded in the formal minutes as defeated amendments to the draft.

Dealing with complaints

Although the Commissioner and the committee each have an important role in preventing problems, their highest-profile activity is ensuring the rules are enforced. The Commissioner can 'self-start' inquiries if there is evidence of wrongdoing, or if the IPSA Compliance Officer asks the Commissioner to do so, but the vast majority of inquiries arise from complaints made by members of the public or, very frequently, other MPs.

When a complaint is made that an MP has broken the rules, the Commissioner decides whether the matter is within her remit or there is enough evidence to justify an investigation. Most cases fall at this stage. Many of the complaints made to the Commissioner are about the handling of constituency cases, which are outside the scope of the Code. Others are about the expression of political opinions, or even actions within parliamentary proceedings, which are not for the Commissioner. Others complain about matters that are not breaches of rules, or are not accompanied by any evidence. It is entirely for the Commissioner to decide whether or not a matter is within her remit or whether the evidence is sufficient to justify starting an investigation. Although some evidence is required to start an inquiry, the Commissioner will usually gather more, particularly in serious cases.

An investigation may result in a finding that no breach of the rules has occurred, or that there has been a minor breach that the MP concerned can put right easily ('rectification'). For example, someone who has inadvertently sent political material in a prepaid envelope may be asked to refund the cost of stationery, or a member who has failed to declare an interest may do so in a point of order on the floor of the House. In such cases, the papers relating to the inquiry are simply published on the internet.

In more serious cases the Commissioner submits a memorandum to the Committee on Standards, accompanied by the evidence gathered during her inquiry. The committee may make further inquiries and report to the House with its conclusions and recommendations, which may include repayment of money, written or oral apologies, or suspension from the House (with loss of pay). It is for the House itself to decide whether or not an MP should be suspended or even expelled.

In principle, the Commissioner and the committee will not deal with criminal matters. But some serious cases still come before the committee. In 2012, it had to deal with a case in which an MP had submitted invoices signed with a '*nom de plume*'. The committee recommended suspension for a year, which resulted in the resignation of the MP concerned, possibly after party pressure. This case had earlier been referred to the police for investigation by the Commissioner (with the committee's consent), but no charges had been brought. When the committee's report was published, the case was reopened, and the person concerned was subsequently jailed. Similarly, in 2014, the committee recommended a suspension of six months for an MP who, as a result of a journalistic sting, accepted a 'consultancy' and tried to found an APPG to further the interests of his fictitious clients. Once again, the member resigned.

Checks and balances

The political class has always struggled to be trusted, and the expenses scandal was a major setback. Whether the current level of distrust is merited is another matter. People in the United Kingdom seem ready to believe the worst: a recent EU anti-corruption report noted:

> *In the case of the UK, only 5 persons out of 1115 were expected to pay a bribe (less than 1%), showing the best result in all Europe; nevertheless, the perception data*

show that 64% of UK respondents think corruption is widespread in the country (the EU average is 74%).

A body without an effective system for policing standards may look cleaner than one where those who break the rules are investigated and punished.

There are real dilemmas in self-regulation. It can, of course, be seen as the political class 'marking its own homework'. But there is already a robust legal framework setting out who can and cannot be an MP, and no blanket immunity for MPs. The Code of Conduct rightly sets higher expectations for MPs than their observance of the law. Handing the right to police compliance (and perhaps even to set such expectations) to an external body would mean non-elected people would decide who should sit in Parliament, whatever the decision of the electorate.

Nonetheless pressure has grown to reform further the standards regime. Perhaps the most significant change came in 2015 when a system of recall of MPs was introduced. Under this system an MP may lose his or her seat, and a by-election is held, if (a) the MP is imprisoned for less than a year (imprisonment for longer means the MP automatically loses his or her seat), (b) the MP is suspended from the House for more than 10 sitting days following a report by the Committee on Standards, or (c) the MP is convicted of the offence of providing false or misleading information for allowances claims. If any of these conditions is met a recall petition may be held in the MP's constituency. If more than 10 per cent of eligible electors sign the petition the MP loses his or her seat and a by-election is held. The MP may stand in the by-election. The Recall of MPs Act 2015 was not universally welcomed. Some think it is open to manipulation, and may reduce MPs' freedom to speak and act in the way that they consider best. There are fears that it may politicise the workings of the Committee on Standards when it considers whether to suspend an MP. If the MP's party would not welcome a by-election it is possible that the party's MPs on the committee would fight hard to have a suspension for fewer than 10 days. The recall process was triggered for the first time in the summer of 2018 following the 30-day suspension from the House of Ian Paisley MP. This followed a report from the Committee on Standards on a finding that he had breached the Code of Conduct in relation to visits he had made to Sri Lanka paid for by the Sri Lankan government. However, the 10 per cent threshold was not met and so no by-election was held.

There are those who believe that all MPs should be full-time; others believe equally strongly that current outside experience makes an MP more knowledgeable and effective. People are distrustful of lobbying and external interests. Many deplore the rise of what they see as the 'professional politician' with no experience outside Westminster (although a conscientious constituency MP sees much more of 'life' than do many of the critics). And we should not underplay the influence of the selectorate and the electorate. Local parties are free to choose candidates without outside interests, and will almost certainly do so if it is likely to increase their vote; and the voters are free to disagree.

No system will satisfy everyone, but if outside interests are to be allowed, then public disclosure of those interests, allied to rigorous investigation of complaints and effective sanctions when the rules are broken, seems a reasonable way to proceed. Whether it commands public confidence, in a society that is distrustful by default, is a separate issue.

The House of Lords

Lords and Commons

Members of the House of Lords are subject to much the same influences as MPs, except that they do not have constituencies. Perhaps the chief influence – constraint even – on the House of Lords is its unequal position in Parliament vis-à-vis the House of Commons. The limitations on Lords' powers to reject or amend bills are fully described in Chapter 6, but it is important to grasp at this stage that the Lords, by not being elected and therefore being unrepresentative, in practice has considerably less power than the Commons. If the Lords always attempted to insist on its will against that of the elected House, especially if the Commons were giving effect to policies endorsed by the electorate as part of the election manifesto of the governing party, there would be a showdown between the two Houses that would almost certainly result in further diminution of the Lords' powers. Because of this, the Lords tacitly recognises the right of the government to govern and of the House of Commons to see its will prevail most of the time. They willingly sacrifice their power in the same sort of compromise as that involved in the supremacy of the government in the House of Commons.

Many thought that the introduction of an elected element into the House under proposals for reform of the House set out in the coalition government's House of Lords Reform Bill in 2012 (see page 396) would have necessitated a readjustment of these assumptions – assumptions that have held good since the House of Commons became a truly representative chamber following the extension of the franchise in the nineteenth and early twentieth centuries. That said, the House of Lords is also subject to government, party, personal and external pressures in just the same way as the House of Commons, although these influences are perhaps less obtrusive in the Lords.

Government

The position of the government in the Lords is not as well entrenched as in the Commons. Following a general election, the party with the majority of seats in the House of Commons forms the government, and it is this party that occupies the government benches in the Lords, too. In October 2017 the government frontbench in the Lords consisted of one Cabinet minister – the Leader of the House; six ministers of state; nine parliamentary under-secretaries of state; and nine whips. Standing at 25, the total is high by historic standards; the fact that five are unpaid indicates that there are more Lords ministers than there are salaries available. Even so, the government presence is, relatively speaking, much smaller in the Lords than in the Commons, and promise of ministerial office is accordingly much less influential. The government's influence over its own backbenchers and over other members of the House is, in the absence of a large 'payroll' membership, that much weaker.

However, there is an understanding that the government can expect to get its business through. As we shall see on page 224, under the Salisbury convention the Lords will not reject at second reading legislation relating to commitments contained in an election manifesto. Indeed, it is rare for the Lords to reject at second reading any government bill. But a more general understanding on business is indispensable for the proper functioning of the House, as there are no procedural devices for curtailing debate on legislation; neither do the Lords' standing orders give government business precedence over other business. In the House of Commons, we have seen that a high proportion of sitting time is reserved for government business. In the Lords, anything up to 60 per cent of sitting time can be occupied with government business, but none of it is formally reserved for government use. In the last resort, a government might try to suspend standing orders in order to give its own business precedence, but fortunately this is rarely necessary. Provided that the government business managers respect the conventions of the House, consult the opposition through the usual channels and do their best to accommodate the demands of individual members, the other parties and private members alike are content to leave the arrangement of business to the Government Chief Whip. Governments are able to get their business through because they make sure that they are seen to deal fairly with the other parties and interests in the House.

The political parties

Although the members of the House are not elected, many of them – but by no means all – belong to political parties. A breakdown appears on page 41. Unlike in the Commons the political composition of the Lords does not change after a general election.

Officially, the House scarcely recognises the existence of the political parties. They are nowhere referred to in standing orders, and they are barely mentioned in the *Companion to Standing Orders*, the House's procedural handbook. But the reality is very different. Each party has its leader and its whips and support staff. We have already seen how opposition parties and the Convenor of the Crossbench Peers receive public funding (so-called Cranborne money) to assist them in their activities. The government party has the advantage of an office manned by civil servants to organise its affairs. Committees of the House tend to reflect the composition of the House, as in the Commons, and the government party negotiates through the whips' offices of the other parties (the usual channels) and, where appropriate with the Crossbench Convenor, in the arrangement of business.

As in the Commons, the party whips send their members statements of forthcoming business in the House, with items underlined to indicate their importance to the party leadership. But discipline is not as strong as in the House of Commons. For some members of the House their political careers are not their principal interest; for many the allure of office carries less weight. There is no pairing system. There are weekly party meetings – every Wednesday afternoon – at which future business is discussed and there is a strong general predisposition to toe the party line. Members of the House do not have to submit themselves to the rigours of selection by the constituency parties or to re-election by constituents. The voting record of members of the House of Lords is not subjected to the same level of scrutiny as is that of MPs. We have seen that party cohesiveness is high when the House votes: but no one has yet measured the effect of strategic absenteeism. The crossbenchers – who profess no party line – are all, theoretically, floating voters though in recent years they have shown remarkable cohesiveness on some votes, particularly when the mover of the proposition is a crossbencher. (An amendment moved by a crossbencher to the Immigration Bill in the 2013–14 session attracted 78 crossbench votes in support and none against!)

The leader of the government party in the Lords is the Leader of the House, who, together with the Government Chief Whip, advises ministerial colleagues on any problems that might be encountered in getting their business through the House. Similarly, the Leader and Chief Whip of the Official Opposition will have regard to the views of the wider parliamentary party and shadow Cabinet in determining their approach to more controversial business.

Personal interests

The composition of the House guarantees great diversity of interest. Table 2.2 on page 37 shows the background from which new members have been drawn over the years. First and foremost, there are the politicians – either those elected hereditary peers who have taken up political careers based in the Lords, or those created peers who have formerly been MPs, MEPs, party officials or prominent in local government. Then there are those, mainly but not exclusively life peers, who are drawn from other walks of life – business, the professions and so on. Very often they are retired or approaching retirement, but they bring valuable experience and sometimes genuine expertise which places them at an advantage where detailed scrutiny of policy is required – say, in debates on academic funding or the operation of the benefits system, or in scrutiny in committee of the lessons to be learned from the banking crisis, for example. The diversity of the members of the House ensures that personal interest and influences are very strong in the Lords.

Members' interests, the Code of Conduct, and the Lords Commissioner for Standards

It was a long-standing custom of the House that members spoke always on their personal honour; and where they decided to participate in debates on matters in which they had an interest, whether pecuniary or not, they were to declare it so that other members and the public might form a balanced view of their argument. These rules were clarified and a scheme of voluntary registration of interests put in place in 1995. Following a review by the Committee on Standards in Public Life, a compulsory registration scheme and a code of conduct came into force in 2001. In the wake of high-profile breaches of that code, a new and more prescriptive Code of Conduct and accompanying guidance came into force in 2010, and a Commissioner for Standards was appointed. Let us now discuss the chief characteristics of the rules on conduct.

Members of the House must as a general principle comply with the Code, act on their personal honour, never accept or agree to accept any financial inducement or reward for exercising parliamentary influence (acting as a 'paid advocate'), or providing parliamentary advice or services (acting as consultants or lobbyists). Any conflict between personal and public interest should always be resolved in favour of the latter. The seven principles of conduct as defined by the Committee on Standards in Public life should be observed. Every member must sign an undertaking to abide by the Code as part of the ceremony of taking the oath of allegiance at the start of every Parliament, or on their first entering the House.

The Code requires every member of the House to register any 'relevant' interests, and keep that registration up to date. A relevant interest is one that might be thought by a reasonable member of the public to influence the way in which the member might discharge his or her parliamentary duties. Interests may be financial, such as a shareholding or paid employment, or non-financial, as with membership of an organisation. In certain cases, they will extend also to a spouse or partner. In addition to registration, members must declare their interests in debate when relevant to the matter under discussion, and when tabling written notices, for instance questions or motions, in *House of Lords Business*.

The Code also requires members to abide by the rules relating to financial support received from the House and the rules on the use of the House's facilities and services.

An investigation of a possible breach of the Code is carried out by the House of Lords Commissioner for Standards. She reaches a finding on whether the Code has been breached. If she finds it hasn't, that is the end of the matter. She can find that the Code has been breached but in a minor way; in which instance the case may be resolved by 'remedial action' – usually involving the member apologising and putting the record straight. In more serious cases where the Code has been breached the Commissioner reports her findings to the Sub-Committee on Lords' Conduct for it to recommend a sanction. The reports of the Commissioner and the subcommittee then go to the parent Committee for Privileges and Conduct, to which the member concerned may appeal. The committee's determination is then reported to the House for final decision. Sanctions for a breach may vary from an apology, or repayment of moneys, to suspension from the service of the House or even expulsion. The power to suspend a member was reasserted by the House in May 2009 at the height of the expenses scandal, which in the Lords chiefly took the form of false claims for overnight allowances. The power of suspension is now unlimited. The power of expulsion was introduced in 2015 and has not yet been used. To date 11 members have been suspended from the House for breaching the Code, for periods ranging from 4 to 18 months.

Territorial

Members of the House of Lords have no constituencies: they are not representatives. As Lord Birkenhead (F.E. Smith) once remarked of a member of the House who had incurred his ire, 'The noble Lord represents no one but himself and I don't think much of his constituency'. It follows therefore that they do not have 'surgeries', or make representations to government or other authorities in respect of individuals' problems or grievances. Neither are they answerable to local party organisations or selection committees.

However, sometimes members of the House will be approached by individuals or interest groups in the locality in which they live or whose title they bear by reason of some long – and sometimes extinct – association, asking them to take up a particular stance on a public matter. Members are undoubtedly responsive to such approaches.

Lobby groups

As we examine in detail later on, all legislation has to be considered in the Lords, as well as in the Commons, and some legislation begins its passage through Parliament in the House of Lords. Members of the House therefore find themselves courted in much the same way as members of the House of Commons by lobby groups either directly, from their government and parliamentary relations officers, or through parliamentary consultants. The dramatic increase in lobbying since the end of the 1970s has been a conspicuous feature of the revival in House of Lords influence in recent years – part cause and part effect. Some lobbyists are skilful and selective in their targets. Others resort to an indiscriminate 'mail-drop'. These organisations will prepare evidence for committees, draft amendments to be moved to bills and provide briefing notes, offer to take peers on visits, or arrange lectures at which their policies are expounded.

As a result of these contacts, some peers form potentially close associations with, for example, local authority organisations, industry groups, charities, bankers, major exporters or libertarian groups. These contacts not only influence members of the House, but also help to provide briefing which is often used in members' speeches. They help to fill a void left by the relatively limited research resources available to peers, who have no separate fund for employing staff.

There are drawbacks to this reliance on third-party organisations. Some members' associations with lobby groups are so close that they can appear to be their mouthpiece; the arguments advanced are inevitably to the advantage of the group, however worthy, often with insufficient regard for the wider consequences; and the lengthy briefing can lead to some debates being unnecessarily long.

Peers, in the same way as MPs, also belong to the all-party and registered special interest and country groups (see page 107).

5

The parliamentary day and the organisation of business

The parliamentary calendar

Before we look at the various items of business that make up a typical day in Parliament, and how members of both Houses are likely to spend their time, it is worth looking more broadly at the parliamentary calendar and the cycle of business in each House.

A parliament

In Chapter 2, we encountered the main division of parliamentary time: *a parliament*. This is the period between one general election and the next. The Septennial Act 1715 set the maximum life of a parliament at seven years. This was reduced to five years by the Parliament Act 1911, although during the First and Second World Wars, to avoid a wartime general election, the life of the 1911 parliament was extended to eight years; that of the 1935 parliament was extended to 10 years. Although the maximum life of a parliament – that is, the period between the day of first meeting and dissolution – was five years, few parliaments ran their course, because the Prime Minister of the day would seek a dissolution at a time that he or she saw as giving the best electoral advantage. The average length of parliaments between 1945 and 2010 was around three years 10 months, with a four-year parliament being the modern norm.

Parliaments are numbered; the 2017 parliament is the 57th parliament of the United Kingdom since the Union with Ireland in 1801.

The Fixed-term Parliaments Act 2011

A significant change was made to the pattern of parliaments by the Fixed-term Parliaments Act 2011. The Act abolished the Prime Minister's power to set the date of a general election and fixed the duration of a parliament at five years (subject to provisions for an earlier, or later, election). It set the date of the next UK general election as Thursday 7 May 2015; thereafter, a general election would normally be held on the first Thursday in May in the fifth calendar year following the previous general election. The dissolution of Parliament was set for a specified period (originally 17 working days, later extended to 25) before the date of the general election. At the time there was debate over whether four or five years was the best length of a Parliament. Four years was closer to the historical average; the then government argued that five years would allow for more long-term decision-making.

The Act was a key element of the 2010 coalition agreement between the Conservatives and the Liberal Democrats. Its main purpose was widely seen as being to ensure the continuance for a full five-year term of the coalition, preventing the Conservative Prime Minister from 'pulling the plug' early and forcing a new election at a time of his choosing (although some commentators and constitutional reformers had been advocating such a change for some time, and the proposal was included in the Liberal Democrat manifesto for the 2010 election).

The Act made provision for early elections when one of the following conditions is met:

- if a motion for an early general election is agreed either by at least two-thirds of the whole House (including vacant seats) or without division; or
- if a motion of no confidence is passed and no alternative government is confirmed by the Commons within 14 days by means of a confidence motion.

For the avoidance of doubt, the Act provided that a no-confidence motion must be in the form 'That this House has no confidence in Her Majesty's Government'. This meant that defeat on other types of motion, such as key parts of the budget or the Address in response to the Queen's Speech setting out the government's legislative programme, which previously would be considered a demonstration of no confidence, would not be enough to trigger an election. It also largely neutered the effect of a government tabling a motion inviting the House of Commons to express confidence in the government or one of its policies (as John Major did over the Protocol on Social Policy to the Maastricht treaty in 1993). In these instances for an election to ensue the government's defeat on the motion would have to be followed by the House of Commons agreeing a motion for an early general election (by a two-thirds majority) or the government then losing a motion of no confidence. In the latter case there would then have to be a further period of 14 days in which no motion of confidence in the government is passed. The likely effect is a government limping on until one of the subsequent motions is passed, having lost much credibility and authority to govern. The scenario may strike many as confusing and inferior to the sharp and dramatic consequences of defeat on a confidence vote which used to prevail.

The Act creates a theoretical possibility of a Prime Minister who commands a majority in the House of Commons engineering a no-confidence vote that will enable a general election to take place at a time of his or her choosing; but the political consequences of attempting such a move make it unlikely.

The alternative route of holding an early election by gaining a two-thirds majority of all MPs was seen as creating a very high bar, which was unlikely ever to be met. However, within an hour of Theresa May calling for a general election in April 2017 the Leader of the Opposition announced that he would support it, thus making a two-thirds majority a formality. (If all Labour MPs had abstained it would have been impossible to get the two-thirds majority.) The motion for an early election was passed by 522 to 13 after a 90-minute debate.

Where an early election has taken place, the date of the next election reverts to the first Thursday in May, either in the fourth calendar year following the early election, if that election takes place before the first Thursday in May of that year, or the fifth calendar year, if the early election takes place after the first Thursday in May of that year. So, because of the early election in June 2017, the next election would be fixed for Thursday 5 May 2022, with the one after that in May 2027. Thus, the usual May date is restored and provision is made so that a parliament cannot last more than five years.

The Act also makes provision for the date of a general election to be delayed by up to two months beyond the date set by the Act. This may happen by an order made by the Prime Minister following its approval in draft by both Houses of Parliament. The draft order laid before Parliament must be accompanied by a statement setting out the Prime Minister's reasons for proposing the change in the polling day. The drafters of this provision presumably had in mind the events of 2001, when the general election expected in, and the local elections set for, May 2001 were delayed for a month as a result of a widespread outbreak of foot-and-mouth disease that necessitated movement restrictions across much of the country.

Given criticisms of the Fixed-term Parliaments Act, and the constraints it imposes on the Prime Minister, it was unsurprising that the Conservatives' manifesto for the 2017 election undertook to repeal it. However, there has been no word of the proposal since the election; it may even be that the difficulty of holding an early election benefits a minority government.

The beginning of a parliament

Some events always happen at the start of a parliament. Both Houses assemble on the day specified in the sovereign's proclamation following the dissolution of the previous parliament. In recent years this has been between five and 12 days after the election. In the House of Commons there is a real advantage in a longer gap between polling day and the day of first meeting, as it allows longer for the induction and initial briefing of what may be a substantial number of new MPs (in 2017 there were 93, or 14 per cent of the House; in 2010 there were 227, or 35 per cent).

On the day of first meeting, the Commons go to the House of Lords, where they are directed to elect a Speaker (see page 49). Having gone back to their own House and done so, the Commons return to the Lords the next day, where the Queen's approbation of the Speaker-elect is signified.

The Commons then return to their chamber, and the new Speaker takes the oath of allegiance, or makes the affirmation required by law, standing on the upper step of the Speaker's chair. Other MPs then take the oath or make the affirmation, starting with the Prime Minister and the cabinet, and the shadow cabinet, then privy counsellors (usually former cabinet and other senior ministers), then other backbenchers. The order of taking the oath is significant only when the longest-serving MPs were elected in the same year; if their seniority is equal, the Father of the House (there has not yet been a Mother of the House) is the member who takes the oath first.

MPs queue up before the Table; the oath is administered by a clerk; under the supervision of the Clerk Assistant each MP then signs the test roll, a bound parchment book, and is then formally introduced to the Speaker by the Clerk of the House. The swearing in of members goes on for three or four hours that day and then continues on the next three or four days.

The wording of the oath and affirmation and the way they are taken was established in the Oaths Act 1978. An MP takes the oath by holding the sacred text in his or her uplifted hand and saying:

> *I [name of member] swear by Almighty God that I will be faithful and bear true allegiance to Her Majesty Queen Elizabeth, her heirs and successors, according to law. So help me God.*

The Act permits the oath to be taken in the Scottish manner, with uplifted hand but not holding the sacred text. Members who want to do so may also take the oath as prescribed in the Promissory Oaths Act 1868, by kissing the book and using the words:

> *I [name of member] do swear that I will be faithful and bear true allegiance to Her Majesty Queen Elizabeth, her heirs and successors, according to law. So help me God.*

Alternatively, members may make a solemn affirmation instead of taking an oath, using the words:

> *I [name of member] do solemnly, sincerely, and truly declare and affirm, that I will be faithful and bear true allegiance to Her Majesty Queen Elizabeth, her heirs and successors, according to law.*

The sacred texts available for those who wish to use them include the King James Bible, the New Testament (in English, Welsh or Gaelic), the Old Testament (in English and Hebrew, or in Hebrew), the Zohar, the Dhammapada, the Gita, the Koran and the Granth. The last three texts are kept in slip-cases so that they are not handled directly by those not of the faith. The oath or affirmation must be taken in English, but it may be said additionally in Welsh, Scots Gaelic or Cornish. An MP must take the oath or affirm before sitting, speaking or voting in the House (except for the election of a Speaker); and if by chance he or she does not, the penalty is severe: the seat is vacated and there must be a by-election. The additional penalty of a £500 fine seems trivial by comparison.

Most MPs take the oath or affirm in these first days of a new parliament, but those remaining may do so in the days following the first Queen's Speech of the new parliament (and, occasionally, much later if prevented by illness). When the 'swearing days' are completed, the House adjourns to the day of the state opening, which takes place at the start of a new parliament and also at the start of each of the subsequent sessions of that parliament.

Similarly, the Lords sit for two swearing-in days for oaths and affirmations, when members also sign an undertaking to abide by the Code of Conduct, and then adjourn until the state opening. For the purpose of taking the oath, they may choose from a variety of religious texts – from the New Testament to the Hindu Gita and Parsee Avesta. Swearing-in in the Lords continues for many days after the state opening, taking up a few moments at the start of business.

A session

This is the period that begins with the state opening of Parliament and the Queen's Speech outlining the government's plans for legislation for the session. It ends with prorogation (see page 135) or with a dissolution (see page 25) if it is the last session of a parliament.

Before the Fixed-term Parliaments Act 2011, a session would normally last from a state opening around early November until prorogation a year or so later. Following a general election in the spring or summer (as has been the case since 1979), the first session of a parliament was usually a long session lasting until the November of the following year. Conversely, the final session of the Parliament was usually a short one, lasting from November until the election the following summer. This pattern had some advantages, providing a long first legislative period for a new government and a foreshortened final period as members' and ministers' thoughts inevitably turned towards the forthcoming election.

Although it was not a necessary consequence of the Fixed-term Parliaments Act, following its passage the government decided that a five-year parliament should contain five sessions of more or less equal length. State opening was moved from November to the spring, in line with the May general election, to last until the following spring. A session is denoted by both years (thus, the '2016–17 session'). The government announced, however, that the session that began in 2010 would last for two years: its 295 sitting days made 2010–12 the longest ever session of the UK Parliament. Similarly, the government announced that the session that began after the 2017 election would last for two years, to allow time for Brexit-related legislation to pass.

The state opening

A session traditionally begins with colourful ceremony, centuries old (Queen Elizabeth I opened Parliament in much the same way), as the Queen drives in procession to

Westminster with an escort of Household Cavalry, normally arriving at 11.30 am. The processional route is lined with troops and thronged with tourists; bands play; the police even wear white gloves. The Queen arrives under the Victoria Tower at the south end of the Palace of Westminster and proceeds to the Robing Room, where she puts on the Imperial State Crown and then moves in procession to the House of Lords, which is a bright theatre of peers' scarlet and ermine, judges' robes and wigs, and ambassadors and high commissioners in evening dress and decorations.

Black Rod ('the Lady Usher of the Black Rod') is directed to summon the Commons. In a symbolic reminder of the right of the Commons to exclude any royal messenger, the doors leading to the chamber are closed in his face; she knocks, is admitted and delivers the summons. Led by the Speaker and Black Rod, and followed by the Clerk of the House, Prime Minister and Leader of the Opposition, and members of the cabinet and shadow cabinet, MPs walk the 100 metres or so to the House of Lords, where they crowd behind the bar of the House (the formal boundary of the chamber) to hear the Queen's Speech.

In 2017 the procession to the Palace of Westminster was dispensed with and the sovereign did not wear robes or the crown, but much of the rest of the ceremony remained in place. It is unclear what form a state opening might take when both chambers are decanted for the restoration of the Palace of Westminster. The Queen

Guests await the Queen in the Royal Gallery; Yeoman Warders line route as the former Black Rod walks through

Source: Copyright House of Lords, 2017. Photography by Mark Duffy

Elizabeth II Conference Centre (the planned decant venue for the Lords) does not have quite the same majesty as the Robing Room, Royal Gallery and throne in the Lords chamber.

The Queen's Speech

The Queen's Speech is the parliamentary core of this state ceremony. The speech is drafted by the government and will have been approved by the Cabinet. It normally refers to any recent or forthcoming royal events or state visits, and it contains some broad policy intentions; the 2017 speech began: 'My government's priority is to secure the best possible deal as the country leaves the European Union. My ministers are committed to working with Parliament, the devolved administrations, business and others to build the widest possible consensus on the country's future outside the European Union'. A sentence in the speech tells the Commons (because they, rather than the Lords, have financial authority) that estimates for financing the public services will be laid before them.

The meat of the speech is the legislative agenda for the coming session: the 2017 speech foreshadowed 24 bills and three draft bills. Bills are usually described in broad terms; in 2017, for example, Parliament was told that 'Legislation will be brought forward to protect the victims of domestic violence and abuse'. Bills do not have to be in the Queen's Speech to be introduced, but the speech outlines the main legislative activity for the year ahead.

The Queen delivers her speech at state opening, 2017

Source: Copyright House of Lords, 2017. Photography by Roger Harris

When the Commons return to their chamber, the sitting is suspended until 2.30 pm. At this point the Speaker will make a statement reminding the House of the duties and responsibilities of members. The details of this statement will vary, but it will usually include a reminder of members' responsibilities under the Code of Conduct, a reference to the ancient privileges by which the House is free to conduct its debate without fear of outside interference, together with a warning about the need to exercise those privileges responsibly, an enjoinder to ensure that all members are heard courteously in debate, regardless of the views that they may be expressing, and a reminder of the need to protect the security of the House and those who work there. The House then gives a formal first reading to the Outlawries Bill 'for the more effectual preventing clandestine outlawries', whose purpose belongs to the distant past but which is a symbol of the right of the House to proceed with its own business before considering what the sovereign has just told Parliament.

The Lords sit at 3.30 pm, when certain sessional orders, including that to prevent 'stoppages in the streets', are passed; some office-holders such as the Senior Deputy Speaker are appointed; and a *pro forma* bill (the Select Vestries Bill) is read a first time.

Debate on the Queen's Speech

This is the first debate of the session, normally lasting four or five days. The debate is formally on a motion to present 'an Humble Address' to the Queen thanking her for the 'most Gracious Speech' addressed to both Houses, but it is in practice a review of the government's policies and intentions. The debate is opened by a mover and a seconder from the government backbenches – the only occasion on which a motion in the House of Commons is seconded. It is something of an honour to be selected (by the whips) to make these first two speeches. The MPs concerned (usually one new and one long-serving) are expected not to be contentious but to be reminiscent and witty, and to extol the virtues of their constituencies.

Then the business gets more seriously under way. The Leader of the Opposition speaks next, with the disadvantage that he gets no advance text of the Queen's Speech and has only a couple of hours to decide on much of what he will say. Then the Prime Minister makes what is, in effect, the keynote speech, outlining the government's plans and programme, and going into much more detail than in the Queen's Speech itself. The leader of the second largest opposition party (currently the SNP) follows and then the debate is open to MPs generally. The first day is a general debate, when any aspect may be raised; the subsequent debates are themed as agreed through the usual channels, perhaps on home affairs, foreign affairs and defence, health, and the economy, and are opened and closed by the relevant ministers or shadow ministers. On the last two days amendments in the name of the Leader of the Opposition are moved and voted on, usually regretting the fact that the Gracious Speech contains no plans to legislate to do this or that. When the government has a comfortable majority, the outcome is not in doubt; but under a minority government or a shaky coalition, these votes, and that on the substantive motion at the very end of proceedings, is the first test of whether the Prime Minister can command a majority in the House. There may be up to four amendments moved in total, with one taken on the penultimate day and up to three on the final day.

In the Lords, the motion for 'an Humble Address' in reply to the Queen's Speech is moved and seconded from the government backbenches, but the debate proper is then adjourned and takes place over the subsequent four days. As with the Commons debate, each day has a theme but, unlike the Commons, it is rare for there to be a vote at the end; and defeat for the government on any vote is embarrassing but no specific consequences would follow.

The pattern of the session

The reference points in any parliamentary session are a combination of the sacred and the secular: the state opening, Whitsun, the summer adjournment, the September sitting, a brief adjournment in November, Christmas, February half-term, Easter and prorogation.

Early business in a session usually includes a government motion to fix the 13 Fridays on which private members' bills will be taken (seven for second readings and six for 'remaining stages'; see page 212). The House does not usually sit on Fridays other than those on which private members' bills are debated, though occasionally the government will arrange for one of the days of debate on the Queen's Speech or the budget (see page 253) to take place on a Friday. With a two-year 2017–19 session the government has undertaken to propose extra sitting Fridays; but at the time of writing the House had agreed only the standard 13 Fridays.

In the first few days of a new session, the first two or three of the major government bills foreshadowed in the Queen's Speech will be introduced (at that stage they will be given a purely formal first reading, with second reading debates on the principle of each bill following 10 or so days later). *Second readings of government bills starting in the Commons* (others begin their parliamentary journey in the House of Lords) in the chamber feature up to the summer break and, again, after the House returns in September and October, usually into November. Also before the summer adjournment, the Commons will normally approve the *departmental estimates* on the first *estimates day* (see page 259).

After their second reading in the chamber, nearly all *government bills will go into public bill committees* (see page 195) and, in the period up until Christmas, public bill committee activity builds up. At its peak, six or seven public bill committees may be sitting for much of Tuesdays and Thursdays, occupying 100 to 150 MPs altogether, with big bills taking several weeks in committee, and each being the main focus of activity for the ministers responsible for each bill and the shadow ministers opposing them. As the bills complete their committee stages, they return to the House for *report stages* and, in the period up to Easter and beyond, this starts to take up time on the floor of the House. Government legislation will usually be contentious between the parties and so will require the presence of MPs to vote even if they are not directly involved in the business.

Most *second readings of private members' bills* will normally be taken from July through to October, but many will fall by the wayside. By November, the successful (up to then!) private members' bills will be coming through their public bill committee stages and queuing up for the *six remaining stages days* in the latter part of the session. An MP's presence on a private members' bill Friday is less likely to be required by the whips (with the exception of the payroll vote of ministers and PPSs), so unless the MP has agreed to support a colleague's bill (or wants to obstruct or kill a bill) these may be days when the MP can work in the constituency, as on other Fridays.

In 2017 the government moved the budget to be held in the autumn rather than the spring (as had been the case for the previous 20 years or so). The budget is debated by the House for four or five days. From 2018 onwards it will be accompanied by a spring statement, the purpose of which is not to make significant tax or spending changes but to provide the government's response to the latest forecasts by the Office for Budget Responsibility (replacing the autumn statement).

From late October onwards *bills that started in the Lords begin coming down to the Commons* and going through all the same stages as those bills that originated in the Commons. By January the government may start to schedule second readings for bills that will be subject to the carry-over procedure – with those that were introduced in the previous session and carried over going into public bill committee or taking their report stages in the early part of the session.

Before Easter the House approves the remaining *supplementary estimates* for the current financial year and any *excess votes* for the previous financial year (see page 262). At a fairly late stage in the session (although increasingly this is spread throughout the year, there is sometimes a queue late in the session), the two Houses consider the amendments each has made to bills that started in the other House: *Commons amendments* and *Lords amendments*, sometimes abbreviated to *CCLA* (Commons Consideration of Lords Amendments) and *LCCA* (Lords Consideration of Commons Amendments). If amendments made by one House are not accepted by the other (most often because the government wishes to reverse a defeat it has suffered in the Lords) a round of 'ping-pong' between the two Houses may ensue, with alternative amendments being offered in an effort to get agreement before the bill is killed by the end of the session.

The end of the session after Easter is usually a final tidying up of the to and fro of bills between the two Houses, often with other business being inserted as a make-weight while waiting for one House or the other to complete proceedings on this or that bill.

We have described the pattern of the session largely in terms of legislation and financial business, but a great deal else is going on. Time must be found for the 20 *opposition days*, each of which is a full day's debate on a subject on which the opposition feels the government may be vulnerable, or for which it wants a parliamentary shop window; the second and third *estimates days*, on which members debate particular aspects of the government's spending plans; time may be needed for private bills; and there are 27 days of *backbench business*: debate on subjects chosen by a committee of backbenchers on the basis of representations made to them by members of the House. And on every day except Friday there is the framework of question time, ministerial statements, urgent questions and the half-hour adjournment debate at the end of each day's proceedings, as well as debates in Westminster Hall on Tuesdays, Wednesdays, Thursdays and occasionally Mondays (see page 278).

Business in the Lords follows a slightly different cycle. Although the business managers make every effort to introduce a certain number of bills in that House to occupy it in the early part of the session, most bills start in the Commons and arrive in the Lords in the late summer or the autumn. This makes for longer sitting hours and more sitting days in the latter part of the session. September sittings have not been as regular a feature in the Lords as in the Commons, but may now have become the norm. If the Lords does not sit in September it often sits later in July than the Commons and returns earlier after the summer break. Other recesses usually follow the same pattern as in the Commons. Unlike the Commons, the Lords have no fixed points in the calendar for consideration of financial matters, except for their formal consideration of the Finance Bill in the spring.

Prorogation

This is the formal end of a session. It is a 'prerogative act' of the Crown, another survival of the early relationship between sovereign and Parliament (when it was used on occasion by monarchs to curb an inconvenient House of Commons). In modern times such royal powers are exercised by the government of the day, so it is the government that decides the length of the parliamentary session. There is no formal requirement for an annual May to April session, but the constitutional convention of an annual session is a strong one. Thus the government came in for some criticism when it announced a two-year session for 2017–19. Were the Fixed-term Parliaments Act 2011 to be repealed it would be open to the government to return to the pattern of November–November sessions, other than in general election years, if they wished.

The timing of prorogation is settled in the last few days of the session; the government business managers want to be sure that they have left enough time to get the last bills through, which may involve a degree of brinkmanship in achieving agreement between the two Houses.

For the prorogation ceremony the House of Commons goes up to the House of Lords just as at state opening, although in rather fewer numbers; but on this occasion the Queen will not be there. The Queen's Speech – a retrospective of the session – and the proclamation proroguing Parliament and setting the date for the state opening will be read out by one of the five peers who form the royal commission to do this on the Queen's behalf. The date to which Parliament has been prorogued may be changed in either direction by a royal proclamation. During the period of prorogation neither House, nor any committee, may meet.

Clearing the decks

A prorogation brings to an end almost all parliamentary business (which is why the business managers are so keen to secure the passage of government bills before the end of the session). The exceptions are those bills that are 'carried over' from one session to the next. This has long been possible for private bills (see page 235) and hybrid bills (see page 237) and, in 1998, the Commons agreed to a procedure whereby public bills may also be carried over. The explicit consent of the House is required for a bill to be carried over, and it requires careful planning by the business managers – it cannot simply be applied at the last minute to a bill that has failed to complete its parliamentary stages at the end of a session. A bill may be carried over only if it is still in the House in which it originated and the procedure applies only to government bills; a bill may only be carried over from one session to the next, and not over again into a further session; a bill may not be carried over from one parliament to the next; and a time limit is set of one year from its introduction within which the bill must complete its passage (subject to the possibility of extension, which can be granted only by the further approval of the House, and not beyond the end of the session into which the bill has been carried over). In most sessions about three or four bills are carried over. In some ways it is surprising that the procedure has not been used more often for government bills. Although it can be convenient for the business managers, it can also allow longer scrutiny of legislation – the pressure of time is both a bone of contention between government and opposition, and a source of criticism of the quality of legislation. It could also smooth the legislative programme by allowing major bills to be introduced later in the session.

The 'sudden death' of parliamentary business at the end of the session is practised by relatively few parliaments. There is no equivalent each year in the devolved legislatures; and in the Australian parliament (which is based on the Westminster model) prorogation exists but is hardly ever used. Prorogation may have disadvantages for handling legislation; but it also acts as a clear-out of the parliamentary agenda and imposes some discipline on the legislative process. Early day motions (of which there may be more than 2,000 by the end of the session) lapse, and private members' bills die – both those that are clearly going to make no progress however much time might be available and those that their backers feel might have had a chance 'if only'.

Adjournments

The standing orders prescribe when the House of Commons sits, both in terms of time and days of the week, so when the House finishes its sitting ('adjourns') on any day, it will automatically meet on the next sitting day. Longer times of adjournment, commonly called 'recesses' – although strictly speaking this word applies only to the time during prorogation – are discussed through the usual channels and decided by the House on the basis of a motion moved by the Leader of the House.

The normal pattern of recesses and sitting periods (sometimes called 'terms') is:

May	State opening
	Whitsun adjournment: one week
June	–
July	House rises in the second half of July (summer adjournment)

August	House adjourned throughout
September	Two-week sitting, after which the House adjourns for the party conferences
October	–
November	Three-day break around the middle of the month
December	Christmas adjournment: about two weeks
January	–
February	'Constituency week' adjournment coinciding with school half-term
March/April	Easter adjournment: two weeks
Late April/May	Prorogation

It should be clear from the earlier account of constituency pressures that recesses are not MPs' holidays. Constituents do not stop writing because the House of Commons is not sitting, and many MPs will do more surgery work, and certainly more constituency engagements, than during a sitting week. But every year when the House rises in July the media remorselessly report that 'MPs are off on *x* weeks' summer holiday'.

Sittings of the Lords follow the same pattern but with occasional small variations. There is a larger variation to the summer pattern if the Lords do not sit in September (they have sat each September since 2015). Proposed recess dates are announced by the Government Chief Whip 'subject to the progress of business', but it is rare for the announced dates not to be followed.

Although the pattern of sitting times has always been broadly predictable to within a week or two, exact dates used not to be announced until a short time before each recess. In 2002 a parliamentary calendar for the next 12 months (something that had long been routine in many parliaments) was introduced, and a motion setting the dates of 'periodic adjournments' is now routinely agreed by the House of Commons in December to cover the whole of the following year. This has proved extremely useful, allowing those who deal with Parliament, as well as those in it, to make long-term plans. There is a tension between announcing sitting times a long way ahead and the wish of business managers to retain flexibility; and any change may lead to criticism.

Recall of parliament

In Chapter 3 we noted the Speaker's role in recalling the House if, as Standing Order No. 13 says, 'it is represented . . . by Her Majesty's Ministers that the public interest requires' that the House should meet during an adjournment. The Speaker always grants such a request. Since 1990 the House has been recalled 15 times, including to debate the invasion of Kuwait (1990), the UK's withdrawal from the European exchange rate mechanism (1992), the Omagh bombing and subsequent emergency legislation (1998), the 9/11 terrorist attacks in New York and Washington (three occasions in 2001), public confidence in the media and police in the wake of the phone-hacking affair (2011), possible military action against Iraq (2002), Syria

(2013) and ISIL in Iraq (2013), and following the deaths of Queen Elizabeth the Queen Mother (2002), Baroness Thatcher (2013) and Jo Cox MP (2016). It was also by an emergency recall that, on 3 April 1982, the House met on a Saturday to debate the invasion of the Falklands. The only Sunday sitting in the last century was on 3 September 1939, on the outbreak of the Second World War.

The Lords is recalled in the same way: formally by the Lord Speaker, but in practice on the initiative of the government. The Lords is invariably recalled whenever the Commons is.

The sitting week in the Commons

From April 1946 the House sat at 2.30 pm each day, with the moment of interruption (see page 147) normally ending the main business at 10.00 pm, and on Fridays at 11.00 am, with the moment of interruption at 4.00 pm. In each case, after the disposal of the business before the House (including business that was exempted and so could proceed after the moment of interruption) there would be the daily adjournment debate (see page 277) for a further half-hour. In 1980 Friday sittings were moved to 9.30 am, with the moment of interruption at 2.30 pm.

In 1994, following the recommendations of a select committee chaired by the former Conservative chief whip Michael Jopling, attempts were made to rein back the amount of business and its effect on the hours the House sat, particularly late at night. One of the changes was the introduction of Wednesday sittings starting at 9.30 am. As with the brief experiment under the 'Crossman reforms' in the 1960s (named after the then Leader of the House, Richard Crossman), these were used primarily for non-contentious business and debates initiated by backbenchers. From 1999 Thursday sittings began at 11.30 am; and at the end of 1999, with the additional backbench opportunities afforded by the establishment of Westminster Hall as a second debating forum, the House went back to sitting on Wednesdays at 2.30 pm.

A new timetable – and second thoughts

As a result of changes recommended by the Modernisation Committee chaired by Robin Cook as Leader of the House, 2003 saw a radical rearrangement of sitting hours. The original hours were kept for Monday (or for a Tuesday or Wednesday if this followed a recess), but with an 11.30 am start Tuesday to Thursday, and an earlier finish on Thursday. The few remaining Friday sittings stayed at 9.30 am. The Modernisation Committee pointed out that historically the House's hours had altered in response to changes in social custom and business practice. Later hours were convenient when MPs were unpaid and could do much of a day's work in the City or the courts and still be at Westminster for the main business of the House. The committee felt that this was no longer appropriate when most members were full-time MPs.

It also observed that major events such as statements and Prime Minister's Questions came relatively late in the day; and the House responded to an agenda of public debate – in effect, media coverage of events – which had already been set by then. Major votes usually came at 10.00 pm, often too late for adequate coverage in the next day's papers.

In making its proposals the Modernisation Committee warned that there was no consensus on sitting hours, and so it proved. Earlier sittings on Wednesdays were approved by 288 votes to 265, and those on Tuesdays by a narrower margin: 274 to 267. Opinion among MPs was sharply divided: some believed that more conventional working hours made Parliament seem less alien, and that a more family-friendly approach would encourage more people with family responsibilities to become MPs. Others disliked earlier starting times for committees and the House sitting during a morning that could be used for constituency and other parliamentary work.

Those with constituencies (and families) in or near London tended to prefer the new hours; those hundreds of miles from Westminster were less enthusiastic.

The new sitting hours remained contentious and, in January 2005, the House reverted to the old sitting hours on Tuesdays, by a majority of 292 to 225. The start of the Thursday sitting was advanced to 10.30 am to allow more substantial business to be taken on that day. Those sitting hours prevailed throughout the 2005–10 parliament, but the advocates of reform did not give up, and early in the 2010–15 parliament the Procedure Committee, picking up the baton from the defunct Modernisation Committee, considered the matter again.

Much the same issues arose as when the Modernisation Committee had considered the matter, and the Procedure Committee largely avoided coming to firm conclusions, stating rather that 'in looking at the sitting hours of the House there are no mainstream options which are necessarily 'right or wrong', 'out-dated or modern', or 'effective or less so'. The whole issue is largely a matter of individual preference', and that 'there are differing views which will need to be resolved by the House'. The eventual result was a narrow vote (256 to 241) in favour of the House meeting earlier again on Tuesdays and a slightly more convincing vote in favour of a further advance, by an hour, of sittings on Thursdays. The existing sitting hours on Mondays and Wednesdays were endorsed without anyone pressing the matter to a vote.

The current sitting pattern is shown in Table 5.1, page 142.

A perverse result of the move to change sitting times is that on only two days of the week is the Commons timetable the same. Most parliaments have a consistent timetable to which members, parliamentary staff, the public and the media easily adapt. The House of Commons does not. Nonetheless a 2017 survey by the Commons Procedure Committee found that a majority of MPs were content with the current sitting hours on each day; and there was no clear consensus among those who were not content as to how the sitting hours should change.

The sitting day in the Commons

This is often complicated and, although the business is taken in a prescribed order and subject to the House's rules, is never entirely predictable. Here we describe both the unchanging parts of the day and events that happen only occasionally. Some of the more important proceedings are described in greater detail later. The order of business for a typical day appears on page 142.

Before the sitting, the *Speaker's conference* will have taken place. Here the Speaker goes over the business for the day with the Deputy Speakers and the Clerk of the House and his senior colleagues, assessing possible problems or procedural complexities – deciding, for example, what will be a reasonable scope of debate on a particular item or what response he will give to a likely point of order. The Speaker will take a view on applications for urgent questions or urgent debates that have been submitted. The Serjeant at Arms is also present and may know of a planned demonstration or mass lobby, which may affect access to the palace or may delay MPs getting to the House to vote.

The start of a sitting

Every sitting begins with the *Speaker's procession* from Speaker's House. The Speaker, preceded by a doorkeeper and the mace carried by the Serjeant at Arms, and followed by his trainbearer, secretary and chaplain, walks to the chamber by way of the Central Lobby. Here the police inspector shouts 'Hats off, Strangers!', though these days it is unlikely that anyone present (except the police officers) will be wearing a hat. This is now a rare use of the term 'strangers' meaning visitors. The Speaker, his chaplain and the Serjeant at Arms then enter the chamber. The Serjeant places the mace on the Table to show that the House is sitting, and the Speaker and chaplain kneel at the Table for *prayers*. These Anglican *prayers for the parliament* take about four minutes and are in private. (A member who wants to reserve a seat in the House for the whole of a sitting may leave a prayer card on a place to show that he or she will be there for prayers.)

As the Speaker rises, the doorkeepers shout 'prayers are over'; the galleries are opened to guests and visitors; the clerks' chairs are set at the Table; and, as the Speaker rises to begin proceedings with 'order, order', television coverage starts.

Up to the end of Question Time

Although infrequent, any *report of the Queen's answer to an Address* (for example, the 'Humble Address', which was formally before the House during the Queen's Speech debate) will come at the start of business. The sovereign's response is normally read out by one of the government whips who holds a post in the royal household (see page 89), and is generally very brief: 'I have received with great satisfaction the dutiful and loyal expression of your thanks for the speech with which I opened the present session of Parliament'.

There may be a *formal communication by the Speaker*. The death of a member is notified to the House in this way: this used to be done in formal terms, but more recently the Speaker has paid a brief tribute. There is normally no opportunity for a eulogy, although the House adjourns on the death of the Prime Minister or a former Prime Minister, or the Leader of the Opposition, after tributes from the party leaders and others (on the death of Baroness Thatcher in April 2013 the House was recalled for a day of tributes). The Speaker may also announce that he has sent or received messages of condolence or congratulation (for example, to the royal family, or to foreign parliaments or heads of state). Early in a parliament there will be arrangements for the election of select committee chairs or Deputy Speakers to make known, and later the Speaker will announce vacancies for those positions as they arise. He may, very rarely, announce the outcome of an 'election court' set up to resolve a dispute about the conduct of an election, which can declare a particular candidate to have been elected or can order a rerun of the election. He may even report the imprisonment of an MP (of which the courts must inform the Clerk of the House).

A *motion for a new writ* may be moved. This triggers a by-election in a seat made vacant by the death, resignation or disqualification of the sitting MP. It is normally moved by the chief whip of the party to which that member belonged but has occasionally been moved by a backbencher wishing to make a point about a delay in holding a by-election, or to frustrate later business. By convention new writs are moved within three months of the vacancy occurring, but there is no formal limit. If a motion for a new writ is opposed at this time, it is taken later in the sitting, after statements but before the main business. There is no statutory provision for cancelling a by-election; when the 2017 general election was called and the announcement made that Parliament was to be dissolved on 3 May, the by-election scheduled to take place in Manchester Gorton on 4 May became otiose. The Commons therefore passed a writ superseding the earlier one setting the date of the by-election.

After these uncommon proceedings comes private business – that is, private bills and related motions (including motions relating to the Selection Committee (see page 329). At this time in the sitting day, only private business to which a blocking motion has not been tabled, or that is not opposed by even one MP shouting 'object', can pass. Much private business is uncontroversial, and it is not unusual for private bills to go through all their stages on different days at this time.

A *motion for an unopposed return* may be moved. It may be that an official inquiry has criticised individuals who might sue if the report were published in the conventional way (for example, Lord Hutton's inquiry into the death of Dr David Kelly in 2004, the Bloody Sunday inquiry in 2010 and the report of the Hillsborough Independent Panel in 2012). This device gives the report the protection of parliamentary privilege.

Even if all the items of business listed above were to take place, they would probably delay the House for only four or five minutes. *Question Time* then follows and continues for an hour (although it may be extended if an *urgent question* has been granted or if a minister has decided to answer a *question at the end of Question Time*). This is described in greater detail in Chapter 9. One issue worth highlighting, when considering the daily routine of the Commons, is the number of urgent questions (UQs) permitted in recent years. The process for granting UQs is dealt with in Chapter 9, but it is notable that under Speaker Bercow the use of UQs has increased dramatically. In

Table 5.1 Programme for a normal sitting week in the House of Commons

	Monday	Tuesday	Wednesday	Thursday	Friday
House sits	2.30 pm	11.30 am	11.30 m	9.30 am	9.30 am
Prayers (every day, for about four minutes); private business after prayers (not on Fridays) Question time (not on Fridays)					
Urgent questions, statements by ministers	3.30 pm	12.30 pm	12.30 pm	10.30 am	11.00 am
(On Fridays, the main business will begin after prayers and will be interrupted if there is a statement or urgent question at 11.00 am)					
Main business (perhaps legislation, an opposition day or a debate on a topic in government time)					
Main business interrupted	10.00 pm	7.00 pm	7.00 pm	5.00 pm	2.30 pm
	After the end of any votes (or of proceedings on 'exempted business'): daily adjournment debate (up to half an hour)				
Sittings in Westminster Hall:					
Begin	4.30 pm*	9.30 am	9.30 am	1.30 pm	
Suspended		11.30 am	11.30 am		
Resume		2.30 pm	2.30 pm		
End	7.30 pm	5.30 pm	5.30 pm	4.30 pm	
Select committees (typically)		9.15 am	9.15 am	9.30 am	
	4.00 pm	2.00 pm	2.00 pm		
Legislative committees (typically)		8.55 am	8.55 am	11.30 am	
	4.30 pm	2.00 pm	2.00 pm	2.00 pm	
(Sittings in Westminster Hall and in committees are suspended for divisions in the House)					

*For debate on e-petitions, if allocated by the Backbench Business Committee

Monday 5 March 2018 Order Paper No.101: Part 1

SUMMARY AGENDA: CHAMBER

2.30pm	Prayers
Afterwards	Oral Questions: **Defence**
3.30pm	Urgent Questions, Ministerial Statements (if any)
No debate	Presentation of Bills
Until 10.00pm	**Data Protection Bill [Lords]: Second Reading**
Followed by	Motions without separate debate:
	■ Programme
	■ Money
No debate	Statutory Instruments **(Motions for approval)**
No debate after 10.00pm	Motions relating to the membership of Select Committees: Joint Committee on Consolidation, &c., Bills; Finance; Northern Ireland Affairs; Petitions; Women and Equalities
Until 10.30pm or for half an hour	Adjournment Debate: **Liquidation of DMB Solutions (Caroline Lucas)**

WESTMINSTER HALL

4.30pm	Debate on an e-petition relating to British Sign Language being part of the national curriculum
	Debate on an e-petition relating to changes to car insurance

Commons Order Paper summary page from Monday 5 March 2018

Source: Copyright House of Commons, 2018

the 2007–08 session (the last full session before John Bercow became Speaker) four UQs were granted; in 2016–17 there were 74. Urgent questions have become part of the Commons' daily routine, rather than exceptional.

After Question Time and up to 'the commencement of public business'

After the first hour of oral questions any new member of the House elected at a by-election is formally introduced to the House and takes the oath or makes the affirmation (see page 128) – normally on the Tuesday following the by-election. He or she waits below the bar of the House (in other words, within the chamber but just outside what is formally the floor of the House; the bar itself does exist, but as it consists of two heavy metal rods that slide back into the woodwork of the benches on each side it is seldom seen). When the moment arrives the new MP, flanked by two members who act as sponsors (perhaps old friends or constituency neighbours), comes forward, clutching paper from one of the clerks in the Public Bill Office certifying that the Clerk of the Crown in Chancery has received the 'return' that is proof of election. He or she bows at the bar, again halfway up the floor of the House, and again at the Table, and then takes the oath (or affirms), signs the test roll and is announced to the Speaker and the House by the Clerk of the House. There will have been considerable political interest in the by-election campaign and its outcome – particularly if the seat has been captured by a different party – and the introduction of the new MP is in some ways the culmination of the campaign, hailed with cheers from MPs of the victorious party and fairly good-natured heckling from other parts of the House.

The main events at this time are *statements by ministers*. These may announce a new policy initiative, inform the House about some international crisis, or perhaps give the government's reaction to the outcome of a court case or an official inquiry. A statement may report on an international meeting, perhaps of the UN or European Council, or developments in Brexit negotiations. Statements are also used to inform the House about serious accidents or terrorist crimes and to set out the government's response. In cases of great urgency, a statement may be made at another time; on 3 March 2011, the Secretary of State for Culture Media and Sport made a statement about News Corporation's proposed acquisition of BSkyB after the main business and before the adjournment debate.

Significant statements are made by the responsible cabinet minister (or by the Prime Minister); less important statements are made by more junior ministers directly responsible for the subject. Ministers notify the Speaker in advance of their intention to make a statement. Although they conventionally begin 'with permission, Mr Speaker', a statement needs neither his permission nor that of the House. Notice that a statement is to be made appears on the television annunciators around the House between one and two hours beforehand, and a minister will as a courtesy give his or her opposition 'shadow' an advance copy of the text an hour or so before it is delivered. Occasionally a statement is planned far enough in advance to be on the Order Paper. However, unless the subject is one that has been simmering on the political agenda, much of the initiative rests with the government (especially if the statement announces a surprise policy development) and the opposition has to be quick on its feet to react effectively.

As we saw in Chapter 3, it is up to the Speaker to decide how long questioning goes on. This will depend on the significance of the statement, and in recent years the Speaker and his deputies have tried to call all those seeking to catch their eye. However, given that more often than not the main business which follows statements (and urgent questions) will have to end at a given point – the moment of interruption – time granted for statements and UQs eats into the time available for the business which follows it.

On Thursdays the Leader of the House's *weekly statement of forthcoming business* is formally a reply to a question from the shadow Leader (and so follows immediately after Question Time) rather than a conventional ministerial statement. However, if on a Thursday there is a statement by a more senior minister, or a statement that needs to be made as soon as possible, the Leader's announcement may follow it and be technically a statement in its own right.

After statements MPs may *request an urgent debate*, sometimes known as 'an S.O. No. 24 application', on what the standing order calls 'a specific and important matter that should have urgent consideration'. The MP must seek the Speaker's permission beforehand and has three minutes in which to make the case for an urgent debate. The Speaker then gives his decision (and is forbidden by the standing order from giving any reasons). If he allows the application and the House agrees, a debate of up to three hours will take place the next day (or the same day if there is sufficient urgency).

Urgent debates can be on constituency, national or international matters, or about issues to do with the operation of Parliament itself. Subjects debated in the 2015–17 parliament included English Votes for English Laws; the refugee crisis in Europe; and the UK steel industry. Since the start of the 2017 parliament matters debated have included the scheduling of parliamentary business; tuition fees; and Yemen. Urgent debates used to be infrequent, but have become less so, as shown below.

Number of urgent debates held since 1979:

1979–83	4
1983–87	6
1987–92	2
1992–97	1
1997–2001	0
2001–05	1
2005–10	2
2010–15	4
2015–17	8
2017–	13

(N.B. figures for 2017 parliament are to June 2018.)

There is then a slot for (rare) *ceremonial speeches* – perhaps on the death of a former Speaker or some other distinguished figure, *motions to give the Speaker leave of absence* for some specific reason and *personal statements*. These may be of apology, perhaps for failing to register an interest or for using 'unparliamentary language', or a minister may apologise for giving the House wrong information; or they may be of explanation after resignation. This second category can be dramatic. Sir Geoffrey Howe's statement after resigning as Deputy Prime Minister in 1990, delivered in an electric atmosphere in the House, was a defining moment just before the end of Margaret Thatcher's premiership. Equally memorable were Norman Lamont's statement in June 1993 after he was sacked as Chancellor of the Exchequer; Robin Cook's in March 2003 after he resigned from the Cabinet on the eve of war against

Iraq (his personal statement was unusually made at 9.45 pm, but that was just after the equally unusual timing of a statement by the Foreign Secretary that talks in the UN had broken down); and Clare Short's attack on Tony Blair's style of government following her resignation in May 2003. Of less immediate impact was Boris Johnson's personal statement after resigning as Foreign Secretary over the government's Brexit policy in July 2018.

Personal statements may be made only with the permission of the Speaker. Because the practice of the House is to hear statements in (near) silence, and not to allow interventions, the Speaker sees the text beforehand (except in the case of ministers who have resigned).

Matters relating to privilege (see page 171) may be taken at this time. Alleged breaches of privilege have to be raised privately with the Speaker, so matters of privilege are raised on the floor of the House only if he is prepared to give them precedence over other business. An opposed motion for the issue of a new writ in a by-election would also be taken at this stage of the day.

Usually at about this time MPs will raise *points of order* with the Speaker (although points of order on the business actually before the House may be raised at any time). The test of a 'genuine' point of order is whether the Chair can actually rule on it because it relates to the rules and practice of the House – for example, whether a phrase is acceptable parliamentary language, or perhaps in some complex business, the order in which the House will take decisions, or whether something was amiss in one of the House's working papers. The Speaker will either give his decision on the spot (particularly if the MP has given him notice of the point to be raised) or undertake to give a decision later. These rulings are part of the case law that is an important element in the practice and procedure of the House.

Even if a point of order is genuine, the Speaker will normally not rule on something that is hypothetical or on something that has happened in committee; that is the responsibility of the occupant of the chair concerned. Neither will the Chair give detailed procedural counsel, normally suggesting that the MP seeks the advice of the clerks.

Genuine points of order sometimes relate to the administrative responsibilities of the Speaker, such as access to the precincts or the use of facilities. But the majority of points raised at this stage in the parliamentary day are, to a greater or lesser degree, bogus in that they make political or debating points. One of the most frequent from the opposition benches is an inquiry as to whether the Speaker has received a request from a minister to make a statement on some contentious subject (usually implying undue reticence on the part of the government). Assertions by ministers, or the content of their replies to parliamentary questions, are often raised. There is a catch-22 in that the Chair has to allow the MP to go some way towards making the point, as it is only then that it becomes clear that it is not a real point of order. However, because of the limited opportunities that MPs have to raise current issues other than in relevant question times or debates (many parliaments have a period each day in which the members may speak briefly on any subject of current concern), these points of order can act as something of a safety valve; the Speaker often acknowledges the point made and says it will have been noted by the ministers present.

'At the commencement of public business'

It may seem strange that this title occurs only at this stage of the sitting day; but for almost all the preceding business most of the very few decisions that arise have to be taken by unanimity, and for much of the time there is no *question* before the House – that is, a matter put forward for decision by the House. Confusingly, there is no 'question' in this technical sense before the House during Question Time.

Three main types of business are taken at this time. The first is the *presentation and first reading of public bills* – a formality, which is explained in Chapter 6. Then may come government motions to regulate the business of the House for that day – perhaps to allow several items to be debated jointly, to allot time to a particular item of business or to allow an urgent bill to be taken through all its stages at one sitting. Such motions may be debated and voted on. To avoid the (perhaps unpredictable) loss of time for the main business, these are usually taken on a previous day.

The best-known category of business 'at the commencement' is the *10-minute rule bill* (strictly a motion, because the member seeks permission to bring in the bill rather than a decision by the House on the bill itself). Every Tuesday and Wednesday, a backbencher has the chance to propose new legislation in a speech lasting not more than 10 minutes; if there is opposition, one MP may put the contrary case, again for no more than 10 minutes, and if necessary there is a vote. These are popular opportunities for backbench MPs, not least because a backbencher's opportunities to initiate business on the floor of the House are limited, but also because they take place in 'prime time', which may be immediately before a major debate. Ten-minute rule bills are discussed further in Chapter 6.

The main business

It is unusual for the events described so far (apart from urgent questions and ministerial statements) to go on longer than 15 or 20 minutes after the end of Question Time. The House then embarks on the main business of the day, which consists of *orders of the day* (typically a stage of a bill) and *notices of motions* (typically a debate either on a substantive motion, as on an opposition day, or a neutral motion that the House has considered a particular matter).

Often the usual channels have agreed that the main business should be in two halves or the Backbench Business Committee has recommended two estimates for debate on an estimates day. In that case, the halfway point is at about 7 pm on a Monday, 4 pm on a Tuesday or Wednesday, or 2 pm on a Thursday ('half days' do not happen on Fridays).

The moment of interruption

At 10 pm on Mondays, 7 pm on Tuesdays and Wednesdays, 5 pm on Thursdays and 2.30 pm on Fridays comes the 'moment of interruption'. This is normally the end of the main business and is when most major votes are taken. Unless there has been a previous decision of the House to the contrary, business still under way when that moment comes will stand adjourned to a future day (or, for adjournment motions or neutral motions, lapse). Thus, an MP can 'talk something out' by continuing to speak as the Speaker says 'order, order' to signify that the business is being interrupted. To prevent this the closure (see page 215) must be moved, which will be granted by the Chair after a full day's debate and is normally agreed without a vote, the House passing straight on to a vote on the main business itself.

Talking out is a traditional weapon used against private members' bills; 100 MPs must vote for the closure for it to be effective, and the sponsor of a private member's bill may find it difficult to round up enough supporters on a Friday. In addition, if the bill is second or third on the Order Paper on a private members' Friday, the Chair may think that there has been insufficient debate to allow the closure to be put to the House. Strictly speaking, 'talking out' happens only when there is opposition to further proceedings. Theoretically, if the Chair detected no objection from any member, debate on 'non-exempted' business could survive the moment of interruption, and the House could then take a decision at the end of that debate; but such cases are extremely rare.

Non-exempted business, which is not expected to be debated, is sometimes described as 'nod or nothing after seven o'clock' (or ten o'clock); in other words, either it is agreed 'on the nod' without any objection, or there is objection and the matter cannot be put to the House. Examples include motions to change the membership of select committees.

Exempted business

Not all business has to end at the moment of interruption. A motion moved may allow an item to be proceeded with 'until any hour' or for a specific time. Such a motion may be moved only by a minister and only if notice has been given on the Order Paper.

Some other business is automatically exempted: finance bills (unlimited time); statutory instruments and European Union documents (an hour-and-a-half – although any that have already been considered in committee cannot be debated again); and some 30 other types of business, although not debatable, may nevertheless be decided.

After decisions and votes taken immediately after the moment of interruption have been disposed of, *public petitions* may be presented. Petitions are described in more detail in Chapter 9. There is then the *half-hour adjournment debate*, which is covered in Chapter 8.

The last words spoken in the chamber are the same as the first: 'order, order'. The occupant of the chair (by this time, usually one of the Deputy Speakers) leaves the chair, and the Serjeant at Arms takes the mace from the Table and joins the Deputy Speaker behind the chair. The Deputy Speaker says '11.30 [or whatever the next day's sitting time is] tomorrow' or '2.30 on Monday', which is repeated by the Serjeant.

The doorkeepers shout 'Who goes home?' – usually abbreviated to a long drawn-out 'ho-oo-me', a relic of days when MPs homeward bound in the same direction would band together as a defence against footpads and highwaymen – the division bells ring for the last time, and the parliamentary day is over.

Late sittings

Late sittings were a regular feature of the House of Commons in the 1970s and 1980s. The average time the House rose in the decade to 1990–91 was well after midnight (so – taking Fridays into account – an average sitting of some nine hours), with some sittings lasting much longer. More than one-fifth of sitting time was after the moment of interruption. Sometimes proceedings were greatly prolonged by backbenchers or by opposition parties to emphasise criticism of the government or its proposals. This occasionally went as far as sitting beyond the House's scheduled time of meeting the next day, thus 'breaking the sitting' and losing the government's planned business for the following day.

By contrast, since 2005 the average sitting day has varied between about seven-and-a-half and eight hours, and the sitting time after the moment of interruption has been less than 10 per cent of the total. There have been various reasons for this change – although all have their critics. They include the *routine programming of bills* (see page 185), whereby time limits are imposed on bills at an early stage in their passage through the House; *the move of a substantial amount of debating time to Westminster Hall* (and, indeed, a net increase in debating time thereby; sitting time in Westminster Hall amounts to the equivalent of nearly two-and-a-half hours for each day on which the House sits); and the taking of *more business in public bill or delegated legislation committee rather than on the floor of the House.*

Time in the House

The Modernisation Committee pointed out that the House of Commons (and by extension the House of Lords, which has similar sitting patterns):

> *spends far less time in recess than most other democratic parliaments. The House of Commons meets for more days than any of the parliaments of the larger Commonwealth countries and indeed for twice as many days as all of them except Canada. The typical pattern among European parliaments is for the legislature to sit around 100 days in the year, compared with 150 days for the UK Parliament.*

Comparisons with continental legislatures, where the work of the plenary is fuelled to a much greater degree by committees, are not exact; but there is no doubt that the Westminster Parliament is one of the longest-sitting parliaments in the world. There are a number of reasons for this: principally the unremitting legislative programme of successive governments; also the number of members and so the pressure for parliamentary time to raise a wide range of issues; even, perhaps, a degree of habit.

Scheduling of time and the Backbench Business Committee

House of Commons Standing Order No. 14 states, 'Save as provided in this order, government business shall have precedence at every sitting'. The business to be taken in the House each day is decided by the government business managers, after consultation through the 'usual channels', and announced by the Leader of the House at the weekly business questions which takes place on a Thursday morning. This announcement of the business is provisional and generally covers two weeks ahead: the business to be taken the following week is usually pretty firm and likely to be displaced only by a serious unforeseen occurrence but the business for the second week may be more likely to change, which would be announced at the next business questions on the following Thursday.

The extent and appropriateness of this government control over the parliamentary agenda were considered by the 'Wright committee' on reform of the House of Commons (chaired by Tony Wright MP), which reported in 2009. The committee examined the system that existed then for scheduling business in the House, and set out for each category scheduled by ministers how far they were really to be regarded as ministerial, as opposed to House or backbench, business. In place of the arrangements by which the government was in control of the vast majority of the House's time and business, the committee recommended an alternative system. Backbench business would be organised by a Backbench Business Committee, responsible for all business that is not strictly ministerial. That committee would then join the representatives of the government and opposition in a House business committee, chaired by the Chairman of Ways and Means and working through consensus, which would come up with a draft agenda for the week ahead. The draft agenda would then be put to the House for its agreement, replacing the weekly business questions.

In 2010, following the general election of that year, a Backbench Business Committee was duly established, and tasked with determining the business to be taken in the chamber and in Westminster Hall on 35 days each year (of which at least 27 are in the chamber). The coalition agreement between the Conservative and Liberal Democrat parties also spoke of establishing a House business committee 'by the third year of the Parliament', but that aspiration was not achieved and was not subsequently pursued by the government. Therefore, in accordance with Standing Order No. 14, the government remains in control of most of the business in the House that is not either determined by the Backbench Business Committee or taken on private members' bill Fridays. The Leader of the House still announces the business for the next two weeks, including which days are to be allocated to backbench business, at the weekly business question. The Backbench Business Committee meets weekly to hear representations from members about the debates that they would like to take place

Table 5.2 Breakdown of sitting time in the House of Commons, session 2016–17

Type of business	Time spent (hours and minutes)	Percentage of total
Addresses other than motions to annul or revoke statutory instruments	34.04	3.2
Government bills	235.20	22.3
Private members' bills	63.19	6.0
Private business	1.45	0.1
Government motions	29.13	2.8
Opposition days	110.08	10.4
Backbench business	121.43	11.5
Private members' motions	11.36	1.1
General debates	22.34	2.1
Daily adjournment debates	69.15	6.5
Emergency debates	6.33	0.6
Estimates (debates on select committee reports under standing order No. 54)	15.31	1.4
Ways and Means motions	21.05	2.0
Motions for approval of statutory instruments	5.29	0.5
Questions to ministers	105.36	10.0
Topical questions	25.53	2.4
Urgent questions	43.38	4.1
Statements	67.37	6.4
Speaker's statements	2.04	0.2
Business statements	32.30	3.1
Points of order	10.00	0.9
Public petitions	2.37	0.2
Miscellaneous (including suspensions of the proceedings of the House)	11.42	1.1
Daily prayers	11.43	1.1
TOTAL	1,057.01	

on backbench business days, which it judges against a published list of criteria. Its decisions on what is to be debated, including select committee statements (see page 346), are reported to the House formally and published in the relevant section of the 'Vote bundle' (see page 158).

Use of time

The amount of time spent on business initiated by the government fell from nearly three-fifths in the 2003–04 and 2004–05 sessions to less than one-third in 2016–17, while time on business initiated by backbenchers rose in the same period from around one-tenth to nearly one-quarter, showing the effect of the creation of the category of 'backbench business' and determined by the Backbench Business Committee. In addition, there were some 410 hours of backbench- and select committee-initiated debate in Westminster Hall. Just under one-third of time on the floor of the House is spent on legislation – not counting the hundreds of hours that are spent on legislation in public bill and delegated legislation committees.

An MP's day

There are as many ways of doing an MP's job as there are MPs. The influences on them, which we surveyed in Chapter 4, and the variety of priorities that they have, mean that there is no standard working week or day, although there are some common ingredients. An MP will normally come to Westminster from midday onwards on a Monday, depending on how far away the constituency is, and go back to the constituency on a Thursday or Friday, subject to the business in the House.

Some of the parliamentary agenda is set by the media, and devouring a variety of websites and newspapers, together with breakfast news or the *Today* programme (or sometimes appearing on it), is a usual start to the day. Time in the office at the House, talking over the in-tray with researcher and assistant, may be followed by attendance at a public bill, delegated legislation or select committee, and then to the House for Question Time (especially on a Wednesday, when Prime Minister's Questions are at noon). Or the morning may be given over to constituency work, perhaps also seeing a delegation representing an important local industry and then taking them to meet a minister in Whitehall.

Lunch – these days for many MPs more likely to be a sandwich than anything more elaborate – may be in the office, hearing the case a pressure group wants to put, or chatting with other members in the Tea Room. The afternoon might include writing the MP's weekly column for the local newspaper, signing letters, an interview with local or national media, telephone calls following up constituency cases, or back to general committee or select committee business – perhaps interrupted by votes in the House. If the MP retains business or professional interests outside the House, he or she may find time for these. Later in the day there may be a meeting of a party committee and an all-party group on a subject in which the MP is involved.

Perhaps the MP wants to speak in the chamber; in that case, most of the afternoon may be taken up waiting on the green benches, leaping up to catch the eye of the Chair at the conclusion of each speech, and then being in the chamber again for the wind-up speeches by the frontbenches at the end. Or possibly he or she has been able to secure the half-hour adjournment debate; in that case, much of the day will be spent preparing notes for the speech and perhaps discussing the issues with the constituent whose case has been raised, or a group interested in the subject to be debated; and, as the parliamentary day nears its end, watching the progress of business so as to be in the chamber in time. Thereafter, a telephone call home to a distant family to exchange news about the day.

Ministers

If the MP is one of the 90 or so ministers in the Commons, the day will be very different. Whitehall, not Westminster, is their focus; their departments' concerns rule their day and their officials feel that they own a minister's time. As well as work at the desk, there will be a range of meetings – with civil servants, ministerial colleagues (for the more senior, in cabinet and in cabinet committees), official visitors and delegations (perhaps led by one of their backbench colleagues). There will be opening ceremonies, keynote speeches at conferences, ministerial visits, international negotiations, press conferences. Their relationship with the House will change; now they are concerned only with one subject area; their time in the House will centre on when their department is due to answer questions (see page 296), when they open or reply to a debate, take 'their' bill through its stages or appear as a witness before a select committee. Their weekends are dominated by red boxes with papers they need to read or approve by Monday morning – in effect, homework set by their department. And they still have to keep up with their constituency work. Most ministers' workloads are very heavy; just how heavy often comes as a surprise to newly appointed ministers.

To a lesser extent the same is true of opposition shadow ministers, who have fewer resources to support them. Although they do not have the burden of departmental work, much of their day is spent in keeping up with developments in their subject brief or perhaps leading for the opposition on a bill in committee or a debate on the floor of the House.

Attendance in the chamber

Most visitors to the galleries, or viewers of coverage of the House of Commons, comment on the relatively small attendance of members in the chamber. Even though the chamber is packed weekly for Prime Minister's Questions and at other times for major debates or statements, the level of attendance for some debates can be embarrassingly low and is often a source of criticism from those who see on television an important subject being debated by only 1 or 2 per cent of the House's membership.

The level of attendance is influenced by various factors: there is continuous television coverage over the annunciator system and there have been improvements in members' office accommodation, both of which have limited the tendency to 'drop in' to the chamber rather than planning to be there for a particular item of business. When debate is predictable and the outcome certain – especially if it is by a large majority – this too will have an effect.

In an effort to increase attendance MPs were recently permitted to use smartphones and tablets in the chamber. Many now live tweet during high-profile debates, but more routinely MPs are simply catching up on emails. It is not clear that it has resulted in a general increase in attendance; the bigger effect has been to enable MPs to continue other work while waiting to be called in a debate.

However, it will be clear from the description of an MP's day that members are also drawn away from the chamber simply because there is so much else to do. For most of the day there is a great deal of formal parliamentary activity going on elsewhere – in Westminster Hall, and in legislative or select committees – in addition to the huge variety of party and group activity, as well as constituency work. Much is sometimes made of 'activity statistics': how many times an MP has voted, or how many times he or she has spoken in debate. These give a rather two-dimensional picture and can be misleading. Whips will score highly on divisions, because they are on the premises most of the time the House is sitting and votes are their business. But they will not feature in debates, because by convention they do not speak. Members with distant constituencies may not score as highly as London members; other MPs may decide that they can do more through select committee work than by interventions in the chamber. And the shift towards constituency casework may be an additional reason why attendance in the Commons chamber is often much lower than in the chamber of the House of Lords.

Sittings and the use of time in the House of Lords

The House of Lords usually sits from Monday to Thursday, and on Fridays about once a month. In 2016–17 it sat for 141 days, averaging 6 hours 38 minutes each day. On Mondays and Tuesdays the Lords meets at 2.30 pm, on Wednesdays at 3 pm, on Thursdays at 11 am and on Fridays at 10 am There are target finishing times – 10 pm on Mondays to Wednesdays, 7 pm on Thursdays and 3 pm on Fridays. The convention of rising at 10 pm was introduced in 2002 and is now fairly well-established, though on occasion due to pressure of business and the need to reach targets it is simply not observed. In 2016–17, 30 per cent of sittings exceeded the 10 pm cutoff. Unlike in the Commons, there is no 'moment of interruption', so if it's necessary to continue past 10 pm the House simply carries on. As in the Commons, Saturday and Sunday sittings have taken place only at times of national crisis.

Sittings of the House and its committees are never impeded by not having enough members present to transact the business: the quorum is only three. This applies to the House as a whole and to select committees (though the joint committees on Human Rights and on Statutory Instruments, and sub-committees of the European Union Committee, have a quorum of two). A higher quorum of 30 is set for divisions on bills and secondary legislation. If fewer than 30 vote – a rarity, but occasionally tactically engineered to delay business – the debate on the question is adjourned and the House proceeds to its next business. So, when the House is considering government bills the government whips always ensure that there are at least 30 government supporters in the House. But attendance is normally far in excess of the procedural minimum.

As in the Commons, the day begins with *prayers*. In the Lords a psalm and prayers are read by a bishop, and many members kneel on the benches. Immediately after prayers, any new members go through their ceremony of introduction and take the oath or affirm, as does any member who has not yet taken the oath or affirmed so far in the parliament. Introduction ceremonies take about five minutes each. The substantive business starts with a 30-minute *question time* when four oral questions are taken. If a private notice question has been allowed by the Lord Speaker it comes immediately after oral questions and lasts 10 minutes. *Business statements* – perhaps to indicate the limit on speaking time in a time-limited debate, or to announce the dates of forthcoming recesses – may follow. *Ministerial statements* come next in theory, but only if the minister making the statement is a peer. Most statements are made in the Commons and repeated in the Lords. Occasionally statements to be made in the Commons are deemed by the usual channels not to be sufficiently important to the Lords to be repeated. When they are important, they will usually have been delivered in the Commons after questions in that House and are repeated in the Lords as soon thereafter as is convenient. In the Lords, brief comments and questions from the opposition frontbenches and from backbenchers of all parties are allowed for up to 40 minutes following the end of the statement. Members value this opportunity to comment and probe the government further on statements.

The timings mentioned above are strictly observed. So when, for example, the 30 minutes for oral questions have elapsed the Clerk of the Parliaments will immediately rise to call the next business. Unlike in the Commons, the Lord Speaker does not have authority to allow business to run past its designated time. As an extreme example of the tradition of promptness in the Lords, in January 2018 a government minister, Lord Bates, dramatically offered his resignation at the dispatch box after arriving a couple of minutes late for an oral question he was due to answer, which was instead valiantly responded to by the government chief whip. Having offered his resignation Lord Bates gathered his papers and swooshed out of the chamber, to shouts of dissent from members who thought it an overreaction and even physical attempts by some peers to drag him back. A few hours later Lord Bates was found and persuaded to withdraw his resignation, after the Prime Minister said she would not accept it.

Turning back to a more standard day, the substantive business usually begins after questions. Discussion of any *private legislation* comes first, followed by *Business of the House motions*, usually moved by the Leader of the House and signifying a change in the timing or order of business. Then, when necessary, comes *Senior Deputy Speaker's business*. This usually relates to the discussion of any reports by committees for which the Senior Deputy Speaker has responsibility – such as a report of the House of Lords Commission on some matter of internal management or the Procedure Committee. Discussion of *public bills, delegated legislation and reports from select committees* come next, followed by other motions. At the end of business, any *questions for short debate* (*QSDs*) that have been tabled for oral answer by the government may be taken. Proceedings on QSDs are time-limited to one-and-a-half hours when taken at the end of business. The closest analogy is adjournment debates in the Commons. QSDs are also taken during the adjournment for dinner of proceedings on a major bill, or in Grand Committee, when they are time-limited to one hour.

The order of business is slightly different on Thursdays when, by standing order, motions have precedence over bills and other business. The practical effect of this is to make Thursday, for most of the session, a day of debates. Any other business comes after.

It would be very unusual to find all these different kinds of business set down for any one day. A typical day might begin with prayers, followed by oral questions; there may then come a business motion or formal approval of some statutory instruments; then would follow the legislative stages of one or more bills. If the principal business consists of a lengthy stage of a major bill, then at about 7.30 pm proceedings may be adjourned for an hour, in which time short items of business – say, an uncontentious piece of delegated legislation or a question for short debate – might be taken. This is referred to as the 'dinner hour'. The proceedings on the major bill will then be resumed and the House might adjourn any time around 10 pm (with the usual channels agreeing the exact point of adjournment). If it is likely that business will finish earlier in the evening, a question for short debate may have been set down as last business.

A fairly typical day's business in the Lords is illustrated by the Order Paper for 24 January 2018 reproduced opposite.

On the day shown, after oral questions a Business of the House motion was moved to enable the second reading of the EU (Withdrawal) Bill to start in the morning on both its days of debate. This was necessary as otherwise a standing order required the House to begin with oral questions on both days. Then there was a committee stage of a private member's bill (the Asset Freezing (Compensation) Bill). As no amendments to the bill were tabled the peer in charge, Lord Empey, had a motion to discharge the committee stage, meaning the bill could move straight to third reading without further debate. These two items would have taken up little time. More substantive was the third reading of the Sanctions and Anti-Money Laundering Bill, a government bill. This would have taken about an hour, so another government bill was scheduled for after it: committee stage on the Secure Tenancies (Victims of Domestic Abuse Bill). This was a narrow bill which did not occupy much time, leaving room for the question for short debate by Lord Cameron of Dillington at the end of business.

The sitting time of the House of Lords in the 1995–96, 2003–04 and 2016–17 sessions broke down approximately as shown in Table 5.3.

The relative apportionment of time in the chamber remains fairly constant, save for a slight increase in the amount of time taken up by government bills and statements relative to other kinds of business.

We conclude this chapter with four topics that are ever-present in a parliamentarian's day: parliamentary papers, voting, the media and the broadcasting of Parliament; and two that form a preface to the more detailed examination of some of the functions of Parliament that follows: privilege and procedure.

HOUSE OF LORDS BUSINESS

No. 84

Items marked † are new or have been altered.

Wednesday 24 January 2018 at 3.00pm

**Oral Questions, 30 minutes*

*__Lord Storey__ to ask Her Majesty's Government what steps they are taking to safeguard children who are not attending school.

*__Lord Strasburger__ to ask Her Majesty's Government what analyses they have carried out of the effect, with regard to the United Kingdom economy, of the potential outcomes of the Brexit negotiations including (1) leaving the single market, (2) leaving the customs union, and (3) leaving the European Union with no deal, on the future trading relationship between the United Kingdom and the European Union; and when they intend to publish those analyses.

*__Lord Ashdown of Norton-sub-Hamdon__ to ask Her Majesty's Government what assessment they have made of Hong Kong's autonomy, rights and freedoms, following recently approved changes to the procedural rules of Hong Kong's Legislative Council, and the refusal of entry into Hong Kong of Taiwanese scholars and the British human rights activist, Benedict Rogers.

*__Lord Ramsbotham__ to ask Her Majesty's Government how many prisons have been given action plans, or are in special measures, following inspection reports.

†**Business of the House** The Lord Privy Seal (Baroness Evans of Bowes Park) to move that Standing Order 40(1) (*Arrangement of the Order Paper*) be dispensed with on Tuesday 30 January to enable the debate on the second reading of the European Union (Withdrawal) Bill to begin before oral questions and, in the event of the debate having been adjourned, on Wednesday 31 January to enable the debate to resume before oral questions that day.

Asset Freezing (Compensation) Bill [HL] Committee [Lord Empey]

†**Lord Empey** to move that the order of commitment be discharged.

Sanctions and Anti-Money Laundering Bill [HL] Third Reading [Lord Ahmad of Wimbledon] *7th, 10th and 11th Reports from the Delegated Powers Committee*

Secure Tenancies (Victims of Domestic Abuse) Bill [HL] Committee [Lord Bourne of Aberystwyth]

Lord Cameron of Dillington to ask Her Majesty's Government what steps they are taking to ensure the availability, and sustainable management, of water in developing countries. (*1½ hours*)

House of Lords Business (the Lords Order Paper), 24 January 2018

Source: Copyright House of Lords, 2018

Table 5.3 Comparison of sitting time breakdowns in the House of Lords

	Percentage of time spent		
	1995–96	**2003–04**	**2016–17**
Prayers	1.2	1.3	1.6
Introductions	0.5	0.5	0.1
Oral questions	6.7	7.4	6.9
Private notice questions	0.0	0.0	0.4
Private bills	0.1	0.4	0.1
Statements	3.1	3.6	4.8
Public bills (government)	47.8	52.7	43.6
Public bills (private members)	4.3	1.9	4.6
Statutory instruments	5.7	5.6	4.7
Debates	25.1	20.1	25.0
Questions for Short Debate	3.0	4.8	7.1

Parliamentary papers

The parliamentary process generates a great deal of written material. Much of it is private and relates only to a particular group – for example, the papers of a select committee – but there is also a central core of printed and electronic material that provides MPs with their bread-and-butter information and that is also available to people outside Parliament.

The Vote bundle

Until recent years every MP received a daily bundle of papers known as 'the Vote'. These papers are now primarily accessed online, although hard copies are made available from the Vote Office on the parliamentary estate. These business papers consist of little more than a few pages in the first few days of the session, but for many sitting days may be as much as 200 pages. The front page is the *Summary Agenda*, which lists the titles of business to be taken in the House and Westminster Hall. Then follows the *Business Today* or Order Paper, a detailed agenda that gives all the items for which notice is required; so, for example, the texts of oral questions and of any motions to be debated (or to be put for decision without debate), in the order in which they will be taken. The agenda for the chamber is followed by that for Westminster Hall. The Order Paper 'freezes' at the moment when the House adjourns on the previous sitting day; nothing can be slipped in thereafter (although, of course, some things are permitted to be done without notice). Statements may appear on the Order Paper but do not have to, and urgent questions are not included; both are in any case notified by way of the television annunciators before the start of the sitting. The Order Paper tries to be informative without being misleading (for example, by implying that a practice normally followed will necessarily be followed). After all, it is often the opposition's aim not to achieve the agenda; and the government does not have to proceed with every item of business simply because it is on the Order Paper.

There is then a list of *written statements* to be made that day (for less important announcements, an alternative to making an oral statement to the House), followed by notice of *committees meeting today*, giving the time and place of each, and the witnesses for public sittings of select committees. This section of the Vote ends with a list of committee reports to be published that day, and a section for other announcements such as the arrangements for future end of day adjournment debates and debates in Westminster Hall.

The next section is *Future Business*, which comes in two parts. Section A is the calendar of business that has been provisionally announced by the Leader of the House or chosen by the Backbench Business Committee for dates in the next two weeks. It also includes private members' bills that have been set down for future Fridays, and notices of motions for leave to bring in 'ten-minute rule' bills on future Tuesdays and Wednesdays. Section B, *remaining orders and notices*, contains items of business that have not yet been scheduled for a specific date.

Other items in the Vote bundle are *lists of amendments* put down to bills to be debated that day, both on the floor of the House and in public bill committee; and the *Votes and Proceedings*. This is the formal legal record of what the House *did* the previous day rather than what was said: decisions on motions, amendments made to bills, papers laid before the House, the record of reports from select committees, and so on. All of the papers listed here are available on the parliamentary website (www.parliament.uk). Also in the Vote bundle are the parliamentary questions and amendments to bills that were tabled the previous day, and new early day motions (or those up to a fortnight old to which new signatures were added the previous day). These are all printed on blue paper to show that they are new notices rather than papers for the current working day.

Hansard

T.C. Hansard was the nineteenth-century printer and publisher whose daily record of the Commons was published privately. From 1909 staff of the House took on the recording of debates, but the name 'Hansard' stuck and was officially adopted in 1943. Properly called *The Official Report*, *Hansard* is the record of what is said in the House. It is substantially verbatim; *Official Report* staff tidy up obvious mistakes and repetitions, but they do not change the substance.

Hansard contains everything that is said in debates in the House and Westminster Hall the previous day, lists of MPs voting in divisions and written statements by ministers. There are two columns on each page of *Hansard* (a column accounts for about three minutes of debate), and references are always to column or 'col.' rather than to page. Unlike some parliaments, Westminster does not allow speeches prepared but not delivered to be put into the record. The full text of each day's *Hansard* is published at 7.30 am the following morning and put on the parliamentary website at 8.00 am. A 'rolling' *Hansard* of the chamber is on the internet, with chunks of text being posted about three hours after the words were spoken. *Hansard* staff also record all the debates in general committees; these appear a little more slowly than the chamber *Hansard*. Evidence given by witnesses before select committees is recorded by *Hansard* or by contractors working for them. Select committee evidence is also posted on the parliamentary website, on the pages of the relevant committee.

Other parliamentary papers

A wide range of papers are presented to Parliament, which MPs may obtain in hard copy from the House's Vote Office. Most papers generated by Parliament itself are also available at www.parliament.uk; those produced by government departments are usually on www.gov.uk.

Bills are published when they are first introduced and again at subsequent stages if they are amended. More than 300 *command papers* (so called because they are formally presented by the government 'by command of Her Majesty') are presented each year. These may be treaties or other agreements with foreign governments, reports of non-parliamentary committees of investigation or royal commissions, *white papers* (statements of government policy) or *green papers* (documents for consultation on possible policy options). *Act papers* are laid before Parliament because an Act of Parliament requires it; the majority are statutory instruments (see page 238) – about 1,500 a year – but this category also includes reports and accounts of a wide range of public bodies, government statistics, and reports by the Comptroller and Auditor General (see page 266).

House of Lords working papers

The most important of these is *House of Lords Business* which is, broadly speaking, the Lords equivalent of the Commons Order of Business, Votes and Proceedings and other notices rolled into one. It is compiled each day, posted on the website that evening and available in hard copy the next morning. It begins with the orders of the day for the next sitting day, which are also printed separately as the *Order Paper* each day (see page 158). Next comes future business – the motions and orders of the day for the coming month in so far as business will have been set down, followed by motions of various kinds awaiting debate but with no day allocated, questions for written answer newly tabled since the last print of *House of Lords Business*, lists of bills and statutory instruments of various kinds currently awaiting consideration, and a list of forthcoming committee meetings. The last item in the document is the Minutes of Proceedings, a formal record of the business conducted in the chamber and Grand Committee that day along with a list of papers laid before the House.

The Government Whips' Office also publishes its own *Today's Lists*. This combines elements of business from the Order Paper with lists of names of speakers in debates and groupings of amendments, as necessary.

The House of Lords has its own *Hansard* and publishes a *Journal* each session, based on the daily Minutes of Proceedings. Two other unofficial documents are useful working papers. The Government Whips' Office publishes each week its *Forthcoming Business*, which contains more information than *House of Lords Business* about what might be taken in coming weeks. Deadlines for tabling amendments and enrolling for debates are also included. It is not as authoritative as *House of Lords Business* – as much of the business is provisional – but gives a fuller picture of what is likely to be on the Order Paper in the coming weeks. The Committee Office publishes online daily a *Committee Bulletin* of all current committee inquiries, their remits and forthcoming programmes.

Nearly all the papers presented to the Commons are also laid before the House of Lords (but not financial statutory instruments (see page 243)).

Voting

Votes are called 'divisions' because MPs 'divide' physically, going through different lobbies depending on which way they are voting. Although during a sitting day many things are decided without a division, disagreement between government and opposition (or dissent by a smaller group of MPs on either side of the House) will produce a vote. Forcing votes as a means of taking time and disrupting the business is a tactic used in every parliament.

Voting in both Houses of Parliament is on the basis of approval or disapproval; there is no provision for formally recording abstentions and no means of ranking competing choices in a single decision; the only exception is in the procedures for the elections of a new Speaker, of deputy speakers and of select committee chairs (see pages 49, 59 and 355).

When a proposition has been put before the House for debate (for example, when a member has moved that a bill 'be now read a second time', or that an amendment be made), after the mover sits down, the Speaker *proposes the question* – in other words, says formally to the House 'The question is, that the bill be now read a second time' or whatever, making clear exactly what it is that the House then has to decide or debate. This may seem a pointless duplication, but it is important as a formality – and vital if the House is proceeding rapidly through a flock of amendments. At the end of a debate the Speaker *puts the question*, saying 'The question is, that the bill be now read a second time. As many as are of that opinion say "Aye". Of the contrary, "No"'. If the matter is uncontroversial, the only response he hears is a muffled 'Aye' from the government whips, and the matter is decided without a vote.

But if there is disagreement and the opposition as a whole, or a group of backbenchers, wants to press the matter to a vote, the two sides will shout out 'Aye' or 'No' in response to the Chair. The Speaker, in what is known as *collecting the voices*, says, judging what he thinks is the louder cry, 'I think the Ayes/Noes have it'. If his decision is challenged by the other side still shouting 'Aye' or 'No', then he says 'Division. Clear the Lobby' (in the singular, this refers not to the division lobbies but to the Members' Lobby beyond the chamber, which the doorkeepers now clear of all but members and House staff to allow MPs easier access to vote). The division bells ring throughout the parliamentary precincts.

After two minutes (sometimes earlier, if the tellers are in place), the Speaker *puts the question again* to check that there is still disagreement between the two sides. He then *names the tellers.* These are usually two whips on each side, although any MP may act as a teller. 'The Ayes to the right, the Noes to the left [referring to the two division lobbies]. Tellers for the Ayes, Mrs Heather Wheeler and Craig Whittaker. Tellers for the Noes, Nic Dakin and Thangham Debbonaire' [or whoever it may be]. If no teller (or only one) has come forward on one side, the Speaker declares the result in favour of the other side.

The tellers, one from each side so that they agree on the numbers, then go to the exit door of each division lobby and count MPs as they emerge (whips will be at the other end of the lobby to encourage their own MPs to vote the right way). Inside the lobby their names will have been recorded by the division clerks on electronic tablets. After eight minutes from first calling the division, the Speaker says 'Lock the doors'; the doorkeepers lock the doors leading into the lobbies and no more MPs can get in to vote. When every member has passed the division clerks and then the tellers, the results are reported to one of the clerks at the Table, who writes them on a 'division slip', which is handed to one of the tellers on the winning side. The tellers then form up at the Table, by the mace and facing the Speaker, with the clerk at the despatch box to one side, and the teller with the division slip reads out the numbers of Ayes and Noes to the House – a soundbite often used on the television news when a major vote has taken place. The clerk takes the slip to the Speaker, who repeats the numbers and declares the result: 'The Ayes to the Right, 307. The Noes to the left, 271. So the Ayes have it, the Ayes have it. Unlock.' The doorkeepers unlock the doors to the division lobbies and the House moves on to the next part of the business of the day. From start to finish, the division has taken anything from 12 to 15 minutes. As noted in Chapter 3, in the event of a tied vote, the Speaker exercises a casting vote in line with firmly established precedents. Lists of which MPs voted which way are published on the parliamentary website and in *Hansard.*

In October 2015 the House changed its procedures, giving effect to the government's policy of 'English votes for English laws' (see page 208) One outcome of those changes is that certain votes need a 'double majority' – where a majority is required not just of *all* MPs, but also all MPs representing constituencies in England (or England and Wales, or England, Wales and Northern Ireland, as appropriate). The procedure for announcing the result of double-majority divisions is the same as for ordinary divisions except that the teller, having got the results for the relevant sub-set from the division clerks, first gives the overall result, then gives the result of the relevant sub-set, and the Speaker repeats both figures.

This House's voting procedure may seem unnecessarily complicated, but there is a good deal of common sense about it. Collecting the voices allows an expression of disagreement but does not commit the House to a division unless the disagreement is persevered with. Putting the question again after two minutes allows for second thoughts; and if no disagreement is expressed (or if it is not enough to provide two tellers for one side or the other) then the matter is decided. This avoids unnecessary votes and in complicated proceedings allows for the occasional mistake – for example, when a group of MPs actually wanted a vote on the next amendment rather than this one. Requiring tellers on each side to agree on the number of votes they have counted also means that the numbers are unlikely to be challenged.

If the result of a division shows that fewer than 40 MPs were present (that is, fewer than 35 actually voting, plus the two tellers from each side and the occupant of the Chair), then the division is not valid and the House proceeds to the next business. In fact, many MPs may be present but not voting; staging an inquorate vote in this way is, for example, a good way of killing a private member's bill.

Electronic voting?

For many people the idea of taking a quarter of an hour of valuable parliamentary time on a vote is inexplicable. Why not vote electronically? There is a good case for it, but also some powerful arguments against. From a practical point of view, the fact that MPs do not have individual seats in the chamber means that there would have to be voting stations outside the chamber. Then, because MPs would have to come to the chamber to vote, perhaps from offices some distance away, and queue up at the voting stations, not much time might be saved after all. Remote electronic voting is canvassed by some; however, for many this goes too far. The public perception of MPs not even having to come to the chamber to vote on some vital issue, at a time when Parliament is struggling to 'reconnect' with the public, might not be favourable. The same might go for a more modest solution, such as voting stations in more distant parts of the precincts.

There is also the question of security; how do you ensure that in every case a vote is registered only by an MP entitled to do so? Swipe cards may not be enough and may need validation by biometric systems such as palm prints or iris recognition. After all, what is at stake may be one of the biggest national issues – whether a government survives a vote of confidence or whether the UK should engage in military action. Any system of electronic voting has to deliver the same confidence in the result as the present system; and the present system is almost never challenged on its accuracy.

Moreover, even if it were possible to devise a quick and secure system, it might not work in favour of MPs. The opposition's ability to call votes so as to slow down progress would be diminished. And there would be a risk that making voting quicker and easier would lead to many more divisions. This would be against the government's interests.

For many MPs the most powerful argument for the present system is that it collects large numbers of members together for a few minutes, often at a predictable time. This brings backbench and frontbench MPs together; many backbenchers do not see very much of those in government. It is a valuable opportunity to buttonhole ministers, or to gather support for some initiative or signatures for an early day motion. For most MPs, this adds a great deal of value to the otherwise often mundane business of voting.

But this may change when Parliament decants to alternative accommodation for the restoration and renewal of the Palace of Westminster; it is likely that the method of voting in its temporary home will be considered. If a move away from division lobbies is agreed, it is not clear that the practice would be resumed when Parliament reoccupies the palace.

Deferred divisions

In 2000 the Modernisation Committee recommended a new procedure to 'reduce the number of occasions on which [the House's] judgements have to be delivered in the small hours of the morning' and to allow debate without requiring other members to be on hand for a vote that might, in the event, not take place. Following an experimental period, this procedure was made permanent in 2004.

The procedure does not apply to bills or to motions that authorise expenditure or charging in relation to bills; neither does it apply to consideration of Estimates and to some types of motion to regulate the business of the House. But where it does apply, if after the moment of interruption (see page 147) an attempt is made to force a vote, that vote is held between 11.30 am and 2.00 pm on the next sitting Wednesday. In one of the division lobbies, members mark 'Aye' or 'No' on a form that lists all the votes to be taken, the numbers are totalled by the clerks, and the Speaker announces the result to the House later that sitting.

The procedure is a departure from the general practice of the House taking a decision immediately following a debate (although this could already happen on Estimates and on some amendments to bills (see page 202)), and it had some strong critics when introduced. To an extent, it reduces the power of the opposition (or dissenters anywhere in the House) to force votes on the spot to demonstrate disagreement and to have that disagreement reflected in inconvenience for the government. Others see it as preserving the opportunity to vote, but at a more sensible time – although this argument is somewhat weakened by the changes to sitting hours.

Some would wish to go further, and have all votes delayed to a single 'decision time'. Although some parliaments have this system, it also has strong critics, on the grounds that it would be seen by the public simply as a means of making MPs' lives easier and would reinforce the image of MPs as 'lobby fodder'. In some types of proceedings, it might actually distort the decision-making process – for example if one amendment to a bill was contingent on another yet they were voted on at different times.

Voting in the Lords

Voting is broadly similar in the Lords, in that members file through lobbies where their names are recorded by clerks on electronic tablets. One difference is that Lords members shout 'Content' or 'Not Content' rather than 'Aye' or 'No'. When a division is called, three minutes elapse for the appointment of two tellers for each side. If tellers are not appointed, the division is called off. The question is then put for the second time and the Contents go to the lobby 'to the right by the throne' and the Not

Contents 'to the left by the bar'. A further five minutes elapse before the doors are locked. When voting in the lobbies is complete, the tellers report their figures to the clerk at the Table who adds in the numbers he or she has recorded as having voted in the chamber. The winning teller takes the result to the Lord Speaker or deputy to be announced. The numbers taking part in divisions are now very high (averaging 396 in 2016–17) and not only do they often take longer than the eight-minute minimum, but it is frequently impossible to lock the doors. Doorkeepers simply prevent latecomers from joining the line. But the frequency of divisions has decreased: there were 250 divisions in 1985–86, 165 in 1992–93, 110 in 1995–96, 89 in 2008–09 and 77 in 2016–17.

As in the Commons, there has as yet been little appetite expressed by members of the Lords to vote electronically or remotely. The present system is reliable and mistakes are rarely made. The sandglasses used by the clerk at the Table to time the vote and the ivory sticks used by the tellers to count their flock through may seem archaic, but the recording of names by the division clerks is now done electronically for *Hansard* and for rapid publication on the internet, along with a breakdown of figures by party. There are no deferred votes in the Lords.

The media

The gallery and the lobby

The relationship between politicians and journalists has always been, and will always be, equivocal. Politics relies on publicity; opinions will gather force and support if they are positively presented to a mass audience. But good political reporting has to be critical; it must show up weaknesses, as well as strengths, which politicians find less attractive. And political disasters make the best copy of all. There is a partnership – or perhaps a fatal attraction: journalists need the stories that politicians provide, and politicians need the oxygen of publicity to further their own aims.

For many years the House of Commons treated reporting of its proceedings with grave suspicion. In 1694 the writer of a newsletter that carried an account of debates was summoned to the Bar of the House and there – on his knees – was rebuked by the Speaker. In 1738 the House resolved:

> *It is a high indignity to, and a notorious breach of privilege of, this House for any news writer, in letters or other papers . . . or for any printer or publisher . . . to give . . . any account of debates or other proceedings of this House . . . and that this House will proceed with the utmost severity against such offenders.*

However, by the end of the eighteenth century, although the resolution still stood, reporters were starting to appear in the gallery of the House (where they had to compete for space with members of the public). The 'press gallery' was established in 1803, when Speaker Abbott directed that seats should be reserved for the press. In the eighteenth and nineteenth centuries literary luminaries appear as parliamentary reporters: Johnson, Hazlitt, Coleridge, Cobbett and Dickens, as well as (before note taking was permitted) 'Memory' Woodfall, a prodigy who could remember hours of debate verbatim and would later return to his office to dictate from memory.

Today there are nearly 500 print, radio and television journalists in the gallery and the lobby. Many of these represent national papers or channels, but some report for a regional audience; given their constituency focus, MPs are particularly keen to establish good relations with these, although with the decline in local journalism the numbers are diminishing. All journalists must be accredited by the Serjeant at Arms before they get a pass – and they, too, must make a declaration of their interests. Members of the gallery used to report proceedings in the House and in committees, and members of the lobby were more concerned with interpreting parliamentary and political events to the outside world; but in practice the distinction has disappeared. Most national newspapers also have sketch writers, who contribute satirical – and more or less witty – pieces about one or two events the previous day. Usually the sketch is the only coverage of Parliament in a newspaper; the era of a detailed report on the day's debates is long past. When they are at Westminster, journalists inhabit cramped and somewhat Dickensian quarters behind the actual Press Gallery in the House.

The lobby have access to a number of places around the palace frequented by MPs but denied to the general public: principally, the Members' Lobby and some of the bars. They receive advance copies of documents, such as government white papers or select committee reports 'under embargo', which allows them a vital 24 to 72 hours to write their stories on what may be a complex subject in time for publication. More importantly, lobby correspondents have access to MPs and ministers in both Houses on lobby terms; the journalists are given information on the basis that it may be disclosed but not attributed. Politicians will use this channel in a number of ways: a secretary of state whose policy has proved damagingly unpopular may be able to hint at a U-turn; public opinion may be prepared for some new initiative; or disenchantment with the party leadership may be aired, and a warning shot fired, without actually putting a head over the parapet.

There are more formal ways in which the lobby is briefed, and ministers and others may be questioned. The Prime Minister's official spokesman or her deputy holds briefings once or twice a day. On Wednesdays after Prime Minister's Questions, there is a rather informal briefing by the PM's special advisers in a huddle outside the Press Gallery, followed by a similar briefing by the Leader of the Opposition's advisers. More generally, press conferences are held by ministers and others as occasion demands.

The lobby system has its critics; it is alleged to be too cosy and open to manipulation by those – especially governments – eager to spin the best story. Partly in response, after the 2001 general election the No. 10 briefings became attributable (although not by name, but as the Prime Minister's official spokesman). Politicians and journalists each have something the other wants – information on one side, and a national or local platform on the other – but journalists can also exercise a great deal of influence on politics. MPs and senior ministers take notice of Laura Kuenssberg's analysis of an issue, or of the results of a mugging in an interview by John Humphrys. But whether the relationship is by turns supportive or critical, suspicious or friendly, the media are an integral part of British politics and, so, of the Westminster Parliament.

Broadcasting Parliament

Although it was as long ago as 1923 that the BBC sought unsuccessfully to broadcast the King's Speech at the State Opening of Parliament, it was not until 3 April 1978 that regular sound broadcasting of both Houses and their committees began. The Lords has been televised since 23 January 1985 and the Commons since 21 November 1989. Both Houses began with an experiment, which was then made permanent. The initial reluctance to be televised – the Commons rejected it in 1966, 1971, 1975 and 1985 – is slightly reminiscent of the House's view of journalists in previous centuries. Even when the Commons approved televising, the majority was not overwhelming: 320 in favour and 266 against; but now it is impossible to imagine Parliament not being televised.

Committees of the two Houses have drawn up rules of coverage concentrating on what is actually being said rather than distractions elsewhere in the chamber: 'a full, balanced and accurate account of proceedings, with the aim of informing viewers about the work of the House'. This means that the use of cutaway shots is limited, which can be frustrating to broadcasters who want more atmospheric coverage; but the pictures ('the clean feed' – in other words, with no captions or other material added) are also used by broadcasters who want brief inserts for a news bulletin and so need pictures of MPs speaking rather than reacting. The rules for the use of material prohibit it being used for comedy or satire, or for advertising.

Proceedings in both the Commons and the Lords are covered gavel to gavel by remote-control cameras in each chamber operated from a control room across the road at 7 Millbank. All sittings in Westminster Hall are televised, but broadcast-quality coverage of committees is arranged on the basis of bids received from broadcasters and is limited to five at any one time. These arrangements, and the rules of coverage and use, are supervised by the Director of Parliamentary Broadcasting, who is an officer of both Houses.

All chamber and committee meetings are streamed live and archived online. BBC Parliament carries the House of Commons chamber live, time-shifted coverage of the House of Lords and unedited coverage of about 10 committees each week. BBC 2, BBC News 24 and Sky News take Prime Minister's Questions live, together with some ministerial statements and committee evidence. The main domestic channels, regional companies and some international organisations use recorded extracts. In 1989, when televising of the Commons began, there were four parliamentary broadcast licence holders. Today, there are in excess of 190 broadcast licence holders and 90 internet licence holders.

All material is archived by the Parliamentary Recording Unit, which keeps the material for about two years before it is deposited at the National Film Archive. This is developing into a fascinating historical record; many will regret that televising or filming was not permitted years before, and that the archive does not show us debates at the time of Munich, during the Second World War or during the Suez crisis; we have only the written word and contemporary recollections to tell us how Chamberlain, Churchill, Bevan, Macmillan, Wilson and many others performed in the House of Commons.

The microphones used in the chambers are highly selective and directional to reduce extraneous noise, especially in the often noisier Commons. Perversely, this makes the coverage slightly less realistic. A minister may be under a great deal of pressure, being barracked as he or she winds up a debate; but if the minister keeps going, talking directly at the microphone, it sounds as though the ride is fairly smooth – and the one-line interjections that spice proceedings are often heard by the House (which reacts) but are inaudible to the listener or viewer.

Privilege

The privilege of Parliament allows the Houses, and their members, to perform their duties without outside threat or interference: rights absolutely necessary for 'the due execution of [Parliament's] powers' as the eighteenth-century Clerk of the House of Commons John Hatsell described them. 'Privilege' is an unfortunate term, as it implies a special advantage rather than a special protection. The word derives from the Latin phrase *privata lex*, meaning private or special law; 'immunity in the public interest' might be a more accurate description.

The privileges of Parliament, and especially of the House of Commons in its struggle for power with the sovereign, have been established over many years in a series of cases that are charted in *Erskine May*. In later years assertion of privilege became less important, and in the nineteenth and twentieth centuries these cases became more a matter of defining the limits of privilege – actions to which it did or did not apply.

From 1997 to 1999, the whole question of privilege was examined by a joint committee of both Houses, chaired by a law lord. The committee made a number of detailed recommendations, including setting out the extent of privilege clearly in an Act of Parliament; its overall approach was that privilege was needed for the proper functioning of Parliament in the public interest, but that it should be limited to what was essential in practice. The difficulty of defining precisely the nature and extent of privilege – and fears that doing so would, perversely, risk increasing the extent to which proceedings in Parliament were open to judicial questioning – meant that the committee's recommendations were largely unimplemented.

Concerns about the possible extent of privilege grew in the wake of the expenses saga when four members accused of fraudulently claiming expenses attempted to argue that the expenses system was covered by parliamentary privilege and that their cases could therefore not be heard in the criminal courts. In anticipation of that case, the 2010 coalition agreement contained a pledge to 'prevent the possible misuse of parliamentary privilege by MPs accused of serious wrongdoing', raising again the possibility of legislation to define the extent of privilege.

In the event, the Supreme Court rejected the (dubious) notion that the House's system of expenses and allowances might constitute a 'proceeding in Parliament' and the government's eventual green paper on parliamentary privilege published in 2012 concluded that there was no need for legislation. As the green paper noted, 'Courts remain respectful of parliamentary privilege and exclusive cognisance; but statute law and the courts' jurisdiction will only be excluded if the activities in question are core to Parliament's functions as a legislative and deliberative body'. It is worth noting that Westminster MPs are less protected than those of many other parliaments, where parliamentary immunity from arrest or civil suit exists.

The green paper was considered by a further joint committee of both Houses which reported in 2013. The joint committee largely endorsed the conclusion of the government's green paper on not legislating, arguing that 'it would be impracticable and undesirable to attempt to draw up an exhaustive list of those matters subject to exclusive cognisance' and that 'legislation should only be used when absolutely necessary, to resolve uncertainty or in the unlikely event of Parliament's exclusive cognisance being materially diminished by the courts'.

Freedom of speech

There are two key elements in modern parliamentary privilege: the first is *freedom of speech*. The classic statement of this is in article 9 of the Bill of Rights 1688–89: 'That the freedom of speech, and debates or proceedings in Parliament, should not be impeached or questioned in any court or place out of Parliament'. This means that no MP or peer can be sued or prosecuted for anything he or she says as part of the proceedings of that House or any of its committees. This ensures that a member of Parliament can speak up on behalf of constituents, or can express any opinion on a public issue, without fear of legal action. Rich and powerful individuals or companies cannot use the threat of writs to silence criticism. Anyone giving evidence to a committee of the House also has the absolute protection of privilege; no civil or criminal action can be brought against them on the basis of what they have said.

The protection of privilege is balanced by a need for it to be used responsibly, as has been emphasised by successive Speakers. Nevertheless, it does happen that individuals are unfairly criticised or even unjustly accused of a crime, but freedom of speech has to include the freedom to make mistakes, and there would be no freedom of speech if everything had to be proved true before it was spoken. However, this freedom of speech is limited to *proceedings*. This includes anything said in debates on the floor, or in general or select committees (including by witnesses to committees); it also includes anything put in writing that forms part of a proceeding, such as the text of any question (or a minister's written answer), amendment or early day motion, written evidence to a committee and, by virtue of the Parliamentary Papers Act 1840, any document published by order of the House (select committee reports, *Hansard* and potentially sensitive reports by outside bodies that are the subject of a motion 'for an unopposed return' (see page 141)).

The privilege of freedom of speech does not include press conferences, letters to constituents or to ministers, or words said at ordinary public meetings (even if they are held within the parliamentary precincts). Strictly speaking, it does not even include distributing a speech from *Hansard*, as the protection applies to the whole of the document rather than excerpts; but, unless the excerpts were selected and edited in a distorting and malicious way, it would be very unlikely that any action would succeed.

Exclusive cognisance

The second key element in modern parliamentary privilege is *the freedom of each House to regulate its own affairs* – to use the language of the Bill of Rights, not to have its proceedings questioned. This freedom is sometimes known as 'exclusive cognisance' and, in practice, it means that the validity of what one House or the other has done – whether in making amendments to a bill, deciding not to proceed with some matter, or in regulating the conduct of its own members – cannot be adjudicated on by any other body.

Exclusive cognisance: the 'Damian Green affair'

The freedom of each House to regulate its affairs extends to control of its precincts. A formal protocol requires that if the police, in the course of investigating a suspected crime, wish to enter the parliamentary estate and access offices or papers, they may do so only on production of a properly executed warrant, with the Speaker taking legal advice before granting access. This principle was not observed in the 'Damian Green affair', when in 2008 the Metropolitan Police arrested Damian Green, an MP and at the time shadow immigration minister, in connection with a series of leaks from the Home Office. No charges were brought against him, but the actions of the police in searching his office, and the actions of the House authorities in not insisting on a warrant, were the subject of criticism and a select committee inquiry. Nearly a decade later, police revelations about what they discovered in the search led to him having to resign as First Secretary of State.

Following these events, a similar protocol was put in place by the House of Lords relating to police access to papers and offices of members of that House. This ensures that the Clerk of the Parliaments and Black Rod are notified beforehand and the authority of the Lord Speaker sought; as in the Commons, procedures are followed to ensure the confidentiality of any material that may be covered by parliamentary privilege.

Parliament and the courts

The scope of exclusive cognisance has contracted in recent years, as Parliament has made certain legislation applicable to itself – for example, on employment protection, anti-discrimination, health and safety, and the Freedom of Information Act 2000. The courts may also find legislation incompatible either with the Human Rights Act 1998 or with EU law; but both these possibilities arise as a result of decisions by Parliament itself, and in both cases what is at issue is the final content of the legislation rather than the way in which Parliament passed it. In addition, following the *Pepper v Hart* case in 1993 (where the Inland Revenue interpreted a piece of tax law in a way at odds with what a Treasury minister had said about it when the bill was before the House of Commons), the courts may try to resolve ambiguities in law by looking at ministerial statements and speeches, and the explanatory notes on a bill, setting out the intention of a piece of legislation.

With the exception of these closely defined categories, the courts are careful to follow the principle set out by the jurist Blackstone in 1830, that 'the whole of the law and custom of Parliament has its origin in this one maxim, that whatever matter arises concerning either House of Parliament, ought to be examined, discussed and adjudged in that House and not elsewhere'. The rules of both Houses seek to return the compliment, through the rules on matters *sub judice* (see page 283) and on criticism of judges.

If the extent of parliamentary privilege were to be set out in an Act of Parliament, as recommended by the 1999 Joint Committee on Parliamentary Privilege, the courts would have a bigger interpretative role (as they do in Australia and New Zealand, for example, whose parliaments have legislated on privilege), which might not make the relationship easier.

Complaints of breach of privilege

Until 1978 complaints that parliamentary privilege had been infringed could be made by any MP in the chamber. This became a regular slot for raising political matters that had nothing to do with privilege (in much the same way as the 'bogus point of order'). Now MPs have to write privately to the Speaker. In the exceptional cases where he agrees that there has been a serious breach he makes a statement to the House and allows the MP the opportunity to move a motion relating to the matter, normally the following day and usually referring the matter to the Committee of Privileges for detailed examination. The most recent reference was in October 2013, after Sussex Police sent a Police Information Notice to a member following a dispute between him and a constituent.

Contempts

The privileges of free speech and exclusive cognisance protect the proceedings of Parliament in the public interest. Attempts to interfere with proceedings in Parliament, or to obstruct or threaten MPs in the performance of their parliamentary duties, are known as 'contempts'. Examples of contempts might include disrupting a sitting; giving false evidence to a select committee; threatening an MP on account of something he or she had said, or intended to say, in the House, or for voting in a particular way; or threatening or taking action against a witness because of what he or she had said to a select committee. A contempt may also be committed by an MP: examples in the last 25 years include the leaking of a draft select committee report to a government department and agreeing to ask parliamentary questions in return for payment. In 2004 the Lord Chancellor and others were found to have committed a contempt by dismissing Judy Weleminsky from the board of the Children and Family Court Advisory and Support Service (CAFCASS) on account of evidence she had given to a select committee.

In December 2017 the Speaker ruled on alleged contempts raised with him in writing by MPs that ministers had misled the House in their accounts about sectoral analyses and assessments they had produced about Brexit; and that the Secretary of State for Exiting the EU had failed to comply with a motion passed by the House to provide those analyses to the Brexit select committee. In both cases the Speaker said that the test he had to apply – that there was an arguable case that there had been a contempt of the House – had not been met. He did, however, express regret at the time taken by the Secretary of State to provide the documents and for having redacted them.

In June 2018 the refusal of Dominic Cummings, the Campaign Director for Vote Leave during the Brexit referendum, to give evidence to the Digital, Culture, Media and Sport Committee's inquiry into *Fake News*, despite the House ordering him to do so, resulted in the incident being referred to the Committee of Privileges.

There is no automatic definition of whether something is a contempt or not. Only if the Committee of Privileges finds that a contempt has been committed, and its view is endorsed by the House, is the matter decided.

Punishment

From early times both Houses have had the power to imprison, fine or reprimand anyone (including an MP), and to suspend or expel MPs from the House. The last time the Commons imprisoned someone was in 1880, and it is difficult to see the House attempting to do so in modern times. The last time the Commons fined someone was in 1666; but the power has never been formally discontinued. The 2013 joint committee recommended that the two Houses re-assert their historic penal jurisdiction – albeit adding that, at the same time, they would need to set up procedures for exercising that jurisdiction which meet modern expectations of fairness and due process.

The sixteenth to eighteenth centuries are dotted with expulsions of members from the House, from the rather grand crime of 'being in open rebellion' through forgery, fraud and perjury to the social discrimination of 'having behaved in a manner unbecoming an officer and a gentleman'. Expulsion became less frequent in the nineteenth and twentieth centuries; the last occasion was in 1954, for a criminal conviction. Suspension, on the other hand, is used more frequently; when an MP is named by the Speaker in the House (usually for disorderly conduct challenging the authority of the Chair), the House suspends the member for five sitting days on the first occasion, 20 sitting days on the second occasion and indefinitely (until the end of the session or until rescinded by the House, whichever happens first) on the third.

Suspensions are also used as punishments for other offences: 20 days for damaging the mace (1988); 10 and 20 days for 'cash for questions' (1995); three, five and 10 days for leaking a draft select committee report (1999); two weeks for conflict of interest, followed by indefinite suspension if an apology was not made (2005); 18 days for misuse of parliamentary resources and failure to cooperate with an inquiry (2006); seven days for misclaiming allowances and supplying misleading information in support of those claims (2011); and 30 days for failure to register and declare visits paid for by a foreign government and related paid advocacy (2018). An MP who is suspended is not paid during the period of the suspension. As described in Chapter 4 (see page 119), the most recent suspension has triggered the recall arrangements introduced in 2015.

In recent times the expectation of a long suspension has tended to prompt a member to jump before he is pushed: although the Committee on Standards stopped short of recommending the expulsion of either Denis MacShane, for misclaiming expenses, or Patrick Mercer, for paid advocacy, both members took the Chiltern Hundreds (resigned as MPs) before the House had the opportunity to consider a motion to apply the lengthy suspension recommended by the committee.

As the Joint Committee on Parliamentary Privilege confirmed in 1999, the House of Lords – as with the Commons – has power to imprison its members, and the House of Lords can also fine them. In fact the House has attempted neither in recent times. Significantly the Lords in 2009 asserted the right to use its inherent powers to suspend its members for serious infringement of its rules, on the basis of advice given to the Committee for Privileges by the former Lord Chancellor, Lord Mackay of Clashfern (see page 123). This power was used several times but has since been overtaken by the statutory power to suspend or expel granted by the House of Lords (Expulsion and Suspension) Act 2015.

Procedure

Procedure regulates the proceedings of the Commons and its committees. It has four sources. *Practice*, sometimes called 'ancient usage', refers to matters so clearly established over centuries that there is no need to set them down formally – for example, the process of moving a motion, proposing the question on it to the House, debating that question and then deciding it by 'putting the question'.

Standing orders are general rules for the conduct of business and are amended or added to as the House alters its procedures. They govern matters as diverse as the election of the Speaker, the appointment and powers of most select committees, and the length of debate on different types of business. It is probably not a coincidence that standing orders became significant in the early nineteenth century when the government began to exert more control over the time of the House. Today, 221 standing orders occupy 248 pages of the blue booklet, which is republished at least once a year to keep up with changes. Their length and complexity increased further with the addition of 13 standing orders to implement English Votes for English Laws in 2015.

Rulings from the Chair are an important part of the 'case law' of procedure. They usually arise because the view of the Speaker is sought on a point of interpretation or some new matter not otherwise covered. The rules on admissibility of parliamentary questions, motions and amendments to bills have grown up in this way. Rulings have a close relationship with precedent – that which has been done before, and judged to have been in order by the Speaker of the day. Rulings and precedents are distilled in successive editions of *Erskine May*.

Finally, some parliamentary proceedings are regulated by *Acts of Parliament*, covering such things as the way Royal Assent to bills is signified to Parliament, how secondary legislation (see page 238) is dealt with, and making an affirmation or taking an oath.

As with the Commons, the House of Lords derives its procedure from practice, from standing orders, and to a limited extent from Acts of Parliament. But as the Lord Speaker has no powers of order, there are no Speaker's rulings in the Lords. Instead, procedure is developed and refined by the House itself by agreeing recommendations from its Procedure Committee. Sometimes these result in amendments to standing orders, but more usually they are set out in the House's procedural handbook, the *Companion to the Standing Orders*.

Why procedure? And why is it complicated?

Every deliberative body, from a parish council to the General Assembly of the United Nations, needs rules to a greater or lesser extent. Rules regulate how business is initiated; they provide a framework for consideration; and they define how a valid decision is reached. Good procedural rules mean the focus is on the substance of the matter at hand, not on the rules of the game.

Many organisations can manage with simple rules, and perhaps no great damage is done if even those rules are not followed very closely. The procedure of Parliament is not simple, for three main reasons.

- *Contention*. If a group of people are in complete agreement about something, rules are barely necessary. The Supreme Soviet in the old USSR had little need of procedure. The Westminster Parliament is a forum where often profound disagreements on politics and principles are argued out and decided. Procedure thus has to provide a means of focusing points for decision, allowing challenge to take place, and balancing the will of the majority against the arguments of the minority.

  In addition, procedure has to protect the rights not only of the opposition parties but also of groups of MPs, or individual members, wherever they may sit in the House. In a House the size of the Commons, this is especially important; one MP out of 650 may be in a very small minority, but he or she may have constituents whose interests might be significantly threatened by a decision of the majority.

  Where the balance should be struck between the will of the majority (in effect, the government of the day) and the arguments of those who disagree is controversial. There has always been an understanding that a government that has a majority will eventually get its way; but governments are impatient.
- *Control*. The standing orders are about setting limits – defining what powers select committees may have, how long various types of business may be debated, when certain things happen, and so on. The more tightly those limits are drawn, and the more circumstances that have to be controlled, the more complex the rules. For example, the standing orders on the programming of bills run to 12 pages.
- *Complexity of business*. Parliament has to deal with a huge range of material: every issue for which the government is responsible and legislation on any subject, often extremely detailed. It approves taxation and grants the government the money required to run the country. At the same time, it must try to fulfil its role of calling government to account. Small wonder that procedures to regulate this business are often complicated.

Consistent, certain and clear

We have seen why there have to be rules and why they are complicated. But rules are not an end in themselves. As the United Kingdom has no written constitution, and as the way Parliament operates cannot be reviewed by any other body, its rules must be robust. Good procedural rules have three qualities:

- They must be *consistent*; things of the same type must be dealt with in the same way; when something is not, that must be on the basis of a formal decision to handle it in a different way.
- They must be *certain*, with notice given of matters for substantive decision and rules enforced firmly but fairly. Punctuality is an important part of this; if the

moment of interruption is 7.00 pm, the Commons Speaker will say 'Order, order' precisely on the stroke of seven o'clock, not a moment earlier or later.

- Rules may be complex, but they must be *clear*. Vagueness will mean that the rules themselves, not what they regulate, will become a source of disagreement; and it will tend to cast doubt on the validity of what has been done.

In his book *Last Man Standing: Memoirs of a Political Survivor*, Jack Straw, the former Foreign, Home and Justice Secretary, and former Leader of the House of Commons, said: 'Procedure may be boring to some, but it's about the distribution and exercise of power. It really matters'.

6

Making the law

Is Parliament 'sovereign'?

Before looking at how Parliament operates as a legislature, we should consider the nature of Parliament's powers. In the past, writers on the constitution would have described these as constituting the 'sovereignty of Parliament', but a better modern term might be 'legislative supremacy', because to call Parliament sovereign is disputable in several ways: much of government's authority derives from the prerogative powers of the Crown, for example, rather than from Parliament. When the government decides to commit the UK's armed forces to military action, it does so formally by exercising a prerogative power, even though there is a recent but robust convention that Parliament's consent will be necessary. More clearly still, when the Prime Minister sacks or appoints ministers – or, indeed, creates or dismantles government departments – she does so by exercising prerogative powers, with no role for Parliament.

Parliament's legislative supremacy

So when people use the phrase 'the sovereignty of Parliament' what they really mean is the *legislative supremacy* of Parliament – that is to say its unique ability, in the words of the nineteenth-century constitutional writer A.V. Dicey, to 'make or unmake any law whatever'.

The principle was set out elegantly in 1844, when Thomas Erskine May published the first edition of his *Treatise on the Law, Privileges, Proceedings and Usage of Parliament* – a work that was to become the authoritative text on the procedures of Parliament (see page 52). He began his second chapter with this paragraph:

> *The legislative authority of Parliament extends over the United Kingdom, and all its colonies and foreign possessions; and there are no other limits to its power of making laws for the whole empire than those which are incident to all sovereign*

> *authority – the willingness of the people to obey, or their power to resist. Unlike the legislatures of many other countries, it is bound by no fundamental charter or constitution; but has itself the sole constitutional right of establishing and altering the laws and government of the empire.*

Parliament no longer legislates for an overseas empire, but Erskine May's words in all other respects still apply.

Characteristics of legislative supremacy

Legislative supremacy is essentially a legal concept, and it manifests itself in a number of different ways. For example, the courts of law are under a duty to apply legislation, even if that legislation might appear to be morally or politically wrong. This is a powerful reason why legislation needs to be technically correct to minimise the possibility of unexpected consequences. Moreover, unlike countries with written constitutions – the United States, for example – it would not be possible to challenge an Act of the United Kingdom Parliament in the courts on the grounds that it was 'unconstitutional'. The 2005 challenge to the Hunting Act (which was appealed all the way to the House of Lords in its judicial capacity) was based on the alleged effects of the Parliament Acts (see pages 222), not on a conflict with the constitution. And, in any event, even the constitution can be subject to statute. New constitutional principles can be established, such as reform of the membership or powers of the House of Lords, or devolved government in Scotland, Wales and Northern Ireland. Moreover, existing constitutional principles can be changed, as in making male and female heirs equal in succession to the throne.

One of the consequences of Parliament's legislative supremacy is that one parliament cannot bind its successor parliaments, which have an equal claim to that legislative supremacy. In some cases, things that Parliament does by legislation are in practical terms so difficult to reverse that successor parliaments are, in effect, bound by those Acts – such as the Acts that gave self-government or confederation to the former dominions, or independence to the former colonies, or votes to women, or even devolution to Scotland and Wales. (Devolution in Northern Ireland, however, has been periodically revoked and restored.)

Limitations on legislative supremacy

Parliament's legislative supremacy is a powerful concept, but it has its limitations. Erskine May put his finger on the chief limitation – 'the willingness of the people to obey, or their power to resist'. Most of the time, in these days of universal suffrage, this manifests itself through the ballot box rather than in mass civil disobedience, but the repeal of the much disliked community charge or poll tax legislation in 1992 was undoubtedly hastened by the mass demonstrations of 1990.

Other limitations derive from the radical changes in society since Erskine May first wrote. On the one hand, the law has covered more and more areas that formerly went unregulated or were considered private matters not deserving the intervention of the state – such as education, working conditions, social security, health, and so on. But on the other hand, modern technology, and in recent years especially information technology, has placed some activities almost beyond the reach of UK lawmaking – electronic international transfer of funds, for example, or intellectual property rights in material placed on the internet.

Apart from the ultimate limitations of public consent and of practical constraint, the legislative supremacy of Parliament has been limited in practical ways in recent years, by:

- the passing of the Human Rights Act;
- accession to the European Union (at that time the European Economic Community); and
- devolution to Scotland and Wales, and, with some qualifications, to Northern Ireland.

We now look at Parliament's legislative function – the means of exercising this legislative supremacy.

Who makes the law?

If asked 'Who makes the law in the UK?' most people would instinctively reply 'Parliament'. It seems to be an obvious feature of our democracy that the law under which it operates has been decided by elected representatives in Parliament. And if we were asked 'Where can one find the law?' we might consult 'statutes' or 'Acts of Parliament', each of which begins with the formula:

> *Be it enacted by the Queen's Most Excellent Majesty, by and with the consent of the Lords Spiritual and Temporal, and Commons, in this present Parliament assembled, and by the authority of the same, as follows:*

However, if we look at the law in operation, the picture is less simple. The way the law works in practice may differ from the intentions of Parliament when the law was passed, or the application of the law may vary in different parts of the country.

For example, the driver of an antique lorry used in a steam fair is stopped by the police as he drives the wrong way down a one-way street. The police find that he has no tachograph in his cab, and they take the view that this is required by law to record his hours of work and the miles he has travelled. The driver is charged with driving the wrong way down the street and with not having the tachograph and is convicted by the magistrates on both counts. He accepts the first but goes all the way to the Court of Appeal on the second, on the grounds that his lorry is an exhibit and is not used for commercial haulage purposes, so it is not required to have a tachograph. The appeal court judges agree and quash the conviction.

What has Parliament to do with this process? The enforcement of the law was the duty of the police. The interpretation of the law was a matter for the courts. The street was not designated as one-way by Parliament but by the local council. The law about tachographs was set out in regulations made by the Secretary of State for Transport, not by Parliament. And all the Secretary of State for Transport had done was to give effect in the UK to European Union legislation brought forward by the European Commission and agreed by the Council of Ministers and the European Parliament.

However, all those involved were operating within a framework that derives from statute law as made by the Westminster Parliament. The local council was able to make the street one-way because an Act of Parliament gave it the power to do so; the European Union was able to legislate because an Act of Parliament – in this case, the European Communities Act 1972 – provided that such European legislation shall apply to the UK (at least at the time of writing); and the Secretary of State for Transport was able to make regulations because the same Act of Parliament allowed the translation of general EU legislation into detailed domestic law. Throughout the UK's membership of the EU the Westminster Parliament retained the power to repeal the European Communities Act 1972 and end the power of the EU to make any law applying to the UK.

This chapter looks in detail at these Acts of Parliament and how they are made. It also examines delegated legislation; that is, legislation made directly by the government and other bodies that have been authorised by Parliament to do so.

Types of legislation

First, some definitions. The *Acts of Parliament* we have been talking about are a level of legislation known as *primary legislation*. A piece of draft primary legislation is a *bill*. When a bill is passed, it becomes an *Act* and part of *statute law*. An Act is referred to by its title and the year it was passed; for example, the Policing and Crime Act 2017.

There are two types of bill and Act: *public* and *private*. The vast majority, and by far the more important, are public. They affect the public general law, which applies to everyone in the UK – although some Acts may apply specifically to England, Wales, Scotland or Northern Ireland (or to London), and the Scottish Parliament and Welsh Assembly have power to make primary legislation for Scotland and Wales on a range of subjects defined by the Westminster Parliament in the Scotland Act 1998 and the Government of Wales Act 2006, as does the Northern Ireland Assembly on 'transferred matters' (those not reserved to Westminster under the Northern Ireland Act 1998).

Private Acts confer private and particular rights, or are local and personal in their effect. A private Act might allow a local authority to close a cemetery, or to confer powers to manage and control access to areas of common land. A private Act may also allow an exception to the general law; for example, to allow an individual local authority to do something within its own area that needs specific legal authority. In recent years, the rare cases of personal legislation (once used for divorces) have been to allow people to marry who otherwise would be prevented from doing so (for example, stepfather and stepdaughter).

Sometimes a public bill contains provisions that do not apply generally but affect particular individuals or bodies differently from others who would otherwise be in the same situation. If these were the only provisions in the bill, it would be a private bill; but combining them with changes to the general law turns the bill into a *hybrid bill*. These are usually bills promoted by the government relating to large-scale infrastructure projects, such as Crossrail and the HS2 London to Birmingham high-speed rail line. Different procedures apply to public bills, private bills and hybrid bills.

Private members' bills are sometimes confused with private bills, but they are public bills to change the general law; their title comes from the fact that they are brought forward by a private member (that is, a backbencher) rather than by the government.

Bills of all types may start their parliamentary passage in either House, although those whose purpose is mainly or entirely financial will generally start in the Commons. At the beginning of a parliamentary session, the government business managers will try to maximise their use of parliamentary time available by deciding which bills will start in the Lords and which in the Commons. A bill that begins in the Lords has [*Lords*] in its title when in the Commons and [HL] when in the Lords.

Delegated legislation is made by a minister (or occasionally a public body) under powers conferred by an Act of Parliament. Individual pieces of legislation may be called *orders*, *rules*, *regulations*, *schemes* or *codes*, depending on what the original Act (called the 'parent Act') says; but they are generally known as *delegated legislation*, *secondary legislation* or *statutory instruments* (SIs). A special type of order, an *Order in Council*, requires the approval of the Queen in the Privy Council.

Delegated legislation is normally used for detailed arrangements that flesh out broader provisions in the parent Act, or to specify matters – for example, the arrangements for licensing some activity – the details of which may need to be changed and for which an amending bill would be a poor use of time. But the balance between what is contained in primary legislation, which can be examined in detail during the passage of a bill, and what is left for ministers to determine in much less scrutinised secondary legislation, is an important issue. We deal with delegated legislation in greater detail on pages 238 to 249, which also cover *legislative reform orders*, *remedial orders* and *Church of England measures*.

Government bills

Origins

After a general election, the legislative programme is normally dominated by *bills reflecting commitments that the winning party has made in its manifesto* or, as happened in 2010, which are the subject of a coalition agreement between parties. Reversing the policy of the previous government on a key issue may also be a priority. During a government's term of office its legislative programme will *reflect new and developing policies* as a result of changing circumstances, subjects moving up the general political agenda, or sometimes the personal priorities of a senior member of the Cabinet in his or her area of policy – although he or she will also need Cabinet support.

Financial bills are required both to raise revenue and to authorise how it is spent. The Finance Bill, introduced following the Budget, authorises taxation, as well as embodying the Chancellor of the Exchequer's proposals for tax changes; and Supply and Appropriation Bills authorise government spending.

Bills may be needed to *give effect to international commitments in domestic law*, such as the European Union (Amendment) Act 2008 to implement the Lisbon Treaty. In general, treaties are not required to be approved by legislation, but the Constitutional Reform and Governance Act 2010 put on a statutory footing the previous convention under which a treaty was laid before Parliament but the government did not proceed with ratification until 21 sitting days had elapsed. Under the new formal arrangements, the government lays a treaty before both Houses with an explanatory memorandum, and the Houses have 21 sitting days in which one or the other may resolve that the treaty should not be ratified. If necessary, there is then a subsequent stage in which a minister lays a statement of why the treaty should be ratified and can be prevented from doing so only by a further resolution of the House of Commons against ratification within a further 21 sitting days.

Government bills may *respond to events*. The Supreme Court's judgment in December 2016 that the royal prerogative gave no power to ministers to trigger article 50 led to Parliament passing the European Union (Notification of Withdrawal) Act 2017, giving the Prime Minister a statutory power. In addition, most government departments will want what might be called *housekeeping bills*. These may or may not be substantial, are often not controversial in party political terms and are about keeping the business of government and public affairs up to date.

Also in the housekeeping category are consolidation bills, which set out the law on a particular subject in a clearer and more up-to-date form without changing its substance, and statute law (repeals) bills, which repeal redundant legislation. Both these bills are prepared by the Law Commissions.

From proposal to bill

Political and day-to-day departmental pressures – to say nothing of proposals from special interest groups – ensure that no government department is ever short of ideas for legislation. When those ideas have been formulated, a process of consultation begins, the length and detail of which depends on what sort of legislation is being considered and how quickly it is needed. Inside government, the Treasury will be consulted, as well as other departments with an interest, together perhaps with the devolved administrations in Scotland, Wales and Northern Ireland. Outside government, the views of pressure groups, public bodies, industries or trade unions affected will be sought.

The process of consulting outside government is covered by Cabinet Office guidance. Consultation documents are widely circulated and available on the internet.

Nevertheless, the process is sometimes open to criticism. Political pressures may mean that there is, in fact, little time for *effective* consultation. The process may sometimes focus too much on 'the usual suspects' – those organisations with a national profile – rather than seeking opinion more widely. Consultation often has to be on the broad intentions of a proposal, but 'the devil is in the detail', and some important elements of a proposal may be decided only when the business of drafting begins. Finally – and crucially – there is no point in consulting if the opinions expressed are ignored and the government of the day steams ahead regardless.

These criticisms are met to a certain extent if legislation follows a Green Paper, where the government has sought views on various legislative options, or a White Paper, where it has made its intentions clear. Increasingly, though, the use of draft bills (see page 188), where a complete legislative proposal can be considered in detail before it begins its formal parliamentary stages, is seen as a way of allowing the widest consultation, as well as resulting in better legislation.

In due course, the sponsoring government department will have proposals to put before a policy committee of the Cabinet. This will often be done by correspondence, and only if disagreements arise or if major issues are at stake will the subject need to be discussed at a meeting of the committee itself. In 2017 there were five ministerial committees of the Cabinet and 11 sub-committees, covering broad areas such as National Security and European Union Exit and Trade, but also specific areas of current concern, such as airports. There were also five 'Implementation Taskforces'.

But even if the relevant ministerial committee endorses a proposal, this does not mean immediate legislation. A minor change may have to wait until a more extensive bill in that subject area comes along. A major policy development, or a series of related proposals, may need a whole bill and so a place of its own in the government's legislative programme.

Parliamentary time is scarce, so further decisions need to be taken centrally about priorities and about balancing the programme of bills for each session of a parliament. This is the task of the Parliamentary Business and Legislation Cabinet Committee (PBL), which includes the Leaders and Government Chief Whips in both Houses. That committee recommends to the Cabinet what proposals will actually find a place in the next Queen's Speech. As the new session approaches, PBL will decide which bills will start in the Commons and which in the Lords, and which should be published in draft; and it makes an assessment of how much parliamentary time will be needed for each and any difficulties on the way – perhaps dissenting government backbenchers in the Commons, or a critical reaction in the Lords.

Meanwhile, those proposals that have been approved for the next session's programme have been moving from concept to detail. The sponsoring department prepares drafting instructions for parliamentary counsel. These instructions will set out what the bill needs to do but not the detail of how it will do it. This is the job of parliamentary counsel, a group of lawyers specialising in legislative drafting. Despite the name, they are servants of the government rather than of Parliament, and they draft all government primary legislation (secondary legislation is normally drafted by lawyers in the government department concerned).

In converting a department's instructions into a bill, parliamentary counsel have a number of tasks. They must achieve clarity and precision, not only so that the bill's provisions will be tightly defined, but also so that, once it is passed, the possibility of legal challenge is minimised. They must ensure that the bill fits with legislation already in existence – both the statute book of primary legislation and any relevant EU or delegated legislation. This may mean that the bill must amend or repeal provisions of UK legislation that may be scattered through a number of Acts of Parliament. Ministers will want them to draft the bill tightly to minimise the possibility of unwelcome amendments in either House being in order – a tough assignment when dealing with major bills with a broad scope. Finally, they must ensure that the provisions of the bill work – in terms of logic rather than political policy. To take a simple example, if you make something illegal you need to ensure that there is an appropriate penalty for doing it, and you also need to define what will constitute evidence that the offence has been committed. Small wonder that it is said to take seven years to acquire the skills needed to draft a medium-sized bill.

This process of turning instructions into drafting often throws up new questions of policy, and for most bills there will be a continuing dialogue between the sponsoring department and parliamentary counsel while the bill is being drafted. Even then the bill may go through several further drafts before it is finally approved by its sponsoring department and minister, agreed by PBL, and is ready to begin its parliamentary journey.

Just before it does so, the text must be submitted to the authorities of the House in which it is to start. In the Commons, the Clerk of Legislation ensures that the bill complies with the rules of the House; that its short title is appropriate and not misleading or sloganising; that everything in it is covered by the long title – the passage at the start of a bill that says that it is 'A Bill to . . .' and then lists its purposes; that any provisions that would require expenditure or would levy charges or taxes are identified (and are printed in italics); whether the royal prerogative or the personal interests of the Queen or the Prince of Wales are affected (in which case the Queen's or Prince of Wales's consent will be required); whether any uncertainties exist as to what sort of amendments might be in order; and whether it conflicts with or duplicates a bill or part of a bill that has already been introduced. In the Lords, the Public Bill Office offers advice on the same range of issues, except on financial matters. Once these consultations are complete, the bill is ready for introduction.

Is a government bill really draft legislation?

Parliamentary and politics textbooks say that a bill is a draft Act of Parliament, but governments do not see it in that way. For each bill, there has been a lengthy process of development and debate between departments and ministers, the government has consulted those it feels have an interest, the contents of the bill have been minutely considered by officials and by parliamentary counsel, and the bill has been through a series of drafts.

So, by the time the bill reaches Parliament it is not so much draft legislation for discussion and amendment as word-for-word what the government of the day wants to see on the statute book. Moreover, ministers identify personally with major bills; 'their' bills are part of their political achievements as ministers, and significant amendment of a government bill – such as the major rewrite of the Health and Social Care Bill in 2011 – can be seen as a loss of face.

The pressure of legislation

This might matter less if there were more time to consider legislation and the lead times were longer. However, governments of both parties are always in a hurry: to demonstrate their dynamism; to seek to deliver on commitments; to respond to events; and to put their stamp on key areas of policy. This means, in turn, that the machinery for preparing legislation is frequently overloaded. The result is that the consultation process is rushed or curtailed, too many large and complex bills are attempted in a session, policy is sometimes not settled well in advance of drafting (and sometimes it changes after introduction of a bill) and instructions from departments to parliamentary counsel are sometimes late.

This often leads to 'drafting on the hoof', when significant amendments to a bill are made not because of effective criticism inside or outside Parliament but in order to reflect the government's changing views. Some government amendments are brought forward to meet such criticism (and one of the strengths of a bicameral system is that it allows an undertaking to amend to be given in one House and the time to bring forward the amendment in the other House).

Although it is difficult, if not impossible, to be sure of the genesis of every amendment that a government puts down to one of its own bills, a large proportion is the result of second thoughts rather than a response to a measured critical process. To give examples of the general and the particular: in the 2016–17 session, 2,200 amendments were made to government bills in the Lords, and only 34 were forced upon the government by a vote. The Investigatory Powers Bill 2016 saw 405 government amendments made in the Lords, and the Higher Education and Research Bill 2016–17 saw 250. It is worth noting that drafting on the hoof has an additional perverse effect in that it occupies the time of parliamentary counsel, who could be working with a longer lead time on the next session's bills.

There has been pressure both from within and outside government to reduce the need for government amendments (especially late amendments), but the results have been patchy. For example, the House of Commons considered 377 Lords amendments, occupying 63 pages, to the Investigatory Powers Bill in November 2016 the day after receiving them.

Programming and guillotines

In the Lords, the normal intervals between the different stages of the passage of a bill are prescribed by a recommendation of the Procedure Committee in 1977: two weekends between introduction of a bill and second reading, 14 days between second reading and committee, 14 days between committee and report for large and complex bills, and three sitting days between report and third reading. Intervals in the Commons are governed by practice and a degree of negotiation between the two sides but are usually much shorter than in the Lords. The 1985 Commons Procedure Committee recommendation for two weekends between introduction and second reading, and ten days between both second reading and committee, and committee and report, was never adopted.

Bills may need little – or sometimes no – debating time if they are narrow and technical, or if they command support on all sides (although all-party agreement may not make for good legislation, as was shown by the oft-quoted cases of the Dangerous Dogs Act 1991 and the Child Support Act 1991). However, for most bills there is pressure, both from the opposition and from government backbenchers, for more debating time than the government is prepared to concede. The purposes and motives of such debate are varied: to set out a contrary political position; to seek explanation and clarification from the government; to explore and criticise the details of the legislation and its likely effects, and to make alternative proposals; and, in the case of the more contentious bills, to make opposition clear, and to inconvenience the government, by delaying the bill.

There are various ways in which debate in the House of Commons may be limited. We have already looked at the closure (see page 148) where, after what in the view of the Chair is a reasonable period of discussion, the use of the government's majority can bring debate to an end and have the particular question before the House at the time put; but this is of little practical use to the government where legislation is concerned. A more draconian power was introduced into the Commons in the nineteenth century following the disruption of proceedings over several sessions by Irish MPs campaigning for Home Rule. It was generally recognised that the rights of the majority needed to be preserved and, despite considerable reservations at the time, the *guillotine* or *allocation of time order* was introduced. In essence, this allows the House to agree, at any stage in proceedings on a bill, strict time limits for the remainder of its progress. A timetable is set out in a motion that is put to the House. If it is agreed, then delaying tactics are of no use; committee and report stages come to an end after a fixed period whether all amendments selected by the Chair have been discussed or not, and sometimes with many clauses of a bill not having been debated at all.

At one time, guillotines were considered wholly exceptional and could arouse outrage both inside and outside the House. The procedure was used just over 70 times in the 90 years 1881–1970. However, from the late 1970s its use increased under governments of both parties, and it was routine for three or four, or more, bills to be guillotined in each session. The highest numbers were in 1988–89 (10 guillotines out of 37 government bills passed), 1998–99 (11 out of 27) and 1999–2000 (13 out of 39).

In 1985 the Procedure Committee argued that the weapon of delay probably does nothing to change a government's mind, and that the guillotine response usually meant patchy scrutiny. It recommended that for controversial bills (those likely to need more than 25 hours in what were then known as 'standing committees') there should be a timetable agreed by a Legislative Business Committee on which all parties were represented, which would allocate time in committee and on report to reflect the importance of different parts of the bill. This proposal had a good deal of support on the backbenches but not on the frontbenches, and in February 1986 it was defeated in the House by 231 to 166. The Jopling Committee (see page 138) returned to this in 1992 and endorsed the earlier approach. In the event, this was introduced in an informal way, with some timetabling agreed through the usual channels and guillotines avoided whenever possible (and, indeed, from 1994 to 1997 there were only six guillotines).

In 1997 the newly established Modernisation Committee returned to the issue. It recommended a halfway house between informal agreement and guillotine, to be known as *programming*. When a bill was selected for programming, there should be discussions that would take account of representations from all sides of the House, including backbenchers. In the light of those discussions, the government would move an amendable motion immediately after second reading specifying the type of committee to which the bill should be sent and the day by which it should be reported. The committee would then decide how to use that time.

A *programme order* differs from a guillotine in that it is imposed on proceedings on a bill immediately after second reading rather than later, when the speed of progress (or extent of delay) is known, and, if taken immediately after second reading, is not debatable (guillotines are debatable for three hours). As noted above, unlike a guillotine it specifies the type of committee to which the bill should be sent. The programme order may be amended later; for example, if the opposition persuades the government to provide more time.

When under a programme order the time allotted for part of a bill expires, only certain specified questions may be put to the public bill committee or the House: in particular, on the amendment already under discussion, on any amendment selected by the Chair for a separate vote (in practice, amendments already debated on which the opposition parties particularly want to register their position); thereafter, government amendments and new clauses may be taken en bloc.

When a programme order applies to proceedings in public bill committee, the number of sittings and allocation of time is proposed by a sub-committee comprising the chair of the committee and seven of its members. The sub-committee's resolution may be debated by the committee for half an hour (and may be amended). A public bill committee can also make proposals to the House for changes in the date for reporting a bill, or in the programming of the report stage and third reading.

Following its introduction early in the 1997 parliament, programming has operated on a fairly consensual basis, even when applied to controversial bills. Though it has on occasion been bitterly disputed, it has become an established, even (as the Procedure Committee put it in 2013) a 'broadly accepted' part of the Commons legislative world. Here the exception rather proves the rule: in 2012 the coalition government dropped its House of Lords Reform Bill because it feared it could not pass a programme motion in the House; and absent a programme motion there was little chance of the bill completing its stages in reasonable time.

Where it does continue to be criticised is when the knives of a programme order fall and large parts of a bill, and many proposed amendments, are undebated (just as with a guillotine). The fact that this has caused particular problems at report stage has been commented on in reports by various House committees, most recently the Procedure Committee in 2013. In the 2013–14 session, when 26 bills were subject to programming, 20 groups of amendments went undebated in this way. The committee proposed that the notice period for amendments be extended to three days, so that programme orders drafted by the government could reflect amendments tabled and selected for debate by the Speaker, with a view to reducing the number of groups which received little or no debate. The House agreed the proposal, initially on a trial and then on a permanent basis, although it is not clear whether it has had the impact sought. Other proposals made by the committee, such as greater use of recommittal of a bill back to committee in cases where large numbers of government amendments are tabled at report stage, did not find favour with the government (unsurprisingly) and have not been introduced.

It is worth noting that although programming offers the prospect of more effective use of time, it can do nothing to increase the total time available; neither in itself can it reduce the pressure of the government's legislative programme. One way of improving scrutiny – and perhaps of saving time in the long run – might be the use of draft bills.

Draft bills and 'pre-legislative scrutiny'

It was the case for many years before the introduction of public bill committees – and remains the case today – that a bill may be sent to a select committee for detailed examination after second reading. The select committee format has several advantages. The committee is not just a debating forum but can take oral and written evidence, involving many more people in a formal process of consultation and making the legislative process more accessible to those outside Parliament. A select committee has to return to the House the text of a bill just as a public bill committee (see page 195) does, but unlike a public bill committee, it can also report its views and the reasons for its decisions. Even on highly contentious issues, select committees have a long history of operating in a consensual rather than an adversarial way, which is likely to make for more effective scrutiny of legislation.

Scrutiny of bills *in draft* by select committees (or joint committees of both Houses) goes several steps further. A draft bill has not begun its formal parliamentary progress, and it really is draft legislation in a way that a bill, once introduced, is not. Ministers have invested less political capital in it and changes will not necessarily be seen as defeats. The Liaison Committee, consisting of the chairs of all select committees, described the scrutiny of bills in draft as 'a development of great significance. It offers the prospect of properly examined, better thought out and so higher quality legislation'.

The numbers of draft bills each session had seemed to be an upward trend: rising from three, four and nine in the sessions 2005–06, 2006–07 and 2007–08, respectively, to 11 in the admittedly long 2010–12 session and 14 in session 2012–13.

However, in 2016–17 only two draft bills were introduced; and only three were announced in the 2017 Queen's Speech. Whatever the number of draft bills, it should be seen against a background of typically more than 20 government bills in most sessions.

However, draft bills are not a panacea – at least, not for governments. They add to the time before a proposal passes into law (and circumstances may change during that time); they tie up more resources in the preparation and drafting of bills, as substantial changes may be needed in the bills eventually introduced; and, as there is the opportunity for criticism well-supported by argument and evidence, they may make it harder for the government of the day to get its way. There is no evidence to suggest that bills which had been scrutinised in draft have an easier passage through Parliament. Unless a way is found of slackening the *overall* pressure on a government's legislative programme, the contribution that draft bills can make may be limited.

For pre-legislative scrutiny to work, it must be allowed enough time. We now follow the passage of a government bill (formally introduced into the Commons and not a draft bill) through Parliament. A chart showing the stages of legislation in the two Houses is overleaf.

Anatomy of a bill

Part of the European Union (Withdrawal) Bill of the 2017–19 session is reproduced on pages 191 to 193 and shows some of the main features of any bill.

Every bill has a *short title*, which is the title by which it is known during its passage and which will normally be the same as the title of the Act that will result. Also on the cover page of the bill will be a statement by the relevant minister as to whether the provisions of the bill are compatible with the European Convention on Human Rights. After the cover page will be a list of contents, if the bill is long enough to need one. At the start of the bill is the *long title*, which sets out the contents of the bill; all the provisions of the bill must fall within the long title. This is followed by the words of enactment: 'Be it enacted by the Queen's Most Excellent Majesty'.

Clauses are the basic units of a bill; they are divided into *subsections, paragraphs and sub-paragraphs*. The European Union (Withdrawal) Bill had 19 clauses, but a long bill may contain 100 to 500 clauses or more and be divided up into several *parts* (which, in turn, may be divided into *chapters*). When a bill becomes an Act the clauses become known as *sections*. To reduce complexity, the *schedules* to a bill fill in some of the fine detail (for example, one of the schedules will usually list amendments and repeals affecting existing legislation). A schedule is always dependent on the clause that introduces it and has no effect unless the clause is agreed to. Any provisions that would cost public money (other than routine administration by the government department concerned), or that would impose taxes or levy a charge, are printed in italics in bills introduced in the Commons, although sometimes a single 'sink' clause will cover all the expenditure implied by the bill.

Table 6.1 The stages in the passing of a public bill

House of Commons		Timing
First Reading	• Formal reading out of title by the clerk at the Table. • Ordered to be printed.	
Second Reading	• Main opportunity to debate the principle of the bill. A 'reasoned amendment' may be tabled. A division at this stage represents a direct challenge to the principle of the bill. • After second reading, government bills are usually timetabled by programme motions which, amongst other things, set an end-date for the committee stage.	Usually two weekends after first reading.
Committee Stage	• Chance to consider and vote on the detail, line by line. • Amendments selected and grouped by the Chair (in practice, for Public Bill Committees, selection and grouping is undertaken by the clerk under the authority of the Chair). (i) Committee of the whole House – for 'constitutional' and some other bills, and parts of the Finance Bill; (ii) Public Bill Committee – most usual procedure; 16–50 members, in proportion to overall party strengths. One or two days of oral evidence in select committee mode is followed by more formal debate on amendments as the committee goes through the bill 'line-by-line'. (iii) Select Committee – infrequently used.	Usually starts shortly after second reading and can take anything from one meeting to two per week for some months.
Report Stage	• A further chance to consider amendments, new clauses and for MPs, including those not on the committee, to propose changes.	Usually shortly after committee stage.
Legislative Grand Committee	• For bills, or parts of bills, certified as relating to England only (or England and Wales only, or England, Wales and Northern Ireland only) an opportunity for MPs representing constituencies in those areas to give or withhold consent to the proposals. If consent were withheld there would be an additional reconsideration stage.	After report stage.
Third Reading	• Final chance to debate the bill, as amended at previous stages. • A vote gives the chance to show dissatisfaction with amended bill. • The bill now goes to the Lords.	Usually immediately after report stage on the same day.

House of Lords		
First Reading	• Formal. • The bill is reprinted in the form finally agreed by the Commons.	No significant delay in the transfer of a bill between the two Houses.
Second Reading	• Debate on general principles of the bill. • Government bills included in the election manifesto are, by convention, not opposed at their second reading, but 'reasoned amendments' may be tabled as a means of indicating dissent and can be voted on.	Two weekends must elapse after first reading.
Committee Stage	• Bills usually go to a Committee of the Whole House or Grand Committee away from the chamber and rarely to other types of committee. • Detailed line-by-line examination. • Unlike the Commons: (i) no selection of amendments – all can be considered, and (ii) no timetabling.	Usually starts at least 14 days after second reading, often taking place over several days.
Report Stage	• Further chance to amend the bill. • May take place over several days. • Normally when divisions on amendments occur.	Usually starts at least 14 days after the end of committee stage.
Third Reading and Passing	• Unlike in the Commons, amendments can be made provided the issue has not been voted on at an earlier stage. • Passing: the final opportunity for peers to comment and vote on bill.	Usually at least three sitting days after the end of report stage.

European Union (Withdrawal) Bill

EXPLANATORY NOTES

Explanatory notes to the Bill, prepared by the Department for Exiting the European Union, are published separately as Bill 5–EN.

EUROPEAN CONVENTION ON HUMAN RIGHTS

Secretary David Davis has made the following statement under section 19(1)(a) of the Human Rights Act 1998:

In my view the provisions of the European Union (Withdrawal) Bill are compatible with the Convention rights.

Typical front page of a bill

Source: Copyright House of Commons, 2017

A

BILL

TO

Repeal the European Communities Act 1972 and make other provision in connection with the withdrawal of the United Kingdom from the EU.

BE IT ENACTED by the Queen's most Excellent Majesty, by and with the advice and consent of the Lords Spiritual and Temporal, and Commons, in this present Parliament assembled, and by the authority of the same, as follows:—

Repeal of the ECA

1 Repeal of the European Communities Act 1972

The European Communities Act 1972 is repealed on exit day.

Retention of existing EU law

2 Saving for EU-derived domestic legislation

(1) EU-derived domestic legislation, as it has effect in domestic law immediately before exit day, continues to have effect in domestic law on and after exit day.

(2) In this section "EU-derived domestic legislation" means any enactment so far as—

(a) made under section 2(2) of, or paragraph 1A of Schedule 2 to, the European Communities Act 1972,
(b) passed or made, or operating, for a purpose mentioned in section 2(2)(a) or (b) of that Act,
(c) relating to anything—

(i) which falls within paragraph (a) or (b), or
(ii) to which section 3(1) or 4(1) applies, or

(d) relating otherwise to the EU or the EEA,

but does not include any enactment contained in the European Communities Act 1972.

(3) This section is subject to section 5 and Schedule 1 (exceptions to savings and incorporation).

Bill 5 57/1

Typical first substantive page of a Bill

Source: House of Commons, 2017

European Union (Withdrawal) Bill

A

BILL

To repeal the European Communities Act 1972 and make other provision in connection with the withdrawal of the United Kingdom from the EU.

continued

Typical back page of a bill: the European Union (Withdrawal) Bill of session 2017–19

Source: House of Commons, 2017

Presented by Secretary David Davis

supported by
The Prime Minister,
The Chancellor of the Exchequer,
Secretary Damian Green,
Secretary Boris Johnson and
Secretary David Lidington.

Ordered by The House of Commons
to be Printed, 13 July 2017

PUBLISHED BY AUTHORITY OF THE HOUSE OF COMMONS

Bill 5 57/1

The last page of the bill is the ***backsheet***, which repeats the long and short titles, gives the bill number and the session it was introduced, and lists the MP or peer introducing the bill (the 'member in charge') and his or her 'supporters'. For a government bill, the member in charge will be the secretary of state heading the relevant department, and the supporters will be senior ministers with an interest in the subject matter. In the Lords there are no names of supporters, only the peer in charge.

Explanatory Notes are a separate document that accompanies a bill. They set out the bill's intention and background, explain the clauses in non-legal language and give an assessment of the bill's resource implications and its impact on businesses (for example, if a bill were to introduce a new system of regulation or licensing). They must be in neutral terms, objectively explaining the bill and not making a case for it.

Commons stages

Introduction and first reading

The most usual method of introducing a bill is by the member in charge giving notice of the bill's long and short titles, and of the intention to introduce it on a particular day. This notice appears on the Order Paper for that day; the MP is called by the Speaker at the commencement of public business (see page 147) and brings the so-called 'dummy bill' (merely a sheet of paper with the short and long titles and the names of up to 12 supporters) to the Clerk of the House at the Table. (In the case of a government bill, a dummy bill is not brought to the Table: it is already there.)

The Clerk reads out the short title and the Speaker says 'Second reading what day?' For all government bills the response is 'tomorrow' (or the next sitting day if there is a break for a weekend or recess) as the government can bring any of its bills forward on any sitting day. For a private member's bill, however, naming a day can be a matter for careful tactics (see page 214).

The bill is now said to have been read the first time; it is recorded in the Votes and Proceedings as having been ordered to be printed and to be read a second time on whichever day has been named. A bill introduced in this way is known as a *presentation bill*; bills may also come before the House by being *brought from the Lords*, by being *brought in upon a resolution* (the Finance Bill is founded upon the resolutions agreed by the House to give effect to the Chancellor's Budget proposals) or when an MP gets *leave to bring in a ten-minute rule bill.*

Second reading

This is the first time the bill itself is debated, and it is a discussion of the principle of the bill rather than the details of individual clauses. In the Commons, it is considered good practice for second reading to be held at least two weekends after the bill's introduction (although, if the bill has not been seen before in draft, even this does not give much time to assess it). The government does not always comply with the 'two weekends' convention; neither, less importantly, do backbenchers with private members' bills. In the Lords, the requirements are more formal.

A second reading debate on a major government bill will normally take a day (in practice, about six hours; on a Wednesday, for example, from about 1.00 pm to 7.00 pm). Less important bills will get less time, and wholly uncontroversial measures (including some private members' bills) can receive their second reading 'on the nod' – that is, without any debate at all. It is also possible – but very unusual – for uncontroversial bills to be referred either to a *second reading committee* 'upstairs'. Second reading committees are also used for bills prepared by the Law Commissions; but these are usually technical reworkings of the law and will normally have started in the Lords and have been considered by a select committee there.

Some major bills have, in the past, had lengthy second reading debates on the floor of the House. In 1972, the bill to enable the United Kingdom to join the then EEC was debated over three days on second reading, and the 1976 bill on Scottish and Welsh devolution (which eventually failed) was debated for 32 hours over four sitting days. In 2017 the European Union (Notification of Withdrawal) Bill and the European Union (Withdrawal) Bill each had a two-day second reading debate.

A second reading debate on a government bill takes place on a motion moved by a minister 'That the bill be now read a second time'. At the end of this debate, on bills that are opposed, a vote is taken. This can be a straight vote against second reading, or a vote on what is known as a 'reasoned amendment' (if it has been selected by the Speaker). This spells out the reasons why the bill's opponents do not wish it to have a second reading. If the reasoned amendment is carried, or the House votes against second reading, the bill can go no further – neither can exactly the same bill be reintroduced in the same session. It is extremely rare for a government bill to be defeated on second reading; the last example was in 1986, when the Shops Bill, which had been intended to relax the law on Sunday trading, was passed by the Lords but defeated in the Commons by a majority of 14. However, as we saw in Chapter 4, voting against the second reading of a controversial bill may be a powerful way for government backbenchers to register dissent.

These days, the second reading of a bill will normally be followed immediately by a *programme motion*, which is decided without debate (although sometimes with a vote), followed if necessary by a motion to authorise government expenditure in relation to the bill (a *money resolution*), or the raising of a tax or charge (a *ways and means resolution*). These also give the committee on the bill authority to consider provisions that would require expenditure or impose a tax.

'Fast-track' bills

Certain types of bill are dealt with on a 'fast-track' procedure. *Consolidation bills* are prepared by the Law Commissions as a sort of housekeeping of the statute book. These bills draw together the law on a particular subject, which may be in a series of Acts of Parliament, and present it in a more logical and user-friendly way. *Statute law repeal bills* remove parts of the law that have become redundant. Bills of both sorts are checked by a joint committee of both Houses to ensure that no change of substance has been made in the process of restating the law, and that no 'live' legislation is to be repealed. If no amendments are put down, such bills are passed without debate. *Supply and Appropriation Bills*, which authorise government spending, have no committee or report stage; the questions on second and third reading are put successively without debate.

'Fast tracking' of these bills is uncontroversial. Occasionally a government will want to expedite the passage of other bills – usually in response to an event or to meet an external deadline. The curtailing of parliamentary scrutiny that results can be controversial, so in these cases Parliament will often want to be convinced that a 'fast track' procedure is necessary.

Committee

As soon as a bill has had its second reading, it is sent to a committee for a detailed examination of the text. The choices are *public bill committee*, *Committee of the whole House* or *select committee*. The Finance Bill is routinely divided between Committee of the whole House for its most important provisions and a public bill committee for the rest ('split committal'), and other bills are occasionally treated in the same way. As public bill committees are the default setting – if no other decision is taken, a bill goes automatically to a public bill committee – we start with this method of consideration.

Public bill committees

A public bill committee (formerly known as a standing committee) is established for each bill. New members, and a new chair or chairs, are appointed to each public bill committee specifically; and, when the committee has reported the bill back to the

Picture of a public bill committee room

Source: Copyright UK Parliament, 2012. Photography by Jessica Taylor

House, it is dissolved. Public bill committees are empowered to receive oral and written evidence, in addition to line-by-line consideration. For the 31 bills considered in public bill committee in the 2016–17 session, there were 123 consideration sittings, 22 oral evidence sessions and 428 written submissions. Government bills starting in the Lords do not have an oral evidence-taking stage, although this is purely government practice rather than a procedural restriction.

Membership

A public bill committee must have between 16 and 50 members but, in practice, the membership is usually between 16 and 30. Its members are chosen by the Selection Committee, which includes whips of the three main parties. Membership of a public bill committee reflects the party proportions in the House; however, a government motion agreed by the House in September 2017 said that for committees with an odd number of members, the government should have a majority (with an equal split for even-numbered committees). Opposition MPs opposed the move, arguing that when there were minority governments in the 1970s those governments accepted that there should be no entitlement to a majority on committees. The government's position was that it would be unable to achieve its legislative programme as set out in the Queen's Speech without a majority in public bill committees, and its motion was agreed. Since the introduction of the English Votes for English Laws (EVEL) provisions, only MPs representing

English constituencies may serve on public bill committees considering bills which effect England alone. Where there is a free vote on second reading (as on the Marriage (Same Sex Couples) Bill in the 2012–13 session), the membership reflects the numbers of supporters and opponents in the House on the second reading vote. The Selection Committee appoints members directly to a public bill committee; the names do not have to be approved by the House, unlike the membership of select committees.

At least one government minister will always be a member of a public bill committee (including public bill committees on private members' bills), together with a government whip, and frontbenchers from the other parties. The backbenchers are a combination of those who are interested in the subject (and who spoke in the second reading debate) and those who are drafted in by the whips but are ready loyally to support their party's line on the subject. Obviously, the strength of the second group becomes more important when very contentious legislation is being considered, but the Selection Committee has generally appointed a spread of MPs, so that dissent within a party is represented as well.

The Law Officers (Attorney General, Advocate General and Solicitor-General) may, if they are members of the Commons, attend a public bill committee and speak (but not vote), although this is in practice very rare. Any minister may do the same in the committee on the Finance Bill but, in practice, this is handled by Treasury ministers. Other MPs not appointed to a committee on a bill may not take part in its proceedings (although they may table amendments – see page 198).

The Chair

Each public bill committee is chaired by a member of the Panel of Chairs. The Panel is a group of 30–40 senior MPs chosen by the Speaker to chair public bill and other general committees. It also includes the Deputy Speakers (and is itself chaired by the Chairman of Ways and Means), thus connecting the business of chairmanship in the House with that of public bill and general committees. The Panel meets from time to time as a committee to consider wider issues affecting general and public bill committees, and also matters relating to Westminster Hall. Public bill committee chairs are paid a salary of £15,509, the same as select committee chairs.

If a public bill committee is taking a big bill, there will normally be two or more chairs sharing the duties. The chair has most of the powers to control proceedings that the Speaker has in the House, including power to select amendments (see page 199), but not including the disciplinary powers listed on page 52. As in the House, he or she does not vote unless there is a tie, and then strictly according to precedent (see page 55). By convention, an MP who has chaired the public bill committee does not take part, or vote, in the bill's subsequent stages on the floor of the House.

Meetings

For any initial oral evidence sessions, public bill committees meet in a select committee room, with the typical horseshoe arrangement. When they proceed to the line-by-line consideration stage, they move to rooms laid out in very much the same way as the chamber, with the two sides facing each other across the floor. The chair sits on the dais at one end, with the clerk on his or her left (see the plan on page 200).

Meetings of public bill committees are open to the public and, as in the House, debates are webcast and recorded verbatim by *The Official Report* (*Hansard*) and published on the parliamentary website. Public bill committees may meet on any day on which the House sits, but committees on government bills normally meet on Tuesdays from 9.25 am to 11.25 am, resuming at 2.00 pm, and on Thursdays from 11.30 am to 1.00 pm, resuming at 2.00 pm. Depending on how keen the government is to make progress with the bill, and how contentious it is, the committee may then go into the evening.

The normal first business of a public bill committee is to consider the resolution of the *programming sub-committee* (the chair of the committee and seven members), which makes proposals about the witnesses who will be giving oral evidence and, sometimes, the time to be allotted to the various parts of the bill and the order in which parts of the bill are to be taken.

Amendments, selection and grouping

Once any oral evidence sessions have been concluded, the committee deals with the clauses of the bill one by one. Any MP may put down an amendment to a bill in public bill committee (or an entire new clause or schedule), but only a member of the committee may actually move it. MPs may supply brief factual explanatory notes for publication with their amendments (and this may also be done at report stage).

Amendments can serve a variety of purposes. If the bill is highly contentious in party political terms, many amendments will be pegs for debate to give publicity to government and opposition viewpoints – although this is more the case in Committee of the whole House (see page 205) as public bill committees get little media coverage. So-called 'probing amendments' are used to get the minister to clarify provisions of the bill and outline the thinking behind them. However, it is extremely unlikely that the opposition will table an amendment, convince the government of its merits and have it agreed to.

The chair of a public bill committee, like the Speaker in the House or the Chairman of Ways and Means in Committee of the whole House, has the power of *selection and grouping*. This is crucial in allowing an orderly and logical debate on amendments, and it prevents the proceedings of the committee being clogged up by hosts of amendments being tabled for their own sake.

Amendments are tabled on the days before the committee first meets (usually by the opposition parties and possibly government backbenchers but the government may even at this stage want to modify its own bill, so amendments may go down in the name of the minister in charge of the bill). The day after they are tabled, amendments will appear on blue paper in the Vote bundle (see page 158); but, on the day the committee first meets, it will have before it a *marshalled list*, printed on white paper, of all the amendments that have been put down up to and including the previous day. This list of amendments is the committee's Order Paper.

The marshalled list sets amendments down by reference to where they apply to the bill. As each amendment is tabled, it is given its own unique reference number, so the numbering will jump about: for example, if the very first amendment tabled was to the last schedule, it will still be 1; and if, after 500 amendments have been tabled, an amendment is put down to the first line of the bill, it will be 501.

The process of selection and grouping, in which the chair is advised by the clerk of the committee, begins with weeding out amendments that are *out of order*. Disorderly amendments include those that are irrelevant or outside the scope of the bill (or of the clause to which they are tabled); inconsistent with a decision that the committee has already taken (or that the House has taken in approving second reading – so-called 'wrecking' amendments); ineffective or incomplete; tabled to the wrong place in the bill, or to a part of the bill that the committee has already considered; 'vague, trifling or tendered in a spirit of mockery'; or that would impose charges outside the scope of any money or ways and means resolutions agreed to by the House. These rules are sometimes complex in their application, but they are a common-sense way of clearing out amendments that are irrelevant or ineffective (although an MP whose pet amendment is ruled out of order may not always see it in that way).

Then begins the process of *selecting* from among the remaining amendments those that will be debated. Selection in public bill committee is fairly generous (at report stage, it is less so), and unless an amendment is fairly trivial, or one of a multiplicity on the same point, it is likely to be selected. Amendments proposed by the member in charge of a bill, whether a minister or a private member, are normally selected automatically provided they are in order. An amendment that has been tabled the previous day or the day before that, rather than the minimum three days in advance, will usually not be selected, although the chair has power even to select a 'manuscript' amendment put forward within the previous few minutes if the circumstances warrant it.

At the same time, the chair and clerk will be looking for themes that will help to *group* amendments. Grouped amendments are debated together. There are three main ways of deciding on groupings: the first is to group amendments that offer *alternative proposals on the same point*. An example might be where the bill proposes that a search can be authorised by any police officer. The opposition think that this is not stringent enough and so have put down an amendment that would require the authorising officer to be of the rank of inspector. Backbenchers on the committee (on both sides) would prefer to go further, and amendments are down variously specifying a superintendent, a magistrate and a High Court judge. If the 'inspector' amendment were selected on its own, the debate would take place only on the issue of whether the minimum authority should be constable or inspector. Separate debates would have to take place on the other proposals – and if the 'inspector' amendment were to be agreed to, then that would rule out debate on any alternative as being inconsistent with the decision the committee had reached. So all the amendments about the level of authorisation are grouped.

The second method is to group *interdependent amendments*. An example here might be where the opposition has an amendment early in the bill to appoint a statutory investigator of complaints. It has a raft of other amendments throughout the bill

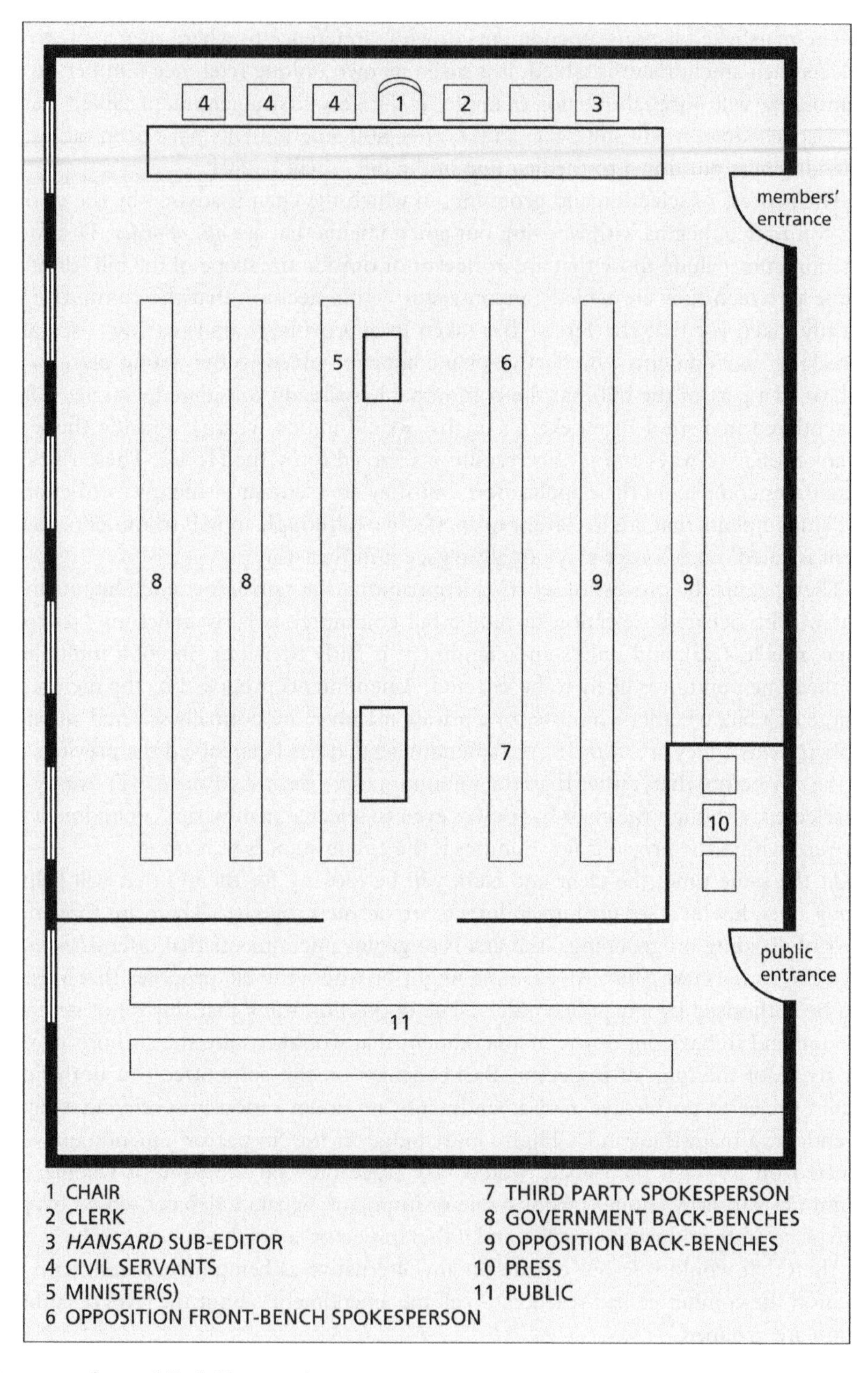

Layout of a public bill committee room

Source: Copyright House of Commons, 2014

that specify how different types of case will come to this investigator. If the principle of appointing an investigator is defeated early on, all the later amendments will fall, so it is sensible to debate them together.

The third method is to group *amendments on a theme*. For example, there might be a number of amendments designed to require the secretary of state to make a regulatory impact assessment before using any of a number of powers that the bill would confer. Grouping these together allows a debate on the principle of requiring such an assessment. If the amendments were not so grouped, the result would be a series of very similar debates as the committee got to each of the clauses that would give the secretary of state each of those powers.

The result of this is a *selection list*, a new edition of which appears for each sitting day. The chair gives no reasons for his or her decisions on selection, and there is no appeal to the Speaker. Two examples of selection lists appear on pages 202 to 204: one for the first day of a public bill committee's consideration of a bill; and one for part of the report stage of a bill in the House. Both of the proceedings were programmed.

How the committee goes through the bill

Once the recommendations of the programming sub-committee have been considered and any oral evidence sessions have been held, the committee begins with the first clause of the bill. Let us suppose that the first amendment in the first group – *the lead amendment* in that group – is to clause 1. That amendment is moved, and the debate on the question 'That the amendment be made' then includes debate on any other amendment (or new clause) that is grouped with it. At the end of the debate the question is decided, on a vote if necessary: after a short interval, the doors of the committee room are locked, the clerk rises and reads out the names of members of the committee. MPs say 'Aye' or 'No' or 'No vote'; the clerk totals the votes and hands the list to the chair. He or she declares the result, says 'unlock' and moves on to the next question to be decided. As in the chamber, the Chair gets a vote only in the case of a tied vote; and must use his or her casting vote in line with firmly established precedent.

If a second group has its lead amendment to clause 1, that group will be dealt with in the same way. But if not, the chair proposes the question 'That clause 1 stand part of the bill'. This gives the opportunity of a 'stand part debate' on the clause as a whole. If debate on a number of amendments to a clause has covered the ground, the chair can decide to put the question on clause stand part without further debate.

An important feature of this way of going through a bill – and one that often causes confusion – is that the *amendments are decided not in the order in which they are grouped for debate but in the order in which they apply to the bill.* This can mean that an amendment to a clause near the end of the bill may be debated with the first group at the first sitting; but it will be put to the vote only when the committee gets to that clause, which may be after many hours of consideration. If amendments have already been debated (unless they are in the name of the member in charge of the bill), they are often passed over in silence when they are reached. But if the opposition or a backbencher wants a vote – a separate division – and the chair agrees, a vote on a specific amendment may take place, but without further debate. Government amendments that are reached in this way are called formally whether or not a vote is expected; the minister says 'I beg to move' and the question on the amendment is put to the committee.

25 OCTOBER 2016

DIGITAL ECONOMY BILL

Chairs' provisional selection and grouping of amendments

Clause 26

92 + 93 + NC3 + NC33

Clause 27

Clause 28

63 + 189 + 64 + 94

Clause 28 stand part + NC14 + NC17

Clause 29

98 + 100 + 99 + 96 + 95 + 105

Clause 30

Gov 108

Clause 31

Clause 32

Gov109 to Gov 117 + Gov120 to Gov 128 + Gov 131 to Gov 139 + Gov 154 to Gov 158

Clause 33

101 + 102 + 103 + 104

Clause 34

Clauses 73 to 75

Clause 76

Gov178 to Gov181

Clauses 77 to 81

Clause 82

Gov182 + Gov184 + GovNC29 + GovNC30 + GovNS2 + Gov187

Gov183 + GovNC27 + GovNC28

Clause 83

Gov185 + GovNC26 + Gov186

Clause 84

continued

A typical selection list for a Commons public bill committee considering a bill under a programme order

Source: The House of Commons 2016

Clause 35

Gov118 + Gov 119 + Gov 129 + Gov 140 + Gov161 + Gov188
106

Clause 36

Clause 37

Clause 38

107 + 97

Clauses 39 to 44

Clause 45

Gov130 + Gov141

Clauses 46 to 55

Clause 56

Gov142 to Gov153 + Gov159 + Gov160 + Gov162 to Gov170

Clauses 57 to 66

Clause 67

Gov171 to Gov176

Clauses 68 to 71

Clause 72

Gov177

New Clauses

NC1 + NC20

NC5

NC13

NC15

NC16

NC19

NC21

NC22

NC23 + NC24

NC31

NC32

New Schedules

Remaining proceedings

Proceedings to be concluded by 11.25 am on

Tuesday 1 November

Chairs: Mr Gary Streeter and Graham Stringer

24 October 2016

DIGITAL ECONOMY BILL

MONDAY 28 NOVEMBER 2016

Consideration on Report

The Speaker's provisional selection of amendments (revised)

[Assumes agreement of the Programme (No.3) Motion]

Safety responsibilities of internet websites and access to broadband and network services

GovNC28 + GovNC29 + NC1 + NC3 + NC10 + NC13 + NC32 + 27 + 28 + 29 + 30 + 2 + 31 + Gov35 + Gov 36 + 32 + 1 + 33 + Gov37 + 34 + Gov38 to Gov42 + NC7 + NC14 + NC20 + NC21 + NC22 + NC25 + NC26 + NC27 + Gov23 + Gov 24
[Two hours after the commencement of proceedings on the Programme (No. 3 Motion)

Television and on-demand services, copyright infringement, digital government, and illicit online trade
NC6 + NC8 + NC17 + NC18 + NC24 + NC33 + NC34 + Gov20 to Gov22 + NC15 + NC16 + NC30 + NC31 + NC5 + NC11 + NC12 + NC19 + NC23 + 3 + Gov4 to Gov 11 + 25 + 26 + Gov12 to Gov 19
[9.00 pm]

---

28 November 2016 By order of the Speaker

A typical selection list for the report stage of a bill in the House of Commons under a programme order

Source: The House of Commons 2016

If no lead amendment is down to any clause, the committee must nevertheless agree whether or not the clause should stand part of the bill. When the committee has got to the end of the bill, any new clauses and new schedules (and any amendments to them) are decided on (and debated, if they have not been grouped with earlier amendments).

When the committee has completed its consideration of a bill, the formal report of the bill appears in the Votes and Proceedings for that day, and the bill – if it has been amended – is reprinted for the *report stage* (see page 207). The process of going through the bill may have taken only a few minutes at a single sitting, or it may have taken 100 hours of often fierce debate over 20 or 30 sittings in the space of several weeks.

Scrutiny by debate and amendment: how useful is it?

Richard Crossman, Labour Leader of the House in the 1960s, wrote 'The whole procedure of standing committees [the old name for public bill committees] is insane . . . under the present system there is no genuine committee work, just formal speech-making, mostly from written briefs'. Consideration in what are now public bill committees occupies a great deal of time: in session 2016–17, public bill committees held a total of 123 sittings, and it is reasonable to ask how good a use of the time of the MPs involved this was, and how effectively the legislation was scrutinised.

Unlike select committees, public bill committees have no research or staff resources of their own (the main concern of the clerk of a public bill committee is the conduct of the proceedings, not the merits of the bill – though, alongside departmental select committee staff and the Scrutiny Unit, they prepare a brief for oral evidence sessions). Other than this, MPs have to rely on input from outside pressure groups (which naturally often advocate for a particular point of view) and their researchers. However, the minister taking a bill through public bill committee has the support of the 'bill team' of civil servants, and behind them the substantial resources of his or her own department.

It is rare for the government to accept opposition (or individual backbench) amendments in public bill committee, although a 2013 study by the Constitution Unit concluded that many ideas raised at this stage go on to be debated at later stages in both Commons and Lords, and often result in government concessionary amendments. But however attractive measured, non-partisan scrutiny may be, one should not lose sight of the role of the Commons as a place where political ideologies clash and where deep divisions between parties (often reflecting different views in the country at large) are played out in an adversarial way.

Committees of the whole House

At one time almost all bills were considered in Committee of the whole House. As its name suggests, it consists of all MPs (although generally only a relatively small proportion will be present during its proceedings) and takes place in the chamber during part of a normal sitting of the House. The only evident differences are that it is presided over by the Chairman of Ways and Means and his deputies and not by the Speaker, that the Chairman sits not in the upper Chair but at the Table in the place of the Clerk of the House (who is absent when the House is in Committee), alongside the Clerk at the Table, and that the Mace is placed on brackets below the Table rather than on it. Votes are taken in the same way as in the House.

The manner of going through a bill is similar to that in public bill committee; and, as in committee, an MP may speak more than once in any debate. Selection and grouping of amendments is the responsibility of the Chairman of Ways and Means.

In recent years Committees of the whole House have been confined to three types of bill. For convenience, *uncontroversial bills* (for which there would be no point in setting up a separate sitting of a public bill committee) are considered in this way to save time, for example, the Telecommunications Infrastructure (Relief from Non-Domestic Rates) Bill 2017–18. Also taken in Committee of the whole House are *bills of great urgency* that need to become law quickly, such as, in November 2017, the Northern

Ireland Budget Bill, to authorise expenditure in Northern Ireland in the continuing absence of an executive there.

The third category is of major *bills of first-class constitutional importance*. Since 1945, governments have been committed to having such bills dealt with in this way, but there is no formal definition, and whether a bill does or does not fall into this category can be a matter of political argument. Legislation to incorporate EU treaties into domestic law, to devolve powers to Scotland and Wales, or to reform the House of Lords clearly qualify. In the 2016–17 session five bills were taken in Committee of the whole House: the European Union (Notification of Withdrawal) Bill, the Northern Ireland (Ministerial Appointments and Regional Rates) Bill, the Wales Bill and two Finance Bills. In session 2017–19 the European Union (Withdrawal) Bill was programmed for eight days' debate in Committee of the whole House.

It may thus be a matter of argument (or negotiation) as to what measures are treated in this way. The opposition will want time on the floor of the House and the higher profile of Committee of the whole House, but the government business managers will generally be reluctant, not only to take floor time on a bill they feel could be dealt with in public bill committee, but also to have the burden of votes taking place in a forum of 650 MPs when they would otherwise take place in a committee of 20 members upstairs. And, historically, Committees of the whole House have presented problems for government business managers: the Parliament (No. 2) Bill to reform the House of Lords was considered for 12 days before it was dropped in 1968; and devolution to Scotland and Wales took up 34 days in Committee of the whole House in the 1976–77 and 1977–78 sessions. Nowadays, the prospect of being able to programme proceedings and so make them much more predictable and controllable may make government business managers slightly less reluctant to take committee stages on the floor of the House. However, this programming function did not prevent the government being defeated on an amendment moved by one of its backbenchers, supported by the official opposition, to require an Act of Parliament to approve the final terms of the Brexit deal.

Select committees

We considered earlier the advantages of scrutinising *draft* legislation in a select committee. A bill that is on its *formal* passage through the House may be committed to a select committee after second reading, although this is rare. The main example is the bill every five years to renew disciplinary law for the armed forces, which is considered by the Defence Committee (most recently in 2015–16).

More frequently, it happens that a select committee seizes the moment and conducts a swift inquiry into a bill (without the bill having been formally committed to it) and reports in time to influence later proceedings upon it, as when in 2014 the Political and Constitutional Reform Committee reported on the Transparency of Lobbying, Non-Party Campaigning and Trade Union Administration Bill twice during its passage through the Commons, the second report being produced in time for Commons consideration of the Lords Amendments to the Bill. However, if the bill has not been formally referred to a select committee by the House, the committee cannot make amendments to it.

Report stage

Except for bills that are considered in Committee of the whole House *and* are not amended there, all bills come back to the floor of the Commons for their *report stage*, properly called *consideration*. The bill returns in the form in which it left committee, and report stage is a further opportunity for amendments to be made. The important difference is that all MPs have an opportunity to speak to amendments on report.

Few bills will have more than two days on report – since 2010 only the Finance (No. 3) Bill and the Legal Aid, Sentencing and Punishment of Offenders Bill were given three days (both in session 2010–12), and only three bills were given that amount of time in all the sessions between 2001–02 and 2009–10. Report stages of government bills in session 2016–17 occupied about 6 per cent of the total time on the floor of the House.

New clauses and amendments for debate on report are selected by the Speaker using the same principles as in public bill committee. However, selection is a little tougher than in committee; the Speaker is unlikely to select amendments on a topic that has been fully aired in committee, unless the government indicated in committee that it was prepared to think again. Even so, major matters of public policy that were debated in committee may reappear, on the grounds that the House as a whole, rather than a small group of MPs, should have the opportunity of expressing a view.

Procedure on report is somewhat different from Committee of the whole House. The Speaker (or one of the deputies) is in the Chair, and the Mace is on the Table. New clauses and schedules are normally taken first (although, as in committee, the minister may propose a particular order in which proceedings should be taken). The House is now revising the bill as a whole rather than going through it clause by clause, so there is no 'clause stand part'.

Legislative grand committee and reconsideration

If the bill, or parts of it, apply to England only (or England and Wales; or England, Wales and Northern Ireland, in the case of Finance bills), it is at this point that a legislative grand committee would consider the bill; and (although to date this has been only a theoretical consideration) reconsideration and consequential consideration stages could be held (see description of EVEL procedures on pages 209 to 211).

Third reading

When all the selected amendments at report stage have been disposed of (or when the time allotted to report stage under the programme order has expired), and any EVEL-related stages have been completed, the House moves on to the third reading (usually at the same sitting). If there are no amendments on report, that stage is omitted and the third reading is taken immediately.

Third reading is the final review of the contents of the bill. Debate is limited to what is actually in the bill rather than, as at second reading, what might have been included. Except on highly controversial bills, where the opposition has the opportunity to fire some last shots, third reading debates tend to be quietly valedictory affairs in which those most closely involved (frontbenchers and other MPs who were on the public bill committee) look back rather sentimentally on the bill's progress through the House. Since the introduction of programming, however, the opposition frontbench has often taken the opportunity to express hopes that the House of Lords will deal in more detail with this or that provision that they feel has had inadequate scrutiny in the Commons.

The procedure is akin to second reading: a minister will move 'That the bill be now read the third time', and a debate takes place on that question. As at second reading, it is possible to move a reasoned amendment (if selected by the Speaker), but this is very rare. As programme orders normally allow no more than one hour for third reading debates, these occupy relatively little time on the floor of the House – under 1 per cent of the total in 2016–17.

Once the third reading has been agreed to, the bill has been passed by the Commons. One of the clerks at the Table then 'walks' the bill to the Lords. The doorkeepers shout 'Message to the Lords', the doors are thrown open, and the clerk proceeds in stately fashion through the Members' Lobby, the Central Lobby and eventually to the Bar of the House of Lords. There, the bill – tied up in Commons green ribbon (known as 'ferret', from *fioretti*, a sixteenth-century Italian name for a kind of silk) – is handed over to one of the Lords clerks.

This may seem a somewhat archaic way of taking a bill from one House to the other, but bill text is compiled and amended using highly sophisticated software and, at the same time, an electronic version of the bill text has gone from the Public Bill Office in the Commons to its counterpart in the Lords. It can happen, though, that near the end of a session, with the 'ping-pong' of amendments between the Houses, the exact moment of a bill's formal arrival is of some importance. Handing it over in the chamber makes this publicly evident in a way that its electronic appearance in a distant office does not.

English Votes for English Laws

In October 2015 the Commons changed its standing orders to give effect to the government's proposals for English Votes for English Laws (EVEL). This was the government's attempt to resolve the asymmetrical quandary posed by devolution, by ensuring that where a proposal affects England only (or England and Wales only; or England, Wales and Northern Ireland in the case of Finance Bills) then the proposal may be agreed only if a majority of MPs representing the constituencies concerned have approved it. In the government's words, the changes 'give English MPs, and in some cases English and Welsh MPs, a power of veto to prevent any measure from being imposed on their constituents against their wishes. No law affecting England alone will be able to be passed without the consent of English MPs'. The process applies to government bills (other than those which relate exclusively to Scotland, Wales or Northern Ireland, or certain types of technical bills, such as consolidation bills), individual parts of such bills, amendments to government bills, as well as secondary legislation. It does not apply to private members' bills.

The procedure requires the Speaker to certify whether a bill is to be subject to the EVEL procedure. In the case of bills, he does this before second reading and again after any stage at which the bill is amended. He may certify that all of the bill, or certain parts of it, should be subject to the procedure. The criteria for certification is that a provision (or the bill as a whole) applies only to England (and Wales), and is within devolved legislative competence in Scotland and Northern Ireland (and Wales for England-only provisions), and that any spill-over effect on the devolved nations would be 'minor and consequential'. A provision is within devolved legislative competence if the same provision could be made by the relevant devolved legislature: the Scottish Parliament, the National Assembly for Wales or the Northern Ireland Assembly. In the case of the very first bill certified, the Speaker's certificate said:

> *The Speaker has certified, in respect of the Housing and Planning Bill, that Clauses 1 to 58, 60 to 70, 72 to 76, 78 to 84, 86 to 88 and 92 to 110 and Schedules 1 to 4 and 6 relate exclusively to England and are within devolved legislative competence; and that Clauses 59, 71, 85, 90, 91, 111 to 139 and Schedules 5 and 7 to 11 relate exclusively to England and Wales and are within devolved legislative competence (Standing Order No. 83J).*
>
> (Source: Votes and Proceedings, 28 October 2015)

Both certified and non-certified bills are considered by the House in same way at second reading. Thereafter, additional procedures apply if the bill (or parts of it) are certified: these are set out in the box below.

Procedures for bills certified as relating to England/ England and Wales only

Committee stage

Bills certified as applying to England only are committed to a public bill committee or the legislative grand committee (England) (the EVEL-equivalent of the Committee of the whole House). Public bill committees nominated to consider such a bill are made up of MPs for English constituencies only. The Legislative Grand Committee (England) comprises MPs for English constituencies only. This applies only to bills which are certified as applying to England only in their entirety.

All other certified bills, or bills containing certified provisions, are committed to a public bill committee to which any MP may be nominated, or to a Committee of the whole House. In committee these certified bills or parts of bills are given no special treatment.

Consideration on report

As with non-certified bills, certified bills are considered by the whole House at report stage.

After report stage, however, the Speaker reviews any changes made to a bill since second reading. If no part of the bill when originally certified before second reading remains, or if nothing added since falls to be certified, the bill proceeds directly to third reading.

If any of the original provisions of the bill, or any changes made to the bill since second reading, are certified by the Speaker as relating exclusively to England, or to England and Wales, and within devolved legislative competence, the bill is considered by a legislative grand committee.

Legislative grand committee

There are three types of legislative grand committee: England, Wales and Northern Ireland; England and Wales; and England only. The membership of each comprises those MPs representing constituencies in the relevant part of the UK only. Legislative grand committees meet in the chamber and MPs who are not members of them may speak but not vote nor move motions or amendments. The legislative grand committee's job is to consent – or not – to those parts of the bill certified as relating to the relevant area. It does so by considering a consent motion, which may be moved only by a minister. Such a motion can propose giving consent to certain parts of the bill and withholding consent from other parts. In either instance it does so by putting all the propositions together in one motion. If a bill is certified in relation to more than one of the geographical categories, debate on a consent motion takes place in the larger of the grand committees concerned, and any votes are taken without debate in the smaller committees.

If the legislative grand committee consents to a bill, then the bill proceeds to third reading.

Reconsideration, veto and consequential consideration

If the legislative grand committee does not consent to a bill, or any part of a bill, there can be no third reading and the bill goes to a reconsideration stage by the House. The purpose of this stage is to resolve any disputed matters of consent, where the legislative grand committee has reached a different view to that of the

House: the Speaker will select only amendments aimed at that effect. He then examines any amendments made to the bill and certifies them. The bill goes back to legislative grand committee, where a consent motion is again proposed. If the motion is agreed to, and all provisions are consented to, the bill moves to third reading. If at this reconsideration stage the legislative grand committee withholds consent from a whole bill, the bill may not proceed. If consent is withheld from any particular parts of the bill, then the bill is amended to remove those parts and may move to third reading.

If removing the disputed parts of a bill at reconsideration stage means that 'minor or technical changes' are required to make sense of the bill, a minister may move that the House consider the amended bill again in an additional 'consequential consideration' stage. This gives the House an opportunity to make those minor or technical changes only. Following completion of this stage the bill moves to third reading. Third reading is then undertaken by the whole House, as with non-certified bills.

Lords amendments and Lords messages

If the Lords amend a bill, the Speaker considers the amendments made and certifies them if they would result in adding or leaving out parts of the bill applying only to England and/or England and Wales. He would also do so if the amendments would cause a previously certified provision to no longer be so, or if they would make part of the bill eligible to be certified in relation to a different territorial extent. Motions on certified Lords amendments need to be supported by a double majority in the House: that is, a majority of all MPs voting and a majority of MPs representing constituencies in England and/or England and Wales.

The new EVEL provisions make an already complicated procedure yet more convoluted. However, in practice the more complex aspects of the procedure have not yet been tested and the impact on the House's operation has not been significant. By December 2016, when the procedures had been in place for just over a year, they had been used on seven bills starting in the Commons and five starting in the Lords. Legislative grand committees met to give consent to the certified provisions of 10 bills, with the total time taken in all legislative grand committees just 1 hour and 23 minutes. Only five MPs other than ministers spoke in those proceedings and on each occasion the motion moved by the minister to consent to certified provisions in the bills was agreed to without a vote. Therefore, the provisions for reconsideration and consequential consideration were not used. Thirty Lords amendments were certified, leading to nine 'double majority' votes, in each of which the majority of members representing constituencies in England, or England and Wales, have agreed with the majority of all members.

The EVEL provisions remain controversial, with SNP MPs in particular highly critical of the arrangements. A review by the Procedure Committee – which called for the procedures to be made more comprehensible and accessible – said that 'EVEL procedures do not command the respect and support across all parties that they should if the system is to be sustainable through the political stresses it must expect to face in the future'. However, in its own review of the new arrangements published in March 2017, the government said that the EVEL provisions were necessary and effective and that the standing orders giving them effect had worked well. It did not propose to change the arrangements and so it is likely that the EVEL provisions will remain in place for the foreseeable future, regardless of the extent to which they are actually used.

Private members' bills

Before we move to the other end of the building to see how the House of Lords considers legislation, let us look at a category of legislation that often attracts publicity even though many more bills in this category fail than ever find their way onto the statute book: private members' bills.

These are not private bills but public bills that aim to change the general law of the land. They are introduced in one of four ways: the first private members' bills in each session appear following the *private members' bill ballot*; then there are *presentation bills* (described on page 193), sometimes called 'back of the Chair bills'; when leave is given under the ten-minute rule; and private peers' bills that have been passed by the House of Lords may be *brought from the Lords* and *taken up* by a private member in the Commons.

Ballot bills

Ballot bills are introduced in the same way as presentation bills, but an MP gets the right to introduce such a bill through success in the ballot, a sort of legislative prize draw. On the Tuesday and Wednesday in the second week of each session, MPs sign a book kept in the No Lobby, being allotted a number in the process. On the Thursday at 9.00 am in committee room 10, normally televised live, the Clerk Assistant draws 20 numbers from a despatch box. The Chairman of Ways and Means matches the numbers to the MPs who have signed in and calls out the names (to increase the suspense, they are announced in reverse order, so the 20th number drawn wins the ballot). The 20 MPs get priority in introducing their own bills – but absolutely no guarantee that any of those bills will become law.

Some MPs are enormously keen to win the ballot; others strenuously hope not to be successful, as they know how much sponsoring a private member's bill may interfere with their daily work. However, the reluctant are 'encouraged' by their whips to sign in, as the whips would prefer to see their own people successful rather than the other side. In most sessions, 400 MPs will enter the ballot. Those whose names are drawn – especially those in the first seven places – are immediately mobbed in person, and by telephone and email by pressure groups who hope to persuade an MP to take on their special cause (and who may happen to have a bill ready for the MP to adopt).

The ballot bills are presented on the fifth Wednesday of the session; and each of the 20 MPs has up to the rising of the House the previous day to decide what sort of bill to introduce. For some, this will be a simple matter; this may at last be the opportunity to introduce legislation for which they have spent much of their parliamentary careers campaigning. For others, there are choices to be made. Should they accept that any bill is unlikely to become law and so produce a sort of manifesto on a subject they think important, hoping that as a bonus they might get a chance to debate it? Or should they temper their ambitions and go for a narrow bill that is likely to be uncontroversial but could make a modest but worthwhile change to the law?

One factor that will help an MP to come to a decision is the extent of outside support likely to be available. A pressure group may be a large and influential body, with resources including lawyers who can help with drafting the bill and people who can write speeches and briefings on hostile amendments. In these circumstances, an MP will feel a little less like David pitted against Goliath.

In a sense, the ultimate pressure group is the government itself. We saw earlier that it can be difficult for a government department to get its bills included in the legislative programme for any session. Persuading a friendly MP (not always from the government party) to take on one of its smaller hoped-for bills can be another route to the statute book. If an MP decides to take on one of these so-called *handout bills*, he or she will act in a similar way to a minister, supported by departmental civil servants; and

Private Members' Bill ballot, 2016

Source: Copyright House of Commons, 2016. Photography by Jessica Taylor

the bill itself will have been drafted by parliamentary counsel. However, the bill will proceed in the same manner as any other private member's bill and will get no special treatment (unless it is one of the very small number of private members' bills to which the government of the day is prepared to give some of its own time; years may pass without this happening).

By the evening before the fifth Wednesday of the session, the MPs successful in the ballot must have given in the short and long titles of their bills (the latter will limit the scope of the bill when drafted), and they will have collected the names of their supporters for the back of the bill. At the commencement of public business (see page 147) the next day, the 20 MPs form a queue at the back of the Speaker's Chair, and as their names are called they come forward and hand their bills to the Clerk, who reads the title. The Speaker says 'Second reading what day?' and the MP names a day.

Tactics and procedure

It is at this point that the tactics essential for success in private members' legislation begin. There are normally seven days for private members' second readings. Obviously, it is best to be the first bill on any day, because that means a full day's debate and the prospect (if 100 MPs can be found to vote for the closure) of getting a second reading and going into committee; and the earlier one can do that, the better. So, if the 20 MPs name the days strictly according to those criteria, the bills will come on like this (the dates of the Fridays below are illustrative):

9 January	16 January	23 January	6 February	20 February	12 March	19 March
1	2	3	4	5	6	7
8	9	10	11	12	13	14
15	16	17	18	19	20	

However, it may be that the sponsor of bill 5 is not too concerned about his or her bill and cannot be in the House on 20 February anyway. So, he or she names 9 January, which leaves a first-place slot open on 20 February. A quick-witted MP with a much lower-placed bill may then be able to get the first slot on 20 February, and a full day's debate. And unless the sponsor of bill 8 has those quick wits, and when it comes to his turn he names 9 January as he had planned, he will find that he is now the third bill on that day and not the second as he had hoped. And once a day is named, there is nothing to be done; a bill can be deferred but not advanced. The picture may be further complicated by MPs guessing that a particular bill will be fairly uncontroversial and may get through quickly, and so putting their bill on for that day rather than the earlier day they could have taken (but when they would have been behind a fiercely contested bill and would have had no chance of getting debating time).

The next step for all the MPs successful in the ballot is to get their bills drafted. They may have the help of an outside body, of parliamentary counsel for a hand-out bill, or the clerks in the Public Bill Office. The drafting does not have to be perfect at this stage. If a bill gets into committee and looks to have a chance of getting further, the government will normally put down amendments so that if the bill is eventually successful it will be in properly drafted and workable form.

For those in the top slots on the second reading days, it will not be enough simply to have a majority of those in the House on the Friday in question. Even a few opponents can 'talk the bill out' by continuing to debate it up to the moment when the Deputy Speaker says 'Order, order' at 2.30 pm. It will be important to muster at least 100 supporters, so that when the closure is claimed by an MP saying 'I beg to move that the Question be now put', it is agreed with at least 100 MPs voting in the majority. (Sometimes the MP in charge of the bill will claim the closure, in order to make sure a decision is taken before the bill is talked out; sometimes a supporter of the second (or subsequent bill) listed for debate will move the closure on the first bill to try to leave some time for debate on their bill.) With most MPs wanting Fridays for constituency work, this may take some silver-tongued persuasion – private members do not have the armoury of the whips at their disposal.

The rule that financial initiative rests with the Crown means that only a minister may bring in a bill whose main purpose is to create a charge. However, if a private member's bill that gets a second reading would incidentally involve an increase in public spending, the government will normally put down a money resolution to authorise such expenditure and to allow the bill to be considered in committee.

As with government bills, the next stage after second reading is public bill committee, where opponents may seek to delay the bill by putting down a great many amendments or – more subtly – may hurry the bill through to report because they can put amendments down at that stage, not to kill this bill but to deny time to the bill that is behind it on report. Not more than one committee on a private member's bill can sit at any one time unless sanctioned by the government.

The next hurdle will be the six 'remaining stages' days. On these Fridays – with Darwinian ruthlessness – the bills are ranked with the most advanced stage first: so, Lords amendments, third readings, report stages, Committee of the whole House (which is an option, although a high-risk one, for the private member) and second readings, in that order. Much the same tactics (and the need for closures) will apply, but at this stage it is much easier for opponents to take up time with amendments rather than on the single question of second reading, and so easier to kill the bill (which may be allowed only one day, because new report stages take precedence over those that have already started). The MP who is successful at this stage and secures third reading will rely on a colleague in the Lords to sponsor the bill there, and he will hope that that House does not amend the bill, as this will produce another chance of 'sudden death' when the Commons considers those Lords amendments. The EVEL procedures do not apply to private members' bills.

When a stage of a private member's bill is on the Order Paper on any of the first twelve private members' days but is not completed (because it is talked out or objected to after 2.30 pm), the member in charge may name one of the later private members' days for continuing with the bill. As the session proceeds, unsuccessful bills are put off from Friday to Friday, until on the thirteenth and last day (widely known as 'the massacre of the innocents') there may be 50 or 60 to be 'called over' at 2.30 pm. Even if an MP is lucky enough to get third reading at this stage, eventual success will depend on the Lords agreeing to the bill without amendment in the relatively short time that then remains in the session.

Presentation, 10-minute rule and Lords private members' bills

Much of what we have said about the procedure and tactics of ballot bills also applies to ordinary presentation bills, to 10-minute rule bills and to bills brought from the Lords. However, all of these have more of a hill to climb, as none may proceed until the ballot bills have been presented (and those will have taken up two or three slots on each of the days devoted to second readings).

Both presentation bills and 10-minute rule bills are thus more often used to make a point than seriously to seek to change the law (although three 10-minute rule bills and two presentation bills have been successful since 2015). Ten-minute rule bills have the additional advantage that an MP has the opportunity to gauge opinion in the House. Beginning in the seventh week of the session, on every Tuesday and Wednesday before the main business of the day, one MP is called to make a speech of not more than ten minutes setting out the case for a bill and seeking the leave of the House to introduce it. Other MPs are alerted to the subject matter by a brief description on the Order Paper. If there is objection to the proposal, one opponent may speak against, again for a maximum of ten minutes; and, if necessary, there is a vote. If the proposer is successful, the bill is introduced in a little ceremony that involves the MP walking from the bar of the House to the Table, bowing three times en route. (In a strange historical survival, the second of those bows, halfway up the chamber, is just at the point where the great chandelier hung in the chamber destroyed by fire in 1834, where MPs presenting a bill would stop and bow two centuries and more ago.)

Ten-minute rule bills are very popular with MPs. They could introduce exactly the same bill by the ordinary presentation method, without seeking the leave of the House. However, 10-minute rule bills come on at prime time immediately after questions and statements, and they are often a high-profile way of floating an idea and getting media attention – and perhaps laying the foundations of a later successful attempt. The right to introduce them is on a first come, first served basis. In the past, an MP would spend the night in a room next to the Public Bill Office in order to be the first to give notice 15 sitting days before the slot came up; but informal arrangements between the parties have, on the whole, ended this 'January sales' tactic.

Success and failure

Even with government backing, the success of a private member's bill is not assured. Against government opposition, failure is virtually certain; and even half a dozen determined backbench opponents can make it exceedingly difficult to get a private member's bill on the statute book.

In recent years, up to ten private members' bills a session have become law; but these figures are skewed by 'hand-out bills' (see page 213) where an MP is, in effect, taking through legislation on behalf of a government department. The numbers of bills passed in the last three complete sessions are shown in Table 6.2.

Table 6.2 Private members' bills dealt with by the House of Commons, 2014–17

Session	2014–15		2015–16		2016–17	
Passed	10	(26)	6	(23)	8	(24)
Not passed	126	(0)	112	(3*)	109	(3**)

Figures for government bills are in brackets.
*Including bills not passed in that session because they were carried over to the next.
** Three government bills were 'lost' because of the early general election

It is difficult to categorise successful backbench legislation. Many are minor pieces of tidying up of the statute book to remove generally recognised anomalies, and a number of these will have been suggested to sympathetic private members by government departments. Other Acts have dealt with small social reforms, particularly in areas affecting the rights of the disabled; marriage, children and the family; gaming and alcohol; care and control of animals; and the environment.

Overall, though, the scope has been very wide. Examples include the British Nationality (Falkland Islands) Act 1983, which gave British nationality to the inhabitants of the islands; the Race Relations (Remedies) Act 1994, giving industrial tribunals new powers in cases of racial discrimination; the Law Reform (Year and a Day Rule) Act 1996, which abolished the old rule of law that a person could not be found guilty of murder if the victim died more than a year and a day after being attacked; the Christmas Day (Trading) Act 2004, which prevented supermarkets and other large stores from opening on Christmas Day; and the Merchant Shipping (Homosexual Conduct) Act 2017, which repealed legislation making homosexuality a disciplinary offence in the merchant navy. Although the scope of these private members' bills may have been relatively small compared with major government bills, they have had important consequences in particular areas.

Some private members' bills have had a much wider application; they have brought about the abolition of the death penalty, the legalisation of abortion and homosexuality, and the end of theatre censorship.

Success can be measured in other terms. Sometimes, the government will take over the intention of a private member's bill and it will appear in a subsequent session as a government bill. In 1994, the then government's embarrassment following its blocking of a private member's bill on disability discrimination led to a government bill being introduced, which became the Disability Discrimination Act 1995. The Wild Mammals (Hunting with Dogs) Bill failed in the 1997–98 session but appeared in the 2000–01 session as the Hunting Bill, was passed by the Commons but overtaken by the dissolution of Parliament in 2001; a similar bill was introduced by the government in 2002–03 but was not passed by the Lords; and in 2004 the Hunting Act, still not passed by the Lords, became law under the Parliament Acts.

It is possible for the government to give a private member's bill government time in the same session that it began as a private member's bill. This was done in the 1950s and 1960s on such subjects as the abolition of the death penalty and the legalisation of abortion, but it is now very unusual – no doubt because of the 'me too' principle; the government would find it hard to pick and choose among worthy bills. In 1976 the Sexual Offences Bill, which provided for anonymity in rape cases, was given government time; so, too, was the Census (Amendment) Bill [*Lords*] in 2002. A slightly different case occurred in 2002, when the Tobacco Advertising and Promotion Bill [*Lords*], a private peer's bill, was taken over as a government bill when it arrived in the Commons. (An identical bill had originally been introduced in the 2000–01 session as a government measure but had been lost at the general election for want of time.) And there are plenty of examples of ideas first proposed in private members' bills which are then taken up in government legislation.

The MP who seeks leave to bring in a 10-minute rule bill rarely expects that his or her bill will get on to the statute book (although three have done so since 2015; before that none were successful since the 2005–06 session); and many bills for which leave is given are never actually printed. The 10-minute rule slot is a way of attracting attention to a subject, gauging opinion and putting it on the future political agenda. In the 2016–17 session, 51 bills were brought in under the 10-minute rule. Only one became law, but the others gave an opportunity to air subjects for possible legislation ranging from a requirement to serve British wines at UK embassies throughout the world to the rights of EU citizens to remain in the UK after Brexit.

Should it be easier?

Private members' bills are fragile vessels. The sponsor of a bill from scratch (rather than a government hand-out) will have to compromise on what is desirable to achieve what is realistic; he or she has to be an astute tactician, must try to ensure that the government is at the least neutral on the proposal, will have to persuade doubters and potential saboteurs, and needs a bit of luck. And even then success is by no means guaranteed.

This process can be frustrating – perhaps never more so than when a bill gets a second reading by a large majority but is then defeated by guerrilla warfare in public bill committee, on report or in the House of Lords. The EU (Referendum) Bill 2013–14 (a private member's bill during the coalition government) is an example; it received a second reading by 304 votes to nil, and was eventually passed by the House of Commons: but it did not become law because it was not passed by the House of Lords.

It may be said that the principle is one thing but the details another, and that scrutinising details is what the committee and report stages are for. And even if the degree of scrutiny – as opposed to obstruction – that a bill gets in those circumstances is open to question, many would argue that protecting the rights of the minority to disagree is especially important in the case of private members' legislation – in contrast to the assumption that a government with a majority will get its bills eventually.

Most proposals for making it easier for private members' bills to pass into law centre on providing more time, although, to make real difference, a substantial amount of time would have to be provided (and in a House that already sits for longer than many other parliamentary chambers).

The Procedure Committee has reported on private members' bills repeatedly, most recently in October 2016, when it reiterated a number of recommendations made in earlier reports, such as:

- Allowing the Backbench Business Committee to nominate up to four private members' bills each session to be given priority on the first four available Fridays, without the need for success in the ballot. This would give a prospect of success for well-drafted bills to become laws, without relying on the vagaries of the ballot.
- Ensuring that each of the bills listed first on the first seven Fridays get voted on, without the need for a closure (requiring at least 100 members to be present).
- Explicitly authorising the Speaker and his deputies to use the powers already available (but never used on private members' Fridays) to apply time limits to speeches).

Despite the committee's depressing prognosis – it argued that only government-backed bills made progress and that it was therefore a pretence 'that there are meaningful opportunities for non-government legislation to be made when that legislation does not have the active support of the government of the day, no matter what the merits are of the legislation proposed or the level of cross-party support it has' – the government rejected the committee's substantive proposals and the House has not yet considered them. A predecessor committee considered, but rejected, moving private members' business to an earlier day of the week; for example, a Tuesday, Wednesday or Thursday evening. Another suggestion previously floated was to make some private members' bills subject to a form of programming that would allow them to be voted on at all their stages and would prevent their simply being 'talked out'.

Opinion is divided, even among MPs themselves. Some believe that taking initiatives to change the law should be a key part of an MP's role, and one in which MPs generally could act more independently of government; others are reluctant to see the amount of legislation already made every year increased, and they take Churchill's view that 'not every happy thought which occurs to a Member of Parliament should necessarily find its way on to the statute book'.

Lords stages

Bills can begin the parliamentary process in either House, and they have to be agreed by both Houses before they can be presented for Royal Assent, unless the Parliament Acts (see page 222) are used. A bill introduced in the Commons, and passed by that House after it has completed the various stages just described, is sent to the Lords. A bill introduced in the Lords will, after going through its stages in that House, be sent to the Commons for similar treatment. Consideration by the two Houses is – unlike the practice in the United States – never simultaneous, although on very rare occasions, when a bill needs to be passed quickly, identical bills are introduced in both Houses. One is later dropped, but the other can then proceed more quickly because its main points have been discussed already by both Houses.

The Lords spend a great deal of their sitting time discussing bills. All stages are normally taken on the floor of the House, despite the development of the grand committee procedure with a view to considering more bills in committee off the floor. Indeed, a greater proportion of time is spent on bills in the chamber in the Lords than in the Commons – around 50 per cent of the total sitting hours as opposed to one-third.

Bills in the Lords go through the same stages as in the Commons – a formal first reading, a substantial debate on second reading, detailed amendments at committee stage and report, and further debate (and, in the Lords only, consideration of amendments) at third reading. There are no EVEL procedures in the Lords. But outward appearances hide substantial differences in style, many of which reflect the more flexible and less constrained procedures that have survived in the Lords long after their demise in the late nineteenth-century House of Commons.

Characteristics of Lords legislative procedure

Lords legislative procedures have some particular characteristics that are quite distinct from those of the House of Commons. First, consideration at committee stage is very different. A bill can, in theory, be committed to five different kinds of committee for consideration but only two are usual – *Committee of the whole House* where most bills are still considered and *Grand Committee*. The Grand Committee was first set up in 1995 following the recommendation of the 1994 Group on Sittings of the House, and in a normal session between six and eight bills will be sent off the floor in this way. The Grand Committee is unselected – any member may attend – and it sits in a specially adapted room near the chamber, the Moses Room. The procedure is exactly the same as in the chamber but, because the committee membership is unselected, amendments may be made only by unanimous agreement; no divisions may take place.

From early and tentative beginnings in the late 1990s, the Grand Committee has evolved into a parallel chamber for many kinds of business in addition to committee stages on bills: motions to consider affirmative or negative statutory instruments, motions to take note of select committee reports, Questions for Short Debate, debates on National Policy Statements, and general motions for debate. In addition, Second Reading debates on Law Commission Bills also now take place in the Moses Room, in an unselected Second Reading Committee different in name only from a Grand Committee. In the 2016–17 session, the Grand Committee sat on 34 days for over 110 hours, equal to about 17 extra sitting days in the chamber. This was, though, a light workload for the Grand Committee; in previous sessions it had sat for more than double the time.

A fourth way for dealing with a committee stage is to commit a bill to a *special public bill committee*. Although in theory any bill could be so committed, in practice the procedure is used exclusively for bills that have been prepared by the Law Commission, implementing normally uncontroversial proposals for law reform emanating from Commission reviews. The committee is selected and may take oral and written evidence on a bill within the first 28 days of its appointment. After a short break, the committee then considers clauses and amendments in the usual way. There is usually one of these bills per session; and they have their second reading off the floor in Second Reading Committee.

Finally, it is possible for a bill to be committed to a *select committee* at any stage between second and third reading, usually after second reading, for consideration of its merits. The committee undertakes detailed investigation of the subject matter and reports on the main provisions, recommending whether the bill should proceed or not and, if so, in what form. If a bill is to proceed, it is recommitted to a Committee of the whole House. The procedure is not used for government bills because of the delay that would be caused and, arguably, because such a bill should not be in need of forensic scrutiny of the policy it enshrines (especially if the bill has been subject to pre-legislative scrutiny). It has been used as a way of considering controversial issues raised by private members' bills, such as the Assisted Dying for the Terminally Ill Bill in 2004. Exceptionally, after the government lost a crucial vote in the House, the Constitutional Reform Bill (a government bill) was committed to a select committee in March 2004. The committee, which included the Lord Chancellor as a member, sat until the end of June, hearing evidence, reporting on the policy of the bill and making amendments. Despite vigorous efforts in the 1990s to move legislative work off the floor, the norm is for the committee stage of bills containing any controversial material to be taken in Committee of the whole House.

A second difference between the Lords and Commons legislative procedures is that there is no selection by the Lord Speaker (or anyone else) of amendments to be discussed. Provided they are relevant to the bill, all the amendments that have been tabled may be considered, even if they have already been discussed at an earlier stage. While this can in some cases lead to a constructive dialogue with ministers – the same points are often made at second reading, committee and report – it also leads to a great deal of repetition of argument. Since the mid-1980s, amendments have been grouped at the initiative of the Government Whips' Office. Groupings are informal and not binding, so every amendment still has to be called and if necessary moved, even if it is unlikely to be further discussed.

Third, there is no guillotine or programme procedure so, in theory, proceedings could be very protracted. Fortunately, filibustering is rare. Most members – and especially the party whips – realise that the excellent opportunities that arise in the Lords to consider all clauses and to take all amendments could not long survive persistent abuse by any one member or any one party. Early in 2011, this longstanding freedom came perilously close to being ended. The Parliamentary Voting Systems and Constituencies Bill (see page 229) took 17 days in committee because of the apparent delaying tactics used by certain opposition members. Parliamentary counsel drafted a timetable motion for the government to use as a last resort. Eventually, it proved unnecessary and the House shied away from the abyss.

Another substantial difference is that, in the Lords, it is possible to move amendments at third reading. The principal purposes of amendments at this stage are to clarify remaining uncertainties, to improve drafting and to enable the government to fulfil undertakings given at earlier stages of the bill. It is not permissible to raise an issue that has been fully debated and decided on at a previous stage. And amendments raising new issues, or amendments similar to ones tabled and withdrawn at an earlier stage, should not be tabled. A general debate may also take place on the motion 'that the bill do now pass', after any amendments have been considered, although this practice is now discouraged.

All government and some private members' bills are considered by the Lords Select Committee on Delegated Powers and Regulatory Reform, which reports to the House whether the provisions of any bill inappropriately delegate legislative powers to ministers using statutory instruments; or whether they subject the use of any delegated powers to insufficient parliamentary scrutiny. All bills are considered – usually on the basis of memoranda supplied by the government – after Lords first reading, and the committee reports quickly so that its findings can, if necessary, be acted on by the House at committee stage. There is no equivalent committee in the House of Commons. All government bills are also scrutinised by the Joint Committee on Human Rights in respect of any human rights issue, and by the Lords Constitution Committee for any constitutional issue. Reports are published by these committees on the issues raised, but the bills themselves are not committed to them and they cannot amend them.

It is worth noting that the government has no formal priority over other peers in introducing or debating legislation. In practice, government business is normally accorded priority, but at the same time – possibly as a quid pro quo – generous provision is made for private members' bills in the Lords. Because there is no limitation on the number of days on which they may be considered, the government has little control on the number of these bills that will actually be considered on the floor of the House. The House now tends to sit on Fridays once a month to consider private members' bills. Since the start of the 2014–15 session, a ballot is held on the day after the State Opening of Parliament to determine the order in which bills handed in on that day will receive a first reading. Although the dates of second reading debates broadly follow that order, it offers no other priority and, of course, it is no guarantee of eventual success. Ultimately, Lords private members' bills rarely cause trouble for the government, because a private member's bill to which the government is opposed and that survives in the Lords can always, if necessary, be blocked in the Commons.

Limitations on Lords powers: ancient practice and the Parliament Acts

Before we consider the impact of the House of Lords on bills, we should note that the Lords do not have free rein in amending certain types of Commons bill. By ancient practice set out in Commons resolutions dating from the late seventeenth century, the

Lords may not amend bills of 'aids and supplies' – a type of bill that includes the annual Finance Bill, which implements the tax proposals made by the Chancellor of the Exchequer in the Budget, and Supply and Appropriation Bills, which sanction government expenditure. Based on this constitutional principle that only the Commons may authorise taxation and spending, any Lords amendment to a bill that has financial implications and that is rejected by the Commons – whether on policy or on financial grounds – will be returned to the Lords with a 'privilege reason': that it offends Commons financial privilege (see page 251). Lords practice is not to insist on such an amendment and, where an amendment in lieu is proposed, it should not be couched in a way that would invite the same response. In fact, the Commons waive their privilege in many cases, particularly in respect of government amendments made in the Lords. Commons financial privilege in respect of Lords amendments is not well-understood and when it has been invoked recently in respect of certain high-profile amendments – for example, to the Welfare Reform Bill in 2012 and to the European Union Referendum Bill in 2015 – some Lords members felt frustrated by the application of these ancient, and fundamental, constitutional principles. They felt that financial privilege has somehow been invoked at the whim of the government, which is not the case. The judgement on whether a Lords amendment has a financial implication is made by the Clerk of Legislation in the Commons, who does so on entirely objective grounds.

If the Lords insist on their amendments to any other public bill in a manner that renders the bill wholly unacceptable to the majority in the Commons and to the point that the bill is lost by the close of the session, or if they reject altogether a bill passed by the Commons, the Parliament Acts 1911 and 1949 may be invoked. These Acts were passed to ensure that important reforming legislation introduced by the Liberal and Labour governments of the time was not frustrated by the then overwhelming Conservative majority in the Lords.

The severest restrictions in the Parliament Acts apply to 'money bills'. These are bills that deal only with certain specified central government finance matters. The most important of them are pure taxation bills or the Supply and Appropriation Bills that formally vote money to the government. These are described in more detail in Chapter 7. (The annual Finance Bill, which implements the budget proposals, is often not certified as a money bill because it contains wider provisions than those defined in the Parliament Acts. This is somewhat paradoxical, since the 1911 Parliament Act was passed as a reaction to the Lords' rejection of the 1909 Finance Bill.) Under the Parliament Acts, money bills passed by the Commons are allowed one month to pass through the Lords. If the Lords do not pass them within a month, they can be sent for Royal Assent without Lords approval. The provisions relating to money bills have never had to be invoked for the purpose of giving Royal Assent. When, through inadvertence or delay caused by a parliamentary recess, a money bill has not been passed within the prescribed timeframe, it has subsequently been speedily passed under normal procedures.

All other public bills passed by the Commons may be delayed for a minimum effective period of 13 months by the Lords. The rule is strictly as follows: any bill that passes the Commons in two successive sessions (whether or not a general election intervenes) can be presented for Royal Assent without the agreement of the Lords, provided that there has been a minimum period of one year between the Commons giving it a second reading for the first time and a third reading for the second time, and provided that the Lords have received the bill at least one month before the end of each of the two sessions. The effect of this is to limit the Lords' power of delay to about 13 months, though it can be longer.

The rigours of these provisions of the Parliament Acts have been taken to their final stage on only four occasions since the 1949 Act (which reduced by one year the delaying time of the 1911 Act) was itself passed without the agreement of the Lords. In 1991, the War Crimes Act received Royal Assent after the bill had been passed by the Commons and rejected by the Lords at second reading in two successive sessions. This bill sought, retrospectively, to create a new criminal offence so as to enable charges to be brought against alleged perpetrators of atrocities, chiefly against Jews, in continental Europe during the Second World War. Many lords felt that such prosecutions would be difficult to secure and that too many legal principles were offended by the proposed legislation. As the bill was not a manifesto commitment by the government, the Lords felt entitled to reject it. In 1998, the European Parliamentary Elections Bill was lost following disagreement over the electoral system proposed. The Lords rejected the reintroduced bill at second reading in the following session, thus enabling Royal Assent to take place in time for the elections to proceed notwithstanding the initial delay. In 2000, Royal Assent was also given under the Parliament Acts to the Sexual Offences (Amendment) Bill, which lowered the age of consent for homosexual activity and buggery to 16. In 2004 the Hunting Bill, which outlawed hunting deer, foxes and hares with hounds, received Royal Assent in the same way.

The Parliament Acts procedures are a fundamental limitation on the legislative power of the Lords. They enable any administration with a majority in the Commons to exert its will and ultimately to pass its legislation without the Lords' agreement. Indeed, when the government introduced proposals to reform the House of Lords in 2012, it based its view of the legislative subordination of the Lords to the Commons in large measure on the continued application of these Acts. But the Parliament Acts operate mostly as a deterrent to the Lords overreaching itself; the infrequency with which they have been used is in part because that involves delay. For practical reasons, government business managers often find it easier to accept Lords amendments than to attempt to overturn them every time, let alone threaten the use of the Parliament Acts. While they may well serve to underscore Commons primacy in legislative matters, as a tool of business management they are clunky.

The Salisbury convention

Members of the House of Lords accept that the elected government of the day must be allowed to get its business through. The nearest that this idea has come to formal expression is in the Salisbury convention – an understanding reached between the Conservative opposition in the House of Lords (led by the fifth Marquess of Salisbury) and the Labour government immediately after the Second World War in 1945. The convention is that the Lords should not reject at second reading any government legislation that has been passed by the House of Commons and that carries out a manifesto commitment – that is to say, a commitment made to the electorate in the government party's election manifesto.

The convention had its origin in the doctrine of the mandate developed by the third Marquess of Salisbury in the nineteenth century. He argued that the will of the people and the views of the House of Commons did not necessarily coincide and that the Lords had a duty to reject – and hence refer back to the electorate at a general election – contentious bills, particularly those with constitutional implications. As did the doctrine of the mandate before it, the Salisbury convention was perhaps more a code of behaviour for the Conservative party when in opposition in the Lords than a convention of the House. The Liberal Democrats – whose precursors, the Liberal party, were not privy to the 1945 agreement – have not considered themselves to be bound by it. Indeed, some have questioned whether, following the passage of the House of Lords Act 1999, the expulsion of the hereditary members and the ending of the overwhelming numerical advantage of the Conservative Party, the Salisbury convention as originally devised has any continuing validity.

In 2006 a Joint Committee on Conventions of the UK Parliament suggested that the Salisbury convention took the following form: that a manifesto bill is accorded a second reading; it is not subject to 'wrecking amendments' that would change the

House of Lords in session

Source: Copyright House of Lords, 2012. Photography by Catherine Bebbington

manifesto intention; and that the bill is passed and sent to the Commons. Interestingly, the Joint Committee also observed that the evidence it had heard pointed to the emergence in recent years of the practice that the Lords usually gave a second reading to any government bill whether related to a manifesto commitment or not.

Some questioned whether the Salisbury convention should apply during the coalition government in the 2010–15 parliament: the government thought it should, the opposition thought it should not – though there was only one opposition attempt to defeat a government bill during the parliament. The convention has come under even greater scrutiny since the 2017 election, with a focus on whether it applies to any government's manifesto, regardless of their strength in the Commons, or whether it applies only during periods of majority government. The Constitution Committee took evidence from the party leaders in the Lords on this matter; perhaps unsurprisingly the government thought the convention continued to apply and the opposition parties thought it did not. But all agreed that of greater significance is the broad acceptance that government bills will usually be given a second reading and dealt with in reasonable time. Whatever one's view of the Salisbury convention, or a broader understanding on government bills, the right of the Lords to amend bills has never been compromised, and this leaves the House with considerable room for manoeuvre, as we shall see.

Lords impact on legislation

House of Lords practice and procedure gives a persistent member far more opportunities and time for getting a point of view across than the equivalent MP has in the House of Commons. We have already observed that, while party voting is very cohesive, the powers of the whips to compel attendance are relatively weak. Since the expulsion of the hereditary members in 1999, the House is more than ever a House of no overall control. In these conditions, members of the House are able, by persuasion or imposition of their will in the division lobbies, to have considerable impact on bills.

But the first thing to remember is that most of the changes that are made to bills in the Lords are by agreement, for the fact remains that most of the Lords work is of a revising character – whether in respect of its own bills or of bills received from the Commons. Detailed examination by a second chamber of legislature is perhaps a unique feature of the UK parliamentary system, allowing time for reflections and time to 'get things right'. Whichever party is in power, this aspect of the Lords' legislative work continues unchanged, and the biggest source of amendments of this kind is the government itself. During the passage of a bill, the government is continually seeking to improve the clarity of drafting of the bill, introducing detailed or even new provisions that were not ready at the time of introduction and – to some degree, at least – making changes in response to pressure within either House of Parliament. In the 2016–17 session 2,270 amendments were made to government bills, of which only 36 were forced on the government on a vote. Practically all of these amendments, which were agreed to consensually, though often after debate, were government amendments moved by a minister.

These instances will have included occasions when the government has been persuaded to bring forward amendments in response to argument in the House at an earlier stage, or in the Commons. For example, in November 2017 the government moved amendments at the third reading of the Financial Guidance and Claims Bill to provide greater clarity on the objectives of the single financial guidance body to be created under the bill, including introducing an objective for it to advise on a debt respite scheme. The amendment followed significant pressure from all sides of the House at previous stages; it is likely that if the government had not undertaken to craft an amendment reflecting members' concerns they would have been defeated in the division lobbies.

Research provides useful quantitative evidence in support of what otherwise would be a series of anecdotes. Meg Russell of the Constitution Unit at University College London has analysed the Lords amendments to 12 varied bills, seven from the 2005–10 parliament and five from the 2010–12 session. She found that 88 per cent of the 498 amendments made in the Lords to those bills were government amendments and, of these, 130 had policy significance. Of these, 84 (or 65 per cent) were traceable to other members' amendments or recommendations of Lords bill scrutiny committees. So, as part of the 'revising' process it is clear that the government does take on board the representations made to it in the House – particularly in those areas where it is prepared to shift, or where it thinks that change will be forced upon it if there were to be no shift. On the other hand, it should be remembered that 2,384 amendments were tabled from all parts of the House to these bills, most of which were successfully resisted.

More dramatic by far than changes secured by persuasion are those forced on a reluctant minister in the division lobbies, though their net effect on a government's legislative programme is not necessarily greater than amendments voluntarily made or conceded. Table 6.3 shows the number of times the government has been defeated on a vote in the Lords in each parliament from 1979 to 2017. It tells us some interesting things. Until the passage of the House of Lords Act in 1999, the House was – at least, on paper – a predominantly Conservative body. All the more remarkable, then, that between 1979 and 1997 the Lords were often highly critical of aspects of government policy. Targeted by lobbyists, the Lords became recognised as the chamber in which Mrs Thatcher's bills were vulnerable. Notwithstanding the departure of most of the hereditary members in 1999 and a great increase in Labour members relative to Conservative members over the period, the years between 1997 and 2010 saw more government defeats than ever before – a reflection of the increased assertiveness of the House following the passage of the House of Lords Act. The 2010–15 parliament saw rather fewer occasions when the government lost votes, despite the fact that the two main parties remain numerically broadly in balance – evidence that when it came to voting, the coalition in the Lords held firm most of the time. But when the Liberal Democrats went back into opposition in the 2015–17 parliament their votes combined with those of the opposition to defeat the government an average of 49 times per session – a record matched only in the 2001–05 parliament.

Table 6.3 Government defeats in the House of Lords

Parliament	Number of defeats
1979–83	45
1983–87	62
1987–92	72
1992–97	56
1997–2001	128
2001–05	245
2005–10	144
2010–15	100
2015–17	98

Many of the amendments made to a bill on a defeat in the lobbies may be reversed in the lobbies during the exchanges between the Houses known as 'ping-pong' (see page 230). But some are not overturned, or will be met with a compromise. Here are some recent examples where the Lords have had a substantial effect on policy.

- *Prevention of terrorism.* The House has been especially vigilant in ensuring that the government's response to terrorism has been proportionate. In the 2001–05 parliament the Lords successfully modified aspects of anti-terrorism legislation that they considered excessive, particularly the Anti-Terrorism, Crime and Security Bill – a 126-clause bill containing measures in response to the terrorist attacks in New York and Washington on 11 September 2001. Although proceedings were accelerated, the Lords spent 53 hours seeking to amend this bill. As a result, changes were made in key areas, in some cases after the Lords had insisted on their amendments. Similarly, the Lords went on to insist on a number of amendments to the Prevention of Terrorism Bill in March 2005, chiefly aimed at making the proposed control orders subject to judicial rather than political decision, under rules of court, consistent with the ECHR and subject to clearer statutory definition. The passage of the bill was eventually secured following the longest sitting of the House in modern times – beginning at 11 am on Thursday 10 March 2005 and ending at 7.31 pm on Friday 11 March. This included four long adjournments for Commons consideration and the necessary negotiations. An attempt to increase the period of pre-charge detention of terrorist suspects (from 28 days to 42 days) in the Counter-Terrorism Bill in the 2007–08 session was rejected by the Lords and the government failed to persuade the Commons to reverse the Lords amendment.
- *Trial by jury.* The Lords have been doughty opponents of attempts to encroach upon the right to trial by jury, going back to their opposition to the Criminal Justice (Mode of Trial) Bill in 1999–2000. These sought to abolish trial by jury in so-called 'either way' cases, which can be heard either by a magistrate or a jury. The provisions were removed by the Lords and the bill abandoned. Reintroduced as a 'No. 2' bill late that session, it was – unusually – rejected by the Lords at second reading when it arrived from the Commons. Further attempts to limit access to

trial by jury in certain cases were effectively seen off by amendments to the Criminal Justice Bill 2002–03 and a final attempt to end jury trial in complex fraud cases was resisted when, in 2007, the Fraud (Trials without a Jury) Bill was rejected at second reading.

- *Constituency boundaries.* In the early months of the 2010 parliament, the government introduced the Parliamentary Voting System and Constituencies Bill. It provided for a referendum to be held on whether or not to change the voting system for a general election to the alternative vote (AV) system; and, following a review by the Boundary Commission, to reduce the number of Commons constituencies by 50, and provide for greater equality in the size of electorates. The Lords failed to make much impact on the bill and it received Royal Assent in 2011. The referendum decisively rejected the AV system. It was expected that the orders making the boundary changes would be made in time for the 2015 election. In 2013, the Lords amended the Electoral Registration and Administration Bill so as to postpone the implementation of the boundary changes until after 2015. Because this amendment – in the opinion of the clerks, not relevant to (in Commons terms 'within the scope of') the bill – had been made with official Liberal Democrat support, it proved irreversible in the Commons. On this occasion, the Lords motives were more than usually political; the Labour Party had vigorously opposed the original bill fearing the loss of many urban seats and the Liberal Democrats sought vengeance against their coalition partners for what they considered to be the premature abandoning of the House of Lords Reform Bill in September 2012.
- *Secondary market for tickets.* Peers have expressed concern about the possibility of profiteering or illegality by reselling tickets to sporting and cultural events on the online secondary ticketing market. After pressure from members with backgrounds in sport and the entertainment industry the House passed an amendment to the Consumer Rights Bill 2014–15 to require more transparency in the market, including the provision of information concerning the seller and value of tickets. Following this defeat the government accepted the amendments. The issue was pursued further in the Digital Economy Bill 2016–17, when the government was defeated on an amendment to require those reselling tickets to provide the ticket reference or booking number, as well as any conditions attaching to the ticket. On ping-pong the government accepted the amendment, albeit with some technical tweaks. Thus the law on the secondary ticketing market is significantly tighter now than a few years ago.
- *Unaccompanied child refugees.* During the passage of the Immigration Bill 2015–16 the House responded to public and media disquiet at the treatment of unaccompanied child refugees at camps in Europe, particularly in northern France, following the migration crisis of 2015. The House agreed an amendment moved by Lord Dubs, himself a refugee from wartime Czechoslovakia, which obliged the government to accept a set number of child refugees into the UK. The amendment was at first rejected by the House of Commons, but a compromise was accepted when it became possible that the government would lose a second vote on it in

the Commons. Now the 'Dubs amendment' obliges ministers to arrange for the relocation of unaccompanied child refugees, with the precise number agreed with local authorities concerned. There remains pressure inside and outside the House for the government to honour the spirit of the amendment.

These case histories make good reading, and there are more of them. Why, one may ask, does the government not reverse all Lords amendments in the Commons? There are a number of reasons why not: occasionally, it cannot muster the votes in the Commons; sometimes, particularly if the amendments have been made with support from its own backbenches, it will seek to compromise or live with the change; sometimes it will have a change of heart and accept the amendment, particularly if public opinion has been engaged; and often, at the end of a busy session when time is of the essence and bills are passing from one House to the other, it will deliberately avoid unnecessary confrontation with the Lords.

And what is the overall success rate? Meg Russell analysed government defeats on bills in the period 1999–2012 and the degree to which the amendments were accepted, overturned in the Commons, or subjected to compromise in the form of 'amendments in lieu'. Of the 406 individual defeats analysed, 33 per cent were accepted, or largely accepted, and a further 11 per cent were met halfway by amendments in lieu. This represents a win or draw rate of 44 per cent. In some sessions, the success rate was higher. In 2008–09, for example, the win or draw rate was as high as 67 per cent.

Disagreement between the Houses: the balance of power

Ping-pong . . . or poker?

The previous section dealt with disagreements between the two Houses on a bill, and we now explore this more fully, together with the constraints on the Lords' powers to amend bills. A bill that passes without amendment through the second House then needs only the Royal Assent – or formal approval by the Queen – before it becomes law. It does not go back to the House where its progress began. However, if the second House makes amendments to a bill, those amendments (but no other part of the bill) must be considered by the first House. If they are agreed, the bill is ready to become law. If they are not, the second House looks at the matter again and can either insist on its amendments, back down entirely or attempt compromise proposals. Theoretically, alternative compromises can be shuttled between the two Houses indefinitely until the session ends. Each time, messages are exchanged between the two Houses. These can become fiendishly complicated.

The final stages of the Prevention of Terrorism Bill in 2005, which we looked at earlier in this chapter (page 228) are an interesting example. The Commons sat from 11.30 am on Thursday 25 March until nearly eight o'clock in the evening of Friday 26 March, and during that time the Bill (which had the previous week gone from the

Lords to the Commons and back again without agreement on the most contentious provisions) went back and forth between the Houses seven times, with proposals and counter-proposals being considered each time (with new working papers being printed on each occasion – even at three in the morning). The Lords finally gave in, and their message to the Commons read:

> *The Lords do not insist on their Amendment to the Prevention of Terrorism Bill to which this House has disagreed and do agree with this House in its Amendments in lieu thereof; they do not insist on an Amendment in lieu of certain other Lords Amendments to which this House has disagreed, and do agree to the Amendments proposed by this House in lieu thereof; and they agree to the Amendments proposed by this House to words so restored to the Bill.*

Shortly after the arrival of this message, Royal Assent to the Prevention of Terrorism Act 2005 was announced to both Houses. Although dressed in archaic language, the exchanges were a classic political struggle between two chambers of a bicameral Parliament, in one of which the government had a majority, and where the second had the power to destroy the government's bill, but was mindful of the possible political consequences of doing so. The process was perhaps more poker than ping-pong.

If a compromise were not reached, the bill would be lost, as happened to the House of Commons (Distribution of Seats) (No. 2) Bill in 1969 (which was not reintroduced); to the Trade Union and Labour Relations Bill and Aircraft and Shipbuilding Industries Bill in 1976 (reintroduced in 1977 and enacted in the conventional manner following compromise); and to the Hunting Bill in 2002–03 (enacted under the Parliament Acts at the end of the 2003–04 session). The point of *final disagreement* is normally thought to have been reached when each House has taken up its position and insisted on it without an alternative proposition being offered (*double insistence*).

In the past, final disagreement has usually been defined with respect to individual amendments even where they may have been grouped for purposes of debate. In the Commons, since 1997 the practice had arisen of grouping amendments together for the purpose of both debate and decision. This Commons practice of 'packaging' created difficulties in the Lords in May 2004 in respect of the Planning and Compulsory Purchase Bill. The Lords authorities took the view that double insistence had been reached on an amendment and that the bill was lost, whereas the Commons intention was that the bill could be further considered because that amendment had been decided as part of a 'package' with another amendment to which an amendment in lieu had been offered. Exceptionally, the bill was further considered by the Lords.

It was, however, subsequently agreed by the House of Lords that it would consider packages of amendments during ping-pong only if they were confined to single or closely related issues, not disparate issues joined together simply for convenience. In the case of the former, the House would be willing to consider such amendments in packages, in which case the double insistence rule would apply to the whole package. This development has the benefit that consideration of Commons amendments has become procedurally easier as the amendments can be printed together, whether consecutive or not. On the other hand, it can mean that exchanges on a package of amendments go on beyond the point at which it is clear that no compromise will be reached, as if one House passes an alternative to one element of a package it keeps the whole package alive.

The language and practice of ping-pong is complicated, but in essence it is relatively simple. It is a means by which the two Houses gradually narrow down their differences on a bill until they either agree on the whole text of the bill or they don't, in which case the bill falls. Importantly, it is not possible to introduce new material at ping-pong nor to reopen matters already decided. This means that the Westminster Parliament does not allow the kind of bargaining and backscratching (sometimes referred to as 'pork barrelling') which is a common feature of other parliaments, especially the US Congress.

Royal Assent and implementation

A bill passed by both Houses needs the Royal Assent – from the sovereign as the third element of Parliament, in addition to the Lords and the Commons – before it may become law. The Queen's agreement is automatic: Queen Anne in 1707–08 was the last monarch to refuse to accept a bill passed by both Houses. Although, in theory, the Royal Assent may be given by the sovereign in person, this was last done in 1854. In 1967 it was decided to stop the procedure by which Black Rod would interrupt the proceedings of the Commons, summoning them to the Lords chamber to hear the Lords Commissioners announcing Royal Assent. This now occurs only at prorogation. At other times, the Speaker in the Commons and the Lord Speaker in the Lords announce the Royal Assent at a convenient break in each House's proceedings.

Although Royal Assent to a bill turns it into an Act and makes it law, the law does not necessarily come into force immediately. The Act will normally contain a *commencement provision*. Typically, this allows the secretary of state concerned to make an order at some future date to bring part or all of the Act into force, although a date may be specified; for example, three or six months after Royal Assent. Sometimes, the appropriate date never comes: the Easter Act 1928, which would have fixed the date of Easter, was never brought into force. In June 2010 a Lords written answer revealed that elements of over 100 Acts of Parliament passed by the Labour government between 1997 and 2010 had not been commenced – ranging from a few sections to whole parts.

The question of whether it was legal for a minister simply not to bring into force something that had been decided by Parliament was considered by the Court of Appeal in 1994. That court decided that, as Parliament had not set a time for commencement, the minister had not acted illegally; but the then Master of the Rolls, in a dissenting judgment, suggested that the power given to the minister was to decide *when* rather than *whether* an Act should come into force. However, it is not clear when delay becomes long enough to regard the Act passed by Parliament as ineffective.

Acts of Parliament in the Parliamentary Archives

Source: Copyright UK Parliament, 2012. Photography by Jessica Taylor

If there is no commencement provision (whether a date, or a power given to a minister), the Act comes into force from midnight at the beginning of the day on which Royal Assent was given.

What is the law?

Acts of Parliament are available in bound copies of the statutes for any particular year, and the government website www.legislation.gov.uk contains Acts of Parliaments as passed and also Acts as currently in force, back to 1267. The website shows the extent to which an Act has been brought into force, or amended or repealed by subsequent legislation (although it is not always entirely up to date: details are given against each individual Act). UK legislation is not codified; in other words, there is no single Act – covering, say, immigration law – which is republished every time there is an amending bill. To some extent, the work of the Law Commissions addresses this problem by compiling *consolidation bills* that bring together the existing law in a more logical and convenient form. For want of resources, the programme of consolidation has produced little in recent sessions of Parliament. So the reader who wishes to know what a particular Act says needs to be careful to consult a fully revised and updated version; as well as www.legislation.gov.uk there are printed publications such as Halsbury's *Laws of England* and online subscription services from law publishers such as Halsbury or Butterworth.

Post-legislative scrutiny

It has always been possible for a select committee to examine the workings of an Act of Parliament relevant to its subject area, but there have been recent moves to make such *post-legislative scrutiny* more systematic. Following various exchanges between Parliament and government, in 2008 the government undertook that in most cases it would produce a memorandum assessing each Act between three and five years after Royal Assent. It is then up to the relevant select committee to decide whether to take up the memorandum and make it the subject of an inquiry. In 2012 the Liaison Committee was able to point to only three specific examples of such inquiries, though there had been wider inquiries that had included evaluations of previous legislation. The House of Lords began setting up select committees to carry out post legislative scrutiny in 2012 when adoption legislation was considered. Since then it has set up a select committee each session to carry out post-legislative scrutiny of an Act – including the Licensing Act 2003 and the Natural Environment and Rural Communities Act 2006. Picking a suitable Act for post-legislative scrutiny is a harder task than it might sound, given complaints about how much legislation Parliament passes. This is mainly because many Acts are amended, repealed or overtaken within a few years, making them unsuitable for post-legislative scrutiny. Overall, post-legislative scrutiny is an initiative that has promised more than it has delivered. This may well be because, if a particular legislative provision is clearly not working and this really matters to the government of the day, it will be dealt with by subsequent legislation; and, if it is a matter of party contention, it may be repealed upon a change of government. A *systematic* assessment of how an Act of Parliament is working is no doubt worthy, but may be better carried out in an academic rather than a parliamentary context. If there is a specific problem with a piece of legislation, a select committee is well-placed to investigate it.

Private legislation

The reader of the House of Commons Order of Business will often see at the beginning of the day's agenda on Mondays to Thursdays references to private business. Occasionally, the words 'Private business set down under Standing Order No. 20' can be seen. The private business is not private in the sense of being confidential or related to the internal affairs of the House; it is business related to private legislation.

As we saw earlier in this chapter (page 212), private bills are nothing to do with private members' bills. Private members' bills seek to change the general law, but private bills affect individuals, groups of individuals or corporate bodies in a way different from other individuals, groups or bodies. Their effect is private and particular as opposed to public and general. For example, the Dartmoor Commons Act 1985 was promoted by Dartmoor farmers to give powers to stop the overgrazing of the moors, the Southampton International Boat Show Act 1997 allowed a park in Southampton to open for one extra day a year, and the City of London (Ward Elections) Act 2002 made changes to the franchise for local elections in the City. The Hereford Markets Act 2003 allowed a livestock market that, by royal charter, had to be held within the city limits to be moved outside and so release a prime site for other uses. Private bills have been promoted by local authorities in recent years to regulate street trading and pedlars in their areas.

The first step in private legislation is for the person or group seeking the legislation to petition for the bill. Private bills are not presented by MPs or peers but by the promoters of the legislation, who are represented by special lawyers known as parliamentary agents. Throughout the bill's passage – but especially before it is even introduced – the promoters will be working to ensure that the bill attracts as little opposition as possible. Promoters need to comply with an elaborate set of standing orders, which try to ensure that interested parties (who may know nothing of the promoters' intentions) are given notice of the bill. When this has been done, the bill is allocated to one House or the other for first consideration, and, after second reading, is sent to a special committee. Private bill procedure is particularly complex but the essence of it is to allow those specially affected by a bill to have their say.

Anyone who is aggrieved by the bill's provisions has the right to petition against it, but only someone directly affected by the bill (who has what is known as *locus standi*) has the right to be heard. If the bill is not opposed by petitions, or if all the petitions are withdrawn because the promoters have been able to meet the petitioners' wishes, the bill is considered by a committee on unopposed bills, through which it usually passes swiftly after an explanation of its purposes by the promoters. Opposed private bills are considered much more elaborately over many days by a committee of four MPs (or five peers), who must have no personal interest in the matter.

The committee acts in a semi-judicial capacity, examining witnesses and hearing barristers who appear for and against the bill. In effect, it displays the character of Parliament both as a court, inquiring into and adjudicating on the interests of private individuals, and as a legislature, safeguarding the public interest. The committee has to decide whether the promoters have demonstrated that the bill is necessary, whether those affected by it have been treated fairly, and whether there is any objection to it on public policy grounds. The committee has the power to make amendments, or even to recommend that the bill should not proceed (as happened with the first Crossrail Bill in 1994, which failed).

After their committee stage, private bills are considered on report (in the Commons, but not the Lords), read a third time and passed to the other House for similar stages to be taken. It is quite usual for a private bill not to complete all its stages in one session; an order is made that allows it to be taken up in the following session at the stage it had reached. Private bills are not covered by the Parliament Acts, so there is no restriction on the power of the Lords to delay them.

Most private bills do not encounter sustained opposition from MPs or peers, but the opportunities for delay are considerable. Each stage of a bill's progress is advertised on the Order of Business 'at the time of unopposed private business' and can be stopped from proceeding further by an MP shouting 'Object!' and then by the tabling of a 'blocking motion'. If this objection is sustained on each appearance of the bill on the Order of Business, the bill cannot proceed without time being found for a debate. This is in the hands of the Chairman of Ways and Means, who has a general responsibility for the way that private bills are handled (but not for the success or failure of any bill). He can set a bill down for a three-hour period, which according to the standing orders is the last three hours before the moment of interruption (for example, from 7.00 pm to 10.00 pm on a Monday), but is usually changed nowadays to a three-hour period at the end of government business.

The government business managers are naturally anxious not to have much scarce parliamentary time taken up with opposed private business, so an MP who objects to an aspect of a private bill has a strong bargaining counter with the promoters. Unless they go some way towards meeting the MP's wishes, he or she can delay the bill by insisting on a debate at each stage, and this may eventually mean that the bill is lost.

In the Lords, private bills that have been reported from a select committee are not usually opposed further on the floor. The Senior Deputy Speaker oversees private legislation proceedings in the Lords in the same way as the Chairman of Ways and Means in the Commons.

The amount of private legislation has fallen dramatically in recent years, especially following the Transport and Works Act 1992. This removed from the parliamentary process private bills dealing with matters such as railway, tramway and harbour building, and other types of development. These were often the most controversial private bills, and there were usually more than 20 bills each session. Nowadays, parliamentary involvement in such projects will occur only when a project is seen by the government as being nationally significant, when a single debate on its desirability will take place on the floor of the House. An example is the debate on the proposal to build a new railway from Leicester to the Channel Tunnel via Rugby, which was rejected by the Commons in 1996.

The timetable for presenting private bills has not yet been amended to match the move of the start of sessions from November to June; petitions for new bills (typically between one and three petitions) are still presented in November.

There will no doubt be private bills in the future that do not deal with transport and works but that will still prove controversial – as, for example, did the City of London (Ward Elections) Bill, which encountered opposition on the grounds that it provided for a weighted franchise, and which took nearly four years to get through Parliament, and the bills relating to street trading, which were opposed by both members and street traders, which also took several years to be passed. Any private bill may be of great importance both for its promoters and for those who will be affected. But, compared with their nineteenth-century heyday, private bills have become something of a parliamentary backwater.

Hybrid bills

These bills – which are fairly unusual – combine characteristics of a public bill and a private bill. Bills that are introduced by the government but that would otherwise be private bills are also treated as hybrid. Examples of hybrid bills include the Channel Tunnel Bill in 1987, the Cardiff Bay Barrage Bill (which was enacted in 1993 after starting out as a private bill and then being taken over by the government), the Channel Tunnel Rail Link Bill in 1994, which became law in 1996, the Crossrail Bill introduced in 2005 and enacted in 2008, and the High Speed Rail (London – West Midlands) Bill, which was introduced in 2013 and became an Act in 2017. One of the classic examples of a hybrid bill was the Aircraft and Shipbuilding Industries Bill of 1976, which was intended to nationalise these two industries. It was discovered that this bill did not apply to one ship building company that otherwise fulfilled the bill's criteria for nationalisation. Because this company was thus being treated differently from all other companies in the same class, the bill was ruled by the Speaker to be hybrid. Although this ruling was set aside by the Commons, the bill was committed to a select committee in the Lords.

Hybrid bills are treated as public bills, and the promoters do not need to prove the need for the bill. Bills are examined to see whether they comply with the standing orders that relate to private bills, and there is an additional stage – they are referred to a select committee in each House, which can hear petitions from those affected. This may be a major exercise; the committee on the Channel Tunnel Bill received several thousand petitions. The Crossrail Bill attracted 358 petitions and the High Speed Rail (London – West Midlands) Bill attracted 1,925 petitions in the House of Commons and 828 in the House of Lords. Following its odyssey through Parliament modest reforms to streamline the petitioning process have been introduced in both Houses.

Delegated legislation

Definitions

Delegated legislation is law made by ministers or certain public bodies under powers given to them by Acts of Parliament, but it is just as much part of the law of the land as are those Acts. The volume of delegated legislation is huge, and this presents particular challenges for parliamentary scrutiny.

Individual pieces of delegated legislation, often called *secondary legislation* to distinguish them from primary legislation contained in Acts of Parliament, or *subordinate legislation*, are found under many different names. They can be *orders*, *regulations*, *Orders in Council*, *schemes*, *rules*, *codes of practice*, *guidance* and *statutes* (of certain colleges rather than in the sense of Acts). Even the Highway Code is a form of secondary legislation.

Delegated legislation may be made by any person or body empowered to do so by an Act of Parliament ('the parent Act'); and although some institutions and professional bodies have this power in particular cases, the bulk of such legislation is made by ministers.

Before the Second World War, there was much less delegated legislation, and parent Acts prescribed a variety of different parliamentary procedures, often designed for a particular case. Most of these were unified by the Statutory Instruments Act 1946, which describes what a statutory instrument is and prescribes the principal procedures for parliamentary approval. Not all pieces of delegated legislation are *statutory instruments*, but this general term (abbreviated to SI, with individual instruments numbered in an annual series; for example, 'SI 2017/875') will serve. About half of the statutory instruments made each year have only a local effect and may be for only a temporary purpose. Our concern is with the general instruments that form part of the law of the land.

In Chapter 11 we discuss the importance of delegated legislation in implementing Brexit and the likelihood of this increasing its volume. A new sifting committee in the Commons will be instrumental in deciding which of the forms of parliamentary control described below will be used for particular pieces of Brexit delegated legislation.

Purpose

The original idea of an SI was to supplement what was set down in an Act of Parliament, for two particular purposes. The first was to prescribe things that were too detailed for inclusion in an Act of Parliament. The second was – again, for fairly minor matters – to provide the flexibility to change the law to meet changing circumstances without the sledgehammer (and the delay) of new primary legislation.

As long as this remained the guiding principle, one would expect there to be little difficulty. However, over the years the boundaries of delegated legislation have been tested. Over the last 30 years there was a significant increase in the number of statutory instruments; although in 2016 and 2017 it declined considerably (see Table 6.4). There is expected to be another increase because of the number of instruments required to implement Brexit. However, the *volume* of delegated legislation is huge: the last set of annual volumes of SIs for which figures are available took up 11,888 A4 pages.

The second area of strain has been in the *use* of SIs. Ministers naturally find it more convenient to be able to legislate in a way that is subject to more limited parliamentary scrutiny than primary legislation, and there is thus a temptation to leave to delegated legislation matters that arguably should be set out in a bill and so in an Act. The most extreme examples of this have been in so-called 'skeleton' or 'framework' bills, where the use of delegated powers is so extensive that the real operation of the bill would be entirely by the regulations made under it. The Childcare Bill 2015–16 and the Sanctions and Anti-Money Laundering Bill 2017–18 attracted criticism on these grounds, as have 'Henry VIII powers', which allow ministers to amend primary legislation by the use of secondary legislation (see also page 246).

The speed of the legislative process encourages overuse of delegated powers. A minister may want to put a new provision into a bill during its passage, but the limited time available to settle the details may lead to the provision being drafted in very general terms, with even quite significant matters being left to delegated legislation. There is also the question of where the threshold should be set between the more important *affirmative instruments*, which Parliament must approve explicitly, and *negative instruments*, which have effect unless Parliament says otherwise.

Since 1992 the House of Lords has sought to address the balance between delegation and control through the Delegated Powers and Regulatory Reform Committee (formerly the Delegated Powers and Deregulation Committee). For each bill introduced into the Lords (and for substantial government amendments), this committee examines

Table 6.4 Number of SIs made in selected years 1950–2017

1950	2,144
1955	2,007
1960	2,495
1965	2,201
1970	2,044
1975	2,251
1980	2,051
1985	2,080
1990	2,667
1995	3,345
2000	3,433
2005	3,602
2010	3,117
2013	3,314
2015	2,059
2016	1,242
2017	1,282

the powers to make delegated legislation that are proposed to be given to ministers. It reports on both whether those powers are justified and whether the level of parliamentary control is appropriate (in other words, which powers should be exercised through negative instruments, which through affirmative instruments, and which should be matters for an Act of Parliament rather than delegated legislation). The vast majority of the committee's recommendations have been accepted, and it plays an important role in striking a balance between executive freedom and parliamentary control.

Two other features of the system should also be mentioned. The first is that the vast majority of SIs are not amendable. This is inevitable in that both Houses must take the same view on an SI, and amendable instruments would be like another class of bills going back and forth for both Houses to agree on any amendments. But it also means an element of 'take it or leave it', especially when an SI is substantial or complex.

The second is that the way the threshold is set between affirmative and negative instruments can become out of date with changes in society. For example, in an Act passed in 1950 it might have been thought essential to require a minister to come back to Parliament for permission to exercise a power that by 2017 would be thought to be routine. But the requirement remains in the 1950 Act, and only further primary legislation will remove it. The phenomenon may also work the other way – something routine in 1950 may have taken on a different significance 60 years later.

Parliamentary control

There are five levels of parliamentary control:

1 Delegated legislation that may be made and come into effect *without any reference to Parliament*. This category includes a large number of SIs with only local effect, and many of these will be printed only if the responsible minister wishes them to be. Among non-local SIs in this category are commencement orders for bringing into force all or part of an Act of Parliament.
2 Delegated legislation that may be made and come into effect, and that *must be laid before Parliament, but on which there are no parliamentary proceedings*.
3 *Negative instruments*: these are *laid before Parliament* and may *come into effect* immediately or on some future date *unless either House resolves that the instrument be annulled*.
4 *Affirmative instruments*: these do not normally (except in cases of urgency) come into effect until they have been *approved by resolution of each House*. (Urgent affirmative instruments come into force before approval but lapse unless approved within a certain time.)
5 *Super-affirmative instruments*, such as *legislative reform orders* (see page 246). These require the minister concerned to have regard to the results of consultations, House of Commons and House of Lords resolutions, and committee recommendations made within a certain period (usually 60 days) of laying the draft instrument, in order to decide whether to proceed with the draft order, whether as laid or in an amended form.

Table 6.5 Instruments considered by the Joint or Select Committees on Statutory Instruments

Type	Session 2015–16	Session 2016–17
Unlaid (general)	151	111
No procedure, laid	21	18
Negative	786	514
Affirmative	131	185
Total	1,088	828

The third and fourth categories are the most significant; in session 2016–17 there were 166 affirmatives and 537 negatives laid.

Procedure

When an instrument has been laid before Parliament, it is examined by the Joint Committee on Statutory Instruments (with members from both Houses), which is supported by specialist lawyers and reports on various technical aspects: whether in making the instrument the minister has exceeded the powers given by Parliament (this is also something that can be challenged in the courts); whether the drafting is defective or unclear; whether the instrument has retrospective effect, and so on. The joint committee also examines instruments not laid before Parliament, but only if they are general, not local. The joint committee reports its conclusions but, even if it finds fault, the progress of the instrument is not automatically halted. Some instruments, on finance and taxation, are laid before the Commons only and are examined by the Select Committee on Statutory Instruments, which consists of the Commons members of the joint committee. In the House of Lords a motion to approve an affirmative instrument may not be moved until the Joint Committee on Statutory Instruments has reported on the instrument.

Negative instruments

In the case of a negative SI, nothing will happen unless an opposition party, or a group of backbenchers, tables what is known as a *prayer*. This has nothing to do with religious devotion but is so called because of the form of the motion: because the instrument has been made by one of Her Majesty's ministers, it is the sovereign who has to be asked to undo what has been done. To take a real example from the 2015–16 session (the SI that replaced means-tested maintenance grants for students with loans), the motion, in the name of the Leader of the Opposition, read:

> *That an humble Address be presented to Her Majesty, praying that the Education (Student Support) (Amendment) Regulations 2015 (S.I., 2015, No. 1951), dated 29 November 2015, a copy of which was laid before this House on 2 December 2015, be annulled.*

Any annulment of an instrument must take place during a period of 40 days (excluding time when both Houses are adjourned for more than four days) from the laying of the SI; this time is known as ***praying time***.

In the Commons, debate on a prayer on the floor of the House is unusual; most are taken upstairs in a ***delegated legislation committee***, which is very similar to a public bill committee on a bill but which debates the prayer on a motion 'That the committee has considered' the instrument, for a period of one-and-a-half hours (two-and-a-half hours in the case of Northern Ireland instruments). Only a minister can move a motion in the House to refer a prayer to a delegated legislation committee, so even debates of this sort are in the gift of the government and are normally granted only to the principal opposition parties, and almost never to backbenchers. Moreover, the committee cannot reject the instrument, so any vote that is not on the floor of the House is purely symbolic; and on the floor of the House no prayer has been carried since 1979.

In recent sessions around five prayers have been taken in delegated legislation committee; but not more than one on the floor of the House.

Affirmative procedure

Because any instrument in this category must be explicitly approved, a decision of each House is required. In the Commons, affirmative instruments are automatically referred to a delegated legislation committee. These operate in the same way for affirmative instruments as for prayers against negative instruments: they offer an opportunity for debate rather than substantive decision. When an affirmative has been debated in committee it returns to the floor of the House for decision, and a vote if necessary, but without further debate.

It is also possible for an affirmative to be 'de-referred': that is, so that it is both debated and decided on the floor of the House. The automatic referral to standing committee has existed since 1995; it was introduced as part of an effort to reduce sitting time on the floor of the House, but there was an understanding that the government would accede to a reasonable request to take particular affirmatives on the floor of the House.

Although, to begin with, substantial numbers of affirmatives were taken on the floor (73 in 1994–95, 47 in 1995–96 and 42 in 1996–97), there was a sharp decline thereafter, and now fewer than a dozen affirmatives are considered on the floor of the House in an average session. Recent subjects taken in the chamber have included: local government finance and the financing of police authorities, up-rating of social security benefits and urgent orders to proscribe organisations under the Terrorism Act 2000.

Every sitting week, the Journal Office in the House of Commons produces a *Statutory Instrument List* showing the state of play on all affirmative and negative instruments and, in the latter case, the number of 'praying days' remaining on each. It is available on the parliamentary website.

EVEL and statutory instruments

The EVEL procedures introduced in October 2015 (see page 208) affect secondary legislation as well as bills. The Speaker is required to apply the certification tests to: instruments subject to affirmative resolution, once an approval motion has been tabled by a minister; instruments subject to negative resolution which have been prayed against and either referred to a delegated legislation committee for debate or set down for debate in the chamber; and draft orders subject to affirmative resolution under the Regulatory Reform Act 2001 or the Localism Act 2011 where the Regulatory Reform Committee has made a recommendation to the House on approval. Certain other instruments do not require certification but apply only to England, or England and Wales, and are covered by the EVEL standing orders, including local government finance reports and police grant reports. In order to be approved by the House (or annulled, in the case of negative instruments) the relevant motion has to be passed by a double majority: only if a majority of MPs for the relevant constituencies vote to approve a measure will a majority of all members also be effective.

Lords proceedings on statutory instruments

Most SIs that are laid before the Commons are also laid before the Lords – except for some financial ones – and the same rules apply (other than the EVEL provisions). The House of Lords spends quite an amount of its time debating secondary legislation, though much of this discussion is off the floor in Grand Committee. In 2016–17, discussion of SIs took nearly 45 hours (or 4.8 per cent) of total chamber time, with a further 20 hours in Grand Committee. Indeed, 18 per cent of Grand Committee time was spent debating 66 SIs. The more controversial debates, any debates potentially leading to a vote, and formal motions to approve affirmative instruments debated in Grand Committee are reserved for taking in the chamber.

Although delegated legislation is not subject to the Parliament Acts, the House of Lords rarely defeats negative or affirmative instruments. As we have seen, they are not amendable, so if the House pressed its opposition to a vote, the result could be the wholesale rejection of the instrument. As the Lords usually consider instruments after they have been taken in the House of Commons, this has constrained opposition parties from pressing their disagreement. Between 1955 and the end of the 2015–16 session, 133 SIs were divided on, but such was the unease of the two major parties while in opposition about using the House's powers to the full that 67 of those divisions were on motions that would not, if carried, have proved fatal to the instrument in question. It is more common for the House to agree a 'non-fatal' motion which expresses regret about an instrument but without rejecting it.

Only six times has the government of the day ever been defeated on a vote which defeats a statutory instrument. The Conservative opposition divided the House against the Southern Rhodesia (United Nations Sanctions) Order 1968 and defeated the government, so provoking a constitutional furore. A virtually identical version of the order was approved a few weeks later. Two other instances occurred in February 2000 on a prayer to annul the Greater London Authority Election Rules 2000 and on a motion to approve the Greater London Authority (Election Expenses) Order 2000. These defeats occurred soon after the removal of most hereditary peers, and were arguably a sign of the newly reformed House wishing to demonstrate its potency. In 2007 the House declined to approve the Gambling (Geographical Distribution of Casino

Premises Licences) Order 2007, following an adverse report from the Merits of Statutory Instruments Committee (as it was then called) questioning the decision-making process for creating the new 'super casinos' to be set up under the order. In December 2012 the House declined to approve the Legal Aid, Sentencing and Punishment of Offenders Act 2012 (Amendment of Schedule 1) Order 2012 on the ground that it did not provide support for welfare claimants at first-tier tribunals.

Undoubtedly the most high-profile and contentious instance of the Lords refusing to pass a statutory instrument was on the draft Tax Credits (Income Thresholds and Determination of Rates) (Amendment) Regulations 2015. The un-catchy title of the instrument masked a significant change to the rules on entitlement to tax credits, which the government estimated would save it around £4 billion a year. The Commons passed the draft affirmative, albeit with reservations amongst some government backbenchers. When the Lords debated it in October 2015 several amendments to the motion to approve the instrument were tabled. One straightforwardly rejected the instrument; one was clearly 'non-fatal'. Neither was passed. However, two amendments stipulated that the House would 'decline to consider' the instrument until certain steps were taken. This was a novel formulation, which had the benefit of falling short of outright rejection of the instrument but the drawback of leaving many confused as to what its effect would be – with proponents arguing that the instrument could live to see another day, and so ideally should be reconsidered by the Commons, and opponents arguing that the amendment was in effect fatal. There was further controversy over whether the Lords would be in breach of convention by rejecting a statutory instrument (or whether it should ever reject one only because it disagreed with the policy, rather than for more profound 'constitutional' reasons); over whether the instrument was financial in nature and so should be the preserve of the Commons only; and over whether the significance of the policy meant it should have been pursued in an Act of Parliament and not in a statutory instrument. Amidst significant media interest the Lords passed the amendments declining to consider the instrument. The government considered that a rejection of the policy and so dropped it.

The next day the Lords narrowly avoided rejecting another statutory instrument. In response the government announced a review of the Lords' powers over secondary legislation, to be undertaken by former Leader of the House, Lord Strathclyde.

The Strathclyde Review

Lord Strathclyde's review set out three options. First, to remove the Lords from statutory instrument procedure altogether, leaving control solely with the Commons. Secondly, for the House to formalise in a resolution or standing orders any convention on how it exercises power over SIs – i.e. to codify the convention. The third option, which the review recommended, was to create a new statutory procedure allowing the Lords to invite the Commons to think again. Under this procedure the Lords could reject an instrument once, but if the Commons subsequently passed the same instrument it would become law.

A similar procedure was recommended by the Royal Commission on Reform of the House of Lords in 2000 (the 'Wakeham Commission') and by the Leader's Group on Working Practices in 2011 (the 'Goodlad Group'). Despite these antecedents the Strathclyde Review received a hostile reception in the Lords. Some saw it as an over-reaction to the tax credits vote; others thought it would give more power to the executive at the expense of Parliament; others thought that it distracted from the greater problems arising from increased use of delegated legislation. Following four select committee reports criticising the review and a change of relevant government ministers when Theresa May became Prime Minister, in late 2016 the government announced that it would not proceed with the proposal. This means that the Lords' powers over secondary legislation remain as they were, only now with the added (but confusing) option of 'declining to consider' an instrument. The controversy over the tax credits regulations may prove to be but a precursor to greater controversy over Brexit-related SIs.

Lords select committees on delegated legislation

The House of Lords, while cautious in the use it makes of its powers to reject affirmative or negative instruments in the chamber of the House, has in recent years taken considerable steps in other directions so as to ensure that delegated powers are appropriately used. We have already noted the major contribution made by the Lords Select Committee on Delegated Powers and Regulatory Reform. Since 1992 this committee has scrutinised all government and some private members' bills so as to establish whether any legislative power is inappropriately delegated to ministers, or whether any delegation is subject to sufficient parliamentary scrutiny. This 'up-stream' policing of the use of delegated powers has been very successful (see page 356). The committee also scrutinises and makes recommendations on draft orders laid under the Legislative and Regulatory Reform Act 2006 (see page 246). By the end of the 2016–17 session, 18 such orders had been considered and, in 2013, it recommended for the first time that one such order – on the regulation of providers of social work services – should not proceed.

In 2004 the House established the Secondary Legislation Scrutiny Committee (formerly the Merits of Statutory Instruments Committee) to sift those instruments of political significance from the rest. The establishment of such a committee had originally been recommended by the Royal Commission on Reform of the House of Lords in 2000 and endorsed by the Group on the Working of the House in 2002 and the Liaison Committee in 2003. The committee finally began its work in April 2004. The committee's remit is to consider every instrument laid before each House subject to parliamentary proceedings. The committee does not consider human rights remedial orders, regulatory reform orders or Church of England measures. The committee draws to the attention of the House any instrument that is important politically, legally or in policy terms; is inappropriate in view of developments since the passage of the parent Act; imperfectly achieves its objectives; is insufficiently explained by the government in explanatory material or was subject to a faulty consultation process;

or inappropriately implements EU legislation. (This latter provision arose out of fears that such regulations were overly elaborate and 'gold plated' the original EU requirements.) The committee was also empowered to conduct inquiries into general matters relating to the scrutiny of merits of instruments and, since 2011, to scrutinise draft orders laid under the Public Bodies Act 2011 where it has power to recommend changes to any draft.

The workload is considerable and the committee is supported by two full-time advisers in addition to the usual clerk and clerical support. The committee reports on around 7 per cent of instruments it considers (51 out of 659 in 2016–17) and usually does so neutrally: rather than recommend the House rejects or accepts an instrument, it draws attention to particular points, thus inviting members to probe further. The policy focus of this committee complements the more technical and legal scrutiny of the Joint Committee on Statutory Instruments. The Commons has no equivalent to the Lords' Secondary Legislation Scrutiny Committee, despite calls having been made for such a body by former Procedure Committees and others.

Legislative reform orders

There are some Acts of Parliament that allow a minister to amend primary legislation by secondary legislation – to amend an Act by an SI. Such a provision in a bill is known as a 'Henry VIII clause' – reflecting that monarch's somewhat broad-brush approach to his powers. It is generally undesirable for a minister to be able to change what normally only Parliament may decide; however, in 1994 the Deregulation and Contracting Out Act gave ministers just those powers, but subject to a stringent system of parliamentary control.

As part of the then Conservative government's wish to lighten the weight of regulation, the 1994 Act allowed ministers to amend or repeal primary legislation that imposed a burden affecting any person carrying on a trade, business or profession. It introduced an entirely new parliamentary procedure whereby a minister had to consult on a proposal, which would then be laid before Parliament and examined by Deregulation Committees of both Houses, which could suggest amendments before the deregulation order was laid as a formal draft for approval. Nearly 90 deregulation orders were made under the 1994 Act, ranging from greyhound racing to the registration of marriages to the selling of salmon roe; but it is in the nature of deregulation that after the early quick hits it becomes harder to find areas to deregulate.

The scope of the procedure was then widened by the Labour government's Regulatory Reform Act 2001 to cover 'burdens affecting persons in the carrying on of any activity'; and some other limitations in the 1994 Act were relaxed. A power to make 'subordinate provisions' (a sort of further delegated legislation, but also to be considered by the committees) was introduced. The committees were renamed: that in the Commons became the Regulatory Reform Committee, and the Lords committee became the Delegated Powers and Regulatory Reform Committee.

Regulatory Reform Orders have now, in turn, been superseded by Legislative Reform Orders under the Legislative and Regulatory Reform Act 2006, which was initially intended to widen considerably the purposes for which such orders could amend previous acts, but which was made more limited following protests during the passage of the bill.

Before a minister may make a legislative reform order, he or she must *consult widely with those who would be affected*. This is part of the procedure on which the committees have been particularly insistent. After the consultation, the minister may lay before Parliament *a draft order, together with an explanatory statement, and a recommendation as to the procedure that should apply (super-affirmative, affirmative or negative)*. There is then a period of time for consideration by the committees (either 40 days or 60 days, depending on the procedure, and, as with praying time, not including recesses). Either committee can 'upgrade' the procedure (strengthen it from negative to affirmative or super-affirmative, or from affirmative to super-affirmative) and then tests the proposal against various criteria, including whether this is the right method of changing the law; the adequacy of the consultation; whether the right balance of burdens and benefits has been struck; and whether the proposal would continue any necessary protection for those affected; whether it would limit any reasonable rights or freedoms; and whether the minister is acting within the powers given by the Act.

In assessing the proposal, the committees often take written or oral evidence, both from the government and from those who might be affected, and they then report separately on whether the proposal should go forward, with or without amendments. If a committee wishes to propose amendments, it will also upgrade the procedure to super-affirmative, to enable the minister to lay a revised draft order, taking into account the views of the committees and of anyone else who has commented during the 60-day period, and setting out what changes have been made, and why. The committees look at the draft order within 15 sitting days and report to each House on it.

In the Commons, there is then a graduated procedure. If the committee has unanimously recommended that the draft order be made, it is put to the House without debate; if the committee had a vote on the matter, there is an hour-and-a-half's debate in the House; but if the committee recommends that the draft order not be approved, there must be a debate of up to three hours on a motion to disagree with the committee. If that motion is successful, the question on approval of the draft order is put without further debate.

Once the draft order has been approved by both Houses (or for the negative procedure, so long as the draft order has not been the subject of a negative resolution in either House), the minister may *make it* and so bring it into law. A list of legislative reform business, and the stages each draft order has reached, is published weekly. The number of draft orders per year has varied and was two in each of the 2015–16 and 2016–17 sessions. This procedure, under all three Acts, has been innovative and effective. It has all the advantages of pre-legislative scrutiny: detailed, evidence-based scrutiny and analysis; wide consultation and public access to the legislative process; and the testing and amendment of proposed legislation to produce a better quality of outcome. Moreover, it is systematic; it is not up to the government of the day to decide, as with bills, whether they should be examined in draft before being formally introduced. If the legislative reform route is taken, then the procedure outlined above applies automatically.

It has been rigorous; indeed, so much so that several government departments decided early on that they would not take this route but wait for an opportunity for the easier ride of primary legislation. It has been effective and has allowed backbenchers to have a real influence on the content of legislation; governments of both parties have almost always accepted the committees' recommendations. And it has been consensual; the committees have worked in a remarkably non-partisan way. The procedure is seen by many as offering lessons that could be applied more widely.

Remedial orders

The Human Rights Act 1998, which came into effect in October 2000, allowed ministers to make a new form of delegated legislation known as 'remedial orders'. These come about when a UK court finds that some provision of an Act of Parliament is incompatible with the Human Rights Act. A remedial order may amend primary legislation; the procedure for considering it is similar to that for a legislative reform order, except that it is the task of the Joint Committee on Human Rights, rather than the two committees described above, to consider and report on proposals and draft orders. Once it has been considered by the Joint Committee on Human Rights, and the statutory periods have passed, a draft order is treated in the same way as any other affirmative instrument.

If swift action is required, a minister may make an order, laying it before both Houses. It has immediate statutory effect, but it must be confirmed by both Houses approving it within 120 days of its being laid (as for praying time, excluding times when both Houses are in recess). During the first 60 of those days, representations may be made to the minister; and if as a result the minister decides to make a new order, it must be approved by both Houses within the remaining 60 days.

Details of remedial orders are included in the Statutory Instrument Lists (mentioned on page 242). There have so far been few remedial orders, the most recent of which was the Human Fertilisation and Embryology Act 2008 (Remedial) Order 2018. Governments have generally tended to address incompatibility with the Human Rights Act using primary legislation.

Church of England measures

As the established church of the state, the Church of England has to have its legislation approved by Parliament, including the Royal Assent of the sovereign. These *measures* are a form of delegated legislation, although they eventually form part of the statute book. They are first agreed by the Church's parliament, the General Synod, which has procedures for debate and amendment very similar to the Commons and Lords. A draft of the measure is then sent to the Ecclesiastical Committee, which consists of 15 members of the House of Lords nominated by the Lord Speaker and 15 MPs nominated by the Speaker. This is not a conventional joint committee appointed by the two Houses but a statutory body set up under the Church of England Assembly (Powers) Act 1919.

The purpose of the committee is 'to determine whether or not the measure is expedient'; it cannot make amendments. To assist the committee in coming to a view, comments and explanations are submitted by the General Synod, and members of its Legislative Committee assist the Ecclesiastical Committee in its deliberations. On difficult issues, a conference with the full membership of the Legislative Committee may be held, but this is rare. The committee presents a short report on each measure, together with its decision on whether the measure in question is 'expedient'. The measure is at the same time laid before each House of Parliament for approval.

The role of Parliament in the governance of the Church is sometimes a cause of controversy. After all, the General Synod as the Church's own representative body has already approved a measure by the time it reaches Parliament. It is arguable that, in its consideration of a measure, Parliament should not seek to second guess the Synod. Very occasionally, the Ecclesiastical Committee has, on some point of principle, suggested that a measure be laid in a slightly different form. Once the Ecclesiastical Committee has found a measure expedient, the proceedings in the two Houses are uncontroversial, although in 1989 a measure dealing with the ordination of divorced men was actually rejected by the Commons.

7

Parliament and the taxpayer

Total government expenditure in 2017–18 was expected to be £802 billion, or about £12,225 for every man, woman and child in the United Kingdom. Taxation and public spending touch everyone's daily lives, from the amount of income tax we pay to the levels of state pensions and benefits we receive, and from standards in our local hospitals and schools to the quality of the environment and the number of police on the beat. It is not surprising, then, that management of the economy and of the nation's finances are always at the heart of political controversy. Are levels of public spending helping or hindering economic growth? What services should be protected from the full effects of reductions in public spending? Is the taxpayer getting good value for money? How will decisions on spending affect levels of taxation and public borrowing?

These questions are central to much of the work of Parliament but, as we shall see in this chapter, while Parliament provides the main forum for debate on the big issues, it exercises little detailed control.

Constitutional principles

The modern role of Parliament (and especially the House of Commons) in financial matters reflects the ancient relationship with the Crown. The sovereign needed the authority and agreement of the Commons for levying new taxes; but from early times the House sought the redress of grievances before approving the Crown's taxation proposals, and this was the cornerstone of Parliament's growing status.

It is now a basic constitutional principle that it is for the Crown (in fact, the government of the day) and not for Parliament to propose expenditure and taxation. This *financial initiative of the Crown* means, in practice, that only ministers may make proposals for spending and taxes. If Parliament agrees to those proposals, then they are given authority through legislation.

The House of Commons has a special role in financial matters, asserted in a resolution of 1671, which stated 'That in all aids given to the King by the Commons, the rate or tax ought not to be altered by the Lords', and reinforced seven years later by a resolution that said in splendidly comprehensive language:

> *All aids and supplies, and aids to his Majesty in Parliament, are the sole gift of the Commons; and all bills for the granting of any such aids and supplies ought to begin with the Commons; and that it is the undoubted and sole right of the Commons to direct, limit and appoint in such bills the ends, purposes, considerations, limitations, and qualifications of such grants, which ought not to be changed or altered by the House of Lords.*

The Lords did not endorse these views, and remained willing to reject tax measures outright.

Thus, in 1860 the Lords rejected the Paper Duty Repeal Bill and, more seriously, in 1909, the Finance Bill, which would have given effect to Lloyd George's controversial Budget. In the latter case, the result was the passing of the Parliament Act 1911 and the permanent restriction of the powers of the House of Lords to thwart the legislative will of the Commons.

One consequence of the *financial privilege* of the House of Commons is that *bills of aids and supplies*, principally Finance Bills, which authorise the government's taxation proposals, and Supply Bills, which authorise government spending, originate in the Commons and are not amended by the Lords. Finance Bills are normally debated on second reading in the Lords, but other proceedings are formal only.

The Parliament Act 1911 defines a *money bill* as a bill whose *only* purpose is to authorise expenditure or taxation, a definition that does not always apply to Finance Bills, but may cover other bills. If the Commons passes a bill certified by the Speaker as a money bill and it is sent to the Lords at least one month before the end of the session and has not been agreed by the Lords within a month, it may be sent directly for Royal Assent. Although it remains, in theory, possible for the Lords to amend money bills – and such amendments have in the past been made – the Commons are not obliged to consider them, and it is now inconceivable that any amendment would be attempted. The stages of money bills in the Lords are abbreviated and no money bill has ever had to be presented for Royal Assent under the terms of the 1911 Act.

A bill whose provisions involve an increase in public expenditure or taxation may begin in the House of Lords, but it may proceed in the Commons only if a minister takes charge of it. In such a case, the constitutional niceties are preserved by a *privilege amendment*: a subsection at the end of the bill that says 'Nothing in this Act shall impose any charge on the people or on public funds' or vary any such charge. This is a fiction, of course; and the provision is removed when the bill is in committee in the Commons.

Another practical effect of Commons financial privilege is that any Lords amendments to a Commons bill that involve a charge upon the public revenue not sanctioned by the Commons money resolution in respect of that bill are deemed disagreed to upon the Speaker's declaration, 'by reason of privilege'. A privilege reason for disagreeing to such amendments should not be questioned by the Lords. This is what is

Table 7.1 Parliament and financial cycles

Month	Budget cycle	Estimates cycle	Reporting cycle
Start of parliamentary session			
May			
June			
July		First and second estimates days Supply and Appropriation (Main Estimates) Bill passed	Annual report and accounts (with audited accounts for year 1 and plans for years 3 and 4) published Select committees may review and report
July/October		Spending review (usually plans for years 3, 4 and 5) published in certain years	
November/December	Budget statement and debate		
December/January	Finance Bill in Committee of the whole House and public bill committee	Presentation of – Supplementary Estimates (for year 2); – Votes on Account (for year 3); – Excess Votes (for year 1); – Ministry of Defence Votes A (for years 2 and 3) (for approval by 18 March)	
February	Finance Bill report stage and third reading Formal consideration by Lords (Finance Act)		
March	Spring statement	Third estimates day Supply and Appropriation (Anticipation and Adjustments Bill) passed (must be by 31 March)	
April		Main Estimates (for year 2) presented (for approval by 5 August)	
End of parliamentary session			

termed 'unwaivable privilege', as such amendments do not simply infringe the Commons financial primacy so that when they are disagreed to the 'financial privilege' reason is given (see page 223), but they have no financial cover and so are disagreed to without formal consideration by the Commons.

The financial pre-eminence of the Commons in matters of legislation does not mean that the Lords are inhibited in discussing or investigating financial subjects. Both in debate and through the work of select committees such matters are frequently pursued. The Economic Affairs Committee usually reports on certain technical aspects of the Finance Bill, rather than on the rates of incidence of tax, and in 2013–14 an *ad hoc* select committee examined the consequences of the use of personal service companies for tax collection. The legislative primacy of the Commons in financial matters rests to some degree on the self-restraint of the Lords. Whether a reformed House of Lords would be equally restrained, and how the Commons might react, have been vigorously debated in the context of Lords reform proposals.

The annual cycles

Financial procedure is hideously complex; this is partly because of the complexity of the subject matter but is also because the process takes place in three largely separate cycles. The *Budget cycle* deals with broad financial issues, the management of the economy and the authorisation of taxation. The *estimates cycle* covers the authorisation of public spending; and the *reporting cycle* provides information on what money has been spent and how effectively it has been used. We will examine these individually (and hope to make them slightly less confusing); but Table 7.1 shows how events in all three relate. The fact that the parliamentary year, which now usually begins around May, does not exactly coincide with the financial year starting in April is a further complication.

Table 7.1 shows the main events in each of the Budget, estimates and reporting cycles. Dates are indicative rather than exact (except for the approval deadlines). The financial year beginning in April is designated year 2; during the session the House will also consider business relating to year 1 (the financial year that ended shortly before the start of the new session) and examine plans for the year 3 (which starts shortly before the end of the session) and beyond.

Some important economic decisions are scrutinised by Parliament but are not under parliamentary control: interest rates are set by the Bank of England rather than by the government; and the level of the public sector net cash requirement (i.e. the budget deficit in any given year) does not require parliamentary authorisation.

The Budget cycle

The word 'budget' comes from the archaic French *bougette*, a little bag, which in English had its literal meaning from the fifteenth century; later, 'to open one's budget' meant 'to speak one's mind'. In 1733 Sir Robert Walpole – then Chancellor of the Exchequer, as well as Prime Minister – was depicted in a satirical pamphlet as a quack doctor opening a bag of pills. The term rapidly became applied to the Chancellor's review of the national finances, given annually from Walpole's time onwards.

The Chancellor of the Exchequer now normally delivers the Budget in the autumn. There will also usually be a Budget not long after a general election if there has been a change of government. In recent years the Budget statement has been on a Wednesday, although for most of the post-war period it was usually a Tuesday. Before 2017 budgets were usually in the spring, though from 1993 to 1996 they were held in the autumn. Budget day is always something of a media event, with the Chancellor being photographed outside his residence at No. 11 Downing Street before leaving for the Commons, holding up the despatch box containing his Budget speech. Customarily the Chancellor briefs the Queen on the Budget the night before and the Cabinet on the morning of the Budget (the Cabinet is informed of the Budget, rather than deciding on it – a significant if understandable departure from the principle of collective cabinet decision-making). In his memoirs Nigel Lawson, Chancellor from 1983 to 1989, thought Budget day was 'best described as an enjoyable ordeal'.

The Budget speech comes immediately after Question Time; in order not to upstage the Chancellor, the ten-minute rule bill slot (which is normally on Tuesdays and Wednesdays) for Budget day is deferred to the following Monday. Before the Chancellor's statement begins, the Speaker's place in the Chair is taken by the Chairman of Ways and Means, a tradition reflecting the fact that until 1967, when it was abolished, taxation proposals were made in the Committee of Ways and Means.

The Chancellor begins with the review of the nation's finances and the economic situation. Some of the form would be familiar to the Chancellor's predecessors over three centuries, but following the creation of the independent Office for Budget Responsibility (OBR) in 2010 – placed on a statutory footing in the Budget Responsibility and National Audit Act 2011 – the economic and public finance forecasts are those of that Office rather than of the Treasury. In the latter part of the speech – in which interventions are not usually taken – the Chancellor moves on to taxation and spending proposals. Modern Budget statements last an hour or so: a far cry from Gladstone's four-and-three-quarter-hour marathon in 1853. When the Chancellor's statement is complete, the motions to give effect to its tax proposals are made available to the House. There are usually around 70 of them. Strict secrecy should be maintained on the Budget proposals until the Chancellor announces them – not least because of their market sensitivity – so, exceptionally, no notice is given of these motions. However, Budget secrecy generally no longer has its former magic and, in the days leading up to the Budget statement, it is now usual to find remarkably authoritative media comment on possible proposals.

The Chancellor then usually moves a motion to give immediate legal effect to certain Budget proposals (three in autumn 2017) to forestall the speculation or bulk-buying that might take place if it were known that the duty on cigarettes or whisky, for example, would be raised, but not for days or weeks. Under the Provisional Collection of Taxes Act 1968, when this motion is agreed to, the proposals it covers have the force of law, but the House must agree to the motions on the individual proposals within ten sitting days. This procedure may apply to any proposal continuing a tax or altering its rate, but not to new taxes.

Philip Hammond, Chancellor of the Exchequer, delivers the autumn Budget, 2017

Source: Copyright House of Commons, 2017. Photography by Jessica Taylor

The Chancellor then usually moves what is known as the 'amendment of the law' motion. This is a general statement that 'it is expedient to amend the law with respect to the National Debt and to make further provision in respect of finance', and it is the vehicle for the very broad Budget debate that follows. In autumn 2017 the government was criticised for not proposing this motion; instead the debate took place on the motion that income tax be charged for 2018–19. It was suggested that this was to prevent backbench rebellions on amendments to the Budget. The Chancellor is followed not by the shadow Chancellor but by the Leader of the Opposition, who must make some shrewd guesses in advance to enable swift reaction to what the Chancellor has said, in addition to setting out the opposition's economic policies.

The Budget debate normally lasts for four or five days, and at its conclusion all 70 or so motions are put to the House, providing the opposition parties with an opportunity to vote against – usually three or four – individual proposals with which they particularly disagree. The Finance Bill is then formally introduced on the basis of what have now become the *founding resolutions*.

The Finance Bill

The Finance Bill is a substantial document, often running to 250 or more clauses with many schedules. Its provisions combine changes to levels and types of taxation with much detailed administration of the tax system, which makes for great complexity. It also provides for the renewal for the financial year just starting of taxes already in force.

The Finance Bill's second reading debate will be a single day, providing a further opportunity for a general debate on the government's fiscal policy. Proceedings on a bill based on founding resolutions such as the Finance Bill need not end at the moment of interruption, which formerly led to many late sittings, but a programme motion agreed at the time of second reading usually now supersedes these open-ended arrangements. (When budgets were held in the spring, the House generally agreed a programme motion to carry over the bill to the next session, but moving the budget (back) to the autumn means that the Finance Bill can be scrutinised and agreed in the same session.) The bill is then divided; clauses dealing with the major, or most controversial, proposals are taken in Committee of the whole House. The rest of the bill is committed to a public bill committee. The report stage and third reading usually occupy a further two days on the floor of the House.

Public bill committees on the Finance Bill have a character rather different from those on other bills. They are larger, often with 30 to 40 members rather than 20 or so; because of the regularity of Finance Bills, and of debates on economic affairs, the participants will know each other well and be old sparring partners; and the level of expertise is high. Both the opposition parties and government backbenchers will be extensively briefed by groups that will be affected by the Chancellor's proposals and assisted by them in drafting amendments to the often highly complex provisions of the bill. In addition to the usual rules about the admissibility of amendments (see page 199), MPs' ability to propose changes is restricted by the scope of the resolutions to which the House has agreed and, where the resolutions simply said 'that provision may be made about the level of' such and such a tax or charge, the levels actually proposed in the bill. For example, if the House agreed to a resolution that said that the rate of corporation tax should be 20 per cent, amendments seeking to raise that rate would not be in order, although it would be possible to move to reduce it.

Governments are usually even less willing to accept substantial amendments to the Finance Bill than they are in the case of other legislation, although disquiet among backbenchers can cause changes, whether following defeat on a vote, as with the scrapping of the second tranche of VAT on domestic fuel in December 1994, or by the government altering its proposals to head off possible defeat, as in the halving of the increase in petrol duty that was proposed in the 1981 Budget. However, to a great extent the Budget is a package and, for MPs of governing parties in particular, voting to defeat one proposal implies voting to increase revenue elsewhere – or to reduce public expenditure. However, less dramatic changes are occasionally made as a result of the committee stage of the Finance Bill. One example in 1998 was the proposal to tax agricultural earnings applied to the upkeep of historic houses. The Historic Houses Association briefed MPs on the committee, they took up the case, and the taxation was phased in rather than being introduced immediately, with considerable benefits for the national heritage.

The Finance Bill then goes to the Lords. A general economic debate is held on second reading of the Finance Bill, and remaining stages are then taken formally, without debate.

Budget information

On Budget day, the Treasury publishes the *Budget Report*, often known as the Red Book. The document, running to 88 pages in autumn 2017, provides an overview of the state of the economy and the public finances, sets out the detail of the Budget measures and their financial implications, and places those measures in the wider context of government policy. It is accompanied by a distributional analysis of the impact of the Budget on households and more detailed policy costings, as well as around 50 documents from HM Revenue and Customs on specific proposals.

At the same time, the OBR publishes its *Economic and Fiscal Outlook*, which sets out the forecasts for the economy and the public finances, and the OBR's assessment of the prospects for the government meeting its targets for the future health of the public finances periodically set in the Charter for Fiscal Responsibility. The OBR also provides a commentary on whether it considers the Treasury's costings to be reasonable.

Although the range and scale of the Budget documentation has fallen back from its peak during the Chancellorship of Gordon Brown, this single parliamentary event is the occasion for announcing a vast array of measures of great complexity, not all of them strictly fiscal. The audience for the proposals is, of course, much wider than Parliament, and the proposals and analysis are closely examined in the financial, commercial and industrial sectors. Nevertheless, the Budget proposals and information set the House of Commons a substantial task of scrutiny, which the legislative stages of the Finance Bill struggle to perform.

However, the Treasury Committee reports rapidly on the Budget in order to inform consideration of the Finance Bill. It takes oral evidence not only from the Chancellor himself and senior Treasury officials, but also from the OBR, as well as from outside financial and economic experts. It often exposes otherwise neglected aspects of the Budget; for example, in 2014 highlighting the proposal to grant HM Revenue and Customs the power to recover money directly from taxpayers' bank accounts.

The Spring Statement

The Chancellor makes a second major economic statement to the House of Commons in the Spring Statement. This provides an opportunity for the Chancellor to update the House on the government's plans for the economy and to set out the economic and fiscal forecasts of the OBR in its second *Economic and Fiscal Outlook* which is published at the same time. As with the Budget, the Spring Statement will be accompanied by substantial documentation. The statement itself is not followed by formal financial proceedings comparable to those after the Budget, although the Chancellor can expect to answer questions after his statement for far longer than is usually the case with a ministerial statement. The Spring Statement is likely to be considered by the Treasury Committee.

From the early 1980s until the early 1990s, there was an Autumn Statement which also reported on the outcome of an annual spending round. From 1993 to 1996 public spending plans and taxation proposals were briefly combined in a 'unified Budget' in November. This was followed, from 1997 to 2010, by a return to the traditional spring Budget, but with a Pre-Budget Report in the autumn including consultation on proposed Budget measures. From 2010 George Osborne reverted to the pre-1993 pattern, although the separation of this statement from the announcement of spending plans, introduced by Gordon Brown, was retained.

In 2010 the government established a tax consultation framework, setting out ideas on prospective tax changes. Although the Autumn Statement was not theoretically as consultative as the Pre-Budget Report, tax proposals in the Budget and Autumn Statement often involved consultation exercises rather than immediate legislative provisions. This enables the government to modify the measures in the light of public responses, or withdraw them altogether.

In 2016 Philip Hammond announced that the government would move to a single 'fiscal event' each year: a Budget in the autumn. This would be accompanied by a low-key Spring Statement which updated Parliament on the latest economic data. Over the last 20 years or so Autumn Statements had become effectively a second Budget, with major fiscal and policy changes announced. It was thought that this caused too much disruption (and temptation for politicking and headline-seeking announcements), so the intention is that the Spring Statement will not contain major announcements. In outlining the change the Chancellor reserved the right to make announcements in the Spring Statement in response to 'unexpected changes in the economy' – time will tell whether Chancellors resist pressure for tax and spending changes in Spring Statements and limit them to economic updates.

The estimates cycle

The process of voting 'supply' has its origins in a time when monarchs needed to spend money that the Crown did not have, usually on wars. Parliament then had to be asked to supply the funds. Initially, Parliament authorised taxation alone and decisions on expenditure were for the Crown, but in the eighteenth century a settled practice emerged whereby separate parliamentary authorisation was required for how money was spent, as well as how it was raised. Thus, even when tax receipts are held in the government's bank account – the Consolidated Fund – distinct statutory authority is needed to spend them. The main method of authorising that spending in the Commons is through 'Supply' proceedings, as distinct from 'Ways and Means' proceedings that relate to taxation. Most public expenditure is authorised annually on the basis of government requests in the form of the estimates.

There are large areas of public expenditure that are not subject to annual parliamentary control based on the supply estimates, either because there is standing statutory authority for such expenditure – for example, for net contributions to the European Union budget – or because the spending is funded by means other than taxation – such as national insurance contributions or council tax.

Resource accounting

Since 2001–02, as a result of the Government Resources and Accounts Act 2000, the estimates have been presented to Parliament on a 'resource' accounting basis (although they still also include a request for total cash (the *Net Cash Requirement*) to give effect to the spending). 'Resource' accounting – also known as 'accruals accounting' – records the economic costs of the provision of services and the consumption of assets (including depreciation and future liabilities such as those for compensation for early retirement). It is designed to give a more accurate picture of how resources are being used and makes government accounts much more like company accounts. It also allows a better assessment of how resources have been applied to the achievement of policy objectives. Cash accounting, the method used until 2001, merely tracked the movement of cash, creating an incentive to bring forward or delay cash payments at year end to stay within voted limits, and thus distorting longer-term spending patterns.

Public spending plans

Since 1998 successive governments have replaced the annual spending round with multi-year spending plans announced every two or three years. Initially, a spending review every other July (in 1998, 2000, 2002 and 2004) announced plans for three subsequent years, including revised plans for the year covered previously. In October

2007 the Labour government set three-year spending plans in a single exercise. In October 2010 the coalition government announced spending plans for a four-year period up to 2014–15, supplemented in June 2013 by a single year spending round for 2015–16. In 2015 there was a combined Autumn Statement and spending review, covering the next five years. In each case, an overall government expenditure ceiling has been set, and departments negotiate with Treasury ministers to agree departmental totals and what will be achieved with such spending. The results are announced in a statement and accompanying publication, but there is no role for Parliament in the negotiation process.

For each department, spending reviews have set a *Departmental Expenditure Limit* (*DEL*) (split between resource and capital totals) within which that department must operate, even though some elements will be demand-led. Spending reviews also set out forecasts for *Annually Managed Expenditure* (*AME*). AME covers expenditure that is less predictable or controllable than DELs; for example, social security and Common Agricultural Policy payments. In 2010, within a context of considerable budgetary restraint, the spending review also sought to bear down on the growing costs of AME (particularly welfare benefits), and this was extended from 2015–16 with a requirement for the House of Commons to approve spending on welfare above a preset 'welfare cap' based on past forecasts of spending from the OBR. Together, the DEL and AME constitute *Total Managed Expenditure* (*TME*).

These multi-year spending reviews provide an important opportunity for debate on expenditure by the House of Commons, and for consideration of departmental priorities by select committees.

Votes on Account

Because the main process for statutory authorisation of departmental expenditure is not completed until nearly four months into the financial year in question, advanced authorisation is given on the basis of Votes on Account presented in January or February. These normally cover about 45 per cent of the amounts already authorised for each government department for the previous financial year. Votes on Account must be agreed by the House within a roll-up motion by 18 March each year (see page 263).

Ministry of Defence Votes A

The Bill of Rights 1688–89 prevented the Crown from maintaining a standing army in time of peace without the approval of Parliament. This control is exercised in part through Supply proceedings, and the Ministry of Defence 'Votes A' laid before the House by the Secretary of State for Defence alongside the Votes on Account and the supplementary estimates invite the annual authorisation by the House of Commons of the maximum numbers of personnel in the regular and reserve armed forces for the coming year, and any modification of those limits for the current year.

Main estimates

The main estimates, one for each government department (and for other bodies such as the Office of Rail Regulation and the NHS Pension Scheme), are published around the start of the financial year to which they relate. They form the principal request from the government to the House of Commons for the resources required to run the state. They vary from small departments such as the Cabinet Office, which in 2017–18 had a combined resource and capital voted budget of £490 million, to major areas of government expenditure: in 2017–18, the Department of Health had an equivalent budget of £104 billion.

Part I of each estimate provides the key information on which the House of Commons is being asked to vote: the net resource and capital totals within DEL, the equivalent totals for AME, any net non-budget requirement (principally the block grants for the devolved governments) and the *net cash requirement*. Even though government accounting is on a resource basis, the amounts sought are expressed in cash terms, as well as in resource terms, to control the cash flowing out of the Consolidated Fund. The estimates now include totals for non-voted expenditure (that not requiring annual authorisation) so that estimates can be aligned with the budgets set in spending reviews and monitored by the Treasury.

Each estimate also contains a formal description of the services to be financed from each relevant budgetary boundary within the estimate (known as the *ambit*). The ambit also specifies the income that may be retained by the department. The ambit is an important part of the process of authorisation because it describes the purpose for which the money is sought, and expenditure must fall within that description. Finally, Part I of the estimate notes any amounts already allocated in the *Vote on Account*.

Part II of the estimate shows the resource requirement from Part I, broken down into more detail of what is going to be provided with the money. This breakdown forms the basis for in-year control of expenditure by the Treasury. If there is an underspend in one area and a requirement in another, funds may be moved between these subheads without further parliamentary authority (a process known as *virement*), although departments need prior Treasury approval to move income between subheads. The rationale for this is that Parliament approves the headline figures but not the detailed breakdown. The flexibility that virement gives also means that there is less need to build in a contingency into each subhead, which would encourage an over-provision in the estimate as a whole. Part II also contains a detailed reconciliation between a department's net resource requirement and the net cash requirement.

Part III provides detailed reconciliation between all expenditure and income within the accounting boundary. It also gives further information on departmental income (which was formerly subject to separate parliamentary control), including income that will be surrendered to the Consolidated Fund rather than used to finance its own expenditure. Finally, Part III states who will account for the estimate; for each estimate there must be an *Accounting Officer*, usually the Permanent Secretary of the government department concerned or the chief executive of an executive agency. Accounting Officers have a personal responsibility for the regularity and propriety of expenditure – including ensuring that money is spent only on purposes authorised by Parliament – as well as for the quality of internal financial controls in the department concerned.

The notes to each estimate describe any *contingent liabilities*: commitments that, if they were to be called upon, would require further expenditure. Although ministers may give guarantees or indemnities, Parliament is not bound in advance to honour any liabilities arising unless by law the liability is charged on the Consolidated Fund. Liabilities outside the normal course of business and above £300,000 or of a nonstandard kind must be reported to Parliament.

When the estimates are published, departments send an explanatory memorandum on their estimates (the Estimates Memorandum) to the relevant select committee. This explains differences between current and previous estimates, the reasons for major changes and the impact of the changes sought, facilitating more rigorous scrutiny of the estimates.

Supplementary estimates

Supplementary estimates seek authority for any additional funds that government departments have found to be necessary since the main estimates were prepared; they can also reduce the amounts sought. They are accompanied by an Estimates Memorandum. *Revised estimates* may be presented in the early summer to replace the main estimate for a department prior to parliamentary approval, usually to reduce the amount sought or vary the way in which it is spent.

If emergencies arise, the government can have recourse to the contingencies fund. This is limited by law to 2 per cent of the previous year's total authorised supply expenditure, and any money drawn out of the fund must be repaid. Alternatively, the House may be asked to agree an out-of-turn estimate at any time. The motion to approve any such estimate would be separately debateable.

Excess Votes

Both main and supplementary estimates are timed to be approved within the financial year to which they relate, in order to set statutory limits that provide the benchmark for audit. Where a department's spending in a financial year is found by that process to have exceeded what Parliament authorised (or has been incurred for a purpose that was not authorised), Excess Votes are presented (usually in February) in the following or a subsequent financial year. These are examined by the National Audit Office (NAO), which advises the Public Accounts Committee; no excess vote may be put to the House for approval without debate unless that committee has no objection.

Roll-up motions and estimates days

In the later Victorian period, Supply motions provided the occasion for exhaustive (although not always relevant) debate, so that the Parliament sat well into August before the main estimates could be approved. In 1896 the Leader of the Commons,

Arthur Balfour, obtained its agreement to a deadline of 5 August for votes on all outstanding estimates to 'give even the hardest worked of us some chance of enjoying, at all events, the end of an English summer'. All outstanding main estimates are now approved without debate on a single 'roll-up' motion prior to 5 August, with matching provision for roll-up motions on supplementary estimates, Defence Votes A and Excess Votes before 18 March. The only estimates that are now debated are those selected for debate on three estimates days each session, the first and second around the day of the summer roll-up, and the third on the day of the spring roll-up (see Table 7.1 on page 252). Given the huge sums involved, and the myriad purposes for which they are used, three days may not seem much, and the process is, indeed, highly selective. Before 2018 the Liaison Committee, consisting of all the chairs of select committees, proposed one or two estimates for debate on each of these days. However, rather than inviting the House's detailed examination of a particular part of the estimate concerned, there was normally a reversal of the process. The estimate was used as a peg for a debate on a select committee report that was usually much more about policy than about the money the government was seeking from the House of Commons. In order to allow debate on the maximum number of select committee reports, estimates days were almost always divided into two parts, each with a different subject. In 2017 (as in earlier election years) there were no such debates before the summer as select committees had not yet been set up following the election; therefore, the House simply agreed all of the Main Estimates in one 'roll up' motion on 4 July.

As noted on page 268, from 2018 onwards, following recommendations made by the Procedure Committee, it is expected that the subjects for debates on estimates days will be determined by the Backbench Business Committee, which will select debates bid for by MPs on issues related to the estimates. In return, the Backbench Business Committee will put three of the days allotted to it at the disposal of the Liaison Committee, for debates on select committee reports.

Because of the financial initiative reserved to the Crown – in effect, to ministers – any amendment proposed to an estimates motion may only reduce the total of a request for resources, not increase it, although amendments to such motions are now rare, the last one that was moved being in June 2002. All questions on estimates day motions are deferred until immediately before the relevant roll-up, even if the debate is on a preceding day.

Supply and Appropriation Bill

Statutory authorisation to the Supply motions agreed at the time of the summer roll-up is given by the *Supply and Appropriation (Main Estimates) Bill*, which is introduced when that motion and any motions arising from the first and second estimates days are agreed. The bill gives parliamentary authority for total resources and capital requested to be used, and cash to be issued from the Consolidated Fund, but also limits the way in which the resources and capital can be used by *appropriating* the specified amounts to particular budgets in order to finance specified services, set out in the ambits that are reproduced in the bill. The bill also sets limits on defence numbers in accordance with Votes A. The questions on second and third reading are put without debate on a day subsequent to the roll-up; and there is no committee stage. Consideration in the Lords is purely formal.

The spring roll-up and any associated motions debated on the third estimates day are given effect in the Supply and Appropriation (Anticipation and Adjustments) Bill. This bill authorises the amounts requested in the supplementary estimates, the Excess Votes and the Votes on Account, appropriates the first two of these and modifies limits on personnel numbers in the Votes A. This bill, too, is passed without debate and is dealt with only formally by the Lords.

The reporting cycle

We have seen so far how the government seeks authorisation for the taxes it wishes to levy and the different stages by which its proposed spending is approved. What about the other side of the process: how does the government account for how it has spent the money?

Departmental annual reports and accounts

The main means by which departments account to Parliament for their spending and performance is their *annual report and accounts* which are usually published in June or July. The first element of these – the annual report – has been produced since 1991 and has developed substantially since then through initiatives by departments themselves and recommendations by select committees. The Treasury exercises general supervision and lays down guidance. Reports vary in format and presentation, but each contains core elements. Each sets out the names and responsibilities of the department's ministers and senior officials and the department's structure and purpose, and surveys the principal activities of the previous year.

Departmental reports also give figures for planned spending over the remainder of the planning period, together with the estimated spending for the current year and the actual spending for the five previous years. Other elements include changes to previously published plans, value-for-money initiatives, and departmental running costs and staffing.

Along with their annual reports departments publish the accounts for the financial year ending in March that year. Accounts are prepared according to government standards adapted from International Financial Reporting Standards and, in many respects, are similar to annual accounts of private-sector businesses. In addition to the standard primary financial statements, the consolidated statement of overall expenditure (equivalent to an income statement or profit and loss account), the statement of financial position (or balance sheet) and a statement of cash flows, there is a *Statement of Parliamentary Supply* comparing voted and non-voted budgets in the final estimate with final audited outturn. These are followed by a number of notes giving further information on categories of expenditure, on income and on assets and liabilities. The format of accounts is reviewed annually – for example, in 2015 changes were introduced to make the accounts more useful to parliamentary and other users, while retaining the components necessary for parliamentary and public accountability.

The accounts of government departments (and many other public bodies, including the BBC) are audited by the NAO, headed by the Comptroller and Auditor General (C&AG) (see page 266). Each set of accounts is preceded by the C&AG's certificate and report which sets out how the NAO has audited the accounts, and whether they represent a true and fair statement of the position. The C&AG may qualify his opinion on the accounts, if there are concerns that the financial statements do not fully comply with accounting standards; for example, spending may be misstated due to large fraud and error rates. In rare cases, the C&AG may even 'disclaim' the accounts or aspects of the accounts if there is insufficient audit evidence to support a 'true and fair' opinion.

In addition to their annual report and accounts, each department must produce a *single departmental plan*. These were introduced from 2015 and describe departments' objectives for the parliament and how they will meet those objectives. They replaced the coalition government's *Departmental Business Plans*, which fulfilled a similar purpose, and which themselves replaced the public service agreements that served as the framework for objective-setting under the 1997–2010 Labour government.

Select committee scrutiny of expenditure and performance

As part of the core tasks for departmental select committees agreed in 2002 and revised in 2012 (see page 346), select committees are expected 'to examine the expenditure plans, outturn and performance of the department and its arm's length bodies, and the relationships between spending and delivery of outcomes'. Some committees conduct inquiries focused on expenditure: the Defence Committee regularly examined the supplementary estimates for the financing of military operations in Iraq and Afghanistan, for example. In 2014, the Justice Committee drew the House's attention to a supplementary estimate from the Serious Fraud Office seeking an in-year increase in budget of over 50 per cent.

In its 2012 report on select committee effectiveness, the Liaison Committee encouraged select committees to broaden their scrutiny of departmental performance, focusing more on future plans and expected outcomes, including alternatives that could be considered. That committee also pressed for financial implications to be considered as a matter of routine when policies are examined. Select committees are aided in their examination by the Committee Office's *Scrutiny Unit*, which, in addition to providing analysis for individual committees, also supports the Liaison Committee in discussions with government on improvements to financial transparency and reporting. All are agreed on the theoretical desirability of greater select committee scrutiny of departments' expenditure. The practice can be different though: such scrutiny can be perceived as dull, and may not engage members unless the expenditure is especially high-profile or contentious. It is easy for this worthy task to be neglected.

The Comptroller and Auditor General and the National Audit Office

Although accounts may be examined by departmental select committees, across government and other public bodies as a whole, audit and control is the task of the Comptroller and Auditor General backed by the Public Accounts Committee (PAC).

The C&AG heads a staff of about 800 (about two-thirds of whom are either professionally qualified or training for professional qualifications) in the NAO, whose main building is about a mile from the Houses of Parliament. The C&AG has a direct responsibility to Parliament and works closely with the PAC. This relationship is recognised by the C&AG's personal status as an Officer of the House of Commons. He and NAO staff are independent of government: they are not civil servants and do not report to a minister.

The C&AG's work has four main elements. In his function as Comptroller, the Bank of England releases money to the government from the Consolidated Fund only on the authority of one of the C&AG's officials, who certifies that the release does not exceed the amount voted by the House. The C&AG also carries out an audit of the propriety and regularity of accounts – around 400 accounts are examined every year, including government departments, executive agencies and associated public bodies. The National Audit Act 1983, which established the NAO (previously the Exchequer and Audit Department), also gave the C&AG the task of examining the economy, efficiency and effectiveness of public spending. This leads to the publication each year of about 60 value-for-money studies. Finally, the NAO supports select committees and individual MPs in their scrutiny of public spending and service delivery.

The C&AG is independent in matters of audit judgement, although (under the Budget Responsibility and National Audit Act 2011) the operation of the NAO is now overseen by a Board. The budget for the NAO is considered by a statutory body, the Public Accounts Commission, composed of MPs.

The Public Accounts Committee

The PAC was first established at Gladstone's instigation in 1861. The committee has up to 16 members and is always chaired by an opposition MP (currently Meg Hillier). The standing orders give it the narrow task of 'the examination of the accounts showing the appropriation of the sums granted by Parliament to meet the public expenditure, and of such other accounts laid before Parliament as the Committee may think fit'; but for some years the committee has ranged more widely, principally drawing on the value-for-money reports of the C&AG. This routinely takes it into areas of policy (which it is always said not to investigate) and produces sometimes unhelpful overlap with the work of departmental committees.

The PAC's consideration of the C&AG's reports enhances their status, and the committee's work is made more credible by the very substantial back-up of the C&AG and his staff. Although the most frequent witnesses at the twice-weekly meetings of the PAC are Accounting Officers, the committee has expanded its range of witnesses in recent years, including contractors and (in the case of high-profile sessions on tax arrangements) individual companies. The PAC publishes some 50 reports a year, achieving a high public profile and keeping many senior mandarins on their toes.

Conclusion

Because the role of the House of Commons in the authorisation of taxation and expenditure is of such long standing and involves so many procedural peculiarities, the House is open to criticism for the imbalance between the ink expended in describing that role and the level of parliamentary engagement in practice. Such criticism has a point, although in forming a judgement it is important to take into account the opportunities for scrutiny, as well as the formal processes of authorisation.

On taxation, the House of Commons does its job quite well, at least in comparison with its examination of expenditure. There are still multiple opportunities for debate on tax measures on the floor of the House, and the public bill committee on the Finance Bill takes its job seriously. However, the Finance Bill has largely escaped the reforms that have benefited legislative proceedings as a whole. Pre-legislative scrutiny is limited and no evidence sessions are held at the start of the public bill committee stage. The Treasury and HMRC continue to use the annual opportunity of the Finance Bill to make manifold changes to the ferociously complex law on tax, sometimes after public consultation, but proposals for systematic pre-legislative scrutiny of the tax administration elements, or for their inclusion in a separate bill, have met Treasury resistance.

From 1996 to 2009 the Tax Law Rewrite project sought to rewrite tax law in more understandable English. It had some success – the special parliamentary procedure for its proposals resulted in five new Acts – but suffered from two drawbacks. First, its remit was to rewrite but not to simplify tax law, as the latter inevitably would result in subtly changing the law. Many think that simplification is desperately needed. Secondly, no sooner had it rewritten the law in an area then a new Finance Bill would amend that law, restarting the cycle of complexity. The Office for Tax Simplification, which was established in 2010 and made statutory in 2016, has on paper a wider remit – but its job is limited to advising the Chancellor; it does not itself simplify the law.

So far as expenditure is concerned, opportunities for debate and consideration closely linked to the formal decisions on authorisation are almost non-existent. The separation between debate and decision is of long standing, and a cause of complaint by select committees for nearly 100 years. In 1981 the Procedure Committee referred to 'the myth of effective control'. The subsequent introduction of three estimates days provided some formal link between debate and decision, but the connection is still tenuous, with the priority for participating MPs invariably being with policies rather than expenditure, and what discussion on expenditure that does takes place seldom arises from the estimates.

Reforms to the process have been proposed. In April 2017 the Procedure Committee recommended a number of changes, including:

- A longer period (at least five weeks) between publication of an estimate and its consideration and authorisation by the Commons.
- Changes to the estimates cycle, so that the main estimates are published before the financial year to which they relate.
- An informal arrangement between the Liaison and Backbench Business Committees, whereby the latter would nominate the subjects to be considered during estimates day debates – so that individual MPs can suggest debates focused on particular areas of government spending rather than having to link the debates to (often tangentially related) select committee reports. In return, the Liaison Committee would be able to nominate committee reports for debates on days allocated for backbench business, removing the need to choose only those reports which have an arguable link with the estimates.
- The provision of clearer information to MPs about the content and implications of the estimates.

With the exception of the informal swap between the Liaison and Backbench Business Committees it is not clear whether these recommendations will come to fruition. The Treasury has historically been opposed to institutional reforms, and it is not necessarily in its short-term interest to give MPs a greater grip on the purse-strings.

8

Debates

The *Oxford English Dictionary* defines the principal meaning of 'debate' as 'to dispute about, argue, discuss, especially to discuss a question of public interest in a legislative or other assembly'. Most proceedings in Parliament, whether on legislation or any other matter, take the form of debates. The main exceptions are questions and the examination of witnesses by select committees. In this chapter, we look at how debates take place on the floor of each House and elsewhere, how motions are moved and amended, and at some of the conventions of parliamentary debate.

Substantive motions

A substantive motion is one that expresses an opinion about something. The subject matter may range from 'That this House welcomes the Natural Capital Committee's first annual State of Natural Capital report; and urges the government to adopt the report's recommendations and to take concerted action to embed the value of natural capital in the national accounts and policy-making processes as early as possible', for which there may be a dozen MPs in the chamber, to 'That this House has no confidence in Her Majesty's Government', which will be a major occasion, with intense media interest and the chamber packed, perhaps to see the Prime Minister of the day fighting for his or her political life and the survival of the government.

A motion is *moved*, or proposed, by an MP who sponsors it. No seconder is required in the House of Commons; the seconding of the motion for the reply to the Queen's Speech is a tradition rather than a requirement.

If the motion requires notice, then the names of that member and any others who are putting the motion forward will appear on the Order of Business (although any minister, including a whip, may move a government motion, and any member of the relevant committee may move a motion in the name of the chair on behalf of a committee). The MP moving the motion argues for its approval by the House. When he or she sits down, the Speaker will *propose the question*, stating to the House what must be decided. Rather than read out a long text, he will normally say 'The question is, as on the Order Paper'. A debate then takes place, with the Chair normally calling MPs alternately from one side of the House and then the other.

If an *amendment* is down to the motion and is *selected* by the Speaker (see page 54), then at some point in the debate the Chair will ask one of the MPs whose names are listed in support of the amendment on the Order of Business to move it (although any MP could do so). It is possible for the Speaker to select a *manuscript amendment* – that is, one that was not tabled before the rising of the House at the previous sitting and so does not appear on the Order of Business, but this is unusual.

Once the amendment has been moved, the Speaker proposes the question on it, saying 'The original question was [as on the Order Paper]. Since when an amendment has been moved [as on the Order Paper]. The question is, that the amendment be made'. Strictly speaking, the debate then takes place on the amendment rather than on the motion that was first moved, but in most cases the scope of debate covers both.

When the time for the debate has elapsed, because the question must be put at any particular time, or because the closure (see page 148) has been moved and agreed to – or simply because there are no more MPs wishing to speak – the Speaker *puts the question* on the amendment first ('The question is, that the amendment be made') and the House decides that question, if necessary, by dividing (see page 161). Once the

Kwasi Kwarteng speaks in the Queen's Speech debate, 2017

Source: Copyright UK Parliament, 2017. Photography by Jessica Taylor

House has made its decision on the amendment, the original motion – whether or not amended – is decided, again by dividing if necessary. If an amendment was moved, the original motion is also known as the *main question*.

The moving of an amendment, whether in the House or in committee, is subject to the Chair having selected it. As we saw in Chapter 3, this is a power through which the Chair exercises great influence on the shape of proceedings. However, the power of selection does not exist in select committees (when, for example, they consider draft reports).

If the motion is agreed to, it becomes a *resolution* or an *order* of the House. The distinction is that a resolution expresses an opinion (for example, 'that this House calls on the Government to pause the roll-out of Universal Credit full service'); an order is something on which the House can exercise power directly ('that a select committee be appointed to examine . . .').

As we saw in Chapter 6, debate on legislation is structured in much the same way: a member moves 'that the such and such Bill be now read a second time'; it is possible to move a 'reasoned amendment'; and at the end of the debate the amendment and the main question are disposed of. Similarly, when an amendment to the text of a bill (or a new clause or schedule) is proposed in committee of the whole House or public bill committee, or in the House on report, the amendment is moved, and the question is proposed and debated. Amendments to amendments or to new clauses or schedules are treated in the same way as amendments to motions.

Debate on leaving the EU

As an example of the House dealing with a substantive motion – in this case, a very high-profile one – let us take the debate on the government's plan for Brexit, which was held on 7 December 2016. It was on an opposition day, so the motion was tabled in the name of the Leader of the Opposition. The motion recognised that leaving the EU was the defining issue facing the UK; recognised that it was Parliament's responsibility to scrutinise the government while respecting the referendum result; confirmed that the government should not disclose material which might damage the negotiations; and called on the government to publish its plan for leaving the EU before invoking article 50. Three amendments to the motion were tabled, by Scottish National Party MPs, by the Prime Minister and other senior ministers, and by all nine Liberal Democrat MPs. The debate began at 12.51 pm with the Speaker informing the House that he had selected the amendment in the name of the Prime Minister. This amendment added text to the end of the Leader of the Opposition's motion which recognised the result of the referendum and called on the government to invoke article 50 by 31 March 2017. Then the Shadow Brexit Secretary opened the debate by moving the motion. He spoke for 36 minutes and took 15 interventions. At the end of his speech the Speaker proposed the question on the motion. The Brexit Secretary then moved the amendment in the name of the Prime Minister and spoke for half an hour. After his speech the Speaker proposed the question on the amendment. Then the SNP frontbench spokesman addressed the House. After his 17-minute speech the Speaker called backbenchers, imposing an 8-minute time limit. After a while that was reduced to 5 minutes. At 6.43 pm an opposition frontbencher wound up the debate, followed at 6.52 pm by a junior Brexit department minister. At the moment of interruption (7.00 pm) the Speaker put the question on the amendment. It was passed by 461 votes to 89. Then he put the main question, on the original motion as amended. The result was similarly overwhelming: Ayes 448, Noes 75. (In both divisions all but one Conservative voted Aye, as did the majority of Labour MPs, and most other parties' MPs voted No.) The motion as amended was therefore formally recorded as a resolution of the House and in due course the government published its plan for Brexit and (after gaining statutory authorisation) invoked article 50 on 29 March 2017.

The sequence of votes on opposition days is often different to that set out above. If a government amendment leaves out words from the opposition's motion and inserts others, the first question put is 'that the original words stand part of the question'; this has the effect of allowing the opposition to record a positive vote for their motion as the first division after the debate. However, in the example above, the government's amendment did not remove words from the original motion, but merely added to it, and so the question on the amendment was put first.

Neutral motions

A different type of motion is tabled when what is wanted is a debate, rather than a decision. These debates used to take place on the motion 'that this House do now adjourn', and this is still done for the half-hour debate at the end of each day in the chamber. The subject for debate is shown on the Order Paper but does not form part of the text of the motion. Since 2007, however, a motion on the floor of the House of Commons that is purely a vehicle for debate has been in the form 'that this House has considered [the matter of] X', and a standing order provides that if the motion is expressed in neutral terms, no amendments may be tabled to it. (This is intended to replicate the rule that an adjournment motion cannot be amended, but it can be a matter of dissension if the government tables a neutral motion when the opposition would prefer an amendable one.) If debate finishes before the moment of interruption (see page 147), a division could still be forced, but this is unusual. Normally, the motion is passed without opposition, or debate is allowed to continue till the moment of interruption, when the motion simply lapses.

Before being replaced by 'has considered' motions, some debates on adjournment motions were great parliamentary occasions. One such in 1940 ('the Norway debate') led directly to the replacement of Neville Chamberlain by Winston Churchill as Prime Minister. In recent years up to 2007, the debates at emergency sittings of the House (for example, on the invasion of the Falkland Islands and on the 11 September 2001 terrorist attacks in the USA) were on motions for the adjournment. But when the House was recalled in June 2016 after the murder of Jo Cox MP the motion was 'That this House has considered the matter of tributes to Jo Cox.'

Disposing of a motion

Once a motion has been moved and the question proposed, it may be disposed of by being decided one way or the other, as outlined above. It may also stand adjourned or lapse because the moment of interruption arrives and there is no provision for it to be debated beyond that hour. It will then have been 'talked out' (see page 148). A motion may also be *withdrawn* or *superseded*.

Withdrawal

Once a motion of any sort has been moved, and before it has been put to the House or a committee for decision, it is possible to seek to withdraw it. But because the motion has been moved, it is in the possession of the House or committee and may be withdrawn only 'by leave' – that is, by unanimous consent. The MP who moved it says 'I beg leave to withdraw the motion [or amendment]'; and the Chair says to all and sundry 'Is it your pleasure that the motion [amendment] be withdrawn? . . . Motion [amendment], by leave, withdrawn'. But even one objection is enough to prevent this happening, and in that case the motion or amendment must eventually be put to a decision.

Superseding

It is possible to supersede debate on a question before the House or committee by what is known as a *dilatory motion*. This may be a motion for the adjournment of the debate, or of the committee, or of the House. In consideration of legislation, it may also be a motion that further consideration of the bill be adjourned, or 'that the Chair do report progress'. The moving of such a motion is subject to the permission of the Chair, who must be satisfied that it is not an abuse. A dilatory motion cannot be moved during programmed business (that is to say, most government bills being dealt with in the chamber) except by a minister. If it proceeds, however, debate on it supersedes the original debate, which is not resumed until the dilatory motion has been decided; (if the dilatory motion is successful debate on the original motion may be resumed only at a subsequent sitting).

A rare and old-fashioned motion similar to a dilatory motion is *the previous question*: a motion 'that the question be not now put'. If it is agreed to, the House immediately moves on to the next business; but if it is not agreed to, whatever matter was interrupted must be decided immediately (as when a closure is agreed to). The motion was moved in November 2014 to demonstrate the opposition's unhappiness about the form of motion the government had tabled to opt-in to certain EU Justice and Home Affairs legislation.

Debate may also be interrupted by a motion 'that the House sit in private'. This might be in earnest if extraordinary circumstances arose during some national emergency; the House sat in secret several times during the First and Second World Wars. Modern use of the motion (formerly in the words 'that Strangers do now withdraw') has been to attempt to disrupt business or express strong objection to some proceeding. The Chair must put the motion immediately to the House for decision; but it may not be moved more than once during a sitting. It is rarely successful; the most recent occasion was in December 2001, during proceedings on the Anti-Terrorism, Crime and Security Bill (as an expression of objection rather than to allow some confidential matter to be discussed). The government was unprepared for such a motion to be moved, the motion was agreed to, and the House sat in private for nearly an hour. As the *Hansard* reporters withdraw when the House sits in private, there is no record of what was said during that time.

Quorum

A motion to sit in private may also be used to test whether a quorum is present, which in the House or Committee of the whole House can be demonstrated only when a vote takes place. If the result of the vote shows that fewer than 40 MPs are present (35 voting, two tellers on each side and the occupant of the Chair), then the business that was under discussion beforehand stands over until the next sitting of the House. If the business is not government business, this may well be fatal, and this tactic is used from time to time to attempt to kill private members' bills.

In general committees and select committees, no such procedure exists; the specified quorum must be present throughout or the chair must suspend the committee. In select committees, the quorum is three or one-quarter of the membership, whichever is the greater; in general committees, it is one-third of the membership (subject to a maximum quorum of 17). In both cases, fractions are rounded up. Somewhat illogically in general committees, the chair is not counted in calculating what the quorum is but does count towards whether a quorum is present. In Westminster Hall (see page 278), the quorum is three.

If the number of members present on the government side of a committee alone does not provide a quorum, the opposition sometimes uses the tactic of removing its own MPs from the room and thus stopping the business. The rule of the business standing over does not apply 'upstairs', however, and as soon as a quorum is again present (provided it is within 20 minutes), debate proceeds.

We now look at several different types of motion.

Motions on opposition days

Each session, 20 days are set aside for debates initiated by the opposition parties. Seventeen of these are allocated to the Official Opposition and three to the second-largest opposition party. Smaller opposition parties sometimes lead opposition day debates. For example, as at December 2017 the DUP have had two half-days, and the Liberal Democrats one opposition half day since the 2015 election, provided by the government as unallotted days – that is to say they did not count towards the total of 20 opposition days provided for in standing orders. Before 2015 the second-largest party often shared some of its allotted days with the other smaller parties. Opposition day debates account for about 10 per cent of the total time of the House.

These days are ring-fenced opposition time; but, although their scheduling is normally agreed through the usual channels (see page 90), exactly when opposition days are taken is formally in the gift of the government. Each is the main business of a parliamentary day, so usually about six hours' debate – although ministerial statements can cut into this (often producing objections from the opposition). Days are often informally divided into two parts of roughly equal length so that two subjects can be debated.

These days are a key opportunity for the opposition parties, and especially for the Official Opposition, to try to expose the government over an issue on which it may be vulnerable, or to provide a shop window for one of its own policies. Among the subjects selected by the Labour Party in 2017 were the NHS and social care funding, prisons, school funding and universal credit roll-out.

The motion moved in the House is usually a strongly worded criticism of government policies. Before the 2017 parliament the government would usually table an amendment that sought to remove all the words of the motion after 'That this House' and substitute a warm endorsement of what the government was doing. The front bench speakers will be the relevant shadow secretary of state and shadow minister, and their counterparts in government. The debate is often combative. Some can be testing for ministers, as well as a proving ground for opposition frontbenchers; and opposition days can give newer MPs an opportunity to shine and perhaps catch the selectors' eye as possible ministerial material.

At the end of an opposition day debate, the question is put in an old-fashioned form that survives only in this case. Normally, the government amendment would be decided first and would, if the government has a majority, no doubt be approved. The next question would be the main question, as amended; so both votes would take place on the government's words, not those of the opposition. The device that is used to avoid this is that the first question put (as long as the government amendment is removing some of the words from the opposition motions, and not simply adding words of its own) is 'That the original words stand part of the question' – in other words, a vote on keeping the opposition motion as it is. When this proposition has been defeated, the second question put is 'That the proposed words be there added' – a vote to approve the government's amendment. When this is agreed to, assuming the government amendment has removed all of the substantive words of the opposition's motion, the Chair declares the main question, as amended, to be agreed to, without a further vote (which would be pointless, as it would be a second vote on the government's text).

This may seem a rather complex minuet, but it is important to opposition parties to be able to put their own proposition to the House rather than to be forced simply to vote on the government's counter-proposition.

Sometimes the government does not table an amendment to an opposition motion and simply votes against it. This happened frequently in the 2010–15 parliament, perhaps because it was not always easy to craft a government amendment with which both sides of the coalition would be happy.

No opposition day debates were scheduled in the first two months of the 2017 parliament, leading to criticism that the government was avoiding parliamentary scrutiny. When they started to be scheduled from September 2017 the government instructed its MPs not to vote on the motions (and did not table amendments to them). This has meant, for example, that motions have been carried unanimously which call on the government to: pause the roll-out of universal credit; halt plans to cap housing benefit; and lift the public-sector pay cap for members of the armed forces. In response to further criticism that the government was downplaying the importance of Parliament by not participating in these votes, ministers undertook to make a statement within 12 weeks of the relevant debate responding to each opposition day motion which is passed.

Opposition days may be used for other types of motions – for example, a prayer to annul a negative instrument or (as in November 2017 with the Brexit sectoral analyses) to instruct the government to lay particular papers before the House. (On that and similar occasions the opposition tabled a humble Address: each House has power to call for papers from the government by the use of a motion for a return – those directed to departments headed by a Secretary of State are done so by means of a humble Address to the sovereign, reflecting the fact that departments are created by royal prerogative.)

Government substantive motions

Most of the occasions on which the government needs to seek the approval of the House of Commons are on legislation or spending. Exceptionally, as in the debate to use armed force against ISIL in Syria in 2015, it may wish to have the backing of an explicit resolution of the House of Commons. On most substantive motions in a session, the government is in the position of defending or explaining in the face of opposition challenge. However, there are some occasions when the government puts a substantive motion before the House for debate. These are often when procedural changes are being proposed; when the Committee on Standards reports on the conduct of an MP; domestic business such as approving arrangements for the summer opening for visitors; or money and ways and means motions that are taken other than immediately after second reading. The four or five days of debates on the Queen's Speech and on the Budget – although each is a special case – may also be counted as government substantive motions.

Backbench business

Until 1995, four half-days and ten Fridays were set aside for motions moved by backbenchers chosen by ballot. As part of the Jopling reforms (see page 138), these were abolished and replaced by extra opportunities for backbenchers to raise subjects on the adjournment on Wednesday mornings (later moved, with increased time, to Westminster Hall). Private members' motion days gave individual MPs an opportunity to put a proposition to the House – which could be as controversial as they wished.

Between 1995 and 2010, there was no way for an ordinary MP to put a proposition to the House and have it voted on (except in a limited way for legislative proposals under the ten-minute rule (see page 216)). However, the Backbench Business Committee, established in 2010 as a result of the Wright Committee recommendations (see page 83), is allotted at least 27 days in each session (and a further eight days in Westminster Hall), and decides the business to be tabled on these days on the basis of proposals made by MPs. This business normally consists either of substantive motions or of neutral ones. Select committee statements (see page 383) are also backbench business.

Daily adjournment motions

Every day, after other business has been disposed of, backbenchers have an opportunity to raise a subject in the half-hour adjournment debate. The government whip on duty formally moves 'That this House do now adjourn', and the backbencher then has 15 minutes or so to speak, followed by a minister replying for the remainder of the time. Brief speeches from other MPs are allowed with the permission of the initiator of the debate and the minister, and either may give way to interventions within their own speech. The Speaker does not allow speeches or interventions from opposition frontbenchers, recognising that these debates are principally a means for backbenchers to engage with ministers, rather than an opportunity for the frontbenches to debate policy.

MPs apply to the Table Office for an adjournment slot (by the end of a Wednesday for the following week), and their applications are put into a ballot operated by the Speaker's Office. The Speaker himself chooses the subject for the Thursday slot, often picking an MP who has an urgent constituency matter to raise or who has been consistently unlucky in the ballot.

Any subject can be raised, provided that it falls within the responsibilities of the government so that a minister can reply to the debate. MPs are, in theory, not allowed to use the half-hour adjournment primarily to call for legislation but, in practice, this rule is not especially restrictive. As an illustration of the topics raised, four successive sitting days in December 2017 produced debates on RBS branch closures in rural areas, the Roadchef Employees Benefit Trust, government policy on local authority housing and cycling fatalities.

The half-hour adjournment is a sought-after opportunity for backbenchers, providing about 150 to 160 mini-debates each year and occupying about 6 per cent of the total time of the House. Unlike the Westminster Hall debates (see below), the timing of the half-hour adjournment is not always predictable because it depends on the main business that precedes it; but many MPs see such debates in the chamber as having a higher status. If the main business finishes early, the debate may nonetheless continue until 30 minutes after the moment of interruption, and therefore could last considerably more than half an hour.

The half-hour adjournment often shows the extraordinary flexibility of the House of Commons. Some great matter may have been decided at the end of the day's main business, eagerly reported by the media; but as MPs stream out of the chamber after a dramatic vote, the House – albeit much depleted – may turn to a very specific local problem: perhaps the difficulties faced by a single constituent.

Recess debates

Before each recess, there is a debate arranged by the Backbench Business Committee on 'matters to be considered before the forthcoming adjournment'. This gives an opportunity for backbenchers to raise topics similar to the half-hour adjournment debates, although in this case they are replied to not individually by the departmental ministers responsible for the subjects but in an omnibus reply given by the Leader or Deputy Leader of the House (although sometimes some of the subjects have been grouped by department and the departmental ministers have replied to those). This is parliamentary time valued by backbenchers, as evidenced by the number of takers, which often means that a time limit on speeches is imposed.

Emergency debates

In Chapter 5 (page 145), we described how an MP can make a case for an emergency debate; if granted by the Speaker, a debate of up to three hours takes place on a motion that the House has considered the subject the MP wishes to raise. Such debates used to be rare, with maybe only one or two in a parliament, but since 2015 they have become increasingly frequent. Debates during a recall of the House (see pages 56 and 137) also have the character of emergency debates, although these happen on the initiative of the government.

Westminster Hall

Following the House's approval of a recommendation from the Modernisation Committee, from the beginning of the session 1999–2000 a 'parallel chamber' was established, known as 'Westminster Hall' but, in fact, in the Grand Committee Room, a large committee room off the northern end of Westminster Hall. The idea had its origin in the 'Main Committee', a parallel but subordinate chamber used by the Australian House of Representatives in Canberra.

The Westminster parallel chamber was intended to allow debates, open to all MPs, on less contentious business for which it would be difficult to find time on the floor of the House. Such business was to be referred by agreement through the usual channels, and decisions in Westminster Hall would be taken only by unanimity. The more consensual approach of Westminster Hall was emphasised by a seating layout closer to the hemicycle found in many other parliaments, with two rows of seats on each side as in the chamber but with two more rows in a semicircle at the end, facing the Chair.

The Modernisation Committee was keen to avoid two possible disadvantages of a parallel chamber: that the additional time available should not simply provide an outlet for more government business – and especially not more legislation – and that the chamber of the House itself should remain clearly pre-eminent.

Westminster Hall sittings take place on Tuesdays and Wednesdays from 9.30 am to 11.30 am, when they are suspended to allow MPs to attend the main chamber, resuming at 2.30 pm until 5.30 pm. On Thursdays, the sitting time is 1.30 pm to 4.30 pm. There is also a Westminster Hall sitting on a Monday from 4.30 pm to 7.30 pm when the Petitions Committee has set down a debate on a petition. Sittings in Westminster Hall are suspended for any votes in the House but have 'injury time' to compensate.

Table 8.1 Distribution of time in Westminster Hall by different types of business (in hours and minutes)

Business	Session 2015–16	Session 2016–17
Backbench debates	342:25	268:09
BBCom debates	56:50	63:12
Liaison Committee debates	4:08	28:39
Petitions	38:01	51:55
Miscellaneous	0:00	0:08
Suspensions of the sitting	19:56	24:19
Total	461:20	436:41
House total	1215:03	1066:34

On Tuesdays and Wednesdays, Westminster Hall is given over to backbench debates, two of one-and-a-half hours each – which are intended for broader subjects on which a number of MPs will want to speak – one of an hour and two of half an hour each. The Backbench Business Committee chooses the subject for one of the longer debates on a Tuesday; the Backbench Business Committee and the Liaison Committee are responsible for determining the business on Thursdays; the Speaker chooses the subject for the longer debate on Wednesday morning; and the remaining slots are determined by ballot. To minimise the disruption to ministers' work, each government department is on call to respond to debates every other week rather than (as in the House) whenever a relevant debate comes up. The business for Thursdays may include debates on select committee reports chosen by the Liaison Committee, which has given the work of those committees a higher profile, or other matters chosen by the Backbench Business Committee, and (not for some time) *cross-cutting oral questions* (see page 299). Forthcoming business in Westminster Hall is set out in Section B of *future business* (see page 159).

In a typical week in January 2018, broader hour-and-a-half subjects included the effect of universal credit on the private rented sector, changes to the Independent Living Fund, mental health in prisons and the Disability Confident scheme.

In Westminster Hall, the chair is taken by a member of the Panel of Chairs under arrangements supervised by the Chairman of Ways and Means (who has overall responsibility for proceedings in the same way as the Speaker in the House). The proceedings are recorded in *Hansard* and published in hard copy and on the parliamentary website in the same way as proceedings in the chamber. Westminster Hall sittings are also televised in their entirety.

Debates in the Grand Committees

The Scottish, Welsh and Northern Ireland Grand Committees (not to be confused with the select committees on each of those parts of the UK) consist of all the MPs sitting for constituencies in each country. Additional MPs from elsewhere are added to the Welsh and Northern Ireland committees. In the years immediately before devolution, the roles of all three committees were widened, allowing them to hear statements from ministers (including ministers in the Lords), to hold sessions of oral questions, to consider bills and delegated legislation, and to hold adjournment debates. Post-devolution, the committees have met less frequently, and the Scottish Grand Committee has not met at all since 2003. The Welsh Grand Committee last met in February 2016 to consider the draft Wales bill. The Northern Ireland Grand Committee last met in September 2013. All three committees may, with the approval of the House, meet away from Westminster in their respective parts of the UK.

The Regional Affairs Committee, while still provided for in the House's standing orders, has not met since 2004. From January 2009 to April 2010, this Committee was replaced by a set of experimental Regional Grand Committees, which could meet either at Westminster or in the relevant region.

Early day motions

Every sitting day, about ten motions are tabled 'for an early day' – that is, for debate on an unspecified day. Almost all these 'early day motions' (EDMs) are tabled by backbenchers (although 'prayers' – see page 241 – first make their appearance as EDMs), so the chances of their being debated are negligible. Very occasionally, as in the case of the 1989 EDM on war crimes, a really significant EDM will be given debating time by the government or may figure in an opposition day debate. In addition, a motion critical of the Speaker will first appear as an EDM but, by convention, the government will normally find time to debate it.

An EDM is simply an expression of a view that could be debated by the House (they all begin 'That this House'). They may be tabled by any MP, must not be longer than 250 words and must conform to other rules of order (for example, no unparliamentary language, and no reference to matters *sub judice*). EDMs are published on the parliamentary website. All EDMs fall at the end of the session.

EDMs are used for a wide variety of purposes: an MP may want to put on record the success of his local football team (perhaps attracting only the signatures of his constituency neighbours – and perhaps a hostile amendment from supporters of a rival team), or criticise somebody's opinion or action – almost like writing a letter to a national newspaper. EDMs are also used by MPs to defuse pressure from constituents and others by being seen to be doing something about an issue, or to put material on the parliamentary record under the protection of parliamentary privilege. EDMs are also used to test and gather support on major issues, and they are a useful source of political intelligence for the whips.

A random selection of EDMs tabled in December 2017 celebrated the centenary of the Education (Scotland) Act 1918, which established in law the principle of state funding for Catholic schools in Scotland; congratulated pupils of Sandwood Primary who took part in the UK Festive #Sumdog competition; expressed concern about intimidation of minorities in Bangladesh; and criticised David Cameron for accepting a new job promoting Chinese investment.

Over 1,000 EDMs are tabled each session and may attract a total of 600 or 700 signatures from MPs on a single sitting day. The number of EDMs, and the fact that many are on relatively trivial matters, have led to criticism of them as 'parliamentary graffiti'. On the other hand, it can be argued that they act as a safety valve, and that MPs (and people outside the House) value them as a means of expressing and testing views – although their increasing numbers are devaluing the currency. Apart from the 'prayers' referred to, none is ever likely to be debated, although it is sometimes suggested that time should be found for those with substantial numbers of signatures. This may be a superficially attractive suggestion, but a good debate needs opposition, and the prospect of a debate on a matter on which all agree does not appeal.

The rules and conventions of debate

An MP is called to speak by the Speaker (or by the chair in a committee). MPs who want to take part in debates in the House or Westminster Hall, but not when a bill is in Committee of the whole House or at report stage, write to the Speaker beforehand. This is not to say that those who do not write cannot be called, but those who do write generally have preference.

When there is great pressure to speak in a particular debate, the Speaker may impose a time limit on speeches, as in the debate on Brexit described earlier (see page 271). This does not apply to the two frontbenches (neither does it apply to one MP per debate speaking on behalf of the second largest opposition party). The time limit is usually somewhere between three and 12 minutes, and may be varied upwards or downwards during the course of a debate. In order to preserve the custom of 'giving way' (see page 282), MPs get 'injury time' for the first two interventions they take from other members; the clock stops while the other member is intervening, and then the MP speaking gets an extra minute so that he or she can reply to the intervention. This injury time can be profitable if the reply to the intervention is very short! On occasions, the chair will suggest an informal time limit for speeches. Unlike the practice in the House of Lords and in many other parliaments, no list is made available of those who are to speak (although there has been some pressure for the introduction of such a list). When the previous MP sits down, all those in the chamber wanting to speak will bob up, hoping to 'catch the Speaker's eye'. The Speaker then says 'Mr Smith' and Mr Smith begins his speech. It is said that the practice of calling out a member's name originated with the corrupt Speaker Trevor at the end of the seventeenth century (see page 113). Up to then, the Speaker merely looked meaningfully at the member he wished to call; but Speaker Trevor had a truly grotesque squint, which is supposed to have led to widespread misunderstanding as to which member he had intended to call. This may be apocryphal, but Trevor's portrait confirms the squint, at least.

MPs must address the House through the Chair, referring to other members in the third person, and by their constituency or the office they hold rather than by name. So, an MP cannot say to another 'What do you mean by that?' but must say 'What does the honourable member for Loamshire East mean by that?'; and an MP cannot talk about 'Jeremy Corbyn' or 'You in charge of the Labour Party' but must instead refer to 'the right honourable member for Islington North' or 'the Leader of the Opposition'. All MPs are referred to as 'honourable members' or 'the honourable lady' or 'the honourable gentleman'; those who are privy counsellors (usually present or former senior ministers) are styled 'right honourable'. This may sound rather antique, but it avoids the direct confrontation of two MPs addressing each other as 'you' and often helps to lower the temperature.

The practice of referring to QCs as 'honourable and learned' and officers retired from the armed forces (or still in the reserves) as 'honourable and gallant' is no longer a convention of debate, but the terms are still used by traditionalists.

When they enter or leave the chamber, MPs are expected to bow to the Chair as a gesture of respect to the House itself (it is not a bow to the Speaker, but almost certainly a survival of the days when there was an altar in St Stephen's Chapel, where the Commons sat from 1547). They should not cross the line of sight between the Speaker and the member who has the floor; and – very important – should sit down as soon as the Speaker or a deputy rises. Dress conventions – business attire, though ties are no longer compulsory for men – are generally upheld. Eating, drinking (except water) and smoking are forbidden: the House of Commons has been a no-smoking area since the resolution of 1696 'That no Member do presume to take tobacco in the gallery of the House or at a committee table'. MPs may not use mobile phones to make or receive calls, but may use hand-held electronic devices (but not laptop computers) in the chamber so long as they do not cause a disturbance and do not 'impair decorum'; in committees laptops may be used.

MPs must speak from the place where they are called, which must be within the formal limits of the chamber (so, not from the crossbenches below the Bar of the House or from the parts of the galleries reserved for members). MPs may refer to notes, but they should not read questions or speeches at length – although notes, and even whole written speeches, are used to a greater degree than was the case a few years ago, with an adverse effect on the quality of debate. An MP should be present for the opening and winding-up speeches of the debate in which he or she takes part, and after speaking should stay in the chamber for at least the next two speeches. The Speaker will not call an MP to ask a question following a ministerial statement (or an urgent question) unless he or she has been there for the whole of the opening statement.

The House of Commons has a long tradition of MPs seeking to intervene in each other's speeches, to ask a question or to make a point. This – different from the practice in many other parliaments – makes debate much more lively than would otherwise be the case and is easier in the relatively intimate style of the chamber than it would be in a large hemicycle (see page 12). Interventions must be brief; and they may be made only if the MP who has the floor 'gives way', although the expectation is that the MP speaking will, indeed, give way. The Chair has the power to stop an MP whose speech is irrelevant or tediously repetitive, although with a certain amount of ingenuity most things can be made relevant and unrepetitive.

In most debates MPs may speak only once but this does not apply, for example, in a committee on a bill. The *sub judice* rule prevents any MP referring to a current or impending court case (more precisely, when someone has been charged in a criminal case or, in a civil action, when a case has been listed for trial). This is to avoid debate in the House – under the protection of privilege – possibly influencing the outcome of a case; but it also reflects the relationship between Parliament and the courts (see page 171). However, the rule may be relaxed at the Speaker's discretion, and it does not apply when the House is considering legislation.

'Good temper and moderation'

The language of debate must be restrained. An MP may not accuse another of lying, or of deliberately misleading the House; the Chair will intervene immediately to require the withdrawal of the charge. In July 2013, Nigel Dodds was ordered to leave the chamber for refusing to withdraw his allegation that a minister's reply had been 'deliberately deceptive'.

However, in June 2012 the Labour MP Chris Bryant was allowed to accuse the then Health Secretary Jeremy Hunt of having lied to the House. Although the style of the accusation was a little immoderate, it was not disorderly because the House was debating a motion that centred on the Health Secretary's veracity before the House; it would have been a nonsense if members could not have addressed the issue directly.

Erskine May no longer lists the words ruled to be 'unparliamentary', although the lists in earlier editions are entertaining. 'Villains' got a red card in 1875, as did 'Pecksniffian cant' in 1928. Rather surprisingly, so did 'rude remarks' in 1887. Animal words of all sorts ('jackasses', 'swine', 'rats' and even 'stool pigeons') have always been required to be withdrawn. The important thing (and the reason why *Erskine May* no longer lists examples) is the context in which language is used. However, *Erskine May's* dictum 'that good temper and moderation are the characteristics of parliamentary language' remains the gold standard. It was for that reason that Dennis Skinner was reprimanded for calling the then Prime Minister (David Cameron) 'Dodgy Dave' in April 2016, and was ordered out of the chamber for refusing to withdraw the term.

MPs are expected to inform their colleagues when they intend to refer to them in the chamber; when they table parliamentary questions that specifically affect the constituency of another MP; and when they intend to visit another constituency (except in a purely private capacity).

All these conventions and constraints may sound a little like school rules, and some occasionally come in for criticism from new MPs and others. But where political views clash and passions can run high, a little formality can make the House more dignified and tolerant. It is a pity that many people judge the House of Commons from what they see on television of the gladiatorial Prime Minister's Questions; the House is actually a much more courteous place than many might think, while still allowing challenge and lively disagreement. At a time when Parliament is seeking to reconnect with the people, this is no bad thing.

The purpose of debate

As has been shown, the House of Commons itself, Westminster Hall and a variety of committees provide a great many different occasions and circumstances where debate takes place. What is the purpose of the millions of words spoken as a result?

Much of debate is, in one way or another, about deploying political argument: seeking to make the case for a particular philosophy or interpretation and applying it to the issue of the moment. Although many in the country at large see a clash of ideologies as rather sterile and negative, it is part of political reality.

But debate is also about challenge, testing and explanation. Parliament is a place where the government should be forced to justify its policies and actions. That process is part of checking an executive that will always tend to be over-mighty. It is also a process that crosses political divides, and it involves both the shadow minister who aspires to be in government and the government backbencher who is uneasy about a course that the government is taking. In these circumstances, debate provides the opportunity to point out the weakness in a case, to offer alternative solutions and to ask 'why?'

Debate is also about exposure. One purpose of this is to force – or provide an opportunity for – the government to set out its view and its policy. This may be on some major issue – the achievement of peace in the Middle East, or the government's plans for leaving the European Union. It may be on something with a lower profile but of great importance to those affected; for example, a school closure, an accident black spot or a local industry. This will produce a statement of government policy, or a response to criticism, but it will also act as a mind concentrator, not only for the minister but also for the civil servants in his or her department, who should be asking 'Is this a reasonable line to take? How vulnerable are we on this? Should we do more?'

The uses of debate

Exposure through debate is a way of attacking and defending – but, above all, testing – policies and ideas. It is also a way of putting subjects on the political (and media) agenda. It may be some abuse – perhaps a holiday timeshare scam, or perhaps an ethical or moral issue – such as stem cell research, battery hens or cluster bombs. It may also be a way of swinging the spotlight on to some injustice – sometimes affecting only one person or one family, perhaps children kidnapped by an estranged father, a disability pension denied or the perverse application of some planning law.

Debate is also about representation: industries, regions, constituencies, pressure groups and individuals have a parliamentary voice through MPs taking up causes, setting out the case and gathering support.

Does debate change minds? On the spot, rarely. On most matters that come to the House of Commons, the parties will already have their view; individual MPs will have their opinions. On a non-partisan issue, a compelling speech may be influential; on a highly charged issue, the trend of debate may change minds (a significant number of MPs said that they finally made up their minds which way to vote on military intervention in Syria only during the debate in August 2013). In the case of most debates, effective advocacy will, indeed, change minds, but more slowly. It may modify the government's view, influence public opinion and put new subjects on the agenda. How effectively it does this is very much down to MPs themselves.

Debates in the House of Lords

Just over one-quarter of House of Lords chamber and Grand Committee time is taken up with debates of various kinds on issues of public policy. In 2016–17, the House spent just over 327 hours in debate – that is, 31 per cent of the total time available to it in the chamber and Grand Committee. Debates take place, as in the Commons, on a motion moved by the initiator. The form of the motion used will vary according to the purpose of the debate. Most debates in the Lords will take place on a neutral motion 'to take note' of a subject: when it is desired that the House express a view on the subject matter under debate, a motion 'for resolution' is moved – usually resulting in a vote at the end. The Lords also has a unique procedure that allows for short debate on a question (a QSD).

A House of Lords debate

Source: Copyright House of Lords, 2012. Photography by Catherine Bebbington

Opposition and backbench debates

Debates on motions moved by opposition parties and backbenchers take place on Thursdays, when motions have precedence over bills and other business. Most of these Thursdays are given over to the political parties to initiate debates, usually on the neutral 'take note' motion. The days for these debates are allocated to the various parties by agreement between party whips, with the majority going to opposition parties and crossbench peers. Although there is no fixed time limit, the Leader of the House usually moves a Business of the House motion limiting the time. This can create the opportunity for two debates to be held. The limit on a single debate is usually five hours: the limits where two debates are held can vary but do not exceed a total of six hours.

In the earlier part of the session, up until the end of December, one Thursday a month is set aside for two balloted debates limited to two-and-a-half hours each and initiated by backbenchers or crossbenchers. The subjects are chosen by a ballot conducted some weeks beforehand by the Clerk of the Parliaments. Members may not hedge their bets by tabling both a motion for the ballot and a QSD on the same topic at the same time. And after the ballot is drawn, all motions fall and have to be retabled, in an attempt to keep the House's debates current.

In the 2016–17 session, Thursday opposition and backbench motions included such themes as defence, NHS funding, the immigration status of overseas students, the Iraq Inquiry report and debates on all aspects of Brexit.

Government motions

Sometimes the government will itself wish to initiate a debate on a matter of public concern or potential concern to the House. Thus, debates on reform of the House in recent sessions have often been held on government motions to take note. Debates on pressing issues of foreign policy fall into the same category. On 18 March 2003, the Lords, as did the Commons, debated the situation in Iraq, but on a take note motion, in the full knowledge that war was probably imminent. Unlike the Commons, however, no vote followed the end of the debate. On 29 August 2013, a similar debate on a take note motion took place on the use of chemical weapons in Syria, following a recall of Parliament. In early July 2016 there was a debate on a motion moved by the Leader of the House to take note of the outcome of the EU referendum.

There have been occasions where the government has sought to test the opinion of the two Houses of Parliament on issues of policy, placing a series of options before each House. Thus, in March 2002 the government itself tabled motions for resolution on a series of options relating to hunting with dogs. In February 2003, although the debate had already taken place, a series of votes were held on seven motions to approve one or other of the options relating to the reform of the composition of the House of Lords that had been proposed by the Joint Committee on Reform of the House. On 12 July 2005 the House resolved, after a short debate, that it should elect its own presiding officer (an issue that had been debated at greater length in early 2004). In March 2007 the House again voted on the seven options for reform of House of Lords membership, with various proportions of elected to appointed members. The Lords rejected all except one – that of an all appointed chamber. (The Commons had already voted the week before in favour of an 80 per cent or 100 per cent elected body.)

Debates on reports of select committees

Select committees on public policy (see page 352) – such as the Economic Affairs Committee, Science and Technology Committee or European Union Committee – make their reports to the House in the expectation that, at some stage, they will be debated. In recent sessions around 5 per cent of sitting time in the chamber and in Grand Committee was spent debating these reports, almost invariably on a motion to take note. In session 2016–17 such debates were especially prominent, as the House debated 16 select committee reports on Brexit – most, but not all, from the EU Committee. Sometimes, motions to take note of reports on similar subjects are debated together. The Economic Affairs Committee's reports on the Finance Bill are usually debated as part of the second reading of the bill.

Chairmen and members of select committees were, in the past, often critical that insufficient time was offered by the Government Whips' Office for debates on select committee reports or that time, when offered, tended to be at short notice or subject to last-minute change. But the availability of Grand Committee time has helped to ease the pressure. There are those who point out that such debates rarely attract interest from the wider House and, save for a few members with knowledge of the subject matter, most of the participants tend to be members of the committee that made the report. In some ways, this does not matter. The dialogue with the government over a committee's recommendations takes place not only on the floor of the House, but also in the direct exchanges between the committees and ministers.

Questions for Short Debate

Many debates take the form of a Question for Short Debate (QSD). These are debates time-limited to an hour or an hour-and-a-half. The running order is for the member who tabled the question to speak for up to 10 minutes, for a minister to answer the question at the end of the debate for up to 12 minutes, and for the remaining time to be split between all others wishing to speak. The mover has no right of reply at the conclusion of the debate. If QSD is taken at the end of the day's business it lasts for up to an hour-and-a-half. QSDs may be held during dinner adjournments in the course of legislative business, when they are limited to one hour. They may also be taken in Grand Committee when either time limit may be applied. Since 2013, up to the end of January in any session, the opportunity exists for a topical QSD to be taken on Thursdays between the two main motions for debate. They are chosen by ballot on the previous Monday and the criterion by which topicality is measured is that of media coverage in two mainstream outlets over the preceding three days. Select committee reports can also be debated in this way provided the topicality criterion is met. Although the topical QSD slot has not always been used, QSDs generally are hugely popular and have proliferated in recent years. In 2016–17, they took up 7 per cent of chamber time and 16 per cent of Grand Committee time. Even though the rules state that QSDs should be limited in scope, they have been used to debate some very significant issues – for example in 2016–17, the Middle East peace process and assisted dying. Such debates can be well-subscribed, sometimes meaning backbenchers are limited to one or two minutes each, with inevitable grumbles resulting. There was a time when QSDs were fitted into the margins of other business, but now they are a central feature of Lords proceedings.

Conventions of debate

Certain conventions apply to all debate in the House, whether on legislative business or on the general motions that are the subject of this chapter. We saw in Chapter 2 that the Chair does not call members to speak in the Lords. Peers usually give advance notice to the Government Whips' Office of their intention to speak in debates, and lists of speakers are prepared by the Government Whips' Office in consultation with the usual channels and published before the debate begins. Any lord not on the list may speak, but only after those already on the list and before the winding-up speeches, and then only briefly. So, there is no problem in the Lords of 'catching the Speaker's eye'. And, of course, the House keeps its own order.

As in the Commons, there are conventions and standing orders – some dating from as early as 1621 – governing the way in which other members are addressed. Thus, remarks are addressed to the House as a whole. Other participants are addressed in the third person, never as 'you'. And the style of address is always 'The Noble Lord, Lord . . .' or 'The Right Reverend Prelate, the Bishop of . . .'. Judges of a certain level and law officers are 'noble and learned'; military officers of a certain rank are 'noble and gallant'. A suggestion in 2011 by Lord Goodlad's Working Group that the forms of address might be simplified was rejected by the House.

Generally speaking, a lord may speak only once in debate, except when the House is in committee on a bill, and should not read (although many do). Unless speaking from the frontbench, where lords speak from a despatch box, members speak in their places. Speeches must be relevant and, indeed, in 1965 the House even resolved that they should be shorter. Today, a rather generous 15-minute rule applies in debates that are not time-limited, with a 20-minute limit for members opening or winding up. Most debates are now time limited and the whips are vigilant to ensure that the limits are observed. Members must avoid 'asperity of speech'. And relevant interests must be declared (see page 122).

In addition to these rules of debate, various rules of conduct apply – such as speaking 'uncovered' (without a hat!) or the custom of making obeisance to the Cloth of Estate behind the throne on entering the chamber. Such customs help to lend the House a veneer of good, even courtly, manners that are sometimes sorely tested in the debates themselves.

Value of debate: the chamber of experience

It is no easier to set a value on Lords debates than it is for the Commons. We take it for granted that debate is free and open. It is, of course, protected by parliamentary privilege. That in itself is something to be cherished. But what purpose is served? Minds are rarely changed, especially not when arguments follow party lines. Given that most speeches are prepared beforehand and then scrupulously read out, that is hardly surprising.

The value of debates is that they offer different opportunities and attractions to different participants. For a backbencher initiating a debate, they offer the chance to air a policy matter of personal interest with the guarantee of a government response that is likely to represent the latest government thinking on the issue. For opposition parties, they offer the chance to set out their wares: to expose some aspect of government policy of which they do not approve, perhaps to say how things might be done better or differently, and to try to put the government on the spot. And for government itself, they offer the opportunity to set out some new policy development or change in world events, and to test opinion across the parties.

A phenomenon which has arisen in recent years is an increase in the number of speakers in debates, sometimes leading to very short speaking times. In large part this is due to the increase in membership and the fact that most members (and almost all new members) regard themselves as 'working peers', regularly attending and participating in the House. But two other factors may operate at the margins. The first is unoriginal but regular media reports on the lack of participation by certain peers. These reports usually view participation solely as speeches in the chamber, ignoring work done in select committees, APPGs, in tabling written questions, and so on. However ill-founded, it would be understandable for members to want to avoid appearing on a list of 'lazy lords'. Secondly, the spectre of reform in the shape of a drastic reduction in membership looms. Although the Burns committee did make proposals for reducing the existing membership of the House (see Chapter 12), an idea frequently cited is to remove members with the lowest participation rates. Faced with this prospect, it would be unsurprising if some members actively spoke more.

So while debates in the House of Lords can attract a lot of speakers, are they of good quality? Many are. In most debates a few speakers can be deemed to have experience that is relevant to the subject matter, and a few may have current and genuine expertise – a rare commodity in a parliamentary body. This high level of knowledgeability stems in part from the fact that the House of Lords has never been a chamber of salaried members. Many, whether life peers or hereditary, have or have had full-time careers elsewhere. And life peerages have been bestowed on a wide range of men and women distinguished in their field – some irrespective of party, others because they have espoused a party cause. Thus, among the speakers in the debate on the second reading of the Higher Education Bill (which significantly reformed the governance structure for universities) in December 2016 were 16 serving or former academics, 17 serving or former chancellors of universities (or the equivalent of a chancellor), three serving or former vice chancellors and eight members of university governing bodies. One would have been hard placed to gather a more expert crowd in any forum.

Some commentators now view the House of Lords as a chamber of experts. This is perhaps to exaggerate the expert element in the House. Most of the peerages bestowed in the last 50 years or so have gone to politicians, active at either the national or local level. And many of the 'experts' have retired, or are about to retire, when they become members of the House. Their expertise might be thought a little dated. It is more apposite to regard the House of Lords as currently composed as a chamber where experience abounds. It is, for the most part, a knowledgeable place in a way that distinguishes it from most other parliamentary assemblies in the world.

9

Calling to account: questions

In this chapter we look at one of the best-known inquisitorial functions of Parliament: parliamentary questions, often known as PQs. This will also be a convenient place to look at public petitions and MPs' letters, which are other ways in which the actions of government can be influenced or exposed.

Questions in the Commons

By comparison with the processes of debate, legislation and examination by select committees, questions evolved relatively late in parliamentary history. Although the first recorded question to a minister was in the House of Lords in 1721, questions in the Commons did not develop until the nineteenth century, when all questions were asked orally. Questions for written answer (or PQs) were not introduced until 1902.

What are questions?

Erskine May states the purpose of a question as 'to obtain information or to press for action'. The people who have the information – and the ability to act on it – are government ministers, and it is they who have to answer questions. Some questions are asked (or, in parliamentary language, 'tabled' or 'put down') of MPs who are not ministers but who speak on behalf of bodies such as the House of Commons Commission (see page 64) or the Church Commissioners. However, well over 99 per cent of all PQs are asked of ministers by backbenchers, and this process is part of the way in which government can be held to account.

Questions are one of the best-known, but often misunderstood, features of the House of Commons, and it is with that House that we start. Questions are also asked in the House of Lords, but in smaller numbers.

There are two types of question: oral and written (which are split into the unrationed ordinary written, and written questions for answer on a named day, of which each member may ask five in a day). Questions for written answer now far outnumber oral questions and the two types of question have steadily grown apart. Questions for written answer are still designed to seek information or press for action; oral questions are increasingly rhetorical in purpose. The introduction of 'topical' oral questions (see page 296) has increased this divergence.

The rules for questions

First and foremost, questions must be about something for which a minister is responsible. In many cases this is clear-cut: the Secretary of State for Defence is responsible for the new aircraft carriers, and the Secretary of State for International Development is responsible for how the UK's aid budget is spent. But, although the government has an overall responsibility for local government finance, it is not responsible for the detail of how local authorities spend their money. Neither, for example, is it responsible for what the courts do or for the operational details of policing.

Ministers are responsible to Parliament for their own policies and actions, not for those of the opposition parties; so a government backbencher could not table a question that asked 'What would be the effect on the economy of the deficit reduction plans announced by the Labour Party', even if the minister were eager to answer. But if the MP were to ask the Chancellor of the Exchequer an oral question such as 'What recent progress he has made on deficit reduction', then that is a matter for which he is responsible, and the reply may well take a side-swipe at the policy of the Labour Party.

There are a variety of other rules. Matters that are *sub judice* (see page 283) cannot be raised. Questions must not offer information 'If she is aware that . . .' or be argumentative 'Does he agree that it is unacceptable that . . .' They must have some reasonable basis in fact, rather than being purely speculative – they cannot, for example, ask whether a press report is correct. Government is treated as a single entity, so it is not in order to ask one minister to intervene with or influence another (although the same result may be achieved by asking the Prime Minister a question about improving coordination between two government departments).

A question that has already been answered in the current session may not be asked again unless there is reason to think that the situation may have changed (although in practice, with the exception of historic statistics, this is interpreted as allowing a question to be repeated after three months). The tabling of numerous but very similar questions is not allowed for the same reason. A related rule prevents an MP asking for information that is readily available – for example, in official publications. Now that huge amounts of information and statistical data are published by the government on the internet, this rule is increasingly applied. The amount of information now published in this way, combined with the impact of the Freedom of Information Act, has altered the role and status of parliamentary questions.

Since devolution to Scotland, Wales and Northern Ireland, ministers at Westminster may not be asked about things for which responsibility has passed to the devolved administrations. They may, however, be asked about matters on which they have power to require information from the administrations, or about concordats or liaison arrangements. The rules about questions have developed over the years; for the most part, they either reflect other rules of the House (such as the *sub judice* rule) or try to ensure that questions keep to their principal purposes of obtaining information or pressing for action. The rules are applied more rigorously to questions for written answer than to questions asked orally. MPs can find the rules frustrating; but it is remarkable how often a slightly different question – or the same question in a different form – avoids running foul of the rules and may get closer to what the MP really wants the answer to.

Tabling a question

Whatever the type of question, whether written or oral, MPs must table questions in writing, either personally with the clerks in the Table Office (a small room behind the Speaker's chair), by post or via a secure electronic tabling (e-tabling) system. Written questions e-tabled are subject to a limit of 20 per day; there is no limit on written questions handed in personally at the Table Office or posted.

An MP's question is examined by one of the clerks, who checks that it does not fall foul of any of the rules for questions and who will, where possible, suggest to the MP how to avoid breaching the rules, or perhaps how to put the question in a more effective form. As well as conforming to the rules that operate for all questions, an oral question should seek no more than three pieces of information and, except in the case of topical questions and questions to the Prime Minister (see page 305), must be precise enough to give an indication of the intended supplementary – 'open' questions are not allowed.

The answers

There is a rather hackneyed story of a minister and a senior civil servant being driven to some remote government establishment. The fog closed down, the car went slower and slower, and finally the driver, dimly seeing a passer-by, rolled down the window and said 'Where are we?' Back came the answer 'You're in a car, in the fog'. 'Do you realise, minister', said the civil servant, 'that's a perfect answer to a parliamentary question. It's short, it's absolutely true, and it tells you nothing you didn't know already'.

In Chapter 4 we quoted the 1997 resolution of the House of Commons on ministerial accountability, which states the duty of ministers to account for policies, decisions and actions. So far as questions are concerned, the key passages are those that require ministers 'to give accurate and truthful information to Parliament' and to be 'as open as possible with Parliament, refusing to provide information only when disclosure would not be in the public interest'. The language of the resolution is reflected in the Ministerial Code, most recently published in December 2016.

The Freedom of Information Act marked a step change in the status of PQs. Before that Act, MPs had a privileged status in terms of access to government information; and journalists, researchers and others quite legitimately had to seek the help of an MP to prise information out of the government. Now, everyone has the right to ask questions of the government and it is legally obliged to answer them. This has devalued the PQ to an extent, and has probably exacerbated the trend for PQs to be used as part of a campaign on a given subject rather than a means of trying to find out information about it. At the time the Freedom of Information laws came into effect the government undertook that answers to PQs would not be more limited than responses provided to freedom of information requests made to departments.

There are some subjects on which few would expect information to be given in answer to a PQ, such as the operations of the security and intelligence services, or where an investigation into major VAT fraud might be under way.

But on many other issues, interpretations and expectations can differ. From a government perspective, it is easy to understand a reluctance to answer particular types of questions – not least because answering one question may produce a flood of questions on a sensitive topic. Nevertheless, MPs find a minister's refusal to answer extremely frustrating when it prevents them pursuing a subject that they see as of political or constituency importance. If a minister refuses to provide information on a particular subject for a stated reason, it usually also prevents the same question being asked for the remainder of the session, which adds to the frustration. Another source of frustration can be the time taken to answer questions. 'Named day' questions should receive a reply on the date specified by the tabling MP, which must be at least three sitting days after tabling. There is no fixed deadline for answers to ordinary written questions, but the government's guidance says that departments should try to answer them within a working week, which is interpreted as five sitting days (including non-sitting Fridays).

Since the 2010–15 parliament the Procedure Committee has monitored unsatisfactory and late answers to parliamentary questions, reporting after each session and receiving from the Leader of the House statistics on departments' performance in answering written PQs within a reasonable time. It appears to have had some success: the proportion of ordinary written questions answered in time rose from 69 per cent in 2010–12 to 92 per cent in 2016–17, with the proportion of 'named day' questions answered on time increasing from 69 to 87 per cent over the same period. These overall figures mask different performances by individual departments: in 2016–17 the Ministry of Justice responded to only 77.7 per cent of PQs on time, but the Department for Transport answered 99.9 per cent on time. The Procedure Committee plans to enhance its monitoring of the quality of written answers in the 2017 parliament, with MPs able to refer answers they consider inadequate to the committee's chair, who may seek observations from the government or refer a case for discussion by the committee as a whole.

Although the form and content of questions is subject to the rules of the House, the content of answers remains a matter for ministers, and in those answers ministers are sometimes not above a sideswipe at the previous administration. And while the majority of questions are seeking information, questions – especially oral questions – are an important dimension of the party clash between opposition and government.

For example, in the 2013–14 session, a question from Hilary Benn about budgets for catering and hospitality in the Department for Communities and Local Government received a detailed answer on the various budget heads and then concluded with the observation that 'his spending in his last year in office is equivalent today to buying 720,479 packets of Jammie Dodgers from Waitrose (albeit, with a free cup of coffee thrown in)'. In the same session, the eagle-eyed would have spotted a number of One Direction song titles hiding in an answer to a question on the contribution to the UK economy of One Direction.

Successive Speakers have refused to comment on the ways in which ministers answer – or avoid answering – and many backbenchers feel that it is unfair that ministers can decide, without any independent check, to refuse to answer particular questions that everyone accepts come within their responsibilities. The reality is that, if questions really are a means of holding the government to account, one cannot always expect answers to involve a friendly volunteering of information.

Cost

Ministers may refuse to provide an answer to a PQ if the cost of doing so would exceed a certain amount, known as the *advisory cost limit*, currently £850. A minister's 'disproportionate cost' answer can be a source of annoyance to MPs: not only may they think that the expenditure limit of £850 does not represent a large amount of civil service time, they may also suspect that estimating the cost of answering is a fairly rough-and-ready business, and that if ministers wanted to answer the question, they would (and, indeed, a minister may decide that a question is to be answered irrespective of cost). However, the government's internal guidance emphasises that even if to give a full answer would cost more than the limit, any readily available information should be given.

In February 2012 the Treasury estimated the average cost of answering a written question at £164, and of answering an oral question at £450. These figures are averages, not the price-tag of each question; it does not cost very much to reply 'No' to a question asking for a particular document to be published, for example. The higher cost of answering oral questions is because of the additional research and briefing needed for possible supplementaries (see page 299), so the extra cost is more that of defending the minister's position than of actually answering the question.

Oral questions

Civil Service guidance for answering oral PQs says of question time:

> *Because supplementary questions vary from the factual to the highly political in content, in briefing for supplementaries we have to try to anticipate every ramification of the original question. While some questions are genuinely seeking action or information, others are designed to highlight the merits of an alternative policy or the shortcomings of the minister's department. It is often the case that*

> *the member can anticipate the answer that will be given before the question is put down. The task facing civil servants is to get behind the question and provide a range of brief subject headings and corresponding short lines to take (drafted in the first person) which the minister can easily pick up and use to answer the supplementaries in the House.*

Some questions for oral answer receive a written reply, either because time runs out before they are reached or because the MP concerned cannot be in the House that day and so asks for a written rather than an oral reply.

But even though oral questions account for a relatively small part of the total, Question Time, when they are answered, is one of the liveliest parts of the parliamentary day, and Prime Minister's Questions (PMQs) each Wednesday is normally the highest-profile event of the week.

Question Time

Question Time takes place every day except Fridays. It begins immediately after prayers are over and any private business (see page 141) has been disposed of. This means that, on Mondays, it runs from about 2.35 pm to 3.35 pm; on Tuesdays and Wednesdays from about 11.35 am to 12.35 pm (although the session with the Prime Minister on Wednesdays often runs to 12.45 pm or later); and on Thursdays from 9.35 am to 10.35 am.

The ministers from each government department answer questions every five weeks according to a rota that the government itself decides. Most departments answer substantive questions (of which they have received notice and which are printed in the Order Paper) for 75 per cent of their slot, and topical questions (of which no notice is given) for the remaining 25 per cent. Members may enter and be successful in both the substantive and topical question ballots. All government departments answer topical questions with the exception of the Attorney General; the Northern Ireland, Wales and Scotland offices; and the non-government answering bodies (such as the House of Commons Commission and the Church Commissioners).

Topical questions were introduced from the 2007–08 session. This took place in response to the perception that the parliamentary question process was unable to react to events on the day of the PQ or just before it. The change resulted from a recommendation by the Modernisation Committee, whose intention was to create the opportunity for 'topical and spontaneous questions' on issues of the day selected by members. The arrangements for topical questions are broadly similar to those for PM's 'engagements' questions. The pro forma topical question is 'if she or he will make a statement on her/his Department's responsibilities'. The minister answers this question once at the start of the topical questions slot – usually with a positive message about the department's activities – and then members who have been successful in the ballot, and others, are called by the Speaker to ask questions. A typical rota for question times and deadlines is below.

DATES AND DEADLINES FOR ORAL QUESTIONS

MONDAY 19 MARCH – THURSDAY 24 MAY 2018

(T) indicates that a topical Question may also be tabled to the answering Department

2017-19, No. 6
(March 2018)

	Monday 19 March	Tuesday 20 March	Wednesday 21 March	Thursday 22 March
Question Time	**Education** (at 2:30pm; T at 3:15pm)	**Health and Social Care** (at 11:30am; T at 12:15pm)	**Northern Ireland** (at 11:30am) **Prime Minister** (at noon)	**Digital, Culture, Media and Sport** (at 9:30am; T at 10:00am) **Attorney General** (at 10:10am)
Deadline at 12:30pm (Date of Question Time)	**Digital, Culture, Media and Sport** (T) (Thu 22 March) **Attorney General** (Thu 22 March)	**Work and Pensions** (T) (Mon 26 March)	**Foreign and Commonwealth Office** (T) (Tue 27 March)	**Chancellor of the Duchy of Lancaster and Minister for the Cabinet Office** (T) (Wed 28 March) **Prime Minister** (Wed 28 March)
	Monday 26 March	**Tuesday 27 March**	**Wednesday 28 March**	**Thursday 29 March**
Question Time	**Work and Pensions** (at 2:30pm; T at 3:15pm)	**Foreign and Commonwealth Office** (at 11:30am; T at 12:15pm)	**Chancellor of the Duchy of Lancaster and Minister for the Cabinet Office** (at 11:30am; T at 11:53am) **Prime Minister** (at noon)	**International Trade** (at 9:30am; T at 9:53am) **Women and Equalities** (at 10:00am; T at 10:23am)
Deadline at 12:30pm (Date of Question Time)	**International Trade** (T) (Thu 29 March) **Women and Equalities** (T) (Thu 29 March)	No deadline this day	No deadline this day	**Home Office** (T) (Mon 16 April) **Treasury** (T) (Tue 17 April) **International Development** (T) (Wed 18 April) **Prime Minister** (Wed 18 April)

	Monday 16 April	Tuesday 17 April	Wednesday 18 April	Thursday 19 April
Question Time	**Home Office** (at 2:30pm; T at 3:15pm)	**Treasury** (at 11:30am; T at 12:15pm)	**International Development** (at 9:30am; T at 9:53am) **Prime Minister** (at noon)	**Transport** (at 9:30am; T at 10:15am)
Deadline at 12:30pm (Date of Question Time)	**Transport** (T) (Thu 19 April)	**Defence** (T) (Mon 23 April) **Scotland** (Wed 25 April)	**Justice** (T) (Tue 24 April)	**Prime Minister** (Wed 25 April)
	Monday 23 April	**Tuesday 24 April**	**Wednesday 25 April**	**Thursday 26 April**
Question Time	**Defence** (at 2:30pm; T at 3:15pm)	**Justice** (at 11:30am; T at 12:15pm)	**Scotland** (at 11:30am) **Prime Minister** (at noon)	**Environment, Food and Rural Affairs** (at 9.30am; T at 10:00am) **Church Commissioners and House of Commons Commission and Public Accounts Commission and Speaker's Committee on the Electoral Commission** (at 10:10am)
Deadline at 12:30pm (Date of Question Time)	**Environment, Food and Rural Affairs** (T) (Thu 26 April) **Church Commissioners and House of Commons Commission and Public Accounts Commission and Speaker's Committee on the Electoral Commission** (Thu 26 April)	**Housing, Communities and Local Government** (T) (Mon 30 April) **Wales** (Wed 2 May)	**Business, Energy and Industrial Strategy** (T) (Tue 1 May)	**Prime Minister** (Wed 2 May)

Notices of Questions may be submitted any time after the previous question time for that Department up to 12.30 pm three days before the day of answering (or five days in the case of Questions to the Secretaries of State for Northern Ireland, Scotland and Wales), excluding Fridays, Saturdays, Sundays and bank holidays. All orderly Questions so submitted will be included in the random shuffle to determine the order of Questions.

In addition to one topical Question (T) to each Department answering them, Members may submit only one Question per Department.

Note: The Secretary of State for Scotland also answers on behalf of the Advocate General.

Continues over

Extract from rota for government departments' oral questions and related deadlines for tabling

Source: Copyright House of Commons, 2018

The day on which a department is top for questions can be a testing time for ministers answering at the despatch box, but can also be a shop window for the department concerned, in which ministers have the opportunity of emphasising their successes and putting on the record their interpretation of events. The balance between the two depends on how quick ministers are on their feet, how well they prepare and how sharp opposition MPs (or, indeed, backbenchers on their own side) are with their supplementaries.

Tabling oral questions

An MP can table a PQ for oral answer any time after the previous Question Time for a particular department up to 12.30 pm three sitting days before that department's next Question Time. So if the department is top for questions on a Tuesday, questions have to be tabled by 12.30 pm the previous Wednesday (for questions to the secretaries of state for Northern Ireland, Scotland and Wales, the notice period is five days because of the extra complication of there being devolved administrations in those parts of the UK). An MP may table only one oral question to a department on any one day, and no more than two in total on that day (which, for example, allows an MP to have a question to the Prime Minister, as well as the secretary of state answering the same day).

Questions are tabled to the responsible secretary of state rather than to an individual minister within a department, although there are slots for government departments and offices that do not have a secretary of state, such as those for the Leader of the House and the ministers for Women and Equalities.

Just after 12.30 pm on the last tabling day, there is a random computer shuffle of the questions that have been tabled to the department or departments concerned. The successful questions are published in Future Day Orals on the parliamentary website in the order in which they will be called on the day. Not all questions tabled are published; if a single department is to answer for the whole of Question Time (in practice, 55 minutes), then 25 questions to that department will be published. If the slot is for 30 minutes, 15 will be published, and so on down to a 20-minute slot, for which 10 questions will be published. The remainder are treated as 'lost', are not published and do not receive answers.

If a question is put down to one government department but is more properly the responsibility of another, it will be transferred and answered by a minister from the second department. This does not matter for written questions, but an MP who has an oral that is transferred after the shuffle has taken place will lose the opportunity to ask the question orally. When this happens, it sometimes results in a row; but it is a matter within the discretion of the government, and the Speaker will not intervene, although Speakers have criticised the transfer of a question where there is some shared responsibility.

Both government and opposition parties are keen to get their MPs to table questions, because it shortens the odds of being successful in the shuffle and so beginning a question exchange with a friendly (or, for the opposition, a critical) supplementary. Both opposition and government front bench teams, through their PPSs and special advisers, will also identify themes they want to raise in a forthcoming Question Time, and encourage their backbenchers to table (sometimes identical) questions on these subjects, a practice known as 'syndication' or 'hand-outs'.

As well as question time in the House, oral questions may be asked at some sittings of the Scottish, Welsh and Northern Ireland Grand Committees (see page 280), although these are not frequent occurrences. The standing orders also provide for 'cross-cutting' oral question times in Westminster Hall, where questions are about a subject that involves a number of departments rather than about the responsibilities of a single department. After a number of such question times in the 2003–04 session – including on youth, domestic violence, drugs and older people – no further cross-cutting question times have been held.

Question Time: on the day

The Speaker announces, 'Questions to the Secretary of State for the Home Department' (or whichever department is top), 'Mr Peter Bone' (or whoever). Mr Bone simply says 'Number one, Mr Speaker' (there is no point in reading out the question because it is printed on the Order of Business), and the minister gets up and replies. Mr Bone is then called to ask a supplementary question, to which the minister replies. Two or three (or more) backbenchers (called alternately from each side of the chamber) ask supplementaries. If the subject is an important one, the opposition shadow minister may ask the final supplementary, and the Speaker calls the name of the next MP with a question down for answer. As we saw in Chapter 3 (page 54), the number of supplementaries called is entirely a matter for the Speaker; on a subject on which the government is vulnerable, calling more MPs to put supplementaries may put the minister under greater pressure; conversely, if fewer supplementaries are called, more questions on the Order of Business will be reached. The current Speaker is very keen to call as many members who have a question on the paper as possible.

Question Time is, above all, a political exchange; it is not primarily about seeking information, which is what written questions are supposed to be for. Oral questions are about exposing and criticising, or helping and supporting. All the ministers in a department – in a large department, the secretary of state, two ministers of state and two junior ministers (parliamentary under-secretaries) – will be present for their slot at Question Time. Which questions they answer will depend on their particular responsibilities within the department, but the secretary of state will usually take the biggest 'political' subjects.

The list of questions on the Order of Business may not be followed exactly. A minister may 'group' similar questions for answer if they are reasonably close together on the list, and the MPs who tabled those questions are called first to ask supplementaries. If an MP is unable to be present, he or she may withdraw a question, or convert it from an oral to a written question (known as 'unstarring' because oral questions were historically denoted by a star against them on the Order of Business).

The art of the supplementary

If Question Time is seen as a duel, the tabling of the question and the minister's often low-key reply are rather like two fencers squaring up to each other before the swords

4 Wednesday 21 March 2018 OP No.112: Part 1 **BUSINESS TODAY: CHAMBER**

BUSINESS TODAY: CHAMBER

11.30am Prayers

Followed by

QUESTIONS

■ **Oral Questions to the Secretary of State for Northern Ireland**

1 **Layla Moran** (Oxford West and Abingdon)
For what reasons the decision was made to publish information about loans and donations given to Northern Ireland political parties dating back to July 2017 rather than 2014. (904409)

2 **Michelle Donelan** (Chippenham)
What recent discussions she has had with Northern Ireland political parties on the UK leaving the EU. (904410)

3 **Carol Monaghan** (Glasgow North West)
What recent discussions she has had with the Irish Government on cross-border trade after the UK leaves the EU. (904411)

4 **Tom Pursglove** (Corby)
What steps the Government is taking to identify opportunities to strengthen Northern Ireland's economy as the UK leaves the EU. (904412)

5 **Gavin Newlands** (Paisley and Renfrewshire North)
What recent discussions she has had with the Irish Government on cross-border trade after the UK leaves the EU. (904413)

6 **Peter Grant** (Glenrothes)
What recent discussions she has had with the Irish Government on cross-border trade after the UK leaves the EU. (904414)

7 **Tommy Sheppard** (Edinburgh East)
What recent discussions she has had with the Irish Government on cross-border trade after the UK leaves the EU. (904415)

8 **Alex Chalk** (Cheltenham)
What recent discussions she has had with Northern Ireland political parties on the UK leaving the EU. (904416)

9 **Jim Shannon** (Strangford)
If she will hold discussions with the Chief Constable of the Police Service of Northern Ireland on recruiting more officers and reducing its overtime budget. (904417)

10 **Kerry McCarthy** (Bristol East)
What steps the Government is taking to ensure that healthcare provision in Northern Ireland is maintained after the UK leaves the EU. (904418)

Extract from oral questions on the Commons Order Paper for 21 March 2018

Source: Copyright House of Commons, 2018

clash. The real conflict of Question Time is in the supplementaries. Thus, an opposition MP may table a question that simply asks the Home Secretary how many police officers there are in England. The Home Secretary gives the figure, and the MP then asks 'But is the right honourable member aware that in the police authority that covers my constituency, police numbers have fallen by 9 per cent over the last three years, and violent crime has increased by 13 per cent? Doesn't that demonstrate that the government is soft on crime? Will the Home Secretary tell my constituents why she is not committed to improving their safety?' This not only makes the political point on behalf of the MP's party, but will play well in the MP's local press.

A government backbencher may table exactly the same question, but the supplementary will be very different: 'Will the Home Secretary accept the thanks of my constituents for the government's commitment to beating crime, for reducing bureaucracy allowing extra officers to be on the beat, and for the reduction of [some category of crime that has gone down rather than up].'

Short and sharp

By comparison with the *tabling* of oral and written questions, there are very few rules for asking oral supplementaries. If they are evidently wide of the original question, or if they refer to matters *sub judice* (see page 283), or if they clearly have nothing to do with the minister's responsibilities, the Speaker will call the MP to order. There is, however, a catch-22 about this; it is not easy to tell that a supplementary is out of order until the MP is a fair way through asking it. However, one type of disorderly supplementary from the government side is usually spotted very quickly: inviting the minister to comment on the policies of the opposition. Ministers are responsible for the government's policies, not those of their opponents. Even in the more knockabout atmosphere of Prime Minister's Questions, the Speaker has stopped the Prime Minister overtly responding to supplementaries that seek criticism of Labour policies.

Long supplementaries are tempting as a way of getting one's point on the record, but they also make things much easier for ministers. Not only is there plenty of time to turn to the relevant part of the briefing file for ammunition in reply, but long supplementaries are less focused and less likely to hit the target. Ministers are much less comfortable with the classic sharp supplementaries like 'Why?' or 'How much?' or 'How many?'

In this respect, Question Time is a perfect example of the law of unintended consequences. There used to be a long-standing rule against any member (other than a frontbencher) reading out a supplementary question; and even a brief glance down to a discreet note was met by cries of 'Reading!' The sensible purpose of the rule was to keep question time moving and to encourage shorter supplementaries. Similarly, the rule against quoting in a supplementary question discouraged long-windedness. The feeling in some quarters that this was too restrictive on backbenchers led to a change in the rule, and the immediate result was to encourage the use of written notes to make

259 21 MARCH 2018 260

House of Commons

Wednesday 21 March 2018

The House met at half-past Eleven o'clock

PRAYERS

[MR SPEAKER *in the Chair*]

Oral Answers to Questions

NORTHERN IRELAND

The Secretary of State was asked—

Political Parties: Loans and Donations

1. **Layla Moran** (Oxford West and Abingdon) (LD): For what reasons the decision was made to publish information about loans and donations given to Northern Ireland political parties dating back to July 2017 rather than 2014. [904409]

The Secretary of State for Northern Ireland (Karen Bradley): The recent publication by the Electoral Commission of donations and loans data for Northern Ireland parties is a positive step that should be welcomed by the whole House. The decision to backdate transparency was taken on the basis of broad support from the majority of political parties in Northern Ireland.

Layla Moran: It has recently been revealed that a portion of the largest ever political donation given to a party in Northern Ireland was spent on services linked to Cambridge Analytica. In the light of that, should not the Secretary of State backdate transparency regulations to 2014 so that we can finally have full disclosure about where that cash came from?

Karen Bradley: As I say, the decision to backdate to July 2017 was taken due to the broad support of the majority of parties in Northern Ireland. My predecessor, my right hon. Friend the Member for Old Bexley and Sidcup (James Brokenshire), took time to consult the parties, and July 2017 was the date that they wished to start the transparency from.

Bob Stewart (Beckenham) (Con): I think that my right hon. Friend has already answered the question I wanted to ask: did all the parties agree not to take it back to 2014?

Karen Bradley: As I say, my predecessor consulted all the parties, and this position was supported by the broad majority of them.

Gavin Robinson (Belfast East) (DUP): The Secretary of State will be able to confirm that even if the regulations did go back to 2014, no information would be published that has not already been published. Will she also confirm that there is a disparity when there is no mention in this Chamber or elsewhere of the dark money received by Northern Ireland parties from foreign jurisdictions? This is the only place where that is allowed to occur, and it should stop.

Karen Bradley: I firmly believe that transparency is the important thing that we have here. We should all know where money is coming from, and I understand the hon. Gentleman's comments.

Lady Hermon (North Down) (Ind): I am very interested to hear the Secretary of State's explanation of why the Northern Ireland Office deliberately and wilfully ignored the advice and recommendations of the Electoral Commission that the publication of donations to political parties in Northern Ireland should be backdated to 2014, not 2017.

Karen Bradley: There was no wilful ignoring or anything else. My predecessor consulted all the parties in Northern Ireland and there was broad support for July 2017.

Deidre Brock (Edinburgh North and Leith) (SNP): We know about one questionable donation that was channelled from Scotland through the Democratic Unionist party to be used in the Brexit referendum. People are rightly asking what the original source of that money was and whether there are others that we do not know about. If the Secretary of State will not consider revising the recent decision to limit transparency by taking it back to 2014, will she bring forward legislation to allow the individual parties to instruct the Electoral Commission to reveal their donation data?

Karen Bradley: As I have said, we are keen to ensure that there is transparency, but the question the hon. Lady asks is a matter for political parties themselves, not the Government.

Leaving the EU: Discussions with Political Parties

2. **Michelle Donelan** (Chippenham) (Con): What recent discussions she has had with Northern Ireland political parties on the UK leaving the EU. [904410]

8. **Alex Chalk** (Cheltenham) (Con): What recent discussions she has had with Northern Ireland political parties on the UK leaving the EU. [904416]

The Parliamentary Under-Secretary of State for Northern Ireland (Mr Shailesh Vara): The Secretary of State and I have regular conversations with the Northern Ireland political parties on a range of issues. This includes matters relating to the UK's departure from the European Union. As we have said repeatedly, these conversations are no replacement for a fully functioning, locally elected and democratically accountable Executive. That is what the people of Northern Ireland need, and that is what we are focused on.

Michelle Donelan: Does my hon. Friend agree that as we leave the EU, it is essential that current levels of security and co-operation between the UK and Ireland, which are so important in the fight against terrorism, are maintained and enhanced?

continued

Extracts from *Hansard*'s reporting of Question Time on 21 March 2018

Source: Copyright House of Commons, 2018

Mr Vara: I agree wholeheartedly with my hon. Friend. All parties have been clear that there will not be any disruption to north-south security co-operation when it comes to policing and tackling the terrorist threat. I applaud the incredible work done by the Police Service of Northern Ireland and the Garda to keep us safe. That will not change after our EU exit.

Alex Chalk: Will my hon. Friend assure the House that as the UK, including Northern Ireland, leaves the EU, this Government's commitment to the Belfast agreement remains steadfast?

Mr Vara: Yes. I can categorically provide my hon. Friend with the commitment that he seeks. Our negotiating strategy puts our support for the Belfast agreement at the heart of our approach to the Northern Ireland-Ireland dialogue. As the Prime Minister and others have said on numerous occasions, we will continue to abide by the UK's commitments in the Belfast agreement.

Nigel Dodds (Belfast North) (DUP): Given the meeting on Monday between the Secretary of State for Exiting the European Union and Michel Barnier, will the Minister confirm that it remains the Government's clear position that the so-called backstop arrangement proposed by the EU Commission is something that no British Prime Minister or Government could ever agree to?

Mr Vara: The Prime Minister has made her views absolutely clear on that. Our country's economic and constitutional integrity will not be harmed.

Nigel Dodds: I thank the Minister for debunking the notion that, as a result of the transition arrangements, somehow the Government have reneged on that pledge, and for confirming that the Government remain firmly committed to the constitutional, political and economic integrity of the UK. Will he ensure that industries such as the Northern Ireland fishing industry are protected after we leave the EU, and that we will take back control of our territorial waters, including our rights for our fishermen?

Mr Vara: The right hon. Gentleman makes some very good points. I can confirm that the agreement reached in December in the joint report remains, and that Britain will do all that it can to ensure that all our industries, particularly fisheries, are maintained, and that our fishermen and the industry are well looked after.

Owen Smith (Pontypridd) (Lab): I am sure that one issue the Minister and the Secretary of State will have discussed with the political parties in Northern Ireland is the problems they see with a hard border returning in Ireland. What are those problems and what does the Minister suggest that we do to avoid them?

Mr Vara: The Prime Minister, the Secretary of State and many others have made it absolutely clear that there will be no hard border.

Owen Smith: That is not much of an answer. The Government should acknowledge that the parties all think that there would be problems with a hard border, as do the Chief Constable, the Northern Ireland Affairs Committee, the Irish Government and many Conservative Members. Should he not therefore acknowledge the problems and tell the House that the only way to avoid a hard border is for us to stay within the customs union and the single market?

Mr Vara: The people of Britain—England, Scotland, Northern Ireland and Wales—collectively agreed to leave the single market and customs union, and that will be the case. As for the border, the December joint report made it absolutely clear that there will be no physical infrastructure and no hard border. There will be a frictionless border, and that is what is being negotiated and discussed.

Leaving the EU: Cross-border Trade

3. **Carol Monaghan** (Glasgow North West) (SNP): What recent discussions she has had with the Irish Government on cross-border trade after the UK leaves the EU. [904411]

5. **Gavin Newlands** (Paisley and Renfrewshire North) (SNP): What recent discussions she has had with the Irish Government on cross-border trade after the UK leaves the EU. [904413]

6. **Peter Grant** (Glenrothes) (SNP): What recent discussions she has had with the Irish Government on cross-border trade after the UK leaves the EU. [904414]

7. **Tommy Sheppard** (Edinburgh East) (SNP): What recent discussions she has had with the Irish Government on cross-border trade after the UK leaves the EU. [904415]

The Secretary of State for Northern Ireland (Karen Bradley): I have regular conversations with the Irish Government. We both recognise the importance of the trade that takes place across the island of Ireland, which is worth £4 billion to the Northern Ireland economy. Equally, Great Britain markets are fundamental to Northern Ireland, with sales worth some £14.6 billion. As the Prime Minister reinforced in her Mansion House speech, we are committed to protecting both these vital markets.

Carol Monaghan: The Tánaiste told the Dáil yesterday that there would be no formal withdrawal agreement between the EU and the UK if the Irish border issue was not resolved. The Under-Secretary of State for Northern Ireland, the hon. Member for North West Cambridgeshire (Mr Vara), has already said this morning that there will be no hard border, but will the Secretary of State explain how that will come about?

Karen Bradley: I do not think that the hon. Lady has said anything that is news to anybody. We are committed to the agreement we made in the joint report, and to the Belfast agreement and all that it stands for. We will ensure that there is no new physical infrastructure at the border and that there is frictionless trade.

Gavin Newlands: Simon Coveney also told the Dáil yesterday that the UK Government had provided a cast-iron guarantee that there would be no physical infrastructure, checks or controls at the border post Brexit. Will the Secretary of State confirm this—yes or no?

lengthy assertions, often backed with quotation, to which ministers were expected to respond. Although this tended to lead to longer questions, the current Speaker has been assiduous in trying to keep questions snappy and will cut off MPs who are verbose.

Preparing for Question Time

For the government, Question Time is an opportunity to tell the story the way ministers see it. It gives junior ministers a chance to show their potential to a busy chamber and senior ministers the chance to demonstrate their mastery of the subject. It can also be a high-risk occasion; government departments prepare very carefully. Ministers will have had briefing meetings with their civil servants and each minister will take into the chamber a ring-binder with the answer he or she is to give to each question, together with a 'survival pack' of information and briefing, according to a fairly standard template:

- *The reason for the question*: why is the MP asking it? Is there a particular constituency focus? What has the MP raised with the department recently? When a government MP puts down a question, he or she will often helpfully let the department know what is behind it, or what he or she plans as a supplementary question. Opposition MPs will also do this on occasion, especially if their intention is to flag up some issue of constituency concern rather than to attack the government. It is much better for them (and for their local media) to have a minister give a full answer on a matter of local concern rather than simply saying that he or she will write to the MP.
- *Elephant traps*: any information that the minister should know about potential gaps in the policy or problems with the figures on the main issues likely to be raised.
- *Positive/defensive*: 3 or 4 key best positive lines and 3 or 4 key defensive lines to take on the main issue . . . covering government achievements and positive activity in the area of policy, and defending against the most likely lines of criticism.
- *Key background facts and figures* and, with a page for each issue, *other issues that may be raised* with bullet-point lines to take.
- *Key quotes*: 'any useful third party endorsements or supportive comments from members of the opposition'.

The official opposition team shadowing the government department will also lay its plans for Question Time, highlighting areas where they believe the government is open to criticism, and seeking the help of backbenchers to reinforce the line being taken by the frontbench team.

Question Times to major government departments end with 10 or 15 minutes of 'topical' questions. For this period, just a list of names of MPs drawn in the shuffle is printed; there is no text of a question. The session starts with a very brief response from the secretary of state to the first topical question setting out some recent initiatives or successes of the department. After this, the rest of the topical question time is a series of spontaneous questions, technically supplementaries. They may be on any topic within the department's responsibility. The ministerial team must make a snap decision as to who is going to answer, and it can be interesting to watch the silent exchanges of body language by which they negotiate in a matter of seconds.

Although there was some trepidation about introducing topical questions in 2007, the House (and ministers) now value them. But topical questions rarely reveal any new information; they are much more of a political joust. In this way, they are a version of Prime Minister's Questions, to which we now turn.

Prime Minister's Questions (PMQs)

The Prime Minister answers for half an hour every Wednesday from 12 noon to 12.30 pm (although in practice the Speaker often allows the session to run until 12.45 pm or later, in order to try to accommodate as many members as possible). Only the top 15 questions in the shuffle are printed, and the vast majority are in the form 'If she will list her official engagements for [Wednesday 9th July]'. Only the first such question is printed out in full on the Order of Business; if other MPs want to ask the same question their names alone are printed alongside the question numbers.

Theresa May's first PMQs as Prime Minister, 2016

Source: Copyright UK Parliament, 2016. Photography by Jessica Taylor

Why the 'engagements question'?

It may seem strange that so many MPs want to ask the Prime Minister what she happens to be doing on a particular Wednesday. The reason is historical but the habit persists even though, in practice, it is not really necessary. Forty years ago, the Prime Minister of the day would transfer a specific question to the relevant secretary of state if the latter had ministerial responsibility for the subject, and the MP concerned would lose the chance of an oral question to the Prime Minister. Prime Ministers are, in a sense, responsible for everything, but there are relatively few things for which they have specific responsibility and a departmental minister does not; examples include coordination between government departments, appointing and dismissing ministers, setting up cabinet committees and the intelligence services as a whole.

So the 'transfer-proof' question was devised by the clerks in the Table Office: either to ask the Prime Minister her official engagements for the day or a related open question – whether she would visit some particular place (usually the questioner's constituency) or country. When she became Prime Minister, Margaret Thatcher indicated that she would not transfer specific questions, as did John Major and Tony Blair when they came to office, and this practice has continued since. However, the open question persisted for two reasons. It allowed MPs to raise the issue of the moment even though the question had been tabled some time before; and it was easy – no thought had to be given to researching and constructing some cunning question when it was odds-against that it would be successful in the shuffle. And even though the period of notice has shortened from 10 sitting days to three with the express purpose of allowing more topical questions, the 'engagements question' is still the norm.

Prime Minister's Questions: on the day

As for departmental questions, the Speaker calls (say) 'Mr Crispin Blunt'; Mr Blunt stands up and says 'Number one, Mr Speaker'. The Prime Minister gives the standard response: 'This morning I had meetings with ministerial colleagues and others. In addition to my duties in this House, I shall have further such meetings later today.' The Prime Minister often takes this opportunity to offer condolences to the families of service personnel who have died on active service, victims of other tragedies or, more cheerfully, to congratulate winning sports teams or other national heroes. Mr Blunt is then able to ask a supplementary on anything that is the responsibility of the government. After the Prime Minister has replied, the Speaker will call other MPs who were successful in the shuffle, interspersed with other backbenchers. Unlike departmental questions, MPs whose names are on the printed list simply ask their supplementary; they do not go through the process of calling out the number and having the Prime Minister repeat her original answer.

If the Leader of the Opposition rises, the Speaker will call him; he has a normal allocation of six questions in PMQs, which he can take either all in a run or split into two groups of three (or any other pattern that he chooses). The leader of the second largest opposition party (currently the SNP) is allocated two questions.

Questions in PMQs are the usual mixture of the supportive and the critical, but the main event is the contest between the Prime Minister and the Leader of the Opposition. The House is full, noisy and partisan; and TV stations and national newspapers carry 'post-match' comment, sometimes rating the encounter in terms of goals scored or punches landed. The Prime Minister of the day has a built-in advantage; she is centre-stage for the whole play, while the Leader of the Opposition has only six appearances; and the Prime Minister can build on questions from her own backbenchers to project a positive presentation of government policy and achievements. The duel between the Leader of the Opposition and the Prime Minister usually lasts 10–15 minutes; after it has concluded, things often settle down and exchanges can be quiet and constructive.

Is PMQs too noisy?

Opinion is sharply divided between those who revel in the heady atmosphere of PMQs, the roars of support or opposition, and the gladiatorial exchanges; and those who see in PMQs the worst of a highly adversarial parliamentary system, with echoes of the junior common room. It would be unrealistic to expect that, having corralled 500 people of deeply held and opposing views in a small room, contentious assertions will be heard in reverent silence; they won't. But in the process it is important not to lose the value of PMQs. It is an opportunity to question for at least half an hour, every sitting Wednesday, the chief executive of the nation. This is a form of accountability that would be unthinkable in many other democracies. It is reasonable for the chamber to be boisterous, but when the volume (and, especially, collective barracking) prevents questions and answers being heard, then the House and the country are the losers. A welcome antidote is the regular appearance of the Prime Minister before the Liaison Committee (see page 324) in a calmer and more courteous atmosphere.

Urgent questions

On any sitting day an MP can privately seek the Speaker's permission to ask an urgent question. These were formerly known as 'private notice questions' (PNQs) because notice of them was given directly to the Speaker and not printed on the Order Paper as for other oral questions. The MP must make a request before 10 am on a day when the House sits at 11.30 am; before 8.30 am on a day when the House sits at 9.30 am; and before noon on a Monday. The Speaker considers the application at the daily conference with the Deputy Speakers, attended by the Clerk of the House, the Clerk Assistant and the Principal Clerk of the Table Office. The Speaker, if he is satisfied that the matter is of public importance and is urgent, grants the application. Warning is displayed on the annunciators around the parliamentary estate, and the MP concerned is called to ask the question at the end of Question Time (or, on a Friday, at 11 am, interrupting the business then under way). Urgent questions on a Friday are rare.

The Speaker's power to grant an urgent question is significant. It brings a minister to the House at very short notice to answer on something on which the government may be in some disarray and may still be deciding how to respond to. It is a way for the House to engage immediately with a high-profile issue of the moment that would not otherwise find its way on to the House's agenda. The mere tabling of an urgent question, of which the government is immediately informed, is sometimes enough for ministers to volunteer a full statement.

The normal format is for the questioner to read out the text of the question. The minister then replies for up to five minutes. Questioning from opposition parties' spokespeople and backbenchers may then last up to an hour, though sometimes less.

As we saw in Chapter 3, the number of urgent questions granted under the current Speaker has increased sharply. In the 2016–17 session the Speaker granted 74 urgent questions. Contrast this with 2007–08, the last full session before John Bercow became Speaker, when four urgent questions were granted. Occasionally, two or more are granted on a single day. The subjects covered can be local, national or international in focus and vary widely. For example, the last three urgent questions in the 2016–17 session concerned: the Nuclear Decommissioning Authority's early contract terminations at the Magnox estate; the persecution and detention of LGBT citizens in Chechnya; and the publication of the government's air quality strategy. In April 2012 the granting of the Question 'if he will refer the conduct of the Secretary of State for Culture, Olympics, Media and Sport [then Jeremy Hunt], in respect of his dealings with News Corporation, to the independent adviser on ministerial interests' brought the Prime Minister himself to the despatch box to answer.

The 'business question' every Thursday morning, in which the shadow Leader of the House asks the Leader of the House to announce forthcoming business in the House, is technically an urgent question, although of a specialised type. The Leader of the House sets out the main items of business on the House's agenda, usually confirmed for the following week, more provisional for the week after, and then answers questions. Strictly speaking, these must relate to the forthcoming business, but more often they are on more general political matters; it does not take much ingenuity to ask for a debate on 'the government's failure to deliver on targets' or on 'the government's successes in carrying through public service reform'.

Since the creation of backbench business (see page 150), the Leader's answer is often to encourage the member to apply to the Backbench Business Committee for a debate. During business questions the Leader will list forthcoming backbench business, but as she has no sway over the allocation of such business she is simply reporting the decisions made by the Backbench Business Committee.

Questions answered at the end of Question Time

A minister may choose to answer an oral question not as it is reached during Question Time, but at the end of oral questions (3.30 pm on Mondays, 12.30 pm on Tuesdays and Wednesdays and 11.30 am on Thursdays). This is relatively unusual, but tends to happen when a question on the Order of Business is a convenient hook for an announcement a minister wants to make, but at greater length than would be permissible in answer to a conventional oral question. As this is, in effect, a mini-statement, the Speaker allows more supplementaries than during Question Time. A minister may answer an oral question in this way even though it would not have been reached during Question Time (and may even answer a written question in this way if it is down for answer on that day).

Written questions

In the 2016–17 session, 3,362 questions received an oral answer in the House. By contrast, 34,711 written questions were tabled during that session. Just over 16 per cent of these – some 5,716 – were to the Department of Health. Seven other departments answered more than 2,000 each. At the other end of the scale, the Wales Office answered 174 and the Attorney General 183.

Written questions are of two types: *ordinary written questions*, which are put down, in theory, for answer two sitting days after they are received but which the government has committed to trying to answer within a working week. There is no limit to the number of this type of question that an MP may table. *Named-day questions* are for answer on a stated day, with a minimum period of three working days, although an answer may be given only on a sitting day. The named-day system was originally intended for genuinely urgent questions (and used to be called 'priority written questions'), but it became greatly over-used, and increasing numbers of questions got holding replies ('I will reply to the hon. member as soon as possible'). In 2003 the House agreed a limit of five named-day questions per member per day.

Written questions have a wide variety of purposes. They are used by MPs to raise the profile of particular subjects, to tease out details of the government's policy on some issue with a view to deploying the material in political debate inside or outside the House, or to press ministers in an area where the government appears vulnerable. They are tabled to gather information in order to be able to respond to constituency concerns or to give a constituent's case wider publicity. Shadow ministers use them to monitor what the government is doing in their policy areas. Outside organisations will ask MPs to put down questions in order to assist a campaign, or to obtain an authoritative statement on a situation or of the government's policy towards it.

Written questions have one great advantage over oral questions: they can be pursued much more relentlessly. Whereas in Question Time an MP gets one supplementary and the moment is past, with the ministers concerned not answering again until one month later, written questions can follow up in detail, almost as a barrister would in cross-examination, the precise conduct of government policy in a particular area.

Although, as we noted, there are rubbing points when MPs see no good reason for the government refusing to answer, replies to written questions put a staggering amount of official information into the public domain, even though some feel that their increasing use has devalued the currency. The total numbers of written answers published per financial year soared from 32,821 in 2000–01 to a peak of 73,601 in 2008–09, but has declined since then to about 30,000–40,000 in an ordinary session.

Such questions used to occupy 40–50 pages of *Hansard* on a typical day. In 2014 the House of Commons stopped printing answers to written parliamentary questions as part of a wider move 'from print to web', making information electronically available to MPs and to the public. Members receive answers to their questions to up to three nominated email addresses. Answers are also fully searchable on the parliamentary website and available in a downloadable daily digest form.

The volume of questions tabled by MPs varies enormously: some will ask hundreds over the course of a session; others a handful, or none. In the 2005–10 parliament there was anecdotal evidence that some MPs were motivated by published 'league tables' showing how busy MPs had been, with media reports on how 'lazy' others were. It appeared that some MPs tried to game the system by tabling scores of questions, regardless of merit. Theyworkforyou.com, the most high-profile source, changed its policy as a result and stopped publishing league tables, and included disclaimers noting that quantity did not necessarily mean quality.

Written statements

It used to be the case that, if the government wanted to put something formally on the record in the House that was not important enough for an oral statement (see page 144), a friendly backbencher would be found to put down an 'arranged question' drafted in the department concerned, for answer the next day, in answer to which the government could make the statement it wanted. These arranged or 'planted' questions were a rather opaque way for the government to make an announcement and, from 2002, a system of written ministerial statements was introduced. In 2013 the House agreed to the Procedure Committee's recommendation that the provision to make written statements should be extended to answering bodies (such as the House of Commons Commission and the Church Commissioners) that already had slots to answer oral questions. Written statements to be made on any day are listed on the Order Paper at the end of the day's business, and statements on a future day appear in Section A of the *Future Business* part of the Vote bundle (see page 159), although advance notification is fairly rare. When made, the statements are published online and are printed towards the end of the next day's *Hansard*.

Are questions effective?

Whereas 30 or 40 years ago an MP would often first write to a government department for information, or seek a meeting to put some point to a minister, and would table a PQ only if he or she had to, in 2018 putting down a question is often the first, not the last, step. As the Procedure Committee has acknowledged, the scale of the increase in written questions risks a reduction in the quality of government replies – although this is not to suggest that if there were half the number of questions the answers would be twice as helpful. Although many PQs engage the efforts of the MP asking them very closely, the sheer number (and the poor level of authentication for 'e-tabling') has led to unease that significant numbers of PQs are actually drafted and tabled by MPs' staff with minimal involvement of the member concerned.

However, as in so many areas of parliamentary life, the determination and hard work of an individual MP can produce remarkable results. For example, it was the written questions tabled by the backbench Labour MP Tam Dalyell in the 1980s that led to the admission from Margaret Thatcher's government that, during the Falklands war, the Argentinian heavy cruiser *General Belgrano* had been torpedoed when steaming away from British forces rather than towards them, as the government had previously implied. There are many less-celebrated examples of assiduous MPs doggedly plugging away at some area of a department's activities until they elicit enough information to reveal that the official account of events is inconsistent with the facts.

Oral and written questions are key functions of the House of Commons. Both can be means of exposing the government to criticism, and of requiring explanation and justification. Oral questions, although inquisitorial in theory, are also part of the political debate. Written questions, on the other hand, are a way of calling governments to account in detail, and should be an important discipline on individual government departments and their ministers – the requirement to reply truthfully to a direct and precise question can mean that the spotlight swings onto something that the government would have much preferred to have kept to itself.

Although, as we have seen, frontbenchers use questions extensively, they are also one of the main opportunities for backbench MPs on all sides of the House to pursue and expose issues, and to get the government of the day to put information on the public record. If the average costs of answering oral and written questions are correct, the system costs about £5.7 million per annum, or about £8,750 for each of the House's members. Set against expected total government expenditure in 2017–18 of some £802 billion, this does not seem excessive.

The great constitutional theorist Ivor Jennings described parliamentary questions as 'of the utmost constitutional importance'. The effect of the internet, digital government and the coming into force of the Freedom of Information Act have all contributed to making PQs a less privileged and special way of eliciting information from the executive. But parliamentary questions still symbolise the ultimate accountability of ministers to Parliament, and in that respect are as important as they ever were.

Questions in the House of Lords

The House of Lords also has a variety of ways of scrutinising the actions of, and eliciting information from, the executive through questions. These questions are always addressed to Her Majesty's Government, rather than to individual ministers. (Questions on domestic House of Lords matters are usually addressed to the Leader of the House or the Senior Deputy Speaker.) It follows that the government must have responsibility for the subject matter of the question. Fewer questions are tabled in the Lords than in the Commons, and the rules governing their content are applied less strictly. It is ultimately for the House itself to determine what is in order and what is not. But there are some conventions, and the guidance for members in the *Companion to Standing Orders* is now much more specific than it used to be. Questions are inadmissible if they cast reflections on the royal family, relate to the Church of England, are on devolved matters, are phrased offensively or if the subject-matter is outside of the government's responsibilities. Questions that are *sub judice* (which are on matters awaiting decision by the criminal or civil courts) are also inadmissible – subject to the discretion of the Lord Speaker, who may allow such a question if the case is of national importance and there is no danger of prejudice to the proceedings. It is undesirable to table hypothetical questions, or to incorporate statements of fact or opinion in the text of a question. And, in the interests of 'comity', questions should not criticise decisions of the House of Commons.

Questions for oral answer (starred questions)

Every sitting day, except on Fridays, four questions for oral answer may be put to the government immediately after prayers and before other business. They are marked on the Order Paper with a '*' and, provided that they are not 'topical questions', may be tabled up to one month in advance. In sessions 2002–03 and 2003–04 the House experimented by taking a fifth question on Tuesdays and Wednesdays, but subsequently reverted to former practice.

As in the Commons, questions in the Lords were losing their currency from being tabled too far in advance and some members were, it was felt, hogging the Order Paper by tabling too many, too far ahead. In recent years, the House has agreed that no member should have more than one oral question on the Order Paper at any one time; that members should be limited to seven oral questions in a year-long session; and that on Tuesdays, Wednesdays and Thursdays one of the questions should be a 'topical question' selected by ballot by the Clerk Assistant two working days before it is to be asked. No oral question may be tabled less than 24 hours before it is to be asked.

Unlike the Commons, questions are not limited to any particular government department on any particular day and there is, of course, no equivalent of Prime Minister's Questions. Every member asking a question is allowed one supplementary before other members' supplementaries are put. Supplementary questions must be confined to the subject of the original question but frequently go wider. They should be genuine questions and not mere points of debate. Question time may not exceed 30 minutes, which usually means 7–8 minutes for each question: this often involves moving on to the next question when several members still want to ask supplementary questions on the previous one. In the 2016–17 session, 508 oral questions were asked – a typical number for a session of normal duration.

When, towards the end of Gordon Brown's premiership, two secretaries of state sat in the Lords (Business and Transport), the House agreed in late 2009 to institute an additional question period for Lords secretaries of state. Three questions to a particular secretary of state would be taken additionally on Thursdays once a month, following a ballot on the previous Monday. The period allotted was 15 minutes. As there are currently no secretaries of state in the House (and have not been since 2010), the procedure is dormant, but it will be revived the next time there is one.

Questions for short debate

A question that may give rise to debate for one hour or an hour-and-a-half may be put down for any sitting day. These may be taken at the end of business, during dinner adjournments or in Grand Committee. Although they take the form of a question, in truth they are as much a peg for a debate as an opportunity to hold the government to account. They are discussed more fully on page 287.

Questions for written answer

Members of the Lords may also table questions for written answer. The same rules on the content of oral questions apply to written questions. They are answered by the relevant minister in writing, appearing online in the Q&A system and in print in a separate volume of *Hansard*. At the request of the Leader of the House, a hard-copy answer with the minister's signature is also sent to the questioner. Answers should be given within 10 working days of the question being tabled; overdue answers feature in a 'naughty list' in *House of Lords Business*. Written answers on matters delegated to executive agencies are filtered through the appropriate Lords minister and printed in *Hansard* in letter form. Each Lord may ask no more than six written questions per sitting day, with a cap of 12 per week. Members should not attempt to evade these limits by tabling multiple requests for information masquerading as a single question. During the long summer recess, written questions may normally be tabled on a couple of specified days, with the precise dates depending on the sitting pattern. In 1961–62, only 72 questions for written answer were tabled; in 1998–99, 4,322; and in 2016–17, 6,872. A general upward trend reached the peak of 8,294 written questions in 2015–16. As in the Commons, written statements may be made by ministers in the Lords – 614 in session 2016–17, most of them repeats of written statements made in the Commons.

Private notice questions

The Lords' equivalent of an urgent question is a private notice question. The Lord Speaker decides whether an application for a question is of sufficient urgency or importance to justify an immediate reply, having consulted the 'usual channels'. The Lord Speaker's decision not to allow a question is final and may not be appealed. Private notice questions may be asked on any sitting day. An application for one must be made to the Lord Speaker by noon if the House is sitting that afternoon, or by 10 am if it is sitting in the morning. If the question is granted, proceedings on it take place immediately after oral questions (or, on a Friday when there are no oral questions, at a convenient time). The member asking it reads the question aloud in the House; the minister replies; then 10 minutes of supplementary questions and answers follow, beginning with a supplementary for the member who tabled the question. Private notice questions used to be rare – from 2006 to 2016 they averaged five per year. But since Lord Fowler became Lord Speaker in September 2016 they have increased greatly. He has announced that his presumption is to grant a question to any application which meets the criteria of urgency and importance. In 2016–17, 19 private notice questions were granted.

Statements

Ministerial statements made in the Commons may be repeated in the Lords. The decision on whether to repeat a statement is taken by the 'usual channels', which in practice means that if the official opposition want the statement repeated, it is; if they don't, it isn't. A repeated statement is read by the Lords minister verbatim – complete with references to 'Mr Speaker' and use of the first person attributed to the Commons minister. (Very long statements, such as the former 'Autumn Statement' by the Chancellor, may by agreement not be read out but simply printed in *Hansard*.) A statement takes place at a convenient time agreed by the usual channels – perhaps between two debates or in-between groups of amendments on a bill. Following the conclusion of the statement, 20 minutes are allowed for questions from the opposition frontbench and the minister's reply, and a further 20 minutes for other members' questions and answers. In rare instances the time for backbench questions may be increased. In 2016–17, 93 oral statements were made, occupying just under 5 per cent of the House's time. Occasionally the relevant principal minister will sit in the Lords; in those instances statements are made first by the Lords minister then repeated later in the Commons.

Answers to many Commons urgent questions are repeated as statements in the House of Lords, by agreement among the usual channels. Questions and answers on repeated Commons urgent questions are limited to 10 minutes and follow the procedure for oral questions.

Petitions

The right to petition Parliament is an ancient one, summarised in a resolution of the House of Commons of 1699: 'That it is the inherent right of every commoner in England to prepare and present petitions to the House of Commons in case of grievance, and the House of Commons to receive the same'. The first recorded petitions date from the reign of Richard II (1377–99); in 1571, a committee with the splendid name of the Committee for Motions of Griefs and Petitions was appointed to examine petitions.

Petitions were originally read at the start of a sitting, and debates could arise on them. Huge numbers were presented during the nineteenth century; for example, 17,000 per year between 1837 and 1841; and 34,000 in 1893. The twentieth century saw a sharp fall in the numbers of public petitions, but they remain a way of giving local or more widespread concerns a higher profile.

There are two ways for the public to petition Parliament: the majority now do so via e-petitions, which we explore below.

The more traditional way is for an MP to present a petition. Public (paper) petitions may have hundreds of thousands of signatures, or only one, but the procedure is the same in each case. The basic rules are that they should state from whom they come, should be in 'respectful language' and should ask for something that it is in the power of the House of Commons to grant. The MP has the petition checked by the Clerk of Public Petitions to make sure it is in order and can then, at any time during a sitting of the House, simply put it in the green baize bag that hangs on the back of the Speaker's chair. The MP may also present a petition formally in the House. Just before the daily half-hour adjournment debate, he or she is called by the Speaker, and briefly introduces the petition and reads the text. The MP then brings the petition to the clerk at the Table and hands the petition to them. The clerk announces the title of the petition and hands it back to the MP, who places it in the petition bag. All petitions are printed in *Hansard* and are sent to the government department responsible for the subject area, as well as the select committee that shadows that department. In October 2007 the House agreed that all 'substantive petitions should normally receive a response from the relevant government department' and select committees should 'formally place them on their agendas'. There is an expectation that observations should be made within two months of the petition being presented to the House. The observations are also printed in *Hansard*. Recent statistics are:

Table 9.1 Number of petitions presented in the House of Commons 2010–12 to 2016–17

Session	Petitions	of which presented formally	Government observations
2010–12 (long session)	187	176	159
2012–13	146	128	132
2013–14	175	163	137
2014–15	104	166	83
2015–16	165	143	173
2016–17	328	296	308

Petitions cover a wide variety of subjects; although they can include national and international issues, there is often a local focus. On the last sitting day before the 2017 summer recess, for example, petitions were presented on Higham Ferrers GP surgery, a particular planning application in Irthlingborough and the continuation of local bus services in Congleton.

Petitions presented in this traditional manner are not formally taken up, either by a committee of the House or by an outside authority such as the Ombudsman. Committees may occasionally write to the member who has presented the petition to share the work that they are doing on that subject area with them. In that sense, they are not a particularly effective way of making a case. On local matters, they indicate that an MP is pressing their constituents' interests and there can sometimes be a snowball effect. On national issues, either the sheer numbers of signatories to a petition, or the fact that similar petitions from scores of constituencies are presented week after week, can be a powerful statement of concern which, for practical political reasons, the government must heed. Sometimes MPs coordinate the presentation of many petitions on the same subject (for example, the school funding formula) in order to increase their impact. It is worth noting that despite the popularity of e-petitions, which we look at below, there has been no reduction in the number of petitions presented in the traditional way.

Petitions may also be addressed to the House of Lords by a member of the House. No speech or debate takes place beyond the formal words of presentation and they are not printed. Though largely defunct, petitions are very occasionally still presented there.

e-Petitions

The House of Commons had, for some years, grappled with whether to introduce an electronic system of petitioning. In 2008 the Procedure Committee recommended that the House of Commons adopt a system of e-petitions, a recommendation that was agreed to by the government in July 2008. But the costs and complexities involved meant that no such system was introduced, despite a follow-up report from the committee calling for government action in 2008–09.

The No. 10 Downing Street e-petitions system was launched on 14 November 2006 and rapidly attracted a large number of petitions and petitioners, and a high level of publicity; however, the procedure had no parliamentary aspect. In 2010 the new coalition government made a commitment as part of its *Programme for Government* 'that any petition that secures 100,000 signatures will be eligible for formal debate in Parliament'. The government gave effect to this commitment through the relaunching of the No. 10 Downing Street petition website in July 2011 as a government petitions website and the Leader of the House notifying the Backbench Business Committee of any petition that had been accepted and had passed a 100,000 signature threshold and was therefore 'eligible' for debate.

By the end of the 2013–14 session, 28 e-petitions on the government website had reached the 100,000 signature threshold, making them eligible for consideration for debate. The topics of 22 had been the subject of debate in the House of Commons, most as a direct result of the e-petition. However, many felt that the system of e-petitioning should be more squarely within the control of Parliament. A debate on petitions was held in the House of Commons in May 2014 and the House supported a proposal for a collaborative e-petitions system. The Procedure Committee made detailed proposals about how such a system might work in December 2014, recommending that the government's e-petition site should be rebranded and redesigned to show that it was owned jointly with the House. An e-petition would need to include a clear statement of the action sought by the government and be supported by at least six people before being opened on the site for others to add their signatures; e-petitions would remain live for six months. The committee also recommended that a new Petitions Committee be set up, responsible for oversight of both the paper and e-petitions system, with the ability to:

- correspond with petitioners on their petition;
- call petitioners for oral evidence;
- refer a petition to the relevant select committee;
- seek further information from the government, orally or in writing, on the subject of a petition; and
- put forward e-petitions for debate.

The House agreed the proposals in February 2015 and the Petitions Committee started its work in July 2015. In its first year it received more than 23,000 e-petitions, of which 6,121 were accepted and published on the committee's webpages. Of the rejected petitions, almost half duplicated an existing petition; another common reason for rejection was that the petition called for an action that was not within the responsibility of Parliament or central government. When a petition has been accepted and achieves 10,000 signatures, the government provides a response to it, and 264 such responses were provided in the Committee's first year of operation. If a petition reaches 100,000 signatures, the Committee considers whether it should be scheduled for a debate; it also has the discretion to schedule debates on petitions that have not reached this threshold. The Committee has the power to schedule debates in Westminster Hall. It scheduled 20 such debates in its first year. In fact, almost all petitions which reach 100,000 signatories are debated, with the exceptions generally being only those where the subject has recently been debated or is already scheduled to be debated. The committee may also inquire into issues raised by petitions, like other select committees. In its first year it inquired into funding for research into brain tumours; high heels and workplace dress codes; and the meningitis B vaccine, in some cases working with other committees to increase impact and expertise. The Committee has also created more informal opportunities for petitioners to have their voices heard in Parliament, including holding discussion events or online conversations to inform debates.

Members of the public engaging with the e-petitions system are sometimes frustrated. As noted earlier, some petitions are rejected. Even if a petition is debated, no change in policy necessarily follows. However, the ability to compel ministers to attend debates and hear the concerns raised, and the requirement for departments to respond to many petitions which are not debated, mean that the concerns of those petitioning have an impact on the executive.

The e-petitions system has helped to engage people with Parliament: in its first year of operation, more than 10 million unique email addresses were used to sign petitions, with over 20 million signatures in total. Debates held in Westminster Hall attracted significant interest: the *Hansard* reports of them are some of the most widely read and it has been estimated that, by emailing petitioners to inform them of debates on petitions they have signed, the committee has brought about a 900 per cent increase in the viewing figures for debates in Westminster Hall. A small number of petitions have led directly to changes in government policy, while others have played a significant role in wider campaigns for change. By any standards, the e-petition system and the work of the Petitions Committee has transformed citizens' ability to connect with Parliament and ensure their concerns are raised in it.

MPs' letters

MPs' letters to ministers can be seen as part of the questioning process, though they are not 'proceedings in Parliament' (see page 169). The level of correspondence between MPs and ministers is very high. The government's figures, from which Table 9.2 is drawn, include correspondence from peers, but the vast majority of letters are from MPs (who in this case also include ministers and the Speaker in their constituency roles).

It is not surprising that the departments that deal with the matters that touch people's lives most closely – health, law and order, education and immigration – have heavy postbags.

Typically, an MP receives a complaint from a constituent, perhaps that he was discharged from hospital too soon, or that he has a partner who is not being allowed to settle in the UK from another country, or that his son is being kept in poor conditions in a remand prison. It would be impossible for the MP to investigate these complaints

Table 9.2 Correspondence in calendar year 2016, selected departments and agencies

Department name	Number of MPs' and Peers' letters
Department for Business, Energy and Industrial Strategy (Business, Innovation and Skills until July 2016)	6,196
Cabinet Office	1,570
Department for Communities and Local Government	6,270
Department for Culture, Media and Sport	4,347
Ministry of Defence	3,367
Department for Education	7,554
Department for Environment, Food and Rural Affairs	7,855
Foreign and Commonwealth Office	8,468
Department of Health	15,483
Home Office	6,628
UK Visas and Immigration/Immigration and Enforcement/Border Force	33,168
Her Majesty's Passport Office	2,961
Department for International Development	1,607
Department for International Trade	1,361
Ministry of Justice	2,073
Office of the Leader of the House of Commons	116
Department for Transport	6,290
Treasury	7,231
Department for Work and Pensions	14,317

personally. He or she could table parliamentary questions or apply for an adjournment debate; but usually the MP begins by forwarding the constituent's letter to the minister responsible for the subject and asking for comments. Not all letters are of complaint. A small firm may want to know what government grants it can apply for, or seek the MP's help in negotiating some tangle of bureaucracy.

The constituent could have written directly to the department, whether with a complaint or query, but the fact that the letter is from an MP means that the issue will be dealt with at a more senior level. The reply – usually from a minister personally, but also from officials with operational responsibility for the subject or the chief executive of an executive agency – will be in a form that the MP can forward to the constituent as a response, but it may also give the MP useful background information if similar cases arise.

Letters from members of the House of Lords to ministers are treated in the same way inside government departments as letters from MPs. No separate figures are published, but the numbers are much lower because peers have no constituency work.

Letters have several advantages over parliamentary questions. They can be sent at any time, whereas questions may be tabled only when the House is sitting or on non-sitting Fridays. They can raise confidential matters, or the personal details of a constituent's case, and can go into great detail about the point at issue. And, unlike questions, there are no rules restricting what an MP may say in a letter. The contents of letters between MPs and ministers are private unless one side or the other releases them; and although by convention the minister does not do this unless the MP does, ministers are always aware that the MP may 'go public' and their letters are, whenever possible, written in a form that can be forwarded directly to the constituent.

One disadvantage of letters is that they are more prone to delay than the answers to PQs. All the departments in Table 9.2 above have targets for replying to MPs' letters, of between 10 and 20 working days. In 2016 the Ministry of Defence responded to 98 per cent of letters within its 20-day target, but the Department for International Trade managed a response rate of only 47 per cent within its 15-day target.

Most matters raised by constituents and taken by MPs to ministers are dealt with by correspondence. However, if the MP is unhappy with the government's response, he or she can seek a meeting with the minister, put down parliamentary questions, or seek an adjournment debate, either in the chamber or in Westminster Hall, to which a minister will have to reply. Proceedings in the House often start with a constituent's letter.

10

Calling to account: select committees

Select committees in the House of Commons

Introduction

People often associate select committees of the House of Commons with the system of departmental select committees set up in 1979; but, in fact, the House has used select committees for centuries to investigate, to advise, to consider complex matters – in fact, for any task that is more effectively carried out by a small group of MPs than by the House as a whole. Indeed, the very name 'select committee' indicates that a task or function has been given, or *committed*, to that body, composed of MPs *selected* to sit upon it.

We have already encountered general committees (see pages 195 and 242), which do not have permanent memberships: each one ceases to exist when it has finished considering the particular item of business committed to it. Some select committees are also appointed for a single purpose – to examine a draft bill, perhaps – and are dissolved when they have completed their work, but most are permanent institutions. They are appointed under standing orders and so do not die at the end of a session or the end of a parliament.

When the House meets after a general election, the permanent select committees are technically in existence but have no members. It can take several weeks before select committees can begin their work. First, the House must decide which party chairs each departmental select committee and some of the other cross-cutting and internal committees. The chairs of these committees are then elected by the whole House, usually within about three weeks of the Queen's Speech. The parties must then nominate the other committee members. Both the Conservative and Labour parties hold internal elections for select committee places. Finally, the names are agreed by the House. Following the 2017 election, parliament first met on 13 June 2017 but most select committees were not appointed until September 2017.

The development of select committees

Select committees have long been a feature of the work of the House of Commons. If you look at the Journals of the House for the end of the sixteenth century, you will find select committees involved in, and advising the House on, some of the most sensitive political issues of the day. In 1571 there was a Committee for the Uniformity of Religion – a matter of life and death in Elizabethan England. The following year there was a Committee on the Queen of Scotts [*sic*] – in this case, a matter of death. In 1571 there was also a Committee for the Examination of Fees and Rewards taken for Voices (that is, votes) in this House – an early example of the House looking at appropriate standards of conduct. Just after the turn of the seventeenth century, select committees dealt with the Confirmation of the Book of Common Prayer and with the Union with Scotland (both in 1604).

Some committees were virtually permanent: committees on Grievances, on Privileges and on the Subsidy (the grant of money to the Crown) were regularly appointed. There were also select committees with wider responsibilities, such as the splendidly named Grand Committee for Evils (1623).

But most committees were ephemeral: something came up that the House wanted looked at, and it set up a committee. These would often operate very informally: the members nominated to the committee would go straight out of the House into another room, would deliberate, perhaps examine witnesses, and then come back to the House (possibly even later in the same sitting), when one of their members would report orally what view they had come to.

Until well into the twentieth century, most select committees were set up *ad hoc* to examine a particular issue of public policy, or often some disaster or scandal (and their appointment was often used as a political weapon). A classic case was the Sebastopol Committee, set up in 1855, which – with some resonances for the aftermath of the Iraq war in 2003 – investigated the conduct of affairs but also sought political scapegoats in the process. The committee sat almost every day for more than two months, asked some 7,000 questions of witnesses and was bitterly critical of Lord Aberdeen, the former Prime Minister (who gave evidence to the committee). Unlike a modern select committee, the Sebastopol Committee had no staff (the role of committee clerks then was largely to ensure procedural rectitude), and the final report was written by one of its members, Lord Seymour (the draft report proposed by the fiery chairman, Mr Roebuck, was rejected by the committee).

The reputation of select committees as a means of inquiring into events was dealt a serious blow by the committee investigations into the Jameson Raid (a botched attempt to overthrow President Paul Kruger of the Transvaal Republic in 1895, often thought to have led to the Boer War) and the Marconi scandal of 1912, involving allegations of insider trading against senior politicians. Both were marked by extreme partisanship and were almost wholly ineffective. The contemporary lack of confidence in select committees as investigators led to the Tribunals of Inquiry (Evidence) Act 1921 providing a non-parliamentary means of investigation (which has since been replaced by the Inquiries Act 2005).

Unsystematic scrutiny

Committees such as the Sebastopol Committee played some part in calling governments to account (often after the event) but, with the possible exception of the Public Accounts Committee (see page 266), set up in 1861 to see whether public money had been properly expended, until the twentieth century there was little use by the House of Commons of select committees to monitor the detail of what the government of the day was actually doing.

A move in this direction was made with the appointment in 1912 of the Estimates Committee, which lasted until 1970, when it was succeeded (until 1979) by the Expenditure Committee. Both committees worked mainly through subject sub-committees, but their coverage of government activity, although occasionally influential, was very patchy. In the late 1960s and 1970s various 'subject' select committees (for example, on agriculture, education and science, and overseas aid) were set up; but there was no real system of select committees; and the Agriculture Committee, for example, was wound up in February 1969 after a campaign of opposition by government departments.

The real change came with the election of the Conservative government in 1979. The new Leader of the House, Norman St John-Stevas, was quick to put before the House the recommendation of the Procedure Committee the previous year that there should be select committees to shadow each government department. The committee had also recommended that eight days per year on the floor of the House should be devoted to debating the committees' reports (and that their chairmen should be paid a small additional salary). These latter recommendations were not adopted by the government, but the key principle of a system of select committees related to government departments was approved in June 1979.

Had St John-Stevas not moved so quickly, the change would probably never have been made; by the autumn the Prime Minister, Margaret Thatcher (who had other things on her mind in the first few months of office), would have realised how inconvenient for the government these committees might be, and would have vetoed the proposal. But, for the first time, the House of Commons now had at its disposal a means of systematic scrutiny of the government of the day potentially much more rigorous than the traditional methods of debate and question.

Today, these departmental select committees account for the majority of select committee activity; but they number only about half of the House's select committees. We now look at what select committees there are and what they do; then at their appointment and powers; and we will then use the example of a departmental committee to see how they work.

The committees

Departmental committees

There are 21 of these. The maximum number of members is given in brackets in the list below (in practice, committees sometimes have vacancies, for example when an MP is made a minister and is taken off the committee, before a replacement is identified and nominated to it):

Business, Energy and Industrial Strategy	(11)
Communities and Local Government	(11)
Defence	(11)
Digital, Culture, Media and Sport	(11)
Education	(11)
Environment, Food and Rural Affairs	(11)
Exiting the European Union	(21)
Foreign Affairs	(11)
Health	(11)
Home Affairs	(11)
International Development	(11)
International Trade	(11)
Justice	(11)
Northern Ireland Affairs	(13)
Science and Technology	(11)
Scottish Affairs	(11)
Transport	(11)
Treasury	(11)
Welsh Affairs	(11)
Women and Equalities	(11)
Work and Pensions	(11)

The departmental committees have a very broad remit: 'to examine the expenditure, administration and policy of [the relevant government department] and associated public bodies'. They are thus concerned not only with the doings of 'their' department, but also with any related executive agencies, and with regulators and inspectorates that operate in their field. All the committees have power to set up a sub-committee.

Because each committee shadows a government department, the system of committees has to change to match alterations in the structure of government. Thus, the Justice Committee followed on from the Constitutional Affairs Committee, which was itself a successor to the Committee on the Lord Chancellor's Department. Similarly, when particular responsibilities move from one government department to another, the task of monitoring them moves from one committee to another.

'Cross-cutting' committees

The departmental committees look 'vertically' at all the responsibilities of a single department and its ministers (although the Scottish, Welsh and Northern Ireland Affairs Committees have a broader range of interests). The cross-cutting committees, on the other hand, look 'horizontally' across Whitehall at themes or actions in which all or most departments are involved:

- Environmental Audit
- European Scrutiny
- Liaison
- Public Accounts
- Public Administration and Constitutional Affairs
- Joint Committee on the National Security Strategy

Environmental Audit Committee

This was set up in November 1997. It has 16 members, and its task is 'to consider to what extent the policies and programmes of government departments and non-departmental public bodies contribute to environmental protection and sustainable development', and 'to audit their performance against sustainable development and environmental protection targets'. The committee inquires into a range of sustainability issues. Recent work has covered issues as diverse as air quality, green finance, the future of chemicals regulation after Brexit and the disposability (or otherwise) of coffee cups and plastic bottles. It has power to appoint a sub-committee.

European Scrutiny Committee

This committee (formerly known as the European Legislation Committee) was established shortly after the United Kingdom joined the EEC in 1973. It examines a range of European Union business: not only European Union policies, spending and draft legislation, but also institutional issues – it reported in detail on the processes that led to the Maastricht, Amsterdam, Nice and Lisbon Treaties. It has 16 members and has power to set up as many sub-committees as it wishes. Since the referendum this committee's status as the pre-eminent body for scrutinising the UK's relations with the EU has been rivaled by the Committee on Exiting the EU. The work of both is covered in Chapter 11.

Liaison Committee

This is an unusual committee whose work includes both detailed housekeeping (and so might be classed with the internal committees) and some of the most high-profile hearings (with the Prime Minister) of any select committee. The committee consists of the chairs of the permanent select committees. The membership thus varies with the number of committees, but at present it stands at 35. It has power to set up two sub-committees, one of which has a limited role in relation to organising the scrutiny of government proposals for National Policy Statements on planning matters.

The Liaison Committee has the general task of considering 'general matters relating to the work of select committees'. This may be a change in the format of committee reports, for example, or the resources available to committees, or the rules of engagement for pre-appointment hearings with senior public officials. The committee also decides how the budget for overseas travel by select committees is allocated, and it chooses reports for debate on the floor of the House and in Westminster Hall (see pages 263 and 279).

In 2000, however, the committee changed its spots entirely and launched into a campaign to make select committees more effective. Its three reports, under the general theme of *Shifting the Balance* (between the executive and the legislature), put forward a reform programme that produced something of a confrontation with the government and with the then Leader of the House, Margaret Beckett. Her replacement by Robin Cook in 2001 led to the adoption of a number of the committee's proposals. The committee has followed up its work by publishing periodic reports on the select committee system, assessing its effectiveness and examining innovations and problems.

One Liaison Committee recommendation produced an important result, although not immediately. In December 2000 the chair of the committee wrote to the Prime Minister inviting him to give evidence to the committee on the government's annual report 'to spell out your policies in an atmosphere very different from that on the floor of the House'. The request was turned down on the grounds of precedent and what was described as 'the important principle that it is for individual Secretaries of State to answer to the House and its individual Select Committees for their areas of responsibility, and not the Prime Minister' – even though the Prime Minister answers on those areas of responsibility every week during Prime Minister's Questions.

However, just over a year later the Prime Minister did, indeed, offer to appear before the committee twice a year to discuss domestic and international affairs, and the first session took place on 16 July 2002. The Prime Minister's appearances have become important parliamentary occasions, televised live and carefully analysed by the media. The size of the committee makes the normal style of examination more difficult, but questioning is focused on themes decided by the committee beforehand, each led by one MP. The Prime Minister is given notice of the themes but not of the detailed questions; the calm questioning in depth at these sessions has been a valuable antidote to the knockabout of PMQs, and it is difficult to see a future Prime Minister being able to discontinue the practice.

Committee of Public Accounts

The work of this committee, usually known as 'the PAC', and of the Comptroller and Auditor General who supports it, is described in Chapter 7.

Public Administration and Constitutional Affairs Committee

The Public Administration Committee was set up in 1997, taking on the functions of two previous committees, the Public Service Committee and the Committee on the

Parliamentary Commissioner for Administration. In its public service role, the committee has conducted inquiries into matters that affect the government as a whole: for example, during 2016–17 it published reports on managing ministers' and officials' conflicts of interest, lessons to be learned from the Iraq Inquiry and the future of relations between devolved and Whitehall/Westminster institutions. The committee has 11 members and the power to appoint a sub-committee.

The committee also considers the reports of the Parliamentary and Health Service Ombudsman. The Ombudsman (currently Rob Behrens) is an entirely independent official who reports to Parliament. Assisted by a staff of around 400, he investigates complaints about maladministration and the actions (or inactions) of government departments and other public bodies that seem to have caused injustice that has not been put right. The main aim of the Ombudsman is to obtain a remedy for those who have suffered injustice, and the secondary aim is to ensure good standards of public administration. If serious faults are found, the Ombudsman can recommend to the public body concerned what redress it should offer and the action it should take to avoid a repetition of the failure. The Ombudsman has no power to enforce recommendations, but they are almost always accepted. There are separate Ombudsman posts in Scotland, Wales and Northern Ireland that report to their respective devolved parliamentary bodies.

The relationship between the Ombudsman and the committee is not unlike that between the Comptroller and Auditor General and the Public Accounts Committee (see page 266). The Ombudsman has the additional clout of the committee's backing, and the committee is able to draw on the work of the Ombudsman's office with its substantial resources. The committee considers the Ombudsman's annual reports; but, rather than following up the details of individual investigations, it draws more general lessons for public administration as a whole.

From the start of the 2015–17 parliament the committee's remit was expanded to include constitutional affairs. In the 2010–15 parliament the Political and Constitutional Reform Committee existed to scrutinise the then Deputy Prime Minister's special responsibility for those areas; on its demise the Public Administration Committee took up the burden.

Joint Committee on the National Security Strategy

This joint committee was established in 2010 to consider not only the National Security Strategy, but also the government structures for decision-making on national security, particularly the role of the National Security Council and the National Security Adviser. It has taken evidence on national security and the EU, the nature of the UK's alliance with the US; and energy security. In January 2014, it took evidence from the Prime Minister. It is chaired by an MP (Margaret Beckett, a former Foreign Secretary) and has 22 members, including the chairs of seven Commons departmental committees with an interest in the subject matter (Business, Energy and Industrial Strategy, Defence, Foreign Affairs, Home Affairs, International Development, International Trade and Justice), and the chair of the Intelligence and Security Committee.

'Legislative' committees

Although most legislation is considered by general committees, several select committees are concerned with different types of legislation:

- Consolidation, &c., Bills
- Human Rights
- Regulatory Reform
- Statutory Instruments.

The European Scrutiny Committee might also be included in this group but, as it deals with a wide range of EU policy matters, as well as legislation, we have treated it as a cross-cutting committee.

Joint Committee on Consolidation, &c., Bills

This is a joint committee of both Houses on which both MPs and peers sit (we look at joint committees more closely on page 357). Established in 1894, the committee has 24 members, half from each House, and is chaired by a retired judge, who does much of the scrutiny work. Its task is to examine bills that 'consolidate' the law – that is, restate it in a more logical and convenient form without changing its substance, although errors and ambiguities may be corrected. Such bills are always introduced in the House of Lords rather than in the House of Commons. The committee considers the form rather than the merits of legislation. It meets only when a bill is referred to it: only five times since 2006.

Joint Committee on Human Rights

Following the enactment of the Human Rights Act 1998, the Joint Committee on Human Rights was appointed in 2001. It has a general remit to consider matters relating to human rights in the United Kingdom (but not individual cases). In 2016–17, its inquiries included mental health and deaths in prison, the human rights implications of Brexit and counter-extremism policies. It also has an important role in legislation. It examines every government bill soon after introduction to assess the implications of the bill on human rights, regularly corresponding with ministers and reporting its views to both Houses. The joint committee also examines draft remedial orders, which come about when a court finds that an Act of Parliament is incompatible with the Human Rights Act and so needs amending (see page 248). The joint committee has 12 members, six from each House.

Regulatory Reform Committee

This is a Commons select committee (the Lords equivalent is the Delegated Powers and Regulatory Reform Committee), consisting of 14 MPs. The committee considers certain orders and draft orders under the Legislative and Regulatory Reform Act 2006, the Regulatory Reform Act 2001, the Localism Act 2011, and the Fire and Rescue Services Act 2004; this process is described in Chapter 6 (page 246). Its staff include legal advisers. The committee has the power to set up a sub-committee. It may also invite members of the House who are not members of the committee to attend oral hearings and ask questions, but they may not vote or count towards the quorum.

Joint Committee on Statutory Instruments

This joint committee is responsible for examining the technical aspects of delegated legislation rather than its merits – unlike the Secondary Legislation Scrutiny Committee in the House of Lords (see page 245). It has six members from each House with an opposition MP as chair. It normally meets weekly when Parliament is sitting, but it reports only when it wishes to draw the attention of both Houses to some defect in a statutory instrument. The analysis of well over 1,000 statutory instruments each year is carried out by a staff that includes three specialist lawyers. Delegated legislation on financial matters, which is laid only before the House of Commons, is examined by the *Select Committee on Statutory Instruments*, consisting of the Commons members of the joint committee. Delegated legislation is described in more detail in Chapter 6 (page 238).

Internal committees

These committees are concerned with the way the House and its members work, both procedurally and administratively:

- Backbench Business
- Procedure
- Selection
- Privileges
- Standards
- Finance
- Administration.

Backbench Business Committee

The Backbench Business Committee was first appointed in 2010, following a recommendation by the Wright Committee on reform of the House of Commons (see page 150). It determines the business to be debated in the House or Westminster Hall on days (or parts of days) allocated to it by the government. There are eight members of the committee. All are backbenchers and are elected by the House at the start of each session. The committee can invite members of the House who are not members of the committee and who either are of a party not represented on the committee, or are of no party, to attend its meetings and take part in its proceedings, although they may not move a motion or an amendment, or vote.

The committee usually meets weekly when the House is sitting. MPs seeking a debate on a subject submit a form to the committee in advance of its meeting. It then hears representations from members, or groups of members, advocating debates, before deciding which to choose. In deciding on which topics to recommend for debate it considers their topicality, how important a debate will be, how many MPs are likely to participate, and whether a debate on the subject has recently been or will soon be held.

Procedure Committee

Procedure Committees used to be appointed *ad hoc* to examine particular aspects of the House's business, or to address some problem. A Procedure Committee was appointed in each parliament from 1979, but the committee did not become permanent until 1997. The committee has no more than 17 members. It considers the practice and procedure of the House in the conduct of public business (so, not including private legislation – see page 235), making recommendations to the House.

The committee considers matters that are referred to it, usually informally by the Speaker or the government rather than formally by decision of the House. It also chooses its own subjects for investigation, although these are often picked because the committee is aware of a general feeling that some topic needs examination. Recently the committee has reported on such things as the arrangements for private members' bills, the EVEL procedures, how delegated legislation to be made under the European Union (Withdrawal) Bill should be considered, and the use of the Welsh language in Welsh Grand Committees. The committee's recommendations must generally be approved by the House before they are implemented.

Selection Committee

The main task of this committee, which meets weekly while the House is sitting, is to select MPs to serve on general committees on bills and statutory instruments and private bill committees. At the beginning of a parliament, it also puts forward names of MPs to serve on all the permanent select committees (except for Liaison, Standards and Privileges), and it nominates any replacements needed thereafter (see page 323). It has nine members, most of whom are whips, but a non-whip is in the chair. As described in Chapter 6 (see page 196), following the 2017 election, the committee was instructed by the House to select a majority of government MPs to serve on each general committee (or an even number of government and opposition MPs if the overall number of members on a committee is even).

Committee of Privileges

The House has long appointed a committee to investigate and report on privilege matters and complaints of breaches of privilege (see page 171). In its current guise, the committee was first appointed in 2012: from 1996 to 2012, the House appointed a Committee on Standards and Privileges that dealt with complaints about members' conduct, in addition to privilege.

The committee has seven members and is chaired by a senior opposition backbencher. It has the power to appoint sub-committees. Unusually, it has the power to order an MP to give evidence to it, or to produce documents; most committees have these powers only in respect of people who are not members of either House. Following the split of the former Committee on Standards and Privileges, the Committee of Privileges has, for the time being, the same membership as the Committee on Standards.

Committee on Standards

There has been a permanent committee to examine issues relating to members' conduct since the Committee on Members' Interests was first established in 1974. The current Committee on Standards was first appointed in 2012. It works closely with the Parliamentary Commissioner for Standards (see page 116), considers reports on complaints against MPs – taking evidence if necessary, and recommends to the House what action (such as suspending an MP for a specified period or withholding salary) should be taken. The committee also oversees the operation of the rules of conduct, and the compilation and publication of the registers of interests.

The committee is made up of seven members of the House of Commons (who are also the members of the Committee of Privileges) and seven external (or 'lay') members, who can make a full contribution to the work of the committee except that they cannot move motions or amendments to reports or vote. However, any comments that the lay members wish to make about a report must be published with that report. The committee is chaired by a senior backbencher and has the power to appoint sub-committees. As with the Committee of Privileges, the Standards Committee has the power to order an MP to give evidence to it, or to produce documents. The operation of the standards regime is dealt with in greater detail on pages 111 to 117.

Finance Committee and Administration Committee

As we saw in Chapter 3 (page 64), the 11-member Finance Committee advises the House of Commons Commission on the financial plans of the House administration and on proposals for expenditure on House services. Although the Straw Committee on Governance of the House (see page 61) recommended that the chair of the committee should be a member of the Commission, the current chair is not, although he does brief the Commission on the committee's activities. The 11-member Administration Committee advises the Speaker and the Commission on the provision of services to members, their staff and visitors.

Ad hoc committees

The House can set up new committees at any time, although the formal initiative to do so is invariably a motion moved by the government (in the nineteenth century and earlier, this was not the case; the Sebastopol Committee described earlier was appointed in the teeth of ministerial opposition, and the approval of the motion to set it up finished the government led by Lord Aberdeen).

In the more recent past, *ad hoc* committees have considered domestic matters such as MPs' pay (1980–82), the televising of the House (1988–90), the sitting hours of the House (1991–92, known as the 'Jopling Committee'), the reform of the House of Commons (2009–10, known as the 'Wright Committee'), an alleged breach of privilege by an unauthorised police search on the parliamentary estate (2009–10) and the governance of the House (2014–15). *Ad hoc* committees have also considered matters of public policy such as the royal family's pay and expenses (1971–72), a possible 'wealth tax' (1974–75), abortion (1974–75) and violence in the family (1975–76). The existence of a permanent Procedure Committee means that select committees are now less likely to be set up to consider individual in-House issues; and the existence of the departmental committees (two or more of which are able to conduct joint inquiries if they wish) means that select committees are also less likely to be appointed to consider specific issues of public policy. However, from time to time, special circumstances arise – usually, but not always, when a particular subject affects both Houses (see pages 168 and 358 for the joint committees on parliamentary privilege and Lords reform).

In July 2012, in the wake of the LIBOR interest-rate rigging scandal, both Houses established the Parliamentary Commission on Banking Standards, to examine professional standards and culture in the UK banking sector and to make recommendations for legislative and other action. Although called a 'Commission' it was, in fact, a joint committee, albeit a rather unusual one. It published five reports over the course of one year, including two relating to the Financial Services (Banking Reform) Bill, the last of which was published in nine volumes in June 2013. The Commission had a number of unusual features. It had the power to use counsel to examine witnesses, which it used on occasion. It established panels to look at specific issues, some of the panels comprising only one or two members of the Commission. The chair was given the power to report to the House matters that had not been agreed by the Commission meeting formally, but on which all members of the Commission had been consulted. These innovations enabled the Commission to operate more flexibly than a select committee, but the call on the time of its members over a considerable period suggests that this may not be a model whose use is easily extended.

These days, most *ad hoc* committees are appointed to consider draft bills. Most recently *ad hoc* joint committees considered the draft Investigatory Powers Bill and the draft Protection of Charities Bill. Other draft bills were considered by departmental select committees (see page 347).

Intelligence and Security Committee of Parliament

The Intelligence and Security Committee was set up under the Intelligence Services Act 1994, and its role was developed in the Justice and Security Act 2013 (including adding 'of Parliament' to its title). It has a parliamentary character but is not a select or joint committee, being created by statute – and so parliamentary privilege does not attach to its proceedings (although it has some protections by statute). It oversees the work of the intelligence agencies and provides broader scrutiny of intelligence and security matters. The committee consists of nine parliamentarians, drawn from both Houses, all backbenchers, and is usually chaired by a former senior minister. When it was first set up, the committee was a government body, made up of parliamentarians appointed by the Prime Minister and reporting to him. Since 2013, Parliament chooses the members of the committee, on the basis of nomination by the Prime Minister after consultation with the Leader of the Opposition. The committee reports to Parliament although, on matters of national security, it may report first to the Prime Minister. Due to its sensitive nature most of its evidence is heard in private, but since 2013 it has taken some public evidence.

How committees work

Although in this section we have a departmental committee particularly in mind, the various functions described apply to most select committees.

Orders of reference and powers

A committee's task is set out in its orders of reference, which also define its powers and specify how many members it shall have. In the case of permanent committees, these orders of reference will be in the House's standing orders; but the House can set up a committee for as long or short a time as it sees fit and can give it other tasks or instructions (such as reporting by a certain date).

Tasks are usually widely defined: for example, departmental select committees must 'examine expenditure, administration and policy', although other committees, such as those on statutory instruments or regulatory reform, are much more circumscribed. Most committees thus have a good deal of latitude; and it is also a basic principle that (subject to any instruction from the House) the interpretation of their orders of reference is a matter for them. Committees generally do not take kindly to being told by the government or by witnesses that they should not be looking at this or that subject; indeed, such comments are normally entirely counterproductive.

Committees are subordinate bodies of the House; they have only those powers that the House gives them and cannot exercise any power that the House itself does not have. The normal menu is 'to adjourn from place to place', which means that they do not have to sit only at Westminster ('within the United Kingdom' is added for those committees that may not travel abroad); to report 'from time to time', which means that they may continue reporting on their subject area rather than making one report at the end of their work; to appoint specialist advisers; (in most cases) to appoint one or more sub-committees; to exchange evidence with other committees (and with the Scottish Parliament, the National Assembly for Wales and the Northern Ireland Assembly); and to meet jointly with any other committee of either House. This last power provides a good deal of flexibility when a subject affects several committees: for example, the Defence, Foreign Affairs, International Development and International Trade Committees form what is, in effect, a joint committee on arms exports. The Welsh Affairs Committee may invite members of any specified committee of the National Assembly for Wales to attend and participate in its proceedings (but not to vote).

The power of compulsion

A key phrase in a committee's powers is 'to send for persons, papers and records' (known as 'PPR'). This means that they have the formal power to compel witnesses 'within the jurisdiction' (that is, within the UK) to attend, answer questions and deliver up any papers that the committee may wish to see.

Most witnesses before select committees are willing, even enthusiastic; they want the opportunity to make their case on a very public stage. But some are not, for a variety of reasons from a generalised reluctance to answer a committee's questions to having something discreditable or damaging to hide. In such cases, the committee may make an order to attend (or produce documents), which is served personally on the witness. If he or she does not comply, the committee may report the matter to the House as a breach of privilege. But there are disadvantages to this: the matter is put into a wider political forum, which means that the committee loses control of events; the procedure is cumbersome; and – especially if the matter becomes a party political football – there is no guarantee that the committee will ultimately get what it wants.

A select committee's strongest weapon is publicity rather than the use of formal powers. A recalcitrant witness looks as though he or she has something to hide; the trick is for the committee to make *not* giving evidence more embarrassing or awkward than acceding to the committee's request. These factors will have influenced the decision by Rupert and James Murdoch to give oral evidence to the Culture, Media and Sport Committee on phone hacking in 2011, both having been formally summoned.

It has sometimes been suggested that the powers of select committees should be formalised in legislation and that a refusal to attend, or the giving of false or misleading evidence, should be punishable by law. This may be superficially attractive, but the practical implications are daunting. Any court, in considering an allegation of refusal to attend, would need to satisfy itself that the summons was fair. Was the witness given alternative dates? Sufficient notice? An indication of why the committee wanted him or her to attend? Was the witness allowed to bring advisers? Even, was the witness really relevant to the inquiry? The issue became a live one again in 2018, with the refusal of Dominic Cummings to attend the DCMS Committee (see page 172).

False or misleading evidence would pose even more problems. Was the committee oppressive in its questioning? Was the witness badgered? Was the committee's behaviour fair? Was the witness allowed to take advice? It is perfectly possible that a court would want to see the video-recording of the evidence session. Turning the process over to the courts would also slow the process down, and would certainly result in witnesses in contentious inquiries coming 'lawyered-up' to give evidence, refusing to answer certain questions on legal advice.

The Joint Committee on Parliamentary Privilege (see page 168) considered these issues and, in July 2013, sensibly came down against the involvement of the courts (as it also came down against the codification of privilege).

Ministers and civil servants have a special status that occasionally leads to conflict with select committees. Civil servants are agents of their secretary of state and carry out his or her instructions; they cannot be forced to divulge information against the secretary of state's wishes. A committee can ask a minister for information but (although the 'embarrassment factor' can come into play here as well) cannot demand it. The House could do so by an address to the Crown, because the information is in the hands of Her Majesty's ministers, as happened with the Brexit sectoral analyses in 2017 – but the House does not delegate this power to select committees.

There have been celebrated tussles between investigating select committees and reluctant governments. In its investigation of the Westland Affair in 1986, the Defence Committee sought to interview the civil servants most closely involved with the selective leaking of an opinion of the Solicitor General. The government refused to allow them to attend, but the Cabinet Secretary appeared twice before the committee, which – because of the political pressure building on the government – also secured internal government documents that had previously been refused. Although the government's internal guidance states that, when there is disagreement between a minister and a committee about the attendance of a civil servant, the minister should appear personally, this issue is still an occasional source of friction. This is particularly the case in relation to the intelligence agencies: several committees have tried and failed to call their heads or more junior intelligence personnel to give oral evidence.

Membership

Select committee members are almost invariably backbench MPs. Committees normally consist of between nine and 18 MPs in as near as possible the party proportions in the House as a whole; thus, in the 2017 parliament, a committee of 11 usually had five Labour, five Conservative and one third-party member. Once MPs are appointed to a committee, they remain on it for the whole of a parliament, unless they resign or become ministers or frontbench spokesmen.

The quorum of a committee – the number of members who must be present for business to be transacted – is three or one-quarter of the number of members, whichever is the larger, with fractions counted as one.

Some committee chairs are elected by the House as a whole – we discuss this in more detail in the next section. The other members (or, where the committee chooses its own chair, all members) are selected by their parties using their own internal procedures. The names are then put to the House for approval in a motion proposed by the Selection Committee. The memberships of the Liaison Committee, the Committee of Privileges, the Committee on Standards, any committees established under a temporary standing order, and the Selection Committee itself, are proposed to the House by the Deputy Chief Whip.

Chairs

Until 2010 committees elected their own chairs. In most cases, among the MPs put on a committee at the start of a parliament was an obvious (or agreed) candidate for the chair. Following the recommendation of the Wright Committee on reform of the Commons, most select committee chairs (including the chairs of the departmental committees) are now directly elected by the House. Candidates must come from the party to which the House has allocated the position of chair, but all MPs may vote. Chairs elected in this way can be removed if their committee passes a motion of no confidence in the chair, either unanimously or with a majority of the members (including at least two members from the largest party represented on the committee and at least one member from another party) voting in favour. This mechanism has not yet been used.

If a chair resigns (by writing to the Speaker), dies, or is subject to a no confidence vote, a by-election is held to replace them.

Under rules agreed by the House in 2002 no MP may chair a committee that she or he has chaired for the two previous parliaments, or for eight years, whichever is the longer. However, in April 2018 the House agreed to recommendations from the Liaison Committee that, during the 2017 parliament, chairs should be allowed to continue for up to 10 years. Without this change, five chairs first elected in 2010 would have had to step down in 2018, as a result of the short 2015–17 parliament. The argument for the revision was that 10 years is the expected duration of two parliaments under the Fixed-term Parliaments Act 2011. While the current situation is a fix for a specific issue in this parliament, the Procedure Committee said it will make proposals for how term limits should apply in future parliaments. The chair is the key figure on any select committee, all the more so since direct elections. He or she takes a full part in the committee's work (unlike the chair of a general committee, who presides impartially over proceedings) and is usually the committee's spokesperson. The committee itself decides subjects for investigation and what witnesses to call, but the chair's views will be highly influential, and the chair has the power of initiative, particularly in relation to the content of draft reports for consideration by the committee.

Chairs operate in a variety of ways: some are less interventionist 'chairmen of the board'; others are much more 'managing directors' driving the committee's work. Whichever style they adopt, the role of a good chair is crucial in keeping the committee together: giving all its members a chance, promoting consensus, foreseeing political problems, establishing good – but not cosy – relationships with ministers in the relevant department, and providing leadership when the going gets tough.

Since 2003, most select committee chairs have been paid a supplement to their salary (currently £15,235 per year), in recognition of their additional responsibilities.

There is no formal post of 'deputy chair'. If the chair is absent, then the senior opposition MP (or government MP, if the chair is from an opposition party) often takes the chair; but the committee can decide to put any of its members in the chair on a temporary basis.

Election of chairs of most select committees by the House as a whole has been widely welcomed, but within select committees it has had a subtle effect on the relationship between chair and members. When it was the committee that elected the chair, they were the power-base and the chair was answerable to them. With election by the House, the relationship has changed, and on several committees the rank-and-file members have resented what they have seen as the high-handed style of a chair who does not feel answerable to the committee.

Staff

Select committees are supported by small teams of staff from the Chamber and Committees Team; some 30 investigative committees are supported by about 280 staff in the Committee Office. A departmental select committee typically has six full-time posts. They are led by the *clerk of the committee*, a deputy principal clerk (equivalent to a Band 1 official in the Senior Civil Service – what used to be called assistant secretary/ grade 5) usually with 15 or more years of experience in the service of the House or, in some cases, an experienced senior clerk (civil service grade 7). In a nutshell, the clerk's job is to help the committee to be as effective as possible in doing the job the House has given it. He or she is the committee's principal adviser, manages the staff team and the specialist advisers, works closely with the chair on all aspects of the committee's work, and will be responsible for some of the committee's inquiries. *The second clerk* deputises for the clerk, manages inquiries and will usually clerk any sub-committee. One or two *committee specialists*, who are subject experts, or generalist *inquiry managers*, provide in-depth research and briefing and manage inquiries. The *senior committee assistant* oversees arrangements for hearings, committee visits, the website, and the publication of reports and evidence. He or she will have the support of a *committee assistant*. Committee teams often work at pace; for example, even substantial committee reports are published extraordinarily quickly; sometimes, agreed one afternoon and published online and in print the next morning.

The committee also has the support of a *media officer*, typically shared with three or four other committees (although some of the most high-profile committees, such as the Treasury Committee, have a dedicated media officer). He or she helps plan communication and public engagement work throughout the course of an inquiry, drafts press notices, promotes reports to the media and organises the chair's media appearances on committee matters. A team of social media officers help committees draw attention to their work and engage with the public on Twitter and other social media channels. There are also a small number of *select committee outreach officers* in the Participation Team who assist select committees with outreach activity, such as meetings away from Westminster or public surveys in particular localities.

The permanent staff are augmented by *specialist advisers*, who work for the clerk of the committee. They are outside specialists, often of great eminence, who assist the committee part-time and are paid on a daily rate. This is a flexible and effective system; a committee can draw on a lifetime's experience in the precise area of what may be a very technical or complex inquiry. Some committees maintain panels of 12 or 15 advisers; others appoint one or two for specific inquiries. There are normally about 120 specialist advisers at any one time.

Committees also draw on the resources of the *Scrutiny Unit*, a group of 20 or so staff who specialise in the analysis of estimates, departmental annual reports (see page 264) and other financial information; and also in the scrutiny of draft legislation (which allows a committee to deal at short notice with a draft bill without having its programme of work blown off course). In addition, a *Web and Publications Unit* helps committee teams with digital publication.

A committee's work

Select committees always meet in private except when they are taking oral evidence; as we shall see later, this has advantages. When a committee meets for the first time at the start of a parliament, its members first make a formal declaration of their registered interests. They will then discuss their working practices and agree a programme of work. The chair will put proposals before the committee, based on their own priorities; work by the committee staff; work outstanding from the last parliament; current and expected events in the subject area (including possible draft bills); previous recommendations on which the committee needs to maintain pressure; policies still in the process of formation, where the committee could have an influence; or perhaps some serious problem where the committee needs to keep up with developments. Committee members will have their own suggestions and, after discussion, the committee will agree and announce its initial programme of work.

In addition, the House has set *core tasks* for departmental select committees. These are listed on pages 347 to 349.

Just as a departmental select committee has wide discretion about *what* it investigates, so it also has great flexibility about *how* it does so. Inquiries may range from an in-depth examination of a complex subject lasting several months to a short sharp inquiry carried out in a week, perhaps with five or six oral evidence hearings crammed into that time. Inquiries may aim to analyse and influence a developing policy, to review a whole subject area, to carry out a 'what went wrong' investigation, or to look at a topical issue of the moment.

Most formal inquiries lead to reports to the House, but a committee may hold hearings without then publishing a report; and most committees hold regular one-off hearings with public bodies, chief inspectors or regulators within their area, or with ministers or senior officials on current issues. However, let us take as an example a typical 'subject area' inquiry.

The start of an inquiry

The committee decides on a subject – let us say the government's policy towards domestic violence. The committee approves terms of reference for the inquiry, which are really to help potential witnesses who want to know what the main areas of interest will be – they do not bind the committee. Indeed, once an inquiry is under way, its focus often changes as the committee identifies particular aspects as more important. The committee publishes a press notice about the inquiry, and it may also publish an 'issues and questions' paper to stimulate debate and the submission of evidence.

As well as issuing a general invitation to submit evidence, the committee will make more specific requests for written evidence. For our example of an inquiry into domestic violence, several government departments – the Home Office, the Department of Health, the Government Equalities Office and the Ministry of Justice – are involved in different aspects of the subject. The committee may ask each department to prepare a paper on its own area of responsibility, or more likely will ask the government to provide a single paper addressing a series of written questions. At the same time, requests for evidence will go out to other key players: the NHS, the British Medical Association as representing GPs, the NSPCC, and national organisations representing social service providers, the police and support groups for those who have suffered domestic violence. Committees usually publish written evidence online shortly after receipt. Sometimes a committee will hold an online forum, encouraging members of the public to share their experiences, or will otherwise seek to engage people on social media platforms.

The committee will, at the same time, draw up a list of likely witnesses. Oral evidence will often start with academics or expert commentators who can 'set the scene' and usually concludes with an appearance by the minister. Committees try to make the process as open as possible, not limiting it to 'the usual suspects'. For example, in an inquiry into the Probation Service, the Justice Committee's star witnesses were a group of former offenders who gave evidence about the support provided to them (or not) by their probation officers; and the Transport Committee has taken evidence from people whose relatives had been killed in accidents at level crossings. On the basis of the written evidence that comes in – often not formal papers from prominent organisations but letters from local bodies or individuals who have heard about the inquiry – committees will select other people to give evidence.

Some time after the call for written evidence first went out, the first oral evidence hearing takes place.

Taking evidence

The members of the committee sit around a horseshoe-shaped table with the chair at the head and the clerk or other member of the committee staff on his or her left. Reflecting the more consensual approach in select committees, the members often do not sit by party affiliation (unlike general committees). Witnesses sit at a table between the arms of the horseshoe. The transcribers who take a verbatim record of the evidence sit either in the middle or at the side of the room.

The MPs on the committee will have a detailed brief prepared by the committee staff. This will cover the background to the hearing, the key points from the witness's written evidence, including areas that could be explored further, anything that the committee especially needs to get on the record for its eventual report, and a list of

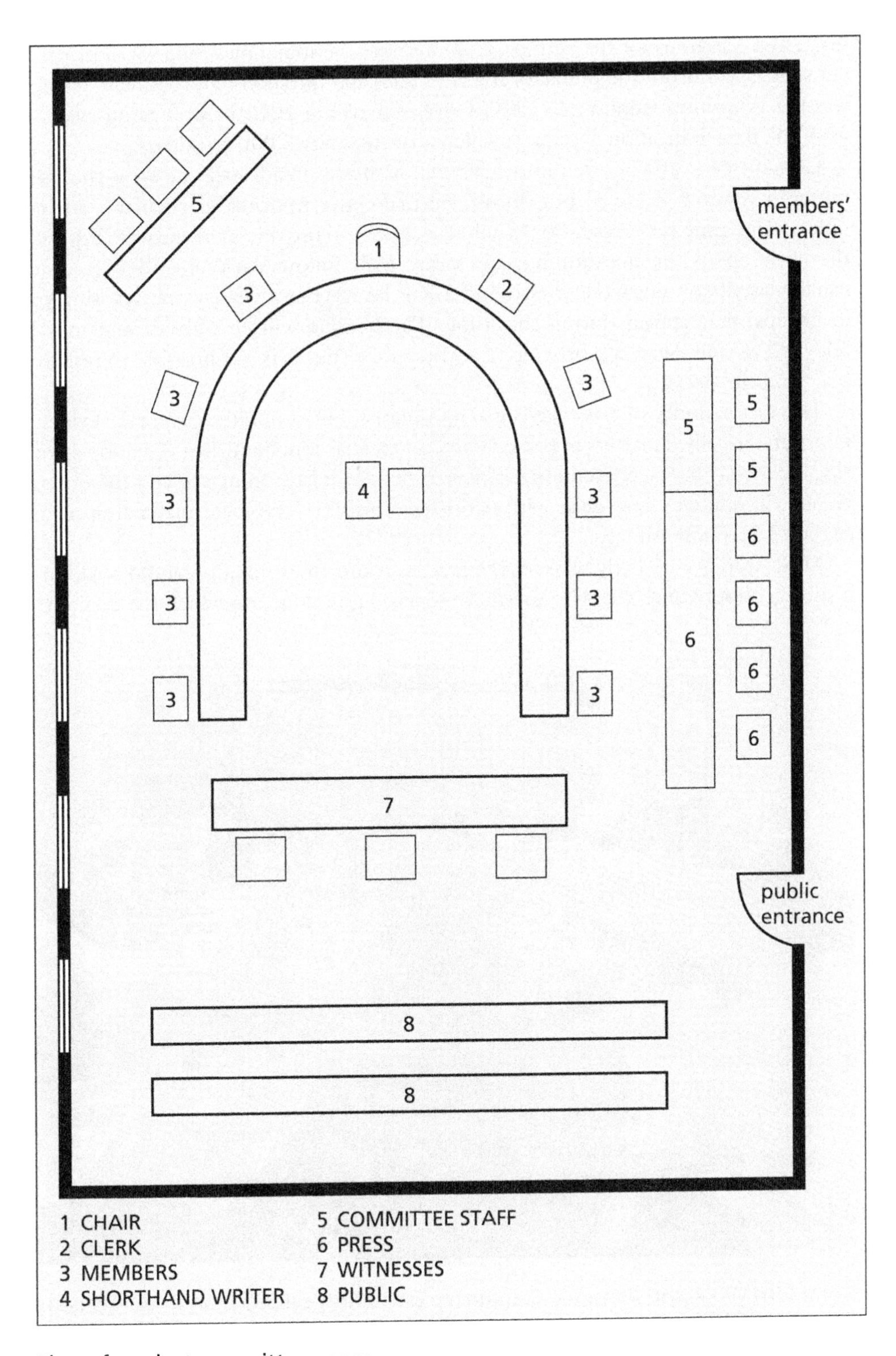

Plan of a select committee room

Source: Copyright House of Commons, 2014

suggested questions for the witness. Committees have sometimes used social media to get suggestions from the public of the key issues and questions: a prominent example was the Education Committee's #AskGove initiative in 2012 before taking evidence from the then Education Secretary, which attracted over 5,000 responses.

Committee staff will often informally tell witnesses in advance the areas the committee may want to cover, but do not normally give notice of particular questions unless some time for preparation would be needed to provide a full answer. Typically, the chair opens the questioning, and other MPs follow. An oral evidence session usually lasts between two and two-and-a-half hours, but several witnesses, singly or in groups, may appear during that time. The hearing will be webcast and may be televised as well. Seats are provided for the public (but it is not possible to reserve a seat) and the press.

The vast majority of evidence is given in public, but committees can take evidence in private, usually if matters of personal or commercial confidentiality, or national security, are involved. Select committees, mainly the Defence Committee and the Foreign Affairs Committee, have dealt with national security or 'classified' material up to the highest levels of sensitivity.

Most hearings are fairly relaxed; the process is one of exploration and discussion of a subject about which the witnesses have special knowledge, on which the committee

Commons Work and Pensions Committee gathering evidence on disability issues, February 2011

Source: Copyright House of Commons, 2014. Photography by Catherine Bebbington

wants to draw. However, some hearings, usually if a committee is investigating something that has gone wrong, or where it believes that a government department or other witness is not being open, can be more adversarial. Committees can take evidence on oath if they wish, although this is unusual, and the witness or witnesses should, as a matter of natural justice, certainly be given notice of a committee's intention to do so.

Those giving evidence before a select committee are taking part in a proceeding in Parliament (see page 170), so they are fully protected by parliamentary privilege – that is, neither their oral nor their written evidence may give rise to a criminal prosecution or civil action, nor, for example, to disciplinary action by an employer.

The transcript of the hearing usually takes a few days to prepare but is sometimes expedited. It is published online straight away.

As the inquiry progresses, the committee will follow up oral evidence with requests for further papers, the staff will research other sources of information or possible evidence, and some thought will be given to possible visits. Committees may also commission research to support their work, such as opinion polling or analyses of a project's business case or likely economic impact.

Travel

Travel by select committees often gets a hard time in the media – but it contributes a great deal to a committee's effectiveness. In the inquiry example we have taken here, the committee may want to make visits within the UK – perhaps to see shelters for the victims of domestic violence in different parts of the country; to talk to social services, the police, GPs and support groups on their home ground; and possibly to take oral evidence. Visits make a select committee inquiry more accessible: they bring the committee to a local community and mean that people can talk informally to the MPs rather than giving evidence in the often daunting surroundings of Westminster.

Visits also mean that MPs see and hear for themselves; the often rather impersonal formal evidence is supplemented by the first-hand experience and opinions of the people actually involved, and a suggestion or criticism by a single individual often finds its way into the committee's final report.

Travel overseas plays a similar role. It may be that policy on domestic violence in Sweden, say, is better coordinated than in the UK; or that the Canadians have the most effective risk registers and techniques for early warning of violence. No amount of background reading and written evidence is a substitute for seeing for oneself, and finding out first-hand about the benefits and the problems.

The report

Towards the end of an inquiry, the staff member who has managed the inquiry will usually prepare a 'heads of report' paper – identifying the possible main themes of the report and recommendations, and questions on which the committee itself will need to form a view. Thereafter, the report will be drafted, sometimes with the assistance of specialist advisers and under the direction of the clerk. The draft report will be submitted to the chair and then, after his or her comments are incorporated, presented to the committee in the chair's name. In a contentious inquiry, other members may want an alternative draft report (and a clerk may be called upon to draft two entirely incompatible reports!). However, most select committee reports are unanimous and are the more effective for it.

Most committees go through draft reports informally and then agree to the whole report as a single decision. However, if amendments are considered formally or there are any votes, these are set out in full in the formal minutes at the back of the published report. The same is true of any alternative draft report that may be put forward (although there is formally no such thing as a 'minority report', the same aim is achieved by publication in the formal minutes).

'Embargoed' copies of reports are often issued to the press a day or two before the publication date so that they can have their stories ready for the moment of publication, and copies will usually go to witnesses and others who have contributed to the inquiry. The committee may hold a press conference, and the chair and individual members of the committee may also give interviews to get their own perspective on the record. (In a sensitive inquiry, they may have to choose their words with care, as an interview or press conference is not a proceeding in Parliament, and there is no protection of absolute privilege.)

A type of report known as a 'special report' is used as a vehicle for publishing government replies to committees, or sometimes for informing the House of some difficulty encountered in the committee's work.

The government reply

Reports are made to the House, although the intended audience includes everyone concerned with the subject, the media and – crucially – the government. Every select committee report should receive a formal government reply within two months. This is a convention rather than a formal rule, but committees have found that asking the minister concerned to appear to explain a delay often means the rapid appearance of the reply.

No one expects a government to put on sackcloth and ashes in this formal reply. If the committee has been highly critical, the government is more likely to be defensive and to restate its case than to say 'It's a fair cop'. If the committee has put forward challenging recommendations, the government is likely to be cautious rather than to accept them right away. But the 'delayed drop' effect of select committee reports should never be underestimated. Ambitious recommendations may change the whole public debate on a subject; they may be taken up by public bodies and pressure groups; and months (or sometimes two or three years) later, they may contribute substantially to a major shift in government policy. Similarly, the effect of justified criticism may not be immediately apparent; but a department may be quietly changing its procedures to avoid making the same mistake again.

Whatever the contents of the government reply, committees are more influential if they follow up on their reports. Most departmental select committees have a 'continuous agenda' in which major policy issues recur, but returning to the detail of previous recommendations, and pursuing vague promises or non-committal responses through further inquiries, maintains the pressure and keeps the subject in the public eye.

Consensus

Select committees seem generally to be held in high regard – perhaps more than anything else that Parliament does. There may be several reasons for this: they provide access to the political process to those outside Westminster; they provide challenge and an alternative point of view based on evidence; but probably most of all they show how politicians of different parties can work together.

A typical inquiry

A timeline for a committee inquiry with four oral evidence hearings and a foreign visit, might look something like this:*

Week 1: Committee agrees to hold an inquiry into a topic (let us say, the future of aspects of social care). Staff are asked to draw up draft terms of reference.

Week 2: Terms of reference are agreed and published in a call for evidence. The chair brings forward a proposal for a visit to Sweden and Finland to investigate social care arrangements there (different models to the UK, generally well regarded). The committee agrees to this proposal and the chair bids for funding from the Liaison Committee (in the Commons).

Week 4: Funding for the visit is confirmed, staff work with the embassies in both countries to draw up a programme.

Week 6: Deadline for written evidence. Committee agrees witnesses for its four oral evidence hearings and agrees to visit social care facilities in Birmingham. A communications plan for the inquiry, including the use of social media to request questions to put to the minister, is also agreed.

Week 7: First oral evidence hearing.

Week 8: Committee visit to Sweden and Finland (three days).

Week 9: Second oral evidence hearing.

Week 10: Committee visit to Birmingham. Third oral evidence hearing.

Week 11: Final oral evidence hearing (with the minister). Chair writes to minister with further questions arising from his or her evidence.

Week 12: Committee agrees on the outline for its report ('heads of report').

Week 14: Draft report, prepared by the staff, is considered and agreed by the chair.

Week 15: Committee considers and agrees the chair's draft report (with amendments). Note, this may sometimes require more than one meeting. The report is finalised for publication. A press notice is agreed by the chair.

Week 16: Report is published. Chair makes a statement about the report on the floor of the House.

Two months later . . . Government sends its reply to the report to the committee, which is considered at the committee's next meeting and published. The committee agrees to apply for a debate on the report in Westminster Hall, which takes place four weeks later.

* This would also be typical of one of the shorter inquiries by a Lords select committee; but both in the Commons and the Lords the complexity of the issues and the amount of oral evidence tend to determine the length of an inquiry. In the Commons many committees would be holding further meetings each week on a different inquiry, or as one-off evidence sessions.

There is no doubt that unanimous committees are more effective. They speak with a single voice, and it is much harder for governments to dismiss cross-party agreement. Some people see consensus as implying flabby compromise, but select committees show time and again that they can reach a tough agreed view on politically hot subjects. Given that select committees are made up of party politicians, how does this happen?

There are three main reasons. *First*, when they are not taking public oral evidence, *select committees meet in private*. Their discussions, working papers and draft reports are private. This means that it is much harder for party political pressure to be put on them – for example, by the whips – and it also means that the MPs can be remarkably frank with each other. For example, an individual backbencher can put forward ideas totally at odds with party (or government) policy; and the readiness to see the other side of the argument is a key factor in getting cross-party agreement.

Second, the members of a select committee usually get to know each other well (even if, as can happen in a House of 650 members, they have never spoken to each other before the committee's first meeting). They will work together over many months, both formally and informally; there will often be a good basis for trust; and some will then, to an extent, see themselves as members of the committee more than as party representatives.

Third, select committees proceed on the basis of evidence (as shown by the wealth of footnotes in most select committee reports!). They do this because basing their conclusions firmly on evidence is part of the due process of investigation, but also because recommendations firmly grounded in fact, and explicitly supported by expert opinion, are much harder to challenge. This approach also helps to maintain consensus; a weight of evidence can lead MPs on a committee to agree on a conclusion even if it does not match their previous personal opinions or their party's position.

Dealing with a select committee

As more and more people in all walks of life come into contact with the work of select committees, it may be helpful to say something about how to have an input into an inquiry (a fuller guide for witnesses is available on the parliamentary website, together with information about current inquiries and planned meetings).

First, *make sure that what you want to say is relevant to the committee's work*. Look at the call for evidence and see what ground the inquiry will cover. If you are submitting written evidence – this goes for government departments and some major national bodies, as well as individuals – do not simply top and tail a paper prepared for some other purpose; make sure it is tailored to the requirements of the inquiry. If the inquiry is already under way, *look on the committee's webpage at transcripts and written evidence that have already been published* to see what others have said to the committee. You can also follow an inquiry via webcasts and sign up to email alerts for a committee.

Keep written evidence concise and to the point; evidence is submitted via an online portal which gives further advice about formatting, but the key message is to be succinct. Do not feel you need to answer all of the questions asked by the committee; focus on those where you have something new to say. Avoid jargon and spell out acronyms. The online portal provides an opportunity to say if any part of the paper should be treated confidentially. Once you submit written evidence, it becomes a committee document and, if you want to use it publicly before the committee publishes it, you should seek permission (which is almost always given).

You can ask to give oral evidence, but remember that the committee will have a full programme for the inquiry and will certainly not be able to accommodate all those who wish to do so. A witness who submits a constructive written paper that suggests solutions rather than simply rehearsing criticism may be more likely to be called to give oral evidence. If you are called, the committee staff will talk to you about the details and will usually be able to give you an indication of the committee's likely areas of interest. When you appear, do not expect to be able to make an opening statement; although some chairs might invite you to do so, this is usually better done in writing in advance, as most committees want to get straight on with questioning. The MPs on the committee will all have name-plates in front of them, but it is best to address your answers to the chair. Remember that giving oral evidence (or submitting a written paper) is not the only chance to contribute. You can provide additional information in writing (for example, if you feel you did not answer a question fully) or comment on the evidence given by someone else. As with written evidence, keep your answers brief and focused. If you want to give any of your evidence in private, talk to the clerk of the committee well before your appearance.

Whether you are contributing to an inquiry or not, you can attend the public hearings (subject to there being space; it is not possible to book seats in advance) either in the Palace of Westminster itself or in Portcullis House, or if a select committee takes evidence elsewhere in the UK.

Select committee activity

Activity is at a high level. More than 1,200 formal meetings of select committees (not including informal meetings, seminars and visits) are held each year, of which some 800 are public evidence hearings. Committees generally publish over 300 reports each year. On average, about 390 MPs are members of select committees of one sort or another. Debates on select committee reports take place in the main chamber and in Westminster Hall (see page 278); and there has been a noticeable increase in the use of committee reports in major debates in the House. Chairs can make oral statements in the House announcing the publication of a report, summarising its contents and answering questions on the report from other members, which has further increased their profile.

Investigative select committees are engaging in a wider range of activity. They hold seminars, often with outside experts, to focus and plan major inquiries; they scrutinise legislation; and they have a role in examining major public appointments. Committees have also widened political debate, taking evidence from opposition spokespeople on their alternative policies and ministers from devolved governments, as well as from UK government ministers. Committees have a constant presence on the news agenda, and it is now routine for high-profile television and radio programmes to turn to select committee chairs and members to comment on current issues, regardless of what inquiries their committees may be undertaking at the time.

Particularly in the context of the core tasks and with the help of the Scrutiny Unit, committees now conduct more financial scrutiny of government departments, particularly the annual estimates and annual reports.

While select committees determine their own agendas, the 'core tasks' developed by the Liaison Committee set out the kinds of work committees undertake. They are listed below, with some recent examples. Inevitably, since the EU referendum, a common theme running through much committee work has been the likely implications

Table 10.1 Number of select committee reports published and meetings held, 2014–15 to 2016–17

	Number of reports published	Number of formal meetings held	Number of meetings at which oral evidence taken
2016–17	384	1,259	810
2015–16	226	1,277	872
2014–15	366	1,214	823

of Brexit for the policy areas concerned. In each case, the examples give only a flavour of the range of activity.

What are select committees doing?

Task 1: strategy

Examples: Global Islamist terrorism (Defence); policing for the future (Home Affairs); and UK–US trade relations (International Trade).

Task 2: policy

Specific areas of policy examined by committees include: business rates retention (Communities and Local Government); alcohol minimum unit pricing (joint inquiry by the Health and Home Affairs Committees); and student loans (Treasury).

Task 3: expenditure and performance

The Public Accounts Committee regularly holds the most senior officials to account over the expenditure and performance of government departments. In 2016–17 it published 65 reports and held 51 oral evidence sessions. Examples of recent topics examined are: mental health and prisons; Hinkley Point C; and delivering the Defence estate. Departmental select committees also look into expenditure and performance, for example: F-35 procurement (Defence); and universal credit rollout (Work and Pensions).

Task 4: draft bills

A recent example is the Business, Energy and Industrial Strategy Committee's work on the draft Domestic Gas and Electricity (Tariff Cap) Bill.

Task 5: bills and delegated legislation

The Joint Committee on Human Rights continues its routine scrutiny of government bills for human rights implications. It is rare for departmental select committees to hold an inquiry specifically on an item of delegated legislation, although in looking at the implementation of broader policy areas they sometimes comment on the content of delegated legislation.

Task 6: post-legislative scrutiny

Committee work often involves assessing how legislation is working, as part of wider consideration of policy or strategy. Although the government now publishes post-legislative memoranda on Acts of Parliament, five years after they passed into law, committees have been sporadic in the extent to which they have examined them. Given many competing demands on their time, committees often prefer to look at pressing issues of current concern, rather than the worthy but generally non-urgent review of legislation agreed five years earlier. Nevertheless, a recent example of a post-legislative scrutiny inquiry was the Environment, Food and Rural Affairs Committee's work on the Flood and Water Management Act 2010, on which it reported in April 2017.

Task 7: European scrutiny

While the European Scrutiny Committee continues its work on legislation and legislative proposals emanating from Brussels, a prime focus for most committees recently has been the likely effect of Brexit on their subject areas. Almost every committee has carried out some Brexit-related work since the referendum, for example: Brexit and local government (Communities and Local Government Committee); Brexit and Northern Ireland (Northern Ireland Affairs Committee); Brexit and the implications for UK business (BEIS Committee, which has also undertaken sub-inquiries on the implications for particular industries). This is on top of the Brexit Committee's scrutiny of the government's ongoing negotiations with the EU.

Task 8: appointments

Scrutiny of public appointments is now routine for many committees. Since the 2017 election pre-appointment hearings have included those with the proposed candidates for: the chair of OFCOM (Digital, Culture, Media and Sport); the chair of the Social Security Advisory Committee (Work and Pensions); and the chair of NHS Improvement (Health). In February 2018, the Digital, Culture, Media and Sport Committee said it could not endorse the appointment of the government's nominee (Baroness Stowell of Beeston) to be Chair of the Charity Commission, but the government made the appointment anyway. It is likely that committees will return to this area, and seek greater powers, such as the ability to trigger a debate in the House, in circumstances where the government rejects their opinion about a candidate.

Task 9: support for the House

Some committee reports are debated in the House or Westminster Hall, or launched in the House, with a short statement by the committee chair. Committees contribute to scrutiny of proposals for National Policy Statements – for example, the Transport Committee's work on the airports National Policy Statement. Very often debates which are not specifically on committee reports or evidence will nevertheless relate to work done by committees; when that happens the committee will usually put a 'tag' on the Order Paper, referring to relevant recent work they have done, which can help inform the debate.

Task 10: public engagement

Committees often build in opportunities for the public to engage with them as part of their inquiries. For example, they might hold online forums (as the Work and Pensions

Committee did recently when looking into medical assessments for various types of benefits) or hold informal meetings away from Westminster.

So far, so good. But what does all this activity achieve?

How effective are select committees?

Objective measurement of the effectiveness or influence of select committees is impossible. Governments have accepted a great many select committee recommendations, even when they have not originally been disposed to do so, but it is always difficult to judge how far this has been down to the committee in each case and how far the committee has been the decisive advocate for a growing body of opinion. Sometimes, the mere fact of an inquiry leads to a change in government policy before the committee reports and public exposure can have wider influence.

There is no point in trying to measure effectiveness by totting up how many recommendations are accepted by the government. This process makes no distinction between 'soft' recommendations, on which the door is already ajar, and 'hard' recommendations, which have no chance of being accepted now, but that change the nature of public debate, and that may end up as government policy – perhaps the policy of an incoming government after a general election – months or years later (the 'delayed drop' effect; see page 342). Nor does it distinguish between the recommendations a committee feel strongly about and the ones about which they are not as concerned.

Having even tough recommendations accepted is not what effective scrutiny is about (although it may be one of the results). Scrutiny of government is the process of examining expenditure, administration and policy in detail, on the public record, requiring the government of the day to explain itself to parliamentarians as representatives of the citizen and the taxpayer, and to justify its actions. As an academic study noted, an important role for select committees is in providing 'an arena within which the credentials of a secretary of state are publicly tested. A competent performance before a committee by a minister may not boost [his or her] standing but a poor performance can certainly damage it'. Perhaps there is no better example of the latter point than the criticism which the then Foreign Secretary Boris Johnson faced when in November 2017 he told the Foreign Affairs Committee that the British national Nazanin Zaghari-Ratcliffe, who was in jail in Iran, was in that country for journalistic purposes, rather than as a tourist. This turned out to be incorrect but was seized on by the Iranian authorities as a justification for her imprisonment. The then Foreign Secretary's mishap led to calls for his resignation from the opposition.

This process of accountability is never comfortable for those being scrutinised; and it should not be. But the fact that the government's actions can be put under the spotlight of public examination at any time makes for better decision-making; as Robin Cook when Leader of the House said, 'good scrutiny makes for good government'.

In this chapter, we have described the role of Commons select committees largely in terms of scrutinising the government of the day. This accounts for much of their activity, but they also have a wider role. Their reports and recommendations may be aimed at particular public bodies, sectors of industry or the professions. Select committees are often good at 'blue skies' thinking; they can examine some difficult topic of public policy and analyse possible courses of action – relaxation of the law on drugs is a good example – that political parties would find more difficult. Where there is controversy about the factual basis of public debate, perhaps on a topic such as climate change or genetic engineering, a select committee is an excellent vehicle for analysing conflicting claims and setting out common ground. As with written questions (see page 309) but to a far greater degree, select committee written and oral evidence puts a mass of information, from both the government and other sources, into the public domain.

Nevertheless, there is scope for select committees to be more effective. In the Liaison Committee's vision for the future:

> *Committees should be respected, listened to and feared by departments and ministers for the quality of their investigations, the rigour of their questioning, the depth of their analysis, and the value of their reports . . . The role of committees – and the powers which they can draw upon – will be understood by the public, and they will engage with a wide diversity of people in gathering evidence . . . Their work will be respected for its integrity and relevance to people's lives and will contribute to reviving faith in the value of parliamentary democracy.*

This is a bold agenda that will require committees to be clearer about their objectives, more strategic in using the resources at their disposal, more agile and inclusive in their inquiry processes, and capable of publishing shorter, sharper reports while still seeking to achieve consensus between different political viewpoints.

Effort equals success: the role of committee members

Whatever a select committee does, its effectiveness depends, above all, on its chair and members. Their commitment and effort are crucial. As the Liaison Committee said in its 2000 report *Shifting the Balance*:

> *no pain, no gain: there is no easy route to success. A determined and hardworking committee, in which members are prepared to devote substantial effort and put the interests of the citizen and taxpayer first, can be extraordinarily effective.*

MPs on select committees need an up-to-date understanding of the subject area. They do not have to be great technical experts – indeed, there is some reason for them not to be; it could be said that one of the strengths of select committees is that they are made up of well-informed lay people who can ask common-sense questions of the experts and make sure they get proper answers. Occasional attempts to browbeat witnesses for some easy headlines do nothing for the select committee system and are usually counter-productive. As a wise select committee chair of another era used to say, 'more flies are caught with honey than with vinegar'.

On individual inquiries, members of a committee need to keep up with the written and oral evidence and to prepare for oral evidence sessions. The committee staff support the committee through briefing, and summarising and analysing evidence, but there is no substitute for individual MPs having command of the subject. Although, as we have seen in earlier chapters, there are many other calls on MPs' time, the most effective oral evidence sessions – especially with difficult and well-briefed witnesses – are those at which all the members of a committee are present throughout; are well-prepared; divide up the areas of questioning between them; ask questions rather than make statements; and follow up each other's questions. It is sometimes suggested that committees should employ counsel to undertake part of the examination of witnesses: counsel was used in this way in the work of the Banking Standards Commission. However, it is relatively rare for this sort of forensic examination to be required. Other types of inquiry are frequently more valuable and play to other select committee strengths; when forensic examination is required, a good many MPs are perfectly capable of effective questioning. Recognising the importance of focused and succinct questioning, some committees have undertaken training by experts to help increase their impact. However, there is also an important principle at stake. MPs are elected by the people to speak in Parliament, ask questions and take part in parliamentary proceedings: they should be wary of delegating these functions to the unelected. Little would be gained by making committees more legalistic.

Being an effective member of a select committee is time-consuming. A chair can easily spend the equivalent of two to three days a week on committee business, having to combine this with all the other pressures on an MP, and the time commitment for members of a busy committee may not be much less (which demonstrates that membership of more than one investigative committee, which happens too often, is not a practical proposition). The average attendances each session for the most well-respected committees routinely top 80 per cent.

A bargain price

The Liaison Committee described the achievements of the select committee system as having been 'at a bargain price'. This is still the case. Staff costs relating to select committees (other than those relating to the National Audit Office and the Ombudsman) run at around £14 million a year, and all other costs, including printing, transcription of evidence, specialist advisers, travel and commissioned work, amount to a little over £3 million. 'Bargain' seems a fair description.

Select committees in the House of Lords

The committees

Since the early 1970s the House of Lords has developed an increasingly elaborate array of permanent select committees reappointed every session to scrutinise various aspects of public policy. (For legislative committees, see pages 245–6; for domestic committees, see page 79.) Some of these committees enjoy a high reputation.

Although the Lords committee structure developed in a somewhat piecemeal way, a principle that has endured is that Lords committees are thematic and cross-cutting rather than shadowing government departments. There is general acceptance that this, in theory at least, should enable Lords committee work to complement rather than compete with or duplicate that of the Commons (as is true of the two Houses more generally).

Sessional (or permanent) select committees

At the beginning of the 2017–19 session, the House of Lords had established the following permanent committees on public policy:

European Union

First established in 1973 and now possessing six sub-committees, this is the most elaborate of all Lords committees involving some 70 members at any one time. Its work is described more fully in Chapter 11. The committee will inevitably take a very different form after Brexit, but in the meantime it has been busier than ever scrutinising the Brexit process.

Science and Technology

Set up in 1979, its remit is to consider science and technology across the board, including public policy that ought to be informed by science, technological challenges and opportunities, and public policy towards science itself. (14 members)

Economic Affairs

Set up in 2001, this committee evolved from an earlier *ad hoc* (temporary) committee to monitor the Monetary Policy Committee of the Bank of England. While it mainly conducts inquiries into topical areas of economic policy, since 2003 it has also established a sub-committee each year to inquire into policy aspects of the Finance Bill. (13 members)

Constitution

Also set up first in 2001, following a recommendation by the Royal Commission on Reform of the House of Lords, the committee inquires into constitutional issues and examines bills for their constitutional implications. (12 members)

Communications

This committee was established in 2007 following on from an *ad hoc* committee on the renewal of the BBC Charter. Set up initially for a series of terms of years, it was made permanent with effect from the 2013–14 session. It conducts inquiries into policy relating to the media, communications and creative industries. (13 members)

International Relations

First established in 2016 following increasing pressure from members to deploy their expertise on foreign affairs in a select committee. It may examine any aspect of international relations, though it tries to avoid duplicating the work of the EU Committee and the Commons Foreign Affairs Committee. (12 members)

Ad hoc *(temporary) committees*

From the 1970s the House occasionally set up temporary or *ad hoc* select committees which ceased to exist once they had reported. They often considered the merits of public bills, invariably private members' bills, that raised important policy issues, such as the Infant Life Preservation Bill in 1987–88 (on abortion), or the Assisted Dying for the Terminally Ill Bill in 2004–05 (on euthanasia). In both cases, the bills did not proceed further though, in theory, after hearing evidence it is open to a select committee on a bill to amend it and report it to the House, whereupon it is re-committed to a Committee of the whole House and continues its passage. The delay and possibility of amendment make the procedure unsuitable for the consideration of government bills, so the setting up of a committee on the government's Constitutional Reform Bill in 2004 – on a motion in the House moved by Lord Lloyd of Berwick, a crossbencher – was most unusual. Committees are also set up *ad hoc* to consider policy matters – embryonic stem cell research in 2001, religious offences in 2002–03, and HIV and AIDS in 2010–12 to name but a few.

Ad hoc committees allow specific contemporary issues to be examined without setting up a permanent vehicle to do it. They have become an established part of the Lords committee structure. Each year the Lords Liaison Committee invites members to submit proposals for *ad hoc* committees for the following session. Dozens of bids are made (of varying quality), invariably reflecting the interests of those members who put them forward. The Liaison Committee then analyses the bids, requesting further briefing on those shortlisted, before making recommendations to the House. Typically four *ad hoc* committees are established for a year-long session, with three on policy issues and one conducting post-legislative scrutiny of an Act or Acts. Thus, at the start of the 2017–19 session three *ad hoc* committees were appointed to look at artificial intelligence, political polling and digital media, and citizenship and civic engagement. One *ad hoc* committee was appointed to undertake post-legislative scrutiny of the Natural Environment and Rural Communities Act 2006. Because there is expected to be a two-year session the Liaison Committee will propose further *ad hoc* committees for 2018–19.

Ad hoc committees are popular with members. They allow an in-depth examination of a subject, usually one which spans several government departments. They enable more members to be involved in committee work than would be the case if there were only permanent committees. And their reports can have considerable impact. However, a recurring problem is the lack of a structure to follow up their recommendations. Permanent committees can return to a subject and keep the pressure on the government (or others). *Ad hoc* committees disband when they report. To prevent their recommendations being forgotten the chairman of the Liaison Committee writes to the relevant minister about a year after an *ad hoc* committee has reported asking about progress on key recommendations. But no one pretends this is a full substitute for proper follow-up work.

The process

How does the House decide when to establish a committee? Following a study of the House's committee work in 1991–92, a Liaison Committee chaired by the Senior Deputy Speaker (previously called the Chairman of Committees) was set up to allocate resources between select committees and to make recommendations to the House on the appointment of committees. Discussions about committee work, which used to take place between the usual channels, now take place in the Liaison Committee, on which the party leaders, the Convenor of the Crossbench Peers and a small number of backbench members also sit. The role of the Liaison Committee is unenviable. The pressure for new committees is high, yet a sessional select committee once established is difficult to abolish or modify. Recently, the Liaison Committee has appeared to be more assertive – reducing the number of EU and Science and Technology sub-committees, and subjecting all *ad hoc* committee activity to an annual review and bidding process. But there have been occasions when the House has rejected the Liaison Committee's advice – in setting up a committee in 2001 on the crash of Chinook Helicopter ZD 576, for example. And sometimes the House has set up committees without reference to the Liaison Committee at all – on stem cell research in 2001, on the Constitutional Reform Bill in 2004. Moreover, the requirement to set up joint committees to give pre-legislative scrutiny to draft bills or, indeed, to respond to any Commons initiative for a joint committee – such as the Parliamentary Commission on Banking in 2012 – cannot always be foreseen.

Sessional select committees are renewed at the beginning of every session, on a motion in the House setting out their orders of reference and powers. *Ad hoc* committees are set up by motion as required. The members are selected by the Selection Committee on the advice of the Whips and Convenor and reflect party balance in the House. While there is no formal rule to this effect, a typical committee of 12 members might have four Conservative, four Labour, two Liberal Democrat and two Crossbench members. Chairmen are usually appointed by the House but, in practice, are agreed through the usual channels. In the Lords, a rotation rule prevents a committee member from serving for more than three sessions on a committee in one stretch. To avoid serial re-appointments to a committee members must be off the committee for at least two sessions before becoming eligible to re-join it. This rotation rule allows for committee membership to be refreshed and for more members to serve on committees, but it can lead to a lack of continuity and institutional memory.

Once established, select committees in the Lords operate in a way that is almost identical to Commons committees and they encounter many of the same logistical difficulties. Each committee or sub-committee is supported by its clerk, a committee assistant, a policy analyst who is usually a specialist in the subject, and receives the assistance of an outside specialist adviser or advisers appointed for each particular inquiry in return for a daily fee. The permanent staff of the Committee Office is about 60 – even more modest than that in the Commons. The total spending of the Lords Committee Office in the financial year 2016–17 was just under £4 million in support of up to 20 active committees and sub-committees, and the average cost of running an extra committee per year is about £225,000. These costs of select committees do not include any element for accommodation, IT, security or utilities. Neither do they have regard to the cost of members, whose expenses are paid by virtue of their attendance at the House. But the fact is that, as with Commons select committees, the monetary costs are modest (especially by comparison with public inquiries and non-parliamentary committees).

Lords committees have powers to send for persons (witnesses) and papers (evidence). Usually, witnesses attend and evidence is provided voluntarily but, were it necessary, a committee could issue a formal summons and failure to respond would be reported to the House as a contempt. Enforcement of the summons would not be easy. As with Commons committees, the prospect of embarrassment and potential adverse publicity in failing to comply has proved to be a powerful persuader. Lords committees have power to meet concurrently with Commons committees, although this rarely occurs. The quorum of a Lords committee is usually three but for two joint committees – on Human Rights and Statutory Instruments – it is two from each House.

House of Lords Constitution Committee taking evidence

Source: Copyright House of Lords, 2014. Photography by Annabel Moller

As in the Commons, there are no minority reports in the Lords. Dissent – which is rare – is recorded by moving amendments to the text and having these amendments printed in the minutes of proceedings. Lords committees usually succeed in achieving unanimity as members know that, unless their conclusions can be supported by all, they are unlikely to achieve the greatest impact. The chairman in the Lords has no casting vote.

The House debates all significant committee reports, although often several months after the committee has reported. Through these debates, the committee seeks to elicit a response from the government. In 2016–17, 26 committee reports were debated, occupying 6 per cent of the House's sitting time, plus a further four debates in Grand Committee. A written response is also provided by the government within two months of publication, unless otherwise agreed with the committee in question. Select committee report debates have notable prominence in the chamber – to the benefit of both.

Outcomes

As with Commons committees, it is difficult to say how far government policy is affected by the findings of Lords select committees, but where those committees produce reports that accord with government thinking, rather than being deeply critical, they seem to have effect.

In some areas of select committee activity, the influence is largely preventative. Thus, the very existence of the Delegated Powers and Regulatory Reform Committee means that the government is more likely to ensure that delegated powers are appropriately used in legislation and, if an adverse report is made, it usually complies with the committee's recommendations. Since the establishment of the Secondary Legislation Scrutiny Committee, precious few instruments have been reported on unfavourably on grounds of 'gold plating'. The bill scrutiny role of the Joint Committee on Human Rights has raised the profile of human rights in government, creating a culture of rights according to some commentators. The Constitution Committee's recommendations on fast track bills (expedited for urgent policy reasons) have been accepted by the government and are now addressed in the explanatory notes accompanying such bills.

In other areas, select committee reports – usually on ethical issues – will have helped to frame the debate. The select committee on the Infant Life Preservation Bill undoubtedly helped to focus the debate on the appropriate maximum period of gestation after which abortion would not be lawful, and its subsequent setting at 24 weeks. More recently, the Select Committee on the Assisted Dying for the Terminally Ill Bill in 2004–05 set the boundaries for a debate on this difficult issue that has continued ever since.

Some committees can point to instances where they have been influential in quite specific ways. For example, in 2012, the Constitution Committee reported on a problem that had occurred at the 2010 general election whereby those queuing outside a polling station when it closed at 10 pm had not been allowed to vote. The committee recommended a change in the law. The government failed to address this issue in its

Electoral Registration and Administration Bill in 2012–13, so members of the committee tabled amendments. Faced with likely defeat, the government brought forward its own amendment to the bill and the law was changed. In 2016–17 the Communications Committee reported critically on the government's plans to privatise Channel 4 and to relocate it outside London. It found that the proposals would put the broadcaster's public service remit at risk. After a change in the Secretary of State for Culture Media and Sport, the new minister decided not to proceed with the plans. The Economic Affairs Committee reported on the housing market in 2016; the government's subsequent white paper on housing specifically adopted over half of the committee's recommendations. The committee's Finance Bill Sub-Committee in 2017 criticised the government's Making Tax Digital plan to require businesses to submit tax returns quarterly (rather than annually), using HMRC software. That criticism contributed to the pressure which led to the government delaying introducing the measure and significantly reducing the range of businesses to which it applied. The Science and Technology Committee's ongoing work on nuclear power has helped change the terms of debate; and its report on Brexit and science policy was widely praised.

Committee members in the Lords, as in the Commons, often identify strongly with their committees and become very committed to the work. It follows that they are most anxious that their reports receive the widest possible publicity. Committee staff maintain webpages containing the committees' programmes of work, publications, and written and oral evidence relating to current inquiries. Part of the House of Lords press and publicity team is dedicated to promoting committee work; meetings are publicised; all public sessions are webcast; the publication of every report is accompanied by a press notice; and, for the more significant reports, press conferences are held and the publication of most reports will have regard to newspaper deadlines and that highly sought after slot on Radio 4's *Today* programme. Coverage in online publications is also sought, and increasingly important. But timeliness is all, particularly when it comes to reporting on Brexit.

Committee work has featured conspicuously in the renaissance of the House of Lords in recent times. It suits the more reflective character of the House, and it is certain to remain a permanent – and most likely ever expanding – feature of its activities.

Joint committees

We have seen elsewhere that the two Houses are able to appoint joint select committees. There was a time when the best-known and most established, such as the Joint Committee on Statutory Instruments and the Joint Committee on Consolidation, &c., Bills were legislative in character (see pages 327–8). But, nowadays, the Joint Committee on Human Rights (see page 327), the Joint Committee on the National Security Strategy and the joint committees established *ad hoc* to scrutinise the policy in draft bills (pre-legislative scrutiny committees, see page 188) are probably better-known because they consider policy matters. First set up in the 1998–99 session at the behest of the new Labour government, 28 pre-legislative scrutiny joint committees had been set up by the end of the 2016–17 session. Joint committees are also occasionally set up for certain kinds of opposed private business – opposed Special Procedure Orders and opposed Scottish Provisional Order Confirmation Bills (though, following devolution, the latter are now seldom necessary).

Joint committees are set up following motions agreed in each House. Formally they are two committees which join together, but in practice they operate much like other select committees. They operate according to Lords procedure – so in the rare instance of a tied vote the chairman has no casting vote. Each House appoints its own members, with usually the same number of MPs and peers. With the right personalities a joint committee can be as cohesive as any other select committee.

Joint committees are also set up *ad hoc* to consider particular issues of concern to both Houses, such as the privileges of the two Houses (see page 168), restoration and renewal of the Palace of Westminster, and reform of the House of Lords.

The first joint committee on Lords reform was set up in July 2002 to report on options for the composition and powers of the House once reform had been completed. After free votes in both Houses on the options, the committee would, it was envisaged, define in greater detail the proposed composition, role and powers of the second chamber and recommend a transition strategy for transforming the Lords into its fully reformed state. The committee's first substantive report, published in December 2002, recommended no change in powers but set out seven options for composition ranging from fully nominated to fully elected. In February 2003, both Houses voted on these options. The Lords voted for 100 per cent nomination and rejected all other options. The Commons rejected all the options.

In a further report published in May 2003, the joint committee reported again, identifying areas of consensus and inviting the government to indicate what view it now took of Lords reform. In its response published in July 2003, the government indicated that, in the absence of consensus, its interest now would be in making the existing House work more effectively and the joint committee was not re-appointed the following session.

Following the 2005 general election and references in the Labour Party manifesto to further Lords reform, a joint committee was set up in April 2006 to examine the conventions of the House (the Salisbury convention and the practices on delegated legislation), the time taken on bills, and the practices governing the resolution of disputes over bills ('ping-pong'). Its report is regarded as the definitive statement on these conventions.

In 2012 a further joint committee was set up to consider Lords reform, this time as a pre-legislative scrutiny committee on the coalition government's draft House of Lords Reform Bill. The draft bill made provision for a largely elected and smaller House. This very large joint committee – with 13 members from each House – was deeply divided on some of the key issues, including the principle of election. Nonetheless, albeit with qualification and on occasion on a majority, the joint committee reported favourably on most of the draft bill's key provisions. The work of all these committees, and in particular the 2012 bill and its eventual fate, are discussed more fully at page 394.

Until recently, it could have been said that joint select committees were seldom, if ever, set up to consider general issues of public policy – issues that would normally fall to a select committee of either of the two Houses to consider. But recently there have been two, on the Joint Committee on Privacy and Injunctions in 2011 and the Parliamentary Commission on Banking Standards in 2012–13. In 2010 and 2011, there was much media comment about so-called 'super-injunctions', which many celebrities were thought to have used to cover up alleged infidelities. Following the naming of one such celebrity under the protection of parliamentary privilege in the House of Commons, the government announced there would be a joint committee to examine the broad area of privacy, injunctions, their connection to parliamentary privilege and the future of media regulation. The Joint Committee on Privacy and Injunctions had 13 members from each House and took an extensive amount of evidence. Early in its life, the 'phone hacking' scandal gained great prominence, leading the committee to focus on the future of media regulation. This aspect of its inquiry had limited influence, though, as the Leveson Inquiry into press regulation was by then the centre of attention. The Parliamentary Commission on Banking Standards (we considered its work earlier on page 331) was also set up as a joint committee at the government's behest.

It is not yet clear how much appetite there is in either House for *ad hoc* scrutiny of policy by joint committee other than in the context of pre-legislative scrutiny. Nevertheless, the possibility remains that from now on, for reasons of its own, the government may well decide on occasion to use its influence to set up a joint committee on a pressing policy issue rather than establish some other kind of inquiry.

11

Parliament and Europe

The relationship between the United Kingdom and the European Union has been central to British politics for nearly 50 years. It has surely never been more controversial than in the run-up to and since the 2016 referendum on the UK's membership of the EU. Although the balance of opinion for and against membership has fluctuated since the UK joined, throughout the topic has raised strong passions inside and outside Westminster.

It is easy to see why membership of the EU has been a divisive issue. On the one hand, the argument runs, our interests are so similar to those of our neighbours that we should act with them, giving up some freedom of action so that we can be more effective and influential as a union of states. On the other hand, this closer union has been seen as an unacceptable loss of sovereignty to an EU in which distinct UK interests will be submerged.

It is certainly the case that the United Kingdom Parliament effectively lost its primacy in law-making in a practical sense. EU regulations automatically became law in this country without the involvement of Parliament. EU directives set out what was to be the effect of the law in all the member states without specifying detailed terms; it was up to each country to decide on the wording. Under the European Communities Act 1972, implementation of EU directives in the UK took place through delegated legislation (see page 238), often with little scrutiny and certainly with no ability to change the legislation. Estimates of how much UK legislation 'comes from Europe' are notoriously difficult to make, but – according to the House of Commons Library – it is possible to justify any measure between 15 and 55 per cent, depending on what is included in the calculation.

The Court of Justice of the European Union in Luxembourg has long held that EU law has precedence over the laws of member states. It was therefore possible for the court to declare an Act passed by the Westminster Parliament to be incompatible with Union law and for a British court then to declare the law to be of no effect. This happened, for example, with the Merchant Shipping Act 1988 in the 1991 *Factortame* case, brought by a Spanish trawler company, and in which the United Kingdom was found to have breached EU law by requiring ships to have majority British ownership if they were to be registered in the UK.

In this chapter we start with an overview of the EU institutions and the history of the UK's relationship with the EU. We then look at the events which led to the Brexit referendum, followed by developments since then. The chapter finishes by exploring what might change in Parliament as a result of Brexit.

Background

On 1 January 1973 the UK joined what were then three 'European Communities': the *European Economic Community* (EEC) or 'Common Market', the *European Coal and Steel Community* and the *European Atomic Energy Community* (Euratom). The 1992 Maastricht Treaty renamed the European Economic Community simply the 'European Community' and made it part of the new European Union. The Lisbon Treaty, which came into force on 1 December 2009, created a comprehensive legal identity and renamed the entire structure the European Union (EU).

Membership

There were six original members of the EEC established by the 1957 Treaty of Rome: Belgium, France, Germany, Italy, Luxembourg and the Netherlands. In 1972 they were joined by Denmark, Ireland and the United Kingdom; in 1979 by Greece; and in 1985 by Spain and Portugal. In 1995 these countries were joined by Austria, Sweden and Finland. The biggest ever enlargement of the EU took place on 1 May 2004, with the addition of Cyprus, the Czech Republic, Estonia, Hungary, Latvia, Lithuania, Malta, Poland, Slovakia and Slovenia; Bulgaria and Romania joined in 2007; and Croatia in 2013. UK governments strongly supported enlargement of the EU, both because it was thought to entrench democracy in new member states and because it was felt to act as a check on the move to ever more integration.

The European Council

The European Council is the highest-level decision-making forum in the EU, its role having been formalised by the Treaty of Lisbon. It consists of the heads of state or government of member states, together with its own President (elected by a qualified majority of the Council) and the President of the Commission. It typically meets four times a year: twice in Brussels and once in each of the member states which holds the six-month rotating presidency. It defines the general political direction and priorities of the EU but does not legislate.

The Council of the European Union

The Council (formerly called the 'Council of Ministers' and not to be confused with the European Council) is one of the two principal legislative and decision-making bodies in the EU, together with the European Parliament. It consists of ministerial representatives from each of the member states' governments, who vary according to the business under discussion. Thus for agricultural matters the Council will consist of agriculture ministers; finance ministers will deal with economic and financial matters, and so on. The great majority of Council meetings are held in private (although under the Treaty of Lisbon it now meets in public when it formally deliberates and votes on legislation); most decisions are taken by consensus, but if votes are necessary they are usually by qualified majority voting (see page 364). Most Council meetings take place in Brussels. The presidency of the Council is held by each member state in turn for a period of six months. The Council is supported by the Committee of Permanent Representatives (member states' ambassadors to the EU), known as COREPER, which prepares Council business and negotiates agreement between member states so that the Council need take only a formal decision.

The European Commission

The Commission (based in Brussels) is the EU's executive – in some ways like a civil service, but with extensive powers of initiative and of decision on a range of delegated matters. There are 28 commissioners (one from each member state), each of whom is responsible for an area of policy. The work of the Commission is carried out by 33 Directorates-General. The Commission President is highly influential, and his or her selection a matter for both the European Council (which proposes a candidate) and the European Parliament (which has the power to approve or reject the Council's nominee). The Lisbon Treaty states that the Council must take the European parliamentary election results 'into account' when making its proposal – wording that was subject to varying definitions following the elections in 2014, especially in the context of David Cameron's opposition to the eventually successful candidate, the former Prime Minister of Luxembourg, Jean-Claude Juncker.

The European Parliament

Since 1979 members of the European Parliament (MEPs) have been directly elected for fixed terms of five years. The total membership is 751, of whom 73 represent UK constituencies (60 in England, six in Scotland, four in Wales and three in Northern Ireland). Following the 2014 elections, the largest party in the parliament was the European People's Party with 221 seats, closely followed by the Socialists and Democrats with 191. The Alliance of Liberals and Democrats for Europe includes the sole British Liberal Democrat MEP. The UK Independence Party (UKIP) has 24 MEPs and is affiliated to the Europe of Freedom and Democracy (EFD) group, which has 48 seats. Labour's 20 MEPs sit with the Socialists and Democrats Group, and the Conservative party's 19 MEPs are part of the European Conservative and Reformist (ECR) group. Other United Kingdom MEPs are Green (3), SNP (2), Plaid Cymru (1), Sinn Féin (1), Democratic Unionist (1) and Ulster Unionist (1).

Most business in European Parliament plenary sessions originates from the 20 permanent committees and their sub-committees, which carry out most of the legislative scrutiny. The European Parliament sits both in Strasbourg, for a week of plenary sittings each month, and in Brussels, for a number of two-day plenaries and the majority of committee meetings.

Other institutions and bodies

The Court of Justice of the EU (also in Luxembourg) has a general duty of ensuring that in the operation of the treaties the law is observed. It decides on cases that challenge the legality of actions of the institutions of the EU, that allege a breach of a treaty by a member state or which seek interpretation on a point of EU law. It is assisted by the *General Court*, which used to be called the Court of First Instance. The *European Court of Auditors* (in Luxembourg) audits EU revenue and expenditure, and reports on expenditure programmes. The 353 members of the consultative *European Economic and Social Committee* are drawn from trade union, employer, consumer and other interests; and the 353 members of the consultative *Committee of the Regions* represent regional and local government. The *European Central Bank* in Frankfurt is the central bank for the eurozone, while the *European Investment Bank* in Luxembourg is the EU's financing institution, providing long-term loans for capital investment.

European legislation: types

There are three forms of European legislation provided for under the Treaty on the Functioning of the European Union (TFEU). *Regulations* have the force of law throughout the EU without member states having to take any action; this is known as 'direct effect'. *Directives* are binding on member states in terms of the result to be achieved by a specified date, but it is up to each country what form and method of implementation are to be used. *Decisions* adopted by an institution are binding on those to whom they are addressed; they are used for a range of matters, but especially to secure fair commercial competition throughout the EU. Regulations and directives must be published in the *Official Journal* of the EU.

European legislation: procedure

The legislative and decision-making processes of the EU are complex. In nearly all cases, the Commission has the exclusive right of initiative to propose draft legislative acts. There are then two categories of legislative procedure: the first is the ordinary legislative procedure (formerly known as co-decision) under which the Council and European Parliament both have to agree before the proposal can come into effect. As in Westminster, this is achieved through 'readings', but in the EU draft legislation is read *up to* three times, and most of the time a deal is concluded at the first-reading stage through informal (and private) discussions between the Council presidency,

European Parliament and Commission known as 'first-reading deals' or 'trilogues'. Other provisions are subject to special legislative procedure, which means that the Council has either to 'consult' the European Parliament or to seek its 'consent'. Under the ordinary legislative procedure the Council normally acts by qualified majority. Where the member states take decisions inter-governmentally, rather than legislatively, they do so through *common positions*, *joint actions*, *declarations*, *common strategies* or *conclusions*.

Closer union

The preamble to the Treaty of Rome set ambitious objectives of 'ever closer union of the peoples of Europe and elimination of the barriers which divide Europe'. However, it also set the EEC apparently less politically sensitive tasks such as 'establishing a common market and progressively approximating the economic policies of member states' . . . harmonious development of economic activities'.

For nearly 30 years the EEC was concerned mainly with commercial and economic affairs; and during that time the Community managed with only modest amendments to the original treaty (such as those required when new member states joined). Subsequent changes were more profound, and fuelled intense political controversy about the balance between national sovereignty and an 'ever closer union'.

In 1986 the *Single European Act* allowed legislation for the completion of the Community's internal market to be made by qualified majority voting (QMV) in the Council of Ministers. The use of QMV, which has since been applied to many other areas of EU legislation, means that the Council makes decisions by a weighted system of voting in which larger countries have more votes. It also means that no individual member state can exercise a veto. The Single European Act also increased the legislative role of the European Parliament and provided for political cooperation on foreign policy.

The *Treaty on European Union* of 1992 (the *Maastricht Treaty*) established three 'pillars' of the EU: the European Communities and two intergovernmental pillars: a common foreign and security policy (CFSP) and cooperation on justice and home affairs (JHA); and it instituted the machinery to bring about monetary union – i.e. the euro, from which Prime Minister John Major negotiated an opt-out for the UK.

The *Treaty of Amsterdam* (1997) formalised for the first time the concept of 'flexibility' in providing for some countries to cooperate on aims that were not necessarily shared by all member states. It moved the free movement of persons from the JHA pillar to the Communities pillar, making it a subject for legislation rather than simply cooperation, and it also incorporated the provisions of the social agreement.

The *Treaty of Nice* (2001) established a European Security and Defence Policy and extended the application of QMV. It made provision for the institutional change that would be necessary on enlargement of the Union, including the size of the European Commission and a new weighting of votes for QMV.

In December 2001 the European Council set up the *Convention on the Future of Europe* to examine how the EU could be made more democratic and efficient, and to propose a constitution for the Union. The convention, which included representatives from national governments and parliaments, both of current member states and applicant countries, as well as representatives of the European Commission and the European Parliament, reported in the summer of 2003. Its draft constitutional treaty, including additional powers for the European Parliament and a longer-term President of the European Council, led to opposition calls for it to be subject to a referendum in the UK – calls which Prime Minister Tony Blair eventually gave in to in 2004.

That referendum never happened, as events superseded it. Although agreed by heads of state and government, and ratified by several member states, the constitutional treaty was rejected in referendums in France and the Netherlands in May and June 2005. There was then a time of reflection and negotiation, after which, in 2007, work began on a new reform treaty, which resulted in the Treaty of Lisbon. Again, the process of ratification by member states was not straightforward and involved a referendum that succeeded only at the second attempt (in Ireland), an appeal in Germany to its Constitutional Court and something of a smorgasbord of caveats, declarations and opt-outs for the Czech Republic, Denmark, Ireland and the United Kingdom. The UK government argued that the Lisbon Treaty was markedly different from the constitutional treaty and so did not need to be put to a referendum. The then opposition, under David Cameron, strongly argued that it should remain subject to a referendum, but once the treaty was ratified in 2009 the matter was settled before David Cameron became Prime Minister.

Thus from the mid-1980s onwards there was a fairly relentless process of change in the EU, with five treaties agreed. The UK obtained a series of opt-outs – for example, on the euro, the Schengen agreement removing border checks within the EU, proposals for measures on Justice and Home Affairs, and on the interpretation of the Charter on Fundamental Rights. The opt-outs were hard won, and many in the EU institutions lamented the special treatment they thought the UK was getting. Yet many in the UK, including in Parliament, remained uneasy with the loss of sovereignty they saw happening and the seemingly never-ending path of integration that the EU was going down.

History of debates about the EU

The European Communities Act 1972, which took the UK into the Common Market, was passed by the narrow majority of 17 (the majority on second reading after three full days of debate was only eight). The UK's relations with the EU have been a matter of political controversy ever since. In 1975 the Labour government led by Harold Wilson held a national referendum on whether the UK should remain a member, following a renegotiation which critics thought superficial. The subject was so divisive that collective Cabinet responsibility was suspended so that senior ministers could campaign for opposite sides of the issue. The referendum was won by the remain side, by 67 to 33 per cent. Outside No. 10 the Prime Minister Harold Wilson, referring to when the UK first sought to join the EEC, said 'It means that 14 years of national argument are over. It means that all those who have had reservations about

Britain's commitment should now join wholeheartedly with our partners in Europe'. That did not prove to be so.

Disagreements about Europe, both between and within parties, continued; but it was institutional change within the European Union that brought them to centre stage. In the 1992–97 parliament John Major's government was dogged by dissent and open rebellion on European issues, made more hazardous by the Conservatives' small majority.

Major came into office with an overall majority of 21, but after the loss of eight by-elections and the defection of four MPs to other parties, the Conservatives lost their overall majority and were in a minority of three before the end of the parliament. This meant that rebels on European issues – and especially on the Maastricht Treaty – had a real prospect of bringing about a government defeat. In July 1992 the government did, indeed, lose a significant vote on the Maastricht Social Protocol, by 324 votes to 316, and had to put a motion of confidence – which it won comfortably – before the House the next day. Serious eurosceptic dissent nevertheless continued, leading to the withdrawal of the whip from eight persistent rebels from November 1994 to April 1995. In June 1995 Major resigned the leadership of the Conservative party, standing immediately for re-election in an attempt to bring matters to a head. Although he won by 218 votes to 89, the size of the minority indicated the level of (largely Europe-fuelled) dissent.

The broadly pro-European stance of the incoming Labour government in 1997 (and also its huge overall majority of 179) meant that European issues were less prominent in the 1997–2001 parliament. In the 2001–05 parliament the Convention on the Future of Europe and the draft EU constitution reopened divisions. Also in this parliament the government undertook to decide on whether to recommend membership of the euro. The official stance was that the UK would join when the moment was right economically, subject to a nationwide referendum. In mid-2003 the then Chancellor of the Exchequer, Gordon Brown, announced that his economic tests for euro membership had not been met, so the issue went off the agenda. In the later stages of the 2005–10 parliament the intense debate about EU integration resumed, this time over the Lisbon Treaty.

Moving towards a referendum

The 2010–15 parliament, under the coalition government, saw some key steps taken domestically towards holding a referendum. By the end of the parliament, following the 2015 general election, it was widely accepted that a referendum was inevitable. Ironically this was a period of relative constitutional (but not economic) stability at the EU level, being the first parliament since 1979–83 when a major treaty was not being negotiated or agreed.

The EU Act 2011 implemented a commitment in the coalition agreement, reflecting an undertaking in the 2010 Conservative manifesto, for a 'referendum lock' on future treaty changes. The Act required a referendum to be held before ministers could agree to transfer powers in a range of areas from the UK to the EU. Other, lesser, powers could not be transferred without an Act of Parliament; and some transfers required merely a resolution of each House. Although several such Acts have been passed they have all been uncontroversial, relating mostly to technical matters. No referendum was held under the Act, but it would certainly have influenced what ministers would have been prepared to agree in future treaty negotiations. And it reaffirmed a view that the referendum was the device to decide on big EU issues.

Aside from publishing a series of technical 'balance of competence' studies, which analysed which powers lay at EU and member-state level, the EU Act 2011 was the only significant EU measure formally agreed by both coalition parties in the 2010–15 parliament. That did not, though, stop either party talking about the future relationship with the EU. In 2013 David Cameron sought to bring matters to a head by announcing at the Bloomberg headquarters that if the Conservatives won the next general election they would seek to renegotiate the UK's membership of the EU then hold an in/out referendum on it. The Liberal Democrats opposed the move so no government action resulted. However, in the debate on the Queen's Speech in 2013 Conservative MPs tabled an amendment regretting 'that an EU referendum bill was not included in the gracious speech'. This was the first time since 1946 that MPs from a government party had tabled an amendment to the Address in reply to the Queen's Speech expressing their disagreement with the government's position. When the amendment was put to a division, the Prime Minister gave Conservative MPs a free vote on it, effectively allowing members of the government to vote against the collective position set out in the speech. In the event, 116 Conservative MPs voted for the amendment and only one voted against it; the amendment was defeated by 277 votes to 130; no Conservative ministers voted in the division, but several parliamentary private secretaries voted for the amendment.

Following that a private member's bill, the European Union (Referendum) Bill, was introduced by the winner of the 2013–14 session ballot, James Wharton. It sought to make provision for a referendum on EU membership before the end of 2017. The bill passed the Commons but ran out of time in the Lords, after it became clear that peers had no intention of passing it. There was talk of passing the bill in the next session under the Parliament Acts, but nothing materialised.

In the 2014 elections to the European Parliament UKIP gained the most votes and seats, which was felt to reaffirm David Cameron's view that without the promise of a referendum the Conservatives would lose votes to UKIP at the 2015 general election.

2016 referendum

The Conservative manifesto at the 2015 general election duly promised an in/out referendum following renegotiation of the UK's membership. When they won a majority at the election, against the expectations of most pollsters and pundits, David Cameron set about renegotiating. The plan seemed to be to prize speed over depth of negotiation, with a view to holding the referendum relatively early. Most people expected the remain side to win, so it was perhaps felt better to get the matter over and done with, such that the government could move on to other priorities.

In the meantime the government introduced the European Union (Referendum) Bill 2015 to legislate for the holding of the referendum. It required a referendum on the question 'Should the United Kingdom remain a member of the European Union or leave the European Union?' before the end of 2017. Although the government was defeated on an amendment in the Commons on 'purdah' rules during the referendum campaign, the bill had a relatively easy passage through Parliament – especially compared to the Wharton private member's bill which preceded it. The official opposition recognised that the government had a mandate for the referendum so did not oppose it in the Commons nor, mindful of the Salisbury convention, in the Lords. Only the SNP opposed holding the referendum; for all other parties the fight moved on from whether to hold a referendum to how people should vote in it. The bill became law in December 2015.

Knowing that a referendum would be held the Prime Minister's renegotiation stepped up a gear. But the message coming from Brussels and many member states was cautious. They were wary of offering too many concessions lest other member states decide to hold their own referendums in pursuit of a more favourable deal. In February 2016 the European Council agreed a package of measures which included a declaration that the UK would not be subject to 'ever closer union' unless it wanted to be; measures for limiting temporarily certain benefits paid to new EU migrants in the UK; the possibility of an 'emergency break' on free movement for EU citizens; and a 'red card' procedure enabling national parliaments to block EU legislative proposals. The proposals, which would come into effect only if there was a 'remain' vote, were concrete but criticised by some as modest.

In a repeat of the 1975 'agreement to differ' it was confirmed that government ministers would be free to oppose the official government position in favour of remain without having to resign. Thus when the referendum date was confirmed for 23 June 2016 five Cabinet ministers announced they would campaign for leave.

Inevitably with a referendum the main forum for debate moved outside Parliament and into the country at large. Indeed, Parliament went into recess for the last week of the campaign. Come 23 June 2016 there was a sense that the arguments had been exhausted. The result and its aftermath is, of course, well known. The leave vote, which most observers did not expect, left many on both sides of the argument asking: what happens next?

Legislating for article 50

At the time of the referendum little was known about the mechanism for leaving the EU; the debate was on the merits of leaving or remaining rather than on processes. It was only in the days following the result that article 50 on the Treaty on European Union became familiar. Many relied on the House of Lords European Union Committee's report on the process of withdrawal, which concluded that triggering article 50 was the only legal route to leave. It was widely assumed that the government would use its prerogative powers to do so; the debate was about when.

However, in autumn 2016 a legal challenge was brought. In summary, the argument went that triggering article 50 would inevitably result in the UK leaving the EU; therefore it would in effect contradict Acts of Parliament (particularly the European Communities Act 1972); and as the royal prerogative could not trump statute it would require a new Act to authorise ministers to deploy article 50. Amid considerable public interest that argument was successful in the High Court and upheld on appeal to the Supreme Court. (Other aspects of the appeal concerning the effect of article 50 on the devolved legislatures, including on the Sewel convention, did not succeed.) Thus the government required an Act before it could begin the formal process of leaving.

It was widely thought that securing such legislation would not be easy. At the start of 2017 the government had a small overall majority in the Commons and was heavily outnumbered in the Lords; and in both chambers the overwhelming majority of members had favoured remain. In the event, though, the European Union (Notification of Withdrawal) Bill 2017 attracted great interest inside and outside Parliament but passed relatively unscathed. In the Commons it was debated for two days on second reading (which is unusual) and had its committee stage, report and third reading over three days. No amendments were passed to the bill.

In the Lords the second reading was also over two days, and attracted the highest number of speakers on record for that stage of a bill: 184. (A record subsequently broken during the second reading of the European Union (Withdrawal) Bill – see page 371.) It too had committee, report and third reading over three days, on an expedited timetable. The House passed two amendments: one requiring the government unilaterally to guarantee the rights of EU citizens currently in the UK; the other to require the approval of both Houses to the final withdrawal agreement between the government and the EU (or, as the case may be, to require both Houses to approve the absence of an agreement). The vote on the latter amendment saw the biggest turnout for a House of Lords division on record: 366 contents and 268 not contents. Liberal Democrat peers, having lost an amendment to require a second referendum, voted against the bill passing in the Lords – a highly unusual move which did not succeed.

Both Lords amendments to the bill were defeated in the Commons by majorities of just under 50 – much more comfortably than the government's then majority of 12. Perhaps because they sensed there was little chance of MPs defeating the government on this bill, the Lords backed down and so did not pursue their amendments through ping-pong. Thus the bill received Royal Assent on 16 March 2017, in time for the Prime Minister to trigger article 50 on 29 March 2017. The government's success in passing the bill was perhaps partly because of the bill's brevity: in two operative sentences it gave the Prime Minister power to deploy article 50, and did nothing else. In part there was also a sense that the battle over Brexit had only really begun and would resume.

Legislating to leave the EU

There is no blueprint for how to leave the European Union. No member state has done it before. (Greenland left in 1985 but as part of Denmark it wasn't a member state, and the EU looked very different then.) One thing that was clear from the beginning, though, is that UK legislation would be needed both to leave and to install whatever future arrangement may be reached between the UK and the EU. So in autumn 2016 the Prime Minister announced that the next session of Parliament would see a 'great repeal bill' introduced to legislate for withdrawal. The bill would also incorporate EU law into UK law in full (so far as possible), thus giving certainty in the short term and allowing that law to be altered by the UK Parliament and government in the longer term. Some parliamentary insiders looked wryly at the proposed 'great repeal bill' name – the short title of a bill is not supposed to be promotional or sloganeering. It was therefore little surprise when, in summer 2017 after the general election, the bill was introduced with the more prosaic short title of the European Union (Withdrawal) Bill.

The bill had three main purposes. First, it repealed the European Communities Act 1972, by which the UK was subject to EU law. Secondly, it transferred the various types of EU law into domestic law. Third, it gave ministers power by secondary legislation to amend transferred EU law and existing UK law in order to make the law work properly and to take account of the terms of the UK's withdrawal.

The bill included broad powers to make secondary legislation, including power to amend Acts of Parliament – known as a Henry VIII power (see Chapter 6). Some thought the powers were more far-reaching than necessary, and could be used by ministers to change the law as they wished with minimal parliamentary involvement. The government was criticised for seeking to return control over lawmaking from Brussels to itself instead of to Parliament. Debate also focused on the bill's proposals for empowering the devolved legislatures. The bill returned powers to ministers in the first instance, with the government saying it intended to agree with the devolved institutions which of those powers would be subsequently devolved. But absent such agreement the government was criticised for a perceived power grab. Another criticism was about the bill not making the EU's Charter of Fundamental Rights part of UK law.

The bill had its second reading in the House of Commons over two days in September 2017. The opposition voted against the second reading but it passed by 326 votes to 290. The bill then had eight days of debate in committee of the whole House. Over 400 amendments and 80 new clauses were tabled, many in the names of Conservative backbenchers. Forty-one divisions took place, of which the government lost only one. That was on an amendment moved by Conservative former Attorney General Dominic Grieve to require an Act of Parliament before the government could use secondary legislation to implement the withdrawal agreement – in effect requiring Parliament to approve the withdrawal agreement. To head off possible defeats the government made other concessions. For example, it undertook to amend the clause on devolution; published a detailed analysis of how the rights in the Charter of Fundamental Rights were recognised in UK law; allowed the date specified in the bill for exiting the EU to be varied if needed; agreed to publish statements on the intended effect of secondary legislation made under the bill; and agreed to create a committee to look at secondary legislation for which the government proposed the negative procedure, to see if they should be subject to the affirmative procedure (the so-called 'sifting committee'). In January 2018 the bill eventually passed the House of Commons, receiving its third reading by 324 votes to 295.

The bill then moved to the Lords, where it had its second reading in February 2018, with a record 190 lords speaking. An amendment which allowed the bill its second reading but regretted that it didn't legislate for a second referendum was tabled but not voted on. The bill proceeded to 11 long days in committee of the whole House. During the six days of report stage and one day of third reading the government was defeated on 15 amendments – a notably high number, if not unprecedented. Amongst the amendments agreed were ones to incorporate the EU Charter of Fundamental Rights into UK law; to limit ministers' discretion in exercising delegated powers under the bill and to subject those powers to greater parliamentary control; to require the government to negotiate to remain a member of the customs union; to require the government to negotiate to remain a member of the European Economic Area; to preserve in UK law EU environmental principles; to remove the exit date of 29 March 2019 from the bill; and to set out a statutory process for Parliament's 'meaningful vote' which may have involved Parliament directing the government on how to negotiate. The House of Lords came in for heavy criticism for the number and significance of the amendments it passed. Many in the House argued that it was simply doing its normal job of scrutinising and revising poorly thought-through legislation, and asking the Commons to think again. Others thought its actions a front for the real agenda of attempting to stifle Brexit, and regardless of that thought this bill different, as it received extensive scrutiny in the Commons – which had previously rejected nearly all of the amendments passed by the Lords – and because the purpose of the bill was to implement a decision taken in a referendum. Proceedings in the Lords were sometimes bad-tempered: one peer was reported to have made an obscene gesture at another across the House, and a longstanding parliamentarian was apparently overheard in the chamber calling a peer from his own party (normally referred to as 'my noble friend') an 'idiot'.

When the bill returned to the Commons in June 2018 the government accepted one of the Lords amendments, made concessions on others and rejected the rest, usually by consistent majorities of 20–25. Perhaps in recognition of the solidity of the Commons majorities against most of the Lords amendments, on ping-pong the Lords returned only one amendment: on the 'meaningful vote'. This was again rejected by the Commons, by a majority of 16, following which the Lords backed down. The European Union (Withdrawal) Act 2018 received Royal Assent on 26 June 2018.

In addition to the withdrawal bill the government proposed legislating for various policy areas which were subject to EU competence. Seven such bills were announced in the 2017 Queen's speech, on: sanctions and anti-money laundering; agriculture; fisheries; nuclear power; immigration; customs and trade. Also the Data Protection Bill was not strictly required by Brexit, but was necessary to maintain alignment with the EU's data protection regime and so enable cooperation post-Brexit. Further legislation will undoubtedly follow.

Brexit and delegated powers

As noted above, one of the controversies about the withdrawal bill was the extent of the powers it gave to ministers and the degree to which Parliament could control those powers. Most observers accepted that significant delegated powers were necessary: the process of leaving would be so complex and potentially fast-moving that it would be impossible to do everything by primary legislation. But, particularly as there was little clarity on how the powers would be used, they were felt to be too wide, resulting in strong criticism from the Lords Delegated Powers and Regulatory Reform Committee and the Constitution Committee. The government expected around 800–1,000 statutory instruments to be needed to implement Brexit – a very large number, but perhaps to be seen in the context of a big decline in the amount of other statutory instruments in recent years. All Brexit statutory instruments would be scrutinised by the Parliamentary Business and Legislation Committee of the Cabinet before they were introduced.

In the Commons the government accepted an amendment moved by the chair of the Procedure Committee to implement that committee's recommendation for greater parliamentary involvement in the secondary legislation. Under the bill the government would, with a few exceptions, decide whether a statutory instrument made under it would be subject to negative or affirmative procedure (see pages 241–2). This replicated a power in the 1972 Act, but aside from that was unusual: normally the primary legislation states definitively what control Parliament will have over its secondary legislation. The amendment allowed for a sifting committee to give its opinion on whether a proposed negative instrument should be made affirmative. The committee would be given 10 sitting days to issue its opinion. Although its advice would not be binding, it was understood that it would normally be followed. A similar system will operate in the House of Lords, with the role carried out by a sub-committee of the Secondary Legislation Scrutiny Committee.

Select committee scrutiny of Brexit

When the Department for Exiting the EU was created by the new Prime Minister in July 2016 a select committee to scrutinise it naturally followed. But the Committee on Exiting the European Union was more than a standard departmental committee scrutinising the department's expenditure, administration and policy. It was the principal committee for scrutinising Brexit.

The committee has 21 members, with the chair elected by the House and other members by their party groups (and formally agreed by the House). The large membership is intended to allow a cross-section of views in the House to be represented (for example, the Liberal Democrats, Plaid Cymru and the Democratic Unionist Party each have a member). But in the past large committees have tended to be less effective. It is harder to get agreement amongst a large group, and members bond less easily. By January 2018 the committee had produced five reports – four on the negotiations and one on the European Union (Withdrawal) Bill – with divisions taking place in the committee on all of them. The committee was the conduit for the publication of the government's sectoral analyses, which collated information about how the existing EU regulatory framework applied to 39 different industrial sectors; a step forced on the government following the humble Address agreed by the House in November 2017 (see page 276).

In the House of Lords no new select committee was necessary. The EU Committee, with its six sub-committees, was already perfectly placed to turn its attention from scrutinising proposed EU legislation to examining the process of withdrawal. The committee initially called for more resources and a change to its terms of reference to carry out this task. Neither followed, but nonetheless it has been remarkably productive. By December 2017, 29 EU Committee reports on Brexit had been published or were in preparation, covering topics such as the options for future trade arrangements, competition law, reciprocal healthcare arrangements and the effect on the Crown Dependencies. Twelve reports on Brexit had been produced by other Lords committees; and Brexit had featured in almost every other select committee report.

Faced with all this committee activity on Brexit in the Lords, it was important to try to avoid duplication or areas falling between the gaps. The Lords Liaison Committee accordingly established an Informal Brexit Liaison Group to coordinate the House's committee scrutiny of Brexit and to keep in touch with Commons committee scrutiny. Its chairman was the Senior Deputy Speaker (Lord McFall of Alcluith) and it comprised the chairmen of all the permanent select committees, plus a Liberal Democrat (because no chairman of a select committee is from that party). The group was informal and had no decision-making powers, but met monthly and published a note of its activities.

Scrutiny of the UK's ongoing membership

The focus of committee and chamber activity has naturally been on the Brexit process. But until the UK's departure it remains a full member of the EU, and even after Brexit may remain subject to some EU laws. In this section we look at how Parliament has scrutinised legislation emerging from Brussels.

The main vehicle for that is two select committees – the European Scrutiny Committee in the Commons and the European Union Committee in the Lords. They examine over 1,000 EU documents each year on behalf of Parliament. For each one, they assess its importance (and seek any additional information or evidence they need in order to form an opinion), report on it and, if necessary, recommend it for debate at Westminster. The Commons committee works quickly, reporting on a large number of documents it judges to be of importance (some 500 each year) and recommending some for debate. Before Brexit the Lords committee reported on many fewer (25 or so each year) but in much greater depth. The two committees operate in rather different ways, complementing each other's work rather than duplicating it.

What is subject to scrutiny?

EU documents subject to the scrutiny process include draft regulations, directives and decisions; Commission green and white papers setting out future policy, including the

Commission work programme; and a range of other papers including proposed actions on foreign affairs and defence and reports of the European Court of Auditors. Any document that is subject to scrutiny must be deposited in Parliament and provided to the committees within two working days of its arrival in the Foreign and Commonwealth Office in London.

The explanatory memorandum

Within 10 working days of deposit, the Whitehall department primarily responsible for the subject matter must submit an *explanatory memorandum* (EM) on the document. The EM contains a range of information on the document, including its legal base, policy implications and likely impact. EMs are an important element of accountability; one is submitted on every document and is signed by the responsible minister as formal evidence to Parliament. The process of producing an EM concentrates minds, both of the civil servants who draft it and the minister who signs it.

Once an EM has been submitted, the two Houses have different ways of dealing with documents.

The European Scrutiny Committee of the House of Commons

This is a select committee of 16 MPs. As well as its main work of scrutinising EU documents, it conducts pre- and post-Council scrutiny, in which ministers involved in particular meetings of the Council explain, usually in writing, their approach to the agenda or the outcome of the meeting and the UK's role in it.

The committee is assisted by the National Parliament Office (NPO) in Brussels, which is staffed by two officials representing the House of Commons and one representing the House of Lords. It acts as the EU committees' 'eyes and ears' in Brussels, gathering intelligence on likely proposals from the Commission, views in European Parliament committees, and so on.

The European Scrutiny Committee meets every Wednesday when the House is sitting, and may consider 40 or more documents at each meeting. In an average year the committee considers about 1,000 documents. It reports on about 500 of them and recommends around 50 debates a year.

The committee must first decide whether it has enough information to make a judgement. A comprehensive EM may be enough; but the committee may ask the government for further written evidence or, occasionally, call a minister to give oral evidence. This dialogue is a crucial part of the scrutiny process and of ministerial accountability. The committee decides whether the document is of political or legal importance. The committee may ask another select committee for a formal opinion on an EU proposal.

If the committee decides that the document is, indeed, of political or legal importance, it will cover it in detail in its report on that week's crop of documents. The committee's weekly reports are in effect a critical commentary on the EU agenda and a useful source of analysis and information for anyone monitoring developments in the EU.

Since the referendum the committee has examined EU proposals with a view to the UK's withdrawal. For example, at a meeting in January 2018 the committee identified an EU decision on cross-border energy projects as an example of UK-relevant legislation which could be negotiated and adopted during a post-Brexit implementation period. It held a document on the .eu domain name under scrutiny, asking the minister to clarify whether workarounds exist which might enable the 340,000 UK-based users of the domain name to continue to use them after Brexit.

Debates

The committee decides whether a document should be debated. It can choose to recommend a debate in one of the three *European committees*, each scrutinising documents in different policy areas. The membership of these committees is appointed afresh for the debate on each document. Any MP can attend and speak (although not vote).

A European committee is a combination of questions and debate. The meeting begins with a brief statement by a member of the European Scrutiny Committee, explaining why the document was referred for debate, following which a minister makes an opening statement. There is then up to an hour of questions to the minister (extendable to an hour-and-a-half), followed by debate on a motion. The committee lasts for a maximum of two-and-a-half hours. The motion is moved by the minister (amendments may be tabled and voted on), and usually formally takes note of the documents with some words supportive of the line the government is taking. European committees can be a testing time for a minister; in addition to the normal debate format, he or she normally has to answer questions alone and without notice. Attendances at European committees are not high, however, and many finish short of their allotted time.

After the committee proceedings the government puts down a motion in the House, which may be the same as the motion agreed to in the European committee (even if that was defeated) or may be an entirely new motion. That motion is taken without further debate, but it may be voted on.

On the most important documents, the European Scrutiny Committee can recommend that a debate should take place on the floor of the House; but it is up to the government to agree to such a recommendation, and it has not always done so. However, if the Scrutiny Committee has recommended a debate, it must take place, in a European committee if not in the chamber. The precise timing is up to the government, but ministers will usually want the debate to take place soon so that they can get 'scrutiny clearance'.

The European Union Committee of the House of Lords

The House of Lords established its Select Committee on the European Communities in 1974. Renamed the European Union Committee in 1999, it scrutinises the government's policies and actions in respect of the EU, focusing now on the Brexit process. Alongside this scrutiny of the government the committee continues to consider the development of EU legislation. It receives the same documents and explanatory memoranda as the Commons committee, but has established a markedly different scrutiny system, in the form of its chairman's sift and the establishment of sub-committees. Each year about one-third of the 1,000 EU documents deposited by the government are referred ('sifted') by the chairman for more detailed consideration by sub-committees. The committee draws the attention of the House to Commission proposals or other documents that raise issues of policy or principle with a recommendation as to whether or not a debate is desirable.

The committee has 19 members and six sub-committees that are divided into broad policy areas: economic and financial affairs; the internal market, infrastructure and employment; EU external affairs; agriculture, fisheries, environment and energy; justice, institutions and consumer protection; and home affairs, health and education. There is a total working membership (including co-opted members) of about 70 lords. The sub-committees consider whatever documents are 'sifted' to them by the chairman of the committee (many are deemed not to require scrutiny and so are not 'sifted'), as well as conducting free-standing inquiries leading to reports.

Some reports of the committee are made for information only, and some for debate. Whether a report is debated or not, it is replied to in writing by the government within two months of publication. However, a substantial number of other documents are considered in detail by way of correspondence with the relevant minister. These exchanges are published on the parliamentary website.

The reports and correspondence are useful as a source of both information and informed opinion. Although their target is, theoretically, the House and, through the House, the government minister and government policies, the Lords reports, as those of the Commons committee, also have a wider market in the EU institutions, including the European Parliament itself and other national parliaments of the EU engaged in the scrutiny process.

Scrutiny clearance and the scrutiny reserve

The 1998 *scrutiny reserve resolution* of the House of Commons, and the 2010 Lords equivalent, constrain ministers from giving agreement in Council to an EU proposal that has not 'cleared scrutiny'. *Clearance* in the Commons means *either* that the European Scrutiny Committee has reported on it but has not recommended debate, *or* that the committee has recommended debate, the debate has taken place and the House has expressed a view on the proposal. In the House of Lords *clearance* means *either* that the chairman of the European Union Committee has cleared the proposal at the weekly sift; *or* that the committee or one of its sub-committees has reviewed the document in more detail and decided to clear it from scrutiny, following correspondence, an inquiry or a debate in the House. A minister may give agreement to an uncleared proposal, but only with the committees' agreement in both Houses, or if the minister believes there are 'special reasons' for agreeing – such as urgency, or if UK interests might otherwise be damaged – in which case the minister must provide an explanation or be called in to explain in person.

The Amsterdam Treaty included a protocol on the role of national parliaments that requires a six-week period of notice before the Council decides on a piece of legislation (now eight weeks); but late changes to proposals often mean that this requirement is circumvented.

Further powers for national parliaments were in the Lisbon Treaty. It gave them a specific role in monitoring whether EU proposals comply with the principle of subsidiarity (that is, whether action at EU rather than national level is necessary). Any national parliament or any chamber of a national parliament may send a reasoned opinion to the Council, Commission and European Parliament stating why it considers that a proposal does not comply with the principle. Bicameral parliaments have one vote per chamber; unicameral parliaments two. Where reasoned opinions on the same proposal received within eight weeks amount to at least one-third of all the votes allocated to national parliaments – one-quarter for proposals in the area of freedom, security and justice – a 'yellow card' is said to have been played, and the Commission has to review its proposal and give a reasoned decision. There is also provision for an 'orange card', with a more stringent review requirement on the Commission, if reasoned opinions are issued in respect of more than half of the allocated votes. If either the Commons or Lords committees decide that a proposal infringes the subsidiarity principle, they recommend a text and the respective House debates a motion on whether or not to issue a reasoned opinion (in the Commons, the debate may take place in a European committee, although the motion then must be approved – without debate – on the floor of the House). This procedure was used several times after it started in 2009, but since the Brexit referendum attention has shifted elsewhere. In addition, national parliaments can challenge EU legislation before the Court of Justice for non-compliance with the principle of subsidiarity.

Other international relations

We should also note the involvement of UK MPs and Lords (and staff of both Houses) in a number of international assemblies. The *Parliamentary Assembly of the Council of Europe*, based in Strasbourg, was established in 1949 as the parliamentary organ of the Council of Europe, in some ways a forerunner of the EU. The Council of Europe has had an important role in a range of social and cultural issues, but especially in human rights matters. It consists of 648 members drawn from the national parliaments of 47 countries (the British delegation has 36 members drawn from both Houses), and in recent years it has acted as a 'waiting room' for the new democracies of Eastern Europe that have become candidates for membership of the EU.

The *NATO Parliamentary Assembly* brings together 266 parliamentarians from the 29 NATO countries. It is based in Brussels but holds its sessions by turn in member countries. The *Parliamentary Assembly of the Organisation for Security and Cooperation in Europe (OSCE)*, based in Copenhagen, was set up in 1991. It consists of

323 delegates from the 57 OSCE participating states. The *British–Irish Parliamentary Assembly* comprises parliamentarians from Westminster, Dublin, and the devolved parliaments and assemblies.

The UK branches of the *Inter-Parliamentary Union* (*IPU*) and the *Commonwealth Parliamentary Association* (*CPA*) are based at Westminster. Although they are not part of the parliamentary administration, they are funded by annual grants from the two Houses. The IPU represents parliaments worldwide; the CPA those within the Commonwealth. Both aim to increase international cooperation and understanding, and they play a considerable diplomatic role: for example, the first formal contact between the United Kingdom and Argentina after the Falklands war was between parliamentarians of the two countries under the auspices of the IPU, and the IPU-organised visit to the UK by Mikhail Gorbachev just before he became leader of the USSR proved hugely significant.

The Overseas Offices of the two Houses also organise a large number of inward visits of officials and members of overseas parliaments, particularly Commonwealth parliaments, to Westminster. And there is increasing demand for staff and members to participate in parliamentary strengthening programmes in the parliaments of new and emerging democracies. These contacts are greatly valued and reflect the wider world beyond the frontiers of the European Union, whose parliaments were in many cases modelled on Westminster principles.

Brexit and the future

It has quickly become a cliché that only a fool now makes political predictions. The Brexit process is fast-moving and uncertain. Political passions run high, and all sorts of outcomes are possible. Nonetheless there are a few parliamentary aspects of the process which are reasonably foreseeable, which we explore here.

First, further legislation to implement Brexit is required. The government has undertaken to introduce a bill to legislate for the withdrawal and implementation agreement. It is likely that this will cover the withdrawal agreement reached between the EU and the UK in December 2017, and, assuming it is agreed, begin a two-year implementation period from 2019 to 2021 during which the UK would largely retain EU rules. Any substantive deal on the future relationship between the UK and the EU will almost certainly require extra legislation. So there is plenty of scope for further parliamentary involvement in the process. As proceedings on the EU (Withdrawal) Bill showed, that will create many opportunities for the government's Brexit plans to be closely scrutinised and amended.

Second, the government has already conceded that the agreements reached with the EU on Brexit are likely formally to be treaties. This means they will be subject to the parliamentary scrutiny process for treaties set out in the Constitutional Reform and Governance Act 2010. In summary, this allows the House of Commons to veto ratification of a treaty and the House of Lords potentially to delay it. In both instances the government can try again, but it seems unlikely that the Commons would refuse ratification in the first instance then later decide it is happy with the same treaty. The Act's scrutiny provisions have yet to be used, so it may be that they are tested for the first time when the stakes are at their highest.

Third, at some point the workloads of the House of Commons European Scrutiny Committee and Exiting the European Union Committee, and that of the House of Lords European Union Committee, will dry up. This may not make a great difference in the House of Commons – select committees occasionally come and go and to some extent the new sifting committee (see page 372) will be the European Scrutiny Committee's natural successor – but in the Lords it will drastically change the committee structure. The EU Committee and its six sub-committees make up just under half of the House's committee activity, occupying 74 members of the House. Committee work is popular among members. While there may be some work in scrutinising the UK's future relationship with the EU, it surely won't be enough for one select committee and six sub-committees. So either the Lords' committee output will be significantly reduced or – more likely – new committees will be created in other policy areas.

Fourth, some parliamentary procedures will cease to exist. There will be no need for European committees to debate EU documents referred to them by the European Scrutiny Committee. There will be no prime ministerial statements after quarterly European Council meetings. There will be no procedures for issuing 'yellow' or 'orange cards' under the Lisbon Treaty for non-compliance with the EU principle of subsidiarity, and no debates on Justice and Home Affairs opt-ins. Bills required under the EU Act 2011 to implement certain EU agreements will cease. Individually none of these will make a great difference, but collectively they show how the daily diet of parliamentary business will alter.

Fifth, the content and amount of legislation will change. The large number of statutory instruments to implement Brexit (see above) may in time be offset by a reduction in the number of statutory instruments required to implement (or 'transpose') EU directives. EU regulations will no longer have 'direct effect' – i.e. operate in UK law without further ado. The powers ('competences') that the EU has in a range of areas – exclusively in some cases; shared with member states in others – will be exercisable solely by the UK Parliament and ministers (and their devolved counterparts). It is possible that this will result in an increase in the amount of legislation coming before Parliament. If so, procedures may have to adapt to cope with the increase.

The above are some of the changes at Westminster which we can at present foresee. We can expect a host of others which cannot be anticipated. The business of Parliament in, say, 2023 may look very different from how it does now. If the Brexit process has proved one thing it is to expect the unexpected.

12

The future of Parliament

Modernisation, reform and effectiveness

Many people would say, usually without thinking, that Parliament needs 'modernisation' or 'reform'. But these are words to be used with care. To the person speaking, they really mean no more than 'change of which I approve'. After all, the 'Balfour reforms' of more than a century ago, which entrenched the government's control over the business and time of the House of Commons, were hardly a milestone in the democratic accountability of the executive. And in the present debate over the role of Parliament, 'modernisation' and 'reform' mean different things to different people.

It is much better to focus on the concept of 'effectiveness'. The traditional roles of Parliament include representing constituents, legislating, authorising taxation and spending, calling government to account, and acting as a forum for the testing of beliefs and opinions and a focus for national feeling. What do we expect Parliament to do for us, and how could it do those tasks more effectively?

Before we look in detail at some of the issues, it is worth establishing a sense of proportion. First, criticising parliaments and parliamentarians is a national sport – all over the world, as well as in the UK. It is also a strange irony that, even though most democratic rights have been purchased with blood, they often seem to be little valued by those who live in democracies. 'Oh, I don't vote', you hear people say, 'I don't know anything about politics, and I'm really not interested'. Yet the stuff of politics, and the business of Parliament, affects every aspect of our everyday lives: peace and war, the education of our children, the safety of our streets, the quality of the air we breathe, our civil liberties. This lack of interest may be a symptom of the disconnection between people and Parliament, but it is also the case that, however Parliament changes, there will always be a significant number of people who 'don't want to know'. This should be taken seriously, but there are no easy answers. The really frustrating thing is that, as we have seen in this book, Parliament is more independent-minded, vibrant and capable than it has been for decades; but this is not itself a guarantee of re-engagement with those it serves.

A reality check

Any proposal for changing the way Parliament – and particularly the House of Commons – works has to take into account the political and constitutional constraints. Here are ten practical factors:

- Some criticisms imply that Parliament should somehow simply stop the government doing things that are misguided or unpopular. As long as the UK has a constitutional system in which the government is *in* Parliament, *the executive is always going to get its way eventually, provided that it has a majority in the House of Commons and can persuade its backbenchers to support it issue by issue.*
- *Parliamentary politics is party politics.* Like it or not, free elections involve a clash of party policies and ideologies, and in any elected House – at Westminster or elsewhere – party discipline will always be a powerful factor.
- *Parliament is by its nature reactive.* It responds to events, to public opinion and constituency pressures, and to the proposals and actions of governments. There are relatively few genuinely parliamentary initiatives: at Westminster, the main ones are private members' bills (though even some of these are government handout bills), policy proposals made by select committees and expressions of view as a result of debates initiated by backbenchers.
- *A wholly fresh start is impossible.* Some think that the restoration and renewal programme should be used to site a new Parliament situated outside Westminster somewhere in the centre of England, breaking the ties with London and shrugging off the burdens of history and tradition. But the executive arm of government would have to move as well, and it is difficult to see much enthusiasm for the establishment of a new administrative capital. Indeed, this option was firmly ruled out by the Joint Committee on Restoration and Renewal. However, as we shall see, the restoration and renewal of the Palace of Westminster may challenge how the two Houses operate.
- *Parliament means different things to different people.* There are many who yearn for a measured, consensual approach to parliamentary politics. But there are also those who revel in the party battle, and see Parliament as an adversarial institution. There is no reason why both cannot be accommodated; but one certainty is that there is no general agreement on *how* Parliament should change.
- *Parliament is not executive.* It approves principles (and, in the case of legislation, detailed instructions) about what is to be done; but it is the government of the day that is responsible for the business and administration of the state and is answerable to Parliament and the electorate.
- *Parliament is an organism rather than an organisation.* It is made up of individual members, often unpredictable, who react to a range of influences but who also have their own views. This means that the law of unintended consequences is a powerful factor in parliamentary reform; it is easy to set out detailed procedural prescriptions but difficult to predict what effect they will have, or how they will be used.

- *Politicians – not just MPs and Lords – but those involved in party and political organisations, and those in a position to bring pressure on them, must see the need for change and support it.* Theorists can propose wonderful schemes for parliamentary reform but, unless they get traction among those who will make things happen, those schemes will be dead in the water. A good example is the history of proposals for House of Lords reform. As we'll see below, even where there is a consensus that the status quo is inadequate it is much harder to agree on how it should change.
- *A constraining factor on all change within Parliament is parliamentarians themselves.* It is pointless to propose new systems of select committees or legislative scrutiny if parliamentarians do not have the time and commitment to devote to making them work. This is especially true in the Commons, where the multiplicity of pressures on an MP may mean that new tasks must displace existing commitments if they are to be done at all.
- Perhaps most important, *Parliament – and especially the House of Commons – cannot easily change itself.* It is the government of the day which largely controls the business. Parliament's interests and those of the government are often at odds; change may come about because of wider political pressure, but it has usually depended on there being something in it for the government, as well as for Parliament. The ability of backbenchers to initiate debate and decision through the Backbench Business Committee has loosened that control, but has not yet altered the centre of gravity.

We now look at the issues as they affect each House.

The House of Commons

The credit side

We need to avoid the 'pre-emptive cringe' – a default setting of apology; the fact is that the Westminster Parliament does many things rather well, and some things better than many other parliaments. This is not an argument for complacency, but for valuing what we have. Westminster is well-regarded by people in the same business, as shown by the constant stream of visiting Speakers, members, committees and senior officials from overseas – from parliaments of all types, not only those in the Commonwealth that use the 'Westminster model'.

Over the last decade or so there have been significant changes in the procedures of the House of Commons, with the pace of change if anything accelerating. And that is before we have left the EU, with all the change to parliamentary processes that is likely to bring.

No survey of the last decade could ignore the savage blow dealt to the reputation of Parliament by the expenses scandal of 2009. However, as we have emphasised, since then the Commons has actively renewed itself, helped by large intakes of new, often younger and more diverse MPs after the 2010, 2015 and 2017 general elections.

We now look at the changes that have recently taken place, the underlying strengths of the institution, and areas of possible future change.

Changes in the Commons

- The Parliamentary Standards Act 2009 created the Independent Parliamentary Standards Authority, entirely separate from the House of Commons, and gave it the task of devising a scheme for MPs' allowances and for determining claims (extended by the Constitutional Reform and Governance Act 2010, see page 69 and below).
- The Joint Committee on the National Security Strategy was established, January 2010.
- Deputy Speakers were elected for the first time (rather than appointed), May 2010.
- The Constitutional Reform and Governance Act 2010 provided for IPSA to be given responsibility for determining MPs' pay and pensions; responsibility for pay was transferred in May 2011 and for pensions in October 2011.
- Election of select committee chairs and members was introduced, June 2010.
- The Backbench Business Committee was created and backbench time allocated in the Chamber and in Westminster Hall, June 2010.
- The Fixed-term Parliaments Act received Royal Assent, September 2011.
- The Committee of Privileges and the Committee on Standards were created from the former Committee on Standards and Privileges; lay members were added to the Committee on Standards, March 2012 with their number increased in 2015.
- Changes were implemented to sitting hours: House sits at 11.30 am on Tuesdays and 9.30 am on Thursdays, July 2012.
- Speaker's Commission on Digital Democracy was established, November 2013.
- Select committee statements were introduced (a statement in the chamber by the chair of a committee about a just-published select committee report, followed by questions), December 2013.
- The notice period for amendments at report stage in the chamber was increased from two days to three, initially on an experimental basis, June 2014.
- Changes to the governance of the House were introduced, including a clearer strategic role for the House of Commons Commission and the introduction of a Director General post, reporting to the Clerk of the House, January 2015.
- Recall of MPs Act was agreed, March 2015.
- Women and Equalities Committee was established, filling a gap in previous scrutiny mechanisms, June 2015.
- A new system of e-petitions was introduced and the Petitions Committee established, with powers to schedule debates on petitions, require responses from the government and inquire into subjects raised by petitions, July 2015.
- English votes for English laws procedures were introduced, October 2015.
- Relaxation of dress code implemented in the chamber, with male MPs no longer required to wear ties, June 2017.

Some changes did not survive: topical debates (introduced in 2007) were not a great success and were, in any event, overtaken by opportunities for backbench business in the 2010 Parliament. The publication by the government of a draft legislative programme in 2007 did not last long and seems unlikely to reappear. Regional committees, to scrutinise public services in the eight English administrative regions outside London, were set up in 2008, as a number of ministers were given regional responsibilities; but they were not a success and did not make it into the next Parliament.

Present strengths

The *close relationship with constituencies* means that Westminster MPs put considerable effort into an ancient function of the House of Commons: representing constituents, and getting their voices heard by ministers who are often seen as remote and inaccessible. Success in solving constituents' problems depends on the tenacity of the MP and the strength of the case, but the 'satisfaction factor' of constituency cases was rated highly by MPs in a recent survey, and this aspect of MPs' work generally gets a good rating from the public.

Select committees are a key part of the work of the Commons. The system is flexible and comprehensive; it encourages independence of view among committee members; it produces well-researched and well-written reports; as well as exposing a wide range of government activity to scrutiny, it publishes a great deal of official information that would not otherwise be in the public domain; and, perhaps most important, it provides public access to the political process. The election of chairs and members of most select committees since 2010 has increased the authority and independence of the system, and innovations in scrutiny techniques and engagement with the public continue.

Parliament attracts and retains high-quality staff; and its work is supported by committed and expert people who are highly regarded by their equivalents in parliaments worldwide. Other parliaments, when faced with a problem, often want to know 'How does Westminster tackle this?'

Parliamentary questions, used on a larger scale than in any other parliament, have their critics but are an important means of requiring governments to put information on the public record and, in the hands of a determined MP, they can be remarkably effective.

The House of Commons is *a natural focus of attention on historic occasions. It is the forum of the nation.* In 2013, it was a forum for tributes to Nelson Mandela and Margaret Thatcher, and more happily in the previous year for celebration of the Queen's 60 years on the throne. It now has the decisive say over decisions to use armed force. Since the 2016 EU referendum it has undoubtedly been the forum in which major decisions on Brexit stand or fall.

Finally, we should not forget the more informal role that the House of Commons fulfils. It is *a place where opinions are exchanged and formed and laid open to the scrutiny of the media and the public*; where pressure groups and campaigners, as well as industries, the professions and a range of other players, put their case or seek a higher profile for their cause.

What next?

We now look at possibilities for the future. This is necessarily a highly selective list and many other proposals for change are considered in the relevant chapters.

Engagement and reconnection

Everyone agrees that Parliament needs to engage better with the people it serves, and to 'reconnect with the public', in the hope that this will raise levels of participation in the democratic process. However, there is no agreement on how to achieve this, beyond a general acknowledgement of the difficulty of making progress and the number of factors involved, which include:

The reputation of Parliament and its members

The foreword to the July 2013 determination of MPs' pay by the Independent Parliamentary Standards Authority (never a soft touch) said of MPs:

> *The importance of the job of an MP should be recognised, something which is all too often overlooked. These are the 650 people we have chosen to represent us. They sit at the pinnacle of our democracy. This is a fact that we ought to record and respect.*

Brave words; but despite the impressive turnaround and change of culture since 2010, there is still work to do. Recent allegations of harassment and bullying by MPs, which followed allegations against Harvey Weinstein and other high-profile figures in the entertainment industry, have further damaged reputations. Unlike the expenses row, it seems likely that only a very small number of MPs are embroiled (although even a small number can cause huge damage to the esteem in which the House and MPs are held) and reforms have been instigated by a working group chaired by the Leader of the House to establish practices which reduce the chances of such behaviour being repeated.

Ease and attraction of voting

Many possible changes have been suggested: *mobile polling stations*, so that people can get to them more easily; *voting on a Sunday* (as in France), as this is the day on which most people can get to the polls; *holding several types of election on the same day*, as has been done for the European Parliament, local and Greater London Assembly elections; *making voting compulsory*, which is superficially attractive but which presents real practical problems and seems unlikely to make much of a difference; *reducing the voting age from 18 to 16*, as was done for the referendum on Scottish independence, and which is Labour and Liberal Democrat policy. *A change in the basis of political party funding* is sometimes canvassed, but agreement on this seems as far away as ever.

All of these ideas have their pros and cons, but in the absence of a dramatic turn of events the lesson from the 2011 referendum to replace first-past-the-post with the alternative vote (which was defeated by 68 per cent to 32 per cent, on a 42 per cent turnout) seems to be that there is little public appetite for great electoral changes. Moreover, the high turnouts in the 2014 Scottish independence referendum, the 2015 general election, the 2016 EU referendum and the 2017 general election perhaps show that electors make the effort to vote when they feel there is much at stake; and so it is not necessarily structures which account for low turnout or political disengagement generally.

Digital democracy

The increase in the use of the internet, and the extraordinary growth in social media, has meant that these are seen as ways of revitalising democracy. Provided that security issues can be dealt with, the possibilities are unlimited. The Speaker's Commission on Digital Democracy made recommendations about the use of new technology. The e-petitions system is a notable success here. But one constraining factor will still be the *digital divide*. The 2015 House of Lords Digital Skills Committee found that around 20 per cent of the population (9.5 million people) lacked basic digital skills, with high proportions of those who are disabled or over 75, and of those with no formal qualifications or who are in social housing. It is obviously important that the use of new technologies does not create new communities of the disenfranchised.

Referendums

No one needs reminding of the potential significance of referendums in our political system. Most democracies use referendums from time to time. In some systems (Switzerland and California, for example) the result has the force of law; but elsewhere, as has mostly happened in the United Kingdom, the result is advisory only (although a government may pledge to abide by the result).

Referendums used to be very infrequent in the UK, but their use has become common in recent decades. The first was in 1973, in Northern Ireland on the province's constitutional future. Then in 1975 there was a UK-wide referendum on continued membership of the EEC. They were used twice, in 1979 and 1997, on proposals for devolution to Scotland and Wales, and again in Wales in 2011 on further devolution of powers. There have been numerous local referendums on proposals for elected mayors, and in 2004 on the setting up of a regional assembly for North-East England. In 2011 there was a national referendum on a change to the electoral system and, in 2014, a referendum on Scottish independence. Plenty of other referendums have been promised or legislated for: had Tony Blair's Labour government recommended joining the euro a referendum would have been held; Tony Blair also promised one on the aborted EU constitution in 2005; the EU Act 2011 stipulated that referendums were required before certain powers were passed from the UK to the EU; and the Localism Act 2011 requires a referendum if a local authority wishes to raise council tax above a set level. Most significantly, of course, in 2016 there was a referendum on the United Kingdom's membership of the European Union.

There are several disadvantages of referendums as a way of supplementing conventional democratic decision-making in the UK. They are normally advisory; in practice they are held only at the government's initiative (and legislation is needed to authorise each referendum). The UK, without a written constitution, has no clear guidance about when referendums should be used; if, say, they should be used on constitutional issues, who decides what a constitutional issue is?

If a referendum is held, what is a valid result? Should a minimum percentage of the electorate vote in favour, or should the requirement be an absolute majority, regardless of turnout? As is evident with the 2016 EU referendum, a close result will not settle the issue in many people's minds. And what should be the question asked? The Political Parties, Elections and Referendums Act 2000 provides that the government should consult the Electoral Commission on the 'intelligibility' of the question, but the final decision is still for ministers. The question asked in the 2014 Scottish independence referendum was criticised for being loaded – 'Should Scotland be an independent country?' – with the 'Yes' side having a naturally more positive ring to it. Mainly because of that criticism the 2016 EU referendum question did not seek a 'yes' or 'no' answer, but instead 'remain' or 'leave'.

However deftly the question may be phrased, what is to prevent the referendum becoming a vote of confidence on the government of the day? Though the 2016 referendum was on the distinct issue of EU membership, it is telling that David Cameron felt he had to resign when he lost.

For many the main objection to referendums is that they are a simplistic device to answer what may be a complicated question. Linked to that, they are thought by some to undermine the concept of representative democracy, where we elect MPs to take decisions on our behalf, holding them to account at the next election for the decisions they have taken.

Whatever individual views on the outcome of the 2016 EU referendum, no one could say that it was not hard-fought or momentous. The flipside is that it was divisive, even bitter. A mechanism to attempt to settle the issue of EU membership once and for all has only opened it right up. Partly for that reason, many who previously advocated greater use of referendums have now questioned their wisdom. But there is a sense of the genie being out of the bottle. In an age which calls for ever greater public involvement in the country's governance, where people have access to more information than ever before, it is hard to see the plebiscite disappearing as a tool for decision-making on major constitutional issues.

A House Business Committee

A committee 'to assemble a draft agenda to put to the House in a weekly motion' was recommended by the Wright Committee on reform of the House and the proposition was endorsed by the House in 2010. In the Coalition Agreement, the government undertook to establish a House Business Committee to consider government business (the establishment of a Backbench Business Committee had already been agreed) 'by the end of the third year of the Parliament' – i.e. by 2014. No further progress was made; the government's stance in the 2010–15 parliament was that there was insufficient agreement on how such a committee might operate, and there was no mention of the idea in the 2015 or 2017 Conservative manifestos. Certainly, a House Business Committee means different things to different people. Would it be 'the usual channels' continuing to meet in private but reporting their conclusions formally? Would it be a committee sitting in public, but largely representing the usual channels? Or would it be the full-strength Wright option of a committee with a broad membership proposing a draft agenda to be voted on (and possibly amended) by the House each week? The last option would bring transparency to the way that the House's business is organised, but it is unlikely to be attractive to any government, as it would considerably reduce its control of the Commons Order Paper. Thus the idea now seems firmly off the agenda.

A fixed calendar?

The introduction of a calendar of sitting dates a year or so ahead, instead of the notice period being a matter of only a few weeks, made a profound difference to the organisation of Commons business, and to the way in which its members could plan their lives. More radical change is sometimes suggested: that there should be fixed sitting and recess times every year; and that there should be a day a week on which the chamber did not sit, in order to create a day for committee activity (although further concentrating committee activity would have serious implications for the availability of committee rooms and other resources). Interestingly, the Scottish Parliament may be moving in the opposite direction, away from set committee and chamber days. Early change at Westminster on this issue seems unlikely; more likely is that the House will continue to tinker with its sitting times for each day of the week.

Restoration and renewal: the effect of moving out

As we saw in Chapter 1, one of the biggest challenges for Parliament will be securing the Palace of Westminster for future generations, and dealing with the deteriorating services of the building. A complete decant of the whole palace for five or six years – the option supported by both Houses in early 2018 – could have a profound effect on Westminster. If the Houses were to get used to sitting in chambers of a different shape and size, what changes in atmosphere and ways of doing business might follow? Many changes will occur organically, but for some a decant should be used for a radical shake up of procedure and practice. Two linked points follow. First, many of those concerned about the implications of a decant will fear it being used as a 'Trojan horse' for dramatic changes which are not strictly consequential on a decant. Secondly, few procedures rely on the physical environs. A change from division lobbies is an obvious example, but many other mooted changes could – if well-argued and attracting a consensus – be made regardless of the decision on a decant.

It would, though, create opportunities for other changes. There will be a powerful case for taking advantage of the disruption and massive expenditure, and not merely

Maintenance of the parliamentary estate, 2017

Source: Copyright House of Commons, 2017. Photography by Mark Duffy

replacing like with like. The possibility of glassing over internal courtyards, and of using space more innovatively, perhaps re-thinking access and visitor routes to transform the visitor experience, will be a huge challenge to both Houses and the ways they and their members work. The cost of any of the options for restoration and renewal are eye-watering; that factor, the scale of the work required and the attachment parliamentarians have to the Palace, mean that, despite both Houses expressing support for the full decant option, actually delivering restoration and renewal will be a formidable challenge.

Legislation: public bills

This is of course a core function of any parliament, and in Chapter 6 we surveyed the Westminster system and some of its strains and inadequacies. A bill needs to be well thought out, properly consulted on, drafted to a high technical standard, challenged as to principles and scrutinised as to detail. This is easier said than done.

There are many ways in which the legislative process could be improved, but there will always be tensions between the opportunities for scrutiny and challenge, and the pressures of the government's legislative programme. The extent to which MPs (for it is in the Commons that the shoe pinches) are willing to devote time to legislative scrutiny and, if they sit on the government side of the House, to challenge the administration they support, are also factors.

Draft bills can make a real difference. Ministers have less political capital invested in them, and consideration by a select or joint committee offers the possibility of real, evidence-based scrutiny and improvement. However, draft bills place extra demands on scarce expert drafting resources and, because of the lead time involved, are less attractive to governments in the first session of a parliament (especially when there has been a change of government, and the new administration wants to press ahead with its legislation). Moreover, there are large categories of bills which will almost never be suitable for publication in draft – for example, most financial bills and bills responding to emergencies.

More bills could be *committed to select committees after second reading* for the same degree of evidence-based scrutiny, but in this case the opportunity of formal amendments would also arise. These would have to be overturned at report stage if the government did not wish to accept them.

Much has been made of a possible *public reading stage*, where those outside parliament could make representations on bills. But it is difficult to see what more this could provide than is already available through the evidence-taking stage of public bill committees (see page 197), so the experiments on three bills in the 2010–15 parliament have not been repeated.

There is scope for tackling the principle of a bill in a different way. In the nineteenth century, it was routine for a bill to be formally introduced only after approval of a *motion to bring in a bill* (a procedure that survives today with ten-minute rule bills). There might be advantages in seeking approval for the essence of a legislative proposal, and for its aims, before embarking on scrutiny of a major bill. Another approach might be *committal to a select committee as to the principle of a bill*, immediately after a bill had been introduced, in order to inform second reading.

There are many other possibilities for improvement, including: *applying the public bill committee procedure to all bills*, not just those starting in the Commons; *more split committals*, where big issues can be dealt with in Committee of the whole House, and details in public bill committee; *much tougher Speaker's selection* (see page 207) *on report*, to limit debate to the big political issues and genuinely new material, rather than revisiting much of what took place in committee; *use of purposive clauses in the body of a bill*, stating what that particular part of the bill aims to achieve; and universal *use of so-called 'Keeling Schedules'*, so that whenever a bill proposes to amend an existing statute, *the text of that statute as proposed to be amended is set out*, rather than the reader having to navigate amendments to other acts. Some time on the floor of the House might be saved by reverting to the practice that *a debate on third reading would take place only if a motion to that effect were tabled*, on the basis that third reading debates have become formulaic and add little to the scrutiny of legislation.

Perhaps we should think more radically about the scrutiny of legislation. How well are parliamentarians equipped for analysis, as opposed to advocacy? Should they concentrate on principles and aims rather than the detailed provisions? Might an independent commission on the quality of legislation be better equipped to deal with details and report to Parliament on how well a bill implemented the political aims that had been approved?

And Parliament also needs to meet the challenge of 'guidance'. We are used to thinking of legislation as a hierarchy: primary, and then descending categories of secondary legislation (omitting the EU dimension). But, today, people's lives are in practical terms often affected more by guidance that has no statutory basis than they are by what is laid down in Acts of Parliament. To take one example: primary legislation sets out, in broad terms, a health and safety regime. Statutory instruments fill in the detail. But it is guidance, usually at local authority level, that determines how the health and safety regime will impact on the individual. If you are running a restaurant, local authority guidance on how many washbasins you should have, of what sort, and how often they will be inspected, is what affects you, and possibly your profit or loss, too.

Delegated legislation

In Chapter 6 we considered the extraordinary volume of statutory instruments and other delegated legislation, and the difficulty of scrutinising them in any meaningful way. The House of Lords has, through its Secondary Legislation Scrutiny Committee, tackled this more effectively than the Commons. It may be time to take a parliament-wide approach to delegated legislation, pooling expert staff to support a joint committee to scrutinise delegated legislation – if necessary, also working through single-House sub-committees to reflect the different political cultures and approach of each House. The Joint Committee on Statutory Instruments could be subsumed in such a body; that committee has expert resources but undertakes narrow technical work (see page 328).

Certainly, longer time needs to be allowed for scrutiny; an increase in 'praying time' from 40 days to 60 has been recommended (see page 241), as has a rule that no affirmative instrument should be put forward for approval until it has received committee scrutiny and has been reported on. There are also calls for Parliament to be able to amend delegated legislation, and not simply accept or reject it.

Private legislation

Although the number of private bills fell dramatically as a result of the Transport and Works Act 1992, this is still something of a parliamentary backwater, really understood only by a few practitioners. Some updating has occurred following the High-Speed 2 Rail Bill, but a fundamental review of private legislation may be overdue. It would need to be carried out by a joint committee, as the interests of both Houses are equally affected.

Parliamentary Questions

Written PQs

In the right hands, these can be a very effective way of calling ministers to account. Too many are tabled, either because they are an easy way of demonstrating activity, or because they are a short cut through the work that MPs and their staff should be doing. They are still dogged by the impression that many written PQs are tabled by MPs' staff without the MP concerned knowing much about it. Together with the sheer numbers tabled and, crucially, the reduction in resources in government departments, which reduces their ability to give timely and detailed answers to PQs, these factors have blunted the effectiveness of written PQs. However, there is no readiness among MPs to have this parliamentary opportunity curtailed or more effectively rationed.

Oral PQs

As we saw in Chapter 9, these have largely lost their inquisitorial character; but, in the right hands, they offer the opportunity to put ministers on the spot. Reintroducing the rule against reading supplementaries or quoting (see page 301) would sharpen Question Time up.

As topical questions (see page 304) have proved effective, now might be the time to turn the whole of Question Time into topicals. MPs would still be able to table substantive oral questions if they wanted to ensure that ministers could not plead lack of notice in giving vague or temporising answers.

Prime Minister's Questions

This is the highest profile event of the parliamentary week, and one which has its passionate supporters and detractors. As we saw in Chapter 9 (page 305), it is not an inquisitorial occasion; no one much expects the Prime Minister to give new information against her will. Almost every new leader of the opposition says they want to move away from the 'Punch and Judy' character of Prime Minister's Questions, but then within a few weeks it tends to revert to its normal raucous atmosphere.

Might another way forward be for every other (or every third, or fourth) PMQs to take place in the relative calm of a select committee room, along the lines of the Liaison Committee sessions with the Prime Minister? The key difference would be that the questioners would be MPs selected by ballot, in exactly the same way that backbenchers are selected to ask questions in the hurly-burly of 'traditional' PMQs. The session would be chaired by the Chairman of Ways and Means, not the Speaker, to mark its distinctive character; it might last for an hour rather than half an hour; and each MP would be able to have several supplementaries.

Reconnecting committees and the chamber

The chamber is the forum in which the House takes its decisions; committees are advisory and preparatory. In most cases – the main exception being when bills (as opposed to draft bills) are referred to committees – the result is *advice* rather than something with which the House has to *agree or disagree*.

One option would be to move from a *committee-advised plenary* to a *committee-fuelled plenary*. This would allow the House to play to one of its acknowledged strengths: select committees. Bills would invariably be referred to the relevant departmental select committees after second reading, for scrutiny in the light of expert testimony and public involvement, and in a more flexible format than that provided by public bill committees. (This would, of course, have implications for the resources of departmental select committees – especially the time of their members.)

The same approach could be used for the estimates, with the House being able to approve them only on the basis of a report from the relevant select committee, which would be able to vary individual components up and down if necessary, provided that the overall totals remained the same.

This radical approach would have a number of implications. Committees would be taking serious decisions that the government, if it disagreed, would have to ask the House to reverse. There would be more political pressure on select committees, and it might be difficult to maintain their generally consensual way of working. The process would demand more time and resources; but it would give much greater power to backbenchers.

Qualified majorities

Not all decisions need be taken by a simple majority. The rights of the opposition parties, and of backbenchers on both sides of the House, might be better protected by requiring certain decisions, such as those suspending a normal rule of the House, to be taken by a qualified majority, perhaps two-thirds. There is a precedent for this in the Fixed-term Parliaments Act 2011, where a two-thirds majority is required to hold an early election (as happened in 2017). But it would be a big change to the way the

House takes decisions, with potential implications for the constitutional practice about a government commanding the majority of the House.

A zero-sum game

Qualified majorities and a mandatory role for select committees in matters of legislation and expenditure are the sorts of things that would cause business managers in governments of either main party to have apoplexy. Most procedural change takes place if there is some balance of advantage and disadvantage to the government of the day. What has become increasingly clear is that a greater role for Parliament usually means a net loss of the power of governments. Whether Parliament takes more power, and how it exercises that power, is in the hands of MPs themselves, just as it is up to MPs how effectively they use the considerable parliamentary opportunities that already exist.

The House of Lords

The background

The changes that have taken place in the Commons in recent years, and the prospects for further change, have been evolutionary in character. The House of Lords, too, has seen evolutionary change and may well see more. But because of a continuing debate about the composition and powers of the House – and, indeed, as to whether the House should exist at all – the Lords has lived with the prospect of fundamental reform of a rather different order for much of the last 100 years. It is useful to see this in historical context.

We saw in Chapter 6 how the powers of the House of Lords over legislation were curtailed by the Parliament Act of 1911 and, again, in 1949 (page 222). Although reform of the composition of the House had been somewhat disingenuously promised by the preamble to the 1911 Act, nothing happened for a very long time. Proposals for an indirectly elected House with a continuing hereditary element were developed by the Bryce Commission in 1918, but these proposals and variations of them found little favour at the time, not least because they would have maintained the Conservative party's majority in the House.

1949

Serious discussion of reform did not resume until 1949, when, in the context of the passage of the second Parliament Bill, an all-party conference discussed powers and composition. No agreement was reached on any wider issue, and the Parliament Act 1949 was confined to reducing the period of operation of the so-called 'suspensory veto' from three sessions to two. But a statement of agreed principles on the future of the House was subsequently published. This statement suggested developments such as the admission of women to the House, some form of remuneration, development of a leave of absence scheme and the elimination of the then permanent majority of the Conservative Party – all of which, in time, were to come about. The most interesting idea of all was that, in future, the membership should be partly hereditary and partly for life. This latter concept was given effect by the Life Peerages Act in 1958, which included life peerages for women. In 1963 the Peerage Act allowed women hereditary peers to sit for the first time and any hereditary peer to disclaim his peerage for life on inheritance.

The Wilson proposals

In 1967–68 the Wilson government made a brave attempt to institute a two-tier House composed of 200 to 250 voting life peers, law lords and some bishops and a remainder of non-voting hereditary peers entitled to sit only for the remainder of their lives. Delaying powers over bills would be reduced to six months, and the government party would have a small majority over opposition parties. Although the proposals were approved in principle by the Lords, a curious alliance of Left and Right in the Commons opposed it, and progress in committee proved to be so slow that the bill was abandoned. The failure of this scheme had the effect of removing Lords reform from the agendas of the two main parties for a generation. The Conservative governments under Margaret Thatcher and John Major showed no interest in the question. Indeed, between 1977 and 1989 Labour party policy was to abolish the House altogether.

The departure of the hereditary peers and a Royal Commission

Not until the election of Tony Blair's Labour government in 1997 did Lords reform reappear on the political agenda, with proposals to eliminate the hereditary members and set up a Royal Commission to consider long-term proposals. Thus, the House of Lords Act 1999 disqualified all hereditary peers from sitting, save for the 92 excepted by the Act (see page 39). In January 2000 the Royal Commission chaired by Lord Wakeham produced its report *A House for the Future*. The Royal Commission supported the continuation of most of the House's existing powers, including that of the suspensory veto under the Parliament Acts.

On composition, however, the Royal Commission made what were its only really radical recommendations. It suggested a chamber of about 550 members, a 'significant minority' of whom would be elected on a regional basis according to a list system of proportional representation, and the remainder appointed. Although the Commission could not agree on the number to be elected – three alternative figures of 65, 87 and 195 were offered – the genie of election had been let out of the bottle and was to dominate the reform debate thereafter. Both elected and appointed members would serve 15-year terms. Existing life peers would become members for life in the new House. Finally, an Appointments Commission established on a statutory basis would vet nominations for membership of the new second chamber and make its own nominations, chiefly of independent members. The report of the Royal Commission was not particularly well-received by reformers, any more than the government's almost equally conservative response to it published as a white paper in November 2001. However, a House of Lords Appointments Commission was established in 2000, on a non-statutory basis, to nominate independent members and to vet political nominations for probity. Despite a steady flow of government papers and consultations, votes in both Houses, and backbench and cross-party studies, there would be no further action until late in the 2010–15 parliament.

The Constitutional Reform Act and the departure of the Law Lords

In 2005 the Constitutional Reform Act was passed, significantly altering the office of Lord Chancellor, making the Lord Chief Justice the head of the judiciary, setting up a Judicial Appointments Commission, and establishing a Supreme Court to take over the appellate functions of the House of Lords. First announced in June 2003, these proposals were aimed at effecting a separation of powers that had previously existed only imperfectly in the United Kingdom. The changes affected the House in three ways. First, they ended the House's judicial role – which was, in the main, exercised away from the chamber. Second, they abolished the role of the Lord Chancellor. Although the office was preserved in name as a result of a vote in the Lords at committee stage, the post-holder is no longer required to be a lawyer or a lord. Since 2007 four of the seven Lord Chancellors have not been lawyers and none has been a peer; the title is now mainly honorific, with the real job being Secretary of State for Justice. This change led to the election by the House of a Lord Speaker for the first time in July 2006 (see page 74). The Lords, ironically, required no legislation to do this but merely the replacement of Standing Order 18 which dated from 1660 and which provided that the Lord Chancellor should be Speaker of the House of Lords. The third effect was to remove serving Lords of Appeal in Ordinary from the House when, in 2009, the Supreme Court finally opened and to end further appointments to the House under the Appellate Jurisdiction Act 1876 (see page 39). This will eventually have the effect of reducing the number of senior lawyers sitting in the House as there is no reason to suppose that all new members of the Supreme Court will, on retirement, be given a seat in the legislature.

The House of Lords Reform Bill 2012

Despite four white papers (in 2001, 2003, 2007 and 2008), and reports from backbench and cross-party groups (Mackay of Clashfern 1999, Hunt of Kings Heath 2004 and Tyler *et al.* in 2005), the administrations of Tony Blair and Gordon Brown failed to deliver on further Lords reform. There was no second stage to the 1999 Act. However, all three major parties promised action on Lords reform in their 2010 manifestos, the Conservatives rather less enthusiastically than the other two major parties. Thus, in the coalition agreement there was a commitment 'to bring forward proposals for a wholly or mainly elected upper chamber on the basis of proportional representation'.

Cross-party talks were held and a white paper and draft bill published in May 2011. After exhaustive scrutiny by a joint committee of 26 members of both Houses, a bill was introduced in June 2012. It received a second reading by 462 votes to 124 on 10 July. But there were 91 Conservative rebels and neither they nor the Labour party would support the necessary programme motion without which progress on the bill would have been impossible. The bill was withdrawn in September 2012.

Ironically, there was very little in the bill that had not been canvassed in the white papers of the previous government or in the reports of some of the cross-party groups – in particular, the group chaired by Paul Tyler MP, as he then was, in 2005, *Reforming the House of Lords: Breaking the Deadlock.*

- The bill proposed a hybrid House, part elected and part nominated. First proposed by the Royal Commission, it was a feature of the 2001, 2007 and 2008 white papers and of *Breaking the Deadlock*.
- The ratio of elected to non-elected members was 80:20, and had been the settled view in the 2008 white paper.
- Election on a regional basis using a proportional system had been a feature of the 2001, 2007 and 2008 white papers; and the proposal to elect by thirds had been trailed by the Royal Commission, *Breaking the Deadlock*, and the 2007 and 2008 white papers.
- The size of the House proposed by the bill was 450, and in the draft bill 300. Neither figure was out of line with earlier proposals.
- Election for non-renewable terms was first recommended by Lord Mackay of Clashfern's *Constitutional Commission* in 1999 and taken up in *Breaking the Deadlock* and in the 2008 white paper.
- The establishment of a statutory appointments commission as set out in the bill had been proposed consistently since the Royal Commission, except for the 1998 white paper which proposed the original non-statutory arrangements.
- The bill made no attempt to modify the House's current powers. This was entirely consistent with the papers and studies since 1998, which had neither called them into question nor sought to modify them.

While the constituent parts had been canvassed before, bringing them together as a whole package of reform awoke old uncertainties. Although in 2007 the Commons had voted for the principle of an 80 per cent or 100 per cent elected second chamber (the Lords, once again, had voted for an appointed House), at the critical moment their will failed them. The chief reason for this was the age-old fear that a mostly elected House would seek to be more assertive, seek to impede Commons bills, and call into question conventions relating to government bills and even Commons financial privilege. A secondary argument was that elected Lords might trespass upon MPs' constituency casework. Furthermore, the assertion relating to Commons primacy over the Lords contained in the draft bill was not convincing (and would have been of no practical effect) and, at the recommendation of the joint committee, was removed from the bill itself. But wider political factors also came into play. Should the all-party talks in 2010 have rolled the pitch better, acceding perhaps to demands for a referendum on the issue of reform? In any event, would the official opposition – sensing Conservative backbench unrest – ever have surrendered an opportunity to drive a wedge between the coalition partners? Who knows.

Small reforms in 2014 and 2015

The lesson many took from the failure of the 2012 bill was that largescale reform was off the agenda, so small evolutionary change was the way forward. Proponents of this argue that it is without prejudice to moving to an elected House in time. Opponents, who for a couple of years after 2012 included the then Deputy Prime Minister, argue that nothing short of an elected House is justified, so there is little point in wasting time on smaller reforms which may only shore up what they view as a fundamentally illegitimate body.

Advocates of incremental reform have had some recent success, starting with the House of Lords Reform Act 2014.

Originally a private member's bill introduced by Dan Byles, the Act allows members of the House of Lords to retire permanently from the House; it compulsorily retires any member – other than those on leave of absence or temporarily disqualified – who failed to attend at all in the previous session; and it permanently disqualifies any member convicted of a serious offence carrying a penalty of over one year's imprisonment, thus bringing the Lords into line with the Commons. These were all the less controversial aspects of a succession of private member's bills introduced in the Lords by Lord Steel of Aikwood, which the coalition government eventually supported. From 2011 to 2014 a voluntary retirement scheme was in place, but it was taken up by only three peers. Many thought the statutory retirement scheme would be no more successful, but it has exceeded those expectations, with 86 retirements by January 2018, including some big names. That said, retirement remains entirely voluntary, and there is an uneven party balance amongst those who have retired. In addition, six members have left the House by virtue of non-attendance for a full session.

The 2014 Act was seen as tidying up some anomalies amongst the composition. A further apparent anomaly was addressed in the House of Lords (Expulsion and Suspension) Act 2015. Introduced as a private member's bill by Baroness Hayman, a former Lord Speaker, this Act enhanced the House's sanctions for punishing members who breach the Code of Conduct. Previously the harshest sanction was suspension until the end of the Parliament then in existence – i.e. a maximum of five years, but usually less. Now members may be suspended for any length of time, or expelled. There was concern about the Act being misused so rigorous procedures were put in place to ensure it covered only serious misconduct.

Another small change was made in 2015, after the Church of England legislated to allow women to become bishops. Under the then rules women bishops would not enter the Lords until they had attained sufficient seniority, which may have taken several years. Instead the Lords Spiritual (Women) Act 2015 allowed women bishops to be 'fast tracked' into the House for the next 10 years. So far two women bishops have become members (the bishops of Gloucester and Newcastle), to be followed by the new Bishop of London.

Size of the House

Encouraged by these successes, those seeking to reform the composition of the House without introducing elections turned their sights on its size. After the majority of hereditary peers left the House in 1999 its membership fell from over 1,300 to under 700. Since then it has gradually crept upwards, as more members entered the House than died (or latterly retired). In March 2018 the total membership was 817, of which 792 were eligible to attend (some, such as judges, are ineligible to attend but legally remain members). As Prime Minister, David Cameron appointed peers at a faster rate than any other Prime Minister – 245 in six years, at a rate of 40 per year; this followed Tony Blair's creation of 374 new peerages, at a similar rate. Some feared that the House's membership might hit 1,000, and worried that its size left it open to ridicule.

Concern grew, led particularly by Baroness D'Souza then Lord Fowler as Lord Speakers. In December 2016 the longstanding and distinguished parliamentarian Lord Cormack sought to address the question of size. He proposed the motion 'that this House believes that its size should be reduced, and methods should be explored by which this could be achieved'. After a lengthy debate the motion was agreed unanimously. Following that, the Lord Speaker established his committee on the size of the House, composed of six members and chaired by Lord Burns. This was an innovation: normally committees are appointed by the House as a whole, such that it gets to decide a committee's remit, powers and membership. Nonetheless the Lord Speaker's committee proceeded as if it were a select committee. In keeping with the tenor of the debate the committee was asked by the Lord Speaker 'to examine practical and politically viable options that might lead to progress on this issue; analyse their implications; and set out any outstanding questions that may need to be answered in order for any proposals to command broad consensus across the House'.

Nearly a year later the committee reported its findings. It agreed that the House was too large and thought the aim should be a fixed cap of 600 members, a size not attained since before life peerages were introduced. But it considered that it would be futile to reduce the size of the House now if the current and future Prime Ministers continued to be able to appoint new members unchecked. Thus the majority of the report sets out a scheme for how the House of 600 appointees should be composed. Until the target is met the current and future Prime Ministers should commit to a 'two-out, one-in' policy for new members, who would be appointed according to a somewhat complicated formula dividing seats amongst the three main parties and the Crossbenchers according to MPs elected and votes won in the last three general elections. New members would serve a 15-year term, with any who don't retire after 15 years being expelled under the Code of Conduct. In the absence of legislation the number of hereditary peers and bishops would remain as at present – 92 and 26 respectively – thus proportionately increasing their strength in the House. Significantly, the committee came up with no scheme for removing existing members. They believed that such members were appointed with the expectation of holding membership for life and that it would be unfair to require any of them to depart. Instead the political parties and the Convenor of the Crossbench Peers were invited to consider how they should reduce the numbers in their groups. The committee hoped that the House might be reduced to 600 members in about 11 years.

The report was naturally of more interest to members of the House than to anyone outside Westminster. In a debate in December 2017 to take note of the proposals the majority of the 95 speakers expressed their approval. Cynics may think that no surprise given that the current members would be untouched by the scheme. The Lord Speaker has been active in support of the ideas, which appear to have momentum behind them. However, implementing them may not be straightforward. For the scheme to work the current Prime Minister and her successors must commit to appointing new members only as determined by the committee, thus limiting their patronage and their ability in extremis to appoint new members to overcome an oppositionist House. Moreover each of the parties and the Crossbenchers must come up with their own schemes for reducing their numbers – something that is unlikely to be popular.

The report's mostly warm reception in the House does not mean it is without its difficulties. Some think it peculiar that the report should offer nothing on how to remove existing members, instead accepting that they have a right to remain for life. It is possible that the prospect of a 15-year term will be unattractive to anyone who is not a career politician or in their dotage. The suggestion that new members be expelled under the Code of Conduct if they serve longer than 15 years makes unexpected use of the power of expulsion, which was designed to deal only with serious misconduct and expected to be used rarely if ever. Others question whether the size of the House is as great a problem as is made out, observing that average daily attendance is under 500 and stable, with many debates sparsely attended. Moreover, they argue that a House supposedly built on the expertise of its members needs a large pool of experts in it. There seems to be an assumption amongst some that the House's size is the sole barrier preventing an ungrateful public from appreciating the good work the House does.

Although the scheme's proponents argue that it is a modest, evolutionary change, in reality a reduction in the size of the House by a quarter, a fixed formula for appointments and 15-year terms are significant constitutional changes.

That was recognised by the Prime Minister in her response to the Lord Speaker in a letter of February 2018. The Prime Minister noted that from her taking office in July 2016 she had acted with restraint, appointing only eight new peers (five of which were Crossbenchers, the other three ministers). The overall size of the House had fallen by 20 over that period. She thought that the House was on a downward course and encouraged all party leaders in the Lords to promote retirements in their groups. Moreover, she undertook to maintain restraint in making new appointments and when doing so to reflect the results of the last general election and the number of retirements amongst the different parties; and she stated that she would not consider any individual who had held high public office to have an automatic entitlement to a peerage. However, the Prime Minister considered the proposal for 15-year terms and annual appointments based on a fixed formula to require 'careful further thought and engagement, particularly with the House of Commons'.

The Lord Speaker welcomed the Prime Minister's response and thought it provided the basis for further steps in reducing the size of the House, though it is hard to see the Prime Minister's response as a clear endorsement of all the Burns committee's proposals.

Future reform of the House of Lords

The Burns committee agenda has somewhat displaced discussion on other reforms to the House. As this book has illustrated, the House of Lords is a busy place, making an active contribution to the parliamentary process. But, to many writers, the only really interesting characteristic of the House is its membership and the only really interesting question is that of reform of its composition.

Election

It is not, of course, necessary to elect both Houses of Parliament. A country's democratic credentials do not rest on whether its second chamber is appointed or elected. But many will continue to argue that a chamber of legislature with the kind of powers that are still vested in the House of Lords should be elected. In the immediate future wholesale reform seems unlikely. It is conceivable that a bill on the same lines as that introduced in 2012 could be introduced into a future parliament, but its chances of success would be slim without the political will to see it through under a government with a clear and biddable majority in the Commons, or else strong cross-party support. Proposals for Lords reform have often floundered due to insufficient political will.

Indirect election or sectoral representation

Some who desire compositional reform but don't want a directly elected chamber which would rival the Commons favour indirect election or sectoral representation. The former might involve local councillors and/or members of the Scottish, Welsh and Northern Ireland legislatures also being members of the second chamber, similar to the composition of the German Bundesrat. While it would change the chamber considerably it might not sate those who want full democratic accountability. Sectoral representation might involve certain industries or groups having ex officio seats in the House – such as representatives of various faiths, trade unions, business sectors, etc. The Hong Kong Legislative Council is partly composed this way. But it would not be easy deciding who is and is not represented, and it risks members taking a narrow sectoral view of the issues before them.

Age limit

The Burns committee ruled out setting an age limit for members, perhaps because the average age of members is just under 70 years. So, if an age limit were imposed it would have to be quite high – likely 80 or 85, way above the national retirement age. The prevailing culture in the House and the contribution made by some older members would make this an unwelcome change and of uneven impact on the political parties.

Phasing out the hereditary members

As we have seen, 90 of the 92 hereditary members excepted under the 1999 Act are refreshed when one of them dies by a by-election procedure, which is criticised as bizarre. The party and crossbench members are elected by sitting hereditary members of that party or group. Those members originally selected by the House as a whole, supposedly to serve as committee chairmen, are elected by the whole House but according to an unwritten presumption that someone of the same party as his or her predecessor will be selected. The candidates are drawn from a list of eligible hereditary peers maintained by the Clerk of the Parliaments and are, by now, often unknown to the electors. The continued presence of the hereditary element was the price of a deal struck between Lord Irvine of Lairg and the Conservative Leader of the Opposition, Viscount Cranborne, to facilitate the passage of the original bill, and was meant to last until the elusive second phase of reform was implemented. Successive private members' bills to phase out the remaining hereditary element – by ending the by-elections – have not attracted government support and have been vigorously opposed by some of those 90 hereditary members, although their own positions in the House would not have been affected. But phasing out the hereditary element is not quite the standalone quick and easy fix it might appear, because a disproportionate number of the excepted hereditary members are Conservative. Over time, as members died and were not replaced, one political party would be especially disadvantaged, perhaps only leading to more life peerages to make up the difference.

House of Lords Appointments Commission

The House of Lords Appointments Commission could be made a statutory body. This would, of course, require legislation. At the same time, it would be possible to widen the commission's remit. In addition to nominating non-party members, it might also be given authority to nominate party members from lists provided to it by the parties – though some would oppose giving the power to determine the whole membership of a House of Parliament to a quango which lacks the accountability the Prime Minister has.

Senators or nobility

At present, the House of Lords is a house of nobility, though it tries hard not to be. Members, other than bishops, receive a writ of summons to Parliament because they have been given a peerage by letters patent, carrying with it the 'style, dignity, title and honour' of a barony, and the right to sit in Parliament. Now that few peerages are granted solely for 'honour', some feel that the link between members of the House of Lords and the peerage is reputationally damaging and should be ended. Here again, legislation would be required. Instead of sitting in Parliament by virtue of letters patent of nobility, members would receive their writs of summons by virtue of a different entitlement – perhaps by simply being entered on a roll maintained by the Clerk of the Crown in Chancery. But this is the kind of change that is far more likely to be effected in conjunction with some other reform.

Where, then, does this leave us? All these possibilities for change would require legislation and are not well suited for private members' procedure. The current government has shown little appetite for Lords reform and has no shortage of other constitutional changes to effect.

Modernisation of practice and procedure in the Lords

As with the Commons, the House of Lords has undergone its own programme of change in working practices in recent years. Many of these changes derive from groups set up by the Leader of the House specifically to review working practices – such as the groups on Sittings of the House in 1995 (the Rippon Group) and on Working Practices in 2001–02 and 2010–11 (chaired by Lord Williams of Mostyn and Lord Goodlad, respectively). The Procedure Committee continually develops the way in which things are done. All changes are ultimately reported to the House for agreement. By these means, the House has made big changes over the years in the way it does things. Many of these have been recounted elsewhere in this book but it is useful to pull some of them together here, along with a few pointers towards further change.

- Since 1997 the House has developed a far more elaborate system of sessional and *ad hoc* select committees than before, when the focus was almost exclusively on European Union and science and technology issues. It has increasingly formalised its processes for appointing *ad hoc* select committees, with four now appointed each session, including one conducting post-legislative scrutiny.
- The Grand Committee procedure has been expanded far beyond the taking of committee stages on bills (see page 220), and in this way more drastic changes to regulate chamber procedure have been avoided.
- Great strides have been made recently in trying to make debates more topical, by requiring motions for balloted debates to be renewed each month, and by instituting topical oral questions and topical Questions for Short Debate.
- While the current pattern of sitting hours had become established by 2002–03, it has now become usual to sit on at least one Friday a month at 10 am, for private

members' business. Regular sittings into the small hours are a thing of the past. When it is known the House will sit longs hours on a day, it now often meets early rather than sits until very late.

- The House has overhauled its Code of Conduct, appointed a Commissioner for Standards and legislated to suspend or expel miscreant members.

How might working practices be developed further? Here are some suggestions.

- The Grand Committee might be developed further. The Goodlad group suggested that the committee stage of all government bills received from the Commons should be taken in the Grand Committee, but the suggestion was rejected by the House. An influx of Brexit-related legislation may force a revisiting of this issue.
- The scope for a Backbench Business Committee in the Lords is fairly limited. The Goodlad Group thought that such a committee could select topics for debates on those Thursdays used for balloted debates, and for some Questions for Short Debate. The idea did not find favour and was rejected on a division in the House. Many members would prefer the serendipity of a ballot to the involvement – indeed, interference – of a committee.
- The committee structure is being reviewed by the Liaison Committee, with the expectation that the EU Committee and its six sub-committees will cease to exist post-Brexit. Committees are popular with the membership, so the House may look to create new committees to replace them.
- Committee members are currently selected by the party whips and the Convenor, and committee chairmen are appointed following agreement between the parties. While most members are prepared to acquiesce in these arrangements, some find the practice to be opaque and unfair. The House could, if it wished, adopt the House of Commons practice of electing chairmen House-wide and of inviting parties and groups to select their nominations for membership through election.
- Finally, just as with the Commons, some unknown – indeed, unknowable – developments in working practices are likely following Brexit and might also come about with a decant of the two Houses of Parliament as part of the restoration and renewal of the Palace.

Conclusion

Parliament is an *organism* as much – or more – than it is an *organisation*. It has all the classic attributes of an organism: reactive, unpredictable, sometimes illogical. But it has much to offer its citizens – and can still play as important a part in the life of the nation as at any time in its history. Parliament has to a large extent bounced back from the expenses scandal of 2009: the increased willingness of backbenchers to act independently and the power wielded by them in circumstances where the government lacks a majority in the Commons mean that Parliament is correctly perceived as active, influential, confident and independent. The citizens of the United Kingdom should feel proud of what their Parliament does for them. There is much still to be done: in ensuring that MPs and others who work in Parliament not only uphold the highest standards of conduct, but are seen to do so; in enhancing public understanding of Parliament and improving the ability of citizens to engage with it; and, most challenging of all perhaps, preserving and updating the physically vulnerable Palace of Westminster, which is symbolically synonymous with Parliament. Ultimately, though, Parliament's future will be assured if parliamentarians themselves have the collective will to tackle these challenges robustly.

Glossary of parliamentary terms

In each definition, words in *italics* are further explained elsewhere in the glossary.

Accounting Officer The individual (usually the *Permanent Secretary* of a government department or the chief executive of an executive agency) who is personally responsible for the regularity and propriety of expenditure voted under a particular estimate.

Act paper Laid before Parliament because an Act of Parliament requires it.

Address A formal communication from either House to the Sovereign. The debate on the Queen's Speech takes place on a motion of thanks for the speech (often called the 'Humble Address').

adjournment The end of a *sitting*. In the Commons, an 'adjournment debate' takes place on a motion 'That this House do now adjourn', usually the half-hour adjournment debate at the end of each sitting in the Commons (where MPs may 'raise a subject on the adjournment'). Major debates formerly on a motion for the adjournment now take place on a motion that the House 'has considered' a specific matter. An adjournment (for example, 'the summer adjournment') is also a more formal name for a *recess*.

Administration Estimate In the Commons, pays for the staff of the House and the services provided by the House departments.

advisory cost limit The estimated cost of answering a parliamentary question (at present £850) above which a minister may decline to answer the question on grounds of 'disproportionate cost'.

affirmation A secular promise of allegiance to the Crown made by MPs or peers who do not wish to take a religious oath.

affirmative instrument A piece of *delegated legislation* that the parent Act requires Parliament to approve explicitly before it can come into effect ('the affirmative procedure').

allocation of time order See *guillotine*.

all-party groups Of greater or lesser formality, these bring together MPs and peers from all parties to discuss matters of common interest. They are established by MPs and peers themselves rather than being creations of either House. The total varies: in 2017 there were some 400 groups. 'Country groups' (about 130) bring together MPs and peers interested in the affairs of particular countries.

ambit of an estimate The formal description of the services to be financed from that *estimate*.

amendment Proposal to change the text of a bill, motion or draft select committee report.

amendment of the law motion Generally moved by the Chancellor of the Exchequer after his *budget* statement: 'that it is expedient to amend the law with respect to the National Debt and to make further provision in respect of public finance'. It is the vehicle for the broad budget debate that follows, although the motion was not moved after the 2017 autumn budget.

amendment in lieu Amendment proposed by one House to the other as an alternative to one that has been rejected by the former.

Annually Managed Expenditure (AME) A category of government expenditure that is less predictable or controllable than that under *departmental expenditure limits*; for example, social security and Common Agricultural Policy payments.

annulment The act of making a *statutory instrument* of no effect. See also *prayer*.

backbencher An MP or peer who is neither a minister, nor (in opposition) a spokesperson for his or her party.

back of the Chair bill See *presentation bill.*

backsheet the last page of a bill, which repeats the *long* and *short title* of the bill, gives the bill number and the session, and lists the MP introducing the bill ('the member in charge') and his or her supporters.

ballot bills In the Commons, the 20 *private members' bills* introduced on the fifth Wednesday of a session following the ballot on the second Thursday of each session.

BBCom Abbreviation for the Backbench Business Committee, a Commons select committee of backbenchers that selects subjects for debate on the (normally) 27 days set aside for backbench business in the chamber (and additional time in *Westminster Hall*), and which also apportions time for those debates.

bill Draft *primary legislation*.

bill of aids and supplies Old name for a bill granting *Supply* and *Ways and Means*.

Black Rod ('the Lady Usher of the Black Rod') An officer of the Lords responsible for aspects of security and ceremonial.

blocking minority The number of votes required to block a proposal in the Council of Ministers of the European Union under *qualified majority voting* (*QMV*) (see chapter 11).

Boundary Commissions The bodies that keep under review the size, boundaries and numbers of parliamentary *constituencies*, especially to take account of population changes.

Budget Oral statement by the Chancellor of the Exchequer, now in the autumn, that reviews the nation's finances and makes taxation proposals.

business questions (strictly, 'the business question') In the Commons, a type of *urgent question* asked of the *Leader of the House* every Thursday, in response to which he announces the business for the next fortnight and answers questions.

by-election An election in a single *constituency* when a seat becomes vacant because the MP dies or is otherwise no longer eligible to sit.

casting vote In the Commons, the vote cast by the Chair to decide the issue when the numbers voting are equal. How the vote is cast is usually dictated by precedent, except in select committees.

CCLA Commons consideration of *Lords amendments.*

Chairman of Committees (or 'Lord Chairman') The formal title of the *Senior Deputy Speaker* of the House of Lords.

Chairman of Ways and Means The principal Deputy Speaker of the Commons, with special responsibilities for Committees of the whole House, *private bills* and *Westminster Hall.* In the House, he is assisted by First and Second Deputy Chairmen of Ways and Means, who act as Deputy Speakers. He chairs the Speaker's Panel of Chairs, which provides chairmen for *public bill committees.*

Chiltern Hundreds The posts of steward or bailiff of Her Majesty's three Chiltern Hundreds of Stoke, Desborough and Burnham, or of the manor of Northstead, are symbolic 'offices of profit' used to allow an MP to resign his or her seat. If an MP is appointed to one, he or she is disqualified as holding an 'office of profit under the Crown' (an MP cannot simply resign).

clause The basic unit of a *bill*, divided into subsections, then paragraphs, then subparagraphs. When a bill becomes an Act, 'clauses' become 'sections' but the names of the other subdivisions stay the same.

Clerk of the House The principal officer of the Commons. Head of the House Service and *Accounting Officer*, as well as the House's principal adviser on constitutional issues and the procedure, practice, law and privilege of the House.

Clerk of the Parliaments The principal officer of the Lords, with functions similar to those of the Clerk of the House of Commons.

closure In the Commons a device for curtailing debate, or for securing a decision on a matter that would otherwise be *talked out.* An MP moves a *motion* 'That the question be now put', which (if allowed by the Chair) is put to a decision immediately, without debate. If a division is forced on it, not fewer than 100 MPs must vote in the majority for the closure, otherwise the motion is lost. If it is agreed to, the question originally proposed from the Chair must be put immediately. Rarely moved in the House of Lords until 2011, when it was moved twice during proceedings on the Parliamentary Voting System and Constituencies Bill, and then in 2014 on the European Union (Referendum) Bill.

collective responsibility The doctrine under which all members of the government – that is, ministers – support the policies of the government and take responsibility for government action, even if there are elements with which they privately disagree. Open disagreement is normally followed by resignation. Under the coalition government the doctrine was modified to allow the coalition parties to take differing views on certain matters.

Command Paper Presented to Parliament by the government, formally 'by Command of Her Majesty'.

commencement The coming into effect of legislation. For Acts of Parliament, this is usually done by an order made by the responsible minister. If there is no commencement provision, the Act comes into force from midnight at the beginning of the day on which *Royal Assent* was given.

Committee of the whole House Used for the committee stage of bills in the House itself rather than in a *public bill committee* in the Commons or, in the Lords, in the Grand Committee. In the Commons, Committee of the whole House is presided over by the *Chairman of Ways and Means* rather than the *Speaker*, and the *Mace* (normally on top of the *Table*) is placed on brackets below the Table to show that the House is in committee. Any MP may take part in proceedings, just as in the House itself.

Commons amendment An amendment made by the Commons to a bill passed by the Lords.

Comptroller and Auditor General A statutorily independent officer of the Commons who heads the National Audit Office (NAO); who approves the release of money from the Consolidated Fund; who audits accounts of government departments and a range of public bodies; and who carries out 'value for money' (VFM) inquiries into the economy, efficiency and effectiveness of public spending. He has a close relationship with the Public Accounts Committee, which considers his reports.

consideration See *report stage*.

Consolidated Fund The government's account at the Bank of England.

consolidation bill One that seeks to set out the law in a particular subject area in a clearer and more up-to-date form without changing its substance.

constituency The area of the country 'returning', or being represented by, each MP.

constituency Friday A non-sitting Friday in a sitting week.

COSAC (known by the French acronym) The Conference of European Affairs Committees that, every six months, brings together representatives of the European Affairs Committees in all the national parliaments of the member states of the EU, and of the Constitutional Affairs Committee of the European Parliament.

Cranborne money Financial assistance to opposition parties in the Lords, named after the then Leader of the House, Viscount Cranborne. The Commons equivalent is *Short money*.

crossbenches Benches in either House facing the Chair rather than on one side or the other of the chamber. In the Lords, crossbenchers are those peers without party allegiance.

crossing the floor Changing party allegiance (even if the MP's new party, in fact, sits on the same side of the House).

decision Any decision of the EU Council of Ministers is binding upon those to whom it is addressed.

deferred division In the Commons, when on certain types of business an attempt is made to force a vote after the *moment of interruption*, that vote is held in one of the division lobbies between 11.30 am and 2.00 pm on the next sitting Wednesday.

delegated legislation sometimes called 'subordinate legislation' or 'secondary legislation' (or 'statutory instruments', which most but not all are): legislation made by a minister, or occasionally by a public body, under powers conferred by an Act of Parliament. Different types of delegated legislation are called variously orders, rules, regulations, schemes or codes, depending on what the 'parent Act' calls them.

Departmental Expenditure Limit (DEL) Total planned expenditure for a government department, but excluding *annually managed expenditure.*

deposit Sum of £500 forfeited if a candidate receives less than 5 per cent of the votes cast at a parliamentary election.

de-referral In the Commons, a motion to take business (typically, debate on a statutory instrument or European Union document) on the floor of the House rather than in the committee to which is has been automatically referred.

despatch boxes At the *Table* of either House, from which *frontbenchers* speak.

dilatory motion A delaying motion, for the adjournment of the debate, committee or House; or to adjourn further consideration of a bill.

directive European legislation binding on member states in terms of the result to be achieved by a certain date.

dissolution The ending of a parliament by royal proclamation, followed by a *general election.*

division A vote 'to divide the House' (or committee) to force a vote. In the Commons, the votes are 'Aye' or 'No'; in the Lords 'Content' or 'Not Content'.

draft bill A bill, not yet formally introduced into either House, that is made available for pre-legislative scrutiny by a select or joint committee.

dummy bill A sheet of paper, with the *short* and *long titles* and list of supporters, presented at the *Table* by a backbench MP introducing a *private member's bill.*

early day motion (EDM) In the Commons, motions set down for 'an early day' and so – apart from *prayers*, which first appear in this form – almost certain not to be debated. EDMs are mainly used to make political points and to test opinion.

elector Someone who has a vote in a parliamentary election.

electoral quota The total number of electors divided by the number of constituencies.

English Votes for English Laws The procedure by which legislation affecting only parts of the UK is subject to scrutiny by MPs from those parts of the UK only. Considered an answer to the *West Lothian question.*

estimate A request from the government to the Commons for the resources required for each main area of public expenditure.

estimates days In the Commons, three days in the course of a session when the *estimates* are approved; select committee reports selected by the Liaison Committee, and linked to particular estimates, provide the subjects for debate on those days.

EVEL *English Votes for English Laws.*

Excess Votes Seek retrospective authorisation when a government department's spending in a financial year has exceeded what Parliament has authorised, or has been incurred for a purpose that was not authorised.

exempted In the Commons, business that may be taken after the *moment of interruption*, either because it falls into an exempted category, or because it is covered by an order (at the initiative of the government) that specifically exempts it.

explanatory memorandum The government's evidence on each EU document, which is subject to the European scrutiny system of each House.

explanatory notes A document accompanying a government bill that sets out the bill's intention and background in neutral terms, explains the clauses in lay person's language and gives an assessment of the bill's effects on public service manpower and costs, and on private sector business.

Father of the House In the Commons, the MP with the longest continuous service.

first-past-the-post The voting system in which the candidate with the most votes – a relative majority – wins regardless of how many other candidates there are or how close they come to the winning number of votes.

first reading The formal first stage of a bill's passage through Parliament, taken without debate when the bill is introduced. The bill is then ordered to be printed.

floor of the House The chamber of either House. A matter debated 'on the floor' is discussed in a plenary sitting rather than in a separate committee.

frontbencher A minister or *shadow minister*.

the gallery Originally the collective term for the journalists primarily concerned with reporting proceedings rather than the interpretation of parliamentary and political events, which was more the province of the *lobby*; in practice, the distinction has largely disappeared.

general election Following a dissolution of Parliament, an election for every seat in the new House of Commons.

giving way Allowing another member to intervene briefly in a speech to make a point or to ask a question.

Grand Committee (1) In the Lords, for considering the committee stage of bills and certain other forms of business off the floor of the House. (2) In the Commons, the Welsh and Northern Ireland Grand Committees may be used for statements from ministers, oral questions, the consideration of bills and *delegated legislation*, and *adjournment debates*. The Scottish Grand Committee has not sat since 2003. (3) In the Commons, the *legislative grand committee* considers bills affecting only parts of the UK under the *EVEL* procedures.

green card Available in the Central Lobby of the Palace of Westminster and filled in by a constituent seeking a meeting with his or her MP.

green paper A document issued by the government for consultation on possible policy options.

grouping The grouping of related *amendments* for debate.

guillotine In the Commons; also known as an 'allocation of time order': at any stage in the passage of a bill, an order that imposes time limits on the remainder of its progress.

hand-out bill A bill that the government wishes to see enacted and that is drafted by *parliamentary counsel*, offered to a backbencher to take forward as a *private member's bill*, usually with the continuing support and briefing of the government department concerned.

Hansard See *Official Report*.

hemicycle A semicircular debating chamber, as in the French *Assemblée nationale* or the European Parliament.

Henry VIII power A power in an Act for ministers by *delegated legislation* to amend *primary legislation*.

hereditary peer A member of the House of Lords by virtue of inheriting a title (usually, a son inheriting from a father, although some hereditary peerages can pass to a daughter); 92 hereditary peers elected from among their own number have seats as a result of the House of Lords Act 1999 (which removed the right of other hereditary peers to sit in the Lords).

House of Lords Appointments Commission A non-statutory commission that makes recommendations to the Queen for non-political peers and vets for propriety all nominations for peerages, including those from the political parties.

House of Lords Business The working papers of the House of Lords, published in advance of every sitting day.

hung parliament After a *general election*, when no one party has a majority in the House of Commons.

hybrid bill A bill that combines the characteristics of a public bill (changing the general law) and a private bill (making provision with local or personal effect). It is subject to a special procedure.

introduction The formal start of a bill's passage through Parliament. The bill is formally given a first reading at the same time and ordered to be printed. Also may refer to the formal introduction of a new MP or peer.

IPSA The Independent Parliamentary Standards Authority, established under the Parliamentary Standards Act 2009, which is responsible for determining and paying the pay and allowances of MPs.

joint committee A *select committee* with a membership drawn from both Houses.

Journal The legal record of the proceedings of both Houses (of decisions and events rather than words spoken).

knives The deadlines within a *programme order*. When a knife falls, only specified decisions may be taken, and it may not be possible to debate or decide on certain clauses or amendments.

Law Commission of England and Wales. A statutory independent body set up by the Law Commission Act 1965 to keep the law under review and to recommend reform where it is needed. The aim of the commission is 'to ensure that the law is fair, modern, simple and as cost-effective as possible'. There is an equivalent body for Scotland.

LCCA Lords Consideration of *Commons Amendments.*

Leader of the House In the Commons, a cabinet minister dealing with House affairs and the organisation of business. The Leader of the House of Lords has a similar role but plays an additional part in guiding the course of business during a sitting.

legislative grand committee Under the *EVEL* procedures, the body formed between report and third reading in the Commons to consider bills which affect only part of the UK. It comprises MPs from England only; England and Wales only; or England, Wales and Northern Ireland only.

legislative reform order An order under the Legislative and Regulatory Reform Act 2006 made by a minister to lift burdens on anyone carrying on any activity. An order may be made only after public consultation on a proposal, which is then scrutinised by committees of both Houses, and may be rejected and then submitted in an amended form. The committees also scrutinise the draft order that is brought forward as a result. A legislative reform order is an unusual type of *delegated legislation* in that it may amend *primary legislation.*

life peer A member of the House of Lords for life, having been appointed under the Appellate Jurisdiction Act 1876 (retired law lords) or the Life Peerages Act 1958 (other peers).

lobby (1) A room, as in division lobbies, the Central Lobby, Members' Lobby or Peers' Lobby; (2) to come to Westminster to put a case, either to an individual MP or as part of a demonstration ('mass lobbies'); (3) the group of parliamentary journalists with special access to the Palace of Westminster, reporting parliamentary and political news and opinion.

lobby terms Information given to journalists on the basis that it may be disclosed but not attributed.

locus standi The position of someone directly affected by the provisions of a *private bill*, who therefore has the right to petition against it.

long title The passage at the start of a bill that begins 'a Bill to . . .' and then lists its purposes. The content of the bill must be covered by the long title.

Lord Speaker Presiding officer of the House of Lords.

Lords amendment Made by the Lords to a bill passed by the Commons.

Mace A silver gilt ornamental mace symbolises the authority of each House. It is carried in procession before a sitting and in the Commons remains on the *Table* (under the *Table* when the House is in *Committee of the whole House*) and in the Lords on the Woolsack while the House is sitting.

main estimates The principal request from the government to the Commons for the resources required to run the state in the following financial year. There is one for each government department (and for other bodies such as the Office of Rail Regulation and the NHS Pension Scheme). Published within five weeks of the *budget*.

main question If an *amendment* to a *motion* has been moved, the original motion is known as the main question.

manifesto Statement of policies and intentions on which a political party fights a *general election*.

measure Legislation of the Church of England, agreed by the General Synod, then considered by the Ecclesiastical Committee (a statutory committee consisting of members of both Houses) and then presented to both Houses for approval.

message Formal communication between one House and the other.

minister of state The second rank of ministers (below secretaries of state).

Ministry of Defence Votes A Published in January or February, these seek the annual authorisation by the Commons of the maximum numbers of personnel in the armed services.

moment of interruption The time at which the main business of the Commons day normally ends (10 pm on Mondays, 7.00 pm on Tuesdays and Wednesdays, 5.00 pm on Thursdays and 2.30 pm on Fridays).

money bill A bill whose only purpose is to authorise expenditure or taxation, as defined by the Parliament Act 1911.

money resolution A motion (when approved, a resolution) to authorise government expenditure in relation to a bill.

motion A proposal 'moved' by a member. When approved, it becomes a *resolution* or an *order*.

named-day questions In the Commons, written questions for answer on a stated day, with a minimum notice period of three sitting days (but including non-sitting Fridays). An individual MP may ask no more than five such questions per day.

naming (of an MP) A power used by the Chair in the Commons, usually for more serious offences, usually including disregard for the authority of the Chair. Following naming, a motion to suspend the MP concerned (to bar him or her from the precincts and stop payment of salary for a stated period) is moved by the senior minister present and invariably agreed to.

National Audit Office See *Comptroller and Auditor General*.

negative instrument A piece of *delegated legislation* that, under the parent Act, may be made and come into effect unless one or other House decides otherwise ('the negative procedure').

new clause A substantial *amendment* to a bill, usually introducing a separate subject or issue rather than seeking to amend the provisions already in the bill (but to be in order a new clause must be within the *scope* of (or, in the Lords, *relevant* to) the bill).

Next Business Motion In the Lords, see *previous question.*

1922 Committee (sometimes called 'the 22') Body consisting of all Conservative MPs but especially important as a reflection of backbench opinion.

nod To secure agreement to something 'on the nod' is without debate or a vote.

Official Opposition The largest opposition party, sometimes known as 'Her Majesty's Opposition'.

Official Report The essentially verbatim report of debates in both Houses, Westminster Hall, standing committees and grand committees. Also contains written answers to questions. Known as *Hansard.*

Ombudsman See *Parliamentary Commissioner for Administration.*

opposition days In the Commons, 20 days in the course of a session on which the subject of the main debate is chosen by the opposition parties.

order A decision of either House or of a committee on a matter within the power of the body making the order; for example, 'That a select committee be appointed to . . .'. See also *resolution.*

Order in Council A type of *delegated legislation*, made in the name of the sovereign rather than that of a minister.

Order Paper The agenda for a day's sitting.

orders of reference *Orders* made by either House when setting up a select committee. They set out the committee's task and define its powers.

ordinary written questions in the Commons, written questions that are put down for answer two sitting days after they are received and that, by convention, the government answers within two weeks.

Outlawries Bill An antique bill 'for the more effectual preventing of clandestine outlawries' given a formal first reading in the Commons as a symbol of their right to deal with their own business before proceeding to debate the *Queen's Speech* after the *State Opening* of Parliament. The Lords equivalent is the Select Vestries Bill.

packaging The grouping of Lords amendments together for debate and decision in the Commons. Even though a particular proposition may have been defeated, its appearance as part of a *package* in which *amendments in lieu* are offered may avoid 'double insistence'; that is, when neither House will give way and the bill in question will be lost.

pairing An arrangement between two MPs on opposite sides of the House not to vote in a particular division, so that their absences cancel each other out.

a parliament The main division of parliamentary time: the period between one *general election* and the next.

parliamentary agent A specialist lawyer who represents the *promoter* of a private bill.

Parliamentary Commissioner for Administration (Ombudsman) An independent officer, reporting to Parliament, who investigates maladministration by government departments and other public bodies that has caused injustice that has not been put right. The holder of this office also holds the posts of Health Service Commissioner for England and for Wales (in the latter role, reporting to the National Assembly for Wales). The Parliamentary Commissioner for Administration has a close relationship with the Public Administration and Constitutional Affairs Committee in the Commons, which considers reports by the commissioner.

Parliamentary Commissioner for Standards An independent officer of the Commons who maintains the Register of Members' Interests and other registers of interests, advises MPs and the Committee on Standards on interests and standards issues, monitors the operation of the Code of Conduct, and investigates complaints about MPs' conduct. The House of Lords Commissioner for Standards investigates complaints that members of the Lords have breached that House's Code of Conduct.

parliamentary counsel A small group of government lawyers who are expert in legislative drafting and who draft all government bills, including *'hand-out' bills. Delegated legislation* is usually drafted not by parliamentary counsel but by the lawyers in the government department concerned.

parliamentary private secretary (PPS) An unpaid MP aide to a *secretary of state* or a *minister of state.*

parliamentary secretary *or* **parliamentary under-secretary of state** The third rank of ministers, below *secretaries of state* and *ministers of state.*

payroll vote Government ministers and *parliamentary private secretaries* – the most reliable supporters of the government in any votes.

PBL The Cabinet Committee on Parliamentary Business and the Legislative Programme, chaired by the *Leader of the House of Commons.* Other members include the *Leader of the House of Lords* and the chief whips in both Houses.

Permanent Secretary (in some departments, more formally 'Permanent Under-Secretary of State') The senior civil servant in a government department. Usually also the *Accounting Officer.*

personal statement A statement (in the Commons, made by permission of the Speaker), usually of apology, or explaining the reasons for a ministerial resignation.

petition Either a *public petition* or, in the case of a *private bill,* a case made against it by someone who would be directly affected by its provisions.

ping-pong The to-and-fro of bills and amendments between the two Houses at the end of a bill's passage through both Houses to enable any remaining disagreements to be resolved.

point of order An appeal to the Chair for guidance or a ruling on a matter of order or procedure, but also a means (through 'bogus points of order') of furthering political argument.

polling day The day on which votes are cast in a *general election* or *by-election.*

PLP Parliamentary Labour Party. Consists of all Labour MPs and peers.

PMQs Prime Minister's Questions (in the Commons, for half an hour every sitting Wednesday).

PPC Prospective parliamentary candidate. Someone selected by a party organisation to contest the next election.

PPR A *select committee's* power to send for 'persons, papers and records'.

PPS See *parliamentary private secretary.*

prayer A motion seeking the *annulment* of a *statutory instrument.*

praying time The period (usually of 40 days, excluding time when both Houses are adjourned for more than four days) during which a motion for the *annulment* of a *statutory instrument* must be taken.

pre-legislative scrutiny See *draft bill.*

prerogative sometimes 'the royal prerogative'. Power of ministers to act in the Queen's name without the approval of Parliament.

presentation bill A bill presented at the *Table*, notice having been given on the *Order Paper.*

previous question An old-fashioned *dilatory motion* in the form 'That the question be not now put'. If it is agreed to, the House moves to the next business; if it is not agreed to, then the matter that was interrupted must be decided immediately, as with a *closure.* The Lords equivalent is now called the *Next Business Motion.*

primary legislation Acts of Parliament.

Prince of Wales's consent Signification by the Prince of Wales that Parliament may proceed to consider legislation that would affect his interests.

private bill A bill that, if passed, will have only local or personal, rather than general, effect.

private business Proceedings on *private bills* and related matters. In the Commons, taken immediately after prayers (the religious prayers at the start of the sitting); if opposed, time for debate is found by the *Chairman of Ways and Means.*

private member's bill A public bill introduced by a 'private member' (not a minister). Not to be confused with a *private bill.*

private notice question In the Lords, a question of urgent importance asked orally of the government and subject to the discretion of the Lord Speaker. In the Commons, the term has been replaced by *urgent question.*

privilege Parliamentary privilege gives the two Houses, their committees and members the protection from outside interference or legal action necessary to perform their roles. The two main elements are freedom of speech and the right of both Houses to regulate their own affairs. Also (as 'financial privilege') used to describe the pre-eminence of the Commons in financial matters.

privilege amendment A polite fiction to preserve the pre-eminence of the Commons in financial matters; a subsection in a bill starting in the Lords that involves an increase in expenditure or taxation says 'Nothing in this Act shall impose any charge on the people or on public funds'. The subsection is removed when the bill is in committee in the Commons.

privy counsellor A member of the Privy Council, consisting of senior politicians past and present, senior judges, some Commonwealth statesmen and certain others of distinction. Members of the Privy Council are styled 'right honourable'.

proclamation A royal proclamation by the sovereign setting a day for the new parliament to meet after a *general election*. Before the Fixed-term Parliaments Act 2011 was used to dissolve parliament.

programming In the Commons, the imposition of a timetable on the passage of a bill immediately after *second reading*.

programming committee In the Commons, when a programme order applies to proceedings in *Committee of the whole House*, *report stage* or *third reading*, a programming committee (chaired by the *Chairman of Ways and Means* and consisting of up to eight other MPs) may propose how the available time should be allocated; in practice such committees are not used, unlike a programming sub-committee (chaired by the chairman of the *public bill committee*, with seven members of the committee), which deals with proceedings in a standing committee.

programme order A timetable for a bill once agreed to by the House.

promoter The body or individual outside Parliament sponsoring a *private bill*.

proposing the question When the Chair states the proposition on which the House or committee must decide.

prorogation The formal end of a parliamentary *session*, which brings to an end almost all parliamentary business.

public bill A bill that, if passed, will have general effect in some or all of the constituent parts of the UK.

public bill committee In the Commons, a committee to which most bills are referred for committee stage. If the bill they are considering started in the Commons, they begin in select committee mode with sessions of evidence from witnesses. Public bill committees meet in rooms laid out in the same manner as the chamber of the House, are chaired by an impartial chair and cease to exist when they have finished considering a bill. A number of public bill committees may be in existence at the same time.

public business Generally, proceedings on the main business of the day (in the Commons, following question time and statements).

public petition An application by one or more people outside Parliament to one House or the other (usually the Commons) for some particular action or relief.

qualified majority voting (QMV) A weighted system of voting in the EU Council of Ministers in which larger countries have more votes. See *blocking minority*.

Queen's consent Signification by the sovereign that Parliament may proceed to consider legislation that would affect her interests.

Queen's Speech Sometimes called 'the Gracious Speech'; written by the government and delivered by the Queen at the *State Opening* of Parliament, it outlines the government's plans for the new session, especially its legislative programme.

Question (as well as the conventional meaning) A matter for decision.

Question for Short Debate (QSD) In the Lords, a debatable question time-limited to one or one-and-a-half hours depending when it is taken. There is no right of reply.

question rota In the Commons, the order in which ministers answer oral questions.

quorum The number of members required to be present to transact business. In the Lords, the quorum for the chamber and any committee is three; but on a division on a bill or on *delegated legislation*, at least 30 peers must vote to constitute a quorum. In the Commons there is no quorum except on a division, when at least 40 MPs must be present (35 voting, the four tellers and the occupant of the Chair).

reasoned amendment One tabled for the *second* or *third reading* of a bill that sets out why the bill should not proceed (or proceed in its current form).

reasons Given by one House to the other for rejecting *amendments* to a bill.

recall The return of Parliament during a recess. In the Commons, it is authorised by the *Speaker* on the request of the government. In the Lords, the power is exercised by the *Lord Speaker*. Also used of a system in which an MP has to face a by-election in certain circumstances (for example, serious misconduct).

recess A longer time of adjournment than over a weekend, usually at Christmas, for a week in February, at Easter, Whitsun, and from late July to early September, for three weeks or so after the September sitting in the Commons, and briefly in November. Strictly speaking, the word applies only to the period of *prorogation* but is rarely used in this sense.

regulation (1) In the UK, a type of *delegated legislation*; (2) in European legislation, regulations have the force of law throughout the EU without member states having to take any action.

remedial order An order made by a minister that amends *primary legislation* when that has been found incompatible with the Human Rights Act 1998. Draft remedial orders are scrutinised by the Joint Committee on Human Rights and are then approved by both Houses. Urgent procedure orders may be made without advance scrutiny but must be confirmed by the approval of both Houses within 120 days.

repeal To make the whole or part of an Act of Parliament have no further effect.

report stage Consideration of a bill in the form in which it left committee, and an opportunity for any member to propose amendments, not just those who were on the committee.

reserved matter One not devolved to Scotland, Wales or Northern Ireland.

resolution A decision of either House, or of a committee, that expresses an opinion (for example, 'That this House has no confidence in Her Majesty's Government'). See also *order*.

resource accounting Records the economic cost of the provision of services and the consumption of assets (including depreciation, the cost of using capital assets, and future liabilities such as those for compensation for early retirement). Resource accounts for each government department are laid before Parliament.

restoration and renewal The project for refurbishing the Palace of Westminster. Expected to involve a decant of the whole Palace for at least six years from around 2025.

revised estimates Change the *ambit of an estimate* if it appears that funds already authorised may have to be spent on something outside the present ambit.

Royal Assent The Sovereign's agreement to a bill passed by both Houses.

Royal Commission Five members of the House of Lords charged with representing the sovereign in Parliament when she is not herself present, for *prorogation* and election of a new Commons Speaker.

ruling A decision by the *Speaker* of the Commons or any other occupant of the Chair (or chairman of a *standing committee*) on a matter of order or procedure.

running whip A requirement for MPs to be available to vote throughout a day or a set period, because the timing of votes is unpredictable (as during a report stage or Committee of the whole House on a bill).

Salisbury convention (dating from 1945 and named after the fifth Marquess of Salisbury). Practice that the Lords should not reject at second reading any government legislation that has been passed by the Commons and that carries out a *manifesto* commitment.

schedule Schedules appear after the *clauses* of a bill and fill in detail.

scope The ambit of a bill. To be in order, *amendments* must not go beyond the purposes of the bill as summarised in the *long title*. The equivalent rule in the Lords is described as 'relevance'.

scrutiny reserve resolutions Constrain ministers from giving agreement in the EU Council of Ministers to a proposal that has not cleared the European scrutiny systems in both Houses.

second reading Approval, in principle, of a bill. A second reading debate is a discussion of the principle rather than the details of individual *clauses.*

second reading committee In the Commons, a (temporary) committee to which an uncontroversial bill may be referred for a *second reading* debate. There is then no debate when the bill is reported to the House for its second reading. In the Lords, an unselected committee (meaning that any Lord may attend) meeting in the Moses Room to give a second reading debate to Law Commission Bills.

secretary of state One of the top rank of ministers; senior minister in a government department; always a member of the cabinet.

section The basic unit within an Act of Parliament, divided into subsections, then paragraphs, then sub-paragraphs.

select committee A committee of members of either House charged with investigating a matter and reporting (*ad hoc* select committees), or of monitoring a government department (Commons departmental select committees) or a subject area, or a category of legislative or other proposals and reporting from time to time. Select committees also advise on the administration of both Houses. Select committees that are not *ad hoc* are normally permanent institutions, with their members nominated for the length of a parliament in the Commons or for a session in the Lords.

selection The decision by the *Speaker*, the *Chairman of Ways and Means* or the chair of a *public bill committee* as to which *amendments* (or, in some cases, *motions*) shall be debated or voted on.

Senior Deputy Speaker The title used by the *Chairman of Committees*; the principal Deputy Speaker of the House of Lords and spokesman in the chamber for the House of Lords Commission, which oversees the Lords administration. He has special responsibility for *private bills* and chairs the Liaison Committee, the Privileges and Conduct Committee and the Procedure Committee.

Serjeant at Arms The officer of the Commons with responsibilities for aspects of maintaining order and ceremonial matters.

session The main subdivision of time during a parliament: the period from the *state opening* to *prorogation* (now usually starting in May or June and lasting a year).

sessional orders Any order of either House that has effect only for the rest of that session of Parliament and, in the Lords, the traditional order passed on the day of the *state opening* for 'preventing stoppages in the streets' and so ensuring access to the House.

shadow cabinet Those opposition frontbenchers who 'shadow' members of the cabinet, presided over by the Leader of the Opposition.

shadow minister An MP who is the spokesperson of an opposition party on a particular subject, mirroring the responsibilities of the 'real' minister in the government.

Short money Financial support for opposition parties in the Commons, named after Edward Short, the Leader of the House when it was introduced. The Lords equivalent is *Cranborne money.*

short title The title by which a bill is known during its passage through Parliament; for example, 'Criminal Justice Bill'. See also *long title.*

sitting A meeting of either House, usually in a single day, at the end of which the House adjourns. Also, a meeting of a committee.

Speaker The presiding officer of the Commons.

special report A report from a *select committee* that is not a substantive report on an inquiry but is used as a vehicle for publishing government replies or informing the House of some difficulty the committee has encountered.

standing orders The rules made by both Houses for the regulation of their proceedings. Standing orders remain in force until they are amended or repealed. 'Temporary standing orders' are typically made for the length of a *session* or *parliament.*

starred questions In the Lords, the old name for the four oral questions on Mondays to Thursdays taken at the start of business. In the Commons, the term is not used, but a star on the *Order Paper* against a question indicates that it is for oral answer.

state opening The ceremonial start to a session of Parliament. The main event is the *Queen's Speech.*

statute An Act of Parliament. 'Statute law' and 'the statute book' are collective terms for all Acts in force.

statute law repeal bill A bill that removes parts of the law that have become redundant.

statutory instrument See *delegated legislation.*

strangers The old-fashioned and rather unfriendly description of visitors to Parliament. Now superseded by 'visitors'.

***sub judice* rule** The rule against referring to a current or impending court case (more precisely, when someone has been charged in a criminal case, or, in a civil action, when a case has been set down for trial), to avoid influencing the outcome. The rule may be relaxed at the discretion of the Speakers of each House in certain circumstances, and it need not prevent the consideration of legislation.

subordinate legislation Another term for *delegated legislation.*

subsidiarity In the European context, the principle that a decision should be taken at national level unless the aim could be achieved only by action at EU level.

substantive motion A motion expressing an opinion or taking a decision; not an *adjournment* motion (even though that involves the narrow decision of whether the House or a committee shall adjourn).

sunset clause A provision in legislation that makes it time-limited (and which may also provide for renewal by Parliament after a prescribed period).

supplementary estimates Seek additional resources for a government department.

supplementary question A follow-up oral question.

Supply The granting of money to the Crown for the running of the country.

Supply Bills Give detailed legislative authority for *Supply*: for the total of resources and capital, and cash to be issued from the *Consolidated Fund*. They set out the *ambit* of each estimate and the amount to be paid ('appropriated') in respect of each, and the numbers of personnel authorised for the armed services. The Lords may not amend Supply Bills.

surgery The time when an MP makes himself or herself available in the constituency for meetings with constituents, usually to discuss their problems.

suspend Informally interrupt the sitting of a House or committee. For suspension of an MP, see *naming*.

table To deposit formally before the House or committee, as 'to table an *amendment*' (or *motion*, question or paper). 'The Table' in both Houses is the table between the frontbenches, and also a collective term for the clerks at the Table.

talking out In the Commons, debating a *motion* or a proceedings on a bill up to the *moment of interruption*, when the business is lost or postponed.

tellers Two members from each side who count the votes at a *division*.

ten-minute rule bill In the Commons (on Tuesdays and Wednesdays), a bill introduced by leave of the House (with a vote if one is forced) following a speech of not more than 10 minutes from the sponsor of the proposal. An opponent may speak for not more than 10 minutes in opposition.

test roll A bound parchment book signed by MPs when they take the oath or make *affirmation* after an election (also in the Lords where the parchment is still kept in roll form).

third reading The final stage of the passage of a bill through one House of Parliament; a final review of the contents of the bill, with debate limited to what is actually in the bill rather than, as at *second reading*, what might be included. Substantive *amendments* are allowed at this stage in the Lords but not in the Commons.

unopposed return A motion for an unopposed return seeks the laying of a report or other paper before Parliament, thus giving it the protection of parliamentary *privilege.*

unstarred In the Commons, a question that has been unstarred has been converted from one for oral answer to one for written answer.

'upstairs' In the Commons, means 'in committee' because legislative committees sit in rooms on the first-floor committee corridor.

urgent debate In the Commons, an application is made to the Speaker under standing order 24 to debate 'a specific and important matter that should have urgent consideration'. Such debates are rare.

urgent procedure order See *remedial order.*

urgent question (formerly known as a *private notice question* (PNQ)). In the Commons, an oral question to a minister on an urgent matter of public importance, granted by the Speaker.

usual channels The informal and private contacts between the *whips* and business managers on the two sides of each House.

virement Moving funds between the subheads of an *estimate* with Treasury approval but without further parliamentary authority.

the Vote bundle The daily working papers of the Commons.

Votes and Proceedings The legal record of the proceedings of the Commons: decisions taken, papers laid and so on. Later becomes the *Journal.*

Votes on Account Come before the Commons in January or February and cover some 45 per cent of the estimated expenditure of each government department over the coming year; they are to tide the government over until the *main estimates* are approved in July. They must be agreed by the House by 18 March.

ways and means resolution A *motion* (when approved, a *resolution*) to authorise the raising of a tax or imposition of a charge in relation to a bill. 'Ways and Means' is an old name for taxation.

West Lothian question Named after Tam Dalyell MP, then member for that constituency: why should Scottish MPs at Westminster be able to speak, question and vote on matters affecting the rest of the UK when, in Scotland, those matters are devolved to the Scottish Parliament and the Scottish Government?

Westminster Hall (1) The Great Hall on the west side of the Palace; the oldest part of the Palace. (2) The parallel Commons debating chamber; 'the House sitting in Westminster Hall', which takes place in the Grand Committee Room off the northern end of Westminster Hall. Used mainly for non-controversial debates on subjects put forward by backbenchers, as well as by the government and for debates on select committee reports

whips Members responsible for parliamentary party organisation and discipline. 'The Whip' is circulated weekly by the whips of each party to their own members; it lists the business for the following week, together with the party's expectations as to when its MPs will be required to vote. The 'All-Party' Whip is generally available; it is a sort of Westminster notice-board of forthcoming events, meetings, etc.

white paper A published statement of government policy (see also *green paper*).

wrecking amendment One designed to frustrate the purpose of a bill already approved at *second reading*, or of a *clause* already approved in committee.

writ An order for an election or by-election, issued by the Clerk of the Crown in Chancery upon a warrant from the Speaker. 'Moving the writ', usually by the chief whip of the party that had held the seat, initiates the process of a by-election.

writ of summons Issued by the Clerk of the Crown in Chancery to every member of the House of Lords at the beginning of a new Parliament, or on first appointment.

written ministerial statements In the Commons, statements by ministers that appear in the next day's *Official Report*, before answers to oral questions. A minister's intention to make a written statement is signalled in the *Order Paper* at the end of the day's business. In the Lords, such statements may be made by ministers and by the *Senior Deputy Speaker*. They are printed in the *Official Report*. No notice is required.

Sources of information about Parliament

Books

This is not a bibliography but a highly selective list of publications that may be of further help to readers of this book.

Companion to the Standing Orders and Guide to the Proceedings of the House of Lords, available from Parliament's website and last updated in 2017.

The chief work of reference on House of Lords practice and procedure. The *Companion* describes every aspect of the House's practice and procedure as established by the standing orders, ancient practice, and decisions of the Procedure Committee and the House itself. It complements *Erskine May* (see below), which for some areas provides more detail and gives precedents.

Contemporary House of Lords, The, Meg Russell, Oxford University Press, 2013.

This comprehensive text concentrates on how the House of Lords has worked since the 1999 reforms. Valuable analysis and insights.

Dod's Parliamentary Companion, Dods, 2017.

The annually published reference work with biographies of MPs and peers, detailed results of the last general election, and a great deal of contact and other information on political parties, government departments, public bodies, the devolved institutions and the European Parliament. It also has a useful website directory.

Erskine May's Treatise on the Law, Privileges, Proceedings and Usage of Parliament, 24th edition, edited by Sir Malcolm Jack, LexisNexis, 2011.

Usually known simply as *Erskine May*, it is technical and comprehensive rather than highly readable, but it is the pre-eminently authoritative textbook on Parliament and the one most used by practitioners.

Exploring Parliament, edited by Cristina Leston-Bandeira and Louise Thompson, Oxford University Press, 2018.

Up-to-date introductory textbook on Parliament, with chapters written by academics, commentators and parliamentary officials. Analyses as well as explains.

House of Lords 1911–2011: A Century of Non-reform, The, Chris Ballinger, Hart Publishing, 2012.

Authoritative history of the many attempts to reform the House of Lords in the 20th and early 21st centuries.

Legislation at Westminster, Meg Russell and Daniel Gover, Oxford University Press, 2017.

Case study of the passage of 12 bills through Parliament examining the difference made by the parliamentary process and the influence of Parliament.

Parliament in British Politics, 2nd edition, Philip Norton, Palgrave Macmillan, 2013.

A clear text covering how Parliament interacts with government, those beyond Westminster (the EU, devolved bodies, courts) and citizens.

Parliament and the Law, 2nd edition, edited by Alexander Horne and Gavin Drewry, Hart Publishing, 2018.

Collection of essays by distinguished academics, lawyers and parliamentary officials examining the intersection between Parliament and the law.

Parliamentary Reform at Westminster, Alexandra Kelso, Manchester University Press, 2009.

Examination of the reforms to Parliament during the Labour government of 1997–2010.

Standing Orders of the House of Commons: Public Business, The, 2017.

Available on the parliamentary website.

Standing Orders of the House of Lords relating to Public Business, The, 2016.

Available on the parliamentary website.

Many peers and MPs have written about their time in the Houses in autobiographies or other texts. Two of the most relevant are *How to be an MP* by Paul Flynn, which provides an entertaining overview of an MP's work, and Chris Mullin's diaries covering 1994 to 2010 which, over three volumes, provide an insight into the role of a backbencher and minister.

Parliament websites

Parliament's website, www.parliament.uk, contains a wealth of information about Parliament. The website publishes:

- What's on: current and future business in both Houses and forthcoming meetings of committees (business is normally updated every Thursday).
- The text of Commons *Hansard* from the session 1988–89 onwards and Lords *Hansard* from the session 1994–95, and the *Hansard* of all committee debates of bills and other matters from the session 1997–98 onwards. *Hansard* for the two chambers is available on the website the following day but a rolling version appears on the day with a delay of around three hours.
- Progress of legislation in the current and previous sessions, including the text of all bills, both public and private, before Parliament, and their current status, along with related documents, Library papers and proceedings.

- Standing orders of both Houses, for both public and private business.
- Lists of: MPs by constituency, gender and party; peers; ministers and PPSs; opposition spokespeople; all-party groups and country groups; together with the state of the parties and by-election results.
- Where to find your MP.
- What is logged on the registers of interests.
- For select committees in both Houses, and joint committees: committee home pages with membership, terms of reference and contact details; press notices; text of reports, all oral and much written evidence (from the session 1997–98 onwards); a guide for witnesses; and weekly bulletins of forthcoming meetings.
- Explanatory notes and factsheets on many aspects of the work of Parliament; films about how Parliament works and images from the Palace of Westminster.
- Commons Library research papers on matters of current interest by topic or searchable, together with research notes and longer papers produced by the Parliamentary Office of Science and Technology.
- Information about the records stored by Parliament in the Parliamentary Archives.
- Current job opportunities in Parliament.

Both Houses have twitter accounts (@UKParliament, @HouseofCommons, @UK HouseofLords) and there are also accounts for individual committees and the Libraries.

All primary and secondary legislation is published on legislation.gov.uk.

Watch proceedings on www.parliamentlive.tv, which broadcasts webcast proceedings of both Houses, Westminster Hall, and select committees taking evidence in public, together with a searchable archive.

The Education Service (www.parliament.uk/education/) has a wealth of material on its part of the website which is searchable by key stages/A Level subject. It has also has details of training opportunities for teachers and education outreach visits. The webpage www.parliament.uk/get-involved/ provides other opportunities for the public to engage with and learn about Parliament, including through free training for individuals and groups, and the Parliamentary Studies module taught at universities throughout the UK.

The government publishes information about Parliament and future business on the website of the Leader of the House of Commons (www.gov.uk/government/organisations/the-office-of-the-leader-of-the-house-of-commons) and the Lords Government Whips Office (www.lordswhips.org.uk/).

Other parliamentary and political websites

Details of EU-related legislation and papers are available from the EU website (http://europa.eu/publications/official-documents/index_en.htm) while UK government explanatory memoranda, as well as ministerial letters to Parliament on EU matters are available from the Cabinet Office (http://europeanmemoranda.cabinetoffice.gov.uk/). 'Votewatch', is an excellent source of information about how EU legislative decisions are made (www.votewatch.eu/).

The Electoral Commission (www.electoralcommission.org.uk) provides information on the regulation of voting, elections and political donations.

IPSA – The Independent Parliamentary Standards Authority (http://parliamentary standards.org.uk/) regulates the pay of MPs; details of claims are published on their website.

www.theyworkforyou.com and www.publicwhip.org.uk are the sites of pressure groups seeking to show constituents MPs' voting records, attitudes to issues, rebelliousness, speed of response to constituents' letters and activity levels. But beware of crude rankings of numbers of questions tabled, speeches made, and so on. Activity is not achievement.

www.w4mp.org is a site designed for all those working for an MP, including guides for MPs' staff, but its material is of general interest, too. It also carries advertisements for jobs as MPs' assistants and researchers.

The Hansard Society (www.hansardsociety.org.uk) describes its mission as 'promoting democracy – strengthening Parliament'. It seeks to explain Parliament and increase involvement in parliamentary politics, and researches and publishes on a wide range of issues, as well as organising a range of lectures, seminars and other events. It also publishes the *Audit of Political Engagement* (www.hansardsociety.org.uk/research/public-attitudes/audit-of-political-engagement/) which is an annual survey of political engagement with, and views on, the political system.

The Constitution Unit, based in the Department of Political Science at University College London (www.ucl.ac.uk/constitution-unit), is an authoritative academic group that publishes briefings on topical constitutional and political issues, organises seminars and other events, and publishes a regular and useful newsletter, *The Monitor*. It also details government defeats in the House of Lords.

www.revolts.co.uk is the website of Philip Cowley, an academic who has made the subject of political revolts and parliamentary voting patterns his own. Essential for anyone researching this subject.

And of course there are many blogs, Twitter accounts and other social media pages on politics and parliament, including those of journalists such as BBC reporters, MPs, political commentators and activists, as well as those related to academia and think tanks.

Television

In addition to normal news coverage, and live broadcasts of Prime Minister's Questions and some other occasions on various channels, BBC Parliament provides a dedicated channel, with real-time coverage of the Commons and 'time-shifted' coverage of the Lords and select committees.

Visiting Parliament

To see proceedings

Both Houses have public galleries, and it is often possible, especially later in the day, to get a seat just by turning up. However, this is difficult on particularly newsworthy occasions (and, in the Commons, for Question Time, and especially Prime Minister's Questions). Then, a public queue forms at the entrance near St Stephen's; but it may not be possible to get in until ticket-holders have left.

To get a ticket for the gallery of the House of Commons, UK residents should write to their MP (www.parliament.uk/mps-lords-and-offices/mps/find-your-mp). Members have only a small allocation of tickets, so it is a good idea to write well in advance. Overseas visitors should write to their Embassy or High Commission.

It is also possible to attend public sittings of public bill committees, select committees in both Houses (see Chapter 10) and debates in the 'parallel chamber' in Westminster Hall. You should go to the Central Lobby and seek directions from the reception desk there. Many of the high-profile Commons committee meetings take place in neighbouring Portcullis House which also provides public access to committee rooms, so if you want to see a specific committee check the location in advance. It is not possible to reserve seats, and high-profile select committee hearings may be crowded. But if you can get in, some select committee hearings can offer the best theatre in London!

To tour Parliament

People who are resident in the UK should contact their local MP (www.parliament.uk/mps-lords-and-offices/mps/find-your-mp/) or a peer they know. At times when both Houses are sitting, tours are available on Mondays, Tuesdays, Wednesdays, Fridays (on Fridays, all day if the Commons and Lords are not sitting, late afternoon if they are) and Saturdays. Timing and access to the chambers is limited on a Tuesday and Wednesday. Tours are normally conducted in English and are free when booked this way but you generally need to book around six months in advance. Further information is available under 'visiting parliament' on the website.

During recesses UK residents can continue to arrange tours through their MP or through a peer they know. During recesses, these tours are generally only available on Fridays. At other times during recess periods, the palace also arranges guided or audio-guided tours at a charge; these are particularly aimed at overseas visitors (who cannot normally arrange a tour on sitting days) but anyone may book tickets. Tours are available in English and other languages. Details are available on the parliamentary website. There are also specialised tours on art and architecture, and tours followed by afternoon tea.

Schools visits

Schools and other educational institutions based in this country may contact their MP to arrange a tour. However, an education programme runs for UK schools covering children aged seven to 18, which includes a tour of the building. A transport subsidy is available for schools outside the South-East. Tours are released in term blocks three days each year and slots book up extremely quickly. Further information is available from the Education section of the website.

Index

Note: Page numbers in italic type refer to photographs, diagrams and documents
Page numbers in bold type refer to tables